Routledge History of
Volume IX

Volume IX of the *Routledge History of Philosophy* surveys ten key topics in the philosophy of science, logic and mathematics in the twentieth century. Each of the essays is written by one of the world's leading experts in that field. The papers provide a comprehensive introduction to the subject in question, and are written in a way that is accessible to philosophy undergraduates and to those outside of philosophy who are interested in these subjects. Each chapter contains an extensive bibliography of the major writings in the field.

Among the topics covered are the philosophy of logic, of mathematics and of Gottlob Frege; Ludwig Wittgenstein's *Tractatus*; a survey of logical positivism; the philosophy of physics and of science; probability theory, cybernetics and an essay on the mechanist/vitalist debates.

In addition to these papers, the volume contains a helpful chronology to the major scientific and philosophical events in the twentieth century. It also provides an extensive glossary of technical terms in the philosophy of science, logic and mathematics, and brief biographical notes on major figures in these fields.

Stuart G. Shanker is Professor of Philosophy and of Psychology at York University, Canada. He has published widely on the philosophy of Ludwig Wittgenstein and artificial intelligence.

Routledge History of Philosophy
General Editors – G. H. R. Parkinson and S. G. Shanker

The *Routledge History of Philosophy* provides a chronological survey of the history of Western philosophy, from its beginnings in the sixth century BC to the present time. It discusses all the major philosophical developments in depth. Most space is allocated to those individuals who, by common consent, are regarded as great philosophers. But lesser figures have not been neglected, and together the ten volumes of the *History* include basic and critical information about every significant philosopher of the past and present. These philosophers are clearly situated within the cultural and, in particular, the scientific context of their time.

The *History* is intended not only for the specialist, but also for the student and general reader. Each chapter is by an acknowledged authority in the field. The chapters are written in an accessible style and a glossary of technical terms is provided in each volume.

Each volume contains 10–15 chapters by different contributors.

Routledge History of Philosophy
Volume IX

Philosophy of Science, Logic and Mathematics in the Twentieth Century

EDITED BY
Stuart G. Shanker

Routledge
Taylor & Francis Group
LONDON AND NEW YORK

First published 1996
by Routledge
11 New Fetter Lane, London EC4P 4EE

Simultaneously published in the USA and Canada
by Routledge
29 West 35th Street, New York, NY 10001

First published in paperback 2003

Routledge is an imprint of the Taylor & Francis Group

Selection and editorial matter © 1996 Stuart Shanker

Individual chapters © 1996 the contributors

Typeset in Garamond by RefineCatch Ltd, Bungay, Suffolk
Printed and bound in Great Britain by
TJ International Ltd, Padstow, Cornwall

British Library Cataloguing in Publication Data
A catalogue record for this book is available from the British Library

Library of Congress Cataloging in Publication Data

ISBN 0–415–05776–0 hbk
ISBN 0–415–30881–X pbk

Contents

Preface to the
paperback edition

The success of the first edition of the **Routledge History of Philosophy**, which has led to the publication of this new paperback edition, fully justifies the thinking behind this project. Our view at the time that we planned this collection was that the history of philosophy has a special importance for contemporary philosophers and philosophy students. For the discipline demands that one develop the rigorous techniques required to grasp the significance of a philosopher's ideas within their historical framework, while constantly assessing the relevance of the problems or theories discussed to contemporary issues. The very persistence of these 'perennial problems in philosophy' is an indication, not just of their enduring relevance, but equally, of how important it is to be thoroughly grounded in their history in order to grasp their full complexity. We would like to take this opportunity to thank once again all of the authors involved, each of whom has produced such a lasting contribution to the history of philosophy, and also, our editors Richard Stoneman and Muna Khogali, for their role in making the **History** such an indispensable resource.

G. H. R. P. Reading, 2002
S. G. S. Toronto, 2002

General editors' preface

The history of philosophy, as its name implies, represents a union of two very different disciplines, each of which imposes severe constraints upon the other. As an exercise in the history of ideas, it demands that one acquire a 'period eye': a thorough understanding of how the thinkers whom it studies viewed the problems which they sought to resolve, the conceptual frameworks in which they addressed these issues, their assumptions and objectives, their blind spots and miscues. But as an exercise in philosophy, we are engaged in much more than simply a descriptive task. There is a crucial critical aspect to our efforts: we are looking for the cogency as much as the development of an argument, for its bearing on questions which continue to preoccupy us as much as the impact which it may have had on the evolution of philosophical thought.

The history of philosophy thus requires a delicate balancing act from its practitioners. We read these writings with the full benefit of historical hindsight. We can see why the minor contributions remained minor and where the grand systems broke down: sometimes as a result of internal pressures, sometimes because of a failure to overcome an insuperable obstacle, sometimes because of a dramatic technological or sociological change and, quite often, because of nothing more than a shift in intellectual fashion or interests. Yet, because of our continuing philosophical concern with many of the same problems, we cannot afford to look dispassionately at these works. We want to know what lessons are to be learnt from the inconsequential or the glorious failures; many times we want to plead for a contemporary relevance in the overlooked theory or to reconsider whether the 'glorious failure' was indeed such or simply ahead of its time: perhaps even ahead of its author.

We find ourselves, therefore, much like the mythical 'radical translator' who has so fascinated modern philosophers, trying to understand an author's ideas in his and his culture's eyes, and at the same time, in our own. It can be a formidable task. Many times we fail in the

viii

historical undertaking because our philosophical interests are so strong, or lose sight of the latter because we are so enthralled by the former. But the nature of philosophy is such that we are compelled to master both techniques. For learning about the history of philosophy is not just a challenging and engaging pastime: it is an essential element in learning about the nature of philosophy – in grasping how philosophy is intimately connected with and yet distinct from both history and science.

The *Routledge History of Philosophy* provides a chronological survey of the history of Western philosophy, from its beginnings up to the present time. Its aim is to discuss all major philosophical developments in depth, and with this in mind, most space has been allocated to those individuals who, by common consent, are regarded as great philosophers. But lesser figures have not been neglected, and it is hoped that the reader will be able to find, in the ten volumes of the *History*, at least basic information about any significant philosopher of the past or present.

Philosophical thinking does not occur in isolation from other human activities, and this *History* tries to situate philosophers within the cultural, and in particular the scientific, context of their time. Some philosophers, indeed, would regard philosophy as merely ancillary to the natural sciences; but even if this view is rejected, it can hardly be denied that the sciences have had a great influence on what is now regarded as philosophy, and it is important that this influence should be set forth clearly. Not that these volumes are intended to provide a mere record of the factors that influenced philosophical thinking; philosophy is a discipline with its own standards of argument, and the presentation of the ways in which these arguments have developed is the main concern of this *History*.

In speaking of 'what is now regarded as philosophy', we may have given the impression that there now exists a single view of what philosophy is. This is certainly not the case; on the contrary, there exist serious differences of opinion, among those who call themselves philosophers, about the nature of their subject. These differences are reflected in the existence at the present time of two main schools of thought, usually described as 'analytic' and 'continental' philosophy. It is not our intention, as general editors of this *History*, to take sides in this dispute. Our attitude is one of tolerance, and our hope is that these volumes will contribute to an understanding of how philosophers have reached the positions which they now occupy.

One final comment. Philosophy has long been a highly technical subject, with its own specialized vocabulary. This *History* is intended not only for the specialist but also for the general reader. To this end, we have tried to ensure that each chapter is written in an accessible style; and since technicalities are unavoidable, a glossary of technical terms is provided in each volume. In this way these volumes will, we hope, contribute to a wider understanding of a subject which is of the highest importance to all thinking people.

G. H. R. Parkinson
S. G. Shanker

Notes on contributors

Joseph Agassi is Professor of Philosophy at Tel-Aviv University and York University, Toronto (joint appointment); M.Sc. in physics from Jerusalem; Ph.D. in general science: logic and scientific method from London (The London School of Economics). Among his major publications in English are: *Towards an Historiography of Science, History and Theory, The Continuing Revolution: A History of Physics From the Greeks to Einstein, Faraday as a Natural Philosopher, Towards a Rational Philosophical Anthropology, Science and Society: Studies in the Sociology of Science, Technology: Philosophical and Social Aspects, Introduction to Philosophy: The Siblinghood of Humanity* and *A Philosopher's Apprentice: In Karl Popper's Workshop.*

James Bogen is Professor Emeritus, Pitzer College, Program Director, Center for Philosophy of Science and Affiliated Professor, Department of History and Philosophy of Science, at the University of Pittsburgh. His publications on Wittgenstein include *Wittgenstein's Philosophy of Language*, 'Wittgenstein and Skepticism' and a critical notice of Bradley's *Nature of all Being*. Having published in several areas, including epistemology, philosophy of science and ancient Greek philosophy, he is now working on a project in the history of nineteenth-century neuroscience.

Rainer Born was born in 1943 in Central Europe. He was educated as a teacher and studied (in Austria, Germany and England) philosophy, mathematics, physics, psychology and pedagogics, leading to degrees in 'philosophy and mathematics', habilitation (venia docendi) for 'Theory and philosophy of science'. He is currently an Associate Professor at the Institute for Philosophy and Philosophy of Science at the Johannes Kepler University, Linz, Austria.

Jeff Coulter is Professor of Sociology and Associate Faculty Member of Philosophy at Boston University. Among his publications are *The Social Construction of Mind* (1979), *Rethinking Cognitive Theory* (1983), *Mind In Action* (1989) and (with G. Button, J. Lee and W. Sharrock) *Computers, Minds, and Conduct* (1995).

Michael Detlefsen is Professor of Philosophy at the University of Notre Dame and editor-in-chief of the *Notre Dame Journal of Formal Logic*. He is the author of *Hilbert's Program*, and editor of *Proof and Knowledge in Mathematics* and *Proof, Logic and Formalization*. He is also the author of various papers in the philosophy of logic.

Oswald Hanfling is Professor of Philosophy at The Open University. He is author of *Logical Positivism, Wittgenstein's Later Philosophy, The Quest for Meaning* and *Philosophy and Ordinary Language*. He is also editor and part author of *Philosophical Aesthetics: An Introduction* as well as various Open University texts.

Rom Harré is a Fellow of Linacre College, Oxford, and the University Lecturer in the Philosophy of Science. He is also Professor of Psychology at Georgetown University, Washington DC, and Adjunct Professor of Philosophy at Binghamton University. He is the author of such books as *Varieties of Realism, Social Being, Personal Being, Laws of Nature*, and with Grant Gillett *The Discursive Mind*. He is also the editor, with Roger Lamb, of the *Blackwell Encyclopedic Dictionary of Psychology*.

Andrew Irvine is Professor of Philosophy at the University of British Columbia. He is the editor of *Physicalism in Mathematics* (Kluwer, 1990), *Bertrand Russell: Critical Assessments* (Routledge, 1999) and co-editor of *Russell and Analytic Philosophy* (University of Toronto, 1993).

Kenneth M. Sayre received his Ph.D. from Harvard University in 1958, and has since been at the University of Notre Dame where currently he is Professor of Philosophy. He is the author of several books, monographs and articles on the topics of cybernetics and the philosophy of mind, including *Consciousness: A Philosophic Study of Minds and Machines, Cybernetics and the Philosophy of Mind, Belief and Knowledge: Mapping the Cognitive Landscape*, and *Intentionality and Information Processing: An Alternative Model for Cognitive Science*. He contributed the article on Information Theory in Routledge's new *Encyclopedia of Philosophy*.

Stuart Shanker is Professor of Philosophy and Psychology at York University, Canada. He is the author of *Wittgenstein and the Turning Point* *in the Philosophy of Mathematics* and *Wittgenstein and the Foundation of AI*, and co-author of *Apes, Languages and the Human Mind: Essays in Philosophical Primatology*. He is also editor of *Ludwig Wittgenstein: Critical Assessments* and *Gödel's Theorem in Focus*.

Acknowledgements

I am deeply indebted to my co-general editor, G. H. R. Parkinson, for all the help he has given me in preparing this volume, and Richard Stoneman, who has been an invaluable source of advice in the planning of this History. I would also like to thank Richard Dancy, who prepared the chronology for this volume, and Dale Lindskog and Darlene Rigo, who prepared the glossary. Finally, I would like to thank the Canada Council, which supported this project with a Standard Research Grant; Atkinson College, which supported this project with two research grants; and York University, which awarded me the Walter L. Gordon Fellowship.

Stuart G. Shanker
Atkinson College, York University
Toronto, Canada

Chronology

The following sources have been consulted for much of the material on science and technology: Alexander Hellemans (ed.) *The Timetables of Science* (New York, Simon and Schuster, 1987); Bruce Wetterau, *The New York Public Library Book of Chronologies* (New York, Prentice Hall, 1990).

	Philosophy (general)	Philosophy of science	Science and technology
1840		Whewell, Philosophy of the Inductive Sciences	
1865	Mill, Examination of Sir William Hamilton's Philosophy		
1866		Lange, History of Materialism	
1872		E. Dubois-Raymond, The Limits of Natural Knowledge	
1873		Jevons, The Principles of Science	Maxwell, Electricity and Magnetism
1874		Kirchoff, Principles of Mechanics	
1877	Peirce, 'The Fixation of Belief'		
1878	Peirce, 'How to Make Our Ideas Clear' Peirce, 'The Doctrine of Chances'		
1881		Helmholtz, Popular Lectures	Michelson–Morley experiment (speed of light found to be the same in perpendicular directions)
1883		Mach, The Science of Mechanics	
1885		Clifford, Commonsense of the Exact Sciences	
1892	Frege, 'On Sense and Reference'	Pearson, The Grammar of Science	
1893	Bradley, Appearance and Reality Peirce, Search for a Method (not completed)	Mach, Popular Scientific Lectures Hertz, The Principles of Mechanics	Lorentz–Fitzgerald contraction (contraction of objects at high speeds)
1894	Peirce, The Principles of Philosophy (not completed)		

Year		Science
1895		Discovery of x-rays (Röntgen), cloud chamber developed (Thomson)
1897		Discovery of electron (Thomson), charge of electron measured (Thomson)
1898	Peirce, *The History of the Sciences* (not completed)	Term 'radioactivity' coined (M. Curie) Alpha and beta rays (radioactivity from uranium) discovered (Rutherford)
1900	Husserl, *Logical Investigations*	Quantum theory initiated: substances can emit light only at certain energies (Planck)
1902	Poincaré, *Science and Hypothesis*	Rutherford and Soddy: 'The Cause and Nature of Radioactivity'
1903	Moore, 'Refutation of Idealism' Moore, *Principia Ethica* Peirce, 'Pragmatism' (Harvard lectures)	
1904	Duhem, *The Aim and Structure of Physical Theory*	Thomson's model of the atom: electrons embedded in sphere of positive electricity
1905	Russell, 'On Denoting' Mach, *Knowledge and Error*	Einstein explains Brownian motion (motion of small particles suspended in liquid); seen as first proof of existence of atoms Einstein's papers on the special theory of relativity Einstein postulates light quantum (term 'photon' coined 1926) for particle-like behaviour of light
1907	James, *Pragmatism* Bergson, *Creative Evolution*	
1908		Minkowski, *Space and Time* (proposes 4 dimensional universe)

	Philosophy (general)	Philosophy of science	Science and technology
1910			Marie Curie, *Treatise on Radioactivity*
1911			Rutherford's atomic theory: positively charged nucleus surrounded by negative electrons
1913	Husserl, *Ideas: General Introduction to Pure Phenomenology*		Bohr's model of the atom: electrons revolve around nucleus in fixed orbits, give off fixed quanta of energy by jumping orbit
1914	Russell, *Our Knowledge of the External World* Bradley, *Essays on Truth and Reality*	Broad, *Perception, Physics, and Reality*	Discovery of proton (Rutherford)
1915			Einstein's general theory of relativity
1917		Schlick, *Space and Time in Contemporary Physics*	Existence of black holes predicted (Schwarzschild)
1918	Russell, *The Philosophy of Logical Atomism* Schlick, *General Theory of Knowledge*		Third law of thermodynamics (Nernst)
1920	Whitehead, *The Concept of Nature*	Campbell, *Physics: The Elements*	Existence of neutron (uncharged particle) proposed (Harkins); discovered 1932 Red shift in spectra of galaxies reported (Slipher) Copenhagen Institute of Theoretical Physics founded (Bohr)
1921	Wittgenstein, *Tractatus Logico-Philosophicus*	Haldane, *The Reign of Relativity*	
1923		Broad, *Scientific Thought*	Particle-wave duality of matter proposed (de Broglie); confirmed 1927 (Davisson)
1924			Bose statistics for light quanta (Bose) Galaxies shown to be independent systems (Hubble)

1925	Whitehead, *Science and the Modern World*	Electron spin hypothesized (Goudsmit and Uhlenbeck)
		Pauli's exclusion principle (electrons of same quantum number cannot occupy same electron)
		Quantum mechanics given first comprehensive formulation (Born, Heisenberg and Jordan)
		'Scopes Monkey Trial' (high-school teacher prosecuted for teaching evolution)
1926		Probability interpretation of quantum mechanics (Born)
		Fermi–Dirac statistics
		Planck's law derived from first principles (Dirac)
		First paper on wave mechanics (Schrödinger); Schrödinger's equation
1927	Heidegger, *Being and Time*	Heisenberg's uncertainty principle (cannot determine simultaneously position and momentum of electron)
	McTaggart, *The Nature of Existence*	First version of 'Big Bang' theory of origins of universe (Lemaitre)
	Russell, *The Analysis of Matter*	
	Weyl, *Philosophy of Mathematics and Natural Science*	
	Bridgman, *The Logic of Modern Physics*	
1928	Carnap, *The Logical Structure of the World*	Dirac's equation combines quantum mechanics with special relativity
	Eddington, *The Nature of the Physical World*	
	Reichenbach, *The Philosophy of Time and Space*	
	Campbell, *Measurement and Calculation*	
1929	Carnap, Hahn and Neurath, *The Scientific World View: The Vienna Circle*	Heisenberg and Pauli's quantum field theory
	Dewey, *Experience and Nature*	Hubble's law (more distant a galaxy, faster it is receding from Earth)
	Lewis, *Mind and the World Order*	

	Philosophy (general)	Philosophy of science	Science and technology
1930		Heisenberg, *The Physical Principles of Quantum Theory*	Dirac, *Principles of Quantum Mechanics* 'Neutrino' postulated (Pauli); term coined 1932 (Fermi); discovered 1955 Discovery of planet Pluto (Tombaugh)
1931	Tarski, 'The Concept of Truth in Formalized Languages'	Neurath, 'Physicalism' Schlick, 'Causality in Contemporary Physics' Carnap, 'Die physikalische, Sprache als Universalsprache der Wissenschaft' (trans. *The Unity of Science*, 1934)	'Positron' (positively charged electron) postulated (Dirac); discovered 1932 (Anderson); first form of anti-matter discovered
1932		Joad, *Philosophical Aspects of Modern Science*	Heisenberg's model of atomic nucleus: neutrons and protons held together by exchanging electrons Discovery of neutron (Chadwick)
1933			Fermi's theory of beta decay (first suggestion of weak interaction) Meisner effect discovered (Meisner)
1934	Carnap, *The Logical Syntax of Language*	Bachelard, *The New Scientific Spirit*	
1935		Popper, *The Logic of Scientific Discovery* Eddington, *New Pathways in Science*	'Exchange particle' causing attraction between particles in atomic nucleus (strong force) proposed (Yukawa); called 'meson' (1939), now 'pion'
1936	Ayer, *Language, Truth and Logic* Schlick, 'Meaning and Verification'	Husserl, *The Crisis of European Sciences and Transcendental Phenomenology*	Bridgman, *The Nature of Physical Theory* Inauguration of *The International Encyclopedia of Unified Sciences* (Neurath, Carnap, Morris)
1937		Stebbing, *Philosophy and the Physicists*	'Muon' discovered (Anderson); initial claim to be Yukawa meson shown false 1945 (Conversi, Puncini and Picconi) Concept of 'charge conjugation' introduced

1938	Reichenbach, *Experience and Prediction* Carnap, 'Logical Foundations of the Unity of Science'	for particle interactions (Kramers); in 1958 is shown to be invalid for some interactions
1939	Blanshard, *The Nature of Thought*	Method of calculating properties of material objects from quantum principles developed (Herring)
1940	Russell, *An Inquiry into Meaning and Truth* Collingwood, *An Essay on Metaphysics*	
1942		Two-meson theory (Sakata and Inoué) First controlled chain reaction (Fermi) First radio map of universe (Reber)
1943	Sartre, *Being and Nothingness*	Quantum electrodynamics (QED) developed (Tomonaga)
1944	Reichenbach, *Philosophical Foundations of Quantum Mechanics*	
1946	Frank, *Foundations of Physics*	Term 'lepton' introduced for light particles not affected by strong force (Pais and Moller) 'V particle' discovered (Rochester and Butler)
1947	Carnap, *Meaning and Necessity*	'Pion' (Yukawa meson) discovered (Powell and team) Lamb Shift discovered; independent development of quantum electrodynamics (QED) four years after similar theory of Tomonaga Two-meson theory developed independently four years after similar theory of Sakata and Inoué (Marshak & Bethe)

	Philosophy (general)	Philosophy of science	Science and technology
1948			Opposed theories of the universe formulated: steady-state theory (Bond, Gold, Hoyle) and Big Bang theory (Gamow, Alpher, Harmon)
1949	Schlick, *Philosophy of Nature*		Atomic nucleus not necessarily spherical (Rainwater)
1950	Strawson, 'On Referring'		
1951	Quine, 'Two Dogmas of Empiricism'; Goodman, *The Structure of Appearance*		
1952		Wisdom, *Foundations of Inference in Natural Science*; Hempel, *Fundamentals of Concept Formation in Empirical Science*	Bubble chamber for study of subatomic particles developed (Glaser)
1953	Wittgenstein, *Philosophical Investigations*; Quine, *From a Logical Point of View*	Toulmin, *The Philosophy of Science*; Braithwaite, *Scientific Explanation*	'Strangeness' quantum number introduced (Gell-Mann, Nakano and Nishijina)
1954	Ryle, *Dilemmas*	Reichenbach, *Nomological Statements and Admissable Operations*	European Centre for Nuclear Research (CERN) founded
1955			Neutrinos observed (Cowen and Reines)
1956	Reichenbach, *The Direction of Time*		Anti-neutron discovered (Cook, Lamberston, Picconi, Wentzel)
1957		Bohm, *Causality and Chance in Modern Physics*	Parity not conserved for weak interactions (Yang, Lee, Wu); 'Boson' (W particle) proposed as mediator of weak interactions (Schwinger)
1958	Polanyi, *Personal Knowledge*	Hanson, *Patterns of Discovery*; Bohr, *Atomic Physics and Human Knowledge*	

Year			
1959	Strawson, *Individuals*		
1960	Quine, *Word and Object*	Bunge, *Causality*	Mossbauer effect discovered (Mossbauer); used to confirm Einstein's general theory of relativity (Pound and Reblan) 'Resonances' (short-lived particles) discovered (Alvarez)
1961		Nagel, *The Structure of Science* Harré, *Theories and Things* Capek, *Philosophical Impact of Contemporary Physics*	First human being to orbit the Earth (Gagarin)
1962	Austin, *How to do Things with Words* Black, *Models and Metaphors*	Kuhn, *The Structure of Scientific Revolutions* Sellars, *Science, Perception and Reality* Maxwell, 'The Ontological Status of Theoretical Entities' Hesse, *Models and Analogies in Science*	
1963	Popper, *Conjectures and Refutations*	Smart, *Philosophy and Scientific Realism* Grunbaum, *Philosophical Problems of Space and Time*	First recognition of a quasar (Schmidt)
1964	Scheffler, *The Anatomy of Inquiry*		Concept of 'quark' introduced (Gell-Mann)
1965		Hempel, *Aspects of Scientific Explanation*	Confirmation of Big Bang theory with accidental discovery of radio-wave remnants of Big Bang (Penzias and Wilson)
1966		Hempel, *Philosophy of Natural Science*	
1967	Davidson, 'Truth and Meaning'	Scheffler, *Science and Subjectivity*	Strong nuclear force shown to violate parity conservation (Lobashov) 'Electroweak theory' unifies weak and electromagnetic forces (Weinberg, Salam, Glashow) First pulsar discovered (Bell)

	Philosophy (general)	Philosophy of science	Science and technology
1969	Quine, *Ontological Relativity*		
1972	Popper, *Objective Knowledge*		Quantum chromodynamics (QCD) initiated (Gell-Mann) Biblical accounts of creation should receive equal attention as evolutionary theory: California State Board of Education
1973			Creation of the universe from absolutely nothing under probabilistic laws of quantum mechanics proposed (Tyron)
1974		Sklar, *Space, Time and Spacetime* Barnes, *Scientific Knowledge and Sociological Theory*	First of GUTs (grand unified theories) unifies strong, weak and electro-magnetic forces (Georgi, Glashow) J/psi particle discovered (Richter; Trug); confirmation of charm theory of quarks
1975	Dummett, *What is a Theory of Meaning?*	Feyerabend, *Against Method*	
1976		Bloor, *Knowledge and Social Imagery*	
1977		Lauden, *Progress and its Problems*	Upsilon particle discovered (Lederman): confirms quark theory of baryons
1978	Goodman, *Ways of Worldmaking*	Feyerabend, *Science in a Free Society*	
1979		Latour and Woolger, *Laboratory Life* Lakatos, *The Methodology of Scientific Research Programs*	
1980	Rorty, *Philosophy and the Mirror of Nature*	van Fraasen, *The Scientific Image*	Neutrinos may have tiny mass, thus representing 'missing mass' thought to hold galaxies together

1981	Putnam, *Reason, Truth and History*	'Inflationary universe' model: universe expands rapidly for short time before Big Bang (Guth) Revival of 'catastrophism': collision between Earth and large body results in mass extinctions, including extinction of dinosaurs, (W. and L. Alvarez)
1983	Cartwright, *How the Laws of Physics Lie*; Hacking, *Representing and Intervening*	'New inflationary universe' theory of the origins of the universe (Linder; Albrecht and, Steinhardt) Discovery of W and Z particles; further confirms electroweak theory (CERN)
1985	Fox-Keller, *Reflections on Gender and Science*	Hole in ozone layer over Antartica discovered
1986	Harding, *The Feminist Question in Science*	Individual quantum jumps in individual atoms observed Fifth fundamental force, hypercharge, discovered (Fishbach); not universally accepted Discovery of 'Great Attractor', a point towards which a number of galaxies (including ours) are moving
1987	Feyerabend, *Farewell to Reason*; Lakoff, *Women, Fire and Dangerous Things* Latour, *Science in Action*; Putnam, *The Many Faces of Realism*	US Supreme Court rejection of equal-time concept of teaching for creationism
1988	Hawking, *A Brief History of Time*	
1989		Controversy over cold-fusion experiments (production of energy through nuclear fusion at room temperature); results subsequently discredited

	Mathematics	Logic	Psychology/Philosophy of mind
1822	Fourier series defined (Fourier)		
1829	First account of non-Euclidean geometry (Lobachevski)		
1837		Bolzano, *Wissenschaftslehre*	
1839			Herbart, *Psychological Investigations*
1843		Mill, *System of Logic*	
1847		Boole, *The Mathematical Analysis of Logic*	
1854		Boole, *Laws of Thought*	
1862	Riemann's non-Euclidean geometry		
1872	Dedekind, *Continuity and the Irrational Numbers*		
1874	Cantor, *Mengenlehre*	Lotze, *Logic*	Brentano, *Psychology from an Empirical Standpoint* Wundt, *Foundations of Physiological Psychology*
1879		Frege, *Begriffschrift*	
1882	Dedekind, 'Was sind und was sollen die Zahlen?'		
1883	Cantor, *Foundations of a General Theory of Manifolds*	Bradley, *Principles of Logic*	
1884	Frege, *The Foundations of Arithmetic*		
1886			Mach, *The Analysis of Sensations*
1889	Peano, *Principles of Arithmetic*		

Year	Logic & Philosophy	Mathematics	Psychology
1890			James, *The Principles of Psychology*
1891	Frege, 'Function and Concept'	Husserl, *Philosophy of Arithmetic*	
1892	Frege, 'Concept and Object'		
1893		Frege, *The Basic Laws of Arithmetic* (vol. 2, 1903)	Freud and Breuer's studies on hysteria
1895		Canton, *Contributions to the Founding of the Theory of Transfinite Numbers* / Peano, *Formulaire de Mathematiques* (final vol., 1908) / Peirce, *New Elements of Mathematics*	
1899		Hilbert, *Foundations of Geometry*	
1900	Hilbert's address to the International Congress of Mathematicians: 'Mathematical Problems'		Freud, *The Interpretation of Dreams*
1901			Titchener, *Experimental Psychology*
1902		Russell's paradox	Pavlov's dog experiments begin
1903	Peirce, 'Some Topics on Logic' (Lowell lectures)	Russell, *The Principles of Mathematics* / Frege, *Basic Laws of Arithmetic*	
1905	Meinong, 'Theory of Objects'		Intelligence test developed, (Binet, Henri, Simon)
1906			Sherrington, *The Integrative Action of the Nervous System*
1908		Axiomatic treatment of set theory (Zermelo)	
1910		Russell and Whitehead, *Principia Mathematica* (1910–13)	
1912		Brouwer, *Intuitionism and Formalism*	Adler, *The Neurotic Character*

Year	Mathematics	Logic	Psychology/Philosophy of mind
1913			Watson, *Behavior*
1918		Lewis, *Survey of Symbolic Logic*	
1919	Russell, *Introduction to Mathematical Philosophy*		Watson, *Psychology from the Standpoint of a Behaviorist*
1921		Keynes, *A Treatise on Probability*	Russell, *The Analysis of Mind* Rorschach's inkblot test introduced
1923	Skolem: 'Some Remarks on Axiomatic Set Theory'		Piaget, *The Language and Thought of the Child*
1924			Watson, *Behaviorism*
1925			Broad, *The Mind and Its Place in Nature*
1926			Piaget, *The Child's Conception of the World*
1927			Pavlov, *Conditioned Reflexes*
1928		Hilbert, *Principles of Mathematical Logic* von Mises, *Probability, Statistics and Truth*	
1929			Kohler, *Gestalt Psychology*; insulin shock treatment for schizophrenia introduced
1930	Gödel's proof of completeness of first-order predicate calculus		
1931	Gödel's incompleteness theorem Ramsey, *The Foundations of Mathematics* Carnap, 'The Logicist Foundations of Mathematics' Heyting, 'The Intuitionist Foundations of Mathematics' von Neumann, 'The Formalist Foundations of Mathematics'		

Year			
1932			Price, *Perception*
1934	Hilbert, *Foundations of Mathematics* (vol. 2 1939)		
1935		Reichenbach, *The Theory of Probability*	Prefrontal lobotomy developed as treatment for mental illness (Moniz) Koffka, *Principles of Gestalt Psychology*
1937		Turing: 'On Computable Numbers' ('Turing machine')	Vygotsky, *Thought and Language* Electro-convulsive treatment (ECT, 'shock treatment') developed for treatment of schizophrenia (Cerlutti, Bini)
1938	Gödel's proof of consistency of continuum hypothesis with basic axioms of set theory	Dewey, *Logic: The Theory of Inquiry*	Skinner, *The Behavior of Organisms*
1939	Witgenstein's lectures on the foundations of mathematics (published 1975) First volume of *Elements de Mathematique* by 'Nicolas Bourbaki' (pseudonym for group of French mathematicians)	Nagel, *Principles of the Theory of Probability* Carnap, *Foundations of Logic and Mathematics*	
1941		Tarski, *Introduction to Logic, and to the Methodology of the Deductive Sciences*	
1942			Merleau-Ponty, *The Structure of Behavior*
1943		Carnap, *Formalization of Logic*	Skinner and Hull, *Principles of Behavior* Rosenblueth, Wiener and Bigelow, 'Behavior, Purpose, and Teleology' Hull, *Principles of Behavior*
1944			Morgenstern and von Neumann, *Theory of Games and Economic Behavior*
1945	Hempel, 'The Nature of Mathematical Truth'	Waismann, 'Are There Alternative Logics?' Carnap, 'The Two Concepts of Probability'	Merleau-Ponty, *The Phenomenology of Perception*

	Mathematics	Logic	Psychology/Philosophy of mind
1948			Wiener, Cybernetics Kinsey, Sexual Behavior in the Human Male
1949		Reichenbach, The Theory of Probability Kneale, Probability and Induction	Ryle, The Concept of Mind
1950		Quine, Methods of Logic Carnap, The Logical Foundations of Probability	Turing, 'Computing Machinery and Intelligence' ('Turing's test')
1951		von Wright, An Essay in Modal Logic	
1952		Strawson, Introduction to Logical Theory Carnap, The Continuum of Inductive Methods	Rapid eye movement (REM) during normal sleep reported (Aservinsky)
1953			Kinsey: Sexual Behavior in the Human Female Skinner, Science and Human Behavior
1954		Goodman, Fact, Fiction and Forecast Savage, The Foundations of Statistics	Thorazine introduced for treatment of mental disorders
1955	Homologic algebra developed (Cartan and Eilenberg)		
1956	Wittgenstein, Remarks on the Foundations of Mathematics		
1957		von Wright, The Logical Problem of Induction	Skinner, Verbal Behavior Chisholm, Perceiving Hamlyn, The Psychology of Perception Geach, Mental Acts
1958			Peters, The Concept of Motivation von Neumann, The Computer and the Brain Malcolm, Dreaming

xxx

Year			
1961	Chaos theory initiated (Lorenz)		Minsky, 'Steps Towards Artificial Intelligence'; Grice, 'The Causal Theory of Perception'
1962			Austin, Sense and Sensibilia
1963	Independence of Cantor's continuum hypothesis from axioms of set theory demonstrated (Cohen)	von Wright, The Logic of Preference; Quine, Set Theory and Its Logic	Kenny, Action, Emotion and Will
1964			Taylor, The Explanation of Behaviour; Hamilton, 'The genetic evolution of social behavior' (beginning of sociobiology)
1965		Hacking, Logic of Statistical Inference	
1966			Masters and Johnson, Human Sexual Response
1967	Putnam, 'Mathematics without Foundations'		
1968			Armstrong, A Materialist Theory of the Mind; Chomsky, Language and Mind
1969		Lewis, Convention	Dretske, Seeing and Knowing
1970		Quine, Philosophy of Logic; Cohen, The Implications of Induction	
1971		Salman, Statistical Explanation and Statistical Relevance	Piaget, Biology and Knowledge
1972		Kripke, 'Naming and Necessity'	Dreyfus, What Computers Can't Do
1973		Lewis, Counterfactuals; Hintikka, Logic, Language Games and Information	

	Mathematics	Logic	Psychology/Philosophy of mind
1974	Wang, *From Mathematics to Philosophy*	Hacking, *The Emergence of Probability* Haack, *Deviant Logic*	Luria, *Cognitive Development*
1975			Fodor, *The Language of Thought*
1977	Putnam, 'Models and Reality' Dummett, *Elements of Intuitionism*		Popper and Eccles, *The Self and Its Brain*
1978			Dennett, *Brainstorms*
1979			Harré, *Social Being*
1980	Exhaustive classification of finite single group completed		
1981			Fodor, *Representations* Dretske, *Knowledge and the Flow of Information*
1983			Searle, *Intentionality* Fodor, *Modularity of Mind* Harré, *Personal Being*
1984			Goodman, *Of Mind and Other Matters*
1985			Harré, Clarke and De Carlo, *Motives and Mechanisms*
1987			Fodor, *Psychosemantics* Johnson, *The Body in the Mind*
1988			Dennett, *The Intentional Stance*

	Biology	Technology
1838	Cell theory established: cell basic structural unit of plant and mammal life (Schleiden, Schwann)	
1832		Babbage's analytical engine
1858	Cell centre of disease processes (Virchow); displaces humoural theory of disease	
1859	Darwin, *The Origin of Species* Role of air-borne bacteria in fermentation (Pasteur); displaces theory of spontaneous generation	First commercial oil well
1862	Spencer, *System of Synthetic Philosophy* ('62-'93)	
1863	Huxley, *Man's Place in Nature*	
1866	Mendel's studies on principles of heredity	
1867		Dynamite patented (Nobel)
1869		Suez canal completed
1871	Darwin, *Descent of Man*	
1876		Telephone patented (Bell)
1880	Germ theory of disease (Pasteur)	
1881	First artificially produced vaccine (Pasteur)	
1885		Electric transformer invented
1891	Ehrlich's diptheria antitoxin establishes field of immunology	
1892	Existence of virus demonstrated (Ivanovsky)	

	Biology	Technology
1900	Rediscovery of Mendel's 1860s work on genetics	Vacuum tube invented
1901	First trans-Atlantic telegraphic transmission (Marconi)	
1902	Human sex chromosome identified	
1903	Chromosomes carry heredity-determining material (Sutton)	First successful airplane flight (Wright brothers)
1906	Existence of 'vitamins' (term coined 1912) postulated (Hopkins); discovered 1928	
1908	Driesch, *The Science and Philosophy of the Organism*	
1909	Term 'gene' coined (Johannsen)	
1912	C. L. Morgan, *Instinct and Experience*	
1913		Henry Ford's assembly line
1914	Driesch, *The History and Theory of Vitalism*	
1915		Sonar developed
1921	Insulin discovered (Banting, Best, McLeod, Collip)	
1923	C. L. Morgan, *Emergent Evolution*	
1925		First analog computer (Bush)
1926	T. H. Morgan, *The Theory of the Gene* C. L. Morgan, *Life, Mind, and Spirit*	First public demonstration of television
1928	Discovery of penicillin (Fleming); production and clinical use not until 1940s	

1929	Discovery of deoxyribose nucleic acids (DNA) Woodger, *Biological Principles*
1930	Immunization against typhus developed (Zinsser)
1931	Haldane, *The Philosophical Basis of Biology*
1932	T. H. Morgan, *The Scientific Basis of Evolution* Particle accelerator first used to split lithium atom (Cockcroft and Walton)
1933	Vitamin C synthesized
1935	Richter scale developed (Richter) First radar developed (Watson, Watt)
1936	Isolation of DNA in pure state (Belozersky) Primitive digital computer (Zuse) ABC (Atanasoff-Berry Computer), first electronic computer begun; completed 1939; operational version 1942
1937	Woodger, *The Axiomatic Method in Biology*
1938	Oparin, *The Origin of Life* Uranium atom first split (Hahn)
1939	DDT insecticide synthesized (Muller)
1940	Penicillin developed as antibiotic (term 'antibiotic' coined 1941)
1941	Zuse's Z2 computer: electromagnetic relays and punched tape for data entry
1943	First all-electronic computer, 'Colossus', developed to crack codes (Turing) First operational nuclear reactor (Oak Ridge, TN)

XXXV

	Biology	Technology
1944	DNA determined as hereditary material for almost all living beings (Avery)	Jet-engine (V-1) and rocket-propelled (V-2) bombs
1945	Lille, *General Biology and Philosophy of the Organism*	Atomic bombs dropped on Hiroshima and Nagasaki ENIAC: first all-purpose, stored-program electronic computer
1946		Radioactive carbon-14 method developed for dating objects (Libby)
1948	Woodger, *Biological Principles*	Discovery of transistor (Shockley, Brattain, Burdeen); will replace vacuum tubes
1950	Sommerhoff, *Analytical Biology*	
1951	Bernal, *The Physical Basis of Life*	UNIVAC I, first commercially available computer Heart-lung machine developed (Gibson)
1952	Plasmid (structure containing genetic material exchanged by bacteria) discovered (Lederberg)	Hydrogen bomb ('H Bomb') developed (Teller)
1952	Polio vaccine developed (Salk); mass innoculation in 1954; superceded by new vaccine in 1957 (Sabine) Woodger, *Biology and Language*	First nuclear reactor accident (Chalk River, Canada)
1953	Double-helix structure of DNA determined (Crick and Watson)	
1955		FORTRAN, first computer-programming language (Backus, IBM) LISP, computer language of artificial intelligence developed (McCarthy)

Year	Event	
1957		Sputnik I, first artificial satellite, launched by USSR
1958		Integrated circuit invented
1960		First laser (Maiman); precursors are Townes' maser (1954), Kastler's 'optical pumping' (1950)
1961	RNA code producing amino acid in cell discovered	First human being in space (Gagarin)
1962	Carson, *Silent Spring* (environmentalist classic)	Disk storage for computer data introduced (IBM)
1964		'Green Revolution' inaugurated with strain of rice generating double yield given sufficient fertilizer
1967		Keyboards used for computer data entry
1968	Discovery of restrictive enzymes (can cut DNA of virus at particular point); would become a basic tool of genetic engineering Becker, *The Biological Way of Thought*	
1969	Single gene first isolated (Beckwith)	First human beings on the moon (Armstrong and Aldrin) First artificial heart used in a human being
1970	First complete synthesis of a gene	
1971	Monod, *Chance and Necessity*	Microprocessor (chip) introduced
1972		CAT-scan (computerized axial tomography) introduced for medical work
1973	Beginning of genetic engineering (Cohen and Boyer)	First Skylab launched

	Biology	Technology
1975		Personal computers introduced (Altair 8800)
1976	Functional synthetic gene constructed (Khorana)	
1977	Earliest known cases of AIDS; disease not recognized until 1981	Apple II personal computer introduced
1978	First 'test-tube' baby (Leslie Brown)	
1979		Partial meltdown of nuclear reactor at Three Mile Island
1980	Bohm, *Wholeness and the Implicate Order*	
1981	First transferrence of genes from one animal to another of a different species	First flight of space shuttle Columbia
1982	First commercial product of genetic engineering (human insulin)	
1984	Baboon heart implanted in human baby	
1984	Genetic fingerprinting technique developed	
1986	First field trials of genetically engineered organisms (tobacco)	Explosion of space shuttle Challenger Chernobyl nuclear reactor explosion
1987		'Warm temperature' superconductor discovered
1989		Exxon-Valdez oil tanker spill off the coast of Alaska

Introduction
S. G. Shanker

In this volume we survey the striking developments that have taken place in the philosophies of logic, mathematics and science in the twentieth century. The very use of a genitive case here bears eloquent testimony to the dramatic changes that have occurred. Prior to this century, few philosophers troubled to break 'philosophy' down into its constituent parts. Nor did they display any pronounced interest in the nature of philosophy *per se*, or the relation in which philosophy stands to science. Indeed, subjects that we now regard as totally distinct from philosophy – such as mathematics or psychology, and even physics or biology – were once all located within the auspices of philosophy.

It is interesting to note, for example, how Hilbert obtained his doctorate from the philosophy department. Now we are much more careful to distinguish between axiomatics, proof theory, categorization theory, the foundations of mathematics, mathematical logic, formal logic, and the philosophy of mathematics. That hardly means that philosophers are only active in the latter areas, however, while mathematicians get to rule over the former. Rather, philosophers and mathematicians move about freely in all these fields. To be sure, it is always possible to distinguish between the work of a mathematician and that of a philosopher: the approach, the techniques, and most especially the intentions and the conclusions drawn, invariably betray the author's occupation. But the fact that philosophers and mathematicians are working side-by-side, that they are reading each other's work and attending each other's conferences, is an intellectual development whose significance has yet to be fully absorbed.

Significantly, the major figures in the philosophies of logic and mathematics this century – Frege, Russell, Wittgenstein, Brouwer, Poincaré, Hilbert, Gödel, Tarski, Carnap, Quine – all moved from logic or mathematics to philosophy. Perhaps more than any single factor, it was this dynamic that determined the nature of analytical philosophy. For it resulted not only in the importation of formal tools but also in the preoccupation with 'logical analysis', in the search for 'regimentation' and the preoccupation with the construction of 'formal models' of language. Increasingly, an undergraduate education in philosophy began not with the writings of Plato and Aristotle but with the propositional and predicate calculus. Where students were once exposed to the subtle nuances in the concept of truth, they were now trained in the art of axiomatizing the concept of truth. Symposia and dialogues were supplanted by truth tables and the turgid prose of late nineteenth-century German scientific writing.

Perhaps the most noticeable effect of this overwhelming logical and mathematical presence is that philosophical arguments began to be conducted at a very high level of technical sophistication. Those who came to these issues straight from philosophy found themselves forced to master the intricacies of formal or mathematical logic if they wished to participate in the debates. But for all the changes taking place, the underlying philosophical problems remained remarkably constant. Questions such as 'What is the nature of truth?', 'What is the nature of proof?', 'What is the nature of concepts?', 'What is the nature of inference?', or even that much-vaunted issue of analytic philosophy, 'What is the nature of meaning?', have all long been the loci of philosophical interest. Thus, it is not surprising that over the past few years there has been a remarkable surge in historical studies, all motivated by the goal of establishing the relevance of some classical figure or argument for contemporary thought – as Professor Parkinson and I point out in our general introduction to this *History*.

Still, it would be imprudent to conclude from the perennial nature of its problems that philosophy has not in fact changed in some fundamental way this century. It is not so much the pervasive influence of formal and formalist thought (which may in fact already be starting to wane), however, as the relation in which philosophy now stands to science. This issue has been a pre-eminent concern throughout this century: indeed, in some ways, it has been a defining issue for the aspiring philosopher of logic, mathematics, or science.

The two main rival positions have been the Russellian and the Wittgensteinian: scientism, and what has been dubbed (by its critics at any rate) ordinary language philosophy. According to Russell, philosophy should 'seek to base itself upon science': it should 'study the methods of science, and seek to apply these methods, with the necessary adaptations, to its own peculiar province'.[1] There are two basic aspects of scientism as conceived by Russell. First, there is no intrinsic difference between philosophy and science: each is engaged in the pursuit of knowledge (albeit at different levels of generality); each constructs theories and generates hypotheses. Second, philosophy plays a heuristic role in the evolution of science. As Russell saw it,

> To a great extent, the uncertainty of philosophy is more apparent than real: those questions which are already capable of definite answers are placed in the sciences, while those only to which, at present, no definite answer can be given, remain to form the residue which is called philosophy.[2]

On this picture, the realm of philosophy is constantly being eroded. The more effective philosophers are, the more imminent becomes their demise. For their success entails the active engagement of scientists, rigorously testing and revising the theories that originated in a priori reasoning.

The appeal of Russell's argument stemmed largely from the fact that he had history on his side. The pattern was set in the mechanist/vitalist debates: in the removal of first the animal heat debate and then the reflex theory debate from the province of philosophy and their resolution in physiology. It was natural for scientistic philosophers to assume that Turing's mechanical version of Church's thesis had set the stage for yet another major step in this process: i.e. the transference of the mind from philosophy's jurisdiction to that of cognitive science. The sentiment began to surface that one could no longer regard philosophy as the driving force behind logical, mathematic and scientific progress. Rather, the feeling was that the 'Queen of the Sciences' had been reduced to the role of handmaiden, initiating perhaps but in no way governing the great advances taking place in logic, mathematics and science. To borrow a term from contemporary concept theory, the fate of philosophy in the twentieth century began to be characterized as the descent from superordinate, to basic-level, to subordinate status.

On the face of it, this argument is rather curious. After all, it takes as its paradigm the displacement of natural philosophy by physics. But the philosophical debates that have been inspired by physics in the twentieth century are amongst the most profound and spirited that philosophy has ever enjoyed. Disputes over the nature of matter and time, the origin of the universe, the nature of experiment, evidence, explanation, laws and theory, the relation of physics to the other sciences: these are but a few of the issues which have been hotly debated this century, and which will continue to stimulate intense debate. And these pale in comparison to the controversies sparked off by Turing's thesis.

If anything, interest in philosophy has grown throughout this century, as is manifest by the rapid growth of philosophy faculties in every liberal arts programme. Like the relation of the Canadian economy to the American, the more science has advanced, the more philosophy has grown. New scientific breakthroughs – indeed, new sciences – seem to create in their wake a host of new philosophical problems. But then the crucial question which this raises, which the scientistic conception of philosophy obscures, is: what renders these problems *philosophical*? Is it just that they arise at a premature scientific stage, before there is an adequate theory to deal with them? But if that were the case, how could we speak of there being *perennial* philosophical problems?

Wittgenstein sought to come to terms with this latter question throughout his later writings. In 1931 he wrote:

> You always hear people say that philosophy makes no progress and that the same philosophical problems which were already proccupying the Greeks are still troubling us today. I read: '. . . philosophers are no nearer to the meaning of "Reality" than Plato got, . . .'. What a strange situation. How extraordinary that Plato could have even got as far as he did! Or that we could not get any further! Was it because Plato was so *extremely* clever?[3]

Wittgenstein's proposed explanation for this phenomenon – viz., 'The reason is that our language has remained the same and always introduces us to the same questions' (Ibid.) – drew from Russell the bitter complaint that this would render philosophy 'at best, a slight help to lexicographers, and at worst, an idle tea-table amusement.'[4] But this criticism rests on a profound misreading of Wittgenstein's conception of the nature of philosophy. Indeed, the very assumption that the philosophers whom Russell cites in *My Philosophical Development* (viz., Wittgenstein, Ryle, Austin, Urmson and Strawson) can be identified as forming a philosophical 'school' is deeply suspect. Admittedly, they all shared certain fundamental attitudes towards the proper method of resolving philosophical problems, but in no way did they all share the same philosophical interests and objectives, let alone subscribe to a common set of philosophical doctrines or theses.

The basic premiss Wittgenstein was advancing is that questions about the nature of concepts belong to logic, and that we clarify the nature of a concept by surveying the manner in which the concept-word is used or learnt. Russell attributed to Wittgenstein the view that philosophical problems can be resolved by studying the ordinary grammar of concept-words. But nothing could be further from the truth. The fundamental principle underlying Wittgenstein's argument is that the source of a philosophical problem often lies in a crucial and often elusive difference between the *surface grammar* of a concept-word and its *depth* or *logical grammar*, or in the philosopher's tendency to treat what are disguised *grammatical propositions* as if they were empirical propositions.

Where Russell was certainly right, however, was in thinking that the later Wittgenstein was fundamentally opposed to the scientistic conception of philosophy. In his 1930 lectures Wittgenstein announced:

> What we find out in philosophy is trivial; it does not teach us new facts, only science does that. But the proper synopsis of these trivialities is enormously difficult, and has immense importance. Philosophy is in fact the synopsis of trivialities.[5]

This means that the task of philosophy is to clarify concepts and theories, not to draw inductive generalizations or to formulate theses. Indeed, Wittgenstein went so far as to insist, 'The philosopher is not a citizen of any community of ideas. That is what makes him into a philosopher.'[6] Wittgenstein did not mean to suggest by this that philosophy does not have a crucial role to play vis-à-vis science. In the *Bouwsma Notes* he remarks that 'the consummation of philosophy' in the twentieth century might very well lie in the clarification of scientific theories: in 'work which does not cheat and where the confusions have been cleared up'.[7] But this would seem to limit philosophy to the task of interpreting scientific prose: the 'history of evolving ideas', as it were. And as the following chapters demonstrate, the philosophies of logic, mathematics and science this century took *Principia Mathematica* not *The A.B.C of Relativity* as their standard-bearer.

What's more, there is a real danger in this thought that the principal role of philosophy is to describe and not explain. For it has a tendency to promote the view that philosophers are armchair critics, akin to theatre critics, both professionally and temperamentally set apart from the scientific writings whose shortcomings it is their chief job to expose. Not surprisingly, one frequently hears the complaint from scientists that philosophers have been seduced by the negative: that they criticize a theory without appreciating the subtle difficulties involved, or without making the necessary effort to master the literature underpinning a scientific issue. Yet philosophers, even scientistic philosophers, are in no rush to lose their distinctive identity. There has thus been marked hostility and frustration on both sides of the 'philosophy versus science' divide.

These are important emotions. For if philosophy were irrelevant to the ongoing development of logic, mathematics and science, there would be neither anger nor impatience: only disinterest. But one constantly hears the demand from scientists for positive philosophical input. So the question which this naturally raises is, what is impeding this union? Is it perhaps the very terms in which twentieth-century philosophy has tried to assess its relation to science? Is it not significant that both scientism and ordinary language philosophy have strong nineteenth-century roots: the former in scientific materialism and the latter in hermeneutics? Indeed, is not the battle between scientism and ordinary language philosophy reminiscent – and perhaps simply a continuation – of the battle between scientific materialism and hermeneutics? If there has not been a decisive victory by either side, is it, perhaps, because each is articulating an important truth: and, perhaps, omitting an important aspect of the development of the philosophy of logic, mathematics and science this century?

We can turn again to Wittgenstein to appreciate this point. At the close of the second book of *Philosophical Investigations* Wittgenstein remarks how, 'in psychology there are experimental methods and *conceptual confusion* ... The existence of the experimental method makes us think we have the means of solving the problems which trouble us; though problem and method pass one another by'.[8] Ironically, a few cognitivists actually greeted Wittgenstein's censure as confirming the importance of the post-computational revolution. For example, F. H. George insisted that:

> [Wittgenstein's] criticism of experimental psychology, at the time it was made, [was] almost entirely justified. Experimental psychologists were, at that time, struggling to unscramble their concepts and clarify their language and models: at worst they believed that as long as a well-controlled experiment was carried out, the mere accumulation of facts would make a science. The relation, so vital to the development of psychology, between experimental results, by way of interpretation and explanatory frameworks, models, used largely to be neglected.[9]

On this reading, the mechanist paradigm that Wittgenstein was attacking was fundamentally displaced by Turing's version of Church's thesis. Hence, Wittgenstein's concerns are now hopelessly dated for:

> Almost everyone now acknowledges that theory and experiment, model making, theory construction and linguistics all go together, and that the successful development of a science of behavior depends upon a 'total approach' in which, given that the computer 'is the only large-scale universal model' that we possess, 'we may expect to follow the prescription of Simon and construct our models – or most of them – in the form of computer programs'.[10]

Ignoring his enthusiasm here for the post-computational mechanist revolution, what is most intriguing about George's interpretation of Wittgenstein's argument is the manner in which he seeks to synthesize scientism with ordinary language philosophy. On this argument, philosophy enters a scientific enterprise at its very beginnings; it serves an important role in clearing away the confusions inhibiting the construction of a comprehensive explanatory framework. But once the new model is in place, philosophy has no further constructive role to play. For, as George puts it, 'much of this conceptual confusion has now disappeared'.[11]

Is this really the case? Has philosophy been even more successful than Russell envisaged? The philosophies of logic, mathematics and science have been driven by five leading problems this century:

1 What is the nature of logic, of logical truth?
2 What is the nature of mathematics: of mathematical propositions, mathematical conjectures, and mathematical proof?
3 What is the nature of formal systems, and what is their relation to what Hilbert called 'the activity of understanding'?
4 What is the nature of language: of meaning, reference, and truth?
5 What is the nature of mind: of consciousness, mental states, mental processes?

I have limited these to five problems to suggest a generational flux. A few philosophers have, of course, been active in all these areas throughout the century, but there is some basis for viewing the development of the philosophies of logic, mathematics and science in the twentieth century in terms of the succession of these five leading problems.

Now, very few philosophers would be willing to consign any, let alone all five, of these problems to the 'History of Ideas'. What the following chapters reveal is not the resolution of these issues, but the deepening understanding we have achieved of the nature of logic, mathematics, language and cognition. Moreover, as the century has progressed, it has become increasingly tenuous to suppose that philosophy is either conceptually prior to science, i.e., that philosophy clears away the confusions so that the proper business of theory-making can proceed – or that philosophy is conceptually posterior to science, i.e., that philosophy is restricted to correcting the errors that occur in scientific prose. For the advances that have been realized in the topics covered in this volume are not simply the result of philosophical reflection, or well-controlled experiments, but rather, are the outcome of a complex interplay of philosophic and scientific techniques as practised by both philosophers and scientists.

Thus, each of the chapters in this volume is as important to science students as the relevant science textbooks are to philosophy students. The point here is not that the categorial difference between philosophy and science – between philosophical and empirical problems, or philosophical and empirical methods – is disappearing, but that the formal, or institutional demarcation of these activities is fast becoming obsolete. All over the world interdisciplinary units are springing up which are specifically designed to train their students in various cognitive sciences as well as in philosophy. This is a reflection of the fact that scientists themselves are constantly engaged in conceptual clarification, while philosophers have grasped the importance of entering fully into the community of science if their efforts are to serve the needs of scientists. What has been consigned to the 'History of Ideas' are the old terms of the 'philosophy versus science' debate. But the following chapters are not just history; more fundamentally, they are a harbinger of the great changes we can continue to expect in the ongoing evolution of philosophy.

∾ NOTES ∾

1 Bertrand Russell, 'On Scientific Method in Philosophy', in *Mysticism and Logic*, London, Longmans, Green and Company, 1918.
2 Bertrand Russell, *The Problems of Philosophy*, Oxford, Oxford University Press, 1959.
3 Ludwig Wittgenstein, *Culture and Value*, P. Winch (trans.), Oxford, Basil Blackwell, 1980, p. 15.
4 Bertrand Russell, *My Philosophical Development*, London, George Allen and Unwin, 1959, p. 161.
5 Ludwig Wittgenstein, *Wittgenstein Lectures: Cambridge 1930–1932*, D. Lee (ed.) Oxford, Blackwell, 1980, p. 26.
6 Ludwig Wittgenstein, *Zettel*, G. E. M. Anscombe and G. H. von Wright (eds), G. E. M. Anscombe (trans.), Oxford, Blackwell, 1967, section 455.
7 O. K. Bouwsma, *Wittgenstein, L. Conversations 1949–1951*, J. L. Craft and R. E. Hustwit (eds) Indianapolis, Hackett Publishing Company, 1986, p. 28.
8 Ludwig Wittgenstein, *Philosophical Investigations*, Oxford, Blackwell, 1953, p. 232.
9 F. H. George, *Cognition*, London, Methuen, 1962, pp. 21–2.
10 Ibid.
11 Ibid.

CHAPTER 1

Philosophy of logic

A. D. Irvine

The relationship between evidence and hypothesis is fundamental to the advancement of science. It is this relationship – referred to as the relationship between premisses and conclusion – which lies at the heart of logic. Logic, in this traditional sense, is the study of correct inference. It is the study of formal structures and non-formal relations which hold between evidence and hypothesis, reasons and belief, or premisses and conclusion. It is the study of both conclusive (or monotonic) and inconclusive (non-monotonic or ampliative) inferences or, as it is also commonly described, the study of both entailments and inductions. Specifically, logic involves the detailed study of formal systems designed to exhibit such entailments and inductions. More generally, though, it is the study of those conditions under which evidence rightly can be said to justify, entail, imply, support, corroborate, confirm or falsify a conclusion.

In this broad sense, logic in the twentieth century has come to include, not only theories of formal entailment, but informal logic, probability theory, confirmation theory, decision theory, game theory and theories of computability and epistemic modelling as well. As a result, over the course of the century the study of logic has benefited, not only from advances in traditional fields such as philosophy and mathematics, but also from advances in other fields as diverse as computer science and economics. Through Frege and others late in the nineteenth century, mathematics helped transform logic from a merely formal discipline to a mathematical one as well, making available to it the resources of contemporary mathematics. In turn, logic opened up new avenues of investigation concerning reasoning in mathematics, thereby helping to develop new branches of mathematical research – such as set theory and category theory – relevant to the foundations of mathematics itself. Similarly, much of twentieth-century philosophy – including advances in metaphysics, epistemology, the philosophy of mathematics, the philosophy of science, the philosophy of language and formal semantics – closely parallels this century's logical developments. These advances have led in turn to a broadening of logic and to a deeper appreciation of its application and extent. Finally, logic has provided many of the underlying theoretical results which have motivated the advent of the computing era, learning as much from the systematic application of these ideas as it has from any other source.

This chapter is divided into four sections. The first, 'The Close of the Nineteenth Century', summarizes the logical work of Boole, Frege and others prior to 1900. The second, 'From Russell to Gödel', discusses advances made in formal logic from 1901, the year in which Russell discovered his famous paradox, to 1931, the year in which Gödel's seminal incompleteness results appeared. The third section, 'From Gödel to Friedman', discusses developments in formal logic made during the fifty years following Gödel's remarkable achievement. Finally, the fourth section, 'The Expansion of Logic', discusses logic in the broader sense as it has flourished throughout the latter half of the twentieth century.

❧ THE CLOSE OF THE NINETEENTH ❧
CENTURY

'Logic is an old subject, and since 1879 it has been a great one.'[1] This judgment appears as the opening sentence of W. V. Quine's 1950 *Methods of Logic*. The sentence is justly famous – even if it has about it an air of exaggeration – for nothing less than a revolution had occurred in logic by the end of the nineteenth century.

Several important factors led to this revolution, but without doubt the most important of these concerned the mathematization of logic. Since the time of Aristotle, logic had taken as its subject matter formal patterns of inference, both inside and outside mathematics. Aristotle's *Organon* had been intended as nothing less than a tool or canon governing correct inference. However, it was not until the mid-nineteenth century that logic came to be viewed as a subject which could be developed mathematically, alongside other branches of mathematics. The leaders in this movement – George Boole (1815–64), Augustus DeMorgan (1806–71), William Stanley Jevons (1835–82), Ernst Schröder (1841–1902), and Charles Sanders Peirce (1839–1914) – all saw the potential for developing what was to be called an 'algebra of logic', a mathematical means of modelling the abstract laws governing formal inference. However, it was not until the appearance, in 1847, of a small pamphlet entitled *The Mathematical Analysis of Logic*, that Boole's calculus of classes – later extended by Schröder and Peirce to form a calculus of relations – successfully achieved this end.

Boole had been prompted to write *The Mathematical Analysis of Logic* by a public dispute between DeMorgan and the philosopher William Hamilton (1788–1856) over the quantification of the predicate. As a result, Boole's landmark pamphlet was the first successful, systematic application of the methods of algebra to the subject of logic. So impressed was DeMorgan that two years later, in 1849, despite Boole's lack of university education, he was appointed Professor of Mathematics at Queen's College, Cork, Ireland, largely on DeMorgan's recommendation. Five years following his appointment, Boole's next work, *An Investigation of the Laws of Thoughts*, expanded many of the ideas introduced in his earlier pamphlet. In the *Laws of Thought*, Boole developed more thoroughly the formal analogy between the operations of logic and mathematics which would help revolutionize logic. Specifically, his algebra of logic showed how recognizably algebraic formulas could be used to express and manipulate logical relations.

Boole's calculus, which is known today as the theory of Boolean algebras, can be viewed as a formal system consisting of a set, S, over which three operations, $\cap$ (or $\times$, representing intersection), $\cup$ (or $+$, representing union), and $'$ (or $-$, representing complementation) are defined, such that for all a, b, and c that are members of S, the following axioms hold:

(1) Commutativity:
    $a \cap b = b \cap a$, and $a \cup b = b \cup a$

(2) Associativity:
    $a \cap (b \cap c) = (a \cap b) \cap c$, and $a \cup (b \cup c) = (a \cup b) \cup c$

(3) Distributivity:
    $a \cap (b \cup c) = (a \cap b) \cup (a \cap c)$, and $a \cup (b \cap c) = (a \cup b) \cap (a \cup c)$

(4) Identity:
    There exist two elements, o and 1, of S such that $a \cup o = a$, and $a \cap 1 = a$

(5) Complementation:
    For each element a in S, there is an element a' such that $a \cup a' = 1$, and $a \cap a' = o$.

The logical utility of the system arises once it is realized that many logical relations are successfully formalizable in it. For example, by letting a and b represent variables for statements or propositions, $\cap$ represent the truth-functional connective 'and', and $\cup$ represent the truth-functional connective 'or', the commutativity axioms assert that statements of the form 'a and b' are equivalent to statements of the form 'b and a', and that statements of the form 'a or b' are equivalent to statements of the form '*b* or *a* '. Similarly, by letting ' represent truth-functional negation, the complementation axioms assert that for each statement, *a*, there is a second statement, not-*a*, such that the statement '*a* or not-*a*' is true and the statement '*a* and not-*a*' is false. A similar interpretation (which identifies electronic gates with Boolean operators) provides the foundation for the theory of switching circuits. Thus, by 1854 the mathematization of logic was well under way.

A second important factor concerning the advancement of logic during this period had to do, not with the mathematization of logic, but with the logicizing of mathematics. The idea of reducing mathematics to logic had been advocated first by Gottfried Wilhelm Leibniz (1646–1716) and later by Richard Dedekind (1831–1916). In general, it amounted to a two-part proposal: first, that the concepts of (some or all branches of) mathematics were to be defined in terms of purely logical concepts and, second, that the theorems of (these same branches of) mathematics were in turn to be deduced from purely logical axioms. However, it was not until the late nineteenth century that the logical tools necessary for attempting such a project were discovered.

Not accidentally, the attempt to logicize mathematics coincided with a process of systematizing and rigorizing mathematics generally. Many commentators had called for such work to be done. Earlier discoveries by Gerolamo Saccheri (1667–1733), Karl Gauss (1777–1855), Nikolai Lobachevski (1793–1856), János Bolyai (1802–60) and Bernhard Riemann (1826–66) in the development of non-Euclidean geometry had led to a new sensitivity about axiomatics and about foundations generally. Thus, by the late 1800s, the critical movement – which had begun in the 1820s – had eliminated many of the contradictions and much of the vagueness contained in many early nineteenth century mathematical theories. Bernard Bolzano (1781–1848), Niels Abel (1802–29), Louis Cauchy (1789–1857) and Karl Weierstrass (1815–97) had successfully taken up the challenge of rigorizing the calculus. Weierstrass, Dedekind and Georg Cantor (1845–1918) had all independently developed methods for founding the irrationals in terms of the rationals and, as early as 1837, William Rowan Hamilton (1805–65) had introduced ordered couples of reals as the first step in supplying a logical basis for the complex numbers. By 1888, Dedekind had also developed a consistent postulate set for axiomatizing the set of natural (or counting) numbers, *N*. Building upon these results, as well as others by H. G. Grassmann (1809–77), Guiseppe Peano (1858–1932) was then able to develop systematically, not just a theory of arithmetic and of the rationals, but a reasonably detailed theory of real limits as well. The results appeared in Peano's 1889 *Arithmetices Principia*.

Beginning with four axioms governing his underlying logic, and the five (now famous) Peano postulates first introduced by Dedekind, Peano defined the set of natural numbers as a series of successors to the number zero. Letting 'o' stand for zero, '$s(x)$' stand for the successor of x, and 'N' stand for the set of natural numbers, the non-logical postulates may be listed as follows:

(1) Zero is a number:
$o \in N$

(2) Zero is not the successor of any number:
$\sim(\exists x)(x \in N \ \& \ s(x) = o)$

(3) The successor of every number is a number:
$(\forall x)(x \in N \rightarrow s(x) \in N)$

(4) No two distinct numbers have the same successor:
$(\forall x)(\forall y)(((x \in N \ \& \ y \in N) \ \& \ x \neq y) \rightarrow s(x) \neq s(y))$

(5) The Principle of Mathematical Induction, that if zero has a property, P, and if whenever a number has the property its successor also has the property, then all numbers have the property:
$(\forall P)(((P(o) \ \& \ (\forall x)((x \in N \ \& \ Px) \rightarrow Ps(x)))) \rightarrow (\forall y)(y \in N \rightarrow Py))$.

Thus, beginning with a few primitive notions, it was in principle possible to derive almost all of mathematics in a rigorous, coherent fashion. Despite this, the task of formally relating most of logic to mathematics remained virtually unadvanced since the time of Boole.

Crucial to further advancement was the introduction of the quantifiers and the development of the predicate calculus. The introduction of the quantifiers resulted from the independent work of several authors, including Peirce and Schröder, but predominantly it came about through the work of Gottlob Frege (1848–1925). It is possible that Peirce was the first to arrive at the notion of a quantifier, although explicit mention of either the universal or the existential quantifier does not appear in his published writings until 1885. Frege, in contrast, first published his account in 1879 in his now famous Begriffsschrift (meaning literally 'concept writing'). Hence the date in Quine's famous aphorism. Subtitled 'a formula language, modeled upon that of arithmetic, for pure thought', the Begriffsschrift took as its goal nothing less than a rigorization of proof itself. Said Frege,

> My intention was not to represent an abstract logic in formulas, but to express a content through written signs in a more precise and clear way than it is possible to do through words. In fact, what I wanted to create was not a mere calculus ratiocinator but a lingua characterica in Leibniz's sense.[2]

The result was the introduction of a very general symbolic language

replace Frege's notation, and further rigorize his logic, that Frege's discoveries began to receive the prominence they deserved. None the less, it is Frege's analysis of propositions into functions and arguments, along with his introduction of the quantifiers, which to this day remain at the heart of the development of modern logic.

Yet a third factor contributing to the revolutionary advancement of logic during the late nineteenth century was Cantor's discovery of set theory. Intuitively, a set can be thought of as any collection of well-defined distinct objects. In Cantor's words, by the idea of a set 'we are to understand any collection into a whole M of definite and separate objects m of our intuition or our thought'.[3] The objects which determine each set are called the elements or members of that set. The symbol '$\in$' is used regularly to denote the relation of membership or elementhood. Thus '$m \in M$' is read 'm is an element (or member) of M' or 'm belongs to M'. Two sets are identical if and only if they contain exactly the same elements; thus, if $A = \{1, 2, 3\}$ and $B = \{+\sqrt{1}, +\sqrt{9}, +\sqrt{4}\}$, then $A = B$.

With little more than these beginnings, Cantor was able to show that the cardinality of the set of all subsets of any given set (i.e. the power set of that set) is always greater than that of the set itself, thus introducing the modern hierarchy of sets. In addition, he showed that the set of real numbers is non-denumerable (or, equivalently, that the cardinality of the continuum of reals, R, is greater than that of N). Cantor proved both results in 1891 by means of a diagonal argument, an argument designed to construct objects, on the basis of other objects, and in such a way that the new objects are guaranteed to differ from the old. Cantor's diagonal argument therefore provides an important example of a modern impossibility proof since, by using it, he proved the non-denumerability of the reals by showing that a one-to-one correspondence between the natural numbers and the reals is impossible. It also followed from Cantor's work that infinite sets could consistently be placed in one-to-one correspondence with proper subsets of themselves, thus disproving Euclid's general axiom that the whole is necessarily greater than the part. Such unintuitive results meant that set theory, like non-Euclidean geometry before it, would soon lead to further questions about the nature of proof. The question of when to rely upon axioms which, up until this point had still regularly been based upon 'clear and distinct ideas', therefore became crucial. The fact that there was also an intuitive identity between the extension of a predicate and its corresponding set meant that developments in set theory were bound to affect logic.

❧ FROM RUSSELL TO GÖDEL ❧

If it is fair to say that by the end of the nineteenth century logic had become invigorated as a result of its connections with mathematics, it is also fair to say that mathematics was becoming similarly invigorated as a result of its connections with logic. In fact, it was the interplay between logic and mathematics which led a host of figures in both disciplines – including most famously David Hilbert (1862–1943), L. E. J. Brouwer (1881–1966), Arend Heyting (1898–1980), A. N. Whitehead (1861–1947), Bertrand Russell (1872–1970), Ernst Zermelo (1871–1953), Kurt Gödel (1906–78), Alfred Tarski (1902–83), Alonzo Church (b. 1903) and W. V. Quine (b. 1908) – to concentrate their efforts upon foundational issues in logic and mathematics. Many were prompted to do so as a result of a problem which affected both logic and mathematics equally, the problem of the antinomies.

In 1900 many of the world's best philosophers met to attend the Third International Congress of Philosophy, held in Paris from 1 to 5 August. Following the Congress, a significant number of philosophers remained in Paris for the Second International Congress of Mathematicians, which was being held immediately afterwards, from 6 to 12 August. It was at these later meetings that Hilbert delivered his famous keynote address welcoming the mathematical world to Paris. Conscious of his place in history, Hilbert took the occasion to remind his audience of the challenges facing them as they entered a new century:

> If we would obtain an idea of the probable development of mathematical knowledge in the immediate future, we must let the unsettled questions pass before our minds and look over the problems which the science of to-day sets and whose solution we expect from the future. To such a review of problems the present day, lying at the meeting of the centuries, seems to be well adapted ... However unapproachable these problems may seem to us and however helpless we stand before them, we have, nevertheless, the firm conviction that their solution must follow by a finite number of purely logical processes ... This conviction of the solvability of every mathematical problem is a powerful incentive to the worker. We hear within us the perpetual call: There is the problem. Seek its solution. You can find it by reason, for in mathematics there is no *ignorabimus*.[4]

To emphasize his challenge, Hilbert presented his now famous list of twenty-three major unsolved logical and mathematical problems. First on Hilbert's list was Cantor's continuum problem, the problem of determining whether there is a set with cardinality greater than that of the natural numbers but less than that of the continuum. Second on the list, but equally important from the point of view of the logician, was the problem of proving an axiom set consistent or, as Hilbert put it, the problem of the 'compatibility of the arithmetical axioms'. Although primarily of theoretical interest in 1900, it was a problem which would, within the year, take on new urgency.

It was also at these meetings that Russell met Peano. By all accounts the meeting was a congenial one. As Russell reports:

> The Congress was a turning point in my intellectual life, because I there met Peano. I already knew him by name and had seen some of his work, but had not taken the trouble to master his notation. In discussions at the Congress I observed that he was always more precise than anyone else, and that he invariably got the better of any argument upon which he embarked. As the days went by, I decided that this must be owing to his mathematical logic.[5]

Thus, impressed by Peano and his logic, Russell returned to England, motivated to begin work on his *Principles of Mathematics* and confident that any problem he might set for himself would quickly be solved. As one might guess, Russell's *Principles* was to be heavily influenced, not only by Peano's *Arithmetices Principia*, but also by Frege's *Begriffsschrift* and *Grundlagen*. Russell finished the first draft of the manuscript, as he tells us, 'on the last day of the century', 31 December 1900.[6]

Five months later, in May 1901, Russell discovered his now famous paradox. The paradox comes from considering the set of all sets which are not members of themselves, since this set must be a member of itself if and only if it is not a member of itself. As a result, one must attempt to find a principled way of denying the existence of such a set. Cesare Burali-Forti (1861–1931), an assistant to Peano, had discovered a similar antinomy in 1897 when he had observed that since the set of ordinals is well-ordered, it therefore must have an ordinal. However, this ordinal must be both an element of the set of ordinals and yet greater than any ordinal in the set. Hence the contradiction.[7]

After worrying about the difficulty for over a year, Russell wrote to Frege with news of the paradox on 16 June 1902. The antinomy was a crucial one, since Frege claimed that an expression such as $f(a)$ could be considered to be both a function of the argument f and a function of the argument a. In effect, it was this ambiguity which allowed Russell to construct his paradox within Frege's logic. As Russell explains:

> this view [that $f(a)$ may be viewed as a function of either f or of a] seems doubtful to me because of the following contradiction.

Let w be the predicate: to be a predicate that cannot be predicated of itself. Can w be predicated of itself? From each answer its opposite follows. Therefore we must conclude that w is not a predicate. Likewise there is no class (as a totality) of those classes which, each taken as a totality, do not belong to themselves. From this I conclude that under certain circumstances a definable collection does not form a totality.[8]

Russell's letter to Frege, in effect telling him that his axioms were inconsistent, arrived just as the second volume of his *Grundgesetze* was in press. (Other antinomies were to follow shortly, including those discovered by Jules Richard (1862–1956) and Julius König (1849–1913), both in 1905.) Immediately appreciating the difficulty, Frege attempted to revise his work, adding an appendix to the *Grundgesetze* which discussed Russell's discovery. Nevertheless, he eventually felt forced to abandon his logicism. A projected third volume of the *Grundgesetze* which had been planned for geometry never appeared. Frege's later writings show that Russell's discovery had convinced him of the false-hood of logicism, and that he had opted instead for the view that all of mathematics, including number theory and analysis, was reducible only to geometry.

Despite his abandonment of logicism, it was Frege's dedication to truth which Russell commented upon in a letter many years later:

> As I think about acts of integrity and grace, I realize that there is nothing in my knowledge to compare with Frege's dedication to truth. His entire life's work was on the verge of completion, much of his work had been ignored to the benefit of men infinitely less capable, ... and upon finding that his fundamental assumption was in error, he responded with intellectual pleasure clearly submerging any feelings of personal disappointment. It was almost superhuman and a telling indication of that which men are capable if their dedication is to creative work and knowledge instead of cruder efforts to dominate and be known.[9]

With the appearance of Russell's paradox, Hilbert's problem of proving consistency took on new urgency. After all, since (in classical logic) all sentences follow from a contradiction, no mathematical proof could be trusted once it was discovered that the underlying logic was contradic-tory. Important responses came not only from Hilbert and Russell, but from Brouwer and Zermelo as well.

The seeds of Hilbert's response were contained in his 1904 address to the Third International Congress of Mathematicians. In this address, Hilbert presented his first attempt at proving the consistency of arithmetic. (Earlier, in 1900, he had attempted an axiomatization of the reals, R, and showed that the consistency of geometry depends upon the consistency of *R*.) Hilbert recognized that an attempt to avoid the contradictions by formalizing one's metalanguage would only lead to a vicious regress. As a result, he opted instead for an informal logic and metalanguage whose principles would be universally acceptable. His basic idea was to allow the use of only finite, well-defined and constructible objects, together with rules of inference which were deemed to be absolutely certain. Controversial principles such as the axiom of choice were to be explicitly excluded. The programme variously became known as the finitary method, formalism, proof theory, metamathematics and Hilbert's programme. Together with Wilhelm Ackermann (1896–1962), Hilbert went on to publish *Grundzüge der Theoretischen Logik* (*Principles of Mathematical Logic*) in 1928 and, together with Paul Bernays (1888–1977), the monumental two-volume work *Die Grundlagen der Mathematik* (*Foundations of Mathematics*), in 1934 and 1939, respectively. This latter work recorded the results of the formalist school up until 1938, including work done following the publication of Gödel's 1931 incompleteness theorems, after which it was concluded that the original finitistic methods of the programme had to be expanded.

Hilbert's finitary method had similarities to a second important response to the antinomies, that of Brouwer and the intuitionists. Like Hilbert, Brouwer held that one cannot assert the existence of a mathematical object unless one can also indicate how to go about constructing it. However, Brouwer argued, in addition, that the principles of formal logic were to be abstracted from purely mental mathematical intuitions. Thus, since logic finds its basis in mathematics, it could not itself serve as a foundation for mathematics. For similar reasons, Brouwer rejected the actual infinite, accepting only mathematical objects capable of effective construction by means of the natural numbers, together with methods of finite constructibility. On this view theoretical consistency would be guaranteed as a result of reformed mathematical practice.

Russell's own response to the paradox was contained in his aptly named theory of types. Russell's basic idea was that by ordering the sentences of a language or theory into a hierarchy (beginning with sentences about individuals at the lowest level, sentences about sets of individuals at the next lowest level, sentences about sets of sets of individuals at the next lowest level, etc.), one could avoid reference to sets such as the set of all sets, since there would be no level at which reference to such a set appears. It is then possible to refer to all things for which a given condition (or predicate) holds only if they are all at the same level or of the same 'type'. The theory itself admitted of two versions.

According to the simple theory of types, it is the universe of discourse (of the relevant language) which is to be viewed as forming a hierarchy. Within this hierarchy, individuals form the lowest type; sets of individuals form the next lowest type; sets of sets of individuals form the next lowest type; and so on. Individual variables are then indexed (using subscripts) to indicate the type of object over which they range, and the language's formation rules are restricted to allow only sentences such as '$a_n \in b_m$' (where $m = n + 1$) to be counted among the (well-formed) formulas of the language. Such restrictions mean that strings such as '$x_n \in x_n$' are ill-formed, thereby blocking Russell's paradox.

The ramified theory of types goes further than the simple theory. It does so by describing a hierarchy, not only of objects, but of closed and open sentences (propositions and propositional functions, respectively) as well. The theory then adds the condition that no proposition or propositional function may contain quantifiers ranging over propositions or propositional functions of any order except those lower than itself. Intuitively, this means that no proposition or propositional function can refer to, or be about, any member of the hierarchy other than those which are defined in a logically prior manner. Since, for Russell, sets are to be understood as logical constructs based upon propositional functions, it follows that the simple theory of types can be viewed as a special case of the ramified theory.

Russell first introduced his theory in 1903 in his *The Principles of Mathematics*. Later, in 1905, he abandoned the theory in order to consider three potential alternatives: the 'zigzag theory', in which only 'simple' propositional functions determine sets; the 'theory of limitation of size', in which the purported set of all entities is disallowed; and the 'no-classes theory', in which sets are outlawed, being replaced instead by sentences of certain kinds. Nevertheless, by 1908 Russell was to abandon all three of these suggestions in order to return to the theory of types, which he develops in detail in his article 'Mathematical Logic as Based on the Theory of Types'. The theory finds its mature expression in Whitehead and Russell's monumental work defending logicism, *Principia Mathematica*, the first volume of which appeared in 1910.

In order to justify both his simple and ramified theories, Russell introduced the principle that 'Whatever involves *all* of a collection must not [itself] be one of the collection'.[10] Following Henri Poincaré (1854–1912), Russell called this principle the 'Vicious Circle Principle' (or VCP). Once the VCP is accepted, it follows that the claim – first championed by Peano and later by Frank Ramsey (1903–30) – that there is an important theoretical distinction between the set-theoretic and the semantic paradoxes, is mistaken. The reason is that in both cases the VCP provides a philosophical justification for outlawing self-reference.

Yet a fourth response to the paradoxes was Zermelo's axiomatization of set theory. In 1904 Zermelo had solved one of Hilbert's twenty-three problems of the 1900 Congress by proving that every set can be well ordered. Four years later, in 1908, he developed the first standard axiomatization, Z, of set theory, improving upon both Dedekind's and Cantor's original, more fragmentary treatments.

Zermelo's axioms were designed to resolve Russell's paradox by restricting Cantor's naive principle of abstraction – the principle that from each and every predicate expression a set could be formed. Specifically, Zermelo's axiom of replacement would disallow the construction of paradoxical sets (such as the set of all sets that are not members of themselves), but would still allow the construction of other sets necessary for the development of mathematics. ZF, the axiomatization generally used today, is a modification of Zermelo's theory developed primarily by Abraham Fraenkel (1891–1965). When ZF is supplemented by the axiom of choice (proved independent by Fraenkel in 1922), the resulting theory, ZFC, may be summarized as follows:

1 Axiom of Extensionality:
   $(\forall x)(x \in A \longleftrightarrow x \in B) \to A = B$

2 Sum Axiom:
   $(\exists C)(\forall x)(x \in C \longleftrightarrow (\exists B)(x \in B \,\&\, B \in A))$

3 Power Set Axiom:
   $\exists B)(\forall C)(C \in B \longleftrightarrow A \supseteq C)$

4 Axiom of Regularity:
   $(A \neq o \to (\exists x)(x \in A \,\&\, (\forall y)(y \in x \to y \notin A))$

5 Axiom of Infinity:
   $(\exists A)(o \in A \,\&\, (\forall B)(B \in A \to B \cup \{B\} \in A))$

6 Axiom Schema of Replacement:
   If $(\forall x)(\forall y)(\forall z)(x \in A \,\&\, \phi(x,y) \,\&\, \phi(x,z) \to y = z)$
   then $(\exists B)(\forall y)(y \in B \longleftrightarrow (\exists x)(x \in A \,\&\, \phi(x,y)))$

7 Axiom of Choice:
   For any set A there is a function, f, such that
   for any non-empty subset, B, of A, $f(B) \in B$.

As a result of the work of many others, including Thoralf Skolem (1887–1963), Leopold Löwenheim (1878–1957), and John von Neumann (1903–57), it is recognized that many additional axioms variously used to formalize set theory may be derived from the above list of axioms. For example, the separation axioms are derivable from the axiom schema of replacement; the pairing axiom is derivable from the power set axiom together with the axiom schema of replacement; and the union axiom is derivable from the axiom of extensionality, the sum axiom and the pairing axiom. (Other axioms, such as an axiom for cardinals, that $\mathfrak{K}(A) = \mathfrak{K}(B) \longleftrightarrow A \approx B$, are also occasionally added to the above list to form extensions of ZFC.)

Overall, these four responses to the antinomies signalled the arrival of a new and explicit awareness of the nature of formal systems and of the kinds of metalogical results which are today commonly associated with them. Specifically, formal systems are typically said to comprise:

1   a set of primitive symbols, which form the basic vocabulary of the system;
2   a set of formation rules, which provide the basic grammar of the system and which determine how primitive symbols may be combined to form well-formed formulas (sentences) of the system;
3   a set of axioms, which articulate any fundamental assumptions of the system;

and

4   a set of transformation rules (or rules of inference), which provide the mechanism for proving formulas of the system called theorems.

Together, 1 and 2 are said to constitute the formal language of the system, 3 and 4 the logic of the system, and 1–4 the primitive basis of the system as a whole. A formal system thus consists essentially of an explicit, effective mechanism for the selection of a well-defined subset of well-formed formulas, known as the theorems of the system. Such systems may be either axiomatic or natural deduction systems, depending upon whether they emphasize the use of axioms at the expense of rules of inference, or rules of inference at the expense of axioms. In either case, each theorem is proved through a finite sequence of steps, each of which is either the statement of an axiom, or is justified (possibly from earlier formulas) by the allowed rules of inference.

Each formal system may be viewed from the point of view of proof theory (i.e. from the point of view of the system's syntax alone), but, following Tarski, it may also be viewed from the point of view of model theory (i.e. from the point of view of an interpretation, in which meanings are assigned to the formal symbols of the system). Given a set, S, of well-formed formulas, an interpretation consists of a non-empty set (or domain), together with a function which:

1   assigns to each individual constant found in members of S an element of the domain;
2   assigns to each n-place predicate found in members of S an n-place relation between members of the domain;
3   assigns to each n-place function-name found in members of S a function whose arguments are n-tuples of elements of the domain and whose values are also elements of the domain;

suitable for expressing the type of formal inferences used in mathematical proofs. By combining expressions representing individuals and predicates (properties and relations) with the propositional connectives ('and', 'or', 'not', etc.) and quantifiers ('all', 'some'), Frege succeeded in producing a language powerful enough to express even the most complicated of mathematical statements. Frege immediately put his language to work, applying it as he did to his project of logicizing arithmetic. By the time his *Die Grundlagen der Arithmetik* appeared in 1884, Frege had arrived at the appropriate logical definitions for the necessary arithmetical terms and had begun work on the essential derivations. The derivations themselves appeared in his two-volume *Grundgesetze der Arithmetik* in 1893 and 1903. Thus, it is Frege, along with Boole, who is generally credited as being one of the two most important founders of modern formal logic.

The *Begriffsschrift* was Frege's first work in logic, but it is a landmark one, for in it he develops the truth-functional propositional calculus, the theory of quantification (or predicate calculus), an analysis of propositions in terms of functions and arguments (instead of in terms of subject and predicate), a definition of the notion of mathematical sequence and the notion of a purely formal system of derivation or inference. Of these contributions, Frege's unique insight with regard to the predicate calculus was to note the inadequacy of the traditional subject/predicate distinction, and to replace it with one from mathematics, that of function and argument. For Frege, once arguments have been substituted into the free variables of a propositional function, a judgement is obtained. In short, a word in a statement which can be replaced by other words is itself an argument, while the remainder of the sentence is the function. The fact that the *Begriffsschrift* additionally contains the first formally adequate notation for quantification, together with the first successful formalization of first-order logic, has guaranteed it a position of unique importance in the history of logic.

Unfortunately, for much of his life, Frege's work was met with indifference or hostility on the part of his contemporaries. Response to the *Begriffsschrift* was typified by a rather caustic review by Cantor, who had not even bothered to read the book. Frege's axioms for the propositional calculus (which use negation and material implication as primitive connectives) turned out not to be independent and, in addition to his one stated rule of inference, detachment (also called *modus ponens*, the rule that given well-formed formulas of the form p and $p \rightarrow q$, one can infer a well-formed formula of the form q), an unstated rule of substitution was also used. However, the most important reason for the *Begriffsschrift*'s poor reception was the difficulty of working with Frege's rather idiosyncratic and cumbersome logical notation, which has not survived. Thus, it was not until others were able to and

4 assigns to each sentence letter a truth value.

Logical constants, such as those representing truth functions and quantifiers, are assigned standard meanings using rules (such as truth tables) which specify how well-formed formulas containing them are to be evaluated. Any interpretation that satisfies the axioms of the system is called a model.

Among the most influential of formal systems to be developed were of course those associated with Frege's propositional and predicate logics. Propositional (or sentential) logic may thus be defined as a formal system or logical calculus which analyses truth-functional relations between propositions (sentences or statements). Any such system is based upon a set of propositional (sentential or statement) constants and connectives (or operators) which are combined in various ways to produce propositions of greater complexity. Standard connectives include those representing negation ($\sim$), conjunction (&), (inclusive) disjunction ($\lor$), material implication ($\to$), and material equivalence ($\longleftrightarrow$). A standard axiomatization consists of several definitions (including the definitions that $p \to q =_{df} \sim p \lor q$, that $p \ \& \ q =_{df} \sim(\sim p \lor \sim q)$, and that $p \longleftrightarrow q =_{df} (p \to q) \ \& \ (q \to p)$), the rules of substitution and detachment, and the following axioms:

1 $(p \lor p) \to p$
2 $q \to (p \lor q)$
3 $(p \lor q) \to (q \lor p)$
4 $(q \to r) \to ((p \lor q) \to (p \lor r))$.

Similarly, Hilbert's positive propositional calculus (which contains all and only those theorems of the classical calculus which are independent of negation), Heyting's intuitionistic propositional calculus (which uses intuitionistic, rather than classical, negation), the several systems of modal logic introduced by C. I. Lewis (1883–1964), and many-valued logics, such as those introduced by Jan Łukasiewicz (1878–1956), are all examples of propositional logics. (As Łukasiewicz also pointed out, logics such as the standard propositional calculus may be reformulated, using so-called Polish notation, in such a way as to avoid the need for scope indicators such as parentheses; thus, letting N represent negation, K represent conjunction, A represent disjunction (or alternation), R represent exclusive disjunction, C represent material implication, E represent material equivalence, L represent necessity, and M represent possibility, sentences such as $\sim(p \to (p \ \& \ q))$ and $\square(p \to p)$ may be represented as $NCpKpq$ and $LCpp$, respectively.)

Like propositional logic, predicate logic may also be defined as a formal system or logical calculus, but one which analyses the relations between individuals and predicates within propositions, in addition to the truth-functional relations between propositions which are analysed within propositional logic. Each such system is based upon a set of individual and predicate (or functional) constants, individual (and some-time predicate) variables, and quantifiers (such as $\exists$ and $\forall$) which range over (some of) these variables, in addition to the standard constants and connectives of the propositional calculus. A standard axiomatization of first-order predicate logic can thus be viewed as an extension of the propositional calculus. One such axiomatization consists of the formulas and inference rules of the propositional calculus, together with the rule of universal generalization (that if A is a theorem, so is $(\forall a)A$) and the following axiom schemata:

1   If A is a uniform substitution instance of a valid well-formed formula of propositional logic (i.e. a formula obtained from a valid formula of propositional logic by uniformly replacing every variable in it by some well-formed formula of the first-order predicate calculus), then A is an axiom;

2   If a is an individual variable, A any well-formed formula, and B any well-formed formula differing from A only in having some individual variable b replacing every free occurrence of a in A, then $(\forall a)A \rightarrow B$ is an axiom, provided that a does not occur within the scope of any occurrence of a quantifier containing b;

3   $(\forall a)(A \rightarrow B) \rightarrow (A \rightarrow (\forall a)B)$, provided a is not free in A.

Other predicate logics include second-order logic (also called the second-order predicate or functional calculus), higher-order logics, in which quantifiers and functions range over predicate (or functional) variables and/or constants of the system, and modal (and other) extensions of both first- and higher-order logics. When the set of individual or predicate constants is empty, a predicate calculus is said to be pure; otherwise it is said to be applied.

With propositional and predicate logic formalized, the systematic metalogical study of formal properties of logical systems, and the investigation of informal, philosophical problems resulting from such results, began to develop. Among the most important metalogical results to be proved at the level of propositional logic are the completeness and soundness results (which show, respectively, that all valid formulas are theorems of the system and that all theorems of the system are valid formulas), the deduction theorem (which states that, if there is a proof from '$s_1, s_2, \ldots, s_n$' to 's_{n+1}', then there is also a proof from '$s_1, s_2, \ldots, s_{n-1}$' to 'if s_n then s_{n+1}'), and the decidability result (which shows that there is an effective, mechanical decision procedure – such as truth tables – for determining the validity of any arbitrary formula of the system).

Among the metatheorems proved for first-order logic are similar completeness and soundness results, Tarski's theorem concerning the undefinability of (arithmetical) truth, and the now famous Löwenheim–Skolem theorems. These are a family of metatheoretical results proved by Löwenheim in 1915, and extended by Skolem in 1920 and 1922, to the effect that if there is an interpretation in which an enumerable set of sentences is satisfiable in an enumerably infinite domain then the set is also satisfiable in every infinite domain and, similarly, that if there is an interpretation in which a set of sentences is satisfiable in a non-empty domain then it is also satisfiable in an enumerably infinite domain. This latter theorem gives rise to the so-called 'Skolem's paradox', the unintuitive (but ultimately non-contradictory) result that systems for which Cantor's theorem is provable, and hence which must contain non-denumerable sets, nevertheless must be satisfiable in a (smaller) enumerably infinite domain.

Despite such impressive results, Hilbert's goal of discovering a consistency proof for arithmetic remained elusive. The explanation came with a paper published by Gödel in 1931. Today Gödel is remembered for several important results, any one of which would have given him a position of importance in the history of logic. Most famously, these included his proofs of the completeness and compactness of first-order logic in 1930, and the incompleteness of arithmetic in 1931. They also include results in constructive logic in 1932 and computation theory in 1933, as well as his 1938 proof that the continuum hypothesis is consistent with the Zermelo–Fraenkel axioms of set theory – in other words, that the usual axioms of set theory could never prove the continuum hypothesis false. (That the negation of the continuum hypothesis is also consistent with the Zermelo–Fraenkel axioms of set theory, and hence that the hypothesis is independent of the standard axiomatization for set theory, was proved twenty-five years later by Paul Cohen (b. 1934).)

Of these results, several require further comment. It was in Gödel's 1930 doctoral dissertation at the University of Vienna that the completeness of the first-order predicate calculus was proved for the first time. Completeness is the property that every valid formula of the system is provable within the system. This turns out to be equivalent to the claim that every formula is either refutable or satisfiable. Building on the results of Löwenheim and Skolem, Gödel succeeded in proving a result slightly stronger than this, a result which also entails the Löwenheim–Skolem theorem. Gödel then generalized his result to first-order logic with identity and to infinite sets of formulas. At the same time Gödel proved the compactness theorem for first-order logic, which states that any collection of well-formed formulas of a given language has a model if every finite subset of the collection has a model.

Equally famous, however, are Gödel's two theorems relating to the incompleteness of systems of elementary number theory. The first of these two theorems states that any ω-consistent system adequate for expressing elementary number theory is incomplete, in the sense that there is a valid well-formed formula of the system that is not provable within the system. (A formal system is ω-consistent if whenever it has as theorems that a given property, P, holds of all individual natural numbers, then it fails to have as a theorem that P fails to hold of all numbers.) In 1936 this theorem was extended by J. B. Rosser (b. 1907) to apply, not just to any ω-consistent system, but to any consistent system of the relevant sort. The second theorem states that no consistent system adequate for expressing elementary number theory may contain a proof of a sentence known to state the system's consistency. Hence, the difficulty in resolving Hilbert's second problem.

Received by the publisher on 17 November 1930 but published the following year, Gödel's theorems were proved in what is, together with *Principia Mathematica*, one of the two most famous logical works of the current century: 'Über Formal Unentscheidbare Sätze der *Principia Mathematica* und Verwandter Systeme I' ('On Formally Undecidable Propositions of *Principia Mathematica* and Related Systems I'). The system Gödel uses is equivalent to the logic of Whitehead and Russell's *Principia Mathematica* without the ramified theory of types but supplemented by the arithmetical axioms of Peano. (A corollary shows that even supplemented by the axiom of choice or the continuum hypothesis, the system still contains undecidable propositions.)

By introducing his famous system of 'Gödel numbering', Gödel assigns natural numbers to sequences of signs and sequences of sequences of signs within the system. This is done in such a way that, given any sequence, the number assigned to it can be effectively calculated, and given any number, it can be effectively determined whether a sequence is assigned to it and, if so, what it is. Metamathematical predicates used to describe the system in this way can be correlated with number-theoretic predicates. For example, the metamathematical notion of being an axiom can be expressed using the predicate $Ax(x)$, which in turn corresponds to exactly those Gödel numbers, x, which are correlated to the axioms of the system. Referring to the set of axioms can then be accomplished simply by referring to this set of Gödel numbers.

Theorem VI of Gödel's 1931 paper states that in a formal system of the specified kind there exists an undecidable proposition (that is, a proposition such that neither it nor its negation is provable within the system). It is this theorem which is commonly referred to as Gödel's first incompleteness theorem (G1). In addition to proving G1, Gödel also proves several other corollaries: for example, that among the propositions whose validity is undecidable are both arithmetic propositions (Theorem VIII) and formulas of pure first-order logic (Theorem IX), and that a statement which expresses the consistency of the system and which can be written as a formula in the system is itself among those formulas not provable in the system (Theorem XI). It is this last theorem, Theorem XI, which is commonly referred to as Gödel's second incompleteness theorem (G2). Both of Gödel's incompleteness theorems required that logicians and mathematicians view formal systems of arithmetic in a new light.

⤳ FROM GÖDEL TO FRIEDMAN ⤳

Hilbert's programme in effect had two main goals concerning the foundations of mathematics. The first was descriptive, the second justificatory. The descriptive goal was to be achieved by means of the complete formalization of mathematics. The justificatory goal was to be achieved by means of a finitary (and hence epistemologically acceptable) proof of the reliability of those essential but non-finitary (and hence epistemologically more suspect) parts of mathematics. Work by both formalists and logicists during the first two decades of the century had effectively accomplished the former of these two goals. Ideally a finitary consistency proof would accomplish the latter.

Gödel's second incompleteness theorem, G2, is often thought relevant to Hilbert's programme for just this reason. Specifically, it is often claimed that G2 implies three philosophically significant corollaries: first, that any consistency proof for a theory, T, of which G2 holds will have to rely upon methods logically more powerful than those of theory T itself; second, that (in any significant case) a consistency proof for theory T can yield no epistemological gain and so cannot provide a satisfactory answer to the sceptic regarding T's consistency; and third, that as a result of this, G2, if not strictly implying the outright failure of Hilbert's programme, at the very least indicates that significant modifications to it are needed. All three of these 'corollaries' are controversial.[11] In fact, Gödel himself explicitly makes the point that the truth of G2 should not be viewed, by itself, as sufficient reason for abandoning Hilbert's goal of discovering a finitary consistency proof:

> I wish to note expressly that Theorem XI (and the corresponding results for M and A) do not contradict Hilbert's formalistic viewpoint. For this viewpoint presupposes only the existence of

a consistency proof in which nothing but finitary means of proof is used, and it is conceivable that there exist finitary proofs that *cannot* be expressed in the formalism of P (or of M or A).[12]

Nevertheless, the formalists themselves drew the moral that radical changes to their programme were required; thus, the 1936 consistency proof by Gerhard Gentzen (1909–45) required the use of transfinite induction up to the ordinal ε_0.

Other consequences also followed. Among them was a renewed interest in the problem of decidability, the problem of finding an effective, finite, mechanical, decision procedure (or algorithm) for determining whether an arbitrary, well-formed formula of a system is in fact a theorem of the system. A positive solution to such a problem is a proof that an effective procedure exists. A negative solution is a proof that an effective procedure does not exist. By 1931 it was already well known that a positive solution existed in the case of propositional logic, that a decision procedure existed in the form of truth tables for determining whether an arbitrary formula was a tautology. However, in 1936 Church proved that there could be no such decision procedure for validity (or equivalently, for semantic entailment) in first-order logic.

Church proved that there does exist a decision procedure for determining that valid first-order sentences are valid. However, at the same time he also proved that there is no corresponding procedure for showing of sentences which are not valid that they are not valid. In other words, although there is an effective, finite, mechanical, positive test for first-order validity, there is, and can be, no such negative test. Thus, given an arbitrary first-order sentence, there can be no effective, finite, mechanical decision procedure for determining whether or not it is valid.

Central to Church's theorem was the idea of computability. Intuitively, a computable function may be said to be any function for which there exists an effective decision procedure or algorithm for calculating a solution. Several suggestions were offered as a means of making this notion more precise, not only by Gödel and Church, but by Emil Post (1897–1954) and Alan Turing (1912–54) as well. One such precise suggestion was to identify effective computability with that given by a Turing machine; another was to identify it with a series of functions identifiable in the lambda calculus; yet a third was to identify it with that of a general recursive function. Perhaps surprisingly, all three notions turned out to be equivalent. As a result, the thesis of identifying computability with the mathematically precise notion of general recursiveness became known alternatively as Church's thesis or the Church–Turing thesis.

Intuitively, a Turing machine can be thought of as a computer which manipulates information contained on a linear tape (which is infinite in both directions) according to a series of instructions. More formally, the machine can be thought of as a set of ordered quintuples, $\langle q_i, S_i, S_j, I_i, q_j \rangle$, where q_i is the current state of the machine, S_i is the symbol currently being read on the tape, S_j is the symbol with which the machine replaces S_i, I_i is an instruction to move the tape one unit to the right, to the left, or to remain where it is, and q_j is the machine's next state. From this rather impoverished set of operations it turns out that a wide range of functions are computable. It also turns out that the decision problem for first-order validity is capable of being modelled via Turing machines since, by assigning unique numbers to first-order sentences, there will be a function which returns 1 if given a number representing a valid sentence and 0 otherwise. The question of whether this function is finitely and mechanically calculable turns out to be equivalent to the so-called halting problem, the problem of discovering an effective procedure for determining whether the appropriate Turing machine will ever halt, given arbitrary input. Church's theorem is equivalent to the result that such a function is not finitely and mechanically calculable.

Equivalent classes of functions turned out to be identifiable in the lambda calculus and in recursion theory. The former gains its name from the notation used to name functions. Terms such as '$f(x)$' or the 'successor of y' are used to refer to objects obtained from x or y by the appropriate functions. To refer to the functions themselves, Church introduced a notation which yields, respectively, '$(\lambda x)(f(x))$' and '(λy) (successor of y)'. Having done so, he then identified a class of functions which turned out to be identical to both the Turing computable functions and the recursive functions.

The latter may be defined as a set of functions whose members are said to be either primitive recursive or general recursive, and which are themselves constructed from a set of more fundamental functions by a series of fixed procedures.

Specifically, a *constant* function is a function that yields the same value for all arguments. A *successor* function is a function that yields as its value the successor of its argument, for example, $s(1) = 2$, $s(35) = 36$. An *identity* function of n arguments is a function that yields as its value the ith of its n arguments. Together, the constant, successor and identity functions are called the *fundamental* functions.

In addition, given a set of functions h_i, each, of n arguments, a new function, f, of n arguments is defined by *composition* such that the value of the new function is equal to the value of a previously introduced function, g, whose arguments are the values of each of the members of the original set of functions when their arguments are the arguments of the newly introduced function. In other words, if f

is being defined by composition and $g, h_1, \ldots h_m$ are previously defined functions, then $f(x_1, \ldots, x_n) = g(h_1(x_1, \ldots, x_n), \ldots, h_m(x_1, \ldots, x_n))$.

Similarly, a new function, f, of n arguments is defined by *primitive recursion* as follows: first, if a designated argument is 0, then f is defined in terms of a previously defined function, g, of $n-1$ arguments whose arguments are taken to be exactly those of f except for the designated argument, 0. In other words, if f is being defined by recursion and g is a previously defined function, then $f(x_1, \ldots, x_{n-1}, 0) = g(x_1, \ldots, x_n)$. Second, if the designated argument is not 0, and is instead the successor, $c+1$, of some number, c, then f is defined in terms of a previously defined function, g, of $n+1$ arguments whose arguments are taken to be exactly those of f except for the designated argument, $c+1$, together with c and the value of f when its arguments are exactly those arguments already given for g. In other words, if f is being defined by recursion and g is a previously defined function, then $f(x_1, \ldots, x_{n-1}, c+1) = g(x_1, \ldots, x_{n-1}, c, f(x, \ldots, x_{n-1}, c))$.

Any function which is either a fundamental function or can be obtained from the fundamental functions by a finite number of applications of composition and primitive recursion is then said to be a *primitive recursive* function.

Next, a new function, f, of n arguments is defined by *minimization* such that its value (whenever it exists) is the least c such that, given a previously defined function, g, whose arguments are exactly the arguments of f together with c, g has the value 0. If there is no such c, then f remains undefined for those arguments. In other words, if f is being defined by minimization and g is a previously defined function, then $f(x_1, \ldots, x_n) = $ the least c such that $g(x_1, \ldots, x_n, c) = 0$, provided that there exists some c; otherwise f is undefined.

Any function which is either a fundamental function or can be obtained from the fundamental functions by a finite number of applications of composition, primitive recursion, and minimization is then said to be a *general recursive* (or simply *recursive*) function.

Examples of recursive functions include familiar arithmetical operations such as addition, multiplication, and others. Thus, letting z refer to the zero function (a constant function which yields the value zero), s the successor function, id_i^n an identity function of n arguments which yields its ith argument as its value, Cn composition, and Pr primitive recursion, such functions can be defined as follows:

1   for sum, where $sum(x, y) = x + y$, we let
     $sum = Pr[id, Cn[s, id_3^3]]$
     or, more intuitively, $x + 0 = x$ and $x + s(y) = s(x + y)$
2   for product, where $prod(x, y) = x \cdot y$, we let
     $prod = Pr[z, Cn[sum, id_1^3, id_3^3]]$

or, more intuitively, $x \cdot 0 = 0$ and $x \cdot s(y) = x + (x \cdot y)$

3 for exponentiation, where $exp(x, y) = x^y$, we let
$$exp = Pr[Cn[s, z], Cn[prod, id_1^3, id_3^3]]$$
or, more intuitively, $x^0 = 1$ and $x^{s(y)} = x \cdot x^y$

4 for factorial, where $fac(y) = y!$, we let
$$fac = Pr[s(0), Cn[prod, Cn[s, id_1^2], id_2^2]]$$
or, more intuitively, $0! = 1$ and $s(y)! = s(y) \cdot y!$.

The proved identification of the class of recursive functions with the other two classes of functions thought to express the intuitive concept of computability lent strong support to the Church–Turing thesis.

Having observed both the incompleteness of first-order theories of arithmetic and the undecidability of first-order validity, questions naturally turned to other issues relating to computability. One such issue is that of computational complexity. Another concerns the extent and nature of arithmetical incompleteness. Recently, advances have been made in both of these areas.

The computational complexity of a problem is a measure of the computational resources required to solve the problem. In this context, the distinction is made between problems solvable by polynomial-time algorithms and problems which, if solvable, have solutions which are testable in polynomial time but which, if not solvable, do not. Problems of the former kind are said to be members of the class of problems P, while problems of the latter kind are members of the class NP. Those problems in NP which are measurably the hardest to solve are said to be NP-complete. Today the problem of whether P = NP remains open. Nevertheless, in 1971 Stephen Cook (b. 1939) proved that the problem of satisfiability (the problem of determining, given an arbitrary set of sentences, whether it is possible for all of the sentences to be jointly true) is at least as difficult to solve as is any NP-complete problem [1.87]. The result is important since it unifies the class of NP-complete problems in a way that was unappreciated prior to 1971.

Similarly, advances have been made concerning the extent and nature of arithmetical incompleteness. Chief among these are the 1981 independence results of Harvey Friedman (b. 1948) [1.58]. Friedman's contributions include the discovery of a series of mathematically natural propositions (concerning Borel functions of several variables) that are undecidable, not just in ZFC, but in the much stronger system of ZFC together with the axiom of constructibility, $V = L$, as well. This is important not simply because such propositions are of a level of abstraction significantly lower than previous results, but because virtually all propositions previously thought to have been undecidable have been made decidable by the addition of the axiom of constructibility to *ZFC*. Importantly, Friedman has also shown that some of these propositions, although undecidable in *ZFC*, are decidable in a competing theory, Morse–Kelly class theory with choice. Such results are important since they indicate in what ways competing axiomatizations of set theory in fact differ.

❧ THE EXPANSION OF LOGIC ❧

As long ago as Galen (*c.* 129–*c.* 199) it was recognized that some sound arguments could not adequately be analysed in terms of either Aristotelian or Stoic logic. For example, neither the argument 'if Sophroniscus is father to Socrates, then Socrates is son to Sophroniscus', nor the argument 'if Theon has twice as much as Dio, and Philo twice as much as Theon, then Philo has four times as much as Dio' is provably valid in such systems.[13] Thus, modern first-order logic can be viewed as a means of extending the ancient idea of formal validity, since it successfully displays many formally valid inferences which ancient logic fails to capture.

One way of understanding the advent of contemporary non-classical and informal logics is to view them in much the same way. Such logics regularly attempt to describe, in a systematic way, additional types of reliable inference not captured in classical first-order logic. They do so in two ways: first, *extensions* of classical logic attempt to exhibit reliable forms of inference in addition to those displayed in first-order logic much as first-order logic exhibits reliable forms of inference in addition to those displayed in ancient logic or in modern propositional logic. Second, *competitors* to classical logic advocate alternative ways of understanding the idea of valid inference itself, rejecting in one way or another the concept of validity as it is described in first-order logic.

Among the most philosophically interesting of the competitors to classical logic are intuitionistic logics, relevance logics and paraconsistent logics. Of these, intuitionistic logics were the first to appear. Motivated by the intuitionistic idea that satisfactory proofs must refer only to entities which can be successfully constructed or discovered, intuitionist logic requires that we find examples, or that we find algorithms for finding examples, of each object or set of objects referred to in a proof. Formalized by Heyting, intuitionistic logic therefore abandons those forms of classical proof (including indirect proof) which do not contain the appropriate constructions. A standard axiomatization consists of rules for substitution and detachment, together with the following axioms:

1    $p \rightarrow (p \wedge p)$
2    $(p \wedge q) \rightarrow (q \wedge p)$
3    $(p \rightarrow q) \rightarrow ((p \wedge r) \rightarrow (q \wedge r))$
4    $((p \rightarrow q) \wedge (q \rightarrow r)) \rightarrow (p \rightarrow r)$
5    $q \rightarrow (p \rightarrow q)$
6    $(p \wedge (p \rightarrow q)) \rightarrow q$
7    $p \rightarrow (p \vee q)$
8    $(p \vee q) \rightarrow (q \vee p)$
9    $((p \rightarrow r) \wedge (q \rightarrow r)) \rightarrow ((p \vee q) \rightarrow r)$
10    $\neg p \rightarrow (p \rightarrow q)$
11    $((p \rightarrow q) \wedge (p \rightarrow \neg q)) \rightarrow \neg p.$

It follows in Heyting's logic that the sentence '$p \vee \neg p$' is not a theorem and that inferences, such as those from '$\neg \neg p$' to 'p' and from '$\neg (\forall x)Fx$' to '$(\exists x)\neg Fx$', are not allowed.

Like intuitionistic logic, relevance logic is a competitor to classical logic which emphasizes a non-classical consequence relation. Like intuitionistic logic, too, relevance logic results from a dissatisfaction with the classical consequence relation. Developed by Alan Ross Anderson (1925–73), Nuel Belnap (b. 1930) and others, the logic stresses entailments which involve connections of relevance between premisses and conclusions, rather than simple classical derivability conditions. It is intended that the relevance consequence relation thereby avoids both the paradoxes of material implication and the paradoxes of strict implication. (The former involve the unintuitive but, strictly speaking, non-contradictory results to the effect that whenever the antecedent is false or the consequent is true in a material implication, the resulting implication will be true, regardless of content; the latter involve the unintuitive, but likewise non-contradictory, results that a necessary proposition is strictly implied by any proposition and that an impossible proposition strictly implies all propositions, regardless of content. Following Lewis's 1912 definition, one sentence, p, is said to strictly imply a second sentence, q, if and only if it is not possible that both p and $\sim q$.)

As it is normally formalized, relevance logic turns out to be a type of paraconsistent logic. Such logics tolerate, but do not encourage, inconsistencies. They do so in the sense that a contradiction (the joint assertion of a proposition and its denial) may be contained within the system; at the same time they are consistent in the sense that not every well-formed formula is a theorem. One example of such a logic (as in [1.146]), which is not a relevance logic, may be outlined as follows: Let $M = \langle W, R, w^{*}, v \rangle$ be a semantic interpretation of a formal system, with W an index set of possible worlds, w_i, R a binary relation on W, w^{*} the actual world, and v a valuation of the propositional constants, i.e. a map from W×P (with P the set of propositional constants) into {{1}, {o}, {1, o}}, the set of truth values. (More naturally, we write $v(w, \alpha) = x$ as $v_w(\alpha) = x$ and read '$1 \in v_w(\alpha)$' as 'α is true under v at w' and '$o \in v_w(\alpha)$' as 'α is false under v at w'.) Valuation v can then be extended to all well-formed formulas as follows:

$\neg$ $1 \in v_w \ (\neg\alpha)$ iff $o \in v_w(\alpha)$
          $o \in v_w \ (\neg\alpha)$ iff $1 \in v_w(\alpha)$

$\wedge$ $1 \in v_w \ (\alpha) \wedge \beta)$ iff $1 \in v_w(\alpha)$ and $1 \in v_w \ (\beta)$
          $o \in v_w \ (\alpha) \wedge \beta)$ iff $o \in v_w \ (\alpha)$ or $o \in v_w \ (\beta)$

$\vee$ $1 \in v_w \ (\alpha \vee \beta)$ iff $1 \in v_w \ (\alpha)$ or $1 \in v_w(\beta)$
          $o \in v_w \ (\alpha \vee \beta)$ iff $o \in v_w \ (\alpha)$ and $o \in v_w \ (\beta)$

$\rightarrow$ $1 \in v_w \ (\alpha \rightarrow \beta)$ iff for all w_i such that $w_i R w$,
          if $1 \in v_{w_i} \ (\alpha)$ then $1 \in v_{w_i}(\beta)$, and
          if $o \in v_{w_i} \ (\beta)$ then $o \in v_{w_i}(\alpha)$
          $o \in v_w \ (\alpha \rightarrow \beta)$ iff for some w_i such that $w_i R w$,
          $1 \in v_{w_i}(\alpha)$ and $o \in v_{w_i}(\beta)$.

Definitions of semantic consequence and logical truth are then introduced in the standard way:

$\Sigma \models \alpha$ iff for all interpretations, M, it is true of the evaluation, v, that

if $1 \in v(\beta)$ for all $\beta \in \Sigma$, then $1 \in v(\alpha)$.

$\models \alpha$ iff for all interpretations, M, it is true of the evaluation, v, that

$1 \in v(\alpha)$.

Given these semantics, some rules of inference, such as disjunctive syllogism (P $\vee$ Q, $\neg$ P $\vdash$ Q), fail. As a result, the logic turns out to be paraconsistent in just the sense outlined above.

Other competing logics include combinatory logic (a variable-free branch of logic which contains functions capable of playing the role of variables in ordinary logic); free logics (logics in which it is not assumed that names successfully refer, hence logics which do not make the kind of existence assumptions normally associated with classical logic); many-valued logics (logics which countenance more than the two possible classical truth values, truth and falsity; historically, such logics have been motivated by the problem of future contingents, the problem first raised by Aristotle but popularized by Łukasiewicz of determining whether contingent statements concerning future states have truth values prior to the time to which they refer); and quantum logics (logics designed to take account of the unusual entailment relations between propositions in theories of contemporary quantum physics; hence, a logic in which the law of distributivity fails).

In contrast to the above logics, extensions of first-order logic typically have as their goal the construction of a broader, more inclusive type of consequence relation than that found in classical logic. Formal extensions, such as modal extensions of both propositional and predicate logic, do so by expanding the concept of formal entailment to include a class of formally valid arguments in addition to those of first-order logic. In contrast, informal extensions do so by expanding the concept of validity to include informal (or material) validity in addition to formal validity. Finally, inductive or non-monotonic extensions do so by expanding the concept of consequence to include, not just entailments, but implications, corroborations, and confirmations as well. Thus it is that logic (in the broad sense) has come to include, not just theories of formal entailment relations, but probability theory, confirmation theory, decision theory, game theory and theories of epistemic modelling as well.

Among the most important extensions to classical logic are the modal extensions. These are extensions emphasizing inferential relations resulting from the alethic modalities, including necessity, possibility, impossibility and contingency. Such logics are obtained from classical propositional or predicate logic by the addition of axioms and rules of inference governing operators such as $\Box$ and $\Diamond$ in '$\Box p$' ('it is necessary that p') and '$\Diamond p$' ('it is possible that p'). The weakest logic generally thought to count as a modal logic in this sense is a logic introduced by Robert Feys (b. 1889) in 1937, system T. A standard axiomatization consists of the axioms and rules of inference for classical propositional logic, together with several definitions (including the definition that $\Diamond p =_{df} \sim\Box\sim p$), the rule of necessitation (to the effect that if p is a theorem, so is $\Box p$), and the following axioms:

1    $\Box p \rightarrow p$
2    $\Box (p \rightarrow q) \rightarrow (\Box p \rightarrow \Box q)$.

Additional modal systems, including the 1932 systems $S1$ to $S5$, introduced by Lewis and C. H. Langford (1895–1964), are normally developed as extensions of T[1.37]. Since a formula, p, is said to strictly imply another formula, q, if and only if it is not possible that both p and $\sim q$, modal logics may be viewed either extensionally as a type of many-valued logic or intensionally as a theory of strict implication. The standard possible world semantics for such logics (in which a proposition is necessary if and only if it is true in all possible worlds, impossible if and only if it is true in no possible world, possible if and only if it is true in at least one possible world, and so on) was developed by Saul Kripke (b. 1940).

Like modal logics, epistemic logics (logics emphasizing inferential relations and entailments which result from epistemic properties of sentences) may be obtained from classical propositional or predicate logic by the addition of axioms and rules of inference governing operators such as K and B in 'Kp' ('it is known that p') and 'Bp' ('it is believed that p'). Similarly, deontic logics (logics emphasizing inferential relations and entailments which result from deontic properties of sentences) may be obtained by the addition of axioms and rules of inference governing operators such as O and P in 'Op' ('it ought to be the case that p') and 'Pp' ('it is permissible that p').

Other extensions include counterfactual logics (logics which are primarily concerned with conditional sentences containing false antecedents); erotetic or interrogative logics (logics emphasizing inferential relations and entailments pertaining to questions and answers); fuzzy logics (logics concerned with imprecise information, such as information conveyed through vague predicates or information associated with so-called fuzzy sets, sets in which membership is a matter of degree); imperative logics (logics emphasizing inferential relations and entailments which result from imperatives); mereology (the formal study of inferences and entailments which result from the relationship of whole and part); theories of multigrade connectives (logics whose connectives fail to take a fixed number of arguments); plurality, pleonotetic or plurative logics (logics emphasizing inferential relations and entailments pertaining to relations of quantity and involving plurality quantifiers such as 'most' and 'few'); preference logics (logics emphasizing inferential relations and entailments which result from preferences); second-order and higher-order logics (logics carried out in higher-order languages in which quantifiers and functions are allowed to range over properties and functions as well as over individual i.e. individuals); and tense or temporal logics (logics designed to be sensitive to the tense of sentences and to the changing truth values of sentences over time).

In contrast to the above logics, informal logic is the study of arguments whose validity (or inductive strength) depends upon the material content, rather than the form or structure, of their component statements or propositions. (The logical form of a sentence or argument is obtained by making explicit the expression's logical constants and then by substituting free variables for its non-logical constants; logical form is thus typically contrasted with the material content – or subject matter – of the non-logical constants for which the free variables are substituted.) Such logics are extensions of formal logic in that they recognize the significance of formal validity, but also recognize the existence of valid arguments which are not instances of valid argument forms. Thus the argument from 'If Hume is a male parent then Hume is a father' and 'Hume is a father' to 'Hume is a male parent', although valid, is not formally so. In fact, far from being formally valid, it is an instance of the invalid argument form of affirming the consequent.

Since all so-called invalid argument forms have valid arguments as uniform substitution instances, the claim is made that formal character-izations alone will never be able to capture completely the concepts of either validity or invalidity.

Finally, mention should be made of formal systems which expand the traditional consequence relation by weakening it to a relation which is less than that of a valid inference. Such systems include inductive and non-monotonic logics, as well as theories of probability and con-firmation. All such systems are concerned with so-called ampliative arguments, arguments whose conclusions in some important sense go beyond the information contained in their premises. Such arguments are defeasible in the sense that their premises fail to provide conclusive evidence for their conclusions and, hence, allow for the later overturn-ing or revision of a conclusion. Ampliative arguments include both inductive inferences and inferences to the best explanation. They may be either acceptable or unacceptable depending upon their (inductive or probabilistic) strength or weakness. Similarly, confirmation theories evaluate the degree to which evidence supports (or confirms) a given hypothesis, emphasizing the rational degree of confidence that a cogni-tive agent should have in favour of a hypothesis given some body of evidence.

Such theories are typically (but not always) based upon prob-ability theory, the mathematical theory of the acceptability of a state-ment or proposition, or of its likelihood. The standard account, first axiomatized in 1933 by Andrej Kolmogorov (b. 1903) [1.160], can be summarized as follows: Given sentences s and t, probability is a real-valued function, Pr, such that

1 $Pr(s) \geq 0$,
2 $Pr(t) = 1$, if t is a tautology
3 $Pr(s \vee t) = Pr(s) + Pr(t)$, provided that s and t are mutually exclusive (i.e. $\sim(s \,\&\, t)$)
4 $Pr(s|t) = Pr\,(s \,\&\, t)/Pr(s)$, provided that $Pr(s) \neq 0$.

Default logics, which permit the acceptance or rejection of certain types of default inferences in the absence of information to the contrary, provide one type of non-monotonic alternative to probabilistic theories.

Defeasible theories often give rise to so-called 'applied logics', including theories of belief revision and theories of practical rationality. Theories of belief revision (for example in [1.123]) are typically designed in such a way as to model changes in one's belief set which come about both as a result of the acceptance of new beliefs and the revision of old beliefs. Thus, if K is a consistent belief set closed under logical consequence, then for any well-formed sentence, S, one of the following three cases will obtain:

1   S is accepted, i.e. $S \in K$ (and $\sim S \notin K$);
2   S is rejected, i.e. $\sim S \in K$ (and $S \notin K$); or
3   S is indetermined, i.e. $S \notin K$ and $\sim S \notin K$.

Epistemic changes may then be of any of the following three types:

1   Expansions: given that S is indetermined, either accept S (and its consequences) or accept $\sim S$ (and its consequences);
2   Contractions: given that S is accepted (or that $\sim S$ is accepted, i.e. S is rejected), conclude that S is indetermined;
3   Revisions: given that S is accepted (or that $\sim S$ is accepted, i.e. S is rejected), conclude that S is rejected (or that $\sim S$ is rejected, i.e. S is accepted).

Theories of practical rationality (for example in [1.159]) typically include both decision theory (the theory of choice selection under various conditions of risk and uncertainty, given that each option has associated with it an expected probability distribution of outcomes, gains and losses), and game theory (the theory of choice selection by two or more agents or players when the outcome is a function, not just of one's own choice or strategy, but of the choices or strategies of other agents as well). Such theories may be either bounded or not, depending upon whether they take account of possible cognitive limitations of the decision-makers.

～ NOTES ～

1 [1.44], vii.
2 Quoted in [1.84], 2.
3 [1.94], 85.
4 [1.183], 1, 7.
5 [1.194], 1: 217–18.
6 [1.194], 1: 219.
7 Much the same difficulty is outlined by Cantor in a 1899 letter to Dedekind (1899).
8 Quoted in [1.84], 125.
9 Quoted in [1.84], 127.
10 Or perhaps equivalently, that no collection can be definable only in terms of itself. See [1.77], in [1.197], 63.
11 For example, see [1.177].
12 [1.65], in [1.62], 1: 195.
13 [1.35], 185.

❦ BIBLIOGRAPHY ❦

Logic Journals

1.1   *Annals of Mathematical Logic*
1.2   *Annals of Pure and Applied Logic*
1.3   *Archive for Mathematical Logic*
1.4   *Argumentation*
1.5   *Bulletin of Symbolic Logic*
1.6   *History and Philosophy of Logic*
1.7   *Informal Logic*
1.8   *Journal of Logic and Computation*
1.9   *Journal of Logic, Language and Information*
1.10 *Journal of Logic Programming*
1.11 *Journal of Philosophical Logic*
1.12 *Journal of Symbolic Logic*
1.13 *Logic*
1.14 *Mathematical Logic Quarterly*
1.15 *Multiple-Valued Logic*
1.16 *Notre Dame Journal of Formal Logic*
1.17 *Studia Logica*

Formal Logic

1.18 Agazzi, E. *Modern Logic-A Survey*, Dordrecht, Reidel, 1981.
1.19 Barwise, J. (ed.) *Handbook of Mathematical Logic*, Amsterdam, North-Holland, 1977.
1.20 Barwise, J. and Etchemendy, J. *The Language of First-Order Logic, including Tarski's World*, Stanford, Center for the Study of Language and Information, 1991.
1.21 Beth, E.W. *The Foundations of Mathematics*, Amsterdam, North-Holland, 1959; 2nd edn, 1965.
1.22 Bochenski, I. M. *Formale Logik*, 1956. Trans. as *A History of Formal Logic*, Notre Dame, University of Notre Dame, 1956; 2nd edn, 1961.
1.23 Boole, G. *Collected Logical Works*, 2 vols, La Salle, Ill., Open Court, 1952.
1.24 —— *The Laws of Thought*, London, Walton and Maberley, 1854.
1.25 Church, A. *Introduction to Mathematical Logic*, vol. 1, Princeton, Princeton University Press, 1956.
1.26 Frege, G. *Begriffsschrift*, 1879, Trans. in J. van Heijenoort, *From Frege to Gödel*, Cambridge, Mass., Harvard University Press, 1967, pp. 5–82.
1.27 —— *Die Grundlagen der Arithmetik*, 1884. Trans. as *The Foundations of Arithmetic*, New York, Philosophical Library, 1950; 2nd rev. edn, Oxford, Blackwell, 1980.
1.28 —— *Grundgesetze der Arithmetik*, 2 vols, 1893, 1903. Abridged and trans. as *The Basic Laws of Arithmetic*, Berkeley, University of California Press, 1964.

1.29 Grzegorczyk, A. *An Outline of Mathematical Logic*, Dordrecht, Reidel, 1974.

1.30 Hilbert, D. *Grundlagen der Geometrie*, 1899. Trans. as *Foundations of Geometry*, Chicago, Open Court, 1902; 2nd edn, 1971.

1.31 Hilbert, D. and Ackermann, W. *Grundzüge der theoretischen Logik*, 1928. Trans. as *Principles of Mathematical Logic*, New York, Chelsea, 1950.

1.32 Hilbert, D. and Bernays, P. *Grundlagen der Mathematik*, 2 vols, Berlin, Springer, 1934, 1939.

1.33 Jordan, Z. *The Development of Mathematical Logic and of Logical Positivism in Poland Between the Two Wars*, Oxford, Oxford University Press, 1945.

1.34 Jourdain, P. E. B. 'The Development of the Theories of Mathematical Logic and the Principles of Mathematics', *Quarterly Journal of Pure and Applied Mathematics* 43 (1912): 219–314.

1.35 Kneale, W. and Kneale, M. *The Development of Logic*, Oxford, Clarendon Press, 1962.

1.36 Lewis, C. I. *A Survey of Symbolic Logic*, Berkeley, University of California Press, 1918.

1.37 Lewis, C. I. and Langford, C. H. *Symbolic Logic*, New York, Dover, 1932; 2nd edn, 1959.

1.38 McCall, S. (ed.) *Polish Logic 1920–1939*, Oxford, Clarendon, 1967.

1.39 Mendelson, E. *Introduction to Mathematical Logic*, London, Van Nostrand, 1964.

1.40 Mostowski, A. *Thirty Years of Foundational Studies*, New York, Barnes and Noble, 1966.

1.41 Nidditch, P. H. *The Development of Mathematical Logic*, London, Routledge and Kegan Paul, 1962.

1.42 Peano, G. *Arithmetices Principia*, 1889. Trans. as 'The Principles of Arithmetic', in J. van Heijenoort, *From Frege to Gödel*, Cambridge, Mass., Harvard University Press, 1967, pp. 85–97.

1.43 Quine, W. V. *Mathematical Logic*, Cambridge, Mass., Harvard University Press, 1940; rev. edn, 1951.

1.44 —— *Methods of Logic*, New York, Holt, 1950; 3rd edn, 1972.

1.45 Risse, G. *Bibliographica Logica*, 3 vols, Hildesheim, Olms, 1965–79.

1.46 Russell, B. *The Principles of Mathematics*, London, George Allen and Unwin, 1903; 2nd edn, 1937.

1.47 Shoenfield, J. R. *Mathematical Logic*, Reading, Mass., Addison-Wesley, 1967.

1.48 Suppes, P. C. *Introduction to Logic*, London, Van Nostrand, 1957.

1.49 Whitehead, A. N. and Russell, B. *Principia Mathematica*, 3 vols, Cambridge, Cambridge University Press, 1910, 1911, 1913; 2nd edn, 1927.

Metalogic

1.50 Barendregt, H. P. *The Lambda Calculus*, Amsterdam, North-Holland, 1981.

1.51 Barwise, J. and Feferman, S. (eds) *Model-Theoretic Logics*, New York, Springer-Verlag, 1985.

1.52 Bell, J. L. and Slomson, A. B. *Models and Ultraproducts*, Amsterdam, North-Holland, 1969.

1.53 Carnap, R. *Foundations of Logic and Mathematics*, Chicago, University of Chicago Press, 1939.

1.54 Chang, C. C. and Keisler, H. J. *Model Theory*, Amsterdam, North-Holland, 1973; 3rd edn, 1990.

1.55 Church, A. 'A Note on the Entscheidungsproblem', *Journal of Symbolic Logic* 1 (1936): 40–1, 101–2.

1.56 Davis, M. *Computability and Unsolvability*, New York, McGraw-Hill, 1958.

1.57 ——(ed.) *The Undecidable*, Hewlett, N.Y., Raven, 1965.

1.58 Friedman, H. 'Higher Set Theory and Mathematical Practice', *Annals of Mathematical Logic* 2 (1971): 325–57.

1.59 —— 'On the Necessary Use of Abstract Set Theory', *Advances in Mathematics* 41 (1981): 209–80.

1.60 Gentzen, G. *The Collected Works of Gerhard Gentzen*, Amsterdam, North-Holland, 1969.

1.61 Girard, J.-Y. *Proof Theory and Logical Complexity*, vol. 1, Napoli, Bibliopolis, 1987.

1.62 Gödel, K. *Collected Works*, 4 vols, Oxford, Oxford University Press, 1986–forthcoming.

1.63 —— *The Consistency of the Axiom of Choice and of the Generalized Continuum Hypothesis with the Axioms of Set Theory*, London, Oxford University Press, 1940; rev. edn, 1953. Repr. in K. Gödel, *Collected Works*, vol. 2, Oxford, Oxford University Press, 1990, pp. 33–101.

1.64 —— 'Die Vollständigkeit der Axiome des logischen Funktionenkalküls', 1930. Trans. as 'The Completeness of the Axioms of the Functional Calculus of Logic', in K. Gödel, *Collected Works*, vol. 1, Oxford, Oxford University Press, 1986, pp. 103–23, and in J. van Heijenoort, *From Frege to Gödel*, Cambridge, Mass., Harvard University Press, 1967, pp. 583–91.

1.65 —— 'Über formal unentscheidbare Sätze der *Principia mathematica* und verwandter Systeme I', 1931. Trans. as 'On Formally Undecidable Propositions of *Principia Mathematica* and Related Systems I', in K. Gödel, *Collected Works*, vol. 1, Oxford, Oxford University Press, 1986, pp. 144–95, and in J. van Heijenoort, *From Frege to Gödel*, Cambridge, Mass., Harvard University Press, 1967, pp. 596–616.

1.66 Harrington, L. A., Morley, M. D., Scedrov, A. and Simpson, S. G. (eds) *Harvey Friedman's Research on the Foundations of Mathematics*, Amsterdam, North-Holland, 1985.

1.67 Hilbert, D. and Bernays, P. *Grundlagen der Mathematik*, 2 vols, Berlin, Springer, 1934, 1939.

1.68 Keisler, H. J. *Model Theory for Infinitory Logic* Amsterdam, North-Holland, 1971.

1.69 Kleene, S. C. *Introduction to Metamathematics*, Amsterdam, North-Holland, 1967.

1.70 Morley, M. D. 'On Theories Categorical in Uncountable Powers', *Proceedings of the National Academy of Science* 48 (1962): 365–77.

1.71 —— (ed.) *Studies in Model Theory*, Providence, R. I., American Mathematical Society, 1973.

1.72 Mostowski, A. *Sentences Undecidable in Formalized Arithmeric*, Amsterdam, North-Holland, 1952.

1.73   Robinson, A. *Introduction to Model Theory and to the Metamathematics of Algebra*, Amsterdam, North-Holland, 1963.

1.74   Rosser, J. B. 'Extensions of Some Theorems of Gödel and Church', *Journal of Symbolic Logic* 1 (1936): 87–91.

1.75   —— 'Gödel's Theorems for Non-Constructive Logics', *Journal of Symbolic Logic* 2 (1937): 129–37.

1.76   —— *Simplified Independence Proofs*, New York, Academic Press, 1969.

1.77   Russell, B. 'Mathematical Logic as Based on the Theory of Types', *American Journal of Mathematics* 30 (1908): 222–62. Repr. in B. Russell, *Logic and Knowledge*, London, Allen and Unwin, 1956, pp. 59–102, and in J. van Heijenoort, *From Frege to Gödel*, Cambridge, Mass., Harvard University Press, 1967, pp. 152–82.

1.78   Shoenfield, J. R. *Degrees of Unsolvability*, Amsterdam, North-Holland, 1971.

1.79   Skolem, T. 'Logisch-kombinatorische Untersuchungen über die Erfüllbarkeit und Beweisbarkeit mathematischen Sätze nebst einem Theoreme über dichte Mengen', 1920. Trans. as 'Logico-Combinatorial Investigations in the Satisfiability or Provability of Mathematical Propositions', in J. van Heijenoort, *From Frege to Gödel*, Cambridge, Mass., Harvard University Press, 1967, pp. 254–63.

1.80   —— *Selected Works in Logic*, Oslo, Universitetsforlaget, 1970.

1.81   Tarski, A. *Logic, Semantics, Metamathematics*, Oxford, Clarendon, 1956.

1.82   Tarski, A., Mostowski, A. and Robinson, R. M. *Undecidable Theories*, Amsterdam, North-Holland, 1969.

1.83   Turing, A. M. 'Computability and λ-Definability', *Journal of Symbolic Logic* 2 (1937): 153–63.

1.84   van Heijenoort, J. (ed.) *From Frege to Gödel*, Cambridge, Mass., Harvard University Press, 1967.

Logic and Computability

1.85   Abramsky, S., Gabbay, D. M. and Maibaum, T. S. E. (eds) *Handbook of Logic in Computer Science*, Oxford, Clarendon, 1992.

1.86   Boolos, G. S. and Jeffrey, R. C. *Computability and Logic*, Cambridge, Cambridge University Press, 1974; 3rd edn, 1989.

1.87   Cook, S. 'The Complexity of Theorem Proving Procedures', in *Proceedings of the Third Annual ACM Symposium on the Theory of Computing*, New York, Association of Computing Machinery, 1971.

1.88   Gabbay, D. M., Hogger, C. J. and Robinson, J. A. (eds) *Handbook of Logic in Artificial Intelligence and Logic Programming*, Oxford, Clarendon, 1993.

1.89   Garey, M. R. and Johnson, D. S. *Computers and Intractability*, New York, Freeman, 1979.

1.90   Rogers, H. *Theory of Recursive Functions and Effective Computability*, New York, McGraw-Hill, 1967.

Set Theory

1.91 Aczel, P. *Non-Well-founded Sets*, Stanford, Center for the Study of Language and Information, 1988.

1.92 Bernays, P. *Axiomatic Set Theory*, Amsterdam, North-Holland, 1958.

1.93 Cantor, G. 'Beiträge zur Begründung der transfiniten Mengenlehre', *Mathematische Annalen* 46 (1895): 481–512; 49 (1897): 207–46.

1.94 —— *Contributions to the Founding of the Theory of Transfinite Numbers*, La Salle, Ill., Open Court, 1952.

1.95 Cohen, P. J. *Set Theory and the Continuum Hypothesis*, New York, W. A. Benjamin, 1966.

1.96 Fraenkel, A. A., *Abstract Set Theory*, Amsterdam, North-Holland, 1954; 3rd edn, 1965.

1.97 Fraenkel, A. A., Bar-Hillel, Y. and Levy, A. *Foundations of Set Theory*, Amsterdam, North-Holland, 1973.

1.98 Hallett, M. *Cantorian Set Theory and Limitation of Size*, Oxford, Clarendon, 1984.

1.99 Moore, G. H. *Zermelo's Axiom of Choice*, New York, Springer, 1982.

1.100 Mostowski, A. *Constructible Sets with Applications*, Amsterdam, North-Holland, 1969.

1.101 Quine, W. V. *Set Theory and Its Logic*, Cambridge, Mass., Harvard University Press, 1963.

1.102 Stoll, R. R. *Set Theory and Logic*, New York, Dover, 1961.

1.103 Suppes, P. C. *Axiomatic Set Theory*, London, Van Nostrand, 1960.

1.104 Zermelo, E. 'Investigations in the Foundations of Set Theory I', 1908, trans. in J. van Heijenoort, *From Frege to Gödel*, Cambridge, Mass., Harvard University Press, 1967, pp. 200–15.

Category Theory

1.105 Bell, J. L. *Toposes and Local Set Theories*, Oxford, Clarendon, 1988.

1.106 Lawvere, W. 'The Category of Categories as a Foundation for Mathematics', in *Proceedings of La Jolla Conference on Categorical Algebra*, New York, Springer-Verlag, 1966, pp. 1–20.

1.107 Mac Lane, S. *Categories for the Working Mathematician*, Berlin, Springer, 1972.

1.108 Pierce, B. C. *Basic Category Theory for Computer Scientists*, Cambridge, Mass., MIT Press, 1991.

Non-classical Logics

General

1.109 Haack, S. *Deviant Logic*, Cambridge, Cambridge University Press, 1974.

1.110 Rescher, N. *Topics in Philosophical Logic*, Dordrecht, Reidel, 1968.

Combinatory Logic

1.111 Church, A. *The Calculi of Lambda-conversion*, Princeton, Princeton University Press, 1941; 2nd edn, 1951.

1.112 Curry, H. B. and Feys, R. *Combinatory Logic*, 2 vols, Amsterdam, North-Holland, 1958.

Logic of Counterfactuals

1.113 Chisholm, R. M. 'The Contrary-to-Fact Conditional', *Mind* 55 (1946): 289–307.

1.114 Goodman, N. 'The Problem of Counterfactual Conditionals', *Journal of Philosophy* 44 (1947): 113–28.

1.115 Harper, W. L., Stalnaker, R. and Pearce, G. (eds) *Ifs*, Dordrecht, Reidel, 1981.

1.116 Lewis, D. *Counterfactuals*, Oxford, Blackwell, 1973.

Deontic Logic and Logic of Imperatives

1.117 Fitch, F. B. 'Natural Deduction Rules for Obligation', *American Philosophical Quarterly* 3 (1966): 27–38.

1.118 Rescher, N. *The Logic of Commands*, London, Routledge and Kegan Paul, 1966.

1.119 von Wright, G. H. *Norm and Action*, London, Routledge and Kegan Paul, 1963.

1.120 —— *An Essay in Deontic Logic and the General Theory of Action*, Amsterdam, North-Holland, 1968.

Epistemic and Dynamic Logics

1.121 Chisholm, R. M. 'The Logic of Knowing', *Journal of Philosophy* 60 (1963): 773–95.

1.122 Forrest, P. *The Dynamics of Belief*, New York, Blackwell, 1986.

1.123 Gärdenfors, P. *Knowledge in Flux*, Cambridge, Mass., MIT Press, 1988.

1.124 Hintikka, K. J. J. *Knowledge and Belief*, Ithaca, Cornell University Press, 1962.

1.125 Schlesinger, G. N. *The Range of Epistemic Logic*, Aberdeen, Aberdeen University Press, 1985.

Fuzzy Logic

1.126 McNeill, D. and Freiberger, P. *Fuzzy Logic*, New York, Simon and Schuster, 1993.

1.127 Zadeh, L. 'Fuzzy Logic and Approximate Reasoning', *Synthese* 30 (1975): 407–28.

Interrogative Logic

1.128 Aqvist, L. *A New Approach to the Logical Theory of Interrogatives*, Uppsala, University of Uppsala Press, 1965.

1.129 Belnap, N. D. and Steel, T. B. *The Logic of Questions and Answers*, New Haven, Yale University Press, 1976.

Intuitionistic and Constructive Logics

1.130 Beeson, M. J. *Foundations of Constructive Mathematics*, Berlin, Springer, 1985.

1.131 Bishop, E. *Foundations of Constructive Analysis*, New York, McGraw-Hill, 1967.

1.132 Bishop, E. and Bridges, D. *Constructive Analysis*, Berlin, Springer, 1985.

1.133 Bridges, D. *Varieties of Constructive Mathematics*, Cambridge, Cambridge University Press, 1987.

1.134 Brouwer, L. E. J. *Collected Works*, Amsterdam, North-Holland, 1975.

1.135 Dummett, M. *Elements of Intuitionism*, Oxford, Oxford University Press, 1978.

1.136 Heyting, A. *Intuitionism*, Amsterdam, North-Holland, 1956; 3rd edn, 1971.

1.137 —— *Constructivity in Mathematics*, Amsterdam, North-Holland, 1959.

Many-valued Logic

1.138 Rescher, N. *Many-Valued Logic*, New York, McGraw-Hill, 1969.

Mereology

1.139 Leonard, H. and Goodman, N. 'The Calculus of Individuals and its Uses', *Journal of Symbolic Logic* 5 (1940): 45–55.

1.140 Luschei, E. C. *The Logical Systems of Lesniewski*, Amsterdam, North-Holland, 1962.

Modal Logic

1.141 Chellas, B. F. *Modal Logic*, Cambridge, Cambridge University Press, 1980.

1.142 Hughes, G. E. and Cresswell, M. J. *An Introduction to Modal Logic*, London, Methuen, 1968.

1.143 Lewis, C. I. 'Alternative Systems of Logic', *Monist* 42 (1932): 481–507.

1.144 Loux, M. J. *The Possible and the Actual*, Ithaca, Cornell University Press, 1979.

Non-consistent and Paraconsistent Logic

1.145 Brandom, R. and Rescher, N. *The Logic of Inconsistency*, Totawa, N. J., Rowman and Littlefield, 1979.

1.146 Priest, G. *In Contradiction*, Dordrecht, Martinus Nijhoff, 1987.
1.147 Priest, G., Routley, R. and Norman, J. (eds) *Paraconsistent Logic*, Munich, Philosophia Verlag, 1989.

Non-monotonic and Inductive Logic

1.148 Besnard, P. *An Introduction to Default Logic*, New York, Springer-Verlag, 1989.
1.149 Ginsberg, M. L. (ed.) *Readings in Nonmonotonic Reasoning*, Los Altos, Cal., Morgan Kaufmann, 1987.
1.150 Hintikka, J. and Suppes, P. (eds) *Aspects of Inductive Logic*, Amsterdam, North-Holland, 1966.
1.151 Jeffrey, R. C. (ed.) *Studies in Inductive Logic and Probability*, 2 vols, Berkeley, University of California Press, 1980.
1.152 Popper, K. R. *Logik der Forschung*, 1935. Trans. as *The Logic of Scientific Discovery*, London, Hutchinson, 1959.
1.153 Shafer, G. and Pearl, J. (eds) *Readings in Uncertain Reasoning*, San Mateo, Cal., Morgan Kaufmann, 1990.

Preference Logic

1.154 Rescher, N. *Introduction to Value Theory*, Englewood Cliffs, N. J., Prentice-Hall, 1969.
1.155 von Wright, G. H. *Logic of Preference*, Edinburgh, Edinburgh University Press, 1963.

Probability and Decision Theory

1.156 Campbell, R. and Sowden, L. (eds) *Paradoxes of Rationality and Cooperation*, Vancouver, University of British Columbia Press, 1985.
1.157 Carnap, R. *Logical Foundations of Probability*, Chicago, University of Chicago Press, 1950; 2nd edn, 1962.
1.158 Hacking, I. *Logic of Statistical Inference*, Cambridge, Cambridge University Press, 1965.
1.159 Jeffrey, R. C. *The Logic of Decision*, Chicago, University of Chicago Press, 1965; 2nd edn, 1983.
1.160 Kolmogorov, A. N. *Grundbegriffe der Wahrscheinlichkeitsrechnung*, 1933. Trans. as *Foundations of the Theory of Probability*, New York, Chelsea, 1950.

Quantum Logic

1.161 Gibbins, P. *Particles and Paradoxes*, Cambridge, Cambridge University Press, 1987.
1.162 Putnam, H. 'Is Logic Empirical?', in R. Cohen and M. Wartofsky (eds), *Boston Studies in the Philosophy of Science*, vol. 5, Dordrecht, Reidel, 1969,

pp. 216–41. Repr. as 'The Logic of Quantum Mechanics', in H. Putnam, *Mathematics, Matter and Method*, Cambridge, Cambridge University Press, 1975, pp. 174–97.

Relevance Logic

1.163 Anderson, A. R. and Belnap, N. D. *Entailment*, 2 vols, Princeton, Princeton University Press, 1975, 1992.
1.164 Read, S. *Relevant Logic*, New York, Blackwell, 1988.

Temporal Logic

1.165 Prior, A. N. *Time and Modality*, Oxford, Clarendon, 1957.
1.166 —— *Past, Present and Future*, Oxford, Clarendon, 1967.
1.167 Rescher, N. and Urquhart, A. *Temporal Logic*, New York, Springer-Verlag, 1971.

Informal Logic and Critical Reasoning

1.168 Hamblin, C. L. *Fallacies*, London, Methuen, 1970.
1.169 Hansen, H. V. and Pinto, R. C. (eds) *Fallacies: Classical and Contemporary Readings*, University Park, Pa, Pennsylvania State University Press, 1995.
1.170 Massey, G. J. 'The Fallacy Behind Fallacies', in P. A. French, T. E. Uehling, Jr and H. K. Wettstein (eds) *Midwest Studies in Philosophy, Vol. 6 – The Foundations of Analytic Philosophy*, Minneapolis, University of Minnesota Press, 1981, pp. 489–500.
1.171 Woods, J. and Walton, D. *Argument, The Logic of the Fallacies*, Toronto, McGraw-Hill Ryerson, 1982.

Philosophy of Logic

1.172 Barwise, J. and Etchemendy, J. *The Liar*, Oxford, Oxford University Press, 1987.
1.173 Carnap, R. *Introduction to Semantics*, Cambridge, Mass., Harvard University Press, 1942.
1.174 —— *Meaning and Necessity*, Chicago, University of Chicago Press, 1947; 2nd edn, 1956.
1.175 Davidson, D. and Harman, G. (eds) *Semantics of Natural Language*, Dordrecht, Reidel, 1972.
1.176 Davidson, D. and Hintikka, J. (eds) *Words and Objections*, Dordrecht, Reidel, 1969.
1.177 Detlefsen, M. *Hilbert's Program*, Dordrecht, Reidel, 1986.
1.178 Field, H. 'Tarski's Theory of Truth', *Journal of Philosophy* 69 (1972): 347–75.

1.179 Gabbay, D. and Guenthner, F. (eds) *Handbook of Philosophical Logic*, 4 vols, Dordrecht, Reidel, 1983, 1984, 1986, 1989.

1.180 Haack, S. *Philosophy of Logics*, Cambridge, Cambridge University Press, 1978.

1.181 Hahn, L. E. and Schilpp, P. A. (eds) *The Philosophy of W. V. Quine*, La Salle, Ill., Open Court, 1986.

1.182 Herzberger, H. A. 'Paradoxes of Grounding in Semantics', *Journal of Philosophy* 67 (1970): 145–67.

1.183 Hilber, D. 'Mathematische Probleme', 1900. Trans. as 'Mathematical Problems', in *Bulletin of the American Mathematical Society* 8 (1902): 437–79. Repr. in F. E. Browder (ed.) *Mathematical Developments Arising from Hilbert Problems (Proceedings of Symposia in Pure Mathematics*, vol. 28), Providence, American Mathematical Society, 1976, pp. 1–34.

1.184 Irvine, A. D. and Wedeking, G. A. (eds) *Russell and Analytic Philosophy*, Toronto, University of Toronto Press, 1993.

1.185 Kripke, S. A. 'Naming and Necessity', in D. Davidson and G. Harman (eds) *Semantics of Natural Language*, Dordrecht, Reidel, 1972, pp. 253–355, 763–69. Repr. as *Naming and Necessity*, Cambridge, Mass., Harvard University Press, 1980.

1.186 —— 'Outline of a Theory of Truth', *Journal of Philosophy* 72 (1975), 690–716.

1.187 Linsky, L. (ed.) *Reference and Modality*, London, Oxford University Press, 1971.

1.188 Martin, R. L. (ed.) *Recent Essays on Truth and the Liar Paradox*, Oxford, Clarendon, 1984.

1.189 Putman, H. *Philosophy of Logic*, New York, Harper and Row, 1971.

1.190 Quine, W. V. *From a Logical Point of View*, Cambridge, Mass., Harvard University Press, 1953; 2nd edn, 1961.

1.191 —— *Philosophy of Logic*, Cambridge, Mass., Harvard University Press, 1970; 2nd edn, 1986.

1.192 —— *Pursuit of Truth*, Cambridge, Mass., Harvard University Press, 1990.

1.193 —— *Word and Object*, Cambridge, Mass., MIT Press, 1960.

1.194 Russell, B. *The Autobiography of Bertrand Russell*, 3 vols, London, George Allen and Unwin, 1967, 1968, 1969.

1.195 —— *The Collected Papers of Bertrand Russell*, London, Routledge, 1983–forthcoming.

1.196 ——. *Introduction to Mathematical Philosophy*, London, George Allen and Unwin, 1919.

1.197 —— *Logic and Knowledge*, London, George Allen and Unwin, 1956.

1.198 Sainsbury, M. *Logical Forms*, Oxford, Blackwell, 1991.

1.199 Schilpp, P.A. (ed.) *The Philosophy of Bertrand Russell*, Evanston, Northwestern University Press, 1944; 3rd edn, New York, Harper and Row, 1963.

1.200 —— *The Philosophy of Karl Popper*, La Salle, Ill., Open Court, 1974.

1.201 —— *The Philosophy of Rudolf Carnap*, La Salle, Ill., Open Court, 1963.

1.202 Strawson, P. F. *Logico-Linguistic Papers*, London, Methuen, 1971.

1.203 Tarski, A. *Logic, Semantics, Metamathematics*, Oxford, Oxford University Press, 1956.

1.204 —— 'On Undecidable Statements in Enlarged Systems of Logic and the Concept of Truth', *Journal of Symbolic Logic* 4 (1939): 105–12.

1.205 —— 'The Semantic Conception of Truth and the Foundations of Semantics', *Journal of Philosophy and Phenomenological Research* 4 (1944): 341–75. Repr. in H. Feigl and W. Sellars, *Readings in Philosophical Analysis*, New York, Appleton-Century-Crofts, 1949, 52–84.

1.206 Wittgenstein, L. *Logisch-Philosophische Abhandlung*, 1921. Trans. as *Tractatus Logico-Philosophicus*, London, Routledge and Kegan Paul, 1961.

CHAPTER 2

Philosophy of mathematics in the twentieth century

Michael Detlefsen

➤ INTRODUCTION ➤

Philosophy of mathematics in the twentieth century has primarily been shaped by three influences. The first of these is the work of Kant and, especially, the problematic he laid down for the subject in the late eighteenth century. The second is the reaction to Kant's conception of geometry that arose among nineteenth-century thinkers and which centred first on the discovery of non-Euclidean geometries in the 1820s. The third is the new discoveries in logic that emerged with increasing rapidity and force during the latter half of the nineteenth century. In one way or another, the main currents of twentieth-century philosophy of mathematics – and, in particular, the so-called logicist, intuitionist and formalist movements – are all attempts to reconcile Kant's revolutionary plan for mathematical epistemology with the equally revolutionary ideas of Gauss, Bolyai and Lobatchevsky in geometry, and the powerful ideas and techniques developed by Boole, Peirce, Peano, Frege and other nineteenth-century figures in logic.

To understand twentieth-century philosophy of mathematics, it is therefore necessary first to have some knowledge of Kant's ideas and of the ideas that were at the heart of the nineteenth-century reactions to his views. We shall therefore devote the remainder of this introduction to surveying these ideas.

We begin with Kant and the *Problematik* he established for mathematical epistemology. This *Problematik* was focused on the reconciliation of two apparently incompatible features of mathematical thought: namely, its rich *substantiality* as a science, which gives it the appearance of something that arises from sources external to the human intellect, and its apparent certainty or *necessity*, which gives it the appearance of something that is independent of the one external source which is best founded and understood – namely, sensory experience.

To resolve this difficulty, Kant formulated a theory of knowledge which imported much of what had traditionally been thought of as information arising from external sources (specifically, the basic spatial characteristics of sensory thought, and the temporal characteristics of both sensory and non-sensory thinking) into the human mind itself, representing it as the product of certain deep, standing traits of human cognition. At the centre of this theory was a certain conception of judgement which represented the intersection of two different schemes for classifying propositions. On the first of these, propositions were sorted according to the type of knowledge of which they admitted; those which required sensory experience were called *a posteriori*, those which did not were called *a priori*. On the second, they were sorted according to whether or not their predicate terms were contained in their subject terms (in the sense that one *thinking* the subject term would, as a part of that very act itself, also *think* the predicate term). Those judgements in which the subject term contained the predicate term in this sense were to be called *analytic*. Those in which no such containment obtained were either falsehoods, because there was no connection between the subject and predicate concepts at all, or they were *synthetic* truths. In true synthetic judgements, the subject and predicate concepts were joined not by a relation of containment, but rather by a relation of *association*. The association of a predicate with a subject provided for their being thought together in tandem, though it did not, like containment, require that a thinking of the predicate term of a judgement be a constituent part of any thinking of its subject term (cf. [2.58] for a good discussion of the Kantian doctrine of concepts, specifically in relation to his conception of intuition).

Kant erected his mathematical epistemology upon these distinctions between a priori and a posteriori and analytic and synthetic judgements. He attempted to explain what he referred to as the 'certainty' or 'necessity' of mathematical judgements by showing that our knowledge of them is a priori. Such knowledge, he argued, derives from two standing capacities of the human mind. One of these, which Kant referred to as our a priori intuition of space, was taken to function as a formal constraint on sensory experience by forcing it to be represented in a Euclidean space of three dimensions. The other, the so-called a priori intuition of time, served formally to constrain both sensory and non-sensory experience by representing it as temporally ordered. Both the a priori intuition of space and the a priori intuition of time therefore functioned to control the senses rather than the other way round. It was because of this that Kant believed judgements arising from them (i.e. the judgements of geometry and arithmetic) to be impervious to falsification by sensory experience.

This, in brief, was Kant's proposal for accounting for the necessity of mathematics. He proposed to account for its substantiality by establishing that its judgements are synthetic rather than analytic in character. If mathematical judgement is synthetic in character, then it cannot be seen as consisting in the mere apprehension of a *containment* relation between its subject and predicate concepts. Rather, it must be seen as the fusion in thought of two analytically unrelated concepts through one of two means: either the conjunction of concepts provided for by repeated sensory experience, or the invariant and inevitable association provided for by an a priori structuring of our minds in such a way as to bring the two together *in thought*. Such a joining of analytically unrelated concepts, in which the thinking of the predicate concept is not, logically speaking, strictly required for the thinking of the subject concept, was, in Kant's view, the essential ingredient of substantiality in judgement. This notion of analytically unrelated concepts necessarily joined in thought enabled Kant to frame an account of the substantiality of mathematical judgements which would allow mathematical judgement to be necessary but, at the same time, not limit the degree and kind of the informativeness of mathematical judgements to the degree and kind of complexity that logical containment relations are capable of displaying. In Kant's estimation, this latter was a limitation that it was important to avoid.

Kant adopted a similarly synthetic view of the nature of mathematical *reasoning*. He maintained that mathematical (as opposed to logical or analytical) inference possesses the same rich substantiality of character that distinguishes mathematical from logical or analytical judgement. He also argued (cf. [2.86], 741–7) that the connection between the premiss(es) and conclusion of a mathematical inference calls for synthetic rather than analytic means of bonding.

To illustrate the point, he elaborated upon an elementary case of geometrical inference; namely, that inference in ordinary Euclidean geometry which takes one from a premiss to the effect that a given figure is a triangle to the conclusion that the sum of its interior angles is equal to that of two right angles. He maintained (Ibid.) that no amount of analysis of the concept of a triangle could ever reveal that its interior angles sum to two right angles. Rather, he said, in order to arrive at such a conclusion (i.e. a conclusion that extends our knowledge of triangles beyond what is given in the definition of the concept itself) we must rely primarily not on the definition of the concept, but on the means by which triangles are presented to us in intuition. In other words, we must construct a triangle in intuition (i.e. represent the object which 'corresponds to' [Ibid., p. 742] the concept of a triangle), and then extract the conclusion not from the mere concept of a triangle but rather from *the universal conditions governing the construction of triangles* (Ibid., pp. 742, 744) in our intuition. 'In this fashion', said Kant, the mathematical reasoner arrives at his conclusion 'through a chain of inferences guided throughout by intuition' (Ibid., p. 745).

These, in brief, are Kant's proposals for the resolution of what he took to be the central problems facing the philosophy of mathematics. But though the problems themselves have remained a staple of twentieth-century thinking on the subject, Kant's particular proposals for their resolution have not. What caused this decline in the popularity of Kant's ideas was, primarily, the emergence of challenges to his conception of geometry and his view of the relation between geometry and arithmetic that arose in the nineteenth century. It is to these ideas that we now turn, beginning with geometry.

On Kant's conception, geometry was the product of an a priori intuition of space which specified the space in which human spatial experience was 'set', so to speak. The character of this a priori visual space was that spelled out in the Euclidean axioms for three-dimensional space. In calling Euclidean three-dimensional space the space of human visual experience, one does not mean, of course, that it is the only space that is intelligible or logically coherent to the human mind. Visualizability is one thing, intelligibility or logical coherence another. Kant's position was that Euclidean three-dimensional space is the only space that is *visualizable* by humans (cf. [2.57] for a useful discussion of Kant's view of geometry).

Not long after Kant elaborated his views in the *Critique of Pure Reason*, mathematicians expressed doubts about them. Gauss, for example, clearly stated his doubts concerning the a priori character of geometry in a letter written in 1817 to Olbers (cf. [2.60], 651–2). He restated the same view in an 1829 letter to Bessel (cf. [2.59], VIII: 200) and added that it had been his view for nearly 40 years. In (my translation of) his words:

> My innermost conviction is that geometry has a completely different position in our a priori knowledge than arithmetic . . . we must humbly admit that, though number is purely a product of our intellect, space also has a reality external to our intellect which prohibits us from being able to give a complete specification of its laws a priori.[1]

Later, in a letter written in 1832 to Bolyai's father (cf. [2.59], VIII: 220–21), he reiterated this view, saying that Bolyai's results provided a proof of the incorrectness of Kant's views.

It is precisely in the impossibility of deciding a priori between

Σ [Euclidean geometry] and S [the younger Bolyai's non-Euclidean geometry] that we have the clearest proof that Kant was wrong to claim that space is only the form of our intuition. [Brackets and translation mine]

There thus arose among nineteenth-century thinkers the belief (given special impetus by the work of Bolyai and Lobatchevsky) that there are fundamental epistemological differences between geometry and arithmetic. Put briefly, the difference is that arithmetic is more and geometry less central to human thought and reason. Arithmetic, on this view, was taken to be wholly a product or creation of the human intellect; geometry, on the other hand, was taken to be determined at least in part by forces external to the human intellect. The difference was implied by a broad epistemological principle (which we might refer to as the *creation principle*) to the effect that what the mind creates or produces of itself is better known to it than that which comes from without.

Belief in the epistemological asymmetry of arithmetic and geometry (though not necessarily Gauss's particular conception of its character) thus became a central tenet of nineteenth-century thinking concerning the nature of mathematical knowledge. It also became a prime force shaping the major movements of twentieth-century philosophy of mathematics. In the main, two basic kinds of reactions emerged, corresponding to the two basic ways of accommodating this asymmetry. One was to retain a Kantian conception of arithmetic (as based on an a priori intuition of time) and adopt a non-Kantian conception of geometry (as based on an a priori intuition of space). The other was to take a non-Kantian view of arithmetic while retaining a Kantian conception of geometry. The former of these two tactics was essentially that which was adopted by the intuitionists Brouwer and Weyl, while the latter became the central idea motivating the logicism of Frege and Dedekind. Hilbert's finitist programme, the third main movement of twentieth-century philosophy of mathematics, in a way adopted and in a way rejected both. It maintained both the epistemological symmetry of arithmetic and geometry and their fundamentally a priori character. It rejected, however, Kant's proposed a priori intuitions of space and time as their bases.

The powerful confirmation of belief in the epistemological asymmetry of arithmetic and geometry that was provided by the nineteenth-century discovery of non-Euclidean geometries was therefore a major factor contributing to the decline of Kant's positive views in the philosophy of mathematics and the emergence of major alternatives in the twentieth century. The second major factor contributing to the weakening of Kant's influence in twentieth-century philosophy of mathematics was the dramatic development of logic during the latter part of the nineteenth and the early part of the twentieth centuries. This included the introduction of algebraic methods by Boole and DeMorgan, the improved treatment of relations by Peirce, Schröder and Peano, the replacement of the Aristotelian analysis of form based on the subject–predicate relation with the more fecund analysis of form based on Frege's general notion of a logical function, and the advances in formalization brought about by the introduction (by Frege, Russell and Whitehead, and Peano) of precisely defined and managed symbolic languages and systems.[2]

These developments took logic to a point well beyond what it was in the time of Kant, and this caused some to judge that it was the relatively underdeveloped state of logic in Kant's time that was primarily responsible for his belief in the need for a *synthetic* basis for mathematical judgment and inference. Russell, for one (cf. [2.120], [2.123], [2.124]), took such a position, arguing that though Kant's views may have seemed reasonable given the sorry state of logic in his day, they would never have been given a serious hearing had our knowledge of logic been then what it is now. (N.B. But though Russell saw the enrichment of the analysis of logical form brought about by the modern logic of relations and the functional conception of the proposition as being of particular importance to the correction of Kant's deficiencies, he also believed that certain developments in mathematics proper were of great importance. Chief among these were (i) the arithmetization of analysis by Weierstrass, Dedekind and others; and (ii) the discovery by Peano of an axiomatization of arithmetic. These led to what Russell regarded as a codification of pure mathematics within a certain axiomatic system of arithmetic (viz. second-order Peano arithmetic), and so provided for its 'logicization'. Russell reckoned the significance of these developments for Kant's philosophy of mathematics to be as great as that of the discovery of non-Euclidean geometries (cf. [2.120], [2.123].).

For the most part, Russell's views on these matters were taken over by the logical empiricists, who, like Russell, were much impressed with the new logic, and who were also attracted to a logicism like Russell's,[3] because it allowed them to resolve the difficulties that mathematics had traditionally posed for empiricist epistemologies.[4] The new logic, then, in being seen as the basis for the working out of Russell's sweeping form of logicism, eventually led to the resurgence of empiricist epistemologies for mathematics, and these, quite clearly, represented a significant departure from Kantian mathematical epistemology. In addition, it posed what has proven to be an enduring challenge to the Kantian view that mathematical *reasoning* is essentially distinct from logical reasoning.[5]

This completes our synopsis of the major influences shaping

twentieth-century philosophy of mathematics. The longer story, which we shall now tell in greater detail, is, for the most part, the story of the ebb and flow of Kant's ideas as they met and interacted with new developments in geometry, logic, science and philosophy.

ᴏᴏ THE EARLY PERIOD AND THE ᴏᴏ DEVELOPMENT OF THE THREE 'ISMS'

We begin our discussion with the first three decades (what we are calling the 'early period'), which, if it was not *the* most active productive period, was certainly one of the most such in the entire history of the subject. The major developments of this period were the three great 'isms' of recent philosophy of mathematics: logicism, intuitionism and (Hilbert's) formalism. All of these, we shall argue, were profoundly influenced by Kantian ideas. In the case of logicism, however, one must take care to distinguish Frege's from Russell's version. Frege's had much closer ties to Kantian epistemology than did Russell's. Indeed, it attempted to retain many of Kant's most important ideas, including, as we shall see, certain of his ideas regarding the nature of reason.

Logicism

Frege was moved by the discovery of non-Euclidean geometries, and dedicated to the task of explaining what he took to be the main upshot of this discovery – namely, the asymmetry between arithmetic and geometry as regards their basicness to human thought. Geometrical thinking, though widely applied in human thought, was not so widely applied as to suggest that it is not based on a Kantian type of a priori intuition. Thus, Frege supported Kant's geometrical epistemology (cf. [2.49], section 89). Arithmetic, on the other hand, was too pervasively applicable in human thought to be ascribed plausibly to the working of a similar faculty of intuition. No, its epistemological source must be sought elsewhere – ultimately, as Frege saw it, in a reconceived faculty of reason.

The basics of this viewpoint were evident in Frege's writings from the very start. Thus, already in his 1873 doctoral dissertation, he emphasized that 'the whole of geometry rests, in the final analysis, on principles that derive their validity from the character of our intuition' (cf. [2.46], 3, my translation). And, in his 1874 *Habilitationsschrift* [2.47], he expanded this observation to include his view of the relation between geometry and arithmetic *vis à vis* their dependency on intuition.

It is quite clear that there can be no intuition of so pervasive and abstract a concept as that of magnitude (Größe). There is therefore a noteworthy (bemerkenswerter) difference between geometry and arithmetic concerning the way in which their basic laws are grounded. The elements of all geometrical constructions are intuitions, and geometry refers to intuition as the source of its axioms. Because the object of arithmetic is not intuitable, it follows that its basic laws cannot be based on intuition.[6]

The same basic point concerning the 'unintuitedness' of the objects of arithmetic is made in the Grundlagen, where Frege remarks that:

In arithmetic we are not concerned with objects which we come to know as something alien from without through the medium of the senses, but with objects given directly to our reason and, as its nearest kin, utterly transparent to it.

[2.49, Section 105]

The same basic contrast between geometry and arithmetic is drawn in sections 13 and 14 of the Grundlagen [2.49]. There Frege broached the question of the relative places occupied in our thinking by empirical, geometrical, and arithmetical laws. His conclusion is that arithmetic laws are deeper than geometrical laws, and geometrical laws deeper than empirical laws. He arrives at this conclusion by conducting a thought experiment in which he considers the cognitive damage that one might expect to be done by denying each of the various kinds of laws. Denying a geometrical law, he concludes, stands to do more extensive damage to a person's cognitive orientation than denying a physical law. For it would lead to a conflict between what people can conceive and what they can spatially intuit. It would bring severe disorientation to a person's cognition. It would force them, for example, to deduce things that formerly they had been able just to 'see'. And it would even make the deductions strange and unfamiliar. It would not, however, result in a global breakdown of their rational thinking. Such global breakdown in one's rational functioning is rather that which would follow from a denial of arithmetical law. Denying an arithmetical law would not only keep one from seeing what he had formerly been able to see, it would, according to Frege, prohibit his engaging in deduction or reasoning of any sort. In his words, it would bring about 'complete confusion', so that 'even to think at all would seem no longer possible' (Ibid.).

Frege sought to explain this projected global breakdown in rational thought by arguing that the scope of arithmetical law, unlike that of physical and geometrical law, is universal. It governs not only that which is physically actual and that which is spatially intuitable, but, indeed, all that which is *numerable* – and that, according to Frege, is the widest range possible, extending to all that which is in any coherent way thinkable or conceivable.[7] The laws of arithmetic must, therefore, he concluded, 'be connected very intimately with the laws of thought' (Ibid.) – that is, the laws of logic.[8]

This alleged difference in the pervasiveness to thought of arithmetic and geometry thus became, in Frege's thinking, the (or at least a) fundamental datum for the philosophy of mathematics. He also believed it to be a datum Kant had overlooked. For, had he been aware of it, Frege felt sure, Kant would never have tried, as he did, to stretch essentially the same epistemology to cover both arithmetic and geometry. Rather, he would have tried to do justice to the 'observable' differences in depth-to-rational-thought of arithmetic and geometry.

Kant's ultimate shortcoming, Frege believed, was that he had acknowledged only two basic sources of knowledge – sensation and understanding. This allowed room only for a distinction between sensory and a priori knowledge. It did not allow for a distinction – at least not a distinction of kind – between different subspecies of a priori knowledge. Frege, on the other hand, distinguished between sensory experience, the source of our knowledge of natural science, intuition, the source of our geometrical knowledge, and reason (cf. [2.49], sections 26, 105), which Frege described as the source of our arithmetical knowledge. This modification of Kant's general epistemology was, Frege believed, necessary if one was to account for the perceivable differences in the relative pervasiveness of arithmetic and geometry.[9]

(N.B. Actually, it is not clear that Kant's epistemology did not enable him to do something of the same sort. Certainly it *did* distinguish two types of experience (cf. [2.86], 37–53), 'inner' and 'outer', and noted that the one (viz., inner) made use of intuitional resources (viz., the a priori intuition of time) that are more pervasive than those (viz., the a priori intuition of space) upon which the other is based. Adding to this the fact that Kant maintained that arithmetical thinking is based on the more pervasive intuition of time and geometrical thinking on the less pervasive intuition of space, it would seem that the distinction between inner and outer experience in Kant is capable of effecting something of at least the same general kind of asymmetry between arithmetic and geometry that Frege believed to be so important to mathematical epistemology. Frege seems never to have considered this point.

We add this remark, however, mainly as an aside. For, clearly, there are important differences between Frege and Kant concerning the pervasiveness of arithmetic. Kant, for example, despite acknowledging arithmetic to be widely applicable, none the less held it to be limited to that which is *experienceable*. He did not take it to apply to the whole of what is (rationally) imaginable or *conceivable*. Consequently, though he judged arithmetical law to be a priori in character, he also judged it to be synthetic. Frege, on the other hand, believed arithmetic to apply to all that is conceivable, and it was precisely in this departure from Kant that he was led to regard it as analytic rather than synthetic in character.)

Frege thus disagreed with Kant concerning the pervasiveness to rational human thought of arithmetical thinking. This disagreement cannot, however, be taken at face value in explaining why Kant held a synthetic and Frege an analytic conception of arithmetic. For the two employed different conceptions of the notions of analyticity and syntheticity. Thus, to comprehend better the true differences separating Kant and Frege, we must look more carefully at the definitions each used in formulating the key notions of his position.

Kant defined an analytic truth as a truth in which the predicate 'belongs to' the subject as something 'covertly contained' in it, and a synthetic truth as one that is not analytic (cf. [2.86], 9–11). He did not characterize the analytic/synthetic distinction, as he did the a priori/a posteriori distinction, in terms of the characters of the possible justifications of a judgement. Frege, on the other hand, did exactly that. In his scheme (cf. [2.49], sections 3, 17, 87–8), both the analytic/synthetic and the a priori/a posteriori distinctions are parts of a classificatory system regarding the different kinds of *justifications* a given judgement might have.

Each truth, Frege believed, possesses a kind of *canonical proof* or justification. This is a proof which, in its ultimate premisses, goes all the way back to the 'primitive truths' of the subject to which the theorem belongs. It gives 'the ultimate ground upon which rests the justification for holding [the theorem proven] to be true' (Ibid., section 3). It thus presupposes an ordering of truths, and its objective is precisely to retrieve that segment of the given ordering which links the proposition to be proven to those ur-truths of its subject which are responsible for its truth. It aims, in other words, at revealing what might be called the *grounds* of the proven proposition's truth – its Leibnizian *Sufficient Reason*, as it were (Ibid., sections 3, 17).

A proposition or judgement is said to be analytical, in this scheme, if its canonical proof contains only 'general logical laws' and 'definitions' (Ibid., Section 3). It is said to be synthetic if its canonical proof contains at least one premiss belonging to 'some special science' (Ibid.). It is considered a posteriori if its canonical proof includes an 'appeal to facts, i.e. to truths which cannot be proved and are not general' (Ibid.). And, finally, it is considered to be a priori if its canonical proof uses exclusively 'general laws, which themselves neither need nor admit of proof' (Ibid.) (in other words, if knowledge of it can arise from the Fregean faculty of reason alone).[10]

Frege believed that finding the canonical proofs of arithmetical truths would reveal an intimate connection between them and the basic laws of thought (i.e. the 'general logical laws').[11] At the same time, however, he was keenly aware of the Kantian objection to such a proposal; namely, that it makes it difficult to account for the epistemic productivity or substantiality of arithmetic. Indeed, immediately after having broached the view that arithmetic is analytic in section 15 of the *Grundlagen* [2.49], Frege went on in section 16 to note that the chief difficulty facing such a view is to explain how 'the great tree of the science of number as we know it, towering, spreading, and still continually growing' can 'have its roots in bare identities'. He thus clearly saw his main task as that of explaining how analytic judgement and analytic inference can yield an epistemic product having the robustness that arithmetic appears to have.

His response can be seen as divided into two parts. The first of these consists in the giving of an account of the 'objectivity' of analytic judgements that does not appeal to sensation or intuition. The second concerns the more general problem of explaining how one might get a conclusion that extends the knowledge represented by the premises of an inference out of premises that can be inferentially manipulated only by purely logical means.

Regarding the former, Frege's idea was to ascribe special properties to concepts, or to the objectively existing *thoughts* which, via the context principle (the principle that it is only in the context of a proposition (*Satz*) that words have meaning, cf. [2.49], section 60), are prior to them. Numbers were then to be defined in terms of concept extensions, and concept extensions to be treated as 'logical objects' (which we somehow grasp by grasping the concepts of which they are extensions). The epistemologically salient features of this arrangement were summed up in the following remark from the *Grundlagen* (Ibid., section 105).

> reason's proper study is itself. In arithmetic we are not concerned with objects which we come to know as something alien from without through the medium of the senses, but with objects given directly to reason and, as its nearest kin, utterly transparent to it.
>
> And yet, for that very reason, these objects are not subjective fantasies. There is nothing more objective than the laws of arithmetic.[12]

In later writings, Frege elaborated a bit – but only a bit – on his notion of concept extensions as *logical objects*. He wrote, for example, that:

> it is futile to take the extension of a concept as a class, and
> make it rest, not on the concept, but on single things ... the
> extension of a concept does not consist of objects falling under
> the concept, in the way, e.g., that a wood consists of trees ...
> it attaches to the concept and to the concept alone ... the concept
> takes logical precedence to its extension.
>
> (cf. [2.53], 455).

Thus, what made a class into a logical object, in Frege's view, was only
its relation to the concept of which it formed the extension. He had
ultimately, however, to establish the sense in which logical objects exist,
since, in his view, they were not actual (i.e. not spatial or 'handleable').
Here he had only analogies to offer, citing such examples as the axis
of the earth and the centre of mass of the solar system (cf. [2.49],
section 26). These illustrated his generally negative characterization of
logical objects as objects 'independent of our sensation, intuition and
imagination, and of all construction of mental pictures, memories
and earlier sensations, but not ... independent of reason' (Ibid.).[13]

Frege had also to establish that logical objects deserve to be called
'logical'. This he did not do in the *Grundlagen*, being at that time
unsure whether he needed concept extensions or just concepts.[14] He
pursued the matter to a (for him) satisfactory end only in the 1891
lecture 'Function und Begriff' [2.51], where he argued (i) that the notion
of concept-extension can be reduced to that of the range-of-values of
a function; and (ii) that this latter notion is clearly a logical notion.

Among the more important things that Frege's belief in the logical
precedence of concepts to their extensions allowed him to do was to
reduce knowledge of infinities to logical knowledge. Along with this
he had also to accept a restriction on how we come to *acquire* concepts;
namely, that we do so by means other than abstraction from the
particulars falling under them (cf. [2.49], sections 49–51). Such a view
of concept acquisition was of the utmost importance to his logicism.
For, were concepts to be obtainable only via such a process of abstraction, knowledge of the number concept would likewise be obtainable
only through prior knowledge of the particulars falling under it. If that
were so, however, one would have to give a prior account of how it is
that we come by knowledge of the particulars from which knowledge
of the abstracted concept is derived. And in order to keep this account
from destroying the 'logical' character of numbers, one would have to
make sure that it made no appeal to the likes of sensation or Kantian
intuition. Moreover, even if it were successful in avoiding appeals to
Kantian intuition, such an abstractive account of concept acquisition
would cause severe problems for the knowledge of infinite sets. For it
is hardly plausible to believe that we could either obtain separate

intuitions for each member of an infinite collection or be given infinite sets of particulars in the space of a single intuition of their members (through devices such as, say, Kant's so-called 'unity of synthetic apperception').[15]

Frege's logicist treatment of number therefore relied heavily on the idea that concepts are given prior to and independent of their extensions. This, indeed, seems to be have been the leading idea behind his notorious Rule V, the principle that every concept ϕ has an extension (or, to put it in its original form, the principle that all and only ϕs are ψs if and only if the extension of ϕ is identical to the extension of ψ).[16]

The discovery by Russell (cf. [2.119]) that this way of thinking of the relationship between concepts and (logical) objects is subject to paradox therefore threw Frege's entire 'improvement' of Kant's arithmetical epistemology into crisis. For without a principle that makes concepts prior to their extensions, a Fregean philosophy of arithmetic would have great difficulty in developing an appropriately non-intuitional model of cognition for our knowledge of concept extensions. And without a non-intuitional model of our knowledge of concept extensions, the major novelty (i.e. the major non-Kantian element) would be missing from Frege's proposed explanation of the epistemic robustness or substantiality of arithmetic.

Russell's discovery thus raised the problem of how we might come to apprehend logical objects (and thus numbers), even if it is assumed that they exist. Without a Frege-type scheme of comprehension, which sees apprehension of numbers as derived from apprehension of concepts, and which allows concepts to be apprehended without any prior non-conceptual apprehension of particulars, one is hard-pressed to avoid at least some minimal appeal to non-conceptually based knowledge of sets or extensions – a knowledge which is hard to account for without making some appeal to sensation or intuition.[17] Russell's paradox therefore raised grave problems for the epistemology of Frege's logical objects.

But even supposing these problems to have been solved, there were, by Frege's own admission (indeed, his own insistence!), serious difficulties still to be overcome in explaining the epistemic productivity of mathematical *inference*. To manage these, Frege appealed to the general phenomenon of *Sinn* and to the possibility of rearranging (or 'recarving') the contents of a proposition in such a way as to expose contents that had been hitherto undetected.

Concepts featured prominently in this explanation too. In particular, it included an appeal to an assumed relationship between concepts and propositions which allows a proposition to be both understood and known even though not all the concepts contained in it are apprehended. This crucially important feature of the relationship between propositions and their constituent concepts was taken to be based on the principles that (i) in order to apprehend a proposition, one need only know a *definition* of its immediate constituent concepts; and that (ii) knowing a definition of a concept does not require that all content tacit in it be apprehended. It is the recovery of tacitly contained content (i.e. discovery of its presence and character) that thus allows the conclusion of an analytic inference to represent something more, by way of cognitive accomplishment, than is represented by the apprehension and knowledge of its premises. As Frege himself put it, the identification and utilization of such content amounts to something more than merely 'taking out of the box again what we have just put into it' (Ibid., Section 88).[18] For what we put into an inferential 'box' is the knowledge of concepts we use in order to arrive at understanding and knowledge of its premises. What, on Frege's account, we are capable of extracting from such a box is not only judgements formed from those concepts, but also judgements formed from concepts identified, indeed *formed*, through the 'carving up' or conceptual rearrangement of the premises.[19]

However, if Frege required analytic inference to be epistemically productive, he also required (at least some of) it to be rigorous. Therefore, in some sense, he demanded that analytical judgement be *incapable* of concealing content. Indeed, he himself insisted that his logicism required the giving of utterly rigorous proofs for the laws of arithmetic. It is 'only if every gap in the chain of deductions is eliminated with the greatest care', he said, that we can 'say with certainty upon what primitive truths' they rest (Ibid., Section 4; cf. also the introduction to [2.52]). And it is only through seeing with certainty the truths upon which the truths of arithmetic rest that we would be in a position to judge whether or not those grounds are logical in character.

What Frege seems not to have seen so clearly, however, is that we can be certain that a canonically proven proposition is analytic only to the extent that we can be certain that its premises do not tacitly contain any synthetic content. At any rate, how certainty on this score is to be attained is something about which he seems to have said little. He firmly believed that there are propositions – the so-called 'basic laws' of arithmetic – that are at once so rich as to be capable of delivering the whole of arithmetic and also so clearly analytic as to self-evidently conceal no synthetic content. What he took to be the justification of this confidence is less clear.

(N.B. Leibniz, the original logicist, also believed in such a layer of analytic truths. However, for him, things were different. For, in the first place, he believed that all propositions are analytic. Second, the propositions he saw as making up the 'basic laws' – namely, the so-called logical identities of the form 'A is A' – were transparently analytic. This is so because, for Leibniz, analyticity consisted in containment of the predicate of a proposition in its subject, and propositions of the form 'A is A' satisfy this containment requirement in a manner in which none clearer or more certain can be conceived. Leibniz therefore had a natural stopping point for his reduction to analytic truth. Frege, on the other hand, having adopted a more complex and sophisticated definition of analyticity, seems to have lost the ability to identify a class of truths which were as clearly and certainly analytic as Leibniz's 'identities'. As a result, he lacked as clear a point at which to terminate the reduction of arithmetic laws to analytic truths.)

Frege's conception of mathematical inference was thus faced with two apparently competing demands: on the one hand, the need to endow analytic judgments with tacit content so as to enable analytic inference to be epistemically productive; and, on the other, the need to restrict the mechanisms producing tacit content in such a way as to guarantee that synthetic content can never be tacitly contained in what passes for analytic content. In the end, I believe, he failed to meet these two demands adequately. He did not succeed in providing a set of basic laws and a criterion of tacit content the pair of which were guaranteed to permit only the production of analytic truths as tacit contents of the basic laws. Nor did he manage to ensure that the epistemic productivity sustainable by means of his mechanisms of tacit content production are capable of matching those which may be observed to hold in arithmetic.

The first failure was clearly illustrated by Russell's paradox, which shows that the latent content concealed by Frege's axioms (in particular, his axiom of comprehension) could include not only synthetic truths, but even analytical falsehoods! The second failure became the pivotal feature of the intuitionists' critique of logicism, which will be discussed later.

Russell's logicism was quite different from Frege's. In the first place, it was not motivated primarily by the discovery of non-Euclidean geometries with its attendant belief in the epistemological asymmetry between geometry and arithmetic. Nor was it based on belief in such things as logical objects, and the associated division of cognition into faculties of sense, intuition and reason. Nor, finally, did it restrict its logicism to arithmetic, but, rather, extended it to the whole of mathematics, and even to certain areas outside traditional mathematics.[20] Rather, it took as its starting points (i) a certain general definition of mathematics; (ii) a methodological principle to pursue ever further generalization in science; and (iii) a belief that pursuing this principle in mathematics would eventually lead one to a most general science of all, namely, logic.[21] It was fuelled in these pursuits by the then rapid and impressive advances in symbolic logic.

In the opening paragraph of *The Principles of Mathematics* ([2.120], 3),[22] Russell offered the following definition of pure mathematics: 'Pure mathematics is the class of all propositions of the form "p implies q", and neither p nor q contains any constants except logical constants'. He then went on to describe his logicist project as that of showing 'that whatever has, in the past, been regarded as pure mathematics, is included in our definition, and that whatever else is included possesses those marks by which mathematics is commonly though vaguely distinguished from other studies' (Ibid.). Russell also maintained that, in addition to asserting implications, propositions of pure mathematics are characterized by the fact that they contain variables (Ibid., p. 5), indeed, variables of wholly unrestricted range (Ibid., p. 7).

Russell planned to defend this last claim, which he acknowledged as being highly counterintuitive, by showing that even such apparently variable-free statements as '$1 + 1 = 2$' can be seen to contain variables once their true meaning and form is revealed. The discovery (or, better, *recovery*) of the true meaning and form of such statements was made possible by the vast enrichment of the basic stock of logical forms made available through the work of Peirce, Schröder, Peano and Frege. Using this work, Russell produced analyses of the deep forms of ordinary mathematical statements. '$1 + 1 = 2$', for example, was analysed as 'If x is one and y is one, and x differs from y, then x and y are two.' Analysed in this way, Russell maintained, the supposedly non-implicational, variable free '$1 + 1 = 2$' is seen both to contain completely general variables and to express an implication, just as his logicist theory predicted would be the case (Ibid., p. 6).

Of course, 'if x is one and y is one, and x and y are different, then x and y are two' does not express a genuine proposition at all since it contains free variables. It expresses instead what might be called a proposition form or a proposition schema. Russell called it a '*type* of proposition', and went on to say that 'mathematics is interested exclusively in *types* of propositions' (Ibid., p. 7) rather than in individual propositions *per se*. On this view, the business of mathematics is to determine which propositions can be generalized (i.e. which constants can be turned into variables), and then to carry this process of generalization out to its maximum possible extent (Ibid., pp. 8, 9). This maximum will have been reached when we have penetrated to a level of propositions whose only constants are *logical* constants and whose only undemonstrated propositions are the most basic truths whose only constants are logical constants (Ibid., p. 8).[23] The logical constants themselves, as a class, were to be characterized only by enumeration. Indeed, by their very nature they admitted only of this kind of characterization, since any other kind of characterization would be forced to make use of some element of the class to be defined.

At bottom, then, Russell's logicism was motivated by a view of mathematics that saw it as the science of the most general formal truths; a science whose only indefinables are those constants of rational thought (the so-called *logical* constants) that have the widest and most ubiquitous usage and whose only indemonstrables are those propositions which set out the most basic properties of those indefinable terms (Ibid). In his view, this provided the only precise description of what philosophers have had in mind in describing mathematics as an a priori science (Ibid). Mathematics is thus in the business of generalization. Its aim is to identify those truths that remain true when their non-logical constants are replaced by variables (Ibid., p. 7). This process of generalization may require some analysis in order to find the genuine form of the sentence to be generalized. But once that form is found, the generalization process should ultimately lead to the realization that the mathematical truth in question expresses a formal truth whose variables are completely general and whose only constants are logical constants.

Ideally, proper method in mathematics requires pursuit of this process of generalization to the ultimate degree.[24] At that point, Russell believed, we will find formal truths of maximum generality – truths of a generality so great as to render them incapable of further generalization – truths, that is, that are so general that they would become non-truths were any of their constants to be replaced, even through conceptual analysis, by variables. This, in Russell's opinion, was the only point at which the method of mathematics (i.e. the pursuit of maximal formal generalization) can properly and naturally be brought to a close. He also believed that it is in this domain of formal truths of the utmost generality, and in this domain alone, that we can rightly expect to meet what are properly regarded as *laws of logic*.

According to Russell, these laws are justified inductively from their consequences.

> in mathematics, except in the earliest parts, the propositions from
> which a given proposition is deduced generally give the reason
> why we believe the given proposition. But in dealing with the
> principles of mathematics, this relation is reversed. Our
> propositions are too simple to be easy, and thus their
> consequences are generally easier than they are. Hence we tend
> to believe the premises because we can see that their
> consequences are true, instead of believing the consequences
> because we know the premises to be true ... thus the method
> in investigating the principles of mathematics is really an inductive

method, and is substantially the same as the method of discovering general laws in any other science.[25]

Thus, contrary to what Kant had maintained, the pursuit of greater generality (or what Kant referred to as 'unification') has a natural and fairly inevitable stopping point; specifically, that level of judgements having broad scope, entirely general variables and utterly ubiquitous constants.

Frege and Russell, then, though they agreed in their rejection of Kantian intuition as the basis of mathematical knowledge, none the less differed with regard to their estimates of the proper scope of logicism and the nature and origins of its basic laws. They also differed on the important question of our knowledge of the infinities with which mathematics deals, and of how, exactly, that knowledge is related to our knowledge of concepts.

Unlike Frege, Russell did not believe that concepts alone can give rise to extensions or sets. Indeed, he responded to his own antinomy by offering a conception of set which assumed a class of individuals as given *prior to* the generation of sets by concepts. In his view, before there can be a rich universe of sets, there must first be a totality of individuals that is given by means other than grasp of a concept. Using this domain of individuals as a base, comprehension by concepts (or what Russell referred to as 'propositional functions') was then supposed to operate according to predicative principles of collection. There was thus an order of 'priority' of *types* or levels induced among entities, with the domain of individuals constituting the lowest level and the upper levels being formed by application of comprehension operations to the entities lying at prior levels.

This way of thinking of set comprehension differs radically from the way Frege thought of it. Fregean comprehension did not presume an ordering of entities according to some 'priority' ranking, and it was not restricted to collection of entities formed at prior levels. Perhaps even more importantly, it did not posit a '0th-level' domain of entities as somehow given prior to all comprehension by concepts. Indeed, in Frege's scheme, the whole idea was to avoid the need of having a 'starting' collection – particularly an infinite one – to serve as the raw material from which comprehension by concepts is to get off the ground. For, in Frege's view, having a non-conceptually comprehended domain of individuals required something like Kantian intuition, and this is exactly what he hoped to avoid (since he did not see how knowledge of such a domain could rightly be seen as *logical* knowledge).

Russell, though he showed some sensitivity to this difficulty, seems never to have settled on a means of resolving it. In his earlier writings he sometimes spoke (cf. [2.120], section 5, ch. 1) as if any statement positing a domain of existents, and therefore any axiom positing a domain of individuals, is not to be regarded as a truth of pure mathematics *per se*, but rather as an hypothesis whose consequences are to be investigated.

Later (cf. introduction to [2.120] (2nd edn) and [2.124]), however, he stated both that he believed such a view to be mistaken and that he himself had never held such a view. There are also systematic elements of his thought that would (or at least should) have led him to reject such a view. Chief in this regard was his belief in the need for the 'regressive' method in the foundations of mathematics (defended in both [2.123] and [2.124]).

Use of the regressive method allows the truth of a principle to be inferred from its usefulness in deductively unifying a recognized body of truths. Hence, to the extent that the postulation of a domain of individuals (e.g. an axiom of infinity) has utility as a means of deductively organizing the recognized truths of mathematics, it, too, inherits a certain plausibility and so deserves to be 'detached' and asserted as a truth on its own right. Russell's 'regressive' method thus elevated axioms of existence to the status of justified assertions, and so made them more than mere 'hypotheses' to be used as antecedents of conditionals whose consequents are propositions whose proof requires their use. There would therefore seem to be a tension between Russell's adoption of the 'regressive' method in mathematics and that part of his logicism (suggested by remarks he made in the second edition of the *Principia* [2.126]) which saw axioms of existence (and, in particular, his axiom of infinity) as mere hypotheses to be put into the antecedents of conditionals.

But if there were differences between Russell and Frege regarding the nature and justification of the basic laws of mathematical thought, there was substantial agreement between them as regards the nature of mathematical inference. In particular, there was agreement on the points that the inferences of mathematics are all to be strictly logical in character, and that this is necessary in order to satisfy the demands of rigour.

It is not always easy to see the similarities between their views, however, because they used different definitions of analyticity and syntheticity. For Frege, a synthetic inference was one in which the conclusion could not be extracted from the premises by any re-carving of their contents, but rather required something like an infusion of intuition in order to connect the conclusion with the premiss(es). For Russell, on the other hand, an inference was synthetic, and, so, epistemically productive (at least in a minimal way), if its conclusion constituted a *different proposition from* its premiss(es). Thus, many inferences that

Frege would have classified as 'analytic', would have been classified by Russell as 'synthetic'.

The standard of syntheticity in inference set forth by Russell was weaker than that set forth by Frege. Consequently, many inferences satisfying Russell's condition would not satisfy Frege's.[26] Indeed, judged by the lights of Russell's definition, even the elementary inferences of syllogistic reasoning, which Frege classified as analytic, would have been counted as synthetic by Russell. This was all to the good so far as Russell was concerned. For it enabled him to meet Kant's challenge to explain the epistemic substantiality of mathematical reasoning while at the same time maintaining, in opposition to Kant, that the inferences involved in such reasoning are of a purely formal, logical nature and make no appeal to intuition (cf. [2.121]). If growth of knowledge through inference is essentially a matter of thereby obtaining a justified judgement whose propositional content is simply *distinct* from those of one's previously justified judgements, then even very elementary logical inferences can be epistemically productive.

The 'logicization' of mathematical inference was thus, in Russell's opinion (cf. [2.120], 4), nothing to be balked at epistemically. What had kept previous generations of thinkers, and, in particular, Kant, from embracing it was simply the relatively impoverished state of logic prior to the late nineteenth century. The old logic with its meagre stock of subject–predicate forms may have been inadequate to the riches of mathematical reasoning, but the new logic with its robust functional conception of form had changed all this. With its help mathematical reasoning could finally be logicized in its entirety, and 'a final and irrevocable refutation' (Ibid.) of the Kantian doctrine that mathematical inference makes use of intuition be given.

Effectively countering Kant's intuitional conception of mathematical inference was thus an important element of both Frege's and Russell's logicist programmes. They seemed to believe that this could be accomplished simply by deriving large bodies of mathematical theorems from specified axioms by purely logical means. On reflection, however, this seems to be mistaken. Kant may well have underestimated the power of logical inference. His main point, however, was not that there are mathematical proofs that have no logical counterparts whatsoever. Rather, it was that such counterparts, even if they were to exist, would not preserve the epistemologically essential features of the mathematical proofs of which they are the 'logicized' counterparts.

Against this essentially epistemological point, detailed *tours de force* (e.g. Frege's *Grundgesetze* and Russell's *Principles of Mathematics* and *Principia Mathematica*) which locate logical counterparts for mathematical proofs on even a grand scale can have but little effect. For the claim to be met is not that there are no counterparts, but rather that they are epistomologically inadequate substitutes for the mathematical proofs they are to replace.

In summary, let us return to our original claim that logicism in this century arose from two very different sources, to wit, the discovery of non-Euclidean geometries and the development of symbolic logic. Frege's logicism owed the bulk of both its motivation and character to the former, while that of Russell was due primarily to the latter. This is the basic reason why Frege's logicism, unlike Russell's, was able to preserve a remarkable degree of fidelity to the precepts of Kantian epistemology.

Frege did not, however, agree with Kant's idealist conception of the faculty of reason (cf. the remark quoted from [2.49], section 105, p. 14 for an expression of this). To get a realist account, though, he had to get the right sorts of objects into the picture. They had to be independent of the human mind in order to insure the objectivity of arithmetic; but they also had to be intimately related to the basic operation of the human mind in order to avoid an appeal to intuition and thus to account for the greater pervasiveness of arithmetic as over against geometry. His solution was the logical object, the ur-form of which was the class-as-concept-extension. Through its essential relation with concepts, it could be brought close to reason. But through the objectivity of concepts it could also be made objective.

Frege's idea of giving a realist rather than idealist treatment of Kant's faculty of reason foundered on Russell's paradox. Russell's reaction to his paradox was rather different. Far from causing him to give up logicism, it led him instead to seek another basis for it – a methodological basis whose chief principle was one enjoining pursuit of maximal generality in one's theorizing, including one's mathematical theorizing.[27] In the presence of his belief that mathematical claims express generalizations, this principle led him in a natural way to a logicist conception of mathematics. In the end, however, Russell's paradox proved to be nearly as great an impediment to Russell's logicism as it was to Frege's. For just as Frege was unable to find a way to fit classes that do not descend from concepts into his realist logicism of logical objects given directly to reason, so, too, was Russell unable to find a satisfactory way of justifying laws asserting the existence of such classes as genuinely logical laws.

Intuitionism

Like Frege's logicism, the intuitionism of the early part of this century was also dominated by (i) the idea that what the mind brings forth purely of itself cannot be hidden from it; and (ii) the belief that the existence of non-Euclidean geometries reveals important epistemological differences between geometry and arithmetic. The direct predecessors of the intuitionists appear to have been Gauss and Kronecker, who interpreted the discovery of non-Euclidean geometries differently than Frege. For whereas Frege proposed a realist modification of the creation principle in order to account for the apparent differences between arithmetic and geometry brought to light by the discovery of non-Euclidean geometry, Gauss and Kronecker, and the intuitionists after them, interpreted the difference between arithmetic and geometry in the light of the creation principle (i.e. principle (i) above), of which they adopted an idealist reading.

Thus, instead of maintaining Kant's synthetic a priori conception of geometry and trying to account for the difference between geometry and arithmetic by establishing arithmetic as analytic, the early intuitionist rejected Kant's synthetic a priori conception of geometry and proposed to account for the differences between arithmetic and geometry by seeing the former as a priori and the latter as a posteriori. As Gauss and Kronecker emphasized, arithmetic is purely a product of the human intellect, whereas geometry is determined by things outside the human intellect.[28] Years later, Weyl (cf. [2.148], 22) would reiterate the same theme, remarking that 'the numbers are to a far greater measure than the objects and relations of space a free product of the human mind and therefore transparent to the mind'.

Brouwer, too, expressed similar ideas, identifying as the primary cause of the demise of intuitionism since the time of Kant (cf. [2.16]) the refutation of Kant's belief in an a priori intuition of space by the discovery of non-Euclidean geometries. At the same time, however, he advocated resolute adherence to an a priori intuition of time, and even argued that from this intuition one could recoup a system of geometric judgements via Descartes' 'arithmetization' of geometry. He considered the 'primordial intuition of time' – which he described as the falling apart of a life-moment into a part that is passing away and a part that is becoming – as the 'fundamental phenomenon of the human intellect' (Ibid., p. 127).[29] From this intuition one can pass, via a process of abstraction, to the notion of 'bare two-oneness', which Brouwer regarded as the basal concept of all of mathematics. The further recognition by the intellect of the possibility of indefinitely continuing this process then leads it through the finite ordinals, to the smallest transfinite ordinal, and finally to the intuition of the linear continuum (i.e. to that unified plurality of elements which cannot be thought of as a mere collection of units since the relations of interposition which join them is not exhausted by mere interposition of new units). In this way, Brouwer believed (Ibid., pp. 131–2), first arithmetic and then geometry (albeit only analytic geometry), via reduction of the former to the latter through Descartes' calculus of coordinates, come to be qualified as synthetic a priori.[30]

The early intuitionists thus retained a semblance of adherence to Kant's belief in the synthetic a priority of arithmetical knowledge while denying his belief in the a priority of our knowledge of the base characteristics of visual space. They were also staunchly Kantian in their conception of mathematical inference. Poincaré and Brouwer, in particular, devoted considerable attention to this point.[31] Indeed, Poincaré, who carried on a well-known debate with Russell in the early years of this century,[32] made the role of logical inference in mathematical proof the centrepiece of his critique of logicism. So, too, in effect, did Brouwer, though his critique was aimed at the use of logical reasoning in classical mathematics generally, and not just at the logicists' programmatic demand regarding the logicization of proof.

At the heart of the view of proof that both criticized is a conception of evidence – the *classical* conception evidence – which sees it as essentially a means of determining the (classical) truth value of a proposition. On this view, evidence is a relatively 'malleable' commodity. Its effects extend to a variety of propositions other than that which forms its direct content. This comes about as a result of subjecting the content of a piece of evidence to logical analysis, which is used to extract 'new' contents from the original content. By this means, the justificatory power which the evidence provided for its content can be transferred to the analytically extracted content. Hence, one and the same piece of evidence can be used to identify the truth value of a variety of different propositions. This holds, moreover, despite the fact that there is no parallel analysis directed at the evidence itself whose purpose is to reveal a separable part of the evidence whose content is precisely the new content brought forward by means of the analysis of its content. On the classical view, then, the propositional content of a piece of evidence can be 'detached' from that evidence itself. Applying logical analysis to that 'detached' content, one can then transfer the warrant attaching to it to any of the new propositions extracted by means of that analysis.

Both Brouwer and Poincaré reacted sharply to this view of inference. Brouwer's reaction was based on the view that mathematical knowledge is essentially a product of introspective experience (cf. [2.17], 488). The extension or development of such knowledge can therefore not proceed via logical extrapolation of its content, since such extrapolation does not guarantee any similar extension of the experience having the extrapolated content as its content. Extension of genuinely mathematical knowledge thus requires the extension of the mathematical experience serving as the evidence for a given content into a mathematical experience of another content. (Here, experience is understood in such a way as to make it capable of serving as the evidence for a given content only if it itself has that content as its content.) In other words, inference is not to be seen as a matter of logically extracting new contents from old and thence transferring warrant from old to new. Rather, it is to be seen as a process of *experientally transforming* an introspective construction having one content into an introspective construction having another.

Brouwer thus held that one can never 'deduce a *mathematical* state of things' (cf. [2.18], 524, emphasis mine) by means of *logical inference*.[33] He memorialized this view in his so-called *First Act of Intuitionism*, in which it he declared that mathematics should be completely separated from 'mathematical language and hence from the phenomena of language described by theoretical logic, recognizing that intuitionist mathematics is an essentially languageless activity of the mind having its origin in the perception of a move of time' (cf. [2.21], 4).

Brouwer thus adhered to a basically Kantian conception of mathematical reasoning according to which extension of mathematical knowledge via inference requires development of a new intuition underlying that inference. Poincaré, too, adopted such a conception of inference, though his view differed in certain respects from Brouwer's. Mathematical reasoning, as he put it (cf. [2.99], 32), has a 'kind of creative virtue' by which its conclusions go beyond its premises in a way that the conclusions of logical inferences do not go beyond their premises. Logical inference from a mathematically known proposition, therefore, though it may yield *some* kind of extension of that knowledge, will none the less typically not yield an extension of the genuinely mathematical knowledge thereby represented. In short, in order for mathematical knowledge that **p** to be extended to mathematical knowledge that **q**, it is not enough that **p** be seen logically to imply **q**. Rather, **p** must be seen both to be mathematically different from **q** and to *mathematically* imply **q** (cf. [2.101], bk. II, ch. 2, section 6; [2.100], ch. 1, section 5). In other words, the 'movement' from premiss to conclusion in a mathematical inference is a case of joint comprehension of the premises and conclusion by a common mathematical 'universal' which is seen to persist in the 'differences' through which it 'moves'.

For Poincaré, then, mathematical reasoning consisted in the synthesis of different propositions by a single, distinctively mathematical structure or architecture. Thus, as with Brouwer, so, too, with Poincaré, we find a view of mathematical reasoning which contrasts sharply with the logicists' conception of mathematical reasoning.

The views of mathematical reasoning or inference of Brouwer and Poincaré are thus Kantian in the sense that they reject the idea that genuine mathematical inference can be logical. They also represent a modification of Kant's views, however. For Kant suggested (cf. [2.86],

741-6) that by means of genuinely mathematical reasoning from a given set of premises, one can obtain conclusions that are actually *unattainable* by means of purely logical (i.e. purely analytical or discursive) reasoning from those same premises. Such an idea, however, seems not to have figured at all in the arguments of Poincaré and Brouwer.[34] What they were stressing was a difference in *epistemic quality* between logical and mathematical reasoning – a difference which, in their view, would persist even if the two types of reasoning might prove to be result-wise equivalent. This emphasis on epistemic quality was based on their belief in a difference between the epistemic condition of one whose reasoning is founded on topic-neutral steps of logical inference and one whose inference rests on topic-specific insights into the given mathematical subject at hand. Reasoning of the latter sort presupposes a knowledge of the local 'architecture' of a subject. Reasoning of the former sort does not. To use Poincaré's own figures of speech, the difference is (i) like that between a writer who has only a knowledge of grammar versus one who also has an idea for a story (cf. [2.101], bk. II, ch. 2); or (ii) like that between a chess player who has knowledge only of the permissible moves of the several players versus one who has a tactical understanding of the game as well ([2.100], pt. I, ch. 1, section V).

The intuitionists were thus at odds with the logicists over the question of the nature of mathematical reasoning. The heart of their disagreement, moreover, was not a dispute concerning which logic is the right logic, but rather a deeper difference regarding the role that *any* logical inference – classical or non-classical – has to play in mathematical reasoning. They were, in other words, divided over the Kantian question of whether intuition has an indispensable role to play in mathematical inference. The intuitionists sided with Kant in holding that it does. The logicists took the contrary view.[35]

In the intuitionism of Brouwer, Poincaré and Weyl we thus find an attempt to work out a modified form of Kant's specifically mathematical epistemology. So far, the modifications noted include (i) the jettisoning of Kant's use of spatial intuition as a fundament for mathematical knowledge; and (ii) the extension and elaboration of his use of temporal intuition as a basis for arithmetic (and, relatedly, the reduction of geometry to arithmetic via appeal to Descartes' 'arithmetization' of geometry).

There is, however, one final modification to be noted, and that concerns the intuitionists' (in particular, Brouwer's and Weyl's) conception of existence claims. It is perhaps the most significant of all the modifications made and consists in a shift from Kant's conception of existence claims and our knowledge of them to a conception of existence claims that is more like that found in such post-Kantian romantic idealists as Fichte, Schelling and Goethe. The basic non-Kantian element of this view was the introduction of a non-sensory, purely intellectual form of intuition (*intellektuelle Anschauung*).[36] This was conceived as a form of self-knowledge whose key epistemic feature was its immediacy – an immediacy expressing the romantic idealists' concern with the epistemic effects of representation. They saw representation as the basic source of error and uncertainty in cognition and therefore advocated its avoidance.

Their reasoning was basically Kantian. That is, they began with the Kantian premiss that no idea or concept (more generally, no representation) contains the being or existence of that which it represents[37] and concluded from this that no concept or idea (more generally, no representation) could, in and of itself, give the existence of anything falling under it. Indeed, representations only tend to increase the epistemic distance between the knower and the object to be known since they leave the being of the object still to be given while adding grasp of the representation to those things that must be accomplished before the object can be known.

What was wanted, therefore, was some kind of representationless knowledge of being. For the paradigm case of such knowledge, the romantic idealists turned to our knowledge of our willing and acting selves. Their model for knowledge of existence thus became one of self-knowledge; in order to know that something exists, the knower must *live* it or *be* it. In other words, she must incorporate it into herself so that her knowledge of its existence becomes that of her knowledge of her own existence. As Schelling said (cf. [2.12], 344), 'the proposition that there are things external to us will only be certain . . . to the extent that it is identical with the proposition I exist, and its certainty can only match that of the proposition from which it derives.'

Brouwer, it seems, adopted this romantic idealist conception of knowledge of existence. His so-called *First Act of Intuitionism* can indeed be seen as issuing a call for the mathematical knower to turn into himself and to shun the epistemic indirection of the classical view of mathematics with its involvement in the representation of mathematical thought – that is, mathematical *language*.[38] Thus he reminded us:

> you know that very meaningful phrase 'turn into yourself'. There seems to be a kind of attention which centres round yourself and which to some extent is within your power. What this Self is we cannot further say; we cannot even reason about it, since – as we know – all speaking and reasoning is an attention at a great distance from the Self; we cannot even get near it by reasoning or words, but only by 'turning into the Self' as it is

given to us. . . . Now you will recognize your Free Will, in so
far [as] it is free to withdraw from the world of causality and
then to remain free only then obtaining a definite Direction
which it will follow freely, reversibly.

([2.14], 2 square brackets, mine)

Here we clearly see the romanticist idea that representation impedes
knowledge – an idea that was expressed in strikingly similar terms by
Fichte, who said:

Look into yourself. Turn away from everything that surrounds
you and towards your inner life. This is the first demand that
philosophy makes on its followers. What matters is not what is
outside you, but only what comes from within yourself.

([2.41], 422)

Though we lack the space adequately to argue for it here, we believe
that Brouwer adhered to this romantic idealist conception of knowledge
in his mathematical epistemology. He believed that mathematical existence consisted in construction, that construction was a kind of autonomous 'interior' activity[39] and that mathematical knowledge was
therefore ultimately a form of self-knowledge. The key point was
summed up well in Weyl's remark (quoted earlier) that arithmetic is a
free creation of the human mind and therefore especially transparent
to it.

For Brouwer, then, existence claims were to be backed by exhibitions of objects (of the type claimed to exist), where these exhibitions
were, at bottom, acts of *creation* by the mathematical subject. He thus
departed from Kant's receptive conception of our knowledge of existence claims whose main idea was that judgements of existence must be
forced upon a passive cognitive agent and not be the product of its
own creative or inventive activity.[40]

Hilbert's position

In the third major 'ism' of the early period, Hilbert's so-called formalism, we find another form of Kantianism, and one which contrasts
with the intuitionist position in at least three important respects. The
first concerns the conception of our knowledge of existence claims that
was adopted. The second concerns the epistemic importance placed on
spatial or quasi-spatial intuition in the foundations of mathematics.
The third concerns the distinction between genuine judgements and
regulative ideals that figured so prominently in Kant's general epistemology.

As was noted above, Brouwer and Weyl conceived of the act of exhibition required for knowledge of an existence claim as, ultimately, an act of creation by the exhibiting subject. The epistemic significance of this act was taken to be based on the special access that a creating subject is supposed to have to his creations. This reduced the epistemic distance between the exhibitor and the exhibited object to that between the willing, acting subject and himself – a distance which, according to romantic idealist lights, is the desirable, optimal or perhaps only tolerable distance to have separating the mathematical knower from the objects of her existential judgements. It also, however, created an irreducible asymmetry between the exhibiting agent and all other agents as regards their knowledge of the exhibited object. Indeed, that was an essential part of the intuitionists' point – namely, that mathematical knowledge is ultimately a form of self-knowledge, and that it is indeed only self-knowledge that possesses the epistemic qualities that we want mathematical knowledge to have.

Hilbert consciously adopted a conception of mathematical knowledge that was more in keeping with what he thought of as the ideal of *objectivity*. He rejected the intuitionists' focus on the inner life and self-knowledge as too subjective a basis on which to found mathematical knowledge. In opposition to the epistemic *individualism* of the intuitionists, Hilbert opted for a more *communitarian* conception of knowledge. Indeed, he believed that it was the very 'task of science to liberate us from arbitrariness, sentiment and habit and to protect us from the subjectivism that already made itself felt in Kronecker's views and ... find its culmination in intuitionism' (cf. [2.77], 475).

In Hilbert's view, therefore, there was to be a public domain of objects to which all members of the human (or at least the human–scientific) epistemic community were to have equal access. Hilbert thus stressed the fact that the objects of finitary intuitions were to be *recognizable* (wiedererkennbar) (cf. [2.75], 171). This meant that those intuitions could be re-enacted and confirmed by other intuitions, including other intuitions of the exhibitor's as well as intuitions of non-exhibitors. Consequently, the exhibitor of a finitary object would have no essential epistemic advantage over the non-exhibitor as regards knowledge of the object exhibited.

In Hilbert's finitism, therefore, the 'constructivist' demand that objects claimed to exist be exhibited was to serve the role of taking the object of exhibition out of the exhibitor's head and putting it in the public domain where both exhibitor and non-exhibitor, alike and equally, would be able (and, indeed, required) to judge the object by its intersubjectively confirmable effects. Intuitionistic and finitistic exhibition were thus two very different things. For while the whole intent of the former was to tap the epistemic power of the supposedly special relation of intimacy that a creative subject was believed to have with respect to his own creative acts and intentions, the latter was intended to function as part of a more communitarian scheme of knowledge – a scheme in which the exhibitor had no epistemic advantage over the non-exhibitor. This parity between exhibitor and non-exhibitor is the kind of thing that is necessary if there is to be meaningful epistemic co-operation (e.g. division of epistemic labour) between them and if there is to be a way of monitoring the quality of each contributor's contribution. Epistemic co-operation, in turn, is desirable because through it the total amount of knowledge at the disposal of the individual community member can be expected to exceed that obtainable by that member himself, acting exclusively on his own.[41]

There are, then, we believe, large and important differences between the finitist and intuitionist conceptions of what is to be accomplished through exhibition. So much so, indeed, that we doubt there is much to be accomplished by describing them both as having adhered to a 'constructivist' conception of existence claims.

The second point of contrast between Hilbert and the early constructivists (which, like the preceding one, we can only mention and not develop here) concerns the very different roles they accorded to spatial intuition. Contrary to both the early constructivists (in particular, Kronecker, Brouwer and Weyl) and Kant, all of whom limited spatial intuition to geometry, Hilbert identified a type of spatial intuition which he took to be the basis of *arithmetical* knowledge. This was the position of his so-called 'finitary standpoint' according to which the basis of our arithmetical (and perhaps also our geometrical)[42] knowledge is a kind of a priori intuition in which the shapes or forms (*Gestalten*) of concrete signs are 'intuitively present as immediate experience prior to all thought' (cf. [2.75], 171; [2.76], 376; [2.77], 464) and 'immediately given intuitively, together with the objects, as something that neither can be reduced to anything else nor requires reduction' (cf. [2.76], 376; [2.77], 465).[43]

Hilbert thus proposed replacing Kant's a priori intuitions of space and time, which he viewed as so much 'anthropological garbage' (cf. [2.78], 385), with a single intuition which was taken to provide a framework of shapes or forms in which our experience of concrete signs was embedded (cf. [2.75], 171). This intuition, being 'prior to' all thought as its 'irremissible pre-condition' (cf. [2.76], 376; [2.78], 383, 385), was the source of all our a priori knowledge.

The third main point at which Hilbert's Kantianism contrasted with that of the early constructivists was in its use of certain key elements of Kant's general (as opposed to his specifically mathematical) epistemology. Of particular importance here is Kant's distinction between genuine judgements and regulative ideals. Hilbert took this distinction as the basic model for his division of classical mathematics into a *real* and an *ideal* part. The real propositions and proofs were taken to be the genuine judgements and evidence of which our knowledge is constituted. Ideal propositions, on the other hand, though they served to stimulate and guide the growth of our knowledge, were none the less not considered to be a part of it. They did not describe things that are 'present in the world' (cf. [2.75], 190). Nor were they 'admissible as a foundation of that part of our thought having to do with the understanding (*in unserem verstandesmäßigen Denken*)' (cf. [2.75], 190). They corresponded instead to *ideas* 'if, following Kant's terminology, one understands as an idea a concept of reason which transcends all experience and by means of which the concrete is to be completed into a totality' (Ibid.).

Hilbert's ideal sentences are therefore not to be likened to the indirectly verifiable 'theoretical sentences' of a realistically interpreted scientific theory familiar to us from logical empiricist epistemology. Rather, they are to be interpreted instrumentalistically, as having the same general regulative function as Kantian ideas of reason. The objects and states of affairs described in the 'theoretical sentences' of a realistically interpreted science clearly do not 'transcend all experience'. Kant's ideas of reason, on the other hand, do.

Hilbert's ideal propositions thus function as regulative devices. They do not 'prescribe any law for objects, and [do] not contain any general ground of the possibility of knowing or of determining objects as such' ([2.86], 362, square brackets mine). Rather, they are 'merely subjective law(s) for the orderly management of the possessions of our understanding, that by comparison of its concepts it may reduce them to the smallest number' (Ibid.).

Hilbert also followed Kant in maintaining that the use of ideal methods should be *epistemically conservative*. They should, that is, be only more efficient means of producing real judgements which could, none the less, in principle (though less efficiently) be developed through the exclusive use of real methods. As Kant put it:

> Although we must say of the transcendental concepts of reason that they are only ideas, this is not by any means to be taken as signifying that they are superfluous or void. For even if they cannot determine any object, they may yet, in a fundamental and unobserved fashion, be of service to the understanding as a canon for its extended and consistent employment. The understanding does not thereby obtain more knowledge of any object than it would have by its own concepts, but for the

acquiring of such knowledge it receives better and more extensive guidance.

([2.86], 385)

Similarly in Hilbert. Ideal methods, he said, play an 'indispensable' and 'well-justified' role 'in our *thinking*' (cf. [2.76], 372, emphasis Hilbert's). They should not, however, be permitted to generate any real result that does not agree with the dictates of real evidence itself (cf.[2.76], 376; [2.77], 471). Their role is rather that of enabling us to retain in our reasoning those patterns of inference in terms of which we most readily and efficiently conduct our inferential affairs (cf.[2.76], 379; [2.77], 476).

These patterns are the patterns of classical logic. Thus, Hilbert's introduction of the so-called ideal elements was ultimately for the sake of preserving classical logic as the logic of our mathematical reasoning. Introduction of ideal methods was made necessary by the fact that there exist certain real propositions (referred to by Hilbert as *problematic* real propositions) that do not abide by the principles of classical logic. By this it is meant that when these propositions are manipulated by the principles of classical logic, they produce conclusions that are not real propositions.[44] In order to obtain, then, a system that both contains the real truths and also has classical logic as its logic, Hilbert believed it necessary to add the *ideal* propositions. He also believed this to be the minimal modification of real mathematics necessary to restore it to its epistemically optimal classical logical state (cf.[2.76], 376–9; [2.77], 469–71).

However, in thus restoring mathematical reasoning to its classical logical state, Hilbert observed that the logical operators were no longer being conceived of and employed in a semantical or contentual way as expressions for operations on meaningful propositions. Rather, they were being used in a purely syntactical way as part of a larger compu-tationo-algebraic device for manipulating formulas. As he put it:

we have introduced the ideal propositions to ensure that the customary laws of logic again hold one and all. But since the ideal propositions, namely, the formulas, insofar as they do not express finitary assertions, do not mean anything in themselves, the logical operations cannot be applied to them in a contentual way, as they are to the finitary propositions. Hence, it is necessary to formalize the logical operations and also the mathematical proofs themselves; this requires a transcription of the logical relations into formulas, so that to the mathematical signs we must still adjoin some logical signs, say

&	v	$\rightarrow$	$\sim$
and	or	implies	not

([2.76], 381)

We thus find here a final step of abstraction from meaning in Hilbert's ideal mathematics – namely, abstraction from the meanings of the logical constants. It was made necessary by the decision to preserve the psychologically natural laws of classical logic as the laws of mathematical reasoning; a decision which, in turn, was the result of trying to preserve the most effective 'canon' available to us for the development of our real mathematical judgements. Ultimately, then, this 'formalism' of Hilbert's, with its radical abstraction from meaning, derived from his Kantian conception of the distinction between the real and ideal propositions according to which he saw the cognitive or epistemic value of the ideal elements as residing in their utility as instruments for extending our real judgements.

At the same time, however, it is also almost certainly this same radical abstraction from meaning that has tempted so many to misdescribe Hilbert's position as a *formalist* position in the sense of one which sees mathematics as a 'game' played with symbols. The idea behind this 'game' imagery, presumably, is that when every trace of meaning is obliterated, as in Hilbert's view of ideal mathematics, mathematics becomes ultimately a symbol–manipulation activity conducted according to certain rules; rules which, moreover, answer not to anything as serious as a concern for objective truth, but rather only to such less weighty concerns as a subjective or psychological urge for logical unity in our thinking. Even such a well-positioned and astute interpreter of Hilbert as Weyl eventually succumbed to the temptations of this description of Hilbert's views (cf.[2.147], 640). In our opinion, however, such an interpretation fails to take account both of Hilbert's overall Kantian epistemology and of certain quite specific remarks he himself made regarding the syntactical character of ideal reasoning. Hence, while we see no particular reason to deny the title of formalism to Hilbert's position, we would none the less insist that it is formalism of a quite different kind than the 'game-played-with-symbols' formalism. Hilbert stated his view forcefully in the following remark.

> The formula game that Brouwer so deprecates has, besides its mathematical value, an important general philosophical significance. For this formula game is carried out according to certain definite rules, in which the *technique of our thinking* is expressed. These rules form a closed system that can be discovered and definitively stated. The fundamental idea of my proof theory is none other than to describe the activity of our understanding, to make a protocol of the rules according to which our thinking actually proceeds. Thinking, it so happens, parallels speaking and writing: we form statements and place

them one behind another. If any totality of observations and phenomena deserve to be made the object of a serious and thorough investigation, it is this one.

([2.77], 475 (emphasis Hilbert's))

This suggests that the rules of the so-called 'game' of ideal reasoning are nothing other than the basic laws of human thought. The heart of Hilbert's proof theory, and the heart of the 'formalism' of his later thought, was thus the belief that much of human mathematical thought is, at bottom, formal-algebraic or syntactical in character. Indeed, as he remarked elsewhere, the custom in mathematical thought, and in scientific thought generally, is to make 'application of formal thought-processes (*formaler Denkprozesse*) and abstract methods' (cf.[2.78], 380). In fact, he noted,

> Even in everyday life one uses methods and conceptual constructions which require a high degree of abstraction and which only become intelligible by means of an unconscious application of the axiomatic method. Examples are the general process of negation and the concept of infinity.

(Ibid.)

What emerges from all this is an idealistically oriented formalism whose goal is to locate and defend (as a sound regulative device) the basic 'forms' of human thought. These forms of thought, which might be thought of as *theory-forms*, represent high-level commonalities of form that our thinking about a wide variety of subjects share. It is less clear whether, in speaking of 'the techniques of our thinking' as being expressible in a 'closed system' of rules that can 'be discovered and definitively stated' ([2.77], 475), Hilbert meant a single system of rules which gives a general algebra of thought, or whether he was thinking of a plurality of different theory-forms, the repository of which is classical mathematics. In either case, however, we obtain a formalism whose forms are fundamentally forms of *thought* – forms of thought, moreover, which, despite their syntactical character, are none the less deep expressions of the nature of human reasoning and therefore much more than a mere 'playing' of a 'game' with symbols.

For Hilbert, then, the ideal methods of thinking constituted a logical mould to whose contours our minds are shaped in their inferential dealings. This makes their use inviting, if not unavoidable. But inviting or not, the legitimacy of ideal reasoning still depends on the satisfaction of a certain condition – namely, its consistency, or, more specifically, its *finitarily demonstrable consistency with the finitarily provable propositions.*[45] As is well known, however, it is precisely the satisfaction of this requirement that was called into question by Gödel's discovery of his celebrated incompleteness theorems in 1931 (cf. [2.62]).

The proofs of these theorems featured a technique (commonly referred to as the 'arithmetization' of metamathematics) for representing the concepts and statements of the metamathematics of a given formal system T[46] in that portion of a formal theory of arithmetic that contains the elementary theory of recursive operations on the natural numbers. For present purposes, the important feature of this fragment of arithmetic is that it appears to be contained in what Hilbert regarded as the *finitary* part of number theory. For that reason, it also appears to be contained in those ideal theories of classical mathematics which it was Hilbert's concern to defend as legitimate.

What Gödel was able to show was first that for any formal system T containing the elementary fragment of arithmetic spoken of above, if T is consistent, then there is a sentence G of the language of T such that neither G nor $\neg G$ is a theorem of T. Using the proof of this *first incompleteness theorem*, Gödel was then able to prove a *second incompleteness theorem* by formulating in T a sentence, Con_T, of which there is reason to say that it expresses the claim that T is consistent, and of which it can be proven that it is not provable in T if T is consistent. From this second theorem, and the assumption that T contains finitary arithmetic, it is then concluded that the consistency of T is not provable by finitary means. From this conclusion it is in turn inferred that no system I of ideal mathematics that contains T is such that its real-consistency can be proven by finitary means, and from this, finally, it is concluded that Hilbert's intended defence of the ideal reasoning of classical mathematics cannot be carried out.

In the beginning, Gödel shied away from this conclusion, maintaining (with characteristic caution) that his second theorem did 'not contradict Hilbert's formalistic viewpoint' since 'it is conceivable that there exist finitary proofs that *cannot* be expressed' in the classical systems for which that theorem had been proved to hold (cf. [2.62], 615). Eventually, however, he was persuaded by Bernays that these reservations were unwarranted, at which time he then accepted the view that his second theorem did indeed refute Hilbert's programme as it was originally conceived by Hilbert (cf. [2.64], 133).

❧ THE LATER PERIOD ❧

This completes our discussion of the developments of the early period. We turn now to the later period (i.e. the period after 1931), where we shall begin by considering the changes it brought to the 'isms' of the early period.

Hilbert's Formalism

The above-stated argument against Hilbert's programme using Gödel's theorems gained nearly universal acceptance in the later period and has indeed become a commonplace amongst twentieth-century philosophers of mathematics. The few challenges there have been to it have been mainly of two types: (i) those that seek to revive Hilbert's programme by arguing for a less restrictive conception of finitary evidence (and, hence, a more potent base from which to launch the search for a finitary proof of the real-consistency of ideal mathematics) than was originally intended by Hilbert; and (ii) those that seek a more restricted body of ideal methods whose real-consistency needs to be proven.

Those belonging to the first camp (e.g. Gentzen [2.61], Bernays [2.8], Ackermann [2.1], Gödel [2.64], Kreisel [2.90], Schütte [2.128], Feferman [2.38]; [2.39] and Takeuti [2.138]), in one way or another have all argued that the means used in giving the proof of real-consistency required by Hilbert's programme ought to be extended to means reaching beyond that which is formalizable in what has commonly been recognized as the natural formalization of Hilbert's finitary standpoint (namely, the theory known as *Primitive Recursive Arithmetic*, or **PRA**).[47] Among those, some (e.g. Gentzen [2.61], Ackermann [2.1], and, on one reading, Gödel [2.64]) have questioned the correctness of identifying the finitary with what is formalizable in **PRA**, arguing that finitary reasoning extends well beyond that which is formalizable in **PRA**, and includes such things as forms of transfinite induction which go beyond even what is provable in ordinary first-order Peano arithmetic (**PA**).

The basic idea of this line of thought is that there are types of reasoning which (a) are not codifiable in **PRA**, but which none the less (b) share the same characteristics believed to give finitary evidence its distinctive epistemological credentials, and which (c) allow us to establish the consistency of much of the ideal reasoning of classical mathematics that cannot be secured by means of proofs formalizable in **PRA**. It is therefore argued that an extension of what is to be counted as admissible reasoning in constructing the required consistency proofs of the various ideal systems of classical mathematics is in order, and that a significant partial realization of Hilbert's original aims can thus be attained.

Others (e.g. Kreisel [2.90] and Feferman [2.39]) in the first camp have argued not so much for a reconsideration of what should be counted as finitary evidence, as for a liberalization and refinement of what are the epistemically gainful means of proving consistency, whether or not they are properly classifiable as finitary. The basic idea here is that the simple distinction between real and ideal methods does not begin to do justice to the rich scheme of gradations in epistemic quality that separate the various kinds of evidence available for use in metamathematical proofs. Hence, this simple distinction should be replaced by a more refined scheme which distinguishes not only the finitary and the non-finitary, but also the various 'grades' of both constructive and non-constructive methods (and the various reducibility relations which exist between the distinguished kinds of non-constructive methods and the distinguished kinds of constructive methods).[48] When this is done, it is claimed, results amounting to a substantial partial realization of a generalized Hilbert's programme can be achieved (cf. Kreisel [2.90] and Feferman [2.39]).

The same basic conclusion is arrived at by a quite different line of reasoning in the so-called programme of 'reverse mathematics' of Friedman and Simpson (cf. [2.134]). The strategic idea of this programme is basically the opposite of that of Kreisel and Feferman. It does not aim at *beefing up* the methods available for constructing the requisite consistency proofs, but rather at *cutting down* the systems of ideal reasoning whose consistency needs proving. This is to be done by giving a more exact characterization of the core of ideal reasoning that is truly indispensable to the reconstruction of the essential results of classical mathematics.

The reverse-mathematical revision of Hilbert's programme thus begins by isolating those results of classical mathematics that are believed to constitute its 'core'. It then seeks to find the weakest possible natural axiomatic theory capable of formalizing this core. The hope is that this minimal system will eliminate unnecessary strength present in the usual axiomatizations of the core (generally, some version of second-order arithmetic) and therefore that its real-consistency will prove to be more susceptible to finitary proof than that of the usual systems.

So far, significant partial progress along these lines has been achieved. In particular, it has been shown that (i) there is a certain subsystem (known as $\mathbf{WKL_0}$) of $\mathbf{PA}^2$ (i.e. second-order Peano arithmetic) which embodies a substantial portion of classical mathematics; (ii) all the II_1 theorems (i.e. theorems equivalent to some formula of the form '$\forall x \, \phi x$' where 'ϕx' is a recursive formula) of $\mathbf{WKL_0}$ are provable in $\mathbf{PRA}$ (cf. [2.133], [2.134]; and (iii) the proof of (ii) can itself be given in $\mathbf{PRA}$ (cf. [2.132].[49] Assuming the codifiability of finitary reasoning in $\mathbf{PRA}$ and the importance of the II_1 class of real truths, this amounts to a finitary proof of the real-consistency of an important part of classical ideal mathematics. This, in turn, would constitute a significant partial realization of Hilbert's programme.

In addition to these two alternatives, it is possible to describe, at least in philosophical outline, a third approach which seems in certain important respects to be closer to Hilbert's original ideas than either of them. The key element of this third alternative, which is absent from each of the other two approaches just described, takes its lead from the Kantian character of Hilbert's conception of ideal mathematics. In particular, it stresses the point that Hilbert's ideal methods, like Kant's ideas of pure reason, are recommended solely by the efficiency that their instrumental use is supposed to bring to the development of our real judgements.

This means, among other things, that ideal propositions and inferences that fail to bring with them discernible improvements in efficiency (when compared to their real counterparts proving the same results) do not belong to that part of ideal mathematics that need, in principle, be defended by Hilbert. In other words, ideal elements that fail in any significant way to increase the efficiency of the development of our real knowledge have, in principle, no claim to be included among those ideal elements whose real-consistency the Hilbertian must defend. Therefore, in identifying the elements (i.e. axioms and rules of inference) of an ideal system I for whose defence the Hilbertian is to be held accountable, it must be borne in mind that they must figure in some significant way in the production of efficiency; that is, each must be an essential ingredient in some ideal derivation Δ_I of a real theorem τ_R such that (i) Δ_I (together with the necessary metamathematical proof of soundness for I[50]) is more efficient than any real proof of τ_R, and (ii) Δ_I is the only derivation in I that significantly improves upon the efficiency of the real proofs of τ_R. If an item (e.g. an axiom, rule of inference, etc.) of I possesses none of the virtues of efficiency for which ideal elements are in general prized, then, in principle, it can and should be eliminated from I. With all such eliminations made, one would expect the prospects for a finitary proof of I's consistency to have been improved. Therefore, the question of whether an ideal system is comprised wholly of elements that are essential in the above-indicated sense ought to be of prime importance in determining the make-up of those ideal theories for whose defence the Hilbertian is ultimately taken to be responsible.

Yet, despite its clear importance for the proper reckoning of the ultimate responsibilities and prospects of Hilbert's programme, this question has been either ignored or overlooked by those writing on the subject. Simpson (cf. [2.134], 360–1), for example, readily admits that the proofs of standard theorems in $\mathbf{WKL_0}$ and $\mathbf{WKL_0^+}$ are sometimes 'laborious' and 'much more complicated than the standard proof(s)'. Yet he takes no notice of the potential this feature of reverse mathematics has to undo its entire rationale for effecting a partial realization of Hilbert's programme. To the extent that the proofs in $\mathbf{WKL_0}$ and $\mathbf{WKL_0^+}$ are *more* laborious than the 'standard' proofs of the same ideal theorems, to the same extent are $\mathbf{WKL}_0$ and $\mathbf{WKL}_0^+$ of questionable worth as models of Hilbert's ideal reasoning. Moreover, were the least laborious ideal proofs of real theorems in $\mathbf{WKL}_0$ and $\mathbf{WKL}_0^+$ to reach levels of laboriousness equal to those of the least laborious real proofs for those theorems, they would cease to be ideal proofs that the Hilbertian should want to preserve, and, hence, cease to be proofs whose soundness he should be obliged to defend.

It is thus important for the 'reverse mathematicians' to answer the following questions: (1) Do the ideal proofs of real theorems in $\mathbf{WKL}_0$ and $\mathbf{WKL}_0^+$ preserve, at least on balance, the kinds of gains in efficiency for which ideal reasoning was prized by Hilbert in the first place?; and (2) Are the ideal proofs of real theorems in $\mathbf{WKL}_0$ and $\mathbf{WKL}_0^+$ less laborious than their most efficient real counterparts? To the extent that either of these questions is answered in the negative, the reverse mathematicians' use of the systems of reverse mathematics to establish partial realizations of Hilbert's programme becomes implausible. So far as I can see, however, the reverse mathematicians have done nothing to allay fears that such questions as (1) and (2) above may have to be answered in the negative.

It would be unfair, however, to lay too much blame on the reverse mathematicians. For the questions they have neglected have been generally neglected by those writing on Hilbert's programme. This includes philosophers, too (indeed, perhaps primarily), and not just logicians. All have failed properly to emphasize two fundamental points: (i) that the prospects for Hilbert's programme can adequately be assessed only when a suitably accurate means of comparing the complexity of real and ideal proofs has been developed and those systems containing the gainful ideal proofs have been identified; and (ii) the complexity metric figuring in (i) is capable of measuring not only the kind of complexity (call it *verificational complexity*) that is encountered when one sets about the task of determining of a *given* item whether or not it is an ideal proof of a certain kind, but also, and, indeed, primarily, a kind of complexity (call it *inventional complexity*) which constitutes the complexity involved in *discovering* an ideal proof of the desired kind in the first place.[51] Failure to appreciate points (i) and (ii) has, it seems to me, led to inadequate attention being paid to the development of *appropriate* metrics for measuring the complexity of ideal proofs and comparing the complexity thus measured to that for the corresponding real proofs. Without the development of such a theory of complexity, however, it does not seem to me possible to render a compelling final assessment of Hilbert's programme – and by that I mean the programme of Hilbert's *original* philosophical conception.

Logicism

Logicism re-emerged in the 1930s and 1940s as the favoured philosophy of mathematics of the logical empiricists (cf. [2.22], [2.23] and [2.66]). I say 're-emerged' because the positivists did not develop a logicism of their own in the way that Dedekind, Frege and Russell did. Rather, they simply appropriated the technical work of Russell and Whitehead (*modulo* the usual reservations concerning the axioms of infinity and reducibility)[52] and attempted to embed it in an overall empiricist epistemology.

This empiricist turn was a fairly novel development in the history of logicism, and it represented a radical departure from both the original logicism of Leibniz, which was part of a larger rationalist epistemology, and the more recent logicism of Frege, which was strongly critical of empiricist attempts to accommodate mathematics (cf. Frege's criticism of Mill in [2.49], sections 9–11, 23–5). It was, perhaps, less at odds with Russell's logicism with its imputation of a common methodology linking mathematics and the empirical sciences.

Like all empiricists, the logical empiricists, too, struggled with Kant's idea that mathematics is immune to empirical revision. More accurately, they struggled with the Kantian problematic concerning how to account for the apparent certainty and necessity of mathematics while at the same time being able to explain its seeming robust informativeness.[53] Their choice of strategies for trying to accommodate these two data was to empty mathematics of all non-analytic content while, at the same time, arguing that analytic truth can be 'substantial' and non-self-evident.

The logical empiricists thus sacrificed the strict empiricist claim that all knowledge is evidensorily based on the senses. Their empiricism was, therefore, a liberal empiricism, an empiricism making use of a distinction like that of Hume's between 'relations of ideas' and 'matters of fact' (cf. [2.83], section IV, Pt. I). The exact distinction they utilized was one calling for the separation of those propositions whose truth or falsity is determined by the meanings of their constituent terms (and is therefore independent of contingent fact) and those propositions whose truth or falsity is dependent upon contingent, empirical matters of fact.[54] They then appealed to this distinction in arguing that the truths of logic are analytic in character. And from this, and the technical work of Russell and Whitehead, they concluded that the truths of mathematics are analytic.[55]

Thus, though they accepted the traditional Kantian idea that mathematical judgements are immune to empirical revision, and though they made central use of something like Kant's analytic/synthetic distinction in formulating their account of mathematics, the logical empiricists none the less rejected the distinctive thesis of Kantian mathematical epistemology; namely, that knowledge of mathematics is synthetic a priori in character. Indeed, the denial that *any* knowledge is synthetic a priori in character was a central ingredient of the logical empiricists' epistemological outlook.

Their mathematical epistemology came under heavy attack by Quine in the 1950s. Quine's attack was based on a criticism of the pivotal distinction of the empiricists between analytic and synthetic truths (cf. [2.109], [2.111]). According to Quine, the basic unit of knowledge or judgement – the basic item of our thinking that is tested against experience – is science as a whole. Since mathematical and logical statements are inextricably interwoven parts of the larger body of science, they therefore too, at least to some extent, must derive their confirmation or disconfirmation from empirical sources. Consequently, the statements of logic and mathematics cannot rightly be regarded as true by virtue of meanings alone, if by that there is intended some contrast with statements regarded as true in virtue of the facts. A distinction between truths of meaning (i.e. analytic truths) and truths of fact (i.e. synthetic truths) cannot therefore be maintained. Yet, without some such distinction, the logicism of the logical empiricists does not have a hope of succeeding.

Within a relatively brief period of time, this critique of Quine's became a major influence in the philosophy of mathematics and, under the weight of that influence, the logicism of the logical empiricists began to sink into oblivion. There have, however, been a few attempts to revive (or, perhaps better, to exhume) logicism along other lines. The most systematic and detailed (if, perhaps, not the most convincing) of these is that given in the two-volume work of David Bostock (viz. [2.12]). This is not, however, so much a defence of logicism as it is an attempt to determine a best case for it, so that its plausibility as a philosophy of arithmetic might finally be judged.[56] Indeed, he ends up concluding that logicism is of strictly limited viability as a philosophy of arithmetic. The main point of his argument is that there is no unique reduction of arithmetic to logic, and that this creates problems for any logicism (like, say, that of Frege or Russell) that wants to identify numbers with *objects*.

More nearly defences are the recent attempts by Hilary Putnam, Harold Hodes, Hartry Field and Steven Wagner to establish the plausibility of modified forms of logicism. Putnam [2.102] and Hodes [2.81] both offer defences of a type of logicist position also known as 'ifthenism' or 'deductivism'.[57] The former argues that, though statements of existence in mathematics are generally to be seen as statements asserting the existence of structures, they are not to be taken as assertions of the actual existence of these structures, but only of their possible existence. Existence statements are therefore, at bottom, logical claims, and they are to be verified by generally logical means (and, in particular, by syntactical consistency proofs).

Hodes takes a somewhat different approach, arguing, in a manner reminiscent of Frege, that arithmetic claims can be translated into a second-order logic in which the second-order variables range over functions and concepts (as opposed to objects). In this way, commitment to sets and other specifically mathematical objects can be eliminated, and, this done, arithmetic may be considered a part of logic.

Field (cf. [2.42], [2.43]) offers what might be regarded as an epistemological form of logicism. He is concerned to defend the claim that mathematical knowledge is (at least largely) logical knowledge. He also argues, contrary to Quine and Putnam (see below), that one can be a realist with respect to physical theory without being a realist with respect to mathematics.[58]

Field begins his argument that mathematical knowledge is logical knowledge by defining mathematical knowledge as that knowledge which 'separates a person who knows a lot of mathematics from a person who knows only a little mathematics' (cf. 2.43], 511, 544). He then goes on to claim that what separates these two kinds of knowers is *not* that the former knows many and the latter knows few' (cf. [Ibid], 511–12; 544–5) of such claims as those for which mathematicians commonly provide proofs of (i.e., of those claims, such that there are prime numbers greater than a million). Rather, he goes on to say, 'insofar as what separates them is knowledge at all, it is knowledge of various different sorts' (Ibid.).

Some of it is empirical knowledge (e.g. knowledge of what is commonly accepted by mathematicians and what they regard as the proper starting point for an inquiry). The bulk, however, is knowledge 'of a purely logical sort – even on the Kantian criterion of logic according to which logic can make no existential commitments' (Ibid., 512). In the end, Field concludes, mathematical knowledge for the most part comes down to knowledge that certain sentences do and certain other sentences do not follow from a given set of axioms.

Generally, such knowledge would either be understood in a semantical way (as knowledge about a class of models) or in a syntactical way (as knowledge about a class of formal proofs or derivations). Neither of these, however, qualifies as logical knowledge in the sense Field wants. For since models are just a particular kind of mathematical object, knowledge of them must be just a particular kind of mathematical knowledge. Similarly for syntactical derivations. For whether they are conceived of abstractly or concretely, they cannot be known to exist on purely logical grounds, since (so the reasoning goes) pure logic cannot assert the existence of things.

Field is therefore obliged to offer an account of logical knowledge that frees it of the need to be knowledge of semantical or syntactical entities. What he comes up with is a kind of 'modal' analysis according to which knowledge that a given sentence S follows from a given set of sentences A is (i) knowledge that N (A → S) (where 'Nφ' is to be read as 'it is logically necessary that φ'), and knowledge that S does not follow from A is (ii) knowledge that M(A&¬S) (where 'Mφ' is to be read as 'it is logically possible that φ'). The key feature of this analysis is that it treats the sentences 'A' and 'S' as *used* rather than *mentioned*. Hence, it treats 'N' and 'M' as operators (indeed, logical operators) rather than predicates that apply to entities like models, possible worlds and/or proofs.

Field identifies the chief task facing this analysis as that of accounting for the applicability of mathematics to physics, and he divides this task into two sub-tasks: namely: (a) that of showing the mathematics applied to be 'mathematically good'; and (b) that of showing that the physical world is such as to make the mathematical theory particularly useful in describing it. Both tasks must be carried out without appeal to the truth of (any parts of) mathematics if Field's logicist ideal is to be met, and it is to the demonstration of this that Field's writings on the subject (cf. 2.42 and 2.43) are primarily devoted.

There is much to question in Field's argument (cf. [2.130], [2.115], [2.27]; but see also Field's responses in [2.44] and [2.45]). For present purposes, however, we shall restrict ourselves to a question concerning the overall place of logical reasoning in mathematical proof. This, we noted earlier, was a point of central concern in Kant's mathematical epistemology, and was taken over as a principal motivating factor of the intuitionist epistemologies of Brouwer and Poincaré. Their belief, and the crux of their disagreement with logicism, was that mathematical and logical inference are fundamentally different – that the former is not only not reducible to the latter, but that it is indeed antithetical to it. As Poincaré put the point: mathematical reasoning has a kind of creative virtue that distinguishes it from the epistemically more 'sterile' reasoning of logic (cf. [2.99], 32–3); the logical reasoner's grasp of mathematics is like the grasp of elephanthood that naturalists would have were their knowledge to be restricted entirely to what they had observed through microscopic examination of their tissue.

> When the logician shall have broken up each demonstration into
> a multitude of elementary operations, all correct, he still will
> not possess the whole reality; this I know not what which makes
> the unity of the demonstration will completely escape him. In the
> edifices built up by our masters, of what use to admire the work
> of the mason if we cannot comprehend the plan of the

architect? Now pure logic cannot give us this appreciation of the total effect; this we must ask of intuition.

([2.101], 436)

Poincaré therefore believed in a distinctively *mathematical* kind of reasoning. Without it one cannot account for the manifest differences in epistemic condition which separate the logical from the genuinely mathematical reasoner.[59] He would, therefore, have denied Field's assumed starting point that mathematical knowledge is largely logical knowledge and also his claim that the modalities pertaining to mathematical reasoning are *logical* rather than distinctively mathematical in character.[60] Both points, we believe, raise serious challenges for Field's position.

Steven Wagner ([2.145]) offers both a different conception and a different defence of logicism. He seeks to root mathematics in what he takes to be the universal needs and urges of (ideally) rational agents. His argument begins with the presumption of an idealized rational enquirer who seeks not only bodily survival but also understanding. He then goes on to say that counting is indispensable to such a being both in the sense of being partially constitutive of that person's rationality and in the sense of being necessary to his or her assimilation and processing of the elementary data of experience and thought. Nobody, he maintains, can get by without answering a host of 'How many?' questions. Thus, the rational agent must develop a system of counting.

From a system of counting there will eventually emerge a system of calculation. This is so because (i) calculation is essentially a refinement of counting (i.e. it functions to advance those cognitive and bodily ends that are served by the capacity to count); and (ii) there is a rational urge to improve those capacities that one possesses, but possesses in what is perhaps only too rudimentary a form[61].

Thus, from counting, the ideally rational agent passes to calculation. And from calculation, the argument continues, he or she will pass to something like number theory. This is due to the facts that (i) part of the urge to understand consists of an urge to unify, simplify and generalize; and (ii) efforts to unify, simplify and generalize one's system of arithmetic calculation will inevitably lead one to something like the arithmetic of the natural numbers. Therefore elementary number theory may be described as a kind of rational necessity.

As a final stage of rational development, the continued need and capacity to simplify, unify and generalize will eventually lead the ideally rational enquirer to some form of analysis and set theory. Wagner's 'second generation' logicism thus states that (i) any ideally rational enquirer will be under pressure to develop forms of arithmetic and set theory; and that (ii) the theorems of such theories as are developed in response to this pressure will be analytic in the sense that *any rational being would have a reason to accept them.*

Wagner's position differs in significant ways from both the metaphysical logicism of Frege and the methodological logicism of Russell. It also differs from Field's logicism – particularly over the question of the in-principle dispensability of mathematics as a device for processing empirical information. Field believes that it is dispensable. Wagner, on the other hand, appeals to an alleged explanatory role that at least certain mathematical theories (e.g. elementary number theory, analysis and set theory) play, and he treats that explanatory role as part of the ultimate justification for those theories. He thus treats mathematics as ultimately indispensable for the full cognitive processing (i.e. the full explanation) of empirical information.

Intuitionism

Turning finally to post-Brouwerian intuitionism, there are two main developments to note: (i) the various attempts, initiated by Heyting's work, to formalize intuitionistic logic and mathematics and to develop it into something roughly comparable in power to classical mathematics; and (ii) the more recent attempts by Dummett and his followers to derive a philosophical justification for intuitionism from a kind of Wittgensteinian conception of the meanings of mathematical sentences.

Since (i) is only very loosely connected with philosophical concerns, we shall say little about it here. The reader desiring a relatively up-to-date presentation of technical findings may consult any of a number of recent surveys (e.g. [2.4], [2.13], or [2.143]) of the subject. We shall confine our discussion of (i) to the idea that seems to have been at the centre of Heyting's attempts to formalize intuitionistic reasoning; namely, the supposed distinction between 'a logic of existence' and 'a logic of knowledge' – a distinction Heyting regarded as fundamental to intuitionistic thought ([2.70], 107).

What Heyting meant by a 'logic of existence' is a logic of statements about objects whose existence is to be understood as being independent of human thought. Intuitionists, and other constructivists too, for the most part, reject the idea of a realm of thought-independent mathematical objects. Likewise, they reject the idea that mathematical propositions are true or false independently of human thought. They hold, instead, the view that mathematical propositions express the results of certain kinds of mental constructions.[62] A logic of such propositions – a 'logic of knowledge', in Heyting's terminology – is therefore one whose theorems express relations between mental constructions; specifically, relations of latent containment among them (where one construction is taken latently to contain another just in case going through the process of effecting the one would automatically either effect the other or put one in a position to effect it).

Given this general outlook, Heyting argued, there is no essential difference between logical and mathematical theorems. Both serve essentially to affirm that one has succeeded in performing mental acts satisfying certain conditions. The former are distinguished only by their relatively greater generality ([2.69], 1–12; [2.70], 107–8).

Intuitionist logic was thus intended by Heyting to serve as an articulation of those most general patterns of latent containment relating our mental mathematical constructions.[63] Since, however, our mental constructional activities constitute 'a phenomenon of life, a natural activity of man' ([2.69], 9), containment relations between them are not conceptually based but rather based on the relations which bind our activities together *behaviourally*, as it were. Thus, a logical theorem to the effect that we know a proof of A only if we know a proof of B would express neither a conceptual connection between our knowledge of a proof of A and our knowledge of a proof of B, nor, except *per accidens*, a conceptual connection between A and B. Rather, it would express a natural fact concerning our (perhaps idealized) mental constructional life, namely, that it is characterized by a disposition to transform proofs of A into proofs of B. As Heyting himself put it, 'mathematics, from an intuitionistic point of view, is a study of certain functions of the human mind' ([2.69], 10). As such, it is akin to history and the social sciences (Ibid.).

Michael Dummett ([2.36], [2.37]) has offered both a different conception and a different defence of intuitionism. He conceives it as a view concerning what is to be regarded as the proper *logic* of mathematics. He argues that an adequate account of the meanings of mathematical propositions reveals that it is intuitionist logic (i.e. the logic set out by Heyting) that is the proper logic of mathematics. This account bears certain affinities to the views on meaning set out by Wittgenstein in his *Philosophical Investigations*. In particular, like Wittgenstein's view, it equates the meaning of a sentence with its canonical use. In mathematics, Dummett believes, canonical use consists in the role that an assertion plays in the central activity of proof. Hence, to know the meaning of a mathematical sentence is ultimately to know the conditions under which it would be proved or refuted.[64]

Dummett's intuitionism is thus far removed from that of Poincaré and Brouwer both in substance and motive.[65] Its defence is also, we believe, open to certain doubts. Dummett argues that since (i) 'that knowledge which, in general, constitutes, the understanding of language ... must be implicit knowledge' ([2.36], 217), and (ii) 'implicit knowledge cannot ... meaningfully be ascribed to someone unless it is possible to say in what the manifestation of that knowledge consists – there must be an observable difference between the behaviour or capacities of someone who is said to have that knowledge and someone who is said to lack it' (Ibid.) – that it therefore follows that (iii) 'a grasp of the meaning of a . . . statement must, in general, consist of a capacity to use that statement in a certain way, or to respond in a certain way to its use by others' (Ibid.).

Premiss (ii), we believe, is inappropriate as a premiss in an argument for (iii). For it seems to beg the crucial question, namely, that concerning whether implicit knowledge (and hence knowledge of meaning) is ultimately to be taken as consisting in a capacity for behaviour or in, say, something like one's being in a mental or psychological or neural state that *underlies* such behaviour. Everyone, it would seem, must agree that (ii′) implicit knowledge cannot legitimately be ascribed to someone unless such ascription is warranted by the best total explanation of his or her observed behaviour.[66] But (ii′) carries with it no guarantee that, as (ii) requires, an ascription of implicit knowledge be traceable to some specific piece or pieces of speaker behaviour or, indeed, that it will even be traceable to the entire corpus of the speaker's behaviour. Speaker behaviour will, after all, typically underdetermine its best total explanation. Nor is there any reason to believe in advance that the best total explanation of the speaker's behaviour will not differ from its rivals in its ascriptions of implicit knowledge to the speaker.

Thus, to avoid begging the question, premiss (ii) of Dummett's argument would seemingly have to be replaced by something like (ii′). Such replacement, however, would block valid passage to (iii), and (iii) is at the heart of Dummett's defence of intuitionism. To salvage his defence would therefore seemingly require finding something like our (ii′) that would (in the company of premiss (i), of course) validly imply (iii). It is not at all clear that this can be done, however.[67]

As noted above, Dummett's defence of intuitionism appeals to certain ideas of Wittgenstein's, or, at any rate, ideas that Dummett and others have attributed to Wittgenstein. It would, however, we believe, be a mistake to identify Wittgenstein's ideas on the philosophy of mathematics too closely with intuitionism.[68] For though it does bear affinities to those forms of constructivism which stress the autonomy of mathematics as a human creation (where creation is understood to consist ultimately of acts of will or decision), it also bears certain affinities to a more conventionalist interpretation. Moreover, in the end, it resists categorization as *either* a constructivist or a conventionalist philosophy.

Wittgenstein's central idea seems to have been that there is a basic kind of construction in mathematics known as a *Beweissystem*. A

Beweissytem is made up of proofs and theorems, but its theorems function as rules of logical syntax rather than descriptive truths concerning the terms of the system. These rules constitute autonomous acts of will by which are laid down the rules according to which we agree to play a certain 'language game' involving the terms introduced by the system. Mathematics as a whole, Wittgenstein maintained, is a 'motley' of such *local* activities or games.

For Wittgenstein, then, mathematical proofs (including even the simplest ones) do not play the role of *compelling* us to accept their conclusions. Nor are mathematical propositions in any other way 'forced' upon us as being true. 'Acceptance' of a mathematical statement does not therefore represent an acknowledgment of its truth, but rather represents a *decision* on our part to count something as a convention of a certain language game. Similarly, proof does not function to *remove* doubt through penetration of the truth, but rather to *exclude* doubt as a logical possibility through the establishment of a theorem as a *norm* governing a certain language game.

Thus, though Wittgenstein saw mathematics as essentially a human creation, he did not understand this in the *descriptive* way that constructivists traditionally have understood it. Nor did his normative conception of our mathematical creations lend itself to any of the usual conventionalist interpretations. For those all call for the reduction of mathematical truths to logical truths and this requires the 'co-operation' of the logical forms of mathematical truths, so to speak (since there are logical forms that a statement might have that would prohibit it from being reducible to a logical truth).

Logical form does not, however, appear to form the same kind of constraint on the institution of norms or rules. Moreover, even if it did, there is a big difference between a statement's being a logical truth and its being a norm of logical syntax. The former has to do with whether a statement passes a certain test of truth invariance (i.e. that it be stable under a certain variety of different semantical interpretations of its semantically variable parts), while the latter has to do with whether something is to be seen as one of the *rules* constituting a certain *rule-governed activity*. Sentences failing the requisite tests of the truth-invariance test could none the less, it seems, still at least in principle play the role of rules of a linguistic game. Consequently, it seems that Wittgenstein is not well classified as a traditional conventionalist, though there is a conventionalist element in his philosophy.[69]

Later Developments

Among later developments not having primarily to do with the three 'isms', perhaps the major one is that stemming from Quine's criticism of the logical empiricists in the 1940s and 1950s mentioned above. This criticism resulted in a new empiricist philosophy of mathematics shorn of even those few Kantian ideas that were retained by the logical empiricists – and this new empiricism has been perhaps the dominant theme in the philosophy of mathematics ever since.

The logical empiricists, as was noted earlier, retained Kant's commitment to the necessity of mathematical truth (though they conceived of this necessity as essentially consisting in immunity from empirical revision). Indeed, it was precisely for the sake of accommodating this 'datum' of mathematical epistemology that the logical empiricists put so much effort into nurturing and preserving the Kantian distinction between analytic and synthetic judgements. In their view, only such a distinction could sustain the division of mathematical judgements into those that are and those that are not subject to empirical revision.

Quine (see [2.108], [2.109]) and Putnam (see [2.105], [2.106]) swept even this final Kantian datum aside, offering instead a general empiricist epistemology in which all judgements, those of mathematics and logic as well as those of the natural sciences, are seen as evidentially connected to sensory phenomena and therefore subject to empirical revision. Central to their argument was an observation borrowed from Duhem; namely, that in order to connect science with sensory evidence, logic and mathematics are inevitably required.[70] They are therefore part of what gets confirmed when connection between a theory and a confirming phenomenon is made, and part of what gets disconfirmed when connection between a theory and a disconfirming phenomenon is made. They are, in sum, of an epistemological piece with natural science and, so, broadly speaking, empirical.

To accommodate the lingering conviction that there is at least some difference regarding sensitivity to empirical evidence between mathematics and logic, on the one hand, and natural science, on the other, Quine argued that while both are subject to empirical revision, the precise extent or degree to which this is true is different in the two cases. He backed this view with a pragmatic conception of rational belief revision, and a view of the totality of our cognitive holdings according to which it forms a 'web' whose various parts are interdependent and ordered with respect to their importance to the preservation of the general structure of the web. At the centre of the web lie logic and mathematics, and the beliefs of natural science and common sense for the most part fan out from this towards the periphery where the entire scheme encounters sensory experience.

According to Quine's pragmatic conception of belief revision, it is to be governed by a concern to at all times maximize our overall predictive and explanatory power. A scheme of beliefs which optimizes predictive and explanatory power also optimizes our ability cognitively to cope with our environment(s), and production of such a scheme is generally aided by policies of revision which minimize, both in scope and severity, the changes that are made to a previously successful conceptual scheme in response to recalcitrant experience. If the beliefs of mathematics and logic are therefore typically less subject to empirical revision than are the beliefs of natural science and common sense, this is because revising them generally (albeit not, in Quine's view, invariably) tends towards greater upheaval in the conceptual scheme than does revision of our common sense and natural scientific beliefs.[71] Quine therefore accommodates the traditional Kantian datum that mathematics is necessary by treating logic and mathematics not as being altogether impervious to empirical revision, but only as being more so, on average, than either natural science or common sense.[72] Quine thus merges the epistemologies of mathematics and natural science into a single, albeit quantitatively differentiated, empiricist whole.

In merging mathematics and science into a single explanatory system, Quine's empiricism also induces a realist or platonist view of mathematics. It sees the world as populated by those entities needed to staff the best theory of the totality of our experience. These include not only the medium-sized objects of ordinary experience and the theoretical entities of our best current physical science, but also mathematical entities, since, as was noted above, mathematical claims play an integral role in our best total theory of experience (see [2.108], [2.109], [2.105] and [2.106]).

Quine's views have been challenged on various grounds. Field, for example, has challenged Quine's claim that the roles played by natural science and mathematics are essentially the same and cannot be differentiated. On his view there is an immense difference between the role played by mathematics and the role played by natural science in our overall conceptual scheme. Mathematics, he believes functions basically as a logic, and its theorems do not make claims that are substantive in the way that the laws of natural science are.

Another criticism is that Quine's epistemology leaves unaccounted for those parts of mathematics that are *not* somehow involved in the explanation of sensory experience. It is not clear, however, how serious an objection this is since it is not clear how much, if any, of even the least elementary, most abstract mathematics would play *no* contributory role in the simplification and explanation of sensory experience.

A final criticism is that by Parsons, who has argued that treating the *elementary* arithmetical parts of mathematics (e.g. the truth that 7 + 5 = 12) as being on an epistemological par with the hypotheses of theoretical physics fails to capture an epistemologically important difference regarding the different kinds of evidentness or 'obviousness' displayed by the two (see [2.95], 151). The kind of evidentness displayed by an elementary arithmetic proposition like '7 + 5 = 12' is not the same as that displayed by even such highly confirmed physical hypotheses as 'The earth moves about the sun', says Parsons. To put it roughly, the latter is more highly *derivative* than the former. Consequently, Parsons concludes, it is not plausible to regard the two claims as based on essentially the same kind of evidence and, so, the empiricist epistemology of Quine and Putnam must be regarded as being of questionable adequacy for at least the more elementary parts of mathematics.

In addition to Quine and Putnam, there have been others who have suggested different kinds of mergings of mathematics with the natural sciences. Of those, some have been empiricists, others not. Kitcher, for instance, has presented a generally empiricist epistemology for mathematics in which *history* and *community* are important epistemological forces (see [2.89]). Gödel, too, offered an epistemology in which mathematical justification was conceived along lines structurally similar to those of justification in the natural sciences.[73] In his own words:

> despite their remoteness from sense experience, we do have
> something like a perception also of the objects of set theory,
> as is seen from the fact that the axioms force themselves upon
> us as being true. I don't see any reason why we should have
> less confidence in this kind of perception, i.e., in mathematical
> intuition, than in sense perception . . .
>
> It should be noted that mathematical intuition need not be
> conceived of as a faculty giving an *immediate* knowledge of the
> objects concerned. Rather it seems that, as in the case of physical
> experience, we *form* our ideas also of those objects on the basis
> of something else which is immediately given. Only this
> something else is *not*, or not primarily, the sensations. That
> something besides the sensations actually is immediately given
> follows . . . from the fact that even our ideas referring to
> physical objects contain constituents qualitatively different from
> sensations or mere combinations of sensations, e.g., the concept
> of object itself, whereas, on the other hand, by our thinking we
> cannot create any qualitatively new elements, but only
> reproduce and combine those that are given. Evidently, the
> 'given' in underlying mathematics is closely related to the
> abstract elements contained in our empirical ideas. It by no

99

means follows, however, that the data of this second kind, because they cannot be associated with actions of certain things upon our sense organs, are something purely subjective, as Kant asserted. Rather they, too, may represent an aspect of objective reality, but, as opposed to the sensations, their presence in us may be due to another kind of relationship between ourselves and reality.

([2.65], 483–4)

Gödel then went on to claim (Ibid., 485) that this use of and need for intuition obtains both in high-level abstract areas of mathematics such as set theory, and in the elementary areas of mathematics such as finitary number theory. He noted, moreover, that even without appeal to intuition, mathematics, like the natural sciences, makes use of what are essentially inductive means of justification.

> even disregarding the intrinsic necessity of some new axiom, and even in case it has no intrinsic necessity at all, a probable decision about its truth is possible also in another way, namely, inductively by studying its 'success'. Success here means fruitfulness in consequences, in particular in 'verifiable' consequences, i.e., consequences demonstrable without the new axiom, whose proofs with the help of the new axiom, however, are considerably simpler and easier to discover, and make it possible to contract into one proof many different proofs. The axioms for the system of real numbers, rejected by the intuitionists, have in this sense been verified to some extent, owing to the fact that analytical number theory frequently allows one to prove number-theoretical theorems which, in a more cumbersome way, can subsequently be verified by elementary methods. A much higher degree of verification than that, however, is conceivable. There might exist axioms so abundant in their verifiable consequences, shedding so much light upon a whole field, and yielding such powerful methods for solving problems ... that, no matter whether or not they are intrinsically necessary, they would have to be accepted at least in the same sense as any well-established physical theory.

(Ibid, 477)

Higher-level mathematical hypotheses are thus taken to be inductively justified by the simplifying, or, more generally, explanatory effects they have on lower-level mathematical truths. In a later remark, Gödel extended this characterization of inductive justification in mathematics to include not only the 'fruitful' (i.e. simplificatory and explanatory) organization of lower-level mathematical results, but also the 'fruitful' organization of principles and facts of physics (Ibid., 485).[74]

This extension is significant because it makes a place in Gödel's mathematical epistemology for what is essentially empirical justification of mathematical truths. This does not, however, make him an empiricist like Quine. For Gödel allowed only that some of our knowledge of mathematical truths might arise from empirical sources. He remained staunchly opposed to any suggestion that all mathematical justification must or even can ultimately rest on sensory experience. Indeed, he described the empiricist view of mathematics as too 'absurd' to be seriously maintained (see p. 16 of the manuscript of his Gibbs lecture). More positively, he maintained that there is a fundamental epistemic phenomenon (viz., that of certain axioms – including certain high-level set theoretical axioms – 'forcing' themselves upon us as 'being true') that cannot be accounted for by an empiricist epistemology for mathematics. This same phenomenon is apparently also that which caused Gödel to reject idealism and accept a Platonist conception of mathematics. In our estimation, neither this phenomenon nor the related question of its status as a 'datum' for the philosophy of mathematics have received the attention they deserve.

Both the empiricist Platonism of Quine and the non-empiricist Platonism of Gödel have been important influences on recent work in the field. So, too, has been an argument given by Benacerraf in the early 1970s (see [2.6]). According to that argument, mathematical epistemology faces a general dilemma. It must, on the one hand, give a satisfactory account of the truth of mathematics and, on the other, offer a satisfactory account of how mathematics can be known. This constitutes a dilemma, in Benacerraf's opinion, because while to get a satisfactory account of the truth of mathematics seemingly requires that we bring abstract objects into the picture as referents of the singular terms used in mathematical discourse, to get a satisfactory account of mathematical knowledge seemingly requires that we avoid such reference. His argument makes use of the following key claims: (i) the semantics for mathematical language should be continuous with the semantics for non-mathematical language; (ii) the deep logical form of a mathematical expression should not be treated as too different from its surface grammatical form; (iii) the semantics for non-mathematical language is referential; and (iv) the best referential semantics for mathematical language uses abstract objects as referents.

As a result of the alleged need to construe the semantics of mathematical language as referential in character, we are obliged to see the *grounds of truth* of a mathematical sentence as residing in the properties of those abstract objects to which its referring terms make reference. Thus, for example, we are obliged to say that what makes '7

+ 5 = 12' *true* are the properties of the abstract objects 7, 5 and 12, the characteristics of the addition operation as an operation on abstract objects, and the features of the identity relation as a relation between abstract objects.

On the other hand, any epistemology for mathematics that is to avoid susceptibility to Gettier-type problems must link the *grounds of truth* of a mathematical sentence with the *grounds of belief* in it. In other words, if a given belief is to count as genuine knowledge, there must be a certain causal relationship between that which makes it true and our state of belief in it. This causes a dilemma because there is seemingly no way of securing the aforementioned causal connection while at the same time securing a reasonable referential semantics for mathematical discourse. There are mathematical epistemologies – in particular, various Platonist epistemologies – which allow for a plausible account of the truth of mathematical sentences. And there are mathematical epistemologies (e.g. various formalist epistemologies) which allow for a plausible account of how we might come to know mathematical sentences. There is, however, no known way of securing both a plausible account of mathematical truth and a plausible account of mathematical knowledge.

A great deal of recent work in the philosophy of mathematics has been devoted to trying to resolve this dilemma. So, for example, there are Field (see [2.42]) and Hellmann (see [2.68]), both of which offer anti-Platonist resolutions of the dilemma, and Maddy (see [2.92]), who attempts to work out an epistemology which is at once Platonistic and yet naturalistic. To date there is no general consensus on which approach is the more plausible.[75]

An earlier argument of Benacerraf's (see [2.5]) on another topic has been similarly influential in shaping recent developments. Perhaps more than any other single source, this paper has served as the inspiration of that recent position known as 'structuralism'. Applied to mathematics generally, structuralism is the view that

> In mathematics . . . we do not have objects with an 'internal'
> composition arranged in structures, we have only structures.
> The objects of mathematics, that is, the entities which our
> mathematical constants and quantifiers denote, are structureless
> points or positions in structures. As positions in structures, they
> have no identity or features outside of a structure.
>
> ([2.113], 530)[76]

Such a view, Resnik claims (Ibid., p. 529), is in keeping with the fact that 'no mathematical theory can do more than determine its objects up to isomorphism', a fact which seems to have led mathematicians increasingly to the view that (i) 'mathematics is concerned with structures involving objects and not with the "internal" nature of the objects themselves' (Ibid.), and that (ii) we are not 'given' mathematical objects in isolation, but rather only in structures.[77]

Benacerraf himself applied the idea only to arithmetic, and, in particular, to the question, raised by Frege and others, of the 'deeper' ontological characteristics of the individual numbers. Frege, as is well known, held the view that numbers are objects. Benacerraf opposed this, arguing that such questions as 'Are the individual numbers really sets?' are spurious. 'Questions of the identification of the referents of number words should be dismissed as misguided in just the way that a question about the referents of the parts of a ruler would be seen as misguided.' ([2.5], 292). He then went on to complement this by noting that:

> 'Objects' do not do the job of numbers singly; the whole system performs the job or nothing does. I therefore argue . . . that numbers could not be objects . . .; for there is no more reason to identify any individual number with any one particular object than with any other.
>
> . . . in giving the properties of numbers . . . you merely characterize an *abstract structure* . . . and the 'elements' of the structure have no properties other than those relating them to other 'elements' of the same structure.
>
> ([Ibid., 290–1)

The primary motivation for such a view, apart from the desire for a more descriptively adequate account of mathematics, is apparently epistemological in nature. Knowledge of the characteristics of individual abstract objects would seem to require naturalistically inexplicable powers of cognition. Knowledge of at least some (e.g. finite) structures, on the other hand, could conceivably be explained as the result of applying such classical empiricist means of cognition as *abstraction* to observable physical complexes. Such abstracted structures would then become part of the general scientific framework and, as such, they could be extended and generalized in all manner of ways as the search for the simplest and most highly unified overall conceptual scheme is pursued.

Though Benacerraf and the other recent structuralists take no note of the fact, the basic idea behind their position enjoyed widespread popularity among philosophers of mathematics in the late nineteenth and early twentieth centuries. Indeed, Dedekind's essay *The Nature and Meaning of Number* ([2.25], section 73) contains an expression of the same basic idea on which the argument of Benacerraf [2.5] is centred. There Dedekind writes:

If in the consideration of a simply infinite system N set in order by a transformation ϕ we entirely neglect the special character of the elements; simply retaining their distinguishability and taking into account only the relations to one another in which they are placed by the order-setting transformation ϕ, then are these elements called *natural numbers* or *ordinal numbers* or simply *numbers*, and the base element is called the *base-number* of the *number-series N*. With reference to this freeing the elements from every other content (abstraction) we are justified in calling numbers a free creation of the human mind. The relations or laws which are ... always the same in all ordered simply infinite systems, whatever names may happen to be given to the individual elements ... form the first object of the *science of numbers* or *arithmetic*.[78]

Similarly, Weyl contains a striking expression – indeed, a strong generalization – of the structuralist idea that mathematical objects have no mathematically important features beyond those they possess as elements of structures. He writes: 'A science can only determine its domain of investigation up to an isomorphism mapping. In particular it remains quite indifferent as to the 'essence' of its objects. The idea of isomorphism demarcates the self-evident insurmountable boundary of cognition' [2.148], 25–6.

Similar, too, were ideas voiced by Hilbert (see, correspondence with Frege in 1899, [2.71] the Paris address of 1900 [2.72] and also by Bernays ([2.9]).[79]

Structuralism as a general philosophy of mathematics is criticized by Parsons [2.98]. There it is argued that there must be some mathematical objects for which structuralism is 'not the whole truth' (Ibid., 301). The objects of which Parsons speaks are those he refers to as 'quasi-concrete'. These are so-called because they are directly 'instantiated' or 'represented' by concrete objects. Examples are geometrical figures, symbols (construed as types) whose instances are written marks or uttered sounds, and the so-called 'stroke numerals' and the like of Hilbert's finitary arithmetic. Such quasi-concrete entities are among the most elementary mathematical objects there are and they are therefore of considerable importance to the foundations of mathematics. Yet they cannot be treated in a purely structuralist way, because their 'representational' function cannot be reduced to the purely intrastructural relations that they bear to other objects within a given system.

❧ CONCLUSION ❧

As noted in the introduction, philosophy of mathematics in this century has been centred on the problematic laid down for the subject by Kant, which is one of the three most important influences. The other two are the discovery of non-Euclidean geometries and the rapid development of symbolic logic.

For the first three decades of the century, the Kantian problematic was for the most part understood in pretty much the way Kant himself had thought of it. That is, necessity was understood as imperviousness to empirical revision, and substantiality was understood as a kind of epistemic non-triviality. What differentiated the rival philosophies of this period, primarily, were the different responses they gave to the discovery of non-Euclidean geometries. Here, three basic alternatives eventually came to be articulated.

The first of these, developed chiefly by Frege, attempted to preserve the basic Kantian judgement that both geometry and arithmetic are necessary. At the same time, however, it sought to distinguish two different kinds of necessity, one for arithmetic, the other for geometry. This it did in response to the discovery of non-Euclidean geometries, which it regarded as having revealed a fundamental asymmetry between geometry and arithmetic – namely, that though there are, at least at the level of conceptual possibility, alternative geometries, there are not alternative arithmetics. Arithmetical thinking was therefore thought to be a more pervasive part of rational thought than is geometrical thinking. Giving a proper account of this asymmetry then came to be seen as the primary duty of a philosophy of mathematics.

The second alternative, favoured by various of the early constructivists, modified the basic Kantian judgement that both geometry and arithmetic are necessary, and maintained instead that only arithmetic is necessary. It therefore also, like the first alternative, regarded the discovery of non-Euclidean geometries as having revealed a fundamental asymmetry between spatial geometry and arithmetic. Unlike the first alternative, however, it took this discovery to be best accounted for by reducing the truly mathematical part of geometry to arithmetic and rejecting its distinctively spatial part as being of an a posteriori rather than an a priori character (which thus means that it is an object *external* to the human mind). Arithmetic, on the other hand, since it admitted of no alternatives like those which non-Euclidean geometries constitute for geometry, was to be seen as arising from a source (viz., a very general kind of temporal intuition) which was wholly internal to the human mind and, so, a priori in nature.

The third alternative, developed by Hilbert, reacted to the discovery of non-Euclidean geometry in a different way still. It sought to put them to the test in order to determine how deeply into geometrical thinking they truly penetrate. The original non-Euclidean geometries were only shown to be independent of Euclid's axioms for plane geometry. They therefore left open the possibility that there are unknown and/or articulated features of the Euclidean plane such that, were they to be registered as axioms, the axiom of parallels *would* follow from them (together with the other axioms). They also left open the possibility that, even supposing the axioms of the Euclidean plane to be 'complete' in the sense just alluded to, the axioms needed to move from a description of the Euclidean plane to a description of Euclidean space are such that the axiom of parallels would follow from them (in conjunction with the other axioms), and would therefore not signify an independent feature of Euclidean *space*.

It was with the resolution of these matters that Hilbert was concerned. He therefore sought to produce a set of axioms so 'complete' that no axiom could be added to them without turning them into an inconsistent theory. In order to do this, he turned to a certain kind of continuity principle (viz., his so-called *Vollständigkeitsaxiom*) which, in Kantian fashion, he reckoned to belong to the domain of pure reason (or what Hilbert referred to as 'ideal' thought) rather than the domain of judgement (which Hilbert referred to as 'real' thought). This distinction between real and ideal elements in our mathematical thinking became the cornerstone of Hilbert's mathematical epistemology, both for arithmetic and, we believe, for geometry.

Hilbert did not, therefore, affirm the necessity of either arithmetic or geometry in any simple, straightforward way. Rather, he distinguished two *different* types of necessity operating both within arithmetic and geometry. One of these – that which attaches to the 'ideal' parts of arithmetic and geometry – he identified with the kind of necessity that attached to Kant's faculty of reason; a kind of necessity borne of the manner in which our minds inevitably work. The other, that applying to the so-called 'real' parts of mathematics, he saw as consisting in the presumed fact that all our thought assumes as a pre-condition the apprehension of certain elementary spatial features of simple concrete objects (cf. [2.76], 376; [2.78], 383, 385).

This, roughly, was Hilbert's complex conception of the a priority of mathematics. Clearly, it represented a significant departure from Kant's 'idealist' explanation of necessity as residing in the supposed inevitable tendencies of our minds to couch all experience in temporal terms, and all spatial experience in Euclidean terms. Clearly, too, it represented a significant departure from the ideas of the logicists and intuitionists. Its response to the discovery of non-Euclidean geometries (and such related discoveries concerning intuition of time as Einstein's theory of relativity) was not to posit an essential epistemological asymmetry between arithmetical and geometrical knowledge, as did (the original forms of) both logicism and intuitionism. Rather, or so it seems to us, it was to try and bring both under the authority of a single type of proto-geometric intuition concerning our apprehension of the elementary shapes or forms of concrete figures.

The 1930s witnessed the demise of Hilbert's Kantian programme at the hands of Gödel's theorems. Frege's Kantian logicism had earlier been vanquished by Russell's paradox, and the Kantian philosophies of the intuitionists, too, were under assault from both philosophical quarters (where their idealism was called into question) and mathematical quarters (where their ability to support a significant body of mathematics remained in doubt). Of the programmes of the early period, perhaps Russell's non-Kantian form of logicism remained most intact, being sustained chiefly through its embodiment of the recent advances in symbolic logic and its selection as the preferred philosophy of mathematics of the then-influential logical empiricist school.

Yet, even though the positive ideas of Kant's mathematical philosophy had largely been abandoned by the 1930s, his basic apparatus remained in effect until the early 1950s. It was only with Quine's attack on the analytic/synthetic distinction of the positivists that its influence, too, began to slip.[80] The dominant trend in the philosophy of mathematics since then, if, indeed, there has been one, has been that of empiricism: an empiricism which denies that there is a difference in kind between the necessity of mathematics and that of the rest of our judgements; an empiricism which sees mathematics as governed by the same basic inductive methodology as governs the natural sciences; an empiricism which sees mathematical inference as reducible to logical inference. The ultimate adequacy of this overall empiricist approach as an explanation of the 'data' of mathematical epistemology, however, remains unclear. So, too, does the justification of its view of what these data are. Indeed, the problem of determining what are the data of the philosophy of mathematics is, I would suggest, among the more serious problems facing the subject as the century draws to a close.

❧ NOTES ❧

1 Years later, in his only philosophical essay (see [2.91]), Kronecker would quote this view with approbation.

2 Ironically, it is probably the continued development of logic in the latter three-quarters of this century that has contributed as much as anything to the blindness of present-day philosophy of mathematics to the Kantian question of whether mathematical proof *can* rightly make use of logical inferences. There are, of course, reasons for this new orientation. There are also, however, some

drawbacks as we see it. Cf. Detlefsen [2.28], [2.30], [2.33] and Tragesser [2.142] for attempts to revitalize the Kantian question.

3 In speaking of a logicism 'like Russell's', we mean a logicism which was applied to the whole of mathematics and not just its arithmetic portion. The very different logicisms of Frege and Dedekind would not have been nearly so attractive to the logical empiricists because, though they would have allowed an analytic treatment of arithmetic judgement, they would not have allowed this account to be extended to geometry. The logical empiricists would therefore have had to deal with the seeming 'necessity' of geometrical judgement in some other way.

4 This it did by allowing them to treat mathematical judgement as analytic judgement, which they then treated as arising from the general phenomenon of linguistic convention. More on this later.

5 It should be noted, however, that the logicism of Frege and Dedekind raised a challenge to Kant on this score too. For it programmatically required that all reasoning appearing in a mathematical proof be reducible to logical reasoning and, indeed, logical reasoning of a sort so clear and perspicuous that it could not conceal anything of a non-logical nature.

6 Cf. [2.47], 50. [My translation.]

7 Frege expanded a bit further on this idea in section 24, where similar ideas in Locke and Leibniz are cited. See also [2.50].

8 In a later remark (cf. the introduction to [2.52], xv), Frege clarified further the connection between the laws of logic and the laws of thought alluded to here. 'The laws of logic have a special claim to be called "laws of thought" only because we recognize them as the most general laws, which prescribe universally the way in which thought ought to proceed when it proceeds at all.' (my translation).

9 This criticism of Kant would apply even more powerfully to Leibniz, since the latter acknowledged only *one* basic source of knowledge (namely, reason) and saw all truth as analytic in character (and, so qualitatively the same). It seems likely therefore that Frege would not have found Leibniz's mathematical epistemology as satisfying as Kant's – and this despite the fact that Leibniz advocated a kind of logicist view.

10 Frege says (cf. [2.49], the first footnote in section 3) that he has tried to capture what earlier writers, and, in particular, Kant, had in mind in their usages of the above terms. This is difficult to accept at face value, however, since Frege insists that *both* the a priori/a posteriori distinction *and* the analytic/synthetic distinction 'concern ... not the content of a judgement but the justification for making the judgement' (Ibid., section 3), whereas Kant held only that the former is a distinction of this sort. Furthermore, Frege later (cf. [2.49], section 88) says that Kant underestimated the potential epistemic productivity of analytic judgements because he 'defined them too narrowly'. What he seems to mean by this is that Kant, because of his impoverished Aristotelian notion of logical form, defined analyticity only for subject–predicate propositions, whereas, of course, the notion applies to a much wider class of propositions. There is, however, no indication that Frege saw Kant as having intended the analytic/synthetic distinction to concern the content of a judgement rather than its justification.

It should also be noted that in the event that canonical proofs are allowed to be non-unique, the definitions of syntheticity and a posteriority would have to be changed to require that every canonical proof involves recourse to a truth of a special science (resp. involves an appeal to facts). Likewise, the definitions of analyticity and a priority would have to be changed to state that some canonical proof contain only general logical laws and definitions (resp. only general laws which neither need nor admit of proof).

11 Cf. [2.49], section 14.

12 Though Frege does not cite the original source of his inspiration, the main idea expressed clearly reverberates a remark from the preface of the first edition of the *Critique of Pure Reason*: 'in an inventory of that which is acquired by us through Pure Reason ... nothing can escape us. For whatever reason brings forth (*hervorbringt*) entirely of itself cannot be hidden from it' (xx).

13 Cf. also section 27 where he says that numbers are neither 'spatial and physical ... nor yet subjective like ideas, but non-sensible and objective' and that 'objectivity cannot ... be based on any sense-impression, which as an affectation of our mind is entirely subjective, but only ... on reason'.

14 Cf. [2.49], sections 69, 107.

15 On this latter, compare [2.49], section 48.

16 Frege's belief in the priority of concepts cannot, however, completely explain his opposition to Kant. For Kant as is well-known, believed in a *form* (as opposed to a *substance* or *content*) of intuition which 'precedes in my subjectivity all actual impressions through which I am affected by objects' (cf. [2.85], section 9, my translation) and held it to be the basis of our mathematical knowledge. He was therefore not committed to a conception of the intuitional basis of our mathematical knowledge according to which it rests on intuitions of particular sensible things. Why, then, did Frege feel that he needed concepts rather than merely Kant's *forms* of intuition? This, I believe, is a difficult question to answer. Such answers as might be given would appear to require recourse to Frege's belief that (i) concepts possess *special* unifying power (and, in particular, unifying power that is superior to that possessed by intuition generally); and that (ii) number is applicable to more than just that which can be sensed. Kant, by contrast, held that

> all mathematical cognition has this pecularity: that it must first exhibit
> its concept in intuitional form ... Without this, mathematics cannot
> take a single step. Its judgements are therefore always intuitional,
> whereas philosophy must make do with discursive judgements from
> mere concepts. It may illustrate its judgements by means of a visual
> form, but it can never derive them from such a form.

> (Ibid., section 7).

17 Of course, quite apart from worries concerning its consistency, one might wonder how Rule V could be defended as a *logical* principle. In his defence, Frege employed his well-known distinction between sense and reference (which is related to his belief in the priority of concepts to their extensions) and constructed an argument to the effect that the two sides of the biconditional in Rule V have the same *sense*.

18 For more on this, as well as some examples, see [2.49], sections 64–66, 70, 88, 91.

19 Frege gives an example of the different ways of carving up content in section 70 of [2.49]. He also discusses it in section 9 of [2.48], where one of the example he considers is the proposition of 'Cato killed Cato'. He remarks there that if we think of this proposition as allowing for replacement of the first instance of 'Cato', we see it as formed from the propositional function 'x killed Cato'. If we think of it as allowing for the replacement of the last instance of 'Cato', we see it as formed from the function 'x was killed by Cato'. And, if we see it as allowing for the replacement of both occurrences of 'Cato' at once, we see it as formed from the function 'x killed y'. No single one of these ways of seeing the proposition is necessary for its apprehension. Hence, each might in its turn be thought of as a 'recarving' of its content.

20 Still, as was mentioned earlier, since Russell believed that the whole of what is ordinarily regarded as pure mathematics can be reduced to (second-order Peano) arithmetic, the distance between him and Frege on this point is not so great as might at first sight appear (cf. Russell [2.123], 275–9 (esp. 276); [2.120], 157–8, 259–60). It should be noted, too, that in these passages, Russell describes the work of the 'arithmetizers' of mathematics (e.g. Dedekind and Weierstrass) as being of greater importance to the cause of logicism than the discovery of non-Euclidean geometries.

21 Even here, of course, one sees vestiges of Kant. For he, too, conceived of reason as impelling one towards ever greater generality in science. He did not, however, think of this procedure as tending towards a terminus – a most general science (the TRUE science!), as it were. Still less did he think of it as tending towards a science of *logic*.

22 Hereinafter we will refer to this as Russell [2.120]. The pagination cited is that of the seventh impression of the second edition, which appeared in 1956.

23 Russell distinguished the level of generality where all constants are logical constants from what we are here referring to as the level of *maximum* generality. The latter was seen as requiring the former. But in addition, it was taken to require an identification of what Russell referred to as the 'principles' of logic; that is, the most basic truths from which all other truths whose only constants are logical constants can be derived by logical means (cf. [2.120], 10).

24 Russell elaborated on this idea and extended a modified version of it to the case of the empirical sciences in [2.122] and [2.123].

25 Russell [2.123], 273–4. Page numbers are those of the reprint in [2.125].

26 It is not obvious that Russell's condition is weaker. Indeed, it is not weaker at all if a suitably stiff standard of individuation for propositions is adopted. For example, if one were to adopt a criterion of individuation which makes all logically equivalent sentences express the same proposition, then Russell's criterion would become considerably more demanding than he wanted it to be. Moreover, the problems intensify the broader one's notion of logical equivalence becomes. Hence, for the logicist, who requires a very broad conception of logical equivalence, a criterion of propositional identity that identifies logically equivalent propositions would make it virtually impossible for a standard of inferential epistemic productivity like Russell's to succeed. Russell did not explicitly propose any standard of individuation for propositions in his discussion of synthetic inference, but his remarks suggest that he would not have

accepted a standard which implies the identity of logically equivalent sentences (at least for any broad conception of logical equivalence).

27 We must leave for another occasion the explanation of how this differs from Kant's understanding of reason as a regulative ideal that leads us to ever greater generality (i.e. unity) in our judgements.

28 The reader will recall that in 1886 Kronecker famously remarked that while God made the whole numbers, everything else is the work of man (*Die ganzen Zahlen hat der liebe Gott gemacht, alles andere ist Menschenwerk*). How do we square that Kronecker with the Kronecker who accepted Gauss's view that the numbers are the product of the human intellect and that geometry is not? The answer would seem to lie in a distinction Kronecker made between arithmetic in a 'narrower' sense and arithmetic in a 'wider' sense. By the former, he meant the arithmetic of the natural numbers, while by the latter he meant to include algebra and analysis as well (cf. [2.91], 265). A resolution of the apparent conflict can be obtained by taking the work of God to be arithmetic in the narrower sense and taking the 'everything else' of Kronecker's remark to refer not to geometry and mechanics and the like, but to arithmetic in the wider sense.

29 Page references to Brouwer's papers are to the reprinting in [2.20].

30 Poincaré, another early constructivist, about whom we shall have more to say later, differed both from Kant, Brouwer and the other early constructivists on this point. He maintained that 'the axioms of geometry ... are neither synthetic a priori judgements nor experimental facts ... They are conventions ... merely disguised definitions' (cf. [2.99], pt. II, ch. 3, section 10). For a statement (not wholly accurate, in my view) of some of the other differences, see [2.21], 2–4.

31 Poincaré, along with Borel and Lebesgue, was described by Brouwer (cf. [2.21], 2–3), as a 'pre-intuitionist'. For present purposes, however, the alleged differences between 'pre-intuitionism' and 'intuitionism' are of no importance.

32 Cf. 'Revue de metaphysique et de morale' 14: 17–34, 294–317, 627–50, 866–8; 17: 451–82; 18: 263–301; [2.121], 412–18, 15: 141–3.

33 As he put it elsewhere, it is a mistake to believe in:

> the possibility of extending one's knowledge of truth by the mental process of thinking, in particular thinking accompanied by linguistic operations independent of experience called 'logical reasoning', which to a limited stock of 'evidently' true assertions mainly founded on experience and sometimes called axioms, contrives to add an abundance of further truths.
>
> (Cf. [2.19], 113)

34 Brouwer, of course, believed that there can be significant differences between the class of theorems provable from a given set S of propositions by means of classical logic and those provable from S by means of intuitionistic mathematical reasoning. He would not, however, have maintained the same for the theorems provable via intuitionist logic from S and the theorems provable by genuine mathematical reasoning from S. Still, he saw an important difference between proving theorems by genuine mathematical means and proving them by means of intuitionist logic. Indeed, the central theme of his critique of classical math-

ematics was that mathematical reasoning is distinct from logical reasoning generally, and not just from *classical* logical reasoning. For more on this, see [2.28].

35 Poincaré was led to his intuitional conception of inference by his belief in what he took to be a fundamental datum of mathematical epistemology; namely, that the epistemic condition of a purely logical reasoner, who sees none of the local architecture that creates the 'channels', as it were, of mathematical inference, is different from that of the genuine mathematician whose inferences reflect a grasp of these channels. Brouwer, in effect, held much the same view. For he insisted that logical inference reflects only a grasp of the channels of belief-movement provided for by the linguistic representation of belief, whereas genuine mathematical inference moves according to the channels provided by that constructional activity which itself is *constitutive* of mathematics.

36 There are, however, foreshadowings of such a notion in the Christian neo-platonists (e.g. Augustine, Boethius and Anselm) and also in Cusanus. The latter even coined a term for the notion – *visio intellectualis*. Kant, too, spoke of such a notion (cf. [2.86], 307, 311–12; and [2.87], vol., VIII, 389), though he thought that only God and not humans could possess it.

37 As Kant said (cf. 1st edn of [2.86] (which was published in 1781), 639, [2.86], 667):

> In whatever manner the understanding may have arrived at a concept, the existence of its object is never, by any process of analysis, discoverable within it; for the knowledge of the existence of the object consists precisely in the fact that the object is posited in itself, outside the mere thought of it.

38 The First Act of Intuitionism says that mathematics is to be 'completely separated ... from mathematical language and hence from the phenomenon of language itself described by theoretical logic' ([2.21], 4–5).

39 'to exist in mathematics means: to be constructed' ([2.15], 96). 'Mathematics is created by a free action' (Ibid., 97).

40 Cf. [2.34] for a more detailed development of these and related matters.

41 Cf. [2.34] for a more detailed discussion of these matters.

42 Conclusive textual evidence that Hilbert intended to use finitary intuition as the foundation for both our geometrical and our arithmetical knowledge may not exist. If we are right, however, in thinking that this was Hilbert's view, then, he not only would have regarded both arithmetic and geometry as a priori, but would have taken both as being based on the *same* a priori intuition.

43 Cf. [2.74], 163, and [2.80], 32 for related remarks.

44 Examples of unproblematic real propositions are variable-free equations of arithmetic and propositional compounds formed from them. The sentences in this class can be manipulated according to the full range of classical logical operations without leading outside the reals. As examples of problematic real propositions, Hilbert offered the following: (i) for all non-negative integers a, $a + 1 = 1 + a$; and (ii) there is a prime number greater than g but less than $g!$ $+ 1$ (where 'g' stands for the greatest prime known at the moment). (i) was deemed problematic because its denial fails to bound the search for a counterexample to '$a + 1 = 1 + a$'. Hence, its denial is not a real proposition, and, so, the law of excluded middle cannot be applied to (i), making it problematic. In

like manner, (ii) classically implies 'there is a prime number greater than **g**'. This was not regarded as a real proposition since it gives no bound for the search for the prime it asserts to exist, and, by the definition of **g** (as being the largest prime known), any such bound would go beyond everything that is known. Hence (ii), too, was regarded as leading to non-finitary conclusions when manipulated according to the principles of classical logic and is therefore problematic. We are not sure that Hilbert's reasoning regarding this last case is ultimately capable of sustaining his conclusion. This does not, however, in our estimation, threaten the cogency of his distinction between problematic and unproblematic reals.

45 To be more exact, what was to be prohibited was the use of ideal methods that conflict with real methods in the sense that they generate real theorems that are *refutable* by finitary means. We will refer to this as *real-consistency*. This may signal a difference between Kant and Hilbert. For while Kant wanted to proscribe all uses of reason that transcend what is determinable by the senses, Hilbert, on the other hand, seems to have been primarily interested in prohibiting uses of ideal reasoning that are refutable by finitary reasoning. What he would have said about ideally proven real theorems that are neither provable nor refutable by finitary means is less clear.

It is also important to note in this connection that there is an asymmetry between the observation sentences of an empirical science and Hilbert's real sentences. This asymmetry consists in the fact that observation sentences are, by their very definition, to be decidable by observational evidence. Real sentences, on the other hand, are not understood as being necessarily decidable by finitary or real means. Thus, while it is possible to pass from a requirement that no observational consequence of an empirical theory be observationally refutable to a requirement that every observational consequence be observationally verifiable, it is not similarly possible to pass from a requirement that no ideally provable real theorem be refutable by real means to a requirement that every real theorem provable by ideal means be provable by real means. For more on this, see [2.29].

46 The salient feature of a formal system for the purposes of this discussion is that its set of theorems is recursively enumerable.

47 **PRA** has as its theorems all logical consequences of the recursion equations for (formalizations of) the primitive recursive functions. In addition, it admits mathematical induction restricted to (formulae formalizing) primitive recursive relations. Cf. [2.135] for an extended argument to the effect that **PRA** is a formalization of finitary reasoning.

48 For a useful discussion of this 'relativized' form of Hilbert's programme, see the very nice expository paper [2.40].

49 **WKL₀** is the theory obtained by adding the so-called *weak König's lemma* (i.e. the claim that every infinite subtree of the complete binary tree has an infinite branch) to a system called **RCA₀**, which contains the usual axioms for addition, multiplication, o, equality and inequality, induction for Σ_1 formulae, and comprehension for Δ_1 formulae (i.e. all instances of the schema $\exists X \, \forall n \, (n \in X \leftrightarrow \phi(n))$ where ϕ is any Σ_1 formula such that there is a Π_1 formula ψ to which it is provably equivalent). It should also be mentioned that the proof of (ii); which is due to Harvey Friedman, actually establishes something stronger than

(ii); namely, that all II_2 theorems (i.e. theorems equivalent to a sentence of the form '$\forall x \exists y\ \phi xy$', where '$\phi xy$' is a recursive formula) of WKL_0 are provable in PRA. Finally, it should be noted that these same results are obtainable for a stronger system WKL_0^+, which contains some non-constructive theorems of functional analysis not provable in WKL_0. For more on this, see [2.134]. Cf. [2.133] for a more thorough bibliography concerning the work establishing (i) and (ii).

50 It is not just the ideal derivation of a real theorem τ_P which, by itself, is to be simpler than any real proof of τ_R. For that ideal derivation of τ_R must be supplemented with a metamathematical proof of I's real-soundness if we are to obtain a genuine justification for τ_R from an ideal derivation of it. For a more thorough discussion of this and related matters, see [2.27], chs 2 (esp. pp. 57–73), 3 and 5, and [2.29].

51 Cf. [2.29], 370, 376 for a bit more on this.

52 Stated intuitively, the axiom of reducibility says that for every propositional function f, there is a predicative propositional function P_f such that f and P_f have the same extension.

53 Ayer stated the predicament of the empiricist well:

> Whereas a scientific generalization is readily admitted to be fallible, the truths of mathematics and logic appear to everyone to be necessary or certain. Accordingly the empiricist must deal with the truths of logic and mathematics in one of the two following ways: he must say either that they are not necessary truths, in which case he must account for the universal conviction that they are; or he must say that they have no factual content, and then he must explain how a proposition which is empty of all factual content can be true and useful and surprising.
>
> ([2.2], 72–3)

54 The former kind of proposition was called *analytic* and the latter kind *synthetic*.

55 In the case of Carnap (cf. [2.24]), this thesis of analyticity was developed by introducing the notion of a *linguistic framework*, which he understood as a system of rules for talking about entities of a given kind. Linguistic frameworks induce a distinction between *internal* and *external* questions of existence. Answers to internal questions, such as the question 'Is there a prime number greater than 100?', come from logical analysis based on the rules governing the expressions making up the framework. Answers to such questions are therefore logically or analytically true. External questions querying the general existence of the entities associated with a given linguistic framework are to be interpreted as questions regarding acceptance of the framework itself (Ibid., 250). Thus, the question 'Do numbers exist?', is to be understood as 'Should the linguistic framework of numerical discourse be accepted?'. Answers to such questions are to be decided on what are basically pragmatic grounds; that is to say, on the basis of the 'efficiency' of the framework in question as an 'instrument', or, in other words, on the basis of 'the ratio of the results achieved to the amount and complexity of the efforts required' (Ibid., 257). This view has often been described as a form of *conventionalism*, though use of this term would seem to disguise its essentially pragmatist flavour. It also tends to confuse the position of Carnap's later writings on the nature of mathematics with that of his earlier

writings, which truly was conventionalist in character. For more on this latter point see [2.116].

56 Sharing some of the general spirit of Bostock, but more concerned to defend (a version of) logicism, are Hodes [2.81] and [2.82].

57 This kind of logicism is closely related to the 'structuralist' position discussed below.

58 The views of Quine and Putnam are stated and discussed below. See also the discussion of Benacerraf's dilemma given there. Field seems mainly to be motivated by a desire to find a physicalist solution to this dilemma.

59 For the beginnings of a defence of the Kantian view, see [2.28], [2.30].

60 Cf. Field [2.43], 516, n. 7, where he cites this as the key feature distinguishing his modalization of mathematics from the earlier one of Putnam [2.102].

61 Basically, the idea is that if one has need of a given capacity, and could also benefit from its improvement, then one will be rationally impelled to bring about such improvements.

62 Heyting referred ([2.70], 108) to this thesis as the 'principle of positivity', and acknowledge that it is the chief determinant of the character of his logic.

63 'a logical theorem expresses the fact that, if we know a proof of certain theorems, then we also know a proof for another theorem' ([2.70], 107).

64 There is some question as to what exactly this means. Does it mean that one who knows the meaning of a mathematical sentence S either knows or can readily obtain either a proof or a disproof of S? Or does it mean, instead, that one knows the meaning of S when and only when he or she *would* recognize a proof or a disproof of S *were* he or she to be *given* it? See [2.93], [2.94] and [2.140] for more on this topic.

65 This is not said as a criticism of Dummett. For he states explicitly that his conception and defence of intuitionism is not intended to comport with that of Brouwer or Heyting or any other particular intuitionist ([2.36], 215).

66 (ii') is not altogether uncontroversial, however. For it equates legitimate ascription of implicit knowledge to a speaker with implication by the best total theory of his or her behaviour. In doing so, it fails adequately to reflect the fact that that theory of a speaker's behaviour which, judged by 'local' standards, qualifies as best might have to be sacrificed in order to obtain the best global theory (i.e. the best total explanation of *all* phenomena – not just those constituting the speaker's behaviour). Changing (ii') in this direction would, however, only intensify the objection to Dummett's argument developed here.

67 On occasion when I've presented this argument I've been met with the charge that it presupposes a holistic view of meaning and that that is something Dummett explicitly rejects. This latter claim is clearly true ([2.36], 218–21). It is, however, a misunderstanding of my argument to think of it as presupposing a holistic view of meaning. Indeed, the alternative I suggested above to Dummett's view of implicit knowledge is one that sees implicit knowledge (and hence knowledge of meaning) as consisting in the occupation of a specific mental or psychological or neural state that underlies the behaviour with which Dummett wants to equate it. Our claim is that even such a non-holistic view of meaning as this is subject to underdetermination by the observed facts of speaker behaviour. The basis of our objection is therefore not acceptance of a holistic view of meaning, but rather acceptance of the general idea of underde-

termination of theory by data. Regardless of whether Dummett has produced convincing reasons for rejecting holism (and we believe he has not), he has provided no reasons for rejecting the idea of underdetermination of theory by data.

68 Indeed, in his 1939 Cambridge lectures on the foundations of mathematics ([2.150], 237), Wittgenstein dismissed intuitionism as 'bosh'.

69 For useful discussions of Wittgenstein's views, the reader should consult [2.35], [2.152], and [2.129]. The latter is especially recommended for the many stimulating questions and challenges it raises for the more influential interpretations of the later writings.

70 Putnam [2.106] strengthens this to say that in order even to *formulate* science, mathematics is needed.

71 On the 'web' metaphor, this is what is meant by saying that they are 'centrally located'.

72 Nor is this merely lip service. For Putnam has argued that the best way of clearing up certain paradoxes in quantum physics may be to revise classical two-valued logic or classical probability theory [2.104].

73 His view was not, however, empiricist. This is so because he rejected the idea that sensory intuition is the ultimate basis for (at least most of) mathematical knowledge. He posited instead a distinctively mathematical form of intuition, though this mathematical intuition was interpreted in a realist or platonist manner, as a means of gaining acquaintance with externally existing objects, and not in a Kantian manner, as an a priori form or condition of thought.

74 Gödel notes in the same place, however, that, at present, so little is known about the lower level mathematical and physical effects of such higher level axioms as those concerning the existence of various kinds of so-called 'large cardinals' that inductive justification of the kind just noted is not possible.

75 My own inclination is to think that Benacerraf's dilemma is not a genuine dilemma. In particular, I am inclined to reject claim (i) of the argument leading to the dilemma – that is, the claim that we are under some sort of obligation to treat mathematical language as semantically continuous with non-mathematical language. What does seem to be an obligation is that we treat mathematical language as a congruous element of our larger linguistic system, conceived of as a device for manipulating representations of the world. In general, I take language to play the role in human thought of allowing us to substitute manipulation of representations of the world for manipulations of the world itself. But schemes for substituting manipulations of representations of the world for manipulations of the world itself (conceived in either realist or idealist terms) can certainly be so fashioned as to make room for sub-devices whose significance within the scheme is that of a calculary or computational device rather than that of a referential device. Sometimes syntactical manipulation of signs might be better than direct semantical manipulation as a way of managing what, in the end, is to be a representation–manipulation. That being so, syntactical manipulation might well play an important role in a greater overall scheme of basically semantical representation–manipulation. At the same time, however, it is hardly to be supposed that such devices are to be treated as semantically continuous with the more referential parts of the linguistic scheme. Nor is there any reason I can see for denying that the role of mathematical language within our overall

linguistic scheme is that of a calculary or computational device. As a result, I see little grounds for accepting Benacerraf's (i) and the ensuing 'dilemma' that is built upon it.

76 For another statement to this general effect, see [2.131], 534.

77 See the remarks from Weyl quoted below for a relatively early statement of just this idea.

78 For more on the ideas expressed here, the interested reader should consult the correspondence with H. Weber in volume III of Dedekind's *Gesammelte mathematische Werke*. For worthwhile discussions of Dedekind's views, see [2.136], [2.137] and [2.98], section 2.

79 The general prevalence of such views around the turn of the century is also noted in [2.148] and [2.10].

80 I would except Hilbert's later philosophy of mathematics (and, in particular, that expressed in [2.78]) from this generalization.

I would like to thank Aron Edidin, Richard Foley, Alasdair MacIntyre, Alvin Plantinga, Phillip Quinn, Stuart Shanker and Stewart Shapiro for reading and helpfully commenting on all or parts of this chapter. The mistakes that remain are mine alone.

❧ BIBLIOGRAPHY ❧

2.1 Ackermann, W. 'Zur Widerspruchsfreiheit der Zahlentheorie', *Mathematische Annalen* 117 (1940): 162–94.

2.2 Ayer, A. *Language, Truth and Logic*, London, Gollancz, 1936.

2.3 —— (ed.) *Logical Positivism*, New York, The Free Press, 1959.

2.4 Beeson, M. *Foundations of Constructive Mathematics*, Berlin, Springer-Verlag, 1985.

2.5 Benacerraf, P. 'What Numbers Could Not Be', *Philosophical Review* 74 (1965): 47–73. Repr. in [2.7].

2.6 —— 'Mathematical Truth', *Journal of Philosophy* 70 (1973): 661–80. Repr. in [2.7].

2.7 Benacerraf, P. and H. Putnam *Philosophy of Mathematics: Selected Readings* 2nd edn, Cambridge, Cambridge University Press, 1983.

2.8 Bernays, P. (1935) 'Hilberts Untersuchungen über die Grundlagen der Arithmetik', 1935, repr. in [2.79].

2.9 —— 'Mathematische Existenz und Widerspruchsfreiheit', 1950, repr. in [2.11].

2.10 —— 'Hilbert, David', in P. Edwards (ed.) *The Encyclopedia of Philosophy*, New York, Macmillan and the Free Press, 1967.

2.11 —— *Abhandlungen zur Philosophie der Mathematik*, Darmstadt, Wissenschaftliche Buchgesellschaft, 1976.

2.12 Bostock, D. *Logic and Arithmetic*, 2 vols, Oxford, The Clarendon Press, 1974.

2.13 Bridges, D. *Varieties of Constructive Mathematics*, Cambridge, Cambridge University Press, 1987.

2.14 Brouwer, L. E. J. 'Life, Art and Mysticism', 1905, repr. in [2.20].

2.15 —— 'On the Foundations of Mathematics', 1907, repr. in [2.20].

2.16 —— 'Intuitionism and Formalism', 1912, repr. in [2.20].

2.17 —— 'Consciousness, Philosophy and Mathematics', 1948, repr. in [2.20].

2.18 —— 'Points and Spaces', 1954, repr. in [2.20].

2.19 —— 'The Effect of Intuitionism on Classical Algebra of Logic', 1955, repr. in [2.20].

2.20 —— *L. E. J. Brouwer: Collected Works*, vol. I, Amsterdam, North-Holland, 1975.

2.21 —— *Brouwer's Cambridge Lectures on Intuitionism*, D. Van Dalen (ed.), Cambridge, Cambridge University Press, 1981.

2.22 Carnap, R. 'The Old and the New Logic', 1930–1, repr. in [2.3].

2.23 —— 'Die logizitische Grundlegung der Mathematik', *Erkenntnis* 2 (1931): 91–121. English trans. in [2.7].

2.24 —— 'Empiricism, Semantics, and Ontology', *Revue internationale de philosophie* 4 (1950): 20–40; repr. in [2.7].

2.25 Dedekind, R. *Was sind und was sollen die Zahlen?* Braunschweig, Vieweg, 1887; repr. in 1969. English trans. in [2.26].

2.26 —— (1963) *Dedekind's Essays on the Theory of Numbers*, New York, Dover Publications, 1963.

2.27 Detlefsen, M. *Hilbert's Program*, Dordrecht, Reidel, 1986.

2.28 —— 'Brouwerian Intuitionism', *Mind* 99 (1990): 501–34.

2.29 —— 'On an Alleged Refutation of Hilbert's Program using Gödel's First Incompleteness Theorem', *Journal of Philosophical Logic* 19 (1990): 343–77.

2.30 —— 'Poincaré Against the Logicians', *Synthese* 90 (1992): 349–78.

2.31 —— (ed.) *Proof and Knowledge in Mathematics*, London, Routledge, 1992.

2.32 —— (ed.) *Proof, Logic and Formalization*, London, Routledge, 1992.

2.33 —— 'Poincaré vs. Russell on the Role of Logic in Mathematics', *Philosophia Mathematica* Series III, 1 (1993): 24–49.

2.34 —— 'Constructive Existence Claims', to appear in *Philosophy of Mathematics Today*, Oxford, Oxford University Press, 199?.

2.35 Dummett, M. 'Wittgenstein's Philosophy of Mathematics', *Philosophical Review* 68 (1959): 324–48.

2.36 —— (1973) 'The Philosophical Basis of Intuitionistic Logic', in H. Rose and J. Shepherdson (eds) *Logic Colloquium '73*, Amsterdam, North-Holland, 1973, repr. in [2.7].

2.37 —— *Elements of Intuitionism*, Oxford, Oxford University Press, 1977.

2.38 Feferman, S. 'Systems of Predicative Analysis', *Journal of Symbolic Logic* 29 (1964): 1–30.

2.39 —— 'Systems of Predicative Analysis, II', *Journal of Symbolic Logic* 33 (1968): 193–220.

2.40 —— 'Hilbert's Program Relativized: Proof-theoretical and Foundational Reductions', *Journal of Symbolic Logic* 53 (1988): 364–84.

2.41 Fichte, J. (1797) *Werke*, III (Wissenschaftslehre), Leipzig, Felix Meiner, 1797.

2.42 Field, H. *Science Without Numbers*, Princeton, NJ, Princeton University Press, 1980.

2.43 —— 'Is Mathematical Knowledge Just Logical Knowledge?' *Philosophical Review* 93 (1984): 509–52, repr. in [2.45].

2.44 —— 'On Conservativeness and Incompleteness', *Journal of Philosophy* 82 (1985): 239–59, repr. in [2.45].

2.45 —— *Realism, Mathematics and Modality*, Oxford, Basil Blackwell, 1989.

2.46 Frege, G. *Über eine geometrische Darstellung der imaginären Gebilde in der Ebene*, 1873, doctoral dissertation, Philosophical Faculty, University of Göttingen. Page references to I. Angelelli (ed.) *Kleine Schriften*, Hildesheim, 1967. Partial English trans. in [2.56].

2.47 —— *Rechnungsmethoden, die sich auf eine Erweiterung des Größenbegriffes gründen*, 1874, Habilitationsschrift, Philosophical Faculty, University of Jena. English trans. in [2.56].

2.48 —— *Begriffsschrift, eine der arithmetischen nachgebildete Formelsprache des reinend Denkens*, Halle, 1879. English trans. in [2.144].

2.49 —— *Die Grundlagen der Arithmetik*, Breslau, Koebner, 1884 English trans. [2.54].

2.50 —— *Über formalen Theorien der Arithmetik*, Sitzungsberichte der Jenaischen Gesellschaft für Medizin und Naturwissenschaft, 19 (suppl. vol. 2) (1885): 94–104. English trans. in [2.56].

2.51 —— 'Function und Begriff'. Lecture presented to the *Jenaischen Gesellschaft für Medizin und Naturwisssenschaft*. English trans. in [2.56].

2.52 —— *Die Grundgesetze der Arithmetik*, vol. I, Jena, Pohle, 1893; repr. Hildesheim, Olms, 1962.

2.53 —— 'Kritische Beleuchtung einiger Punkte in E. Schröder's Vorlesungen über die Algebra der Logik', *Archiv für systematische Philosophie* 1 (1895): 433–56. English trans. in [2.56].

2.54 —— *The Foundations of Arithmetic*, Evanston, IL, Northwestern University Press, 1974; English trans. of [2.49].

2.55 —— *Philosophical and Mathematical Correspondance*, G. Gabriel *et al.* (eds), H. Kaal, (trans.), Chicago, University of Chicago Press, 1980.

2.56 —— *Gottlob Frege: Collected Papers on Mathematics, Logic and Philosophy*, B. McGuinness (ed.), Oxford, Basil Blackwell, 1984.

2.57 Friedman, M. 'Kant's Theory of Geometry', *Philosophical Review*, 94 (1985): 455–506.

2.58 —— 'Kant on Concepts and Intuitions in The Mathematical Sciences', *Synthese* 84 (1990): 213–57.

2.59 Gauss, K. *Werke*, Vols I–XI, Leipzig, Teubner, 1863–1903.

2.60 —— *Briefwechsel mit H. W. M. Olbers*, Hildesheim, Georg Olms, 1976.

2.61 Gentzen, G. 'Die Widerspruchsfreiheit der reinen Zahlentheorie', *Mathematische Annalen* 112 (1936): 493–565.

2.62 Gödel, K. 'Über formal unentscheidbare Sätze der *Principia Mathematica* und verwandter Systeme I', *Monatshefte für Mathematik und Physik* 38 (1931): 173–198. English trans. in [2.144].

2.63 —— 'What Is Cantor's Continuum Problem?' *American Mathematical Monthly* 54 (1947): 515–25.

2.64 —— 'Über eine bisher noch nicht benützte Erweiterung des finiten Standpunktes', *Dialectica* 12 (1958): 280–7. English trans. in *Journal of Philosophical Logic* 9 (1958): 133–42.

2.65 —— 'What Is Cantor's Continuum Problem?', rev. version of [2.63]; rep. in [2.7].

2.66 Hahn, H. 'Logik, Mathematik und Naturerkennen', vol. 2 of the *Einheitswis-senchaft* series (Carnap and Hahn (eds)), Vienna, Gerold, 1933. English trans. in [2.3]

2.67 Halsted, B. *The Foundations of Science*, Lancaster, PA, The Science Press, 1946.

2.68 Hellman, G. *Mathematics Without Numbers*, Oxford, Oxford University Press, 1989.

2.69 Heyting, A. *Intuitionism: An Introduction*, Amsterdam, North-Holland, 1956. Page references are to the 3rd rev. edn, 1971.

2.70 —— (1958) 'Intuitionism in Mathematics', in R. Klibansky (ed.) *Philosophy in the Mid-Century*, Firenze, 1958.

2.71 Hilbert, D. Letter to Frege, 29 December, 1899. English trans. in [2.55].

2.72 —— 'Mathematische Probleme', lecture presented to the International Congress of Mathematicians in Paris. English trans. in *Bulletin of the American Mathematical Society* 8 (1902): 437–79.

2.73 —— 'Axiomatisches Denken', 1918, in [2.79].

2.74 —— 'Neubegründung der Mathematik (Erste Mitteilung)', 1922, in [2.79].

2.75 —— 'Über das Unendliche', *Mathematische Annalen* 95 (1925): 161–90.

2.76 —— 'On the Infinite', 1925, English trans. of [2.75] in [2.144].

2.77 —— 'The Foundations of Mathematics', 1927, in [2.144].

2.78 —— 'Naturerkennen und Logik', 1930, in [2.79].

2.79 —— *Gesammelte Abhandlungen*, vol. 3, Berlin, Springer, 1935, repr., New York, Chelsea, 1965.

2.80 Hilbert, D. and P. Bernays *Grundlagen der Mathematik*, vol. I, Berlin, Spinger, 1934.

2.81 Hodes, H. 'Logicism and the Ontological Commitments of Arithmetic', *Journal of Philosophy* 81: (1984) 123–49.

2.82 —— 'Where do the Natural Numbers Come From?' *Synthese* 84: (1990) 347–407.

2.83 Hume, D. *Enquiry Concerning Human Understanding*, Oxford, Clarendon Press, 1748.

2.84 Kant, I. *On the Form and Principles of the Sensible and Intelligible World*, 1770, in G. B. Kersferd and D. E. Walford (trans. and eds) *Kant: Selected Pre-Critical Writings and Correspondence with Beck*, New York, Barnes and Noble, 1968.

2.85 —— *Prolegomena zu einer jeden künftigen Metaphysik die als Wissenschaft auftreten können*, Riga, 1783. English trans. in P. Carus (trans.), *Kant's Prolegomena*, Chicago, Open Court, 1929.

2.86 —— *Kritik der reinen Vernunft*, 2nd. edn, Riga, J. F. Hartknoch, 1787. English trans. in [2.88].

2.87 —— *Gesammelte Schriften*, Berlin, Reimer, 1900.

2.88 —— *Critique of Pure Reason*, N. K. Smith (trans.), New York, St Martin's Press, 1965.

2.89 Kitcher, P. *The Nature of Mathematical Knowledge*, Oxford, Oxford University Press, 1983.

2.90 Kreisel, G. 'Hilbert's Programme', 1958, in [2.7].

2.91 Kronecker, L. 'Über den Zahlbegriff', *Journal für reine und angewandte*

Mathematik 101 (1887): 261–74. Repr. in *Werke*, vol. 3, Part I, 1932, pp. 249–74.

2.92 Maddy, P. *Realism in Mathematics*, Oxford, Oxford University Press, 1990.

2.93 McGinn, C. 'Truth and Use', in M. Platts (ed.) *Reference, Truth and Reality*, London, Routledge and Kegan Paul, 1980.

2.94 —— 'Reply to Tennant', *Analysis* 41 (1981): 120–3.

2.95 Parsons, C. 'Mathematical Intuition', *Proceedings of the Aristotelian Society* 80 (1980): 145–68.

2.96 —— 'Quine on the Philosophy of Mathematics', repr. in [2.97].

2.97 —— *Mathematics in Philosophy*, Ithaca, Cornell University Press, 1983.

2.98 —— 'The Structuralist View of Mathematical Objects', *Synthese* 84 (1990): 303–46.

2.99 Poincaré, H. *La science et l'hypothese*, Paris, Ernest Flammarion, 1903. English trans. in [2.67].

2.100 —— *La valeur de la science*, Paris, Ernest Flammarion, 1905. English trans. in [2.67].

2.101 —— *Science et méthode*, Paris, Ernest Flammarion, 1908. English trans. in [2.67].

2.102 Putnam, H. 'Mathematics without Foundations', *Journal of Philosophy* 64 (1967): 5–22, repr. in [2.107] and [2.7].

2.103 —— 'The Thesis that Mathematics is Logic', in R. Schoenman (ed.) *Bertrand Russell: Philosopher of the Century*, London, Allen and Unwin, 1967, repr. in [2.107].

2.104 —— 'The Logic of Quantum Mechanics', in R. Cohen and M. Wartofsky (eds) *Boston Studies in the Philosophy of Science*, vol. 5, Dordrecht, Reidel, 1968, repr. in [2.107].

2.105 —— *Philosophy of Logic*, New York, Harper and Row, 1971.

2.106 —— 'What Is Mathematical Truth?' 1975, in [2.107].

2.107 —— *Mathematics, Matter and Method*, Cambridge, Cambridge University Press, 1979.

2.108 Quine, W. V. D. 'On What There Is', *Review of Metaphysics* 2 (1948): 21–38, Repr. in [2.110].

2.109 —— 'Two Dogmas of Empiricism', *Philosophical Review* 60 (1951): 20–46, repr. in [2.110]

2.110 —— *From a Logical Point of View*, New York, Harper and Row, 1953.

2.111 —— 'Carnap and Logical Truth', *Synthese* 12 (1954): 350–79. Repr. in [2.7].

2.112 Resnik, M. *Frege and the Philosophy of Mathematics*, Ithaca, NY, Cornell University Press, 1980.

2.113 —— 'Mathematics as a Science of Patterns: Ontology and Reference', *Nous* 15 (1981): 529–50

2.114 —— 'Mathematics as a Science of Patterns: Epistemology', *Nous* 16 (1982): 95–105.

2.115 —— Review of H. Field's *Science Without Numbers*, *Nous* 27 (1982): 514–19.

2.116 Runggaldier, E. *Carnap's Early Conventionalism: An Inquiry into the Historical Background of the Vienna Circle*, Amsterdam, Rodopi, 1984.

2.117 Russell, B. 'Recent Work on the Principles of Mathematics', *International Monthly* 4 (1901): 83–101.

PHILOSOPHY OF SCIENCE, LOGIC AND MATHEMATICS

2.118 —— 'Is Position in Time and Space Absolute or Relative?' *Mind* 10 (1901b): 293–317.

2.119 —— Letter to Frege, 1902, in [2.144].

2.120 —— *The Principles of Mathematics*, Cambridge, Cambridge University Press, 1903. Page references to the 7th impression of the 2nd ed, London, George Allen and Unwin, 1937.

2.121 —— 'Review of *Science and Hypothesis* by H. Poincare', *Mind* 14 (1905): 412–18.

2.122 —— 'Les paradoxes de la logique', *Revue de métaphysique et de morale* 14 (1906):, 627–50. English trans. under the title 'On "Insolubilia" and their Solution by Symbolic Logic' published in [2.125].

2.123 —— 'The Regressive Method of Discovering the Premisses of Mathematics', read before the Cambridge Mathematical Club, 9 March, 1907. First published in [2.125]

2.124 —— *Introduction to Mathematical Philosophy*, London, George Allen and Unwin, 1919.

2.125 —— *Essays in Analysis*, D. Lackey (ed.) London, Allen and Unwin, 1973.

2.126 Russell, B. and Whitehead, A. N. *Principia Mathematica*, Cambridge, Cambridge University Press, 1910.

2.127 Schelling, F. *System des transcendentalen Idealismus*, Hamburg, Felix Meiner, 1800.

2.128 Schütte, K. *Beweistheorie*, Berlin, Springer-Verlag, 1960.

2.129 Shanker, S. *Wittgenstein and the Turning-Point in the Philosophy of Mathematics*, Albany, NY, State University of New York Press, 1987.

2.130 Shapiro, S. 'Conservativeness and Incompleteness', *Journal of Philosophy* 80 (1983): 521–131.

2.131 —— 'Mathematics and Reality', *Philosophy of Science* 50 (1983b): 523–48.

2.132 Sieg, W. 'Fragments of Arithmetic', *Annals of Pure and Applied Logic* 28 (1985): 33–72.

2.133 Simpson, S. 'Subsystems of Z_2 and Reverse Mathematics', 1987, in [2.139]

2.134 —— 'Partial Realizations of Hilbert's Program', *Journal of Symbolic Logic* 53 (1988): 349–63.

2.135 Tait, W. 'Finitism', *Journal of Philosophy* 78: (1981): 524–46.

2.136 —— 'Truth and Proof: The Platonism of Mathematics', *Synthese* 69 (1986): 341–70.

2.137 —— 'Critical Notice: Charles Parsons' *Mathematics in Philosophy*', *Philosophy of Science* 53 (1986) 588–606.

2.138 Takeuti, G. *Proof Theory*, Amsterdam: North-Holland, 1975.

2.139 —— *Proof Theory*, 2nd. edn, Amsterdam, North-Holland, 1987.

2.140 Tennant, N. 'Is This a Proof I See Before Me?', *Analysis* 41 (1981): 115–19.

2.141 —— 'Were Those Disproofs I Saw Before Me?', *Analysis* 44 (1984): 97–195.

2.142 Tragesser, R. 'Three Insufficiently Attended to Aspects of most Mathematical Proofs: Phenomenological Studies', 1992, in [2.32].

2.143 Troelstra, A. and van Dalen, D. *Constructivism in Mathematics*, 2 vols, Amsterdam, North-Holland, 1988.

2.144 van Heijenoort, J. *From Frege to Gödel: A Sourcebook in Mathematical Logic 1879–1931*, Cambridge, MA, Harvard University Press, 1967.

2.145 Wagner, S. 'Logicism' 1992, in [2.31].

2.146 Webb, J. *Mechanism, Mentalism, and Metamathematics*, Dordrecht, Reidel, 1980.

2.147 Weyl, H. 'David Hilbert and his Mathematical Work', *Bulletin of the American Mathematical Society* 50 (1944): 612–54.

2.148 —— *Philosophy of Mathematics and Natural Science*, Princeton, Princeton University Press, 1949 rev. and augmented English edn, New York, Atheneum Press, 1963.

2.149 Wittgenstein, L. *Philosophical Investigations*, New York, Macmillan, 1953.

2.150 —— *Wittgenstein's Lectures on the Foundations of Mathematics: Cambridge 1939*, C. Diamond (ed.), Chicago, University of Chicago Press, 1976.

2.151 —— *Remarks on the Foundations of Mathematics*, G. H. von Wright et al. (eds), Cambridge, MA, MIT Press, 1978.

2.152 Wright, C. *Wittgenstein on the Foundations of Mathematics*, Cambridge, MA, Harvard University Press, 1980.

CHAPTER 3

Frege

Rainer Born

∾ LIFE IN INTELLECTUAL CONTEXT ∾

Gottlob Friedrich Ludwig Frege was born on 8 November 1848 at Wismar Mecklenburg, Germany and died on 26 July 1925 at Bad Kleinen (south of Wismar). He was initially a mathematician and logician and finally became a very important philosopher in the field of analytical philosophy (depending of course on one's understanding or conception of philosophy).

Today it is usually undisputed that Frege was the real founder of modern (mathematical) logic, i.e. he is considered to be the most important logician since Aristotle. In his philosophy of mathematics (more precisely his philosophy of arithmetic), the so-called 'logizism', in which he attempted to reduce arithmetic to logic alone, depending on one's understanding of logic), Frege was concerned with the foundations of mathematics and provided the first contribution towards a modern philosophical discussion of mathematics.

Furthermore, Frege is considered to be the founder of philosophical logic and analysed language from a philosophical–semantic point of view (philosophy of language). In this respect he can be considered to be the grandfather of a modern, linguistically orientated analytical philosophy.[1]

Frege studied mathematics, physics and philosophy at Jena and Göttingen. Among his teachers was Hermann Lotze, who by some (e.g. Hans Sluga) is considered to have influenced the development of Frege's 'functional' conception of logic.[2] He wrote his doctoral thesis in 1873 at Göttingen about a geometrical representation of the imaginary entities in the plane (*Über eine geometrische Darstellung der imaginären, Gebilde in der Ebene*)[3] and was appointed University Lecturer in mathematics in 1874 at Jena with a second dissertation about 'Methods of calculation founded upon an extension of the concept of magnitude', (*Rechnungsmethoden, die sich auf eine Erweiterung des Größenbegriffes gründen*).[4] He was professor at Jena from 1879 to 1918 and in 1879 he was made extraordinary (and in 1896 ordinary) honorary professor.

During his lifetime Frege received little scientific acknowledgement and he died an embittered man.

Russell, Wittgenstein and Carnap, tried to promote Frege's ideas, but entitled the chapter *Gottlob Frege* in Philip E. B. Jourdain's 'The Development of The Theories of Mathematical logic and the Principles of Mathematics', which drew attention to Frege's work. It was not until the publication of the 'Philosophy of Arithmetic' (*Grundgesetze der Arithmetik*), which Frege himself read and supplemented with commentaries, that his reputation was established. Frege considered it to be his life's work to produce incontestable foundations for elementary number theory and analysis.

Frege's published work can be divided into three important periods:

Early period:	*(1879–1891)*	*Reference number*
Begriffsschrift (*BS*)	(1879)	[3.3]
Grundlagen der Arithmetik (*GLA*)	(1884)	[3.6]
Mature period:	*(1891–1904)*	
Grundgesetze der Arithmetik I (*GGAI*)	(1893)	[3.11]
Grundgesetze der Arithmetik II (*GGAII*)	(1903)	[3.14]
Funktion und Begriff (*FB*)	(1891)	[3.8]
Sinn und Bedeutung (*SB*)	(1892)	[3.9]
Über Begriff und Gegenstand (*BG*)	(1892)	[3.10]
Was ist eine Funktion (*WF*)	(1904)	[3.15]
Late period:	*(1906–1925)*	
Der Gedanke (*LUI*)	(1918)	[3.16]
Die Verneinung (*LUII*)	(1918)	[3.17]
Das Gedankengefüge (*LUIII*)	(1923)	[3.18]

Further important insights can be gained by studying the *Nachlaß* (*NL*) [3.19] and the *Briefwechsel* (*BW*) [3.19]. These abbreviations are used internationally.

☙ FREGE AND MODERN LOGIC ❧

Summing up Frege's contribution to logic retrospectively speaking, i.e. from a modern point of view and with the knowledge of modern developments, one could say that Frege in his *BS* [3.3] for the first time produced a logical system with formalized language, axioms and rules for inference. The later logical system of the *GGAI* [3.11][6] is concerned with what today we call the second-order predicate calculus (quantification over objects and properties). The fragments of sentence and predicate logic of first order contained in the *BS* build – as we know today – a complete formalization of deductive logical theories. Frege's achievement in logics is comparable to Aristotle's with respect to 'syllogistics'. From the point of view of philosophy of science one can interpret the *BS* as a sort of preparation for the logical foundation of arithmetic, as the development of the instruments to achieve this aim.

In this section, I shall give a short survey of Frege's achievements in formal logic from a modern point of view.[7] Then, I shall deal with some philosophical considerations, which are especially important for our investigations. Finally, I shall briefly touch upon predicate logic and the transition from Frege's *BS* to his *GGA*. In doing so, I would like nevertheless to emphasize that one first has to make oneself familiar with a given field of knowledge,[8] so that one has a fund of examples at one's disposal and, while analysing and thinking about it, is able to gain new insights.[9] This is in accordance with posthumus interpretations of Frege's procedures, with what might be called his constructivist approach,[10] and which one should distinguish from Husserl's abstractivistic approach.

Frege's essential contribution to modern logic consists in the introduction of (logical) quantifiers, which helped to solve problems that hitherto had turned up in the logical analysis of general sentences, i.e. sentences containing expressions like 'for all', 'some', 'there exists one' (and perhaps only one), 'there exists at least one', etc.[11] The unsatisfactory attempts to analyse these sentences in a formal logical way had prevented substantial progress in logics since Aristotle.[12]

One can argue that from a logical point of view Frege analysed these sentences in such a way that they could be considered as names for truth-values. This means that he considers just judgeable expressions, i.e. sentences which possess a 'judgeable content', an idea that later, in connection with problems concerning the identity-relation between statements, led to the invention of the term 'sense' (*Sinn*) as distinct from 'reference' (*Bedeutung*).

One can interpret this in the following way: when Frege uses '–' in front of some A (he calls '–' the content stroke) this means (to

Frege, reconstructively speaking) that in analysing A one is abstracting from everything except from the fact that the expression A must be judgeable and that one can positively assert it, i.e. turn it into a statement, whereby the sentence (in the logical sense) thus 'created', i.e. being considered as a sentence,[13] can be true or false. In this case Frege uses what he calls judgment-stroke '|' and writes '⊢A' (asserting *that* A).

The way in which A is related to its content −A is then (explanatorily speaking) simulated by relating it to (letting it refer to) ⊢A, to a truth value. Thus '⊢A' (in modern language) can (very cautiously and for reasons of reconstruction) also be considered as an expression for a truth value variable. The 'truth values' themselves can be interpreted/considered as belonging to the 'realm of the objective' (in Frege's sense).

From an external, theoretico-explanatorical point of view, we are here concerned with simulations, and the truth values are so-called 'constructs'. From an internal, so-to-speak philosophical point of view, we have to consider that the idea of sentences as 'names for truth values' can be useful or not, i.e. as an explanatory concept which can be projected onto our understanding of what it is to be a sentence.

Kutschera, however, insists that Frege's logical operations are not defined for truth values or judgeable contents but for sentences, and sentences are not analysed as names but are names for truth-values ([3.46], 24).

Perhaps one should empasize that in the context of logic the expression 'sentence' has a primarily technical meaning, i.e. grammatical sentences are replaced (thought of) in such a way that their relation to real objects (our intimate experience of where it makes sense to talk of real objects) is simulated by the relation of sentence signs (names) to truth values, i.e. a sentence can be a name for a truth value. So the point is that sentences are analysed *as* functions.

The greatest difficulty in presenting Frege's 'logic' – especially if one analyses the original papers – is that one cannot simply immerse oneself in the background knowledge of Frege's time. We cannot really ignore our so-called modern knowledge, it will always influence our interpretation, as Kutschera illustrates in [3.46].

In the following considerations, I shall therefore resort to an approach that does not rest purely on linguistic means.

Frege in *BS* starts by introducing the distinction between variables and constants, then introduces an expression for judgements and goes on to introduce 'functions' as a new means for analysing linguistic expressions (a means distinct from the classical subject – predicate analysis). He is thus able to circumvent the classical approach to logic, which starts with concepts, goes on to judgements, and ends with inferences.

Frege explicitly starts with judgements and later, after extending the mathematical concept of functions, shows that concepts can be analysed as special functions. In regarding a linguistic expression as a function, he considers the expression as the result of the application of a function, i.e. as the value of a function (in the modern sense).

In *BS* Frege talks only of signs and sign sequences which announce the content of a judgement, i.e., if A is such a sign in our language (a meaningful linguistic expression that refers to some fact in the world), then ' −A'[14] is an expression for the idea to consider the sign A under the aspect that A expresses some content. Frege himself circumscribes this in normal language as 'the sentence that' or 'the fact that'. Later in *GGA* Frege very precisely distinguishes between a sign and what it designates and develops a logic of terms. In *BS* a judgement seems to be a statement that claims to be true or false.

But not every 'content' ' −A' can be turned into a judgement (using the judgement stroke '|' as a means of expression, '⊢A'), i.e. turned into a claim about a fact that obtains/contains (or not) a true or false statement. According to Frege, one has therefore to distinguish between 'contents' that can be turned into judgements and contents for which this is not the case. The following remark by Frege in the *BS* is important:

'The horizontal stroke "−" in the sign "⊢" combines the signs or sign sequences following upon it into a *whole* (my emphasis). And the affirmation which is expressed by the vertical stroke at the left of the horizontal line concerns the sign sequence considered as a whole' [3.3], 2.[15] 'What follows upon the content stroke therefore must always be a "judgable content" ' (Ibid.).[16] Thus, '⊢A' expresses the fact that the content ' −A' is claimed or can be claimed.

In Frege's calculus one more or less stays within the given language. One considers linguistic expressions under a certain aspect of analysis but has to enrich the ontology, i.e. to locally refine the express-ive power of the means of expression, the language. In other words, we are talking within a language about that language.

One can understand this procedure as a sort of simulation, i.e. as the picture that, just as a language is referring to the/some world, the claim '⊢A' refers to some content ' −A' as existing within the world our natural language refers to from the beginning. This means that the special matters in a natural language are simulated by some mapping or assignment '⊢A ↦ −A' within the given language.

It is interesting to see how Frege introduces what today are known as logical operators. Frege uses only two: negation and what today is called material implication, and uses a two-dimensional notation in analogy to arithmetics, as he explains in 'Berechtigung, 54' ([3.4]). The logical operators are defined for sentences or for linguistic expressions.[17] To my mind, however, and for matters of analysis, one should distinguish between a 'sentence' in the logical reconstruction/analysis and a sentence as element of a natural language.

Today, even in working with natural languages we regard the concatenation of sentences to form new sentences (with the help of some copula like and, or etc.) as produced by operators 'and', 'or', 'if, then', which from a logical point of view are considered as two-place operators that combine two given (logical) sentences into a new one, such that, considered as a whole, this new sentence possesses a definite truth value. It is clear that the theoretico-explanatory logical analysis is somehow (mis-)projected as descriptive of (or operative within) the inner process of a natural language. Language does not work in that way, but it can be *analysed* in that way, though not in a global manner and only under restrictive assumptions.

Summing up that part of *BS* which makes up sentential logic one can transcribe Frege's result in the following way:[18]

Axioms:
(A_1) $A \rightarrow (B \rightarrow A)$
(A_2) $(C \rightarrow (B \rightarrow A)) \rightarrow ((C \rightarrow B) \rightarrow (C - A))$
(A_3) $(D \rightarrow (B \rightarrow A)) \rightarrow (B \rightarrow (D \rightarrow A))$
(A_4) $(B \rightarrow A) \rightarrow (\neg A \rightarrow \neg B)$
(A_5) $\neg\neg A \rightarrow A$
(A_6) $A \rightarrow \neg\neg A$
Derivation rule:
R 1: $A \rightarrow B$, $A \vdash B$

Frege was important in developing predicate logic. In *BS* he introduces a general concept of functions where his mathematical experience may have been essential. He had the idea that it is possible to express the utmost generality with respect to the *truth* of statements/propositions by using the analytical and expressive power of functions (as generalization of the mathematical use the latter). Thus, the introduction of functions amounts to introducing a new means and aspect of analysing linguistic expressions, in so far as the latter refer to or are concerned with the world, i.e. refer to a judgeable content. This method of analysis ought to be considered (with some qualms, of course, cf. G. Patzig vs. J. Łukasiewicz with respect to interpreting Aristotelian logic[19]) as a generalization of the subject-predicate analysis as exemplified by Aristotelian syllogistics.

Logic should – with respect to mathematics – be able to solve problems which hitherto could not be solved. Thus, a sentence such as 'there are infinitely many prime numbers' cannot even be analysed in

Boolean logic. Anyway, the merit of Frege's approach was to be able to exhibit Aristotelian logic as a sort of borderline case (e.g. [3.3], 22–4, where syllogistics is reconstructed).

Usually the sentence 'all men are mortal' is analysed (with respect to subject and object) as '$(Bx \rightarrow Ax)$'. The functional analysis is $(\forall x)$ $(Bx \rightarrow Ax)$ meaning that 'for all x, if x is human then x is mortal'. But according to Patzig ([3.50], 47) there is more to it, since in the Aristotelian case the subject of a sentence is not the universal class of individuals but the class of individuals of which B holds, i.e. the class B. A is the predicate. In Aristotle the 'universe of discourse' is restricted to objects of which B holds.

The Transition from the Logic of Concepts and Functional Expressions (BS) to a Logic of Value Ranges (GGA)

In *GGA* ([3.11], [3.14]), Frege's main *oeuvre*, which is explicitly concerned with his so-called logicist programme of 'reducing' arithmetic to logic (given his conception of logic), Frege once more formulates his logic (cf. sections 1–48). The main differences with respect to *BS* concern:

1 The introduction of so-called value ranges for functions (see below).[20]
2 Sentences are consistently considered as names for truth (values), i.e. a logic of terms is developed.
3 Syntax and semantics are defined much more precisely.

Preparatory works for *GGA* ([3.11]) are *Funktion und Begriff* ([3.8]) in which Frege introduces value ranges, *Über Sinn und Bedeutung* ([3.9]), and *Über Begriff und Gegenstand* ([3.10]), which are all generally regarded as already belonging to Frege's linguistic philosophy.

In [3.8] Frege minutely dissects the concept of function (and its generalization) and for the first time introduces value ranges of functions (actually as undefined basic concepts). He also formulates a first version of what later became the notorious Axiom 5 in his *GGA*, opening up the possibility for the derivation of Russell's paradox. In the introduction to the *GGA* Frege discusses exactly that axiom and its possibilities as problematic.

To pick out just a few aspects which are interesting for shedding additional light on Frege's conception of logic in the later stages of his life, consider the following: Amongst other things, Frege shows how one can get from expressions for functions (remember they are values of the application of a rule of ascription/assignment) to the 'actual essence of a function'. Taking expressions like '$2 \cdot 1^3 + 1$', '$2 \cdot 2^3 + 2$', '$2 \cdot 4^3$

+ 4', one can see what those expressions have in common, namely, what in the 'unsaturated' (see below) expression '$2 \cdot x^3 + x$' is present besides the 'x' and what could be written in the following way: '$2 \cdot (\ )^3 + (\ )$'.[21] Into the empty slots one can insert names of numbers, such that again, a name of a number is the result. Thus a function by itself can only be *alluded to* but cannot be (literally) denominated.

The expression '$2\xi^3 + \eta$', and thus any *function* ξ, η (which today would be called dummy variables), is therefore incomplete or, as Frege calls it, 'unsaturated', which means it is in need of supplementation.

And it is this property that principally distinguishes functions from objects, or from what, in a model, can play the role of an object. So, if one wants to be clear about what is meant when we talk about an object, one could say that an object is something that can be put into an empty slot in a function, is able to play the role of an argument in a function, is something to which a name can refer.

Only in applying a function to an object does a function yield something independent in itself, namely the value of the function, which again is something that can play the rôle of an object or, in Frege's diction, is an object, though this 'is' need not be interpreted in a Platonistic, realistic way but can also be understood as being simply explanatory with no ontological commitment.[22]

Nevertheless it makes sense to say that for Frege the distiction between function and object plays the rôle of a basic ontological distinction.

Concepts especially (remember that Frege's starting point are judgements) are considered as special functions, whereas propositions (thoughts) are considered as objects. Thus, the unsaturatedness of functions means that functions are not objects. Any value of a function, however, is an object.

With respect to the plainly mathematical concept of functions it is essential to note that not only numbers are admitted as arguments and values. In Frege's 'technical' language 'truth values' especially are admissible as arguments and values, which means that concepts (technically speaking) can be characterized as specific functions, i.e. as functions whose value is always a truth value [3.8], 15.

Frege therefore insists that we should see how close what in logic is called concept is connected with what he (and we today) call functions. Especially the idea of the extension of a concept, i.e. the characterization of something as 'falling under a concept', can be grasped by the idea of a function (or be realized/actualized in a different way) in a more general way, i.e. as being the value of a function where the concept of 'value range' proves decisive.

We say, for example, that the value of the function $2x^3 + x$ for the argument 1 is 3. As we can see in Figure 3.1 below, we can identify the value range for two functions, which also allows us to talk about equivalence of function (i.e. if they produce the same value ranges).

	argument	0	1	2	3	4	5	6	
$x\,(x-4)$	value (1)	0	-3	-4	-3	0	5	12	value range (1)
$x^2 - 4x - 2$	value (2)	0	-3	-4	-3	0	5	12	value range (2)

Figure 3.1

～ REFLECTIONS ON FREGE'S PHILOSOPHY ～ OF ARITHMETIC

With the previous chapters at the back of our mind, we can now concentrate on the definition of numbers. I shall be very explicit in order to convey what it means to give a logical definition and once more shall shed some light upon Frege's concept of logic in general[23]. It is essential here to get a feeling for the formal tools in use, especially the epistemic resolution level provided by them, which I think is distinct from the epistemic resolution level of ordinary language. As background, I shall use primarily *GLA* and *GGA* and discuss the important distinction between sense and reference, into which Frege's *beurteilbarer Inhalt*[24] decomposed in the *GGA* and which is essential for his philosophy of language. I shall also briefly touch upon the so-called Axiom 5 (from the *Grundgesetze*, the principle of abstraction, cf. *Grundgesetze*, pp. 36, 69, 240 and 253 ff.), which led to Russell's paradox with respect to consequences for Frege's programme.

First, I shall try to develop a technical, theoretico-explanatory understanding of Frege's definition of a number, which is deliberately not to be understood in historical terms but rather as an explanatory reconstruction. The picture thus developed should assist in an understanding of how to understand the philosophical significance of Frege's definition.

Frege's starting point in his context of conveyance, i.e. the presupposition he uses to get off the ground in a discussion, is that the realms of application for the concept of number are usually one-place concepts (i.e. predicates), which means that he already presupposes his analysis/understanding of concepts *as* functions. In short: since one-place concepts can be empty as well, the number zero [o] can be defined as a statement (actually a number statement) concerning an empty concept, i.e. a concept under which no objects fall or belong.

Furthermore, since a concept to which there belongs one and only one object is definitely distinct from that object, one can consider the number one [1] as the *property* of a concept, and thus primarily not as the property of an object. And if one knows what it means to ascribe the number n to a concept, one also knows what it means to ascribe the number $n + 1$ to a concept.

Now all this is not as simple as it sounds. An essential presupposition for an understanding of the approach is to have a 'logical picture' of what it means to talk about the immediate succession in a series/sequence of objects (cf. [3.3] *Einiges aus der allgemeinen Reihenlehre*). This logical analysis can be used to make clear in a most general way what the succession of one number to the next one in the sequence of natural numbers amounts to (cf. [3.6], 67, section 55). One can then very clearly express what it means to talk about the ascription of the number $n + 1$ to a concept F. From a purely logical point of view it means that if there is at least one object a belonging to F, such that one can build the following concept G, defined as 'belongs (also) to F but is distinct from a', then the number n is ascribed to G; in symbols, the cardinality of G is n (card (G) = n).

This construction can be applied to any a, even those not belonging to F.[25] Therefore one can define G more precisely as G[a; F] and then the following holds: for any a from the extension ext(F) = [F] of F it is the case that card (G[a; F]) = n. This means that by using purely logical means, i.e. in the most general way, one has expressed what it means that the number $n + 1$ is ascribed to a concept F. And this logical understanding is independent with respect to its claim of validity of any *Anschauung* in the Kantian sense and therefore, as Frege claims, not synthetic a priori but, as he still claims in *Logik in der Mathematik*, analytically a priori.

Let us now informally come back to the case of the number zero: one can choose an inconsistent concept Λ (e.g. αx $(x \neq x)$, the concept of all x distinct from themselves) and recognize that it does not make sense to consider any object as belonging to that concept – which means that we cannot conceive of the existence of such an object. Now we may consider the 'class of all concepts F which have the same extension as Λ' (I shall write [Λ]). We assume that there exists a one-to-one mapping between the elements of the extensions [Λ] and [F] of the concepts Λ and F, respectively. This mapping defines an equivalence relation between concepts and the class [Λ] is an equivalence class of second order and as such an expression of the extension of the concept 'equinumerous to L'. It is only by a detour via this class [L] in its entirety that one ascribes the numeral 0 as a number to the concept Λ. In n: card: $\Lambda \mapsto [\Lambda]$ such that card (Λ) = 0.

This kind of reconstruction factually corresponds very closely to Frege's ideas, since his concern is to define the number which should belong to a concept as the extension of the concept 'equi-numerous to the concept F' (cf. [3.6], 79/80).

It definitely does not mean, however, that one needs to count the elements of [Λ] or needs to know [Λ] in its entirety or to understand, in a plainly logical manner, what is intended by a number. The logical 'intuition' behind all this seems simply to be that one can say someone has grasped what is meant by some number card. (F) ascribed to a concrete concept F, if they have grasped the latter for all concepts with the same extension as F, which means that that kind of grasping is independent of the choice of a special representative as element of [Λ].

Now all this talk of 'grasping a concept' (e.g. the concept of a number) is not intended as empirical psychological talk. It rather aims at showing that it is not necessary to be concerned with philosophical introspection (or, for that matter, a private language) in order to grasp what in general is meant by a number. What is claimed is that this kind of grasping is independent of the special choice of an empirical visualization/intuition (in Kant's sense of *Vorstellung*), or of an empirical ability to understand mathematics.

Let us return to zero and consider the transition from 0 to 1. If one wants to understand Frege's approach, one has to try to recognize something as succeeding immediately upon zero; something which will be able to play the rôle of 1. Frege uses a one-place concept (a predicate) '$\Psi(x)$' defined as $\Psi :=$ 'equal to 0'. But since 'equal to 0(0)' holds true of 0, we can see that 0 belongs to Ψ.[26]

Consider the concept 'equal to 0'. This does only mean that some object 1 immediately succeeds upon 0. One can then determine that 1 is the number which belongs to the concept 'equal to 0'.

Counting thus is reduced *qua* logical understanding of what is going on to a simple procedure of ascription f, contrary to an introspective understanding of how one personally perceives oneself in the process of counting – how one actualizes counting – or how one tries to teach children to count properly.

Presupposing Frege's functional interpretation or rather reconstruction of the idea of a concept, a number is attached to a concept in the sense that the objects which need to be counted fall under (belong to) that concept. (The objects are put together under a concept. The number attached to the concept is itself an object in two ways: first, as a sign to which we are accustomed, i.e. as something we have learnt to manipulate; second, as an abstract object such that any kind of realization/actualization will help us to use the abstract concept (of number) correctly.)

What seems important is the logical step of abstraction that is explicated by Frege's analysis. Already in his habilitation/second dissertation ([3.2], 1) he is concerned with a similar problem concerning measurements of length. Length should no more be considered as some kind of 'matter' filling up a line between its starting point and its end point. This means that what is important (in modern terms) is solely the beginning and end point and the attachment of a value, as was later clearly elaborated by Hausdorff, Frêchet and others[27], when they were defining distance 'functions' d(a,b), if a and b designate points.

One clearly sees how Frege is against 'introspection' as an intuitive (visualizable, *anschaulich* in Kant's way of talking) source of logical knowledge and how he, despite remaining extensional in his logical outlook, is able to grasp what goes on in mathematical thought, considered as an abstractum.

Frege therefore insists, for example, that the number 1 assigned to the concept 'moon of the earth' does not express any content about the moon, but only means that there is just one object falling under the concept, no statement about the moon as such.

The role of abstraction in the process of counting becomes clear in the following way: corresponding to a concept (but not identical with it, it should be considered rather as a replacement or expression of a concept) there is the extension of a concept, a sort of class of well-defined objects (at least considered in that way) belonging to that object. Counting amounts to identifying a concept F such that the objects to be counted fall under this concept (considered as a function!) and then to ascribe a number to that concept; a function $f(x)$ is actualized as card (F).

The intuition explicated by Frege consists of the idea that what counting *amounts to* is the fact that one subsumes the objects to be counted under a concept (remember this talk is to be understood interpretatively or explanatorily and is not literally descriptive) and then one can say that to the so identified concept there belongs that number which we in our practice regard as the result of a process of counting, or have learnt to generate as such.

Now if one thinks that this is really essential for a theoretical understanding of the idea of number, then it is good for a start to be clear about what it means that no number belongs to a concept or further, that there is exactly one object falling under a concept. This is exactly what we said before, namely that one formulates a logical analysis about what it means, e.g., that no object belongs to F – but need the extension of the concept be given literally?

According to Frege, numbers are (simply) objects and not concepts, i.e. they should be regarded as arguments in a function and one should be able (logically speaking) to quantify over them.

In order to be able to define numbers as objects in a logical sense, Frege invents what today is called definition by abstraction. In [3.6], 74 ff. he illustrates his idea by the transition from the concept of two parallel lines to the concept of the direction of lines in the Euclidian plane.

In principle, such a definition by abstraction (generation of equivalence classes) works in the following way:[28] one starts with a basic domain B of some kind of entities one is intimate with and of which one has practical experiences. It should be possible that one is able to experience there the fact of a real partition of that domain, i.e. of subclasses/aggregates of objects consisting of elements of the original domain, which under a certain aspect of consideration, i.e. *modulo* this aspect (which means by disregarding other distinguishing features), are considered as equal, i.e. identical with respect to some value of a function, or indistinguishable for a certain aim, demand, application or whatever one wants to do with these entities.

Consider again the set of parallel lines (replaced by 'lines of the same direction' in *GLA*) in the Euclidean plane (here the basic area B) or perhaps a set of small wooden blocks for children, which can be distinct in size, thickness, colour, roundness, etc., such that only length is the essential aspect to choose in order to regard them as equal or not (cf. Frege's Habilitation).[29] If one wants to generate an object with the length of, say, 7 units and considers two groups of objects of length 3 and 4, respectively as characteristic length, then it is inessential which special representatives of the corresponding groups one chooses and places together such that the length of the concatenation will be 7 units.

The point in question, which leads to definition by abstraction with the help of equivalence classes, is exactly the explication of just that procedure, i.e. the steps of abstraction involved, a procedure that does not rest upon introspection or upon an intuition built upon inner perception.

Abstractly speaking, this means that one assumes the existence of an equivalence relation 'R' between the elements of B (in our case, identity or indistinguishability with repect to some evaluation) in that domain.[30]

One can define such equivalence classes $[x]$ as the sets of all those elements y which are in relation R to some chosen x, i.e. by setting $[x] := \{ y / x \mathrel{R} y \}$. [or written as $\{ y / x \sim y \}$].

In this way one can attach to each element x from B a (new abstract) object $[x]$ (from M). One can understand this especially as a mathematical function

$$f : B \rightarrow M; x \mapsto f(x) = [x].$$

This means that the elements x and y are in the relation R $[x \mathrel{R} y]$ if and only if they are assigned the same 'value' $f(x) = f(y)$, i.e. $x \mathrel{R} y : \Leftrightarrow f(x) = f(y)$, i.e. if and only if $[x] = [y]$. The relation R thus induces a partition of objects in B.

The result is that one can choose a more or less abstractly distinguished or even constructed set of objects as a replacement of some concretely chosen realm B and use the replacement to talk (simulatively) about the situation, relations and concerns in the original realm B. This is, more or less, the theoretico-explanatory understanding underlying Frege's whole approach as it is used today in many areas of mathematics (definition by abstraction).

As a point of departure for his construction, Frege chooses the concept 'equinumerosity' of concepts, i.e. as an equivalence-relation upon some realm containing concepts referring to some realm of effective experience. Equinumerosity is constructed as a one-to-one mapping between the objects falling under some concepts F and G, respectively. For tactical reasons I use [F] as an abbreviation for the equivalence-class of all the concepts with the same extension as F, such that $[F] := \{ G / F_R G \}$. This class [F] is then mapped onto card (F). If one introduces the mapping 'card', i.e.

$$[F] \mapsto card (F) : = \{G / F \text{ equivalent to } G \} = [F],$$

One can say that

F is equinumerous to G if and only if card (F) = card (G)

In the *NL* paper *Erkenntnisquellen der Mathematik und der mathematischen Naturwissenschaften*, Frege retrospectively writes:

> The disposition to produce *proper names not corresponding to any object* is a property of language that proves disastrous for the reliability of our thinking. If it happens in the context of art or literature where anybody knows that they are dealing with literature it does not lead to disadvantages ... An especially remarkable example however is the creation/formation of a proper name following the pattern of '*the extension* (Umfang) *of the concept F*', e.g. in the case 'the extension of the concept fixed star'. This expression seems to designate an object because of the use of the definite article 'the'. But *there is no such object which in a linguistically correct manner could be designated as such* (i.e. as literally corresponding to the expression). From thence the paradoxa of set theory developed, which killed this set theory. I myself have been deceived in that way as well, i.e. when I tried to produce a logical foundation for the numbers, *in so far as I wanted to conceive of numbers as sets*[31]
>
> ([3.19], Vol. 1, 288, my emphasis)

It surely was the use of classes/value ranges within logic (i.e. quantification over value ranges) that actually paved the way for the possibility of the derivation of Russell's paradox by using the abstraction principle (cf. [3.11], [3.14] and addendum: 253).

Perhaps one should pay attention to some minor points in GLA and not only to the fact that Frege in GLA still uses his old conception of 'judgeable content' (to which correspond BS expressions, i.e. concept–script expressions as logical analysis of ordinary language expressions), which later, due to the introduction of sense and reference, decomposed into 'thought and truth value'.[32]

First, however, one might explain the intuition in order to grasp the concept of number in the context of a general strategy and try to make available the meaning of abstract knowledge by means of using our logical/analytical abilities. This makes the claim of 'general validity' (*Allgemeingültigkeit* or general truth) of knowledge (cf. Kant) a matter of controlled reproduction and therefore to be generally obligatory even in thinking of ethics.

The intuition is that one thinks that one has understood or grasped what, e.g., the number 'three' amounts to if one has grasped the equivalence class of sets of three elements each. This means that speaking of 'three' can be represented by a set of three elements.

In the GLA definition this is chosen in such a way that the 'number of F' [card (F)] is defined by means of the extension (used as an undefined basic concept) of the concept 'equinumerous to F(X)'.[33] But 'equinumerous to F(X)' can be given by an equivalence-class of concepts: – what does it amount to to talk about someone having grasped the concept of number or at least of having grasped what it means to detect that a certain quantity of objects belongs to or falls under a concrete concept F*? – independently of the special choice of a concrete concept (a special representative from the repertoire [F]), one can always decide whether F* belongs to the extension of 'equinumerous to F', which means that there is a G from [F] such that G is equinumerous to F*, i.e. one should be able to ascribe the correct number to F*.

Actually, one explains the behaviour of a person in the process of counting by saying that this person needs to have grasped the equivalence class [F] (in one go, so to speak) and by providing a necessary condition (as the 'condition for the possibility of knowledge' in the Kantian sense) which (theoretico-explanatorily speaking) needs to be actualized in order to be able to count.

Now all this may sound extremely complicated and hardly any one will claim that they have learned to count in just that way. One of the problems in philosophy of science is that we look for (universal) explanations which at the same time can be understood as descriptive, i.e. as (even introspectively) action-guiding, even if they are not. So the problem of 'grasping' in our case the meaning (here sense) of numbers by grasping the equivalence class [F] in one go may lead to a lot of basic empirical misunderstandings in ordinary-language reception. Of course, in philosophy one has the impression that one seeks a theoretical understanding (e.g. of numbers) that just allows for a descriptive projection into ordinary language, without doing much harm as long as we stick to ordinary realms of experience. But sometimes we need to be able to see those misapplications and be able to correct them – provided we do not presuppose some universal, god-given, pre-established harmony between language and the world. Frege paved the way for stepping out of (a universal) language. A diversity of local language games, which are not to be considered as language-relativism, may be a good thing to which to remain alert, i.e. sensitive to reflective correction and prepared to overcome the problems just hinted at, without, however, falling into the traps of scepticism.

So again, all this may sound extremely complicated and again hardly anyone will claim that they have learned to count in that way, but that is not the point. Actually one only expresses what (theoretico-explanatorily, i.e. from a logical point of view) it means to say of someone that they can count. The real problem is whether this theoretical explanation is close enough to our everyday understanding to be helpful.[34]

So the point is that our theoretico-explanatory talk must not be projected in an action-guiding way upon reality/experience, i.e. it must not be considered as a description of our effective actions or thinking. Otherwise one would really have to be able to grasp the whole class [F] in one go and for all times. In principle there are many actions which may be compatible with one theoretical explanation.

In this context a short discussion of Frege's distinction between sense and reference may be of interest.[35] In the sequel I shall use the special expressions F-sense (F-*Sinn* = Frege-*Sinn*) and F-reference (F-*Bedeutung* = Frege-*Bedeutung*) for Frege's special use of them.

Frege uses a discussion of claims of equality (as different to the position in the *BS*) to introduce the distinction – between sense and reference as two technical/theoretical components for the determination of meaning (as the general expression for an undifferentiated understanding) of linguistic expressions.

I shall here try to link up with the former discussion, especially the relevance to build equivalence classes. A very good discussion of the technical reasons for introducing the distinction between sense and reference in the transition from the logic of the *BS* to the logic of the *GGA* can be found in [3.46]. A discussion that links the logical and the philosophical aspects from a philosophical point of view can be found in Stekeler-Weithofen ([3.56], 272), whose approach I would like to adapt and modify.

The F-reference of a name is the named object.[36] Truth values as F-references are therefore attributed to the 'sentences' in logical concept-script–notation (expressions of a logical analysis, eternal sentences). The F-sense of a name or a sentence consists in the way (of being given) in which the F-reference of a sentence is determined. i.e. the reference of a name towards an object is mediated by the F-sense. Thus: a sign *expresses* its F-SENSE and *designates/gives/provides* its F-REF-ERENCE.

One can understand this in the following way: in the realm of the names (anything that can act/work as a name in some distinguished realm) the F-sense stipulates an *equivalence-class* of names with the same 'F-reference'.[37] The sign 'morning star' expresses its F-sense (F-*Sinn*) (i.e. the way of givenness of the object Venus, e.g., as morning star) and assigns (literally gives to us, provides us with) its F-reference (F-*Bedeutung*) (i.e. designates the object 'Venus'). The expression 'the number of children in this room' thus designates, e.g., the *number 3* and it *gives* '3' as an application of the *concept* 'children in this room (x)'. Expressions with the same F-reference thus should allow for a replacement *salva veritate*.[38]

In grasping the sense-component of the meaning of a linguistic expression, as it should show itself (explanatorily speaking) in the grasping of the corresponding equivalence class, first of all the so-called 'context' (of knowledge) is brought in. Thus, with the help of the mediating rôle of sense in determining the reference, it becomes clear how it is possible (i.e. in which way it is meaningful or in which way one can talk about it meaningfully) to refer to an object unambigously (in so far as it is an actual object), even without knowing the object as such.[39]

Anyhow, one can explain what it means to say that there is attributed one and only one truth value to a sentence without knowing which value that may be. Of course that does not mean that this is possible in all contexts (cf. intuitionistic or constructive mathematics today).

Frege's logical investigations are quite often of a theoretico-explanatory kind, as I have tried to emphasize several times. But many of his papers (like 'Sense and Reference' [3.9]) seem to deal with the context of the so-called ordinary language, though he just uses it to introduce technical terms with the help of nice-sounding commonsens-ical names. In understanding the philosophical consequences (depending on the aim of the philosophical investigations) one should also do justice to the technical meaning and not purely the commonsensical reception of expressions like 'sense' and 'reference'. Still, the philo-sophical interests in the latter have proved fruitful, even though sometimes they are put out of context and seem to have gained a life of their own.

Understanding the theoretico-explanatory moment of Frege's idea of sense can help us to focus not just on questions concerning the meaning of linguistic expressions in the 'ordinary language context', but also to take into account some constructive elements of, say, ascending definitions of concepts ([3.19], vol. 1, 217–72). This can help to counter the tendency to universalize common sense and to correct dogmatisms of any given time. It can help to produce flexibility and adaptability to new situations and positively influence and balance the interplay between science and common sense – ordinary life. Frege himself explicitly emphasized that talk about numbers is talk concerned with content. The constructions used to grasp the sense of mathematical expressions or claims are not literal descriptions of what one thinks if one uses certain words. Meanings usually are not given literally. The constructions used are 'objects of comparison' which surely need to be supplemented by some 'approximation from within' the actual use of language. But only the interplay between both sides can lead to a rewarding 'reflexive dealing' with some realm of objects.

❧ REMARKS CONCERNING THE CONTEXT ❧ OF FREGE'S PHILOSOPHY OF LANGUAGE

One starting point for an approach to Frege's philosophy of language can be the question, 'how one could talk or communicate about abstract entities/objects in such a way that one can understand what abstract objects are' and also in such a way that one can *handle* those objects (so to speak) reasonably.[40] This presupposes an evaluation by both common sense and scientific understanding and furthermore a connection between both, since via his prose, even a scientist uses common sense when making sense of his findings. If one poses the question in such a way, one clearly has a picture, a sort of understanding, in mind of how language actually works.

It is to Michael Dummett's credit that he has focused especially on the linguistic interests of Frege's *oeuvre*, i.e. the philosophical origins and consequences of Frege's philosophy of language, and thus to have led to philosophy of language, although his presentation or emphasis is controversial and not everyone wants to follow in his footsteps.

Dummett emphasizes the rôle of the so-called 'context principle', which, roughly, says that only in the context of a sentence does a word have a proper meaning, and thus contradicts any understanding of

Frege that elaborates his conception of language as naive and as simply a picture of the world.

The context principle plays an important part in Frege's *GLA*: 'to fix the ... conditions of sentences in which numerical terms occur'.[41] In the *GLA* it is finally quoted in [3.6], section 106, 'to remind the reader of an indispensable step in the preceding argument' ([3.37], 200). The consequences of the context principle for the philosophy of language, i.e. the consequences it has for our modern understanding of language and thus for our 'understanding of meaning', leads towards a 'truth-functional semantics', i.e. one needs to know the truth conditions of sentences containing 'expressions of interest', i.e. expressions, whose meaning we want to grasp.[42]

The context principle can be used and applied in this sense as a theoretical starting point to produce a modern, linguistically orientated reconstruction of Frege's philosophy.

There is another sense in which the significance of Frege's 'semantic theory' can be viewed. Truth-functional semantics can be used only as the result of a technical necessity to understand the meanings of the parts of sentences from *outside* (by way of meaning partitions of sentences) because in the course of logical analysis and reconstruction of the sentence one has attributed exactly one truth value to the sentence as a whole. This does not mean that the extension of the context principle is wrong or unimportant; the aim is rather to focus, in a stronger sense, on Frege's anti-psychologism and the possibilities for a non-introspectivistic philosophy, a philosophy not resting upon psychological abstraction, in contradistinction to Husserl who might be interpreted in this way.

The problem especially concerns the discussion about the determination of the domain of reference of some language – talking, for example, about abstract objects. Dummett writes: 'there *is* a further question to be settled, especially when a term-forming operator, and therewith a whole range of new terms (or items/entities), are being introduced: the question of suitably determining the domain of quantification,' [3.37]. This, however, argues Dummett, was 'persistently neglected [by Frege], a neglect which, as we shall see, proved in the end to be fatal' (Ibid.).

Stekeler-Weithofer puts this straight in arguing that Frege was shifting to and fro between two incompatible points of view:

> (1) that the universe of all objects of speech be pregiven such that (e.g.) the meaning of equality has (already) a fixed/precise/ ready meaning and (2) that the meaning of a name be given purely by its use within sentences.

([3.56], 272)

The problem concerns the constructive character of Frege's means of expression – his language, i.e. its characteristic of being constitutive for objects both in the case of the abstraction principle and in the case of the talk of equality.[43]

If not for reasons of defence, at least to put matters straight, one should point out the fact that Frege again and again is wavering between a mathematical use of language, between mathematical practice and its projection onto commonsensical matters. This holds especially for originally logico-technical concepts like sense and reference, which only later (in the context of introducing the terms and giving examples from ordinary language to show their applicability and importance) gain an enormous significance for philosophy of language.[44]

Later in his life Frege was well aware of this fact of language division. In his posthumus paper concerning 'logics in mathematics' (cf. [3.19], 1: 219), Frege explicitly talks about a distinction between technical terms and commonsensical expressions. In this context, one could talk of a sort of 'split semantics' ([3.28] and [3.29]), which Dummett somehow seems to admit when he writes: 'The language of the mathematical sciences differs markedly from that of everyday discourse: it could be said that the semantics of abstract terms bifurcates, according as we are concerned with one or the other' [3.37].

Phrased more generally, our problem is the *constitution of objects* by means of using a language – considering Frege's experience and background as a mathematician, one can interpret his findings in the following way. Frege provides us with a theoretico-explanatory analysis of how language works, an analysis which then is compatible with several concrete and effective procedures to determine, e.g., a 'domain of quantification' (a favourite problem in modern linguistically orientated philosophy – 'To be is to be the value of a bound variable' [3.52]).

Expressed, however, in Kantian terms, i.e. in the way that is relevant to Frege considering his philosophical background and upbringing, one could say that Frege tried to formulate the 'conditions for the possibility of' determining the realm of reference (the [logical] domain of quantification), or in a more modern way: giving formally determined *necessary conditions* for just that. In interpreting and trying to understand Frege, one has to take into account the language of his time and his background of experience, and therefore need not take everything too literally when viewed from a modern understanding of language.

Considering the determination of the reference of 'numbers', it is, from a mathematical point of view, essential first to state/identify the formal properties that must be fulfilled by something that should be able to work as a number (presupposing that they link up to our ordinary intuitions or those of the mathematicians, just in case one wants to reconstruct those intuitions).[45] Afterwards, say after the definition of 'zero', some entities – quite often not a single object – will be presented in a way that the possibility is formulated as to how to identify and use something as 'zero'. One more or less keeps an open mind about what might be expected as a definite determination of a realm of reference.

Dummett is concerned with this in so far as he writes:

> On the *Grundlagen* view, we can ask whether the truth-conditions of sentences containing a term of the kind in question have been fixed, and (we can ask) for a statement of those truth-conditions; *we cannot ask after the mechanisms by which the truth-values of those sentences are determined, nor, therefore, after the rôle of the given term in that mechanism.*
>
> ([3.37], 207, my emphasis)

The aim of a logical definition (e.g. of numbers), however, should be that it should hold in any possible world (as it is usually attributed to Leibniz and taken up by Frege), which means it should be *independent* of the *special choice* of the *mechanisms* for the determination of the truth value of a sentence containing a word for designating, so to speak, a number.

This also means, however, that it is enough to know one single counter-example, one single concept, such that there does not exist a mechanism to determine whether an object falls under the concept, to quash the claim for utmost generality, i.e. for universal logical validity.

Now if one presupposes that in demanding (Frege's proposal) to start logic with 'judgements'[46] means that a sentence (as a whole) gets attributed a truth value and that one determines 'meaning' starting from the outside, with the surface, so to speak, and not by abstracting from introspective experiences, i.e. by decomposing a sentence into meaningful components (only in the context of a sentence do words have a meaning/reference), then one can understand this matter in the following way. One expresses only what it means (theoretico-explanatorily speaking) to talk about a word having reference, what it means to ascribe some reference to a word, but still has to determine or define the truth conditions for the sentence containing the word in question. So one (might) know that it should have some reference but has not yet specified it. One knows what it means/amounts to look for some reference, but one still has to determine compatible mechanisms, which may be context-dependent and which attribute the truth values by way of judgement.

This can either (wrongly!) lead to projecting the theoretico-explanatory structures onto the world, i.e. turning them into effective procedures, as it is sometimes the case in classical philosophy – although there 'theories' tend to be rather introspective–abstractive. Alternatively, one can deal with unreflected (?) skills, which are then considered to make up for the effective use of some language.

According to Frege, the distinction between sense and reference can be extremely important, especially in the context of philosophy of language, in so far as on the one hand it can help to systematize the referring habits of human beings in a theoretico-explanatory way. On the other hand, this distinction can, if it does not just project a theoretical understanding, help to take care of the actual mechanisms to fix the reference of the expressions of something used as a language. These actual mechanisms stand in contradistinction to those one seems to *use* consciously (or one appeals to), and which enable one to keep in mind those many facets of understanding and communicating 'meaning' (in a modern sense) that seem to be relevant today.

❧ REFLECTIONS ON THE CONSEQUENCES ❧ OF FREGE'S WORK

Apart from perhaps the second section in this chapter, I have placed the emphasis on the philosophy of logic because I think that the other important aspects of Frege's work, such as the philosophy of mathematics or the philosophy of language, become more or less self-explanatory if one has a clear picture of Frege's conception of logic. This, however, is not true of the history of Frege's influence, especially if one tries to distinguish between a logical or objective core of Frege's philosophy and its reception.

Though many of Frege's ideas, for example, his notation of logic, were taken up and transformed outside Germany (by, for example, Jourdain and Russell) he might have suffered a fate similar to Wittgenstein with regard to Austria. Perhaps the best-known influences and effects of his work can be found in 'analytical philosophy', of which he has been considered the 'grandfather' by Dummett (with Wittgenstein as the link between).

I shall now leave the well-trodden paths of traditional analytical philosophy and consider Frege from a meta-philosophical point of view. In doing so, I shall closely analyse Frege's anti-psychologism.

Let us presuppose that one can interpret/reconstruct Frege so that we can say that it was his aim to gain access to an *understanding of the meaning* of mathematical or of abstract knowledge in general. Furthermore, this access should not be considered to *rest upon* synthetical (empirical) sources of knowledge and especially not upon some introspective perception.

In order to do this, one tries to make use of an analytical source of knowledge, which, in the Kantian sense, should also produce the justification of something as knowledge. Thus, one could interpret Frege's approach as a new method, or rather, way of reflective thinking, leading to a new kind of actualization/realization of an essential act of philosophy, namely the provision of a possibility for a *correction of knowledge by reflection* with the help on an analysis of meaning. In other words, Frege's approach would lead to a literal understanding of how knowledge comes/is brought about.[47]

With respect to a reconstructive interpretation, i.e. trying to make sense (of Frege's approach) within a modern perspective (on philosophy) and with hindsight (of the experiences of this century), we simply cannot abandon, these considerations and presuppose an understanding or perhaps conception of philosophy that is at least twofold (see below) and definitely goes beyond the idea that even modern philosophy is nothing but footnotes to Plato:

1   In our thinking about and in viewing the world, we have to do justice to philosophical attitudes in attributing an important quality to them, namely that philosophical thinking should help us reflectively to correct mistakes and guide our view towards possible solutions if we are stuck; i.e. if we do not know how to go on (in Wittgenstein's sense).

2   This means that one presupposes that occasionally we can be deceived (or experience being deceived), that we can have the insight into mistakes and the experience of errors and again, at least occasionally, we can reduce these experiences to the fact that in some cases in our behaviour we are misguided by some false picture or wrong sort of information about the world.

But it is exactly the second point which already presupposes some sort of explanation (eventually leading to a locally applicable theory) why and how some behaviour in others and ourselves, experienced as a mistake, came about. It aims at a reflective correction (of both the theory and the behaviour) in trying to correct the cause (the picture in use).

Loosely speaking, in developing such a (reflective) theory, we will eventually turn it into 'effective use', i.e. the theory will be projected upon the level of individual acting and finally will be activated in an action-guiding manner.

At the level of daily life there may turn up philosophically motivated but individually coloured questions. These questions about the pictures that (might) have seduced us (in our actions) will have a rather constitutive character and, if we want to talk about them consciously, it will be unreflected skills (classified as such from 'outside') which guide our behaviour; skills that may be replaced by other, more successful or effective ones according to the tasks we have to settle. If those skills are reflected they will become effective, i.e. can be 're-' followed/ re-instantiated consciously.

On the other hand, one can characterize the (research?) pro- gramme of classifical/traditional philosophy quite crudely as 'philo- sophical reflection' – whether at a theoretical level or in the context of daily life. In any case it takes 'inner perception' as a point of departure. This is the situation when one asks to *understand* the content of some 'message', of something intended for communication. Then it seems to be essential to understand what it is that is 'meant'. If one asks 'what is actually the case?' (if one is insecure) one is more or less said to be trying to grasp the truth by getting behind the screen of the appear- ances, trying to tear (away) the veil hiding reality from our view (to use the old metaphor).

But the aim of this enterprise (whether conscious or not) was to provide knowledge for *correcting* mistakes, so that explanatorily one might speak of corrective reflection.

Especially with respect to logic and the coming about of math- ematical knowledge, Frege seems to reject a plainly introspective– abstractive access to an understanding of the content of the meaning of arithmetic or, more generally, abstract knowledge (given the interpre- tation proposed in this article). For an understanding of the so-called content of arithmetical knowledge, Frege presupposes an 'analytical source of knowledge', which in the case of arithmetic should accomplish what in the the case of the 'psychologistic logicians' was achieved by the use of 'inner perception'.

Frege's method can now be regarded as having consisted in provid- ing the general core (meaning), resting on objective thought, of 'abstract/mathematical entities' by using a 'logical' (i.e. a concept script) analysis (presentation). Frege tried to achieve it by cutting up 'truth' (*from outside so to speak*) and building up meaning (understanding the content of an expression) externally, by realizations in a model, as one might say today. This procedure of building up meaning should help to make *accessible* (in a controlled and reproducible way) the meaning of abstract concepts (of mathematics), which leads to the problem sometimes called 'paradox of analysis'.[48]

Given this understanding,[49] the problem is now how fruitfully to apply Frege's methodology to the 'reflective' concern of modern 'philosophical thinking' as described above, thus getting from the so- called 'What is (really the case)?' question and the question, 'What can I know?' to the more promising questions, 'What can I understand?' and 'How (depending on the language in use) is understanding brought about?'

This last question is important for the 'coming about' of an 'understanding of scientific knowledge', in which abstract knowledge plays an essential part, especially so with respect to 'reflective corrections' in the context of the application of science and technology.[50]

Frege's approach can now be understood (with respect to interpreting the consequences of his work and taking care of some misunderstandings and the historical context of his achievements) as pointing towards a new way of dealing with reflection; a new way of *actualizing* reflection.

Occasionally one has equated this approach with a purely 'logical analysis' of language, an interpretation which some of Frege's remarks at the end of the introduction to *BS* somehow seem to support.[51] The question should rather be 'How can the task of "reflective correction" be met by or, methodologically speaking, be instantiated by linguistic analysis?'

I think one can credit Wittgenstein with having executed the turn to linguistic analysis as a philosophical programme, though the method needs some elaboration or maybe improvement (given the road to linguistically orientated analytical philosophy).

A very good analysis concerning the connections between Wittgenstein's *Tractatus-logico-philosophicus* and Frege (primarily with respect to logic!) can be found in Stekeler Weithofer ([3.56], 248).

The *replacement* of the reflective–abstract method assumed to be characteristic of the primarily classical/traditional approach in philosophy as, for example, demonstrated in Husserl, by the method of *linguistic analysis* (as demonstrated by the 'Wittgenstein of the Philosophical Investigations') leads to a *replacement* of Frege's 'concept script' analysis of 'expressions', produced by using and thus provided by the 'objective' language of *BS*, by a meaning analysis within ordinary language.[52]

This kind of replacement of the original Fregean approach can now, as a system of rules for its use, be followed up on its own as a new programme for doing philosophy. Today, though, one sometimes has the impression that the programme serves just 'as an end in itself'. Not only the general context and aims of philosophy but also the connection to Frege's original aims, and thus to the idea of Wittgenstein's theory of names as a reaction to Frege (cf. [3.58]), have been lost from sight.

The possibilities of newly actualizing the reflective task(s) of philosophy with the help of an analytical approach, especially in the sense of Wittgenstein's later philosophy, are not yet exhausted. Though we have to keep in mind that in comparison with the traditional (introspectively abstractive) approaches these possibilities are just one-side-of-the-coin 'philosophy' and must not be treated dogmatically, i.e. be taken as an absolute method for pursuing philosophy (just as on the other hand, performing philosophy in the traditional way sometimes gives that impression).

I think that today, perhaps more than ever before, it is essential to take into account the interplay of both sides, analytical and traditional philosophy, science and everyday-life, analysis and tradition, because otherwise we – considered as flies in Wittgenstein's famous picture – will definitely not be able to find our way out of the fly-bottle and will perhaps end up on a Möbius strip[53], the prototype of a 'single or just one-sided surface'.

❧ NOTES ❧

1 Cf. [3.36], (11–12) and [3.37], 111.
2 Cf. [3.53] and [3.54] for the use of 'functional', cf. [3.47], 47.
3 Repr. in [3.24], 1–49.
4 Repr. in [3.24], 50–83.
5 Repr. in [3.19], 2: 275–301.
6 The *GGA* contains decisive developments with respect to Frege's logical ideas, i.e. the introduction of value ranges and the distinction between sense and reference (first introduced in *SB* [3.9]).
7 In doing so, I follow the rather technical presentation of Frege's achievements in [3.46] fairly closely.
8 I use the term 'epistemic resolution-level' for this phenomenon and it may be interesting that Frege was befriended by Ernst Abbé who developed the formula for the resolution level of microscopes (working with Zeiss) and that Frege did use the metaphor of the microscope in the introduction of the *BS* [3.3], xi and later in *SB* [3.9].
9 Cf. the problem of the *Paradoxon der Analyse* as discussed in [3.49], and in [3.35] and [3.37], 141. This paradox concerns a fundamental difference about the basics of traditional and analytical philosophy, which can be illustrated aptly with a comparison between Husserl's and Frege's.
10 I refer to his 1914 paper 'Logik in der Mathematick' in [3.19], I: 219–72, esp. p. 277.
11 Cf. Frege's dealing with Boole in *Boole's rechnende Logik und die Begriffsschrift* (1880/81) in [3.19], I: 9–52 and *Boole's logische Formelsprache und meine Begriffsschrift* (1882) in [3.19], I: 53–9.
12 As an example take the sentence 'There are infinitely many prime numbers, i.e. to each prime number there exists a greater one.' This sentence could not be analysed in classical logic nor in Boolean logic either.
13 To consider a sentence as a sentence means to regard it under a special aspect, i.e. not to consider the content of the sentence as such but solely whether it is true or false (as a sort of attributable property of a sentence, i.e. if an expression is classified as a sentence).
14 I mention that particular sign combination here but the use of quotation marks as a metalinguistic way of talking 'about' was not known to Frege, although

there are hints in a later paper, *Logische Allgemeinheit* (not before 1923) [3.19], I: 278–83; esp. p. 280, where he uses the expressions *Darlegungs-und Ililfssprache*.

15 'Der waagrechte Strich, aus dem das Zeichen "⊢" gebildet ist, verbindet die darauf folgenden Zeichen zu einem *Ganzen* und auf dies Ganze bezieht sich die Bejahung, welche durch den senkrechten Strich am linken Ende des waagrechten ausgedrückt wird' ([3.3], 2; my emphasis).

16 'Was auf den Inhaltsstrich folgt, muß immer einen beurteilbaren Inhalt haben' (Ibid.).

17 That seems to be the prevailing interpretation, e.g. [3.46], 24.

18 [3.46], 14.

19 Cf. [3.48] and [3.50], Figs 2/3.

20 [3.11], 15: 'Die Einführung der Bezeichnung für die Wertverlaufe scheint mit eine der folgenreichste Ergänzung meiner Begriffschrift zu sein' (From the way in which we talk about abstract entities it can follow what abstract entities are for us, what they mean, how we should treat them).

21 It is interesting to see that Frege himself here already uses quotation marks in the modern sense and therefore shows an intuitive understanding of the difference between object language and meta language.

22 An ontological problem arises: Is it possible to understand 'is' just in an explanatory manner?

23 One needs to get a feeling from the definition to understand what he means by logical.

24 Judgeable content.

25 If a is not element of ext(F), then G[a:F] = card (F) or $n + 1$ according to our presupposition. We will need that below in connection with Russell's paradox.

26 0 is an element of [ψ] or rather [equal to o[(X)], the extension of the concept ψ. But 0 is not an element of [equal to o].

27 [3.39], [3.40].

28 Taking up an idea from *Mathematik in der Logik*, I would like to call these definitions 'ascending' and not 'constructive', as the term *aufsteigend* is sometimes translated in this context.

29 [3.24], 2: esp. p. 51.

30 The formal conditions for an equivalence relation are: if a, b and c designate elements of B such that the relation may hold between them, then the relation R [a R a] obtains between any element with itself: 'a R a' (reflexivity), further: 'a R b implies b R a' (symmetry) and last but not least: 'a R b and b R c imply a R c' (transitivity).

31 'Eine für die Zuverlässigkeit des Denkens verhängnisvolle Eigenschaft der Sprache ist jhre Neigung, *Eigennamen zu schaffen*, denen kein Gegenstand entspricht. Wenn das in der Dichtung geschieht, die jeder als Dichtung versteht, so hat das keinen Nachtei.... Ein besonders merkwürdiges Beispiel dazu ist die Bildung eines Eigennamens nach dem Muster "*der Umfang des ßegriffes a*", z. B. "der Umfang des Begriffes Fixstern". Dieser Ausdruck scheint einen Gegenstand zu bezeichnen wegen des bestimmten Artikels *aber es gibt keinen Gegenstand, der sprachgemäß so bezeichnet werden könnte*. Hieraus sind die Paradoxien der Mengenlehre entstanden, die diese Mengenlehre vernichtet haben. Ich selbst bin bei dem Versuche, die Zahlen logische zu begründen, dieser läuschung unterlegen, *indem ich die Zahlen als Mengen auffassen wollte*'.

[3.19], I: 288, my emphasis, I have deliberately produced a very free translation here!)

32 The picture or idea that sentences are ascribed a truth value as their *Bedeutung* = 'reference' will then be projected upon our natural language and eventually leads to a holistic conception of the *meaning* (t can be instantiated as reference/ *Bedeutung* or sense/*Sinn*) of sentences and finally to the context principle in determining the *Bedeutung*/reference of expressions by decomposition.

33 I sometimes deliberately use the language of functions to highlight the theoretical, i.e. functional, understanding of concepts.

34 It is definitely helpful if we want to construct computers and if we want to be clear about ascribing the ability of counting or computing to them. But even there the physical operation is quite distinct from our way of talking about or ascribing some property to it. What may be interesting, however, is whether a certain mental disposition or attitude may be helpful if we interact with machines, i.e. if we want to handle them, if we want to use them appropriately – whatever that may be.

35 Explicity introduced in [3.9] but indicated already in [3.8].

36 Name is here considered as attributed 'value' like f(x); an object x being something that can be an argument in a function.

37 To such a class can be attributed a truth value. All this does not concern indirect speech!

38 Cf. the famous Leibniz principle (e.g. [3.6], 76 ff.).

39 Remember that in mathematics and even physics there are defined/calculated objects (finite groups, positrons) which one knows exist, though it sometimes takes years to find examples of them.

40 I.e. makes uses of them or applies them in accordance with everyday needs or perhaps in agreement with arguments to show the necessity of the application of some scientific tools as the means to gain results that are desirable by standards of daily life. Now all that is a tricky matter and only makes sense with hindsight from this point in time.

41 According to Dummett, this leads to essential consequences for the philosophy of language in general ([3.37], 209–22), although in the *GGA* it is only used in a generalized form. (Ibid., ch 17, 'The Context Principle in *Grundgesetze*'.)

42 'The context principle in fact also governs terms for actual objects, since a grasp of a proper name involves an understanding of its use in sentences' (Ibid., 207).

43 Stekeler-Weithofer ([3.56]) thinks that Frege did not give up the context principle in the *GGA*, while Kutschera ([3.46]) believes that it does not play any further role in the *GGA*, cf. also [3.37].

44 In Frege's paper *Der Gedanke* [3.16], which is concerned with logical investigations. This paper has been taken up in modern 'philosophy of mind'.

45 One may wonder of course whether 'numbers' are anything we encounter in an ordinary life that is not guided by our cultural upbringing with its set of instituted knowledge.

46 Remember that the classical approach to logic was the partition into: concept, judgement, inference (in syllogistics: deduction, induction, etc.).

47 The expression 'coming about' needs some consideration: its meaning is ambiguous, i.e. it can be understood as literally descriptive, i.e. as the presentation of a set of rules about how to achieve a result (like an algorithm in a computer

program) but also as theoretico-explanatory. In the latter case several ways to turn the theoretical understanding into advice for action (making it an action-guiding device) are compatible with the theory.

48 Cf. [3.35]. This means that, as in the case with Plato, a mathematical method in a more general sense has been made fruitful for philosophy.

49 This presentation of the problem situation is of course not 'true to the historical facts'. Frege was interested in anti-psychologism (from our point of view) and as we see from his thesis in analytical sources of knowledge.

50 Except one has the opinion that human beings cannot make mistakes and therefore reflective corrections are inessential and only disturb the peace of the ordinary mind on the positivistic pillow. – 'Everything is what it is' as Bishop Buttler is reported to have said – and so we need not care to think about the world.

51 Cf. [3.3], vi-vii, introduction.

> Wenn es eine Aufgabe der Philosophie ist, die Herrschaft des Wortes über den menschlichen Geist zu brechen, indem sie die *Täuschungen* aufdeckt, die durch den Sprachgebrauch über die Beziehungender Begriffe oft fast unvermeidlich entstehen, indem sie den Gedanken von demjenigen befreit, womit ihn allein die Beschaffenheit des sprachlichen Ausdrucksmittels behafet, so wird meine Begriffschrift, für diese Zwecke weiter ausgebildet, den Philosophen ein brauchbares Werkzeug werden können.

Freillich gibt auch sie [die *BS*], wie es bei einem *äußeren* Darstellungsmittel wohl nicht anders möglich ist, den Gedanken nicht rein wieder ...

> If it is one of the tasks of philosophy to break the domination of the word over the human spirit by laying bare the misconception that through the use of language often almost unavoidably arise concerning the relations between concepts and by freeing thought from that which only the means of expression of ordinary language, constituted as they are, saddle it, then my ideography, further developed for these purposes, can become a useful tool for the philosopher. To be sure, it too will fail to reproduce ideas in a pure form, and this is probably inevitable when ideas are represented by concrete means.

([3.57], 7)

52 Cf. [3.59], 43 'The meaning of a word is its use within the language.'

53 Or some sort of topological generalization of it, e.g. Klein's bottle: a closed, one-sided surface that penetrates itself.

❧ BIBLIOGRAPHY ❧

Selected Bibliography of Frege's Writings

3.1 *Über eine geometrische Darstellung der imaginären Gebilde in der Ebene* (On a Geometrical Representation of Imaginary Forms in the Plane). Inaugural dissertation of the Faculty of Philosophy at the University of Göttingen, submitted as a doctoral thesis by G. Frege of Wismar, Jena, 1873 (75pp. + appendix of diagrams).

3.2 *Rechnungsmethoden, die sich auf eine Erweiterung des Größenbegriffs gründen* (Methods of Calculation based on an Extension of the Concept of Magnitude). Dissertation presented by Dr Gottlob Frege for full membership of the Faculty of Philosophy at the University of Jena. Jena 1874 (26pp. + curriculum vitae).

3.3 *Begriffsschrift, eine der arithmetischen nachgebildete Formelprache des reinen Denkens* (Concept-Script: A Formula Language of Pure Thought modelled on Arithmetical Language). L. Ebert, Halle, 1879 (88pp.).

3.4 *Über die wissenschaftliche Berechtigung der Begriffsschrift* (On the Scientific Justification of Concept-Script). In *Zeitschrift für Philosophie und Philosophische Kritik* (Journal of Philosophy and Philosophical Criticism) LXXXI (1882): 48–56 (repr. in BS/Darmstadt).

3.5 *Über den Zweck der Begriffsschrift* (On the Purpose of Concept-Script). In *Jenaische Zeitschrift für Naturwissenschaft* (Jena Journal of Science) XVI (1883), (suppl.): 1–10. Lecture delivered at the meeting of the Jena Society for Medicine and Science, 27 January 1882

3.6 *Die Grundlagen der Arithmetik* (The Foundations of Arithmetic). A Logico-mathematical Enquiry into the Concept of Number, W. Loebner, Breslau, 1884 (119pp.). New impression: M. and H. Marcus, Breslau, 1934. Facsimile reprint of the new impression: Wissenschaftliche Buchgesellschaft (Scientific Book Society), Darmstadt, 1961, and G. Olms, Hildesheim, 1961 (119pp.).

3.7 *Über formale Theorien der Arithmetik* (On Formal theories of Arithmetic). In: *Jenaische Zeitschrift für Naturwissenschaft* (Jena Journal of Science) XIX (1886), (suppl.): 94–104. Lecture delivered at the meeting of the Jena Society for Medicine and Science, 17 July 1885.

3.8 *Funktion und Begriff* (Function and Concept). Lecture delivered at the meeting of the Jena Society for Medicine and Science, 9 January 1891. H. Pohle, Jena, 1891 (31pp.).

3.9 *Über Sinn und Bedeutung* (On Sense and Reference). In *Zeitschrift für Philosophie und Philosophische Kritik* (Journal of Philosophy and Philosophical Criticism) C (1892): 25–50.

3.10 *Über Begriff und Gegenstand* (On Concept and Object). In *Vierteljahresschrift für wissenschaftliche Philosophie* (Scientific Philosophy Quarterly) XVI (1892): 192–205.

3.11 *Grundgesetze der Arithmetik* (The Basic Laws of Arithmetic: Following the Principles of the Concept-Script. Vol. 1). H. Pohle, Jena, 1893 (253pp. with revisions). Facsimile reprint: Wissenschaftliche Buchgesellschaft (Scientific Book Society), Darmstadt, 1962, and G. Olms, Hildesheim, 1962.

3.12 *Über die Begriffsschrift des Herrn Peano und meine eigene* (On Peano's Concept-Script and My Own). In *Berichte über die Verhandlungen der Königlichen Sächsischen Gesellschaft der Wissenschaften zu Leipzig, Mathematisch-Physikalishe Classe* (Reports on the Proceedings of the Royal Saxon Society for Science in Leipzig, Mathematics/Physics Division) XLVII (1897): 361–78. Lecture delivered at the extraordinary meeting of the Society held on 6 July 1896.

3.13 *Über die Zahlen des Herrn H. Schubert* (On H. Schubert's Numbers), H. Pohle, Jena, 1899 (32pp.).

3.14 *Grundgesetze der Arithmetik* (The Basic Laws of Arithmetic: Following the Principles of the Concept-Script, vol. 2), H. Pohle, Jena, 1903 (265pp. with revisions and glossary of terms). Facsimile reprint: Wissenschaftliche Buchgesellschaft (Scientific Book Society), Darmstadt, 1962, and G. Olms, Hildesheim, 1962

3.15 *Was ist eine Funktion?* (What is a Function?). Festschrift dedicated to Ludwig Boltzmann on the Occasion of his Sixtieth Birthday, 20 February 1904. J. A. Barth, Leipzig, 1904, pp.656–66.

3.16 *Der Gedanke* (The Thought). A Logical Enquiry. In *Beiträge zur Philosophie des deutschen Idealismus* (Contributions to German Idealistic Philosophy) I (1918): 58–77.

3.17 *Die Verneinung* (Negation). A Logical Enquiry. In: *Beiträge zur Philosophie des deutschen Idealismus* (Contributions to German Idealistic Philosophy) I (1918): 143–57.

3.18 *Logische Untersuchungen* (Logical Investigations). Part 3: Sequence of Thought. In *Beiträge zur Philosophie des deutschen Idealismus* (Contributions to German Idealistic Philosophy) III (1923): 36–51.

3.19 *Gottlob Frege: Nachgelassene Schriften und wissenschaftlicher Briefwechsel* (Gottlob Frege: Posthumous Writings and Correspondence), Hans Hermes, Friedrich Kambartel and Friedrich Kaulbach Posthumous (eds), Hamburg, 1969. Vol. 1: Writings (1969); Vol. 2: Correspondence (1976).

Important Sources

3.20 *The Foundations of Arithmetic.* A logico-mathematical enquiry into the concept of number. Oxford, Blackwell, 1950 and New York, Philosophical Library, 1950, 2nd rev. edn 1953, repr. 1959. XII, XI, 119pp. + XII, XI, 119pp. Dual-language German/English edn. Transl., foreword and notes by J. L. Austin. Repr. of the English text of this edn: New York, Harper, 1960.

3.21 *Funktion, Begriff, Bedeutung* (Function, Concept, Meaning). Five Studies in Logic, edited and with an introduction by Günther Patzig, Göttingen, Vandenhoeck und Ruprecht, 1962 (101pp.). 2nd rev. edn, 1966 (103pp.).

3.22 *Bergriffsschrift und andere Aufsätze* (Concept-Script and Other Essays), 2nd edn annotated by E. Husserl and H. Scholz, ed. Ignacio Angelelli. Darmstadt Wissenschaftliche Buchgesellschaft (Scientific Book Society), dt, 1964, and Hildesheim, G. Olms, 1964 (124pp.). (BS/Darmstadt)

3.23 *Logische Untersuchungen. Herausgegeben und eingeleitet von Günther Patzig*

(Studies in Logic, edited and with an introduction by Günther Patzig), Göttingen, Vandenhoeck und Ruprecht, 1966 (142pp.).

3.24 *Kleine Schriften. Herausgegeben von Ignacio Angelelli* (Minor Works, edited by Ignacio Angelelli). Darmstadt, Wissenschaftliche Buchgesellschaft (Scientific Book Society), 1967 and Hildesheim, G. Olms, 1967 (434pp.) (Contains doctoral thesis and dissertation [3.1 and 3.2.]

3.25 *Begriffsschrift: A Formula Language, Modelled upon that of Arithmetic, for Pure Thought*, in Jean van Heijenoort (ed.) *From Frege to Gödel. A Source Book in Mathematical Logic*, 1879–1931, Cambridge, Mass., Harvard University Press, 1967, pp.1–82.

3.26 *The Thought. A Logical Enquiry*; in P. F. Strawson (ed.) *Philosophical Logic*, London, Oxford University Press, 1967, pp.17–38.

General Bibliography

3.27 Benacerraf, P. 'Frege: The Last Logicist', in *Midwest Studies in Philosophy* 6 (1981): 17–35.

3.28 Born, R. 'Schizo-Semantik: Provokationen zum Thema Bedeutungstheorien und Wissenschaftsphilosophie im Allgemeinen', in *Conceptus, Jahrgang* XVII. (41/42), (1983): 101–16.

3.29 —— 'Split Semantics', in *Artificial Intelligence – The Case Against*, London, Routledge, 1987.

3.30 Church, A. *Introduction to Mathematical Logic*, Princeton, Princeton University Press, 1956.

3.31 Dedekind, R. *Was sind und was sollen die Zahlen?* Braunschweig, Vieweg and Sohn, 1888.

3.32 Dummett, M. 'Frege, Gottlob', in P. Edwards (ed.) *The Encyclopedia of Philosophy*, London, Collier MacMillan, 1967, pp.225–37.

3.33 —— *The Interpretation of Frege's Philosophy*, London, Duckworth, 1981.

3.34 —— *Frege. Philosophy of Language.* London, Duckworth, 1981.

3.35 —— 'Frege and the Paradox of Analysis', 1987, in *Frege and Other Philosophers*, Oxford, Clarendon Press, 1991.

3.36 —— *Ursprünge der analytischen Philosophie*, Frankfurt/M, Suhrkamp, 1988.

3.37 —— *Frege. Philosophy of Mathematics*, Cambridge, Masses, Cambridge University Press, 1991.

3.38 Fischer, K. *Geschichte der neueren Philosophie*, 2nd rev. edn, Heidelberg, Basserman 1869.

3.39 Fréchet, M. 'Relations entre les notions de limite et de distance' in *Trans. American Mathematical Society* 19 (1918): 54.

3.40 Hausdorff, F. *Grundzüge der Mengenlehre*. Leipzig, Veit and Co., 1914 (1927); Mengenlehre (zweite stark veränderte Auflage), Berlin-Leipzig, Walter de Gruyter, 1927. (Goeschens Lehrbuecherei, Gruppe 1, Reine Mathematik, Vol. 7.)

3.41 Husserl, E. *Die Philosophie der Arithmetick*, Halle, Martinus Nijhoff, 1891.

3.42 Jourdain P. E. B. 'The development of the theories of mathematical logic and the principles of mathematics', *Quarterly Journal of Pure and Applied Mathematics* 43 (1912): 237–69.

3.43 Kitcher, P. 'Frege, Dedekind and the Philosophy of Mathematics', in L. Haarparanta and J. Hintikka (eds) *Frege Sythesized*, Dordrecht, Reidel, 1986, pp. 299–343.

3.44 Klein, F. 'Zur Interpretation der komplexenElemente in der Geometrie', *Annals of Mathematics* 22 (1872); repr. in R. Fricke and A. Ostrowski (eds) *Gesammelte Mathematische Abhandlungen*, vol. 1, Berlin, Julius Springer, 1922, pp. 402–5.

3.45 —— F. *Vorlesungen über Nicht-Euklidische Geometrie*. Berlin, Julius Springer, 1928.

3.46 Kutschera, F. V. *Gottlob Frege. Eine Einführung in sein Werk*, Berlin, Walter de Gruyter, 1989.

3.47 Lotze, H. *Logik. Drei Bücher von Denken vom Untersuchen und vom Erkennen*, Leipzig, S. Hirzel, 1880b.

3.48 Łukasiewicz, J. *Aristotle's Syllogistic* (From the Standpoint of Modern Formal Logic), Oxford, Clarendon Press, 1958b.

3.49 Moore, G. E. *Eine Verteidigung der Common Sense* (Fünf Aufsätze aus den Jahren 1903–1941), Frankfurt/M, Suhrkamp, 1969.

3.50 Patzig. G. *Die Aristotelische Syllogistik.* (Logisch-philosophische Untersuchungen über das Buch A der 'Ersten Analytiken'. Göttingen, Vandenhoeck and Ruprecht, 1969c.

3.51 Putnam, H. *Renewing Philosophy*, Cambridge, Mass., Harvard University Press, 1992.

3.52 Quine W. V. O. *From a Logical Point of View*, Cambridge, Mass., Harvard University Press, 1961.

3.53 Sluga, H. *Gottlob Frege*, London, Routledge and Kegan Paul, 1980.

3.54 —— 'Frege: the Early Years', in R. Rorty, J. Scheewind and Q. Skinner (eds) *Philosophy in History. Essays on the Historiography of Philosophy*, Cambridge, Cambridge University Press, 1984, pp. 329–56.

3.55 Staudt, C. V. *Beiträge zur Geometrie der Lage. Erstes Hef*, Nürnberg, F. Korn, 1856.

3.56 Stekeler-Weithofer, P. *Grundprobleme der Logik*, Berlin, Walter de Gruyter, 1986.

3.57 Van Heijenoort, J. (ed.) *From Frege to Gödel: A Source book in Mathematical Logic 1879–1931*, Cambridge, Mass., Harvard University Press, 1967.

3.58 Wittgenstein, L. *Tractatus Logico-Philosophicus*, London, Routledge and Kegan Paul, 1922.

3.59 Wittgenstein, L. *Philosophical Investigations*, Oxford, Basil Blackwell, 1953.

CHAPTER 4

Wittgenstein's Tractatus

James Bogen

➤➤ I INTRODUCTION ➤➤

Containing material (mainly on logic and language) dating back at least to 1913 when Wittgenstein was twenty-four, the *Tractatus* was first published in 1921. In 1922 a somewhat revised version was published with a translation by C. K. Ogden and an introduction by Bertrand Russell. The last significant correction to the German text was made in 1933. The second major English translation (by Pears and McGuinness) was published in 1960.[1] It is a short, oracular book. Much of it is aphoristic; some of it, formidably technical. Few of its claims are explained or argued in any detail. Its core is a theory of language which Wittgenstein applies to topics as diverse as ethics, religion, the foundations of logic and the philosophy of science.

The major components of the *Tractatus* theory of language are:
(T1) a theory of meaning and truth for elementary propositions (*Elementarsätze*) (*T*4.03, 4.0311; 4.21–4.24).[2]
(T2) a *construction thesis*, which holds roughly that because all meaningful statements are truth functions of elementary propositions, if we were given all of the elementary propositions, there is no proposition (*Satz*) which could not (in principle at least) be 'constructed' or 'derived from' them (*T*4.26–5.01; 5.234–5.45; 5.5–5.502; 6–6.01); and
(T3) a development of the idea that propositions can express every possible fact.
All of this applies only to language as used to say what is true or false. The *Tractatus* does not deal with questions or commands, jokes, riddles, etc – a limitation emphasized in the early sections of *Philosophical Investigations* [4.47].

All three of these involve problematic notions which Wittgenstein criticized harshly in his later work. For example, elementary propositions are supposed to be composed of names which refer to objects, but the *Tractatus* supplies no examples of names, and its characterization of objects is fraught with difficulties (see Section XI below). There are neither examples nor clear characterizations of the propositions of T1 and constructions of T2. Indeed, the very notion of a Tractarian proposition is problematical (see Section IX below). To get started, I will use a simple, idealized model which departs from the *Tractatus* as needed to postpone consideration of the difficulties.

～ II ELEMENTARY PROPOSITIONS ～

The model features language which describes 'states of affairs'. Tractarian states of affairs (*Sachverhalte*) are possible concatenations of simple elements. A state of affairs obtains (*besteht*) if the relevant objects are concatenated in the right way; otherwise, it does not obtain (2–2.01). For now pretend that states of affairs are arrangements of two-dimensional objects with the following shapes.

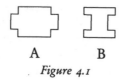

A   B

Figure 4.1

Any B-shaped object can connect at either end to any A. Objects of the same shape cannot connect to each other. No object can curve around to connect to itself or to both ends of another object.

    Names are signs which refer to objects. Elementary propositions are strings of names (cp. *T*4.21, 4.22, 4.221). Figure 4.2 assigns names ('a_1', 'b_1', etc.) to objects and illustrates three states of affairs (possible concatenations).

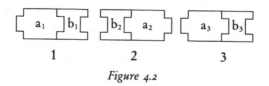

1   2   3

Figure 4.2

The syntax of a Tractarian language allows as elementary propositions all but only arrangements of names which are isomorphic to possible concatenations of the objects they refer to. In our model the isomorphism is spatial: for example, what we get by writing 'a_1' to the left of 'b_1' is an elementary proposition because object a_1 can be connected to the left side of object b_1. 'a_1a_2', and 'a_1a_1' and '$b_1a_2b_1$' are not elementary propositions. Neither is a single name; the model does not talk about objects apart from concatenations. Thus, the syntax of elementary propositions mirrors the geometry of the states of affairs.

Each elementary proposition pictures the isomorphic concatenation of the objects it mentions. Thus 'a_1b_1' pictures

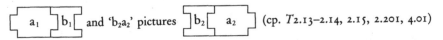

and 'b_2a_2' pictures (cp. $T2.13$–2.14, 2.15, 2.201, 4.01)

An elementary proposition is true just in case the objects it mentions are concatenated as it pictures them; otherwise it is false (cp. $T2.21$, 4.022, 4.25). An elementary proposition has a sense just in case it portrays a state of affairs (i.e. a concatenation which can obtain). Thus, the relation between the geometries of elementary propositions and states of affairs established by the syntax of our model guarantees a state of affairs (hence a sense) for every elementary proposition and an elementary proposition for every state of affairs. This corresponds to the Tractarian doctrine that elementary propositions cannot portray anything which is impossible, and can portray all possible concatenations of objects because the constraints which determine how symbols can be combined into elementary propositions are identical to the constraints which determine how objects can combine with one another ($T2.151$, less 2.17–2.182).

I emphasize that this model is non-Tractarian. Its names and propositions are *marks* (signs) while Tractarian names and propositions are not (see Sections IV and IX below). Two dimensional spatial objects are not Tractarian simple objects (see Section XI below). Bearing this in mind the foregoing illustrates T1 – including some crucial features of the *Tractatus* picture theory of language (see Section VIII below) – for elementary propositions.

❧ III T3 AND THE CONSTRUCTION THESIS ❧

The *Tractatus* says reality is the totality of all 'positive' and 'negative facts'. Positive facts are obtainings of states of affairs and negative facts are their non-obtainings ($T2.06B$). For example if a_1 is connected to the left of b_1, it is a positive fact that a_1b_1. If they are not concatenated it is a negative fact that they are not.[3] Possible worlds are collections of possible facts. The positive facts a world includes, and its including no others, determine which negative facts belong to it ($T1$–1.13; 2.04–2.06).[4]

To illustrate T2 and T3, let p be 'a_1b_1', the elementary proposition which pictures the obtaining of state of affairs 1 in Figure 4.2. Let q be 'b₂a₂'. Let r picture the obtaining of 3 in Figure 4.2. If a_1, a_2, a_3, b_1, b_2 and b_3 are the only objects, and 1, 2 and 3 are their only possible concatenations, the possible worlds are:

w8 in which no objects are concatenated and all the elementary propositions are false.

According to T3 and the construction thesis, every positive and negative fact in every possible world can be pictured by propositions included in or constructed from a complete list of elementary propositions. To show how this could be, the *Tractatus* employs the truth table, a gadget which is known and loved by every beginner logic student.[5] In a truth table 'T' indicates truth, and 'F', falsity. Each elementary proposition can be true or false independently of the others. The first three columns of Figure 4.3 represent the possible combinations of truth values for p, q and r. (The ordering of the permutations is idiosyncratic to Wittgenstein. (*T*4.31 ff). Thus in line 1, columns 1, 2, 3, represent the possibility that all of our elementary propositions are true. In line 2, columns 1, 2, 3, p is false while q and r are true. Etc. Each subsequent column represents the truth conditions of non-elementary propositions. Thus ¬p is true whenever p is false, and false whenever p is true, regardless of the truth values of q and r, p&q is true whenever both p and q are true, regardless of whether r is true, etc.

	p	q	r	¬p	¬q	¬r	pvq	pv¬q	p&q	p⊃q	(pvq)⊃(p&q)		Taut.	Contr.
1	T	T	T	F	F	F	T	T	T	T	T		T	F
2	F	T	T	T	F	F	T	F	F	T	F		T	F
3	T	F	T	F	T	F	T	T	F	F	F		T	F
4	T	T	F	F	F	T	T	T	T	T	T		T	F
5	F	F	T	T	T	F	F	T	F	T	T		T	F
6	F	T	F	T	F	T	T	F	F	T	F		T	F
7	T	F	F	F	T	T	T	T	F	F	F		T	F
8	F	F	F	T	T	T	F	T	F	T	T		T	F

Figure 4.3

Each row corresponds to a different possible world. If p is 'a$_1$ b$_1$,' q is 'b$_2$a$_2$,' and r is 'a$_3$b$_3$,' row 1, represents w 1 in which p, q and r are all true, row 2 corresponds to w2, etc. For each different proposition there is a column which specifies its truth value in each world. Thus, by column 10, p⊃q is true in w1, w2, w4, w5, w6, w8, and false in w3 and w7. A proposition is contingent if it is true in at least one world and false in at least one other. Necessarily true propositions ('tautologies') are true in every world. Necessarily false propositions ('contradictions') are false in all worlds (T4.46). Because objects are extra-linguistic entities whose natures determine which states of affairs (and therefore which possible facts) there are, the *Tractatus* does not think that all necessity and impossibility is propositional (T2.014, 2.0141; cp. section XI). But tautology, contingency and contradiction exhaust its propositional modalities.

If (as in our model) there were only a limited number of truth possibilities for elementary propositions, we could prove the construction thesis by simply writing a truth table with a column for every possible proposition. Wittgenstein offered no such proof, presumably because he thought he could not list all of the elementary propositions, and could not rule out the possibility that there are infinitely many of them (T4.2211, 5.571). Instead, he suggested that every proposition (elementary as well as non-elementary) can be expressed by one or more applications of an operation he called joint negation and symbolized 'N (ξ̄)'. ξ is a variable whose values are collections of propositions. The bar indicates that the order of the propositions is indifferent. The joint negation of any ξ is the conjunction of the denials of every proposition in ξ (T5.5–5.51). For example, N(p,q,r) =

(1) ¬p&¬q&¬r,

and N([¬p&¬q&¬r], p, q, r) =

(2) ¬(¬p&¬q&¬r)&(¬p&¬q&¬r), a contradiction (cp. 5.5–5.51)
$\bar{\xi}$ can be a one-member collection. For example, we can jointly
negate (2) to obtain a tautology,

(3) ¬[¬(¬p&¬q&¬r)&(¬p&¬q&¬r)].

The first step in the construction of any proposition is the joint denial
of all of the elementary propositions (T5.2521–5.2523, 6–6.6001). Wittgenstein doesn't say what comes next, but we could proceed as follows.
At each successive step replace $\bar{\xi}$ by any proposition or propositions
you feel like choosing from the elementary propositions and whatever
non-elementary propositions have already been constructed. By
common sense we shouldn't replace $\bar{\xi}$ with propositions whose joint
negation will duplicate results already obtained, and we should keep
trying different substitutions until we get a proposition for every
column.[6] Such policies might enable someone with enough ingenuity
to construct all of the truth functions of a finite number of elementary
propositions. But since the choices for $\bar{\xi}$ (and therefore the outcomes
of joint negation) are not determined after the first step, Wittgenstein's
construction procedure is ill-defined.[7]

In addition to this there is the possibility that there are infinitely
many elementary propositions.[8] Wittgenstein mentioned this later as an
insurmountable problem for his account of universal and existential
quantification. [4.24], 279 The *Tractatus* treats universally quantified
propositions of the form ∀x(Fx) as if they were conjunctions expressing
agreement with every value of Fx and existentially quantified propositions as if they were disjunctions which are true just in case at least
one value of Fx is true. Since the values of the function are propositions,
they must themselves be elementary propositions or their truth functions. Suppose the truth conditions of each value of Fx involved a
different elementary proposition. If there were infinitely many of them,
Wittgenstein argued, they could not be enumerated, and Wittgenstein
thought this would rule out constructing universally and existentially
quantified propositions by treating them as conjunctions and disjunctions.[9] Indeed, if there were infinitely many elementary propositions,
the first step in the construction of any proposition whatever – unquant-
ified or quantified – would have to begin with the joint denial of
a group of propositions whose members could not be enumerated.
Wittgenstein apparently decided the *Tractatus* could not be adjusted to
allow for this. Why didn't he consider construction methods which
would not require enumerating all of the elementary propositions? It is
plausible that by this time changes in Wittgenstein's ideas about elementary propositions (see section IX below) had not only complicated the
problem, but had also led him to doubt whether it was worth pursuing.

If *all* propositions can be constructed (T4.51, 4.52, 5) we must be able to construct elementary as well as non-elementary propositions. In effect that would mean detaching each elementary proposition from the set of all elementary propositions. How can repeated applications of joint negation accomplish this? If p, q and r were the only elementary propositions we could construct a proposition with exactly the same truth conditions as p as follows.[10] Having obtained (1) by jointly negating p, q and r, select (1) together with all of the elementary propositions to form the collection [(¬p&¬q&¬r), p, q, r)]. Its joint negation is the contradiction (2) obtained above. Now the joint negation of (2) and p is the conjunction of ¬p and a tautology:

(4)   3&¬p. Finally, N(4) =
(5)   ¬(3&¬p). This expression is true just in case (3) is false or ¬¬p is true. Since ¬3 is false in all worlds, (5) is true exactly when ¬¬p is true. Thus (5) has exactly the same truth conditions as p (column 1, Figure 4.3). But this is not the only way to express the truth conditions of p. For example, after the mandatory joint denial of the elementary propositions we can substitute p for $\bar{\xi}$.[11] N(p) = ¬p and N (¬p) =
(6)   ¬¬p

which has the same truth values as p.

❧ IV 'A PROPOSITION IS A QUEER THING!'[12] ❧

But in constructing (5) and (6) did we really construct p, or just different propositions with the same truth conditions? I was pretending that propositions were sentences but if they are, the construction of (5) and (6) does not give us p, even though they have the same truth conditions. Furthermore, if propositions are sentences, then, contrary to Wittgenstein, the order of the propositions in $\bar{\xi}$ is not indifferent; N(p, q, r) = ¬p&¬q&¬r, and N(r, q, p) = ¬r&¬q&¬p have the same truth conditions but '¬p&¬q&¬r' and '¬r&¬q&¬p' are different sentences. Apparently, then, propositions are not sentences. Wittgenstein says that what is 'essential' to a proposition is not the shapes of its signs but rather, the features 'without which the proposition could not express its sense' (T3.34B) and which are common to 'all propositions which can express the same sense' (T3.341A). Because the sense of a proposition is its truth conditions (T2.221, 4.022–4.03, 4.1) propositions with the same truth conditions must have the same essential features. If propositions whose essential features are identical, are themselves identical, Wittgenstein need not worry: p would differ no more from pv2 than Thelonius wearing a hat would differ from Thelonius bare-headed (cp. T5.513A, 5.141). Thus, differences between sentences used to express the same truth conditions need not constitute an objection to the construction thesis.

But if different sentences (marks and sounds) can be counted as one and the same proposition, what *is* a proposition? One thing Wittgenstein says a proposition is is a written or spoken sign in use ('in its projective relation to the world') to picture the world as including a particular situation (*Sachlage*) ($T3.11$, 3.12). A situation is a congeries of obtainings and non-obtainings of states of affairs ($T2.11$). But if different sentences are used to picture the world as including the same situations, they have the same truth conditions and therefore, they must have the same essential features. How can exactly the same essential features belong to all the different sentences which can be used to say the same thing? For example, since a proposition must contain 'exactly as many distinguishable parts as ... the situation which it presents' ($T4.032A$) sentences presenting the same situation must somehow have the same number of distinguishable parts. This applies to the 'propositions of our everyday language' for Wittgenstein considered them to be 'in perfect logical order just as they stand' ($T5.5563A$) even though their outward form completely disguises their logical form ($T4.002CD$). Thus, all artificial and natural language sentences which can say the same thing must have the same number of distinguishable parts when they are so used. The question of what these parts are and how to count them exemplifies the difficulty of understanding what propositions are and what they have to do with sentences.[13]

Wittgenstein says other things about propositions which seem to promise help with the counting problem. First, at $T3.31$ propositions and their parts are said to be 'symbols' or 'expressions'. And the symbol (expression) is said to be everything 'essential to their sense' which propositions expressing the same sense 'can have in common'. Thus, where sentences of different lengths are used to express the same sense, the number of words in a sentence need not equal the number of symbols in the relevant proposition. Second, Wittgenstein says pictures, propositions and sentences are not just words or symbols, but facts – the facts that their elements stand to one another in certain relations ($T2.141$, 2.15, 3.14ff). Thus what pictures or asserts that a stands in some relation to b is not the complex sign 'aRb', but the fact that 'a' stands in a certain relation to 'b' ($T3.1432$). The sign 'R' is not treated as a part of the fact (that 'a' and 'b' stand to one another in a certain relation) which says that aRb. This promises some help with the counting problem, for if the symbol is a fact, the number of elements it contains need not be the same as the number of words used make the assertion. But how are the parts of such facts to be counted, and why is not their number directly determined by the number of signs they involve? The third characterization of the proposition suggested in the *Tractatus* is relevant to this.

As a group of names arranged to depict the world as including a concatenation of the objects to which they refer (*T*4.0311) the elementary proposition resembles what is supposed to have suggested the picture theory to Wittgenstein – a model[14] composed of toy cars, pedestrians, etc, representing real automobiles, people, etc., and used to allege that an accident had occurred in a certain way.[15] But it is an important fact about such representations that one and the same picture or model can be used to claim that this is how an accident occurred, or that this is how it *did not* occur. (It can also be exhibited as a representational sculpture which makes no claim at all.) Strictly speaking, truth conditions belong to assertions ordinary pictures can be used to make. By itself, apart from any such use, the picture has no truth conditions. By the same token if propositions represented facts in the same way the model represented the accident, they would have no truth conditions. The reason the proposition has a sense is that, in addition to picturing, it asserts that the world is as pictured (*T*4.022, 4.023E, 4.06). If the proposition is an assertion which can be made with more than one sentence instead of a sentence used to assert, the number of its parts would depend upon the number of things done with signs instead of depending on the number of signs used. For example, the countable parts of the an elementary proposition would be references to objects. At *T*3.3411 'the real name of an object is what all symbols which designate it have in common'. The suggestion is that what they have in common is their use to refer. Indeed this promises a way to disregard as inessential not just the number of signs in sentences used to say the same thing, but *any* features possessed by some of those sentences but not others.[16]

How do the different things the *Tractatus* says about propositions hang together? The later Wittgenstein thought they do not. In the *Philosophical Investigations* [4.47], he spoke of the tendency to think of the proposition as 'a pure intermediary between the propositional *signs* and the facts. Or even to try to purify, to sublime, the signs themselves'.[17]

It is plausible that the Tractarian symbol exemplifies the first tendency. It is plausible that the conception of a proposition as a sign or a fact involving signs whose essential features are determined by what it is used to say exemplifies the second. It is plausible that the picture theory of language exemplifies both.

❧ V FALSE ASSERTIONS ❧

The *Tractatus* attempts to solve a puzzle about falsehood dating back
to Plato's Theaetetus:

> [If] ... a man who is judging some one thing is judging
> something which is ... that means that a man who is judging
> something which is not is judging nothing ... But a man who
> is judging nothing is not judging at all ... And so it is not
> possible to judge what is not, either about the things which are
> or just by itself.[18]

To get the problem of false assertion Wittgenstein addressed, replace
Plato's talk of judgement and what is judged with talk about assertion
and what people assert. To say that some specific state of affairs or
situation ('some one thing') belongs to the actual world a proposition
must tell us *which* state of affairs or situation its truth value depends
on. Otherwise, for example, state of affairs ab would have no more
bearing on the truth or falsehood of the proposition 'ab' than any other
concatenation of a and b or the concatenation of other objects. But a
proposition is false only if what it claims to be the case is not one of
the positive or negative facts which make up the actual world. The
problem of false assertion is the problem of explaining how a proposition can specify the putative fact it claims is the case (as it must do
to have a sense) if it is false and there is no such fact. For example,
how can a proposition say that ab obtains when it is false and the
actual world does not include that concatenation? And if ab obtains,
how can '¬ab' specify the negative fact required for its truth?

The picture theory solves the problem by rejecting the assumption
(which generates it) that a proposition cannot specify which fact its
truth requires unless that fact is actually there to be specified. Elementary propositions are pictures whose elements are names of simple
objects (T3.203). 'One name stands for one thing, another for another
thing, and they are combined with one another. In this way the whole
group – like a *tableaux vivant* – presents a state of affairs' (T4.0311).
Instead of naming (standing in a referring relation) to a putative fact,
a proposition specifies what its truth requires by 'picturing' it, where
picturing does not require the actual existence of the putative fact. In
order for an elementary proposition to say that ab, the names 'a' and
'b' must refer to objects a and b, respectively, and those objects must
be *able* to be arranged as the proposition shows them to be. But this
does not require the state of affairs (ab) to actually obtain. And because
the possibility of its obtaining consists of nothing more than the pos-
session by a and b of the abilities required for concatenation, the state
of affairs (the possible fact that ab obtains) is not an entity the propo-

sition must refer to in order to claim that ab is the case. Thus the proposition 'ab' can be false as long as there are objects (capable of concatenating) for its names to refer to, and an actual world which fails to include the obtaining of ab.

Complex situations, including non-obtainings of states of affairs, are pictured by non-elementary propositions whose construction – Wittgenstein thought – requires nothing more than the joint negation of collections of propositions. Whatever difficulties this may involve, there is no reason to think, e.g., that the construction of '¬ab' should require ab to obtain any more than would the assertion 'ab'. Thus, Wittgenstein can say that 'a proposition which speaks of a complex' is false rather than 'meaningless (unsinnig) if the complex does not exist' as it would be if complexes had to be named in order to be mentioned (T3.24B). With regard to the problem at hand, the non-existing complexes are the putative facts mentioned by false propositions.

The notion of picturing involved in this solution is a primitive. Instead of trying to define it Wittgenstein designed his account of elementary propositions and their truth functions to secure that, as long as there are objects for names to refer to and an actual world for the proposition to represent, the proposition can picture the world as including a putative fact regardless of whether it belongs to the actual world. In order to appreciate the elegance of this solution to the problem of false assertions and also to introduce some of its difficulties it helps to look at the competition.

❧ VI SOME REJECTED ACCOUNTS OF FALSE ❧ JUDGEMENT

Wittgenstein intended his account to avoid problems he found in the solutions of Frege and Russell, and a theory of Meinong's they all rejected. Before he became Wittgenstein's teacher Russell entertained and rejected Meinong's idea that a proposition has meaning by virtue of doing what amounts, ignoring details, to referring to the fact whose existence is required for its truth.[19] Meinong called these 'Objectives'. The Objective signified by a false proposition like 'Napoleon was defeated at Marengo' must enjoy a shadowy grade of existence – robust enough to give meaning to the proposition, but not robust enough to make it true. Russell rejected this because he believed philosophy must be constrained by a 'vivid sense of reality', and was convinced that 'there is no such thing as [the fact that] Napoleon was defeated at Marengo'.[20] In addition to dispensing with the Objective, his treatment of the Theaetetus problem[21] was (like Wittgenstein's) intended to avoid the ontological commitments of the account Frege devised before the turn of the century.[22] Let us look at Frege's before turning to Russell's.

In Fregean semantics propositions can have meanings of two sorts – sense and reference. All propositions have senses. Frege calls the sense of a proposition a 'thought' – an unfortunate term because his 'thoughts' are structures which are as they are quite independently of anyone's psychological states. Their study belongs not to psychology, but to logic and the philosophy of language. Logical relations (like entailment) are grounded in structural features which Fregean thoughts possess regardless of whether anyone grasps them, and which they would have had even if there had never been any minds. Frege says the existence and structure of a thought depends no more upon anyone's thinking than the existence of a mountain depends upon anyone's travelling over it.[23]

According to Frege not all propositions have truth values.[24] Those that don't have sense but no reference. A proposition is true if its referent is an object Frege calls The True, and false if its referent is The False. Which (if either) a proposition refers to depends upon the thought it expresses together with how things are. For example, the sense of 'Bud played faster than Thelonius' is such that this proposition refers to The True if Bud actually did play faster (he did) and to The False if Thelonius played faster (he did not).[25] Which thought a string of words is used to express depends upon the psychology of those who use it. But once this is established its truth conditions, i.e. what is required for it to name The True (and what is required for it to name The False), depend entirely upon the structure of the thought. The judgement (assertion) that a proposition is true commits one to its naming The True. If it does, the judgement (assertion) is true; if not it is false. But whether or not the proposition is true does not depend upon whether it is judged or asserted.

This solution is Platonistic. But because it does not posit different grades of existence it is not Meinongian. Consider the false proposition 'Thelonius played faster than Bud'. Its referent (The False) and its sense enjoy exactly the same kind of existence as Thelonius Monk, Bud Powell and the proposition itself.[26] Thus, the price Frege pays to avoid Meinong's two grades of existence is Platonism required to posit Fregean thoughts, The True, and The False.

Wittgenstein rejected the Platonism of Frege's account, and along with it, the Fregean idea that propositions are names, let alone names of The True and The False (T3.143, 4.063, 4.431, 4.442).[27] He tells us not to say propositions have senses – as if a sense were a Fregean thought which could exist even if no proposition had it, and as if having a sense involved a two-term 'having' relation between a proposition and its sense. Instead of saying a proposition has a sense we can simply say it pictures the world as including the situation it presents ($T4.031$B). For a proposition to be true is not for it to name The True but rather, to picture the world as containing a situation it actually contains. Russell's alternative to Frege and Meinong was to maintain that truth and falsity belong primarily to complex structures assembled by a person in the course of believing, disbelieving, doubting, understanding, questioning, or any of the other mental states which Russell later called 'attitudes to ideas' and which are now called 'propositional attitudes'.[28] In what follows I will use the term 'judgement' generically for all of these attitudes. A Russellian judgement is not a mind's attitude toward a pre-existing, pre-structured Fregean thought. Russell eschewed these as well as Meinongian Objectives. Instead, he treats judgement as consisting of a many-termed relation between the judging mind and a number of (what he considered less exotic) items. In judging that one of these items, a, stands in some relation, R, to another item, b, one puts together what Russell calls a proposition. Unlike Fregean propositions whose constituents were words, and Wittgensteinian propositions composed of symbols, a Russellian proposition is composed in this case of the objects a and b themselves, the relation, R, and a gadget which orders them into a proposition and thereby determines its structure.[29] These constituents exist on their own whether or not anyone makes a judgement about them.[30] If they actually are as judged (e.g. if someone believes that a is louder than b, and a actually is louder) the proposition is true. But since their collection into a proposition requires nothing more than judgement, false propositions can be put together in exactly the same way as true propositions. This treatment of the problem of false judgement does not commit Russell's ontology to anything beyond the minds which judge, the relation which constitutes judging, and the constituents which judgement puts together to form propositions. Thus, Russell avoided positing the Meinongian Objectives and Fregean thoughts which offended his ontological sensibilities by plucking out of his account of judgement the notion of prefabricated contents of judgement (Objectives, Fregean thoughts) which do not depend upon judgement for their existence, their logical structures, or their truth conditions. The development of the picture theory was driven by Wittgenstein's dissatisfaction with this no less than with Frege's and Meinong's theories.

In 1913 Wittgenstein argued that Russell's theory was inadequate because it could not rule out the possibility of judging nonsense, i.e. believing, affirming, etc., what lacks truth conditions. The problem was that Russell's account does not constrain the items which can belong to propositions or the ways in which judging can arrange them as needed to rule out such nonsense judgements as 'that this table penholders this book'.[31] This defect is hard to remedy. Even if Russell had a principled way to limit the selection of constituents to items which could belong to a fact his theory would not know how to prevent someone from judging a disorganized jumble.

Well then, how does Wittgenstein avoid the possibility of nonsense judgements? He says what is needed to avoid Russell's mistake is a correct 'explanation of the form of the proposition, 'A makes the judgement p' . . . [which shows] that it is impossible to judge a nonsense (*einen Unsinn*)' (5.5422). The mistake, says Wittgenstein, was to analyse 'A believes that p is the case', 'A thinks p', etc.', as claiming that a proposition p stands in some relation 'to an object, A' (*T*5.541C-D).[32] Properly analysed, 'A judges p' and the rest turn out to be . . . of the form ' "p" says p' (5.542). In 'A judges p', 'A' appears to be a name which refers to a judging subject. But the only names the Tractarian analysis of a proposition can include refer to Tractarian objects, and Wittgenstein believes that judging subjects are not objects (*T*5.5421). Thus neither 'A' nor anything else which purports to name a judging subject can occur in the analysis of 'A judges p'. More surprisingly Wittgenstein's analysis does not mention judgement either. If ' "p" says p' is the proper analysis of 'A judges p' then the situation Russell analysed as including a judging subject, the judging, and a Russellian proposition consisting of objects arranged by the judging reduces to a situation consisting just of a picture, sentence, or proposition, 'p', and its expression of its sense. 'p' says that it is the case that p because its elements are 'correlated with' the elements of the putative fact that p (*T*5.5421). Thus, where Russell purged his ontology of Meinongian Objectives and Fregean senses by reducing the content of a prop-ositional attitude to a collection of objects assembled by judging, Witt-genstein reduced judging (believing, and all other sorts of thinking) to a proposition's (picture's, or sentence's) expression of a sense.[33] Instead of analysing someone's judgement that ab as a relation between a judging subject (mind, soul, etc.) and objects a and b, Wittgenstein analyses the judgement as consisting essentially of a Tractarian picture (proposition or sentence) which depicts a and b as concatenated.[34] This reduction of judgement to the expression of a sense transforms the problem of explaining why there can be no nonsense judgements into the problem of explaining why propositions cannot assert nonsense on the order of 'the table penholders the book'.[35] Because Tractarian names can only combine to form elementary propositions which picture possible concatenations of their referents (*T*2.16–2.17, 2.18–2.203)[36] elementary propositions cannot lack senses. Since all non-elementary propositions are truth functions of elementary propositions, no propo-sition can be nonsensical. If judgement can be analysed as the *Tractatus* proposes, this rules out the possibility of nonsense judgements.

❧ VII UNASSERTED PROPOSITIONS ❧

The question of how there can be false propositions has a counterpart in the question of how there can be judgements about and logical relations between propositions which are not themselves judged. How can I believe that (p) Theophrastus wrote the book we know as Aristotle's *Politics* only if (q) Theophrastus held inexcusably stupid political views, even though I disbelieve p and have no opinion about q? How can it be the case that every conjunction entails its conjuncts regardless of whether anyone ever has or will ever even grasp the sense of a given conjunction, its conjuncts or the claim that the one entails the others?

Frege's theory allows for all of this by treating the sense of a proposition as a structure whose composition does not require judgement. Thus I do not have to believe that Theophrastus wrote the *Politics* in order for the sense of p to be such that p is true only if he did. The same holds for q. I happen to believe the hypothetical but my doing so is not what gives it the truth conditions it has. And if logical relations depend upon senses whose existence and structure are quite independent of judgement, no judgement is required for the entailment of p by p&q.[37]

Hypotheticals and entailments raise problems for non-Fregean accounts which provide no contents to judge apart from someone's judging them. One such account is Kant's theory that the antecedents and consequents of hypothetical judgement are themselves judgements, rather than pre-existing contents.[38] Because the contents of Russell's judgements are creatures of the judging mind, it is astonishing to find the multiple-relation theory of judgement in *Principia Mathematica* whose very programme assumes that logical relations are not psychological and that their explanation requires no reference to the judging mind.[39]

By reducing judgements to the expressions by propositions of their senses, the *Tractatus* turns our questions about hypotheticals and logical connections into questions about unasserted propositions. For example, the question of how I can believe a conditional without believing its antecedent and its consequent becomes a question about how a conditional proposition can fail to assert its antecedent and its consequent. Since Wittgenstein holds that '... propositions occur in other propositions only as bases of truth operations' ($T5.54$) – i.e. as members of jointly denied collections of propositions ($T5.21$) – he need not worry, e.g., about how propositions p and q can occur unasserted in p⊃q; his answer is that they do not. But the construction of any proposition requires the joint negation of the elementary propositions. Therefore just as Kant needs to explain how we can judge that a hypothetical is true without judging the truth of its component judgements, Wittgenstein must interpret an expression like 'N(p,q, . . .) as including p and q without including the assertion that it is the case that p (or that q).

Tractarian operations take us from propositions to propositions (T5.21–5.23). Even though we can express a negative proposition without using the sign for the proposition it denies, the negative proposition must still be constructed 'indirectly' from the positive proposition (T5.5151). Thus, in order to say that state of affairs ab does not obtain, we must use the *proposition* 'ab' (in joint negation, I suppose) not just the sentence (sign) customarily used to say that ab obtains. But elementary propositions do not just show states of affairs; they also say that they obtain (T4.022, 4.023E, 4.06). The *Tractatus* does not address the question of how to use the proposition 'ab' to construct '¬ab' without asserting what we wanted to deny – that ab is the case.

Since we can write down a sentence without asserting anything, things would be easier if Wittgenstein had treated joint denial as taking us from sentences to sentences instead of propositions to propositions. But he does not, and it is not clear how he could have. The joint denial of p and q has no definite truth conditions unless p and q each have definite truth conditions (T5.2314). For Frege, propositions were sentences which could have truth conditions without benefit of assertion just by virtue of their assignment to Fregean thoughts. But Wittgenstein rejected Frege's account of the senses of propositions and treated sentences as having senses only as used to assert.[40] It seems to follow that if the 'p' and the 'q' in 'N(p, q)' are sentences, then 'N(p, q)' has no definite truth conditions unless 'p' and 'q' are used to assert something. It would be nice if a sentence could have the obtaining of ab as its truth condition just in virtue of its employment in the construction of the proposition which says that ab does not obtain. But the *Tractatus* does not set out a mechanism for this.

In the 1913 theory of knowledge manuscript which Wittgenstein criticized, Russell himself said the 'chief demerit' of his theory of judgement was that it could not explain logical relations among unjudged propositions.[41] But Wittgenstein's objections centred on the problem of nonsense judgements. I find no record of objections based on the question of logical relations between unjudged propositions. This is surprising, for Wittgenstein certainly knew the relevant parts of Frege's work. No less surprisingly, the *Tractatus* does not indicate how to avoid the analogous problem of how logical relations can obtain between unasserted propositions.

VIII LOGIC, PROBABILITY, AND THE CONSTRUCTION THESIS

In spite of this difficulty, the construction thesis provided an interesting and influential treatment of logical and probabilistic relations between propositions. By the construction thesis, the truth value of every proposition is determined by the truth values of elementary propositions, and elementary propositions are truth functions of themselves ($T5$). Wittgenstein calls each combination of truth values of elementary propositions sufficient for the truth of a proposition a truth ground of that proposition ($T5.1241$C, 5.01). Thus, for elementary propositions p, q, r_1, r_2, ... r_n, the truth grounds of p&q are ⟨true p, true q, true r_1⟩, ⟨true p, true q, false r_1⟩, ⟨true p, true q, true r_2⟩, ⟨true p, true q, false r_2⟩, and so on for every r_i. Since the truth values of the rs are irrelevant to the truth value of the conjunction we can write '⟨true p, true q⟩' as an abbreviation for the full list of its truth grounds. The truth grounds of p⊃q are ⟨true q, true p⟩, ⟨true q, false p⟩ and ⟨false q and false p⟩. And so on.

Wittgenstein explains deductive inference as resting on nothing more than relations between truth grounds ($T5.12$). For example, since the truth ground of p&q, includes ⟨true p⟩, p is true in every possible world in which p&q is true. This explains why p&q entails p, and accounts for the validity of the argument: p&q; therefore p. On the other hand, because p is made true by ⟨true p, false q⟩ as well as by ⟨true p, true q⟩, p&q is false in some worlds in which p is true. That is why p does not entail p&q and we cannot infer the latter from the former. ¬p entails p⊃q because both its truth grounds (⟨false p, true q⟩ and ⟨false p, false q⟩) are truth grounds of p⊃q. One proposition contradicts another just in case their truth grounds exclude one another.

Russell called this, 'an amazing simplification of the theory of inference, as well as a definition of the sort of propositions that belong to logic'. ([4.33], xvi). The simplification consists of the fact that if Wittgenstein is right there is no need for laws of logic as traditionally conceived. Russell's idea that '(p or p) implies p' is analogous to such '... particular enunciations in Euclid' as '... let ABC be an Isosceles triangle; then the angles at the base will be equal' is an example of the traditional view.[42] According to this the inference of the disjunction 'John Carter played the clarinet' from the disjunction 'John Carter played the clarinet or John Carter played the clarinet' is justified by its falling under the law '(pvp)⊢p' in the same way that the claim that the angles at the base of a particular isosceles triangle are equal is justified by its being an instance of the Euclidean principle. Without such maximally general truths (axioms and their consequences) it would be impossible to explain entailment or inference. But if Wittgenstein is right and logical relations are nothing more than relations between truth grounds, what justifies the inference of one proposition from another is the propositions themselves and ' "laws of inference" ... supposed to justify inference ... [by] ... Frege and Russell ... [are] ... superfluous' ($T5.132$). The connections between truth grounds which constitute logical relationships between propositions can be established and exhibited by constructing them from the elementary propositions. And this would suffice to establish whether one entails or contradicts the other. And given a logically perspicuous notation, propositions could be written down in a form which clearly exhibits relations between their truth grounds ($T5.1311$). Finally, the propositions (like '(pvp)⊣ p' and *modus ponens*) which Russell called laws of logic turn out on Wittgenstein's view to be nothing more than tautologies ($T6.113$ff.) whose truth can therefore be fully explained by construction.

Wittgenstein applies the same strategy to the explanation of probabilistic relations between propositions.

> If T_r is the number of the truth grounds of a proposition 'r', and if T_{rs} is the number of the truth grounds of a proposition 's' that are at the same time truth grounds of 'r', then ... the ratio T_{rs}: T_r is the degree of *probability* that the proposition 'r' gives to the proposition 's' ($T5.15$).

For example, by rows 1,2,5 in Figure 4.3, three of the four truth grounds of r are also truth grounds of (pvq) ⊃ (p&q), and its probability given r is ¾. By rows 1, 3, (p&q) is probabilistically independent of r: (p&q) shares half of the truth grounds of r. The fact that the probability of q given p is 1 if p entails q, and 0 if p contradicts q is similarly explained, as is the fact that conditional on any consistent proposition, the probability of a tautology is 1 and the probability of a contradiction, 0 (cp. $T5.152$ C, D).[43]

Elementary propositions are probabilistically independent because the truth value of each one depends on the obtaining of a different state of affairs. 'States of affairs are independent of one another'; the obtaining or non-obtaining of any given state of affairs has no influence whatever on the obtaining or non-obtaining of any other ($T2.061$, 2.062). If r and s are elementary propositions, their respective truth grounds will be {⟨true r, true s⟩, ⟨true r, false s⟩} and {⟨true s, true r⟩, ⟨true s, false r⟩} (ignoring irrelevant propositions). r and s share just one truth ground so $T_{rs} = 1$. Since r has two truth grounds, $T_r = 2$, and the probability of r conditional on $s = T_{rs}/T_r = ½$ ($T5.252$).

This makes all probability conditional and construes conditional probability as a logical relation determined by the truth grounds of the relevant propositions. Since truth grounds are completely determined by meanings, Wittgenstein's account makes probability assignments a priori and analytic. Tractarian probability is objective as well. The probability you assign to a proposition will depend upon what you take the relevant truth grounds to be. But there is an objective fact of the matter as to what the relevant truth grounds actually are, and that makes real probabilities objective and independent of subjectively influenced assignments.[44]

This sort of approach dates back to Jacques Bournoulli (1713) and Laplace (1812). It was revived by Keynes in 1921. As discussed by the Vienna Circle from 1927 on, and modified by Waisman, Wittgenstein's version gained its influence by attracting Carnap's interest.[45] Its importance turns in part on Wittgenstein's second thoughts about the independence of elementary propositions. By 1929 his thinking about 'the logical analysis of actual phenomena' persuaded him that in order to explain, e.g., why the same colour cannot have different hues or degrees of brightness at the same time, he must suppose that numbers can occur in elementary propositions.[46] This would make some elementary propositions mutually incompatible. But if one elementary proposition can confer a probability of 0 on another, it is natural to ask whether elementary propositions can entail one another,[47] and more to the point, to consider the possibility of conditional probabilities among elementary propositions ranging all the way from 0 to 1. These possibilities became essential to Carnap's thought, and thus to the development of the logical treatment of probability in this century.

Despite a number of attractive features (including its conformity to standard conditions on a probability calculus)[48] the *Tractatus* story has two remarkable drawbacks. First, it is silent about what empirically observed frequencies could have to do with probability estimates. This renders it incapable of application to statistical reasoning from sample populations and to learning from experience. Second, if probabilistic relations between natural language propositions (including those of the sciences) depend upon relations between their truth grounds, the assignment of probabilities to them is impossible unless they can be analyzed to determine which elementary propositions and states of affairs are involved in their truth conditions. As will be seen below, the *Tractatus* discussion of objects and names, states of affairs and elementary propositions does not indicate what such an analysis would involve, how, or even whether it could be accomplished.[49]

❧❧ XI TRACTARIAN PHILOSOPHY OF ❧❧ SCIENCE

If states of affairs are mutually independent there are no causal connections (deterministic or stochastic) between them (T5.135–5.1361, 6.37).

If elementary propositions are mutually independent, they cannot influence each other's probabilities any more than they can entail or logically exclude one another. Thus, the *Tractatus* is no place to be a realist concerning laws of nature.

But although states of affairs are independent of one another, complex situations – patterns of obtainings and non-obtainings of states of affairs – are not. If they were, non-elementary propositions would be as logically and probabilistically irrelevant to one another as elementary propositions. By allowing non-trivial, logical and probabilistic connections between truth functions, Wittgenstein leaves open the possibility, e.g., that universal gravitation might be a law of nature which embodies probabilistic and logical connections between non-elementary propositions and objective dependencies among complex situations.

Instead of denying this possibility, Wittgenstein says the belief that 'the so-called laws of nature' explain natural phenomena is an illusion (*Täuschung*) (*T*6.371). This is because he thinks 'the so called laws of nature' (a mixed lot including 'laws of conservation' (*T*6.33), the 'law of least action' (*T*6.3211), 'the principle of sufficient reason' and 'laws of continuity in nature' (*T*6.34), as well as the laws of Newtonian mechanics (*T*6.341A, 6.342B) and other such theories) are creatures of convention. Here is why.

If states of affairs are mutually independent, scientifically interesting deterministic and stochastic dependencies can hold only between complex situations. But complex situations are collections assembled by linguistic practice from a fixed stock of possibilities for obtainings and non-obtainings of individual states of affairs. In the absence of natural connections between the obtainings and non-obtainings of any states of affairs, the only connection the *Tractatus* allows, e.g., between ab and cd, would be constituted by linguistic conventions. Different natural and artificial languages need not allow for the expression of all or of the same truth functions of elementary propositions. Thus, one language might enable its speakers to say things whose truth values depend on the joint obtaining of ab and cd while another language does not. Wittgenstein thinks of scientific theories as embodying conventions for describing the world. These conventions determine how states of affairs will be collected and thus what complex situations the science will treat. Thus Newtonian 'mechanics determines one form of description of the world by saying that all propositions used in . . . [its] description must be obtained in a given way from . . . the axioms of mechanics' (*T*6.341A). Wittgenstein illustrates this by analogy to a procedure for describing a surface covered with an irregular pattern of black spots by laying a square-meshed net over it and saying for each square whether it is black or white. The coarseness of the net will influence the accuracy of the descriptions, but in different ways for differently shaped meshes. But even so we can allow for this by adjusting the degree of coarseness to the shape of the mesh, and equally accurate descriptions can be obtained through the use of at least some different nets. Thus, even if some meshes would not permit accurate enough descriptions for our purposes, the pattern of spots does not uniquely favour any one net. By analogy the world is nothing more than the obtainings and non-obtainings of situations which do not uniquely favour the descriptive conventions of any particular scientific language. The laws of Newtonian mechanics do not explain the obtainings or non-obtainings of any of the states of affairs of which any world is composed. Instead, they constrain their organization into complex situations by requiring, e.g., that we describe motions in terms of mass, force and acceleration – all of which involve convention-driven groupings of naturally independent states of affairs.

So much for Newtonian laws of motion. Laws like the principle of sufficient reason do not explain anything either; they are higher-level constraints on description (T6.35B).[50] We can learn something about the world from the fact that it 'can be described more simply with one system of mechanics than with another' and by 'the precise *way* in which it is possible to describe it' by Newtonian mechanics (T6.342B).[51] That is because obtainings and non-obtainings of states of affairs which do not depend upon linguistic conventions constrain the scientist's ability to construct and use theories and the results their use can bring. But all the same 'the possibility of describing the world by means of Newtonian mechanics tells us nothing about the world' (T6.342B). The possibility of describing the spotted surface did not require the shapes or spatial arrangements of the spots to resemble the shapes or arrangements of the mesh of the net chosen to describe them. By analogy, if states of affairs are mutually independent and if theory and theory choice are conventional as Wittgenstein thinks they are, the possibility of Newtonian descriptions does not require states of affairs to fit any more naturally into Newtonian groupings than into complex situations resulting from the groupings of any other theory.

The idea that regimenting and organizing descriptions of phenomena is the real function of the explanatory principles of physics is a venerable one held by philosophers who understood and respected the sciences no less than Duhem did. But motivated as it was by Wittgenstein's conventionalism and his views on mysticism (see Section XII below), Tractarian philosophy of science contains the seeds of what became an increasingly unsympathetic attitude towards the natural and behavioural sciences. The 'whole modern conception of the world', said Wittgenstein, 'is founded on the illusion ... that the so-called laws of nature' and by extension, the sciences which invoke them 'explain natural phenomena' (T6.371–6.372). People who hold this conception treat the laws of nature 'as something inviolable, just as God and Fate were treated in past ages'. Wittgenstein preferred the 'view of the ancients' for its acknowledgement of the inexplicability of God and Fate over 'the modern system ... [which] tries to make it look as if *everything* were explained' (T6.372). Time brought no rosiness to Wittgenstein's opinion of 'the modern system'. According to the later works, science is grounded just as much in 'forms of life' and social practices as any other activity involving language use. And it is no better justified by such grounding. This picture, along with Wittgenstein's distaste for the arrogance he attributed to science descends directly from the philosophy of the *Tractatus*.[52]

❧ X TROUBLES WITH OBJECTS ❧

Unlike the two-dimensional objects in my simplification (see Section II above), the objects Tractarian names refer to are 'simple' and 'indivisible' (T2.02), unalterable and unchanging, and eternal (T2.022, 2.024–2.0271). Sense data, ideas, sensations, direct experiences and other such mental items posited by psychologists and philosophers lack these virtues. According to the theories which appeal to them they are all evanescent, most of them are complex, and some are changeable. This marks a crucial difference between the *Tractatus* and a good deal of the empiricist philosophy commonly associated with it. G. E. Moore, Bertrand Russell, members of the Vienna Circle and others Wittgenstein encountered both before and after the *Tractatus*, held that the analysis of ordinary and scientific language terminates in perceivable objects which belong to the foundations of empirical knowledge. For Russell these were sense data. He believed that only statements whose fully analyzed versions mention sense data can be empirically tested. And he believed we could not understand our own utterances unless they made reference to such objects of direct acquaintance. In contrast to all of this and to Wittgenstein's later work as well, the *Tractatus* is not greatly concerned with epistemology.[53] Tractarian objects belong to an ontological theory about the ultimate composition of the world rather than an epistemological theory about our knowledge of it. Tractarian objects are the ultimate components of the facts we form beliefs about rather than the evidence we use to justify empirical beliefs. And even though they are the ultimate objects of reference according to Tractarian semantics, the *Tractatus* does little or nothing in the way of appealing to objects to explain how languages are actually learned and utterances understood.[54] Wittgenstein's later remark concerning Socrates' dream of analysing complexes into simple components that '[e]xperience certainly does not show us these elements' is quite faithful to the objects of the

Tractatus, and was probably meant to apply to them [4.47], 59; [4.25], 202 A–C).

Things were not always so. Wittgenstein's pre-*Tractatus*, notebooks sometimes suggest that 'patches in our visual field' might be the referents of genuine names.[55] Wittgenstein's conversations with Schlick and Waisman, after his return to Vienna clearly suggest an epistemological development of Tractarian ideas. Around 1930 Waismann wrote 'Theses', an epistemologically oriented adaptation of the *Tractatus* which appears to have had Wittgenstein's (temporary) blessing.[56] But the notebooks also consider the possibility of objects as non-Russellian as watches and mass points.[57] The *Tractatus* is remarkable for its lack of any such suggestions. In spite of Wittgenstein's willingness to speculate elsewhere about what objects might be, the *Tractatus* leaves this as an exercise to the student. It is plausible that this is because Wittgenstein had hit upon an approach to semantics which required objects without providing any guide whatever to what they might be.[58] It is also plausible that the *Tractatus* is not driven by interests which required Wittgenstein to continue his pre-Tractarian speculations about what the objects are (see Section XII below).

Because states of affairs are just concatenations of objects, we cannot know what the states of affairs are unless we know what the objects are. But if we do not know what objects there are, we cannot know the meanings of simple names. But then we cannot understand elementary propositions either, for an elementary proposition is an arrangement of names whose sense is a function of their meanings. Furthermore, although the *Tractatus* speaks of knowing 'on purely logical grounds' that there must be elementary propositions ($T5.5562$), it says it is impossible to determine a priori what the elementary propositions are ($T5.5571$) or what their forms might be (i.e. how many different names they can contain, and in what arrangements) ($T5.5541$–5.555). Instead, ' ... the application of logic decides what elementary propositions there are' ($T5.557$). I suppose this means the only way to discover the elementary propositions would be to try analysing non-elementary propositions (cp. $T4.221$A). You might start with a list of arbitrarily chosen candidates for elementary propositions and try to express the truth conditions, for example, of colour claims, by joint negation, modifying the original list of putative elementary propositions as needed to obtain the required results. If that worked you could repeat the process, adjusting the list as needed to construct other propositions, and so on.

Be that as it may, no such project is undertaken in the *Tractatus*, and the *Tractatus* does not provide the materials for any of the reductions or analyses the construction thesis might lead us to expect (including, e.g., the application of its treatment of logic and probability to natural language claims (see Section IX above)).

A survey of the kinds of features Tractarian objects are supposed to have raises questions about whether one object (hence one state of affairs) can be discriminated from another. If they cannot be discriminated, it is hard to be optimistic about the prospects for undertaking the constructions the *Tractatus* neglects. The features of Tractarian objects are of three kinds.

1 Each object has trans-world, 'internal features' constituted by its ability to concatenate with one or more other objects (and its inability to concatenate with still others). Thus, the internal features of objects determine which states of affairs they can belong to (*T*2.0123B). The natures of all of the objects taken together determine what worlds are possible; possible worlds differ from one another just in virtue of the concatenations of objects they contain and fail to contain. Although configurations of objects change from world to world, the internal features of an object remain constant over all possible worlds including even worlds in which no situation to which it can belong obtains.

2 Wittgenstein mentions 'external' properties (*T*2.01231, 2.9233, 4.023). He doesn't say much about what they are, but we can guess. Since an object's internal properties are features it has in all worlds (*T*4.123), its external features should be properties it has in the actual world but lacks in some other worlds. What would these be? Because no elementary proposition is true in every world, no concatenation to which an object can belong obtains in all worlds. Thus the external features of an object should consist of its belonging to whatever concatenations it actually belongs to along with the non-obtaining of other states of affairs to which it can belong. Perhaps there are other sorts of external features, but Wittgenstein does not mention them.[59]

3 The *Tractatus* needs to ascribe features of another sort to objects in order to allow for colours and other properties which Wittgenstein calls 'material' (*T*2.0231). Since it is impossible for 'two colors to occupy the same place in the visual field' or for a particle to have two different velocities or spatial positions at the same time (*T*6.3571) being red and being blue (being here and being there, having this velocity and that velocity) exclude one another and therefore cannot *all* be states of affairs. It is plausible that according to the *Tractatus* none of them are. Colour, velocity and position are material properties and it is 'only by the configuration of objects that ... [material properties] ... are constructed (*gebildet*')' (*T*2.0231). Thus, the fact that my Dodger cap is Dodger blue should reduce to complex situ-

ations made possible by the natures (concatenation abilities) of the objects they involve. The natures of the relevant objects must also rule out complex situations which would give my cap different colours (or give its colour different degrees of brightness) all over at the same time. This is an example of how 'empirical reality is limited by the totality of objects' (T5.5561A). I will call the features of objects which make possible and constrain the material properties of familiar things 'material capacities'.[60] These are, or should reduce to internal features of objects.

In the next section, I suggest that objects with no features but these cannot be discriminated one from another as required to understand their names.[61] If so, it will be impossible to interpret sentences used to picture states of affairs or complex situations. Because states of affairs are simply concatenations of objects, it will also be impossible (for theoreticians as well as speakers) to discriminate between states of affairs which constitute the truth grounds of different propositions. The meaning of a Tractarian name is exhausted by its reference to an object (T3.203) and elementary propositions are nothing more than names arranged to picture states of affairs which are nothing more than arrangements of the bearers of the names. Thus, it looks as though we will not be able to determine the truth conditions of elementary propositions. That makes it hard to see how we could construct (or interpret constructions of) their non-tautologous, logically consistent truth functions – including the truth functions expressed in technical and everyday natural languages. Over and above the fact that no construction is actually undertaken in the *Tractatus*, this makes it look as though the construction of any informal or technical natural language proposition would require considerable adjustments in its theory of objects.

❧ XI TRACTARIAN ANTI-DISCRIMINATION ❧

A first thing to say about this is that while Tractarian objects neither are nor possess material properties, these are the only features which our senses and instruments of observation and measurement are capable of registering or recording (at least in any form that we can recognize). Thus, there is no reason to think that our senses or our equipment can observe perceive, photograph or otherwise register or record any particular object or its features. If we have any empirical access to objects, it must be by way of the analysis of whatever states of affairs or situations we (and our equipment) can observe and record.[62]

The next thing to notice is that objects cannot be discriminated unless they have different features ($T2.02331$) and all features of objects are external or internal (including material capacities). But even if we could pick out an object by way of its external features, they would not suffice for its re-identification. Setting aside the fact that our senses and our equipment are not attuned to objects suppose we could somehow examine single states of affairs and give the name 'a' to the object we find presently concatenated with another object, to which we give the name 'b'. This gives us one external feature of a and b – the fact that they are concatenated. But that will not enable us to recognize a in any other state of affairs. And even if it did, we would not be able to tell whether or not any other object concatenated with a in any other state of affairs (in this or any other world) is the object we originally called b. (Since we do not know any internal properties we have no reason to think a and b cannot belong to other states of affairs, and no idea of which ones they can belong to.) The fact that b was concatenated with a will not allow us to discriminate b from any other object concatenated with a in any other state of affairs. Thus, Wittgenstein seems to be quite right to say we cannot know an object unless we know its internal properties ($T2.01231$).

How could we detect the internal features of an object? If a and b are concatenated we know that they can concatenate with one another; that's one internal feature. But to find out what other internal features they have, we must find out what other objects they can or cannot concatenate with. Suppose we knew somehow that ac does not obtain, where c is yet another object. ac might fail to obtain because the concatenation is impossible. (That would be an internal feature of a and c.) But its non-obtaining could be just a contingent fact (external feature). To decide between these possibilities, we would have to find out whether ac obtains in any non-actual world. But there is no way to find that out unless the objects have marks which enable us to identify them across worlds. External features are limited to properties objects have in the actual world, and so they cannot serve this purpose. Internal features (including material capacities) would do the job, but they cannot be detected without marks by which objects can be identified across worlds. If we cannot detect the internal features which distinguish a from b, we will not be able to discriminate state of affairs ab from ba, or bc, where c is any other object you please.

If (as seems impossible) we had some way to assign names (i.e. signs to be used as names) to objects belonging to actual facts, we might try to avoid trans-world identity questions by stipulation. For example, in thinking about how the object concatenated with b in this world might be situated in other possible worlds, we would give it a name and stipulate its inclusion (under the same name) in the relevant alternative worlds. On this approach possible worlds are constructed by the theoretician, and their contents are *'stipulated,* not *discovered* by powerful telescopes'.[63] But because states of affairs are completely independent, there are any number of possibilities for different systems of stipulations. We could not discriminate between different objects called by the same name and states of affairs portrayed by the same sentence under different stipulations. But Wittgenstein was a realist about objects; according to the ontology of the *Tractatus* our inability to detect their differences would not make the differences any less real. The *Tractatus* considers no such possibility, let alone how such stipulations might be constrained.

If the identities of objects rest on stipulation, so do the senses of elementary propositions. Different stipulations will allow the same propositions to be analysed as truth functions of different elementary propositions. Under different stipulations material properties will reduce to deployments of different objects. This need not sound so bad from the standpoint of model semantic techniques which do not require discriminations to be made among all of what the *Tractatus* would count as different collections of possible worlds. But this is not Wittgenstein's point of view; the relevant semantic techniques were developed after the *Tractatus*.

It need not sound so bad from the standpoint of programmes of reduction and construction developed by the logical positivists. These programmes allow the theoretician's purposes to dictate the choice of items to be treated as objects. For example, although Carnap's epistemological concerns led him to choose 'experiences' as the basic elements of the *Aufbau*, he thought that given other interests, 'physicalistic' items could have been treated as basic.[64] Wittgenstein rejected this approach, at least in so far as the choice of basic elements involves stipulations or assumptions concerning the forms of elementary propositions. In 1931 he said it had always been clear to him that 'we cannot assume from the very beginning, as Carnap, does, that the elementary propositions consist of two-place relations, etc'.[65]

It is ironic that such construction programmes are still commonly associated with the *Tractatus*. It is historically important that their treatment of objects, states of affairs, and the interpretation of names and elementary propositions is profoundly non-Tractarian.

❧ XII THE MEANING OF LIFE, THE ❧ UNIVERSE, AND EVERYTHING

If Wittgenstein did not mind the incompleteness of the *Tractatus* treatment of topics so many readers believed it taught them about, what did he want his book to accomplish? Its preface (echoed by its closing line) says what the *Tractatus* shows is that the posing of philosophical problems:

> rests on the misunderstanding of the logic of our language. One could capture (*fassen*) the whole sense of the book in something like the words: What can be said at all can be said clearly; and that whereof one cannot speak, thereof one must be silent.
>
> ([4.45], 3; cp. p. 7)

This applies, for example, to 'mystical' questions about why there is a world (*T*6.44), the nature and concerns of God (*T*6.432) and the source of ethical and aesthetic value. (*T*6.41–6.421) It applies to questions about the meaning of life (*T*6.52) and why we should do what is good rather than what is wrong (*T*6.422). It applies to questions raised by philosophical skepticisms (*T*6.51), solipsisms and realisms (*T*5.62–5.641). Propositions can represent everything which can be the case (*T*3, 4.12A). But philosophical problems are not questions about what is the case (*T*6.52, 6.4321, 4.1, 4.11). For the *Tractatus*, philosophy properly understood is an activity aimed at resolving problems by the clarification of thoughts, rather than a body of doctrine (*T*4.112ff.). The *Tractatus* and Wittgenstein's later works agree as much on this as they disagree about the nature of the activity.[66]

For the *Tractatus* a crucial part of the activity would involve setting out propositions in a logically perspicuous symbolism (*T*4.1213) which reveals the essential features of the relevant symbols which must be exhibited to clear away a philosophical problem. There are illustrations of this for the case of problems whose resolution does not require us to construct natural language propositions, use names for objects or grasp the truth conditions of elementary propositions. For example, the notation for joint negation resolves questions about what sorts of things such logical constants as '¬', '⊃', '&' represent by showing that the expression of truth functions does not require these signs to represent anything (*T*4.0312, 5.4). Similarly for any p and q, the connections between the truth grounds of q and (p & p⊃q) which explain why the latter entails the former can be exhibited without interpreting any elementary propositions. This allows Wittgenstein to dissolve questions generated by the assumption that *modus ponens* reports very general extra-linguistic facts – and similarly for other logical laws (see section VIII above).

Wittgenstein thinks the cure for these and all other philosophical problems (including the mystical ones) lies not in what propositions *say*, but rather, in what is *shown* by various uses of signs – including the use of logically perspicuous notations to say the same things as less perspicuous ones. The employment of signs shows what the signs fail to say (*T*3.262). While the employment of signs tells us (*spricht*) 'what the signs conceal' (T3.262) it does not literally say it: 'what *can* be shown *cannot* be said.' (T4.1212). It looks as though these ineffables are conveyed in a number of different ways. For example, although we cannot say of a proposition (symbol) that it has such and such a sense, the proposition shows us what its sense is by picturing it (T4.022). But presumably if the way Newtonian mechanics allows us to describe the world shows us something about world, it does not show us in the same way (T6.342) – or in the same way that a proposition displays its pictorial form (T2.172). All that these and other sorts of showings need and have in common is (a) that what is conveyed is not the obtaining and non-obtainings of states of affairs, and (b) that it is not conveyed in the same way that a proposition expresses its sense.

A particularly important kind of showing is required for the sentences of the *Tractatus* which Wittgenstein says 'clarify' (*erläutern*) the functioning of language even though they are 'nonsensical' (T6.54). This includes, e.g., the sentences which present the picture theory, the ontology and the method of construction by joint negation. It would include any locution offering any semantical or syntactical analysis. Wittgenstein's treatment of identity illustrates the difference between this and another sort of showing. 'Roughly speaking, to say of *two* things that they are identical is nonsense' (T5.5303). This does *not* mean such expressions as 'a = b', '$\forall x(fx \supset x = a)$' convey nothing. Instead, they convey what they convey by showing rather than saying it. But the employment of a notation with no identity sign can show the same thing in another way which 'also disposes of all the problems that were connected with such pseudo-propositions' (T5.535). A logically perspicuous notation would employ exactly one name for each object. The differences between the names would dispense with the need to write down anything like 'a = b' (T5.53). The number of different names would show the same thing a non-perspicuous notation would show (in a different way) by means of such nonsense expressions as 'there are (are not) infinitely many objects' (T5.535). And it would show us that identity is not a relation if it provided a way to analyse identity signs away from formulas which contain them.[67] This – as opposed to the showing done by some nonsense sentences – is the sort of showing illustrated by the use of joint negation to show that the logical constants do not represent and that the justification of an inference does not depend upon laws of logic (above). Wittgenstein appeals to these (and other sorts of showing) in hopes of avoiding the need for a hierarchy of languages, each one of which is described by expressions belonging to the next language up. Instead of constructing a metalanguage to *say*, e.g., that 'ab' is true just in case a is concatenated with b, Wittgenstein's idea was that this could be *shown* by nonsense sentences in the same language we use to say 'ab' or by features of that language.

In effect, Wittgenstein appeals to different ways of communicating (saying and showing) in place of metalanguages constructed to describe object languages.

But I do not think this is the only, or the most important, motivation for the doctrine of showing. Wittgenstein was deeply concerned with mystical issues including those the logical positivists called 'metaphysical' and hoped to eliminate by employing methods they believed the *Tractatus* contained. Carnap said Wittgenstein gave him the 'insight that many philosophical sentences, especially in traditional metaphysics are pseudosentences devoid of content'.[68] This sounds like something you could learn from the philosopher who wrote that because answers to *'all possible* scientific questions' would leave the 'problems of life ... completely untouched ... there are then no questions left, and this itself is the answer.' (*T*6.52).

But Wittgenstein wrote to an editor to whom he had submitted the *Tractatus* that its 'point is an ethical one'. It consists, he said:

> of two parts: the one presented here [i.e., the complete text of the *Tractatus*] plus all that I have *not* written. And it is precisely the second part that is the important one ... I believe that where *many* others today are just *blathering (schwefeln)* [about the sphere of the ethical] I have managed ... to put everything firmly into place by being silent about it.[69]

This suggests that when Wittgenstein spoke of the vanishing of mystical problems (*T*6.521) all he really meant was the vanishing of the blather about them. He says 'the sense of life' has become clear to people after long periods of doubt even though 'they have been unable to say what constituted that sense' (*T*6.521)[70] Far from denying the reality of what these people could not express, the next passage affirms it: 'there are, indeed things that cannot be put into words. They show themselves. They are the mystical' (*T*6.522).

In contrast to these, what we can say, namely: '... *[h]ow* things are in the world is a matter of complete indifference for what is higher' (*T*6.432).

Wittgenstein seems to have felt that what can be said is insignificant in comparison to what can be shown.[71] If this is so, what Wittgenstein's readers thought they learned was not what he hoped to teach. The *Tractatus* exerted its greatest influence through the works of empiricists who thought that what cannot be said is nothing at all. They believed that what is important can be discovered and expressed by the natural sciences. They believed the mystical concerns of the unwritten part of the *Tractatus* were delusions. They valued the *Tractatus* as a cache of weapons to combat them.[72]

❧ NOTES ❧

1 [4.45]. The original title was *Logisch-Philosophisce Abhandlung*. The title *Tractatus Logico-Philosophicus* was suggested by G. E. Moore. For a composition and publication history, see [4.48], 1–33, 255ff. For the history and circumstances of its composition, see [4.22] chs 7–8 and [4.23], chs 5–8.

2 Numbers in parentheses marked *T* are *Tractatus* section numbers.

3 Wittgenstein's usage differs from Russell's. For Russell, G. E. Moore's having recorded with Thelonius Monk is a negative fact. For Wittgenstein it is not a fact of any kind and the relevant negative fact is that Moore did not record with Thelonius.

4 I use 'world' for what [*T*2.06] calls 'reality'; Wittgenstein's worlds include only positive facts.

5 Wittgenstein wrote a version of the truth table in 1912 on the back of a paper Russell presented to the Cambridge moral sciences club [4.22], 160. Quine says truth tables were used to set out truth functions independently of the *Tractatus* in papers by Łukasiewicz, and Post in 1920–1, and that Peirce described a non-tabular version of essentially the same method in 1885 [4.26], 14.

6 For example since N (3) has the same truth conditions as (2), we had best pick another ξ once we have got (3). For a complete discussion for the case of two elementary propositions see [4.1], 133ff.

7 See [4.38], 480ff.

8 For details, see [4.1], 135ff.

9 [4.24], 297.

10 Cp. [4.1], 133–4.

11 [4.2], 312. We need the next steps because merely to select p as a value of ξ is not to construct it by joint denial.

12 [4.47], section 94.

13 For a discussion of this problem for the case of quantified propositions, see [4.19].

14 A model according to von Wright; a diagram according to Malcolm. [4.21], 8, 57.

15 Cp. [4.46], 7, 27.

16 Cp. [4.37], [4.38].

17 [4.47], Section 94.

18 [4.25], 321. Anachronistically speaking, to judge 'one thing' is to believe something definite enough to determine the truth conditions of the belief. Wittgenstein's quotation of some of this in connection with picturing at [4.47], section 518, makes it plausible (without proving) that he knew the passage when he wrote TS. For another version of the argument see [4.3], 6ff.

19 [4.28], 28–33, [4.30], 528–33, [4.35], 193ff.

20 [4.6], 144.

21 [4.31], ch. XII, [4.34], 43, [4.36], part II, chs i–iii.

22 [4.12], 56–78. For a concise statement of Frege's version of the problem, see [4.14], 117ff. See also [4.1].

23 [4.14, 127].

24 For example, if there is no such person as Odysseus, the name 'Odysseus' lacks

a reference and propositions like 'Odysseus was set ashore at Ithaca...' have sense but no reference [4.12, 63].

25 [4.12]. This ignores many important details, most notably Frege's treatment of indirect reference.

26 See [4.8], 197, 280–1.

27 The last sentence of 4.442 rejects (and mis-states) Frege's idea that to assert a proposition is to commit oneself to its naming the True. For other points of contact with Frege, see [4.2], 182–3.

28 [4.3], 104ff.

29 The constituents of Russell's propositions are not the constituents of Tractarian states of affairs. For example, (section X) Russellian objects are sense data, not Tractarian simples and Tractarian situations contain no relational constituents. For this and other differences between Russellian and Tractarian atomism see [4.4], ch. 1.

30 Russell depends upon the theory of descriptions to analyse judgements which seem to involve non-existing things. Thus my judgement that unicorns live outside of Boulder, Colorado, relates me not to non-existent unicorns – but to a collection of existing things at least one of which would be a unicorn *if* my judgement were true.

31 [4.22], 174. Wittgenstein's pressing of this point was not only decisive, but remarkably harsh. In 1916 Russell wrote to Ottoline Morrell that they 'affected everything I have done since. I saw he was right and I saw that I could not hope ever again to do fundamental work in philosophy. My impulse was shattered like a wave... against a breakwater'. [4.22], 174–7.

The following from a letter to Russell from Austria in 1913 is a good place to start trying to imagine what it might have been like to be personally involved with Wittgenstein.

> The weather here is constantly rotten, we have not yet had two fine days in succession. I am very sorry to hear that my objection to your theory of judgement paralyses you. I think it can only be removed by a correct theory of propositions.

([4.49], 24)

32 I assume Wittgenstein is using 'proposition' here for collections of objects to which Russell thought judging relates the mind of the judger. This would accord loosely with both Russell's and Moore's usage during this period.

33 [4.27], 13.

34 Cp. 3.11: If 'the method of projection' by which signs are used to picture possible situations is identical to 'the thinking of the sense of the proposition' and if the sense of the proposition is that such and such is the case, then judging, thinking, believing, etc. that such and such is the case should be reducible to the relevant uses of signs. A 1919 letter to Russell says that the elements of the thought are 'psychical constituents which have the same sort of relation to reality as words', [4.49], 72.

Wittgenstein's analysis has its problems. Wittgenstein does not say what 'p' has to do with the person who judges, thinks, etc., that p. Thus, if all claims of the form 'A believes p' are to be analysed as ' "p" says p', how is the analysis supposed to capture the difference between the claim that Thelonius believes p and the claim that Bud believes p? What sorts of signs are involved in judging? Ramsey thought (quite plausibly) that they should belong to some sort of mentalese, but Wittgenstein does not go into this. Presumably, we can say that Thelonius believes that p, and what we say is contingently true or false. But the *Tractatus* seems to treat such claims as that such and such proposition has such and such a sense as unspeakable, and what is unspeakable should not be contingently true or false.

35 See note 43.

36 This would be much easier to understand if it were a matter of syntactical constraints on signs than it is to understand in connection with Tractarian symbols.

37 See [4.41], 1–36 for an enlightening discussion of this and the importance of Frege's approach.

38 [4.17], 109.

39 [4.6], 145–6.

40 Cp. [4.45], Shwayder discusses this in detail, suggesting that part of Wittgenstein's point (at *T*3.5) in calling the applied propositional sign *der Gedanke* (which should be translated '*the* thought', rather than '*a* thought') and then saying that the thought is the meaningful proposition (4), was to show how he proposed to get along without the Fregean sense ('the thought') [4.38], vol II, 4–7).

41 [4.36], 115.

42 cp. [4.34], 93.

43 For example, the ratio of truth grounds common to p⊃q and p&¬q (there are none) to truth grounds of p&¬q is true is ⚬. Since tautologies are true in every world, their probability is 1, given any non-contradictory proposition. Wittgenstein does not tell us what to do about the fact that the probability of any proposition given a contradiction will be ⚬.

44 Or so it seems; see section XI.

45 Not only in *Tractatus*, but also in discussion from 1927 on, and as expanded and modified by Waismann in 1929 [4.5], 71ff.

46 [4.44], 33, 35.

47 Cp. [4.43], 93.

48 For example, by requiring every probability to equal 0, 1, or some number in between.

49 Cp. [4.2], 256.

50 It is important that Wittgenstein's conventionalism does not require him to think that developing, accepting or using a scientific theory requires anyone actually to find out what states of affairs there are and decide how to group them, or to inspect the elementary propositions and decide which sorts of truth functions to construct from them. The construction of truth functions and complex situations is something the scientist must accomplish in order to do his work. But just as people can speak without having any idea of which muscles must be made to contract in order for them to utter words, the scientist – like any other language user – can construct and employ languages to describe phenomena 'without having any idea of how each word has meaning or what its meaning is' (*T*4.002). This does not explicitly mention science but there is no reason to think it does not apply to scientific language.

51 I suppose 'the precise way' involves, e.g., how the Newtonian physicist must

think of time and space, what he must do, e.g., in choosing and employing a reference system to locate bodies in the space and describe their motions – as well as what must be done to calculate values of such quantities as Newtonian force, acceleration and mass from observational data, what kinds of computations are required for prediction, etc. See [4.2], 354–60.

52 See, for example, [4.50], 5–7, 10, 17, 27, 62, 63, and [4.23] ch. 23.

53 [4.1], 25–9.

54 4.062 is typical of what little he does say on such subjects: it contrasts propositions which we can understand without having their senses explained with 'the meanings of the simple signs (the words)' which cannot be understood without explanation. But he has just said that foreign language dictionaries help us translate propositions by translating 'substantives, . . . verbs, adjectives, and conjunctions, etc.', rather than whole propositions (4.025). Since these are not Tractarian names, it is not clear whether 4.062 is a remark about Tractarian names.

55 [4.46], 65

56 [4.42], Vienna Circle, pp. 233 ff. Among other things, this includes the 'verification theory', (one of the most important ideas attributed by the logical positivists to Wittgenstein) in the form of the claim that 'a proposition cannot say more than is established by its method of verification' and that 'to say that a statement has sense means that it can be verified' (p. 244). No such thing occurs in the *Tractatus*. But cp. 'On Dogmatism' (1931) in which Wittgenstein decides that writing the 'Theses' was not such a good idea after all [4.43], 182

57 [4.46], 60, 67

58 Ibid., 60, 62

59 Constituted for example, by the way states of affairs an object belongs to are collected into complex situations

60 This may explain why 'space, time, and color . . . are forms of objects' (2.0251). Even though Tractarian objects neither are nor have colours Wittgenstein may think that certain objects figure uniquely in states of affairs which determine colour possibilities, and have colour as their form in just this sense. Similarly, objects which figure uniquely in the construction of (physical) spatial facts could be said to have space as their form even though they are not themselves either physical spaces or spatial objects.

61 [4.16], ch 2 is an excellent (and as far as I know, the first) discussion of difficulties in the individuation of *Tractatus* objects.

62 Ibid., 15–19.

63 [4.20], 44.

64 [4.5], 18.

65 [4.43], 182 This passage also eschews 'hypotheses' (i.e. 'law[s] for constructing statements' (p. 255) concerning elementary propositions).

66 This may be one reason Wittgenstein wanted the *Tractatus* and the *Investigations* to be published together [4.47], x.

67 Wittgenstein's example of replacing (1) '$\forall x(Fx \supset x = a)$' with (2) '$(\exists x)(Fx) \supset Fa)$ & $\neg(\exists x,y)(Fx \& Fy)$' (5.5321) is troublesome unless he can rule out the substitution of 'a' for both variables to obtain '$Fa \supset Fa$ & $\neg(Fa \& Fa)$' as an instance of (2). For other issues involving the elimination of identity see [4.10], 60–9; [4.11], *passim*.

68 [4.5], 25.

69 Adapted from McGuiness' translation in [4.9], 143.

70 Wittgenstein's use of the word 'sense' is surely intended to make us contrast this sort of meaningfulness with the meanings of propositions.

71 [4.10], 90. [4.9] includes sympathetic and persuasive support for this reading.

72 My understanding and appreciation of Wittgenstein's early work has been greatly enhanced by conversation with and help from David Shwayder, Robert Fogelin, Jack Vickers, Jay Atlas, and David McCarty. I am also indebted to Howard Richner for spotting disasters in an earlier version of this chapter.

ᕁ BIBLIOGRAPHY ᕁ

4.1 Anscombe, G. E. M. *Introduction to the Tractatus*, Hutchinson, 1959.

4.2 Black, M. *A Companion to Wittgenstein's Tractatus*, Cornell University Press, 1964.

4.3 Bogen, J. *Wittgenstein's Philosophy of Language Some Aspects of its Development*, London, Routledge and Kegan Paul, 1972.

4.4 Bradley, R. *The Nature of all Being*, Oxford, Oxford University Press, 1992.

4.5 Carnap, R. 'Intellectual Autobiography' in P. A. Schilpp (ed.) *The Philosophy of Rudolf Carnap*, LaSalle, Open Court, 1963.

4.6 Coffa, J. A. *The Semantic Tradition from Kant to Carnap, To the Vienna Station*, Cambridge, Cambridge University Press, 1991.

4.7 Copi, I. M., Beard, R. W. (eds) *Essays on Wittgenstein's Tractatus*, London, Routledge & Kegan Paul, 1966.

4.8 Dummett, M. *Michael Dummett, Frege, Philosophy of Language*, London, Duckworth, 1973.

4.9 Engelmann, P. *Letters from Ludwig Wittgenstein with a Memoir*, trans. L. Furtmüller, Oxford, Blackwell, 1967.

4.10 Fogelin, R. J. *Wittgenstein*, London, Routledge and Kegan Paul, 1976.

4.11 —— 'Wittgenstein on Identity' *Synthese* 56 (1983): 141–54.

4.12 Frege, G. (1892) 'On Sense and Reference' in [4.15], 56–78.

4.13 —— 'The Thought: a Logical Inquiry' in [4.18], 507–36.

4.14 —— 'Negation' in [4.15], 117–36.

4.15 —— *Translations from the Philosophical Writings of Gottlob Frege*, ed. and trans. P. Geach, and M. Black, Oxford, Blackwell, 1970, pp. 56–78.

4.16 Goddard, L. and Judge, B. 'The Metaphysics of Wittgenstein's Tractatus', *Australasian Journal of Philosophy* Monograph No. 1, (June, 1982), ch. 2.

4.17 Kant, I. *Critique of Pure Reason*, trans. N. K. Smith, Macmillan, 1953.

4.18 Klemke, E. D. *Essays on Frege*, Urbana, University of Illinois Press, 1968.

4.19 Kremer, M. 'The Multiplicity of General Propositions' in *Nous* xxvi(4) (1991): 409–26.

4.20 Kripke, S. *Naming and Necessity*, Cambridge, Mass., Harvard University Press, 1980.

4.21 Malcolm, N. *Ludwig Wittgenstein, a Memoir*, Oxford University Press, 1984.

4.22 McGuinness, B. F. *Wittgenstein, a Life, Young Ludwig, 1889–1921*, Berkeley, University of California Press, 1988.

4.23 Monk, R. *Ludwig Wittgenstein The Duty of Genius*, New York, Free Press, 1990.

4.24 Moore, G. E. 'Wittgenstein's Lectures in 1930–33' in Moore, G. E., *Philosophical Papers*, New York and London, George Allen and Unwin, 1970.

4.25 Plato *Theaetetus* trans. M. L. Levett, in M. Burnyeat, *The Theaetetus of Plato*, Indianapolis, Hacket, 1990.

4.26 Quine, W. V. O. *Mathematical Logic*, Cambridge, Harvard University Press, 1979.

4.27 Ramsey, F. P. '*Review of Tractatus*' in [4.7], 9–24.

4.28 Russell, B. (1904) 'Meinong's Theory of Complexes and Assumptions' in [4.35], 21–76.

4.29 —— (1905) 'Review of: A Meinong', *Untersuchungen zur Gegenstandstheorie und Psychologie* in [4.35].

4.30 —— 'The Nature of Truth', *Mind* 15 (1906): 528–33.

4.31 —— *The Problems of Philosophy*, London, Williams and Norgate, 1924.

4.32 —— *Human Knowledge, its Scope and Limits*, New York, Simon and Schuster, 1948.

4.33 —— 'Introduction', in [4.45].

4.34 —— *Principia Mathematica to *56*, with A. N., Whitehead, Cambridge, Cambridge University Press, 1962.

4.35 —— *Essays in Analysis*, in D. Lackey, (ed.) New York, George Braziller, 1973.

4.36 —— *Theory of Knowledge*, in E. R. Eames and K. Blackwell (eds), London, Routledge, 1992.

4.37 Schwyzer, H. R. G. 'Wittgenstein's Picture Theory of Language' (1962) in [4.7].

4.38 Shwayder, D. *Wittgenstein's Tractatus vols I and II*, unpublished doctoral dissertation on deposit, Bodleian Library, Oxford, 1954.

4.39 —— 'Gegenstände and Other Matters: Observations occasioned by a new Commentary on the Tractatus', *Inquiry* 7, (1964): 387–413.

4.40 —— 'On the Picture Theory of Language: Excerpts from a Review', in [4.7].

4.41 Vickers, J. *Chance and Structure An Essay on the Logical Foundations of Probability*, Oxford, Clarendon Press, 1988.

4.42 Waismann, F. 'Theses' in [4.43], 233–61.

4.43 —— *Wittgenstein and the Vienna Circle*, ed., B. McGuinness, trans. B. McGuinness, and J. Schulte, New York, Barnes and Noble, 1979.

4.44 Wittgenstein, L. 'Some Remarks on Logical Form', 1929, in [4.7].

4.45 —— *Tractatus Logico-Philosophicus*, London, Routledge & Kegan Paul, 1961.

4.46 —— *Notebooks 1914–1916*, ed., G. H. von Wright and G. E. M. Anscombe trans. G. E. M. Anscombe, New York, Harper, 1961.

4.47 —— *Philosophical Investigations*, 3rd edn, trans. G. E. M. Anscombe, New York, Macmillan, 1968.

4.48 —— *Prototractatus*, ed. B. F. McGuinness, T. Nyberg, G. H. von Wright, Ithaca, Cornell, 1971.

4.49 —— *Letters to Russell, Keynes, and Moore*, ed. G. H. von Wright, Ithaca, Cornell, 1974.

4.50 —— *Culture and Value*, ed. G. H. von Wright trans. P. Winch, Chicago, University of Chicago Press, 1984.

CHAPTER 5

Logical Positivism
Oswald Hanfling

⸎ I INTRODUCTION ⸎

'Logical positivism', writes a leading historian of twentieth-century philosophy, 'is dead, or as dead as a philosophical movement ever becomes' (Passmore [5.42]). Most philosophers today, and indeed for some time past, would endorse this statement. In one sense it is absolutely dead, for it lost its cohesive membership with the break-up of the group of philosophers known as the 'Vienna Circle', due to political pressures in the 1930s. It was here that the philosophy known as logical positivism had been initiated, developed and energetically propounded to the philosophical community throughout the world.

The 'death' of the movement was due, however, not only to the dispersal of its members, but also to a widespread recognition of the defects of its ideas. Now in this sense, probably most of the philosophy studied in our universities is dead, for most of it is open to more-or-less fatal criticisms; and criticism is regarded as one of the main approaches to the great philosophers and movements of the past. However, what hastened the widespread rejection of logical positivism was not merely the (unsurprising) discovery that its doctrines were open to criticism, but the aggressive and even arrogant way in which those doctrines were propounded to the world. Chief among these was the 'elimination of metaphysics'. It was claimed by members of the movement that they had noticed something about existing and traditional philosophy, which would completely overturn it and render it largely otiose. There appeared articles with such titles as 'The Elimination of Metaphysics through the Logical Analysis of Language' (Carnap [5.5]) and 'The Turning Point in Philosophy' (Schlick [5.24]). Carnap posed the question: 'Can it be that so many men, of various times and nations, outstanding minds among them, have devoted so much effort, and indeed fervour, to metaphysics, when this consists of nothing more than words strung together without sense?' International conferences were called with a view to disseminating the new 'insights', and a grandiose project, *The Encyclopedia of Unified Science*, was launched to give definitive expression to the new 'scientific' era in which philosophical and other discourse would become part of the discourse of science. In these circumstances it was not surprising that critics of the new ideas were more than usually prompt, forthright and thorough in their criticisms.

Nevertheless, logical positivism has an established place in the history and continuing development of philosophy. At least three reasons might be given for this. One is purely historical, regarding the considerable impact and influence of the movement in its heyday. A second lies in the intrinsic interest of its ideas, which I hope to bring out in what follows. A third lies in the fact that even if no one today would call himself a logical positivist, some of its main positions, such as verificationism, and emotivism in ethics, are still referred to as parameters within which discussions of particular topics, such as ethics or the philosophy of religion or of science, are to be conducted. Again, it can be argued that even if the parent plant is dead, many of its seeds are alive and active in one form or another. In an interview in 1979, A. J. Ayer, a leading philosopher of our time, who had been an advocate of logical positivism in the 1930s, was asked what he now saw as its main defects. He replied: 'I suppose the most important... was that nearly all of it was false'. Yet this did not prevent him from admitting, shortly afterwards that he still believed in 'the same general approach' ([5.70], 131-2).

In a number of ways 'the same general approach' is still widespread today, and indeed was so long before the advent of logical positivism. Empiricism, in one sense or another, is a major thread running through Western philosophy since the seventeenth century, including logical positivism and much of the philosophy of today. The same is true of 'reductionism', and especially the assumption that mental phenomena can be reduced, in some sense, to the vocabulary of the material or physical. Another idea, which was central to logical positivism and remains of central importance today, is that philosophical questions are largely questions of language, and that theories of meaning are therefore of central importance.

The movement originated in the 1920s among philosophers and scientists of the 'Vienna Circle', under the leadership of Moritz Schlick, professor at the University of Vienna. After some years of writing and discussion, the Circle organized its first international congress in 1929, attracting sympathizers from many countries. In 1930 it took over a journal, renamed *Erkenntnis*, for the publication of its ideas. The British philosopher A. J. Ayer attended its meetings in 1933 and made its ideas widely known in the English-speaking world with the publication of *Language, Truth and Logic* in 1936 [5.1].

By that time the dispersal of the Circle was already under way, a number of members having emigrated, mainly to the United States and Britain. But there were also fundamental intellectual differences within the Circle. One of these, between Schlick and Carnap and Neurath, will be described below in section V.

An important influence was that of Wittgenstein, though he was not a member of the Circle. Having retired from philosophy after the publication of his *Tractatus Logico-Philosophicus* in 1922 [5.28], he was coaxed back into the subject by Schlick in 1927 and had regular meetings with Schlick and Waismann, another member of the Circle. (Their conversations are recorded in [5.27].) But from 1929 he declined to meet with other members of the Circle, whose views he found unsympathetic – a sentiment that was reciprocated by Otto Neurath, for one. Nevertheless, the *Tractatus* was regarded by the Circle as a classic statement of the new outlook in philosophy, and the work was read out and discussed sentence by sentence in the period 1924-6. It was, moreover, Wittgenstein who first formulated the 'verification principle' by which the new philosophy became known. Nevertheless it was he who made the most decisive break from these ideas when embarking on his 'later' philosophy in the early thirties.

The philosophy of the Circle became known as 'logical positivism' or 'logical empiricism'. The former name is more usual, but the latter, preferred by Schlick, seems to me to be more appropriate. It has the advantage of indicating the affinity of the Circle's ideas with those of the empiricist tradition begun by Locke in the seventeenth century, and later represented by such thinkers as Mill and Russell. It is also readily connected with the Circle interest in empirical science. Hence, although this article is entitled 'logical positivism', I shall prefer to use the term 'logical empiricism'.

The term 'logical' indicates a primary interest in language and meaning, as opposed to knowledge. The main questions for such philosophers as Locke and Descartes had been about the sources and extent of knowledge, and the empiricist Locke claimed that sense experience was the only source. In the new empiricism, by contrast, the primary question was not 'How do we know that *p*?', but 'What does "p" mean?'

The new approach may be illustrated by the problem of 'other minds'. How can I know that other people really have thoughts and feelings, when I can only observe their bodily movements and the sounds they utter? In the new philosophy this problem of knowledge is transformed into one about meaning. What does it *mean* to say that another person has such and such a feeling? According to the new philosophy, it can mean *no more* than what is observable. Any statement about feelings as distinct from what is observable will be meaningless. 'It is not false, be it noted, but meaningless: we have no idea what it is supposed to signify' ([5.24], 270).

The logical empiricists recognized two, and only two, kinds of meaningful statements. They are, first and mainly, empirical statements, verifiable by observation. Second, there are statements, such as those of logic and mathematics, whose truth can be known a priori; but these were regarded as not presenting 'new' knowledge, but merely an analysis of what was known already. Any other statements were to be dismissed as meaningless 'pseudo-statements'.

❧ II THE VERIFICATION PRINCIPLE ❧

'The meaning of a proposition is the method of its verification.' So ran the principle as formulated by Wittgenstein and Schlick. (It was first formulated by Wittgenstein, but its most frequent use occurs in the writings of Schlick.)

In this sentence we have an answer to a long-standing question of philosophy, namely, What does meaning – the kind of meaning that language possesses – consist in? This question has sometimes been answered in terms of words and sometimes in terms of sentences or speech-acts. Locke answered it by reference to mental entities corresponding to words, claiming that 'words ... signify nothing but the Ideas that are in the mind of the speaker' [5.78], 3.2.4). Wittgenstein, in the *Tractatus*, had postulated 'names' as the fundamental units of meaning, these 'names' being correlated with fundamental 'objects' in the world; with a further 'picturing' relation between propositions and corresponding 'states of affairs' in the world. The verificationist answer, as I have said, was in terms of the method of verification of a given proposition. Here was an apparently simple principle which could provide a focus for both adherents and critics of the new movement.

As well as providing an answer to the question 'What is meaning?', the principle was intended to provide a criterion to distinguish what is meaningful from what is not. Thus, if there is *no* method of verification – no way of verifying the proposition – then it must be meaningless.

It seems obvious that there is something right about the verification principle; that there is, at least, an important connection between meaning and verification. Thus, if we are unsure what someone means by his words, we can often find out by asking how one would verify what he said. And sometimes, at least, the admission that there is no conceivable method of verification will lead us to conclude that what was said is meaningless.

On the other hand, there are a number of difficulties with the principle, which may be divided into three, corresponding to the terms 'proposition', 'is' and 'method of verification'.

The original German word for 'proposition' is *Satz*, and the straightforward translation of this is 'sentence'. There is a difficulty, however, about treating sentences as objects of verification. Such a sentence as 'It is raining' cannot be regarded as true or false in itself. It is only when someone *uses* the sentence on a particular occasion that *what he says* is true or false. In answer to this and other difficulties philosophers have used the term 'proposition' to mean, roughly, what is asserted by means of a declarative sentence. It is, according to this usage, propositions that are true or false, and not the sentences by means of which they are asserted.

But now another difficulty may arise. 'Proposition' is sometimes defined as meaning an entity that is necessarily true or false. But if this is so, then the question of meaningfulness has already been decided in using the term 'proposition', for only what is meaningful can be described as true or false. In other words, it would be self-contradictory to speak of a meaningless proposition.

One way of overcoming this would be to put 'putative' before 'proposition'; another, which I shall adopt, is to use the word 'statement'. In ordinary English we can ask of a statement, made by someone, both whether it means anything and, if so, whether it is true. Some philosophers have also defined 'statement' to mean what is necessarily true or false (and hence meaningful), but there is no need for a verificationist to follow this usage. In this article I shall prefer the word 'statement', but will sometimes follow the writers under discussion in using 'sentence' or 'proposition', as the case may be. This seems the least confusing way of proceeding. (For further discussion of the difficulty about sentences and propositions, see [5.59] and [5.42].)

My next difficulty was about the word 'is', in the claim that meaning 'is' a method of verification. How are we to understand this identification? 'Meaning' and 'method' are concepts of different types. 'One can sensibly talk about *using* a method, but [not] "using a meaning"' ([5.52], 36). A method may be easy or difficult to carry out, it may take a long or a short time, etc.; but these things cannot be said about the meaning of a statement.

Nevertheless, it was thought essential to account for the meaning of verbal expressions by reference to something other than verbal expressions. Otherwise what would be the connection between language and reality? This need was expressed as follows by Schlick:

> in order to arrive at the meaning of a sentence or proposition
> we must go beyond propositions. For we cannot hope to

explain the meaning of a proposition merely by presenting
another proposition ... I could always go on asking 'But what
does this new proposition mean?' ... The discovery of the
meaning of any proposition must ultimately be achieved by some
act, some immediate procedure.

([5.24], 219–20)

A similar thought was sometimes expressed with reference to words as
distinct from propositions, and here the notion of 'ostensive definition'
(as distinct from verification) was invoked, as when we point to an
object to explain the meaning of a corresponding word, such as the
word 'red'. Wittgenstein expressed this thought as follows: 'The verbal
definition, as it takes us from one verbal expression to another, in a
sense gets us no further. In the ostensive definition however we seem
to take a much more real step towards learning the meaning' ([5.79],
1). This passage, however, was written after Wittgenstein's break from
verificationism, and in the ensuing pages he argued that such appeals
to 'reality' as distinct from language could never supply the desired
detatchment from language. He imagined someone trying to explain
the word 'tove' by pointing to a pencil and pointed out that, in the
absence of all verbal information, this act might be taken to mean all
sorts of different things.

   This brings us to the third difficulty; about 'method of verification'. What would be the relevant method in the case of, say, the
statement 'It is raining'? I might verify this by putting my hand out
of the window. But this act might serve to verify all sorts of statements;
and, on the other hand, all sorts of methods might be used to verify
the statement.

   I began with a difficulty about identifying meaning with a method,
as indicated by the word 'is' in the verification principle. Suppose now
that we removed this word and spoke instead of a 'correspondence'
between meaning and method. This would still leave us with the difficulty just mentioned. It is hard to see how Schlick's requirement of
'going beyond propositions' – breaking out of the circle of language –
could ever be satisfied.

❧ III THE CRITERION OF VERIFIABILITY ❧

Not every verificationist was concerned, or mainly concerned, about
the question of what meaning consists in. One of the main aims of the
movement, as I said, was to distinguish what is meaningful from what
is meaningless, with the special aim of showing statements of metaphysics to belong to the latter class. Now such a criterion can easily be

deduced from the verification principle. If the meaning of a statement is the method of its verification, then it will follow that if it lacks such a method – if it is not verifiable – then it will, likewise, lack meaning. It is possible, however, to advocate this criterion independently, without deduction from the verification principle. Thus, one might claim that unverifiable statements are meaningless, without putting forward an account of what meaning consists in; and this was the position of A.J. Ayer. He expressed the *criterion of verifiability*, as I shall call it, as follows:

> We say that a sentence is factually significant to any person if, and only if, he knows how to verify the proposition that it purports to express – that is, if he knows what observations would lead him, under certain conditions, to accept the proposition as being true, or reject is as being false.
>
> ([5.1], 48)

(Sometimes the term 'verification principle' has been used for the criterion of verifiability, but the two tenets should not be confused.)

It should be noted that the word 'verify' is used here in the sense of 'verify whether...' and not 'verify that...' The latter would presuppose that the proposition in question is *true*. But a proposition that is known to be true is, by the same token, known to be meaningful; so that the criterion would be redundant. The relevant sense of 'verify' is that in which this is *not* known, so that, as Ayer implies, we do not yet know whether the proposition will turn out true or false. Moreover, either of these results would satisfy the criterion: what is at stake is not the truth of the proposition, but whether it has meaning. Unverifiable propositions, being meaningless according to the criterion, would be neither true nor false.

By means of such a criterion it was hoped to proceed immediately to the 'elimination of metaphysics', without getting involved in questions about what meaning consists in. The discovery that the propositions in question are meaningless would explain why philosophers who had wrestled with them through the ages had never, apparently, succeeded in getting anywhere, while, at the same time, providing the key to a resolution of their problems.

It soon appeared, however, that the criterion was beset with difficulties. First, there is simply the question of acceptance. In a broadcast debate with F. C. Copleston, A. J. Ayer introduced the word 'drogulus' to stand for 'a disembodied thing' whose presence could not be verified in any way. He put it to Copleston: 'Does that make sense?' But Copleston replied that it did make sense. He claimed that he could form an idea of such a thing and that this was enough to give it meaning ([5.50], 747).

Second, it proved difficult to formulate the criterion in such a way as to yield the desired results – to exclude the statements of metaphysics while admitting those of 'science' (including everyday empirical statements). The formulation I quoted from Ayer was too weak, because all sorts of observations might 'lead' someone to regard a proposition as true or as false. In a further formulation he introduced the more rigorous notion of 'deduction'. A statement is meaningful, he held, if 'some experiential propositions can be deduced from it', the latter being defined as propositions 'which record an actual or possible observation' ([5.1], 52). A typical example would be 'This is white', which might result from the fact that it is snowing. But while it is clear that this fact and this statement are related, the relation does not seem to be one of deduction. There is, for example, no logical deduction from the statement 'It is snowing' and, say, the fact that I am looking out of the window, to the conclusion that 'this is white', or the conclusion that I am seeing something white.

Suppose, however, that this difficulty could be resolved. In that case 'It is snowing' would be vindicated because 'This is white' is deducible from it. But clearly there is more than that to the meaning of 'It is snowing'. And might not the remainder be merely pseudo-meaning, for all that Ayer's criterion has shown? This difficulty was illustrated in a striking way by Carl Hempel, who supposed that some straightforward empirical statement, such as 'It is snowing', had been *conjoined* with a piece of 'metaphysical nonsense', such as 'The absolute is perfect'. This conjunction would yield the same deductions as the empirical component by itself; so that the conjunction as a whole would have to be declared meaningful ([5.14]).

Various formulations were attempted by Ayer and others to escape these and other difficulties, but it seems that what is required is not merely deduction, but *analysis*. There must be a way of showing that the *whole* meaning of a statement is, somehow, accounted for by observations and the corresponding observation statements. Moreover, as we shall see, this affects all kinds of ordinary statements and not just the rather fanciful example constructed by Hempel.

⚈⚈ IV ANALYSIS ⚈⚈

According to Waismann, ordinary empirical statements were to be analysed into 'elementary propositions', whose whole meaning would consist in corresponding verificatory experiences.

> To analyse a proposition means to consider how it is to be verified. Language *touches* reality with elementary

propositions ... It is clear that assertions about bodies (tables, chairs) are not elementary propositions ... What elementary propositions describe are: phenomena (experiences).

([5.27], 249)

There is a difference between this and verification in the ordinary sense. The latter is an activity of some kind, and hence it made sense to speak of a *method* of verification. But what seems to be meant in the passage just quoted is that elementary propositions are to be verified by *having* the corresponding 'experiences', as distinct from any activity.

But how is such analysis to proceed? From the true statement that there is a table in my room, it would not follow that anyone is having a relevant experience, since there may not be anyone in the room. The view adopted, known as 'phenomenalism', allowed for this possibility. According to it, a crucial role is played by *hypothetical* statements, such as 'If someone were in the room, he would have such and such experiences'. But in what sense are such statements entailed by the statement under scrutiny? Even if I am in the room, and endowed with normal eyesight, I may fail to see the table. 'You can't miss it' is notoriously unreliable.

There was also a difficulty about entailment in the other direction. From the fact that I am having the experience of seeing something brown, etc., it would not follow that there is a table in the room; and neither would it follow from my having the experience of seeing *a table*, for I might have these and other experiences in the course of a dream or hallucination. Just how far this kind of scepticism may be taken is a matter for debate, but the sceptical view is encouraged by the empiricist reliance on 'experience', conceived as something that occurs in us, is 'imprinted by the senses', etc. This problem has been recognized from the beginnings of empiricism, and in the case of logical empiricism it led to the view that statements about tables and chairs are not 'conclusively' verifiable. Wittgenstein spoke of them as 'hypotheses' which could not be 'definitively verified' ([5.80], 282–5).

A similar development took place with regard to general statements, such as 'All men are mortal'. The 'all men' in this statement is not analysable into any finite conjunction of names, and the truth of the statement would not follow from any finite number of verificatory experiences. The same is true of scientific laws, such as 'Water expands below 4°C', whose meaning is not confined to any finite number of observations.

The discovery that the meaning of scientific laws, in particular, went beyond any finite verification, was especially serious for a philosophy which regarded scientific statements as paradigms of meaningful discourse. One solution, advocated by Schlick, was to deny that a scientific law is a statement: it is really, he maintained, 'an instruction for the forming of statements'. A genuine statement must be 'conclusively verifiable', and this would be true only of the particular experiential statements which would be produced under that 'instruction'. A statement, he insisted, 'has a meaning only in so far as it can be verified; it only *signifies* what is verified and absolutely *nothing* beyond this'; there cannot be a 'surplus of meaning' beyond that ([5.24], 266–9).

Another approach was used to deal with statements whose verification is impossible for technical reasons. Consider a statement about the far side of the moon. When Schlick and Ayer considered this example, verification was impossible and, for all they knew, might always remain so. The same is true, for us, about speculations concerning life on other planets. But it would seem absurd to claim that whether such questions have meaning depends on the present technology of space exploration. The answer was to describe the relevant statements as 'verifiable in principle'. 'I know what observations would decide it for me, if, as is theoretically conceivable, I were once in a position to make them' ([5.1], 48–9).

But what should we say about scientific statements or theories whose meaning seems to go far beyond their verificatory content, even 'in principle'? Consider the statement that the universe is expanding, and assume that it is based on the observation of a 'red shift' in the light emitted from remote galaxies. It seems clear that the statement is not merely about red shifts. Yet such a 'reduction' of meaning seems to be required by the verificationist analysis. In this connection verificationists enlisted P. W. Bridgman's idea of 'operationism'. On this view, the meaning of statements about distant parts of the universe, for example, would indeed correspond to the relevant scientific 'operations'; there would be no more to it than that. This meant, as Bridgman pointed out, that ordinary words might change their meaning when used in a scientific context. The meaning of 'length', he claimed, 'has changed completely in character' in the context of astronomy. 'Strictly speaking, length when measured ... by light beams should be called by another name, since the operations are different' ([5.4], 3).

A further difficulty arose about the analysis of statements about the past. The statement 'It rained yesterday' might be verified, in the ordinary sense, by present evidence including, perhaps, asking other people. But the statement obviously does not *mean* any of these present things ([5.67], 329). Ayer offered a variety of analyses in attempting to meet the difficulty, including the bold claim that the tense of a statement is not part of its meaning, so that there would be no difference of meaning between 'George VI was crowned in 1937', 'George VI is being crowned in 1937', and 'George VI will be crowned in 1937' ([5.1], 25, [5.3], 186).

❧ V THE ELIMINATION OF EXPERIENCE ❧

In one way or another, the analysis of different kinds of statements would lead to the ultimate 'elementary propositions', variously described as 'experiental propositions', 'observation-statements' etc., whereby, as Waismann put it, 'language *touches* reality'. At this stage the speaker or hearer passes from linguistic activity to the occurrence of a suitable experience or sensation which is supposed to give meaning to the words. But here arose a problem which produced a serious split in the ranks of the Circle. Experience and sensation are personal and in some sense private; must not the same be true, then, of meaning? On this view, the sentence 'I am thirsty', as Carnap argued, 'though composed of the same sounds, would have different senses when uttered by [different people]'. But what, in that case, becomes of the claims of science, and of language itself, to be communal activities? There was, thought Carnap, a ready way of disposing of such awkward questions. 'These pseudo-questions', he declared, 'are automatically eliminated by using the formal mode.' By the 'formal mode' he meant a discourse that confined itself to statements and did not try to go beyond these, to what he called 'the material mode'. There was, he held, no need to talk about 'the content of experience', 'sensations of colour' and the like; we should instead refer to the corresponding *statements*, which he called 'protocol statements'. These, and not the corresponding experiences, would occupy the fundamental role in the system – that of 'needing no justification and serving as the foundation for all the remaining statements of science' ([5.7], 78–83).

Carnap was uncertain about the form that these protocol statements should take, proposing such expressions as 'Joy now', 'Here now blue' and 'A red cube is on the table' (Ibid., 46–7). But Otto Neurath argued that such expressions could not be fitted into the system of science, unless the reference of 'now' and 'here', and the identity of the speaker, were known to others. He gave the following as a suitable example: 'Otto's protocol at 3:17 o'clock: [At 3:16 o'clock Otto said to himself: (at 3:15 o'clock there was a table in the room perceived by Otto)]' ([5.17], 163). This example, however, is still not sufficiently purged of personal elements. We who read it today would not know where in the system to place '3:17' or 'the room'; and the same would be true of 'Otto', were it not for independent knowledge of who Otto was. But perhaps Neurath was indicating the way towards a still more complex kind of statement, which would be wholly independent of reflexive reference.

Now it is clear that Neurath's example is meant as a protocol statement, because the term 'protocol' is used in it. But, now that the connection with experience has been cut, what entitles it to this designation? Why should such statements be regarded as 'needing no justification and serving as the foundation' of science? Neurath's answer was that there are, indeed, no statements having this status. 'No sentence', he declared, 'enjoys the "*Noli me tangere*" which Carnap ordains for protocol sentences' (Ibid., 164–5). To illustrate the point he asked the reader to imagine an ambidextrous person writing down two contradictory protocols at the same time.

After the elimination of experience, what becomes of verification and truth? Neurath proposed that we might think of the system of science as a kind of 'sorting machine, into which the protocol sentences are thrown'. When a contradiction occurs, a bell rings, and then some exchange of protocol sentences must be made; but it does not matter which (Ibid., 168). This conception of truth, known as the 'coherence theory', would strike most people as paradoxical and is open to various objections. An objection made by Schlick was that on this view we 'must consider any fabricated tale to be no less true than a historical report' ([5.24], 376).

Schlick, describing himself as 'a true empiricist' (Ibid., 400) was resolute in his opposition to the elimination of experience. 'I would not', he declared, 'give up my own observation propositions under any circumstances ... I would proclaim, as it were: "What I see, I see"' (Ibid., 380). In a number of writings he tried to overcome the difficulty about the subjectivity of experience without giving up this cardinal tenet of empiricism. In one of them he maintained that statements have both a 'structure' and a 'content'. The former they share with corresponding facts; and 'my propositions express these facts by conveying to you their logical structure' (Ibid., 292). But there is also a private 'content', which 'every observer fills in' for himself, and which is 'ineffable' (Ibid., 334).

In this matter too, logical empiricism was anticipated in the writings of 'classic' empiricists. According to Locke, we commonly think that words have shared meanings, but this is a mistake, given that meaning is tied to mental entities which he called 'ideas':

> Though words, as they are used by men, can properly and
> immediately signify nothing but the Ideas that are in the mind
> of the speaker, yet [men] ... suppose their words to be marks
> of the ideas in the minds also of other men, with whom they
> communicate.

([5.78], 3.2.4)

Locke accepted this difficulty rather lightly, claiming that it was not a serious obstacle to communication. Such a treatment may seem acceptable for a philosophy which concerned itself primarily with questions of knowledge. But in the new *logical* empiricism the matter could not be passed over so lightly.

A further development, beyond the scope of this article, was the celebrated 'private language' argument of Wittgenstein's later work, in which he made a decisive break from empiricist ideas about language, arguing that the alleged 'private' meaning would not be meaning, in the required sense, at all ([5.29], 1–243ff.).

❧ VI THE UNITY OF SCIENCE ❧

Another common feature that the new empiricism shared with the old was its 'reductionism'. Locke, for example, had insisted that the various kinds and aspects of knowledge could all be reduced to a single type and source, namely the 'sensations' with which our sense organs furnish us in 'experience' ([5.78], 2.1.24). In the case of the new empiricism a similar but linguistic reductionism led to a grandiose project known as the *International Encyclopedia of Unified Science*. In this work it was hoped to show that all the different sciences, including the physical, biological and human sciences, could be expressed in a fundamental common vocabulary. Carnap's proposal for this purpose was what he called the 'thing-language' – that which we use 'in speaking about properties of the observable (inorganic) things surrounding us': such words as 'hot', 'cold', 'heavy', 'light', 'red', 'small', 'thick' etc. (It will be noticed that this proposal, unlike the verification principle, is about words rather than statements.)

One aspect of the 'unity of science' that is of particular interest is its application to human beings. It was thought that descriptions of human feelings, for example, could be reduced to statements about observed behaviour ('behaviourism'), or other physical occurrences such as those in the brain. (Here we see the beginnings of the 'physicalism' which, in various forms, is prominent in the philosophical literature of today.) The difficulties of behaviourism can be brought out by their effect on Wittgenstein in his 1930–33 lectures as recorded by G. E. Moore. 'When we say "He has toothache" ', asked Wittgenstein, 'is it correct to say that his toothache is only his behaviour, whereas when I talk about my toothache I am not talking about my behaviour?' This cannot be so, because 'when we pity a man for having toothache, we are not pitying him for putting his hand to his cheek'. Again, 'is another person's toothache "toothache" in the same sense as mine?'. He now saw that according to the verification principle, the meanings, following the difference in methods of verification, must indeed be utterly different. Indeed, the difference was not merely *between* methods of verification, since there is no verification at all in case of the first person:

'there is no such thing as verification for "I have", since the question "How do you know you have toothache?" is nonsensical' ([5.16], 307).

Carnap tried to accommodate such difficulties in a number of writings. In one of these he admitted that a person N_1, 'can confirm more directly than N_2 a sentence concerning N_1's feelings, thoughts etc.'; but, he went on, 'we now believe, on the basis of physicalism, that the difference ... is only a matter of degree' ([5.10], 79).

❧ VII THE 'ELIMINATION OF METAPHYSICS' ❧

One of the main objectives of logical empiricism was to provide a way of demarcating the meaningful statements of science and ordinary life from the 'pseudo-statements' of metaphysics. Now the word 'metaphysics' may mean various things. The verificationists used such examples as Heidegger's statement 'The nothing nothings', and F. H. Bradley's talk about 'the Absolute', as in the statement: 'The Absolute enters into, but is itself incapable of, evolution and progress'. This, said Ayer, was 'a remark [he had] taken at random' from Bradley's *Apperance and Reality*. It was, he claimed, 'not even in principle verifiable', and therefore nothing more than a 'metaphysical pseudo-proposition' ([5.1], 49).

Now such a sentence, plucked 'at random' out of its context, might well strike the reader as meaningless. But is this so because it is unverifiable? Perhaps, if we read Bradley's argument, we would find there the means of assessing the truth of his statement. *That* would be the appropriate method of verification in this case. In taking the statement out of its context, Ayer had merely denied us access to the relevant method of verification.

Perhaps what Ayer had in mind was that the method of verification would not be *empirical*. Now this might well be true; but what would it show? It might show that the statement itself is not empirical; but perhaps it was never intended to be so. Merely to classify it as non-empirical is not to show that it is a 'pseudo-proposition', nor even that it is unverifiable.

Another class of statements to which verificationists turned their attention were those about God. Such statements, it was argued, were not necessarily meaningless, but the meaning ascribed to them should not exceed their verificatory content. Carnap spoke of an early phase of the concept of God, in which He was conceived as a corporeal being dwelling, say, on Mount Olympus. Such statements would satisfy the verificationist criterion, but this would not be true of the metaphysical accretions of later phases of the concept. Ayer put the matter thus:

If the sentence 'God exists' entails no more than that certain types of phenomena occur in certain sequences, then to assert the existence of a god will be simply equivalent to asserting that there is the requisite regularity in nature.

([5.1], 152)

Here again the requirement is that of sense experience, of the observation of phenomena by means of the senses. But is this the only kind of experience? In a further passage Ayer spoke of 'mystical intuition'. He would not, he said, deny that 'the mystic might be able to discover truths by his own special methods'. But, he went on, the mystic's statements, like others, 'must be subject to the test of actual experience'. But is not the mystic's experience itself a kind of 'actual experience'? Some further argument would be needed to show that such experiences cannot count as verificatory.

This difficulty is part of a fundamental problem about the whole empiricist programme. How is their preference for empirical statements, and empirical methods of verification, itself to be justified? John Locke, the father of empiricism, posed the question: 'Whence has [the mind] all the materials of reason and knowledge?', to which he replied: ' . . . in one word, from *experience*: in that, all our knowledge is founded; and from that it ultimately derives itself' ([5.78], 2.1.2). But if this were so, how could this knowledge itself have been obtained? The claim that all knowledge comes from experience cannot itself be derived from experience.

A similar difficulty arises if we turn the verification principle or the criterion of verifiability on themselves. They are not themselves empirical statements: must they not suffer the same fate as other non-empirical statements? As Bradley observed, 'the man who is ready to prove that metaphysics is wholly impossible . . . is a brother metaphysician with a rival theory of first principles' ([5.77], 1).

This difficulty was recognized by verificationists, who made various proposals to overcome it. Schlick claimed that the verification principle was 'nothing but a simple statement of the way in which meaning is *actually* assigned to propositions, both in everyday life and science' (5.24], 458–9); while Ayer said that his criterion of verifiability was to be regarded 'not as an empirical hypothesis, but as a definition' [5.1], 21). But what reason would there be for accepting this definition or Schlick's claim? As we have seen, they are not confirmed by the various ways in which the word 'meaning' is actually used.

Another idea was to describe the principle or the criterion as a 'proposal' or 'methodological principle'. This would exempt them from self-application, since a proposal cannot be described as true or false, verified or unverified. But what would it mean to adopt the proposal in question? According to it, I am to describe certain statements as meaningless. But how can I do that unless I *believe* them to be meaningless? (Of course I could *say the word* 'meaningless', but that is a different matter.)

Leaving this difficulty aside, we may ask what would be gained if such a proposal were to be adopted. One of the motives behind it, as we have seen, was that of reductionism and the 'unity of science'. It was thought, and hoped, that the multifarious jungle of human discourse could all be reduced to a single type. Wittgenstein, in his later writings, spoke disparagingly of such aspirations as due to a 'craving for generality'. He now maintained that the uses of language – 'language-games', as he called them – are irreducibly various, and that the philosopher's task was to notice and expound the differences, resisting any temptation to impose an artificial uniformity.

VIII THE ACCOMMODATION OF ETHICS

How are ethical statements to be accommodated under verificationist criteria? Should they be accommodated at all? Carnap, at one stage, declared: 'we assign them to the realm of metaphysics'. But while it might be thought that metaphysical discourse can safely be set aside as unnecessary for the conduct of human life, this could hardly be so in the case of moral discourse. Could the latter be regarded, perhaps, as a kind of empirical discourse?

According to Schlick, this was the proper way of regarding it, as is clear from the first sentence of his book on the subject: 'If there are ethical questions which have meaning, and are therefore capable of being answered, then ethics is a science' ([5.22]). He went on to maintain that all of these conditions are fulfilled in the case of ethics. Words such as 'good', he claimed, are used to express desires; and these belong to the science of psychology. The 'proper task of ethics' was to examine the causal processes, social and psychological, which would explain why people have the desires they have.

But cannot something be described as morally good or desirable even if people do not desire it? According to Schlick, this would make no sense. 'If ... I assert that a thing is desirable simply in itself, I cannot say what I mean by this statement; it is not verifiable and is therefore meaningless' ([5.22], 19). There is no place in Schlick's account for the aspect of morality on which Kant laid so much emphasis: the conflict between desire and duty, which is such a familiar aspect of moral life. He rejected Kant's account of moral discourse, accusing him of being out of step with the ordinary meaning of 'I ought' (Ibid., 110). Yet it makes good sense for a person to say, for example, that he ought to do X because he promised, even though it is contrary to his desire.

A more common approach among logical empiricists towards moral statements was to deny that they are really statements. In a paper published in 1949, Ayer referred to his earlier view, 'which I still wish to hold, that what are called ethical statements are not really statements at all, that they are not descriptive of anything, that they cannot be either true or false'. This view, he now admitted, 'is in an obvious sense incorrect', since in ordinary English 'it is by no means improper' to speak of ethical statements as statements or descriptions, or to describe these as true or false. Nevertheless, he continued, 'when one considers how these ethical statements are actually used, it may be found that they function ... very differently from other statements'. Yet, after all, 'if someone still wishes to say [they] are statements of fact, only it is a queer sort of fact, he is welcome to do so' ([5.3], 231–3). Here again is the craving for uniformity – a wish to deny that ethical facts are facts, because they do not conform to a preferred model.

To support his denial Ayer resorted to the existence of moral disagreement. 'Let us assume that two observers agree about all the circumstances of [a] case ..., but that they disagree in their evaluation of it.' In that case, he claimed, 'neither of them is contradicting himself' (Ibid., 236). Now in such a case we might indeed conclude that there is 'no fact of the matter'. But there are many other cases in which this is not so. If I have said I will do you a favour, then I *would* be contradicting myself if I denied responsibility for doing what I said. In that case it would be true, and a fact, that I am under an obligation to do what I said. And, as Ayer recognized, the word 'true' is freely used in moral discourse, in various contexts.

As we have seen, Schlick regarded moral statements as factual and verifiable, while Carnap and Ayer tried to dispose of them in other ways. Another writer tried to analyse them into factual and non-factual components. This was the moral philosopher C. L. Stevenson, whose works were cited with approval by logical empiricists. According to the first of Stevenson's 'working models', the statement 'This is wrong' means 'I disapprove of this; do so as well'. (He dealt similarly with the words 'ought' and 'good'.) The first part of this, he pointed out, is amenable to verification, while the second, being an imperative, is not ([5.25], 21, 26).

A difficulty with which Stevenson wrestled was about applying this account to someone who is *asking* himself whether X is wrong. This would not be a factual psychological question, about whether he does in fact approve of X; the question for him would be whether he *ought* to approve of it. Another difficulty is that of making sense of the imperative 'do so as well'. A person can be requested to do something only if he can choose to do it; but this is not the case with approval. If you give me suitable reasons, I may *come to see* that X is wrong; but I cannot do so at will, in response to an imperative.

The connection with reasons was, however, denied by Stevenson. He admitted that 'a man's willingness to say that X is good, and hence to express his approval, will depend partly on his beliefs', but pointed out that 'his reasons do not "entail" his expression of approval' ([5.26], 67). Now this is true enough; indeed, it is not clear in what sense an expression can be 'entailed'. But it remains the case that on the basis of suitable reasons I may come to see (recognize, know it to be a fact) that X is wrong and ought not to be done. If such facts do not conform to the reductionist programme of logical empiricism, then it may be the programme that should be questioned, rather than the status of moral facts.

✦ BIBLIOGRAPHY ✦

Texts by Logical Positivists and Related Writers

5.1 Ayer, A. J. *Language, Truth and Logic*, 1936. Penguin, 1971.
5.2 —— *The Foundations of Empirical Knowledge*, Macmillan, 1940.
5.3 —— *Philosophical Essays*, Macmillan, 1965.
5.4 Bridgman, P. W. *The Logic of Modern Physics*, Macmillan, 1927.
5.5 Carnap, R. 'Überwindung der Metaphysik durch logische Analyse der Sprache', *Erkenntnis*, 1931.
5.6 —— *Der Logische Aufbau der Welt*, F. Meiner, 1962.
5.7 —— *The Unity of Science*, transl. M. Black, Kegan Paul, 1934.
5.8 —— *Philosophy and Logical Syntax*, Kegan Paul, 1935.
5.9 —— *The Logical Syntax of Language*, trans. A. Smeaton, Routledge, 1937.
5.10 —— 'Testability and Meaning', H. Feigl (ed.) *Readings in the Philosophy of Science*, Appleton, 1953.
5.11 Hempel, C. 'Some Remarks on Facts and Propositions', *Analysis* 1935.
5.12 —— 'On the Logical Positivists' Theory of Truth', *Analysis* 1935.
5.13 —— *Fundamentals of Concept Formation in Empirical Science*, Chicago 1952.
5.14 —— *Aspects of Scientific Explanation*, Collier, 1965.
5.15 Juhos, B. 'Empiricism and Physicalism', *Analysis* 1935.
5.16 Moore, G. E., 'Wittgenstein's Lectures in 1930–33,' G. E. Moore, *Philosophical Papers*, Allen & Unwin, 1959.
5.17 Neurath, O. 'Protocol Sentences', in O. Hanfling (ed.) *Essential Readings in Logical Positivism*, Blackwell, 1981.
5.18 —— The Scientific Conception of the World – The Vienna Circle', M. Neurath and R. S. Cohen (eds) Otto Neurath: *Empiricism and Sociology*, Reidel, 1973.
5.19 —— *Foundations of the Unity of Science*, Vols I and II, University of Chicago Press, 1969.

5.20 Reichenbach, H. *The Rise of Scientific Philosophy*, University of California Press, 1951.
5.21 Rynin, D. 'Vindication of L*G*C*L P*S*T*V*SM', ed. O. Hanfling, *Essential Readings in Logical Positivism*, Blackwell, 1981.
5.22 Schlick, M. *Problems of Ethics*, Dover, 1962.
5.23 —— *Gesammelte Aufsätze*, Olms, 1969.
5.24 —— *Philosophical Papers*, Vol. II (1925–36), Reidel, 1979.
5.25 Stevenson, C. L. *Ethics and Language*, Yale, 1944.
5.26 —— *Facts and Values*, Yale, 1963.
5.27 Waismann, F. 'Theses', ed. F. Waismann *Wittgenstein and the Vienna Circle*, Blackwell, 1979.
5.28 Wittgenstein, L. *Tractatus Logico-Philosophicus*, Routledge and Kegan Paul, 1922.
5.29 —— *Philosophical Investigations*, Blackwell, 1958.

Anthologies of Texts

5.30 Ayer, A. J. *Logical Positivism*, Allen and Unwin, 1959.
5.31 Hanfling, O. *Essential Readings in Logical Positivism*, Blackwell, 1981.

Critical Discussions

General

5.32 Berghel, M. (ed.) *Wittgenstein, The Vienna Circle and Critical Rationalism*, Reidel, 1979.
5.33 Church, A. 'Review of Ayer's *Language Truth and Logic*', *Journal of Symbolic Logic*, 1949.
5.34 Feibleman, J. K. 'The Metaphysics of Logical Positivism', *Review of Mataphysics*, 1951.
5.35 Feigl, H. 'Logical Positivism after Thirty-five Years', *Philosophy Today* 1964.
5.36 Gower, B. *Logical Positivism in Persepctive*, Barnes and Noble, 1987.
5.37 Haller, R. 'New Light on the Vienna Circle', *The Monist* 1982.
5.38 Hanfling, O. *Logical Positivism*, Blackwell, 1981.
5.39 —— 'Ayer, Language Truth and Logic', in G. Vesey (ed.) *Philosophers Ancient and Modern*, Cambridge University Press, 1986.
5.40 Kraft, V. *The Vienna Circle*, Greenwood, 1953.
5.41 Macdonald, G. F. (ed.) *Perception and Identity*, Macmillan, 1979.
5.42 Passmore, J. 'Logical Positivism' (three parts), *Australasian Journal of Psychology and Philosophy* 1943, 1944, 1948.
5.43 —— 'Logical Positivism', ed. Paul Edwards, *Encyclopedia of Philosophy*, 1972.
5.44 Sellars, R. W. 'Positivism and Materialism'. *Philosophy and Phenomenology Research* 1946.
5.45 Sesardic, N. 'The Heritage of the Vienna Circle', *Grazer Philosophische Studien* 1979.

5.46 Smith, L. D. *Behaviorism and Logical Positivism*, Stanford University, 1986.
5.47 Schilpp, P. A. (ed.) *The Philosophy of Rudolf Carnap*, Open Court, 1963.
5.48 Urmson, J. O. *Philosophical Analysis*, Oxford University Press, 1967.

On Verification and Meaning

5.49 Alston, W. P. 'Pragmatism and the Verifiability Theory of Meaning', *Philosophical Studies* 1955.
5.50 Ayer, A. J. and Copleston, F. C. 'Logical Positivism – A Debate', eds P. Edwards and A. Pap, *A Modern Introduction to Philosophy*, Collier, 1965
5.51 Berlin, I., 'Verification', ed. G. H. R. Parkinson, *The Theory of Meaning*, Oxford University Press, 1968.
5.52 Black, M. 'Verificationism Revisited', *Grazer Philosophische Studien* 1982.
5.53 Brown, R. and Watling, J. 'Amending the Verification Principle', *Analysis* 1950–1.
5.54 Copleston, F. C. 'A Note on Verification', *Mind* 1950.
5.55 Cowan, T. A. 'On the Meaningfulness of Questions', *Philosophy of Science* 1946.
5.56 Evans, J. L. 'On Meaning and Verification', *Mind* 1953.
5.57 Ewing, A. C. 'Meaninglessness', *Mind* 1937.
5.58 Klein, K. H. *Positivism and Christianity: a Study of Theism and Verifiability*, Nijhoff, 1974.
5.59 Lazerowitz, M. 'The Principle of Verifiability', *Mind* 1937.
5.60 —— *The Structure of Metaphysics* Routledge, 1955.
5.61 O'Connor, D. J. 'Some Consequences of Professor Ayer's Verification Principle', *Analysis* 1949–50.
5.62 Ruja, H. 'The Present Status of the Verifiability Criterion', *Philosophy and Phenomenology Research* 1961.
5.63 Russell, B. 'Logical Positivism', ed. R. C. Marsh, *Logic and Knowledge*, Allen and Unwin, 1956.
5.64 Russell, L. J. 'Communication and Verification', *Proceedings of the Aristotelian Society* suppl. vol., 1934.
5.65 Wisdom, J. O. 'Metamorphoses of the Verifiability Theory of Meaning', *Mind* 1963.
5.66 Malcolm, N. 'The Verification Argument', N. Malcolm, *Knowledge and Certainty*, Cornell, 1963.
5.67 Waismann, F. 'Meaning and Verification', ed. F. Waismann, *The Principles of Linguistic Philosophy*, Macmillan, 1965.
5.68 —— 'Verifiability', G. H. R. Parkinson (ed.) *The Theory of Meaning*, Oxford University Press, 1968.
5.69 White, A. R. 'A Note on Meaning and Verification', *Mind* 1954.

Historical Accounts

5.70 Ayer, A. J. *Part of my Life*, Oxford University Press, 1978.
5.71 Baker, G. 'Verehrung and Verkehrung: Waismann and Wittgenstein', ed. C. G. Luckhardt, *Wittgenstein: Sources and Perspectives*, Cornell, 1979.
5.72 Magee, B. (ed.) 'Logical Positivism and its Legacy' (with A. J. Ayer), *Men of Ideas*, London, BBC, 1978.
5.73 Morris, C. 'On the History of the International Encyclopedia of Unified Science', *Synthese* 1960.
5.74 Schilpp, P. A. (ed.) *The Philosophy of Rudolf Carnap*, Open Court, 1963.
5.75 Wallner, F. 'Wittgenstein und Neurath – Ein Vergleich von Intention und Denkstil', *Grazer Philosophische Studien* 1982.
5.76 Wartofsky, M. W. 'Positivism and Politics – The Vienna Circle as a Social Movement', *Grazer Philosophische Studien* 1982.

Other Works Referred To

5.77 Bradley, F. H. *Appearance and Reality*, OUP, 1893.
5.78 Locke, J. *Essay Concerning Human Understanding*, P. H. Nidditch (ed.), Oxford University Press 1975.
5.79 Wittgenstein, L. *Blue and Brown Books*, Blackwell, 1964.
5.80 —— *Philosophical Remarks*, Blackwell, 1975.

CHAPTER 6

The philosophy of physics
Rom Harré

One convenient way of dividing up the investigations that make up
the philosophy of physics could be the following:

1   Analytical and historical studies of the development and structure
of the leading concepts used in the science of physics, such as
'space–time', 'simultaneity' and 'charge'.
2   Naturalistic and formal studies of the methodologies that have been
characteristic of physical science, including experimentation and
theory–construction, assessment and change.
3   Studies of the foundational principles of significant examples of
physical theory.

These three sorts of investigations can be found throughout the long
history of philosophical reflection on the nature of physical science.
For instance, in the writings of Aristotle [6.2] (c. 385 BC) there are
extensive discussions of many of the questions that still concern philosophers of physics about the nature of the properties of matter. Con-
flicting views about the methodology of physics are easily identified in
the writings of the ancients. For example, Plato's remark that the task
of astronomers is to 'save the appearances' has been contested, interpreted and reinterpreted. In Lucretius' *De rerum natura* [6.31] there is
a sketch of a metaphysical foundation for a general physics supposedly
applicable everywhere in the universe based on the idea of a world of
unobservable material atoms.

It seems that these three clusters of studies could also be found
in the philosophy of chemistry. To disentangle what it is that is characteristic of studies in the philosophy of physics, I shall have to say
something about what distinguishes physics from all other natural

sciences. Nowadays, one would be reluctant to try to draw a hard-and-fast line between physics and the other sciences. But for the purposes of this article, a rough division might be effected as follows. Physics is the study of the most general properties of matter. In chemistry and biology the unique properties of particular kinds of matter are examined. With this rather vague prescription in mind, we can pick out as physics studies of such ubiquitous features of the material universe as its spatio-temporal structure, and of the common properties that every material being shares with every other, such as mass–energy and mobility. This way of distinguishing subject by scope is rather simplistic. It is only very recently that matter and radiation have been found to be mutually convertible and so to have common properties. But the study of optics and the study of mechanics have always been or almost always been branches of physics.

It is worth emphasizing the antiquity of philosophical investigations of the science of physics. It has never been free of some philosophical content. In times of crisis questions about ontology and about method come to the surface. By a time of crisis, I mean a moment in the history of the investigation of the physical universe in which the best theories that we can construct according to the local criteria for identifying a good theory, are in apparently irresolvable conflict with one another while they are indistinguishable by reference to the results of observation and experiment. In these circumstances, philosophical speculation returns to the centre of the stage. Physics, more dramatically than any other science, develops through the interplay between philosophical analysis of conceptual foundations and what, at first sight, seems to be an independent scientific research programme. I shall illustrate this feature of the history of physics from time to time in the course of making my more detailed remarks.

Before I turn to sketching some particular examples of conceptual analysis, there is one further general distinction to be borne in mind. Since the days of Euclid's formalization of the science of geometry, mathematics has played a central role in the development of physics, but this role has not been uncontroversial. There is an important distinction between different ways of interpreting mathematical formalisms [6.47]. Is the abstract mathematical representation of the laws of physics auxiliary or representational? Auxiliary mathematics consists of formal devices by which the knowledge of the physicist can be conveniently summarized and manipulated. I owe to John Roche a very simple example of auxiliary mathematics. This is the grid of lines of lattitude and longitude which geophysicists have laid over the earth. A more complex example is the system of deferent circles and epicycles with which Ptolemy calculated the ephemerides, the risings and settings of the heavenly bodies. We are not justified in assuming a priori that all the technical devices employed in some mathematical formulation of a law or theory have physical counterparts. The laws and principles of quantum mechanics can be expressed mathematically in terms of vectors in Hilbert space. But what could the physical meaning of the leading concepts of the Hilbert space representation possibly be? What physical sense could one give to the idea of a vector rotating in an infinite dimensional 'space'? Equally, it is a misunderstanding of the second Bohr theory of the atom to ask for the physical counterparts of the charged oscillators which replaced the planetary electrons of the earlier theory. On the other hand there are plenty of theories in physics, such as the Clausius–Maxwell theory of the behaviour of gases in which every element in the mathematical representation is taken to be the counterpart of some determinate feature of the physical system. Each variable in $pv = \frac{1}{3} nmc^2$ can be given a physical meaning in terms of the molecular model of gas.

I shall illustrate the three branches of the philosophy of physics by outlining some recent discussion of topics of perennial interest. To illustrate analytical and historical studies, I shall draw on problems of the interpretation of relativity theory. An alternative example could have been the concept of 'mass' which has also had a long and interesting development. It has been sharpened, subdivided and differentiated in response to experimental and theoretical advances ([6.28]). To illustrate methodological studies I shall take some very recent work on the role of experiments in physics ([6.20]). I shall also outline the debates between realists and anti-realists, concerning the interpretation and role of theories in physics. Do they describe unobservable but real entities and processes or are they merely devices for predicting more phenomena ([6.46])? If the former, how could we ever know whether we are getting a better and better picture of the hidden world of causal processes if we can never observe it directly ([6.33], [6.12], [6.3])? To illustrate foundational questions I shall turn from the development of the dispositional treatment of the foundations of Newtonian matter theory to debates about the meaning of the leading concepts of quantum field theories ([6.10]). An alternative example could have been the discussions of the significance of the Bell inequality and the status of the EPR experiment ([6.16], [6.6], [6.5], [6.4]).

❧ THE ANALYTIC AND HISTORICAL ❧ STUDIES OF CONCEPTS

I shall divide the topics that fall under this heading into two broad groups. There are those which are concerned with the analysis of concepts which at first sight are taken to be independent of the particular theories within which they fall. So there are analyses of space, time, causality, property, etc., which, though influenced by particular theories in physics seem to be in some respects, independent of them. On the other hand, there are analyses of leading concepts such as mass, momentum, charge, force, etc., which it is hard to imagine being carried out independently of the particular theories in which they have, from time to time, been embedded.

These analyses, whether generic or specific, are usually conducted with respect to larger questions. So, for example, developing and arguing for analyses of concepts such as space and time, are part of long-running controversies between absolutists and relationists. Do the concepts of 'absolute space' and 'absolute time' make sense? Some relationists would argue that these hybrid concepts are logically incoherent. Discussions about the proper interpretation of the concepts of mass, charge, force and so on, are related to the broad issue of whether the physical properties of things are best understood as dispositions, powers and propensities ([6.23], [6.43]). I shall take up this question again in the foundations section.

In investigating the status of the kinds of concepts that I have mentioned, it is important to bear in mind that these analyses are relative to the state of physical science at the time that they are being carried out. Yet they bear upon such general questions as whether we should favour an absolutist or a relationist theory of space and time, or whether all physical properties are really dispositions. Debates such as that between Leibniz and Clarke ([6.1]) over the nature of space and time, though set in the context of Newtonian physics, nevertheless have universal significance.

One cannot say that there is no philosophy of physics independent of the state of physical theory. The generality of the concepts involved sometimes allows us to investigate concepts and to develop arguments which transcend particular epochs in the history of the science itself.

At the beginning of this century relativity theory seemed to present a radical challenge to a well-established conceptual system for expressing spatial, temporal and causal relations. The community of physicists had become accustomed to the idea of an absolute frame of reference, though it was hardly ever necessary to invoke it in solving any actual problem in physics. According to the popular myth, relativity theory was something extraordinary and utterly radical. I hope to show that such a picture is far from an adequate portrayal of the way in which theories of space, time and space–time had evolved in the course of the development of post-Aristotelian physics. Among many deep questions that can be asked with respect to space and time is whether there is a relation between the spatial and temporal location of an experimenter or observer and the forms that experimenters or observers would use to express the laws of nature. Are they or are they not the same when an experimental apparatus is run at one place and time rather than another? Would the laws of nature seem to be the same if studied on a moving platform as on one which was stationary relative to some apparently fixed frame of reference? Or on one which was accelerating with respect to some other platform on which stood the apparatus with which the experiments had previously been done? Ultimately the deepest question would be – could we discover which system of bodies was moving or accelerating and which was *really* stationary by looking for indicative changes in the laws of nature?

There are two ways in which absolutist views on space and time have been challenged. Relativity theory challenges the idea that there is a privileged reference frame, absolutely at rest, to which all motions uniform or accelerating could be referred. There is also the 'relationist' challenge to that idea which can be mounted independently of the question about reference frames. Relationists believe, with Leibniz, that space and time do not exist independently of the material system of the world. They are among the relational properties of that system. Absolutists (lately called 'substantivalists' to distinguish them from those who favour ultimately a non-relativist position in physics) believe that the space–time manifold is a substance which exists independently of the material world of charges, forces and fields ([6.11]). My illustrative example concerns the absolutist/relativist issue, not the substantivalist/relationist debate.

Let me briefly sketch how one now sees the historical progression that leads to the contemporary interpretation of relativity theory. The idea that the forms of laws of nature are independent of spatio-temporal location is expressed in the technical notion of covariance of the law under a coordinate transformation. To take a simple example: changing the coordinates of a location in a Cartesian plane each by a fixed quantity is a transformation. If the coordinates were x and y before the transformation and are $x-a$ and $y-b$ after, it is as if we moved the whole reference frame a units to the right and b units upwards. If a law of physics has the same form before and after the transformation is applied to the coordinates, we say that it is 'covariant under the transformation'. However, that technical idea is a version of a more fundamental conception. It expresses the idea that the forms of the laws of nature are indifferent to (that is unaffected by) changes in location, epoch or relative velocity of the frame with respect to which they are studied. We can detect the very beginnings of the covariance or indifference to location idea in the writings of Nicholas of Cusa ([6.4]). Contrary to the Aristotelians, who believed that space and time had instrinsic structures, the laws of nature differing with the location in which they are studied within that structure, Cusa introduced a general principle of indifference. His elegant epigram ran as follows: 'the centre and the circumference of the universe are the same', or in other words, physical laws are indifferent to their location in space and also, he believed, in time.

The next step in freeing physical processes from the influence of space and time came with the work of Galileo ([6.18]). In a striking image, he asked us to imagine conducting experiments inside a ship on a smooth sea. He argued that it would be impossible to discover whether the ship was in motion or at rest relative to the sea, by experimenting in a closed cabin. The relative motion between ship and ocean would have no effect upon the results of our experiments. Physics would always be the same inside the ship, no matter what its uniform velocity was relative to the ocean. This is the principle of Galilean relativity. Newton certainly subscribed to this principle. The laws of mechanics were thought to be indifferent, or covariant, as we might say to the Galilean coordinate transformation. In that transformation we can change the mathematical expression for uniform motions by any amount we like, the mathematical equivalent of slowing down or speeding up the ship by a definite amount relative to the ocean, and the laws of nature will preserve their form when expressed in the new coordinates.

All went merrily until the development of a comprehensive set of laws for electromagnetism by Clark Maxwell. Voigt showed in 1891 that Maxwell's laws were not covariant under the Galilean transformation. This implied that it might be possible to find electromagnetic evidence of our real or absolute motion through some uniform and universal background. It seemed that, in principle, one could find one's way about and perhaps even determine one's velocity with respect to some absolute frame of reference. Since it was the electromagnetic laws which were not covariant under the Galilean transformation, perhaps an electromagnetic aether might serve as just the absolute background that physicists needed. This was the project of Michelson and Morley (for an exposition of the work of Michelson and Morley, emphasizing the importance of the apparatus see [6.22]).

By the end of the nineteenth century, however, it had become clear that there was a coordinate transformation under which the laws of electromagnetism were covariant. This was the Lorentz transformation. The situation had now become very interesting. The Maxwell laws of electromagnetism are covariant with respect to the tranformation of Lorentz but not with respect to that of Galileo. The laws of mechanics are covariant with respect to the transformation of Galileo but not with respect to that of Lorentz. Both are covariant with respect to the Cusan transformation, but this was taken to be so obvious as not to be worth remarking. This was the situation that Einstein confronted.

Essentially, Einstein had to solve two problems ([6.15]). How to make a reasoned choice between electromagnetism on the one hand and mechanics on the other as the most basic physical science. His reasons for choosing the electromagnetic option have to do with the need he felt to preserve a thorough-going symmetry between the process of electromagnetic induction that occurs when a moving conductor cuts the lines of force of a stationary magnetic field and that which occurs when a moving magnetic field interacts with a stationary conductor. If we assume an electromagnetic aether, the processes will be different in each case. He thought this intolerable. So he chose to privilege electromagnetism by denying the necessity to postulate an aether. This choice served not only to eliminate the aether from physics but to elevate the Lorentz transformation to be the dominant principle of covariance. His second problem was to find a new form for the laws of mechanics so that they too would be covariant under the Lorentz transformation. If this could be done, physics would be unified. There would be one physics and all its laws would be independent of the place, moment and relative velocity of the material system in which they were tested. He found these laws and they are none other than the laws of the special theory of relativity.

But now we can see that there was a third problem. With respect to what spatio-temporal structure are the new laws of mechanics, together with the laws of electromagnetism, indifferent? Einstein did not solve this problem himself. We owe its solution to Minkowsky ([6.36]). In the Minkowsky manifold, space and time are not independent systems of locations and moments. There is a four-dimensional manifold in which physical processes are imagined to take place. Minkowsky coordinate systems, moving with uniform relative velocity with respect to one another, now become the frames of reference with respect to changes between which the laws of nature must be indifferent. Wherever and whenever an experiment is conducted in the Minkowsky manifold, the result should be the same.

General relativity simply extended the same idea one step further. Einstein pursued the project of finding a formulation for the laws of nature which would leave them covariant under the general coordinate transformation, including that between frames of reference accelerating with respect to one another. Corresponding to the Minkowski manifold of special relativity came the famous curved space of general relativity which represents a manifold, with respect to which the laws of nature are absolutely indifferent.

The story of relativity is the story of one programme progressively developed, acquiring a more and more sophisticated form as the history of physics has unfolded. It begins in 1440 with Cusa's *Of Learned Ignorance* ([6.41]) and culminates in general relativity. At each step yet another candidate for the one absolute space–time manifold was deleted from physics.

There is a connection with the absolutist (substantivalist)/relationist debate. Clearly, if the laws of nature are indifferent to their presumed locations in manifolds of space or time or space-time, then those manifolds can play no role whatever in the physical sciences. Absolute space, absolute time and absolute space–time are redundant. Experimental proof of this redundancy by Michelson–Morley is not in fact part of the history of relativity theory. It was, so to say, a comforting result that confirmed Einstein in the wisdom of privileging electromagnetic laws and their properties in his programme of research.

Relativity has turned out to be a cousin of relationism. But the triumph of relationism is by no means the foregone conclusion. There are still some reasons for thinking that there may yet be a place for an absolutist space–time in the physical sciences. These have to do with the status of the space–time manifold as required by general relativity. It is argued ([6.38]) that even in the absence of all matter-fields this manifold would still have a structure. Therefore, it cannot be just one of the sets of relations that order the material stuff of the world.

Exemplary cases of conceptual analysis of other physical notions have occurred throughout the history of physics. One notices in the Clarke–Leibniz controversy, as a footnote, a conceptual investigation into the notion of quantity of motion, in which the distinction between momentum and energy is foreshadowed.

❧ METHODOLOGICAL PROBLEMS IN THE ❧ SCIENCE OF PHYSICS

From the earliest days of mathematical astronomy, the nature of physical theory has been a matter of perennial dispute. The arguments have turned on the balance that one can draw between epistemology and ontology. Clearly, in some sense, that which is known through perception, the observable, has some kind of privileged ontological status, even though we know that many of our ontological claims made on the basis of perception are disputable and have sometimes had to be revised. Physical theory, however, characteristically seems to refer to processes such as the orbiting of the planets, entities, such as subatomic particles and structures, such as the curvature of space–time, that lie beyond perception. What, then, is the status of our knowledge of these beings and what of their standing as existences alongside and perhaps as components of that which we can perceive? Anti-realists have tended to privilege the deliverances of the senses, particularly the sense of sight, both ontologically and epistemologically. Realists, more cautious epistemologically, have nevertheless been bolder ontologically, and have tried to find ways in which attributes of physical theories, particularly their power to engender new kinds of experiments, have been taken as grounds for interpreting them realistically, and thereby adding to our ontology, enlarging the list of kinds of things we believe to make up the world. However, sceptics have little difficulty in finding grounds for pressing the interpretation of physics back in the anti-realist direction. They ask how we can be sure of the truth of our laws, when we have very limited grounds for accepting them, the classical problem of induction. How we can be satisfied with theories when our grounds for accepting them are only their predictive and retrodictive powers, since it is easy to demonstrate that there are infinitely many theories with the same predictive and retrodictive power, the problem of under determination, first formulated by Christopher Clavius. Quite recently a new mood has spread among philosophers of physics. Diagnosing the source of the weakness of realism as a commitment to the principle that science aims to establish the truth of the propositions of physical theory, a new school of neo-pragmatist philosophies of science animated to some extent by a reading of the philosophy of Niels Bohr ([6.27], [6.37]) has appeared. These philosophers have argued that a realist interpretation of physical theory should be taken as doctrine that theories are good in so far as they give us just sufficient understanding of the unobservable to allow us to manipulate it ([6.21]). Manipulability is the concept which allows us to penetrate beyond the bounds of perceptibility.

There are some important consequences that flow from the new 'pragmatic' realism. In one respect it harks back to an eighteenth century conception of the logical status of physical properties. At that time, the popular philosophy of physics decreed that our knowledge of the physical world was a knowledge of the powers and disposition of otherwise unknown entities. We knew them through what they could bring about. In very much the same way, the Bohrian philosophy of physics asks us to consider the world in so far as it appears to us through the dispositions it displays in apparatus of our own devising. There is another consequence which follows from this point of view. The early ecologists developing concepts to understand the way in which species of animals are related to their physical environment have coined the concept of *umwelt*. The *umwelt* of a species is that region of the world which is available to the species by virtue of its biological endowments. The physical world is broader and richer than the sum of the *umwelten* of the animals which inhabit it. This concept was used to explain how it was possible for different species of animals to occupy the same physical environment. Each carved out its own *umwelt*. In a similar way, one could treat the worlds of physics as *umwelten* and the development of the physical ontology as the successive marking-out of an ever-changing *umwelt* for humankind with respect to the experimental apparatus and conceptual systems with which they explored it. So the new philosophy of science is realist in a new way. The world is that which we make available to ourselves and our knowledge of it is our knowledge of what it is capable of doing and being made to do by our manipulations.

The next question that obviously arises in relation to the move from anti-realist to realist conception of physical science concerns the nature of physical theory. If we think of physics in the anti-realism manner as the statistics of perceptual experiences or even the statistics of the performance of instruments, while all else is of no ontological significance and merely serves the role of intervening variables to carry us from one empirical statement to another, we would be inclined to follow the philosophies of science of Mach ([6.32]) and Duhem ([6.14]). According to these philosophers theory performs only a logical role: an inference machine for Mach, a taxonomical system for Duhem. However, when one examines physical theory and considers the development of the theorizing in a certain field of enquiry, one is struck by the fact that the theories of physics do not seem to be about the world at all. They are at least, ostensibly, about models of the world. A model, in this sense, can be either an abstract representation (a homeomorph) or a paramorph, which is an analogue of something we do not yet know but believe to exist. A law of nature like $pv = $ a constant, is an idealised description of the behaviour of an abstract version of a real gas. The corresponding theoretical proposition, $pv = \frac{1}{3} mc^2$, is a description of the molecular model of what a gas might be like. This view of theory has been about for more than three decades ([6.48], [6.26]). It is now becoming popular again. A philosophical question that is immediately evident if we think about theory in this way, is how this view fits with realism. Thinking it through, the fit is rather nice. Having given up the idea that realism must be defined in terms of the truth of propositions but rather thought out with reference to the manipulability of objects to which theory guides us, the idea of theory centred on a model of reality is very attractive. Model and reality are, so to say, beings of the same sort, and we can consider the fit of a model to that of which it is a model in terms of similarities and differences. The problem of which similarities are to be counted as important is itself readily soluble by reference to the structure of the theoretical concepts which constitute the discursive part of the theory. Some properties will appear as essential and some as accidental. Similarities and differences gain their importance from the extent to which they are drawn from the real and nominal essences of the beings in question, that is from our ideas about their inner constitutions and from our criteria for assigning them to kinds on the basis of their observable properties.

The shift from positivism to realism to what one might call post-realism or neo-pragmatism also involves rethinking of the role of experiments. In the logistic account of science, whether positivistically conceived or developed in the fallibilist mode by Karl Popper ([6.42]), gives a logical account of experiment. An experiment is done in order to provide a rational being with a proposition of the form 'Some A are B' or alternatively, if it so turned out, 'Some A are not B'. The significance of the experiment is determined by logical relations between those propositions which describe the experimental results and the general hypotheses to which they are considered relevant. So the logical account requires us to accept either inductivism or fallibilism. In the former we would have to accept the force of some pattern of inductive reasoning, in which the result in some cases, those that have been studied, are generalized to all cases, a notoriously shaky inference. In the latter we would have to rely upon the fallibilist pattern, that while we can draw no certain conclusion from a positive result, a prediction that turns out to be false justifies us in rejecting the hypothesis from which it was drawn. Neither is satisfactory.

The evident mismatch between the logicist way of construing experiments with the neo-pragmatist view of science, suggests the possibility of conceiving of experimentation in a much broader fashion. If we are endeavouring to see by experiment how well our models match reality, then we should not think of experimenting as a way of producing propositions to stand in a logical relation to a theory. We should think of the performance of an experiment as doing work in the world directed towards producing a certain outcome under the guidance of the theory. The question is not whether the theory in use is true or false, but whether, read as a set of instructions, it enables us to do what we aim to do. There is a sense to be given to the verisimilitude of a theory, but not in the propositional mode, not centred on truth. In particular we are concerned with manipulating the world as if it were well-matched to our model. Indeed, there are specific model-matching experiments, some of which have been of enormous importance in the development of science. One which I find particularly instructive is the Fage and Townsend experiments, by which a model of the flow of fluids with respect to bounded media is matched against a subtle experimental revelation of what the structure of such fluid motion 'actually' is (that is what the motion appears to be by the use of an ultramicrosope). Interesting cases arise where our faith in the iconicity of our models is based only upon their power to suggest manipulations. It seems to me that our main reason for believing in the reality of the magnetic field is the set of effects we can bring about by procedures which, we believe, act directly on that field. Changes so induced then bring about effects we can observe, such as the swing of the pointer of a galvanometer.

The notion of 'model' which I have been assuming in this discussion so far is the familiar one of analogue. One system is a model of another if it is analogous in relevant ways. But there is another, connected, sense of 'model' which has also been prominent in the writings of some philosophers of science ([6.49], [6.50]). In logic a model is a set of entities and relations which can be used to interpret an abstract calculus. If the formulae of the calculus, interpreted as meaningful sentences by the use of such a domain of entities and relations, are all true when used of that domain, then that set of entities and relations is a model for the calculus. In logic there is a calculus and a model is needed to give it meaning; in physics a model or analogue of reality is imagined and a theory is subsequently created by describing the model. At the end of the day, so to say, the relation between calculus, theory and model is the same in both cases. However, in the order of creation, logic and physics run in opposite directions.

Disputes about how physical theory should be presented can be found throughout the history of physics. They were particularly prominent in the sixteenth century when many philosophers treated the heliocentric and geocentric astronomies, many versions of which were on offer in the mid-sixteenth century, as alternative mathematical systems. Ways of answering the question as to which formal system was to be preferred were interestingly divided between those who thought that anti-realist criteria, like simplicity and logical coherence, were of prime importance and those who favoured realist criteria, like the ontological plausibility of the model of the solar system that the mathematical structure represented.

In the late eighteenth, through the nineteenth century, Newtonian mechanics became the focus of a considerable effort to rework its formal representation. This was in part animated by the discovery of Maclaurin's paradox, perhaps more justly attributed to Boscovich. Boscovich [6.8] noticed that the grand Newtonian theory was internally incoherent, indeed, self-contradictory. The concept of action, 'force × time', which was essential to setting up Newton's third law, that in action by contact action and reaction are equal and opposite, required all such action to take place in a finite time. But the Newtonian ontology required the ultimate material particles to be truly hard, that is incompressible. It follows that all action by contact must be instantaneous, since the ultimate contacting surfaces cannot deform. Forces in instantaneous Newtonian impact would, according to the mechanical definition of action, be infinite. But there is no place for

PHILOSOPHY OF SCIENCE, LOGIC AND MATHEMATICS

infinite forces in the Newtonian scheme. A variety of strategems were developed to try to resolve the difficulty. In general physicists in France tended to favour theories without forces ([6.13]), whereas the English and some of their continental allies tended to favour a mechanics without matter, the so-called dynamical interpretation ([6.24]).

Great advances were made in the mathematics of physics, in the course of the working out of these alternatives. The Lagrangian formulation, the Hamiltonian formulation and Hertz's immensely influential reformulation of mechanics were all attempts in one way or another to come to terms with the same fundamental problem.

But there is another kind of investigation which we could classify as foundations of physics. This is the project of finding the minimal or most elegant formal representation of a scientific theory. In these cases, the mathematician–philosopher is driven by an interest in the aesthetics of formalisation rather than by some metaphysical paradox, such as the one uncovered by Boscovich and Maclaurin. In the present century some very interesting developments have hinged on attempts to provide alternative formal representations in which the very foundations of a theory are revealed in a clear and unambiguous way. For example, the matrix theory of Heisenberg and the wave mechanical formulation by Schrödinger of the laws of quantum mechanics, though they were shown to be mathematically equivalent in some sense, were animated, in part at least, by ontological differences between their authors. Lucas and Hodgson [6.30] sum up an enormous variety of ways of arriving at the Lorentz transformation. There are many different paths by which this important group can be arrived at. Sometimes exercises of this sort, the formulation of an alternative mathematical representation, are significant. But sometimes they seem to be little more than formal exercises, mere auxiliary mathematics.

The way that the results of experimenal manipulations enter into the record of physics as *phenomena* is exceedingly complicated. Goodings [6.20] has analysed the paths by which the personal experience of the discoverer of a new phenomenon makes it available, conceptually and manipulatively to the community of scientists and ultimately to everyone. A key move in the transformation of personal experience into public phenomenon is the elimination of all traces of the human hand that was involved in the early occasions of its production. Goodings shows that the circularity of the motion Faraday demonstrated as a natural electromagnetic effect was extremely difficult to produce on the laboratory bench, let alone understand. To explain how this transformation is achieved Goodings introduces the idea of a 'construal'. It could be a way of describing, a picture, a diagram or anything by which a scientist, in interaction with others, makes the phenomenon available as such. In applying construals the great scientists of history transform complex chains of fragile steps into simple sequences of sure-fire manipulations. Faraday describes seventy-five steps in recording how he first produced circular electromagnetic motion in his own laboratory. The published description of the procedure mentions only forty-five steps. The final simplification to a mere twenty steps occurs in his set of instructions for anyone to reproduce the effect.

❧ FOUNDATIONAL DEBATES ❧

The indeterminacy of subatomic processes that had first appeared in experiments with electrons was eventually canonized rather than resolved in the mathematical theory of quantum mechanics. Quantum mechanics has been the source of one of the major conceptual problems which has beset physical science for the last seventy years. At the heart of Newtonian physics was an assumption of the strict causality of all physical processes and the determinate character of all physical effects. Quantum mechanics provides a formalism by means of which a description of the state of preparation of a system can be linked to predictions about the probabilistic distribution of the effects of certain treatments of that system. The theory provides no way in which determinate outcomes can be predicted from knowledge of the original state of the system. Here is the dilemma. Is this because the way we now understand the state of any physical system is actually complete? This would seem to imply that there are real propensities to vary the outcomes of identical operations performed on identically prepared systems, contrary to the ordinary notion of determinate causality. Or is there something missing in our knowledge of electrons and other subatomic particles, knowledge which would restore the determinate structure of physical theory? Perhaps there are 'hidden variables' which do behave deterministically.

Arguments about the viability of hidden variable theories are almost as old as quantum mechanics itself. Can we find a theory based on the assumption of the existence of a set of attributes which we can ascribe to subatomic particles and their states of preparation from the determinate mathematics of which we could recover the probabilistic results for quantum theory as it is now understood?

So far, the answer has been equivocal. It is now clearly understood that there is no way in which a theory employing the familiar classical concepts of momentum, energy and so on, could be formulated, to provide a determinate hidden variable theory ([6.5]). Every experiment so far conducted has only given stronger and stronger support to the 'Bell inequality', the mathematical condition that expresses the principle of no hidden variables. On the other hand, there

PHILOSOPHY OF SCIENCE, LOGIC AND MATHEMATICS

have been hidden variable theories constructed using exotic concepts from which the existing quantum mechanical results can be recovered [6.44]. However, they lack any serious degree of physical plausibility.

In quantum field theory, another and yet more fascinating conceptual problem has arisen. It is now some fifty years since the idea of expressing field interactions as the exchange of particles was first proposed. The idea has been, one might say, extremely successful, at the cost of the development of theories of incredible mathematical sophistication. The quantum theory of fields is now a very well-developed speciality in physics, but it leaves us with a tantalising conceptual problem. The particles which are exchanged in interactions, say, the photons that are exchanged in an interaction between two electrons, are not identical with the photons, the flux of which is the light with which we are familiar. These photons are virtual, that is, they exist in and only in the interaction, if they exist at all. Furthermore, as imagined, they have properties which differ from the familiar properties of the photon of light. They are like light quanta, but not quite like light quanta. Are they real?

Recently, the idea of using the analogy between the light photon and the photon of quantum electrodynamics as a basis for developing theories of other kinds of fundamental interaction, the weak interaction, the strong interaction and even gravity has led to the proliferation of such 'virtual particles'. I think it would scarcely have crossed the minds of most physicists to ask about the reality of virtual particles, were it not for the use of the structure of reasoning through which the light quanta became the models for quantum electrodynamics. In quantum electrodynamics, the virtual photon is modelled on the real photon, if I may be permitted to put the matter that way. Then weak interaction particles, the w+ and w-, and z_0 particle are modelled upon the virtual photon. They are all species of the same genus. Then, in a reversal of the reasoning which led to the conception of the virtual photon, the idea of a real w particle, or a real z particle seemed to be a natural development from the quantum field theory of the weak interaction. The programme for hunting the w's and z's was defined, and in the manner in which such events are achieved, they were eventually 'discovered'.

I believe that this pattern of reasoning which is characteristic of quantum field theory was at least in part responsible for raising the question of the reality of the intermediate vector particles which carry the forces of interaction. If there are real versions of these particles, then surely there is some sense to the reality of the particle as the physical bearer of the field ([6.10]).

A clear formulation of the idea that there is a distinctive set of properties, the behaviour of which defines the subject matter of physics first appears in the seventeenth century. At that time the perceptible attributes of material things were classified as primary or secondary depending on their relation to human sensibility. Those which existed only in the act of perceiving were classified as secondary. Those which were thought to exist independently of the perceptual capacities of human beings were taken as primary. Galileo [6.17] seems to have so tightly tied the primary qualities to the science of physics as to make the one definitive of the other. Secondary qualities were marked by the way that they varied in quality, intensity and duration with the state of the human perceiver. Locke [6.29] completed the philosophical treatment of the distinction by carefully analysing the relation that must be supposed to obtain between secondary qualities, such as the power of a body to induce a colour sensation in a human observer, or an observable change in another material body, such as the power of fire to melt ice, and states of material bodies by virtue of which they had these and other powers. He sharply distinguished between ideas and qualities. Ideas are mental, including, for instance, sensations of colour. Qualities are material, including the properties of coloured things. This distinction enabled Locke to come at the distinction between primary and secondary qualities by a different route from that followed by Galileo. Ideas of primary qualities resembled the qualities as they existed in the material world. But the ideas of secondary qualities did not. Red, as a perceptible quality, does not resemble whatever property it is that causes a human being to see an old Soviet flag as red in hue. Generalizing the theoretical use of the concept of primary quality, Locke took the qualities that 'in the material body' caused corresponding ideas of secondary qualities as just those which are central to the conception of matter as it is used in the science of mehanics. All this is tied together by the thesis that the quality in the perceived thing that corresponds to the idea of colour, say, that is the secondary quality itself, is nothing but a power, a power to induce the relevant sensation. What the word 'red' refers to in the thing that is seen as red is a disposition. But it is grounded in an occurrent state of the perceived thing. According to this metaphysical scheme that state must be some combination of primary qualities.

For the scientist–philosophers of the seventeenth century, physics was mechanics. It was the study of the primary qualities of material bodies. Friction, for instance, as a mechanical disposition, must be grounded in the atomic structures of the interacting bodies. Mechanics, the basic science, was based on an absolutist metaphysics. Locke's philosophical account of the foundations of physics required two main categories of concepts. One set of concepts were relational. Many of the qualities of material things are dispositions to cause perceptible effects in a human being or in other material things. Whether they are activated or not depends on the contingent existence of suitable targets for their activity. The other category of qualities was absolute. The properties on which the dispositions are grounded are primary. Primary qualities are so defined as to be independent of the relations between the material things which possess them and human beings or to anything else. Boyle [6.9] sums them up as the 'bulk, figure, texture [arrangement] and motion' of the elementary material things or corpuscles. The word 'corpuscle' was preferred to the word 'atom' by the sophisticates of the period, since it left open the question of whether the constituents of matter that were elementary for chemistry or mechanics were truly atomic, that is, indivisible in principle. Though Newton listed many dispositions amongst the primary qualities of matter, he shared the assumption of his contemporaries that there were *some* absolute physical properties. In the second edition of the *Principia* the list of the mechanical properties of matter are a mixture of the occurrent and the dispositional. Newton (1690) writes of the 'extension, hardness, impenetrability, mobility, and inertia of the whole [body] which 'result from' the corresponding properties of the parts. To have inertia, says Newton, is 'to be endowed with certain powers' [6.39]. Inertia appears in the list of primary, mechanical properties as the power to resist acceleration. But inertia is not mass in Newton's metaphysics. Mass is an occurrent property. It is that which grounds the disposition identified as inertia. To give mass its occurrent character Newton defines it as 'quantity of matter'. Since the mass per unit volume differs from material to material, a universal matter, serving as a basic common substance, would have to exist in different states of diffusion. In a substance of low density the matter is rarefied, while in a substance of high density it must be compressed. One physical scheme to accommodate this difference would be basic atoms in a void with more or less pores between them. There would be fewer such atoms in a given volume of a light substance than in a similar volume of one that was more dense. Newton seems to favour this account. The basic atoms would be full, and so of uniform density. Lacking pores they must be incompressible and impenetrable. I have emphasized above the problem this thesis raised for Newton's general mechanics.

Though most of Newton's primary qualities are dispositions, they are nevertheless absolute in one of the dimensions on which the notion of the absolute figures. In Rule III Newton asserts that they 'are to be esteemed the universal qualities of all bodies whatsoever' whether or not they are 'within the reach of our experience'. As primary qualities they are not relative to human sensibility, but by the same token they are a mix of the relational and the absolute. In Newton's scheme mass, inertia, extension and mobility must exist even in a body wholly isolated from all other material beings. It seems to follow from the definition of mass that Newton's physics includes at least two absolute properties of matter. The quantity of matter would seem to be unaffected by the presence or absence of other material things. Since the quantity of matter of a body is related to its spatial extension, and that to absolute space, it would seem that extension and mass are both absolutes in Newton's scheme. The close conceptual tie between absolute space and mass is further underlined in Newton's argument for the intelligibility of the concept of absolute motion:

> if two globes, kept at a given distance one from the other by means of a cord that connects them, were revolved about their centre of gravity, we might, from the tension of the cord, discover the endeavour of the globes to recede from the axis of their motion.
>
> ([6.39])

By testing to see in which direction impressed forces bring about the greatest increase in that tension, we can find not only the angular velocity of the globes in absolute space but also the true plane of the motion with respect to that space. To suppose that a force will appear in the cord when the globes are set rotating, Newton must be assuming that the masses of the globes are unaffected by the absence of all other matter. The masses are absolute qualities. If mass is a quantity of matter, then indeed that assumption seems natural and also inevitable.

The generality with which Newton uses the notion of 'power' is evident in Query 31 of the *Opticks*.

> And thus, Nature will be very conformable to herself and very simple, performing all the great motions of the heavenly bodies by the attraction of gravity which intercedes those bodies, and almost all the small ones of their particles by some other attractive and repelling powers which intercede the particles.
>
> ([6.40])

There is yet another root idea in Newton's conception that gravity cannot be a primary quality because it suffers 'intensification and remission of degree'. So there must be a more basic power, 'an agent acting constantly' which is the absolute, because non-relational element, in the physics of gravity.

Mach's (1883) criticism of Newton's metaphysics is usually presented as an attack on the assumption that mass is an absolute property ([6.32]). But Mach's argument develops in two steps. He first shows that mass is best considered as a relational property in his analysis of the basic laws of mechanics. The argument goes as follows: consider an impact of tensions. The body A is falling under gravity. When the string joining it to the body B, resting on a smooth surface becomes taut, A will decelerate and B accelerate. Since the string is taut at the moment of 'impact' the force decelerating A will be equal to that accelerating B, so Mach argues. Let that force be 'F'. Then if the mass of B is m_b, the mass of A is m_a, and the accelerations f_b and f_a respectively, the equation of motion for the whole system is $m_a.f_a = -m_b.f_b$

Mass appears here, and in all other contexts of mechanics, as a ratio. In this case the ratio is equal to the negative inverse of the quotient of the accelerations. Mass and inertia are the very same relational disposition. Given this prior analysis, Mach's treatment of the experiment of the globes (and of the more complicated argument of the thought experiment we call Newton's bucket, which involves a refutation of the Cartesian conception of locally real motion) in which the assumption of the persistence of inertial properties into the isolated system of the globes is entirely consistent. It simply involves the generalization of the relationality of the mass concept to the components in the simple system of the impact of tensions to the structure and contents of the universe as a whole. Mach completes a trend that began in the sixteenth century, a trend to replace absolute versions of the properties of material things with relational properties. Not only are these properties dispositions, manifested only in the interactions between material bodies, they are also relational in the sense that they are not grounded in some intrinsic property of isolated material individuals but in their relations to all the rest of the bodies of the universe.

One can tie together the seemingly disparate mechanics of Newton (read relationally) with quantum field theory by the realization that there is a common structure to their deep ontologies. In what sense do *any* of the 'particles', actual or virtual, exist? It seems obvious that only a dispositional account of their manner of being makes any sense. By that I mean that our claims about the world-in-itself made on the basis of the experiments by which apparatus, has (permanently) a disposition to display itself in such and such a way in the behaviour of that apparatus. Or to put it in Popper's terms only the set-up has propensities to yield this or that phenomenon. The phenomena are ephemeral, but it is they which are particulate or wavelike or whatever it might be. In this treatment we have both of Bohr's famous principles, that of complementarity and that of correspondence. Complementarity because set-ups which exclude each other produce, as a matter of fact, disparate and complementary phenomena; correspondence because the state of an apparatus-world set-up can be described for a human community only in the terms made available in classical physics, the physics the concepts of which are paradigmatically defined by the things and events of the ordinary world.

⚬⚬ BIBLIOGRAPHY ⚬⚬

6.1 Alexander, H. G. *The Clarke-Leibniz Correspondence*, Manchester, Manchester University Press, 1956.

6.2 Aristotle, *Metaphysics*, trans. W. D. Ross, *The Works of Aristotle*, vol. VIII, Oxford, Clarendon Press (*ca.* 335 BC), 1928.

6.3 Aronson, J. L. 'Testing for Convergent Realism' *British Journal for the Philosophy of Science* 40 (1989): 255–60.

6.4 Aspect, A., Grangier, P. and Roger, C., 'Experimental realization of the E-P-R-B paradox', *Physical Review* (le Hess), 48 (1982): 91–4.

6.5 Bell, J. *Speakable and Unspeakable in Quantum Mechanics*, Cambridge, Cambridge University Press, 1987.

6.6 Bohr, N. 'Discussion with Einstein', in P. Schilpp (ed.) *Albert Einstein: Philosophes Physicist*, vol. 1, New York, Harper, 1949, pp. 201–41.

6.7 Bohr, N. *Atomic Physics and Human Knowledge*, New York, Wiley, 1958.

6.8 Boscovich, R. J. *A Theory of Natural Philosophy*, Venice, 1763.

6.9 Boyle, Hon. R. *The Origin of Forms and Qualities*, Oxford, 1666.

6.10 Brown, H. R. and Harré, R. *Philosophical Foundations of Quantum Field Theory*, Oxford, Oxford University Press, 1990.

6.11 Butterfield, J. 'The Hole Truth', *British Journal for the Philosophy of Science* 40 (1989): 1–28.

6.12 Cartwright, N. *How the Laws of Nature Lie*, Oxford, Clarendon Press, 1983.

6.13 D'Alembert, J. d'*Traité de Dynamique*, Paris, David, 1796.

6.14 Duhem, P. *The Aim and Structure of Physical Theory*, Princeton, Princeton University Press, 1906 (1954).

6.15 Einstein, A. 'On the electrodynamics of moving bodies' in H. A. Lorentz *et al.*; (eds) *The Principle of Relativity*, New York, Dover, 1905 (1923), pp. 53–65.

6.16 —— 'Remarks to the Essays Appearing in this Collective Volume,' in P. A. Schilpp (ed.) *Albert Einstein: Philosopher–scientist*, New York, Harper, 1959.

6.17 Galileo, G. *Il Saggiatore*, (1623) in G. Stillman Drake (ed.) *The Discoveries and Opinions of Galileo*, New York, Doubleday, 1957.

6.18 —— *Two New Sciences*, 1632, trans. H. Crew and A. de Salvio, New York, Dover, 1914.

6.19 Giere, R. *Explaining Science*, Chicago, Chicago University Press, 1988.

6.20 Goodings, D. *Experiments and the Making of Meaning*, Dordrecht, Kluwer, 1991.

6.21 Hacking, I. *Representing and Intervening*, Cambridge, Cambridge University Press, 1983.

6.22 Harré, R. *Great Scientific Experiments*, Oxford, Oxford University Press, 1985.

6.23 Harré, R and Madden, E. H. *Causal Powers*, Oxford, Blackwell, 1975.

6.24 Heimann, P. M. and McGuire, J. E. 'Newtonian Forces and Lockean Powers', *Historical Studies in the Physical Sciences* 3 (1971): 233–306.

6.25 Hertz, H. *The Principles of Mechanics*, 1894, New York, Dover, 1956.

6.26 Hesse, M. B. *Models and Analogies in Science*, London, Sheed and Ward, 1961.

6.27 Honner, J. *The Description of Nature*, Oxford, Clarendon Press, 1987.
6.28 Jammer, M. *The Concept of Mass*, Cambridge, Mass., Harvard University Press, 1961.
6.29 Locke, J. *An Essay Concerning Human Understanding*, ed. J. Yolton, London, Dent, 1961.
6.30 Lucas, J. R. and Hodgson, P. E. *Spacetime and Electromagnetism*, Oxford, Clarendon Press, 1990.
6.31 Lucretius, *De Rerum Natura* c. 50 BC trans. R. E. Latham Harmondsworth, Penguin, 1954.
6.32 Mach, E. *The Science of Mechanics*, (1883), La Salle, Open Court, 1960.
6.33 —— *The Analysis of Sensations*, Chicago, Open Court, 1914.
6.34 Maxwell, J. C. *The Scientific Papers of J. C. Maxwell*, ed. W. D. Niven, Cambridge, Cambridge University Press, 1890.
6.35 Miller, A. *Imagery in Scientific Thought*, Boston, Birkhauser, 1984.
6.36 Minkowski, H. 'Space and time' (1908), in H. A. Lorentz *et al.* (eds) *The Principle of Relativity*, New York, Dover, 1923.
6.37 Murdoch, D. *Niels Bohr's Philosophy of Physics*, Cambridge, Cambridge University Press, 1987.
6.38 Nerlich, G. *The Shape of Space*, Cambridge, Cambridge University Press, 1976.
6.39 Newton, Sir I. *Mathematical Principles of Natural Philosophy* (1686), Berkeley, University of California Press, 1947.
6.40 —— *Opticks*, (1704), New York, Dover, 1952.
6.41 Nicholas of Cusa *Of Learned Ignorance*, (1440), trans. G. Heron London, Routledge and Kegan Paul, 1954.
6.42 Popper, K. R. *The Logic of Scientific Discovery*, London, Hutchinson, 1959.
6.43 —— *A World of Propensities*, Bristol, Thoemmes, 1981.
6.44 Ptowski, I. 'A Deterministic Model of Spin Statistics,' *Physical Review*, 48 (1984): 1299.
6.45 Rae, A. I. M. *Quantum Physics: Illusion or Reality*, (1986), Cambridge, Cambridge University Press, 1994.
6.46 Redhead, M. *Incompleteness, Non-locality and Realism*, Oxford, Clarendon Press, 1987.
6.47 Roche, J. Personal communication, 1990.
6.48 Smart, J. J. C. 'Theory Construction', in A. G. N. Flew (ed.) *Logic and Language*, Oxford, Blackwell, 1953, pp. 222–42.
6.49 Sneed, J. D. *The Logical Structure of Mathematical Physics*, Dordrecht, Reidel, 1971.
6.50 Stegmüller, W. *The Structure and Dynamics of Theories*, New York, Springer-Verlag, 1976.

CHAPTER 7

The philosophy of science today

Joseph Agassi

THE PHILOSOPHY OF SCIENCE HAS A REMARKABLY LOW STANDARD

Science began in Antiquity as a branch of wisdom, and philosophy (= the love of wisdom) was distinguished from wisdom only by philosophers. Cultivators of science in its early modern times (*c.* 1600–1800) called themselves philosophers, and their activity was called not science but natural philosophy. What we call today the philosophy of science includes the theories of knowledge (epistemology) and of learning (methodology), as well as the study of the principles of science (metaphysics, the philosophy of nature). The first two disciplines were at the time neglected as they were considered marginal; the third, metaphysics, was deemed distinctly dangerous. Natural philosophers did not consider their work impractical; they called themselves 'benefactors of humanity', as they were convinced that their activities, in addition to their intrinsic merits, will bring peace and prosperity to the whole world. But they insisted that the practical aspects of science, significant as they surely are, can only appear as by-products, not as the outcome of study directed to any goal other than the search for the truth: any other goal will render research biased and so worse than nothing.

It is not that applied science evolves all by itself, as the application of knowledge for practical purposes certainly requires efforts, including research. But the research for any practical purpose need not, it was taken for granted, be a search for knowledge. To make this clear, it may be useful to contrast the classical, typically eighteenth-century view with today's view: today we recognize within science not two but three categories; we recognize basic research in addition to the classical pure and applied research, where pure research is disinterested and applied research is the use of the fruits of pure research for practical ends; basic research is pure research directed at material which is not very interesting in its own right but which is expected to be very useful in practice. There is little doubt that today research claims prestige for itself because of its potential usefulness. That is to say, all research is claimed to be more-or-less basic.[1] In the classical vein this was unthinkable, the value of science was deemed almost exclusively personal and research was deemed edifying.

Obviously, of the many thousands of citizens engaged in research proper, most are engaged in small tasks – which Thomas S. Kuhn has labelled 'normal'. And, he stresses, normal science is practical. He probably means by this that normal science is all practical, but let us admit that it can also be basic. The practical attitude to science is very modern; it is at most the result of the industrial revolution, and so nineteenth-century at the earliest; more likely it is post-Hiroshima. Kuhn is a historian of science and so he should know the obvious fact that normal science in the eighteenth century was more for individual entertainment than for practical ends. This was not always so: anyone familiar even with the mere illustrations in the literature in the history of science in the eighteenth century will know that. This is reflected in the third edition of *Encyclopedia Britannica* of the early nineteenth century. The article 'Science' there is extremely brief, reporting that an item of knowledge belongs to the body of science if and only if it is certain. Though the article gives no instances, clearly, the best instances are either from logic and basic mathematics or from extremely common and undoubted experiences, though, of course, some high-powered scientific theories should count as well. Today, incidentally, it is generally acknowledged that of these seemingly most certain items, none is exempt from doubt and revision (except perhaps logic; this is still a contested matter). Next to that brief third-edition *Britannica* article on science is a long article on science as amusement, in which the contents of a famous popular eighteenth-century book (by Ozanam) is reported. We would recognize today the contents of this article as vaguely within the domain of high-school sciences, as it includes somewhat amusing experiences with mechanics, electricity, magnetism and the like. Probably these two articles were not conceived of together and they were put together by sheer lexicographic rules.

The picture which emerges from this description presents a concern with science which is pre-critical. It was at times purely intellectual, at time practically oriented, always with great implication for life in general, for daily life and for peace, but with hardly any concern for the problems and issues in the philosophy of science as recognized today. Today, many of the concerns of the field, epistemological, methodological and metaphysical, are traced back to writers of the classical era, especially David Hume and Immanuel Kant. There was a major difference between these two thinkers. Hume is typical of his class: he was a private scholar who was clearly concerned with the social sciences (politics and economics, in particular), whose contributions to the philosophy of science he himself saw as marginal and preparatory. Not so Kant, who was most uncharacteristic; he was a university professor, who was on the side of science, and who was reputed to be a polymath proficient in fourteen different branches (some of which he inaugurated as academic subjects, such as geography and anthropology). He was still primarily a philosopher, and even primarily a philosopher of science.[2]

It is hard to examine this, quite generally received, assessment, since the expression 'the philosophy of science' is new. To repeat, traditionally the word 'philosophy' designated learning in general and empirical science in particular. After the defeat of the French Revolution, some fashionable reactionary philosophers swore allegiance to unreason. Other, more old-fashioned philosophers understandably attempted to distance themselves from the new advocacy of unreason, and one way they did this was by naming their own views 'scientific philosophy'. This name usually designated mechanistic philosophy; its adherents considered theology to be typically metaphysical and so they branded all metaphysics evil; this enhanced their claim for scientific status for their own, mechanistic metaphysics. This way the philosophy that upheld the traditional esteem of reason centred mainly on science and on reasonability in the moral life of the individual and the nation. It naturally tended to centre increasingly on epistemology, methodology and rational metaphysics as a main tool to combat unreason. The philosophers of unreason had – still have – their own philosophy of science, but this is scarcely recognized: the philosophers who defend reason against the attack on it from the advocates of unreason took a monopoly on science and its defence.

The philosophy of science thus evolved into a specific activity of philosophers of the rationalist persuasion – the activity of defending science against its detractors. This explains the poverty of the field today: today science has no worthy detractors to combat; and no dragons to slay, no heroic deeds.

Even the philosophers of science themselves are aware of this fact, as they defend science not only by singing its praise, but also by attempting to solve problems in epistemology and in methodology, and by seeking newer and better arguments to combat metaphysics with. They do this as a mere pious act, paying no heed to the possibility that the problems they pose are insoluble, at least insoluble as long as they are presented in the traditional manner and settings. They cling to the pre-critical, optimistic view of science in the face of the risks to

the very survival of humanity which scientific technology has originated: they relegate these risks to the new field of the philosophy of
technology (which is less than half a century old), as if their philosophy
of science does not include the philosophy of technology and as if their
philosophy of science does not credit science with scientific technology
as a great achievement. It really is a cheap trick to admit to the field
of the philosophy of science the praise for science as the source of the
benefits from scientific technology and its great achievements, and to
banish to the philosophy of technology the possible and actual ill-
effects of the same scientific technology.

David Stove is exceptional. The efforts to solve the traditional
problems of the philosophy of science, he says, are commendable even
if these should turn out to be insoluble. For, he explains (in his book
against those who have given up the traditional struggle, including Sir
Karl Popper and Thomas S. Kuhn), the struggle is the ongoing defence
of science and thus of traditional rationalist philosophy and thus of
rationalism as such.

This is a charming admission, but of a position that is obviously
pathetic.[3]

∾ PUBLIC RELATIONS FOR SCIENCE IS ∾
MEANINGLESS

In the year AD 1600 St Roberto Cardinal Bellarmino consigned Girdano
Bruno to be burnt at the stake – allegedly because he taught that the
universe is infinite, so that in all likelihood there exist other worlds
like ours. Later on the said Saint issued an official threat to Galileo.
Science was then rightly militant. Today science is triumphant; even
the Church of Rome has recently admitted the superiority of Galileo's
case over that which was contrived against him and officially endorsed
there and then. However embarrassing this repudiation was, science
became too strong to continue evading it.[4] Today, science surrounds us
and appears on all levels from the sublime, through the mundane to
the abject.

In the sublime mood science is what Bertrand Russell called
([7.53]) 'Promethean madness' and what Albert Einstein considered to
be the scientific undertaking: 'tracing the Good Lord's blueprint of the
universe'. In the mundane world of the modern industrialized metrop-
olis, the impact of science on the intellectual, political, social and technical aspects of life is overwhelming; especially, the impact of scientific
technology is so very prominent. The abject aspect of the impact of
science on daily life has attracted a certain kind of philosopher
of unreason, whose hostility to reason is expressed as a hostility to

science, transformed into a hostility to scientific technology – on the grounds of prophecies of gloom and of apocalypse that should be blamed on scientific technology, *the* cause of the alienation of Modern Man. These prophets of unreason identify science with the foolish attempt to conquer and subjugate Nature and they are confident that Nature will soon avenge this treatment by devastation. They advocate the replacement of the Western harsh, indifferent attitude to Nature with a soft, intuitive, irrational, oriental attitude. This mixture invites very urgently the sifting of the grain from the chaff.[5]

This quick survey of the impact of science on society that goes from the sublime to the ridiculous, has omitted the ridiculous. This dimension is normally absent: science is no cause for levity. The entertainment world is as much under the influence of science as any other component of our small universe, in its shaping of our tastes and opinions and values and in its stupendous media technology. But not as an object of hilarity; even as sedate entertainment it is almost entirely confined to the juvenile. Yet they raise in a fresh manner the question, what is science? The question seems to require an answer that is easy to apply to what we usually call science, including high-school science and nuclear physics and electronic engineering. This is an error: we may have a thing and the received model of that thing, and the two need not agree. In the literature on social anthropology, this is taken for granted. In that literature, the paradigm for the difference – between a thing and the received idea of it – is the difference between magic and the received idea of it: in every society that has been described by some anthropologists, there are magicians, and yet (unless we deem the scientists as powerful magicians as did Sir Francis Bacon in the early seventeenth century), we all agree that real live magicians never fitted the characterization of magic admitted in their society (except possibly contemporary modern society). Magicians like Merlin do fit the image of the magician, but they never existed (except perhaps among modern scientists). Do the modern scientists fit the image of science?

It is the image of science that is rather ridiculous, as it is put forward by the spokespeople for the public relations of science. This is not peculiar to science. The practice of public relations evolved unawares and uncontrolled as a part of the advertising world of the free market, where the shortest of the short-term interests govern, so that the most cynical opportunists set the tone. This is harmless enough when pertaining to the sales of soap, but not to the sales of the higher things in life, be they the arts, the sciences or religion. Whoever the individuals are who take upon themselves to express the social concerns of science, they are these days powerful individuals and they control the appointment of suitable individuals to the positions of spokespeople of science. The leading positions in this matter are well-paid professorships in the leading universities in the subject called the philosophy of science.

In brief, official philosophy of science, the philosophy of science boosted by the scientific establishment, is much less tolerable than the commercials on television which sell soap and other cosmetics. They are as remote from the Promethean madness of the search for the secret of the universe as eroticism is from the (intellectual) love of God.[6]

If we grant this, and it is hard to deny it as we will soon have the occasion to notice, then we may begin by denying that there is anything more specific to science as such than to cosmetics as such. And the best characterization of science that can be given is in that vein: science is the Promethean madness, the attempt to trace God's blueprint of the universe, the search for the secret of the universe.[7]

SCIENCE IS A CULTURAL PHENOMENON

There are some immediate, obvious objections to the view of science as a quest, and they centre on the missing object of the quest and on its trail, expressed in the following two questions. What will satisfy the scientific quest? Which way does one turn to be on its trail? These questions are reasonable and should be taken seriously, but they are presented as objections, and as objections, I will now show, they are residues from the pathetic public-relations department – by illustrating their immediate socio-political implications – on the assumption that there are no competitors within human culture.

The first objection is dominant in the semi-official literature on the matter: what exactly are we in search of? Are we in search for information or for knowledge? If for mere information, will any information do? If yes, why not be pleased with the information contained in primitive lore and in Scriptures? This series of questions looks so straightforward, but it is not. It begins well and degenerates: what exactly are we looking for? This is the right question even though obviously we do not know: we know what we look for when we look for a lost penny, but not when we look for a masterpiece while roaming in a foreign museum, much less when we seek the secret of the universe. The question is right, but we should not expect too much for an answer: anything remotely resembling a possible answer may be a tremendous excitement. But look where the series of questions ends. It ends with an insult to the competition. This is not serious; it is public-relations frivolity – especially since repeatedly the self-appointed public-relations spokespeople of science often find the quest formidable and even exasperating, so that they finally settle for the mere physical comforts that science-based technology has to offer to the modern world. (The leading public-relations spokesperson of science in the previous generation was Rudolf Carnap, the famous debunker of all speculations; his *magnum opus* was his *The Logical Foundations of Probability* of 1950; it starts with the formula for finding the truth about the world and ends by giving up the task, with the excuse that science is a mere instrument.) And so, when the circle is closed and science is praised as a mere instrument, the conclusion is not drawn but remains all the same: the mere physical comforts that science-based technology has to offer the modern world is superior to the primitive lore and to the Scriptures. This is hard to take seriously. Primitive lore and the Scriptures do not compete with modern science-based technology as conveyors of physical comforts, but they still are very interesting and deserve attention in many ways and on many levels. This is the end of the objection from the hostility to the idea of science as a quest from popular lore and the Scriptures: the quest is obviously not replaced by the study of popular lore and of the Scriptures; rather, the study is a part of the quest.

The public-relations spokespeople do not allow themselves to be dismissed so easily, and they respond with forceful objections to the dismissal here suggested: they want reason, namely science, to be the guide for life; they want science to offer but better technology and better education, and the two should go together (as the proper education for the next generation is essential for the technological challenges they will face), yet the competition will not agree. Admittedly taking the Scriptures as a science substitute is frivolous. Yet, however frivolous the competition is, its hostility to scientific technology and to scientific education must be taken seriously in the interest of the wellbeing of us all.

This rejoinder seems very serious and very responsible, but it is not. Responsibility will be served if the question of education and of the place of technology in the modern world be discussed not apropos science but apropos the design of a better education policy, the study of education and its purposes. And the same holds for the problems that are specific to high-tech society. Here we are discussing science, and as the search for the secret of the universe, not the implication this has for education and for the training for high-tech. True, science shares with other domains the search for the secret of the universe, including magic and religion. Do the public-relations spokespeople of science want to distinguish between the search conducted in a manner becoming science and in alternative ways? Or will the comparison suffice of the results of the search along different lines? Today it is agreed that the results tell the important tale: by their fruits ye shall know them. Do we know the difference in the results? Of course we do: even the most ignorant among the public-relations spokespeople of science have no difficulty in telling a magic text from a scientific one! To be precise, the semi-official literature of the public-relations spokespeople of science is not that advanced: only a few philosophers of science discuss magic proper in a manner which is up to the standard of current social anthropology, the scientific field of study which retains an exclusive claim over magic. Rather, the semi-official literature of the public-relations spokespeople of science is concerned to a large extent with the unmasking of items of pseudo-science as merely pseudo, namely, not the genuine articles they masquerade as.

❧ SCIENCE NEEDS NO PROMOTERS ❧

It should be granted that this is more challenging: the public-relations spokespeople of science can easily distinguish a genuine amulet or talisman from a page of a scientific paper, but lamentably all too often they cannot distinguish a phony page of a manuscript that deserves publication in a scientific journal from one that is not. This is why the public-relations spokespeople of science are never invited to act as referees for judging the merits of scientific research any more than the public-relations spokespeople of a financial concern will be asked to adjudicate on matters financial. This is why the public-relations spokes-people of science are so pleased and so proud when a scientist proper joins their ranks, even though they should know better. For, a scientist can contribute to the philosophy of science without joining the ranks of the philosophers, as many scientists often do. Hence, scientists become philosophers only as an admission of defeat as scientists, often after retirement. Max Born, the great physicist of the early twentieth century, who was also a somewhat less-great public-relations spokesperson of science, said that all able-bodied researchers should devote all their energies exclusively to science and permit themselves to turn to philo-sophy, if at all, only after retirement.[8]

All this sounds rather evasive, yet it is the heart of the matter: analysing the means for distinguishing between the genuine research from the pseudo sounds a reasonable task, yet it clearly is very ques-tionable, and probably it cannot be done: even scientists of the best repute are not very good at it. Proof: young Albert Einstein was deemed phoney by many scientists, and he was taken as suspect for well over a generation – while those who took him seriously debated hotly the question, was he right?

The great historian of physics, Sir Edmund Whittaker, who was himself a serious scientist (he was the Astronomer Royal for Northern Ireland) was hostile to Einstein all his long life, and as late as in the mid-century, long after the heated debate had subsided, he declared that there never was an Einsteinian revolution and overlooked the heated debate completely. In a review of Whittaker's book Born said, I was there, I witnessed the heated debates and took part in them.[9]

To return to the items that may be masqueraded as parts of science. These items are, among others, magic, theology and metaphysics. What is so pathetic about all the many studies dished out year in and year out by the public-relations spokespeople of science is precisely this: were they right, then there would be no regular problem in refereeing, and in the rare cases of such a problem, these very public-relations spokespeople of science should be the experts to consult. Such cases do not exist.

To be precise, one such case does exist: in the long history of the public relations of science, one such spokesperson was invited to speak as an expert on the matter at hand. It was the second 'monkey trial' so-called, the court case a few decades ago, in which a judge in Little Rock, in the State of Arkansas, USA, was called to adjudicate between the education department of that state and a religious sect which demanded that the official biology text books should include proper reference to scripture. It is a priori obvious that both parties were lamentably in the wrong: the education department was in error in proscribing such reference and the other party was in error in trying to bring in, not the Scriptures, but a certain dogmatic attitude.[10] The judge had little choice but to side with the education department, simply because the public-relations spokespeople of the religious sect in question were even more inept than the public-relations spokesperson of science who was invited to speak for the department. He argued that the religious are dogmatic and the scientists are not. Even apart from the fact that many individuals are religious scientists, this is a naked falsehood: there are non-dogmatic religious sects and dogmatism is lamentably too common among scientists, religious and non-religious, and more so among science teachers. When it comes to the curse known as science-education inspectors, it seems that for them dogmatism is obligatory, though, as many obligations, it is at times not carefully observed.[11] This is no complaint about the judge: he was facing in court dogmatism on both sides and had to choose the lesser evil. In that Arkansas court on that day, science appeared the lesser dogma and the lesser evil; but with the help of the public-relations spokespeople of science this will soon change – unless something is done about it. These public-relations spokespeople of science are not powerful at all, but they may do harm anyway, as they cover up some powerful evils: the more powerful science is, the more success it brings about, the more the dangers of its abuses, and unchecked it will be abused. This, after all, is the major lesson we learn from all science fiction, and Mary Shelley, H. G. Wells and Isaac Asimov spun yarns to let us absorb this lesson. Except that under the pious guidance of the public-relations spokespeople of science, readers of science fiction take the lesson to be mere fiction with no moral to it or as fiction with futile moral against the abuse of magic, not a real moral against the abuse of science.[12]

We have arrived back at the claim of the self-appointed public-relations spokespeople of science that the evil of magic is in its masquerading as science, in its being pseudo-scientific. This is most parochial as an attitude: most magicians and theologians, even most metaphysicians, operated (and still do) in societies in which there is no familiarity with science so that they do not masquerade as scientific and so they do not qualify as pseudo-scientific. Even cargo cults, the magic rituals involving wooden copies of aeroplanes and other modern artefacts in the hope of inducing the gods to grant them to the worshippers, scarcely qualify as pseudo in any sense.[13] To say of Moses the Law-giver and of Jesus Christ that their theology masqueraded as science defies the imagination. Only in response to the assertion of Maimonides, that Moses the Law-giver was a scientist, could anything like the charge of masquerading be launched – validly or not.[14] *The* philosophers of science, however, that is to say, the semi-official public-relations spokespeople of science, are not interested in all this: they care little about societies overseas; they are here to advertise science here and this task includes the discrediting of the competition here. They therefore permit themselves at times to be agreeably tolerant to theology and to metaphysics – after proof is issued to their own satisfaction that the parties involved do not compete with science. Usually, that is, theology and magic are deemed competitors, and then *the* philosophers of science, that is to say, the self-same semi-official public-relations spokespeople of science, find themselves acting as bouncers for the exclusive club of science. The leading sociologist of science, Robert K. Merton, prefers the term 'gate keepers', as he deems it the less offensive of the two; it is more offensive, as will be clear when we find the answer, which should guide the bouncer, to the central question of the philosophy of science: who is and who is not a *bona fide* member of the club? What is science? Is there a quality of science that sets it apart from what the bouncers consider as the competition? For, clearly, science is open and gate-keeping makes it a closed club.

❧ SCIENCE IS NOT SUPER MAGIC ❧

What is science? Science is a body of knowledge; science is what scientists do *qua* scientists; science is a tradition; science is any empirically involved research activity; science is a faculty in the university. All these answers are true and meet the question, yet they are highly unsatisfactory. Hence, the question was ill-put. Here it is in its proper wording: what is the essence of science?

This is a tricky question; without entering the hoary matter of the critique of essentialism we can re-word it: what differentiates science from . . . . . .? Taking it seriously requires the study in depth of many competitors to science. The study of alien cultures is, of course, highly recommended and even the bouncers will not object to it unless it is done from the viewpoint of the competition. Yet controversy about alien cultures abounds in the scientific departments devoted to it, and consequently the task of characterizing science in opposition to them gets increasingly harder. Example: is Claude Lévi-Strauss, who has created a revolution in the current view of myth and of magic, is he a bouncer or a competitor? He says he is a friend of science, a scientist indeed. Is he? The question is very difficult to settle and the anthropological literature is still struggling with it.[15] Let us try to alter our strategy, then. Can we look at science rather than at the competition and find there some clear-cut characteristic that sets science clearly apart from all the competitors? If so, what is it?

This is the problem of the demarcation of science as semi-officially understood.[16] The most traditional answer to it, to repeat, is that science is a body of theories, and what characterizes them is their certitude, our ability to prove their perfection and finality. The more modern answer is the theory that science is a prestigious social class which lends prestige to its ideas. These two answers are contested these days, though the first is advocated mainly by philosophers of science and contested mainly by sociologists and historians of science, and the second suffers the reverse role – we have here two groups of self-appointed public-relations spokespeople of science competing for the same territory. Let us take the first answer first.

In the twentieth century the impact of logic led to a shift on this matter. The scientific character of a sentence shifted: it was deemed not proof but provability. Now generally one cannot know if a sentence will prove true or false before it is compared with experience. So, a sentence was deemed not quite provable, but merely decidable; a sentence is decided if it is either proved or disproved.[17] This doubled the number of entries: not only a proven sentence but also its negation is scientific, as the negation of a proven sentence is disproved, and the couple of sentences taken together is decidable. Now the claim was that though generally a sentence cannot be declared a priori provable, it was declared that every well-formed sentence is a priori decidable. The justification for the relaxation of the criterion of demarcation of science to the extent of letting the negation of scientific claims be scientific was the wish to corner the competition once and for all by permitting the competition to contradict science openly. If the competition does contradict science, they will put themselves to ridicule, and if not, we will be able to expose them as saying nothing. The very idea that one can permit the competition or not, and decide that they say something or not, shows that the advocates of this view took anti-science to be passé, that they were serving science in the supposition that it is winning anyhow. In any case, they met the surprise of their lives when they learned (from Kurt Gödel) that even in mathematics decidability is unattainable. In computer science it is at times an empirical affair: many tasks given to a computer for deciding the truth or falsity (called the truth value) of a sentence are performable, and demonstrably so; at times the demonstration is purely abstract, as when the time the task takes to complete is much too long. And some tasks are not known to be performable or not. And then, if such a task is given to a computer, then, if the computer finishes the task, it is performable and the truth or falsity of the sentence in question is decidable; but until the task is completed it cannot be decided whether the task will be completed soon or not.[18]

At this juncture the story of contemporary philosophy of science gets much too involved. First, there are modified conceptions of the empirical character of science: the requirement from a sentence that may claim (empirical) scientific status is lessened by leaps and bounds. The exercise of the lessening of the requirement is curious: the input into it increases all the time, yet the output becomes less and less satisfactory, to the point that its own advocates are too unhappy about it to conceal their displeasure with it. Briefly, the idea of certitude is replaced by probability, by a limitation on the domain of the validity of the proof, and by the abandonment of the very concept of proof, which imports finality, in favour of the concept of relative truth.[19] What all of these substitutes for the idea of decidability share is the following incredibly fantastic idea: though a sentence is not usually decidable, its scientific character is. (In other words, though finding the truth or falsity of a sentence is not generally assured, the truth or falsity of the claim that it is scientific is easily assured.) This is a fantastic idea, since one way or another science is linked to truth, no matter how tenuously. Yet it is accepted upon faith. What accepting a sentence on faith means is not clear, but its political implication usually is: the society of the elect are known by their faith.

This is how the first answer, the idea of decidability, upheld by philosophers of science, slowly degenerates into the second answer, the idea that science is a social status of sorts, upheld by the sociologists of science.

Can we ignore all this? Can we ask as curious observers, what is the root of the success of science? Is there some activity peculiar to science?

~~ SCIENCE IS PUBLIC AND EMPIRICAL ~~

Our question has undergone some transformations. First we asked, what is science? This was replaced by, what is the essence of science? And this was translated to, what differentiates science from other intellectual matters? And this was narrowed down to, what characteristic is peculiar to science? And rather than go over the same exercise yet again we should translate this into the following, final wording: what is the specific characteristic of science? (The word 'specific' in the question by tradition hides an essentialist gist, but let us not be too finicky.)[20]

There are two very generally accepted answers to this last question, what is the specific characteristic of science? This would be very comforting, except that the two answers do not overlap. The one is, science is public; the other is, science is empirical.[21]

Take the public character of science first. The claim made here is that most intellectual activities are esoteric, closed to the general public, that entry is conditioned – whether on some natural gift or some specific preparation not given to all or both. Is this true? If so, then by what virtue do the public-relations spokespeople of science dare bounce people who wish to be or appear scientific? More than that: if science is open – exoteric – then why does science need public relations in the first place? It needs recruiting officers, talent scouts, instructors; but why bouncers? What does it matter to science that some esoteric groups appear to be exoteric and other groups have esoteric reasons to oppose science? What does it matter to science, asked Einstein, if this or that church opposes it? If it is necessary to expose and unmask those who masquerade as scientists, is it not best to do so by examining the question, how open are their clubs? Perhaps the bouncers suggest that this is not such a good idea as it may deprive them of their jobs; if so then they are disqualified from debating this question because of a conflict of interests![22]

The second answer is that science is empirical. Now surely Sir Karl Popper is quite right when observing, as a matter of historical fact, that astrology and alchemy and even parapsychology, are empirical as well. The public-relations spokespeople of science are outraged by this observation, and they protest that the empirical evidence in question is highly questionable, and often it is simply lies. This complicates matters immeasurably by raising two tough questions. What evidence is not questionable? Are all scientific reports honest and all parapsychological ones lies? It has been reported that some people pose as parapsychologists and are liars; it has also been reported that some people are genuine parapsychologists and are not liars. Are the reported liars not simply pseudo-parapsychologists? Since people who falsely call themselves scientists are unmasked as pseudo-scientists, and science is free of responsibility for them, surely the same privilege should be granted to parapsychology! The question here is not who is a liar (this question belongs to sociology, to criminology, to cultural history), but, what grants a theory the right to scientific status, namely, what is the characteristic of science? Supposing it is claims to empirical character. Are we to alter this supposition in the light of criticism to say that it is the employ of scientific empirical evidence?[23] This, surely, is hardly helpful, unless we know what makes evidence scientific. Whatever it is, two obvious, extreme answers are unacceptable. The one is that scientific evidence is true: history is full of (historically important) empirical evidence that is known to be false. The other is that empirical evidence is *bona fide*. For it is undeniable that some parapsychology is *bona fide*; indeed, some famous individuals whose contributions to empirical science is unquestionable were known parapsychologists. William Crookes is the standard example for that.

The matter of alchemy or of astrology is even more complex: historians of alchemy and of astrology tell us that the better practitioners of these activities were *bona fide*, and that some of them even contributed to what is now deemed chemistry and astronomy.[24] And we have still not said whether all the *bona fide* empirical evidence should count as scientific. There is a vast literature, going back to the writings of Galileo Galilei as to this question. It is called the literature on theory-ladenness, and for the following reason: if empirical evidence is based on theoretical suppositions, then it may be false unless the suppositions are known to be true. Suppose they are known to be true. On what grounds? Suppose they are known to be true a priori? Then science cannot be said to be thoroughly empirical; assuming, as we often do, that no intellectual activity is utterly devoid of some empirical component, and empirical character ceases to be the differentiating characteristic of science. Suppose, then that the theocratical suppositions are known to be true on some empirical grounds. Then, are these free of theoretical supposition? If no, then the question returns full strength. If yes, then there is some empirical evidence based on nothing but experience. Can this exist? If so, do we have an instance of it?[25]

Public-relations spokespeople of science hardly ever stay to hear all of these objections. Usually they or their seniors are in charge of (politically significant) discussions and they curtail them long before they are exposed that much.[26] They have a strong technique to justify their impatience: no matter how abstract and distant from real life their discussion is, they sooner or later turn the complaint that their opponents are remote from real life. In real life, they intimate, science is successful. This success should be analysed. And profound analysis tells us that the success is predictive, i.e. it yields successful forecasts.

Thus, if we have no proof, we have systematic probability: the earthly success of science is too systematic to be merely accidental; rather, this systematic earthly success is due to the systematic success of science in its efforts to confirm its theories.

SCIENCE POWER WORSHIP IS HILARIOUS

The discussion thus leads to the question, how come science is so systematically successful in its efforts to confirm its theories? What is the trick? Can it be learned? Can it be emulated by parapsychology? The answer must be, it can be learned, or else the success would not be so systematic. How can it be learned? There are two answers to this question, that of the traditional philosophers of science and that of the sociologists of science led by Michael Polanyi and his follower Thomas S. Kuhn. The one is exoteric, and so should be able to describe the formula that makes science an ongoing success; the other is esoteric and describes the knowledge of the formula an ineffable personal knowledge of the trade secret which is transmitted by master to apprentice.[27] This is the worst aspect of the philosophy of science as currently practiced, as public-relations mulch: science is predictive success or it is nothing. If the worse comes to the worst, then scientists are better viewed as exoteric magicians who simply deliver the goods and no questions asked. But the trick is to take as much time as possible getting to the worst, and in the meantime perform the real function as bouncers. Let us review the discussion which leads to this blind ally and see clearly that it is but killing time, that the only serious, *bona fide* ideas involved in the time-killing activity are long dead.

There are two schools of thought in the establishment of the philosophy of science, inductivists and instrumentalists, so-called. Inductivism is the preferred view, as it suggests that scientific theories are probable, even if not provable. It is not clear what this probability of theories means, and, regardless of what exactly it is, it is not clear which evidence raises it and how. It will soon be shown that this is all sham. When inductivism is relinquished, its touchstone, the idea that the goodness of science is shown as it yields useful predictions, or probable forecasts, becomes more than a touchstone; it becomes the criterion of goodness: science, it is then suggested, is nothing but applied mathematics; its merit is practical. Consequently, it turns out, its merit is not theoretical but merely practical – it is merely instrumental.[28]

Assuming for the moment that the value of science is nothing but true forecasts does not yield the conclusion that all true forecasts are desirable. The approval of true forecasts runs against the very well-known very commonsensical facts, first, that some forecasts are terrible and are better not fulfilled and second, that a true forecast may mislead.

There is no question that this is the case, and the public-relations spokespeople of science are not in the least unaware of it. They do not deny this either. They only ignore it. What this oversight amounts to is clear: we are in control and there is no reason to fear that our forecasts are alarming or that we are misled by them. This *is* establishment talk. The world is threatened by destruction from pollution, from the proliferation of nuclear weapons, from population explosion and from the ever-increasing gulf between the rich nations and the poor nations. But there is nothing to worry about. All will turn out to be well.

Query: is this a scientific forecast or false prophecy? It is neither; it is cheap public-relations mulch.

To see how unserious this mulch is one only needs see the low level of the current debates in the leading literature on the matter. The topic common to both inductivists and instrumentalists is the question, are there any items of empirical information free of theoretical bias? Is there any 'pure' evidence? Or is all evidence theory-laden?

The onus here is on the party that says there is 'pure' evidence: they should offer instances. There are none. The only candidates in history were Bacon's naive realism and Locke's sensationalism. Naive realism is refuted: the naive see the sun rise and set, and, to cite an example of Erwin Schrödinger, the sun appears as not bigger than a cathedral, which means, given some simple trigonometry, that the distance between east and west is less than one day's walk. In an attempt to replace naive realism in view of the criticism from Copernicanism, Locke revived sensationalism, claiming that motion is not perceived. It is. Sensationalism is refuted, anyway, by myriads of experiments. This is the end of that discussion.

The next discussions concern theories. There is hardly a debate between the inductivists who ascribe to theories informative contents and the instrumentalists who deny that and read the theories as a mere *façon de parler*. Rather, each struggles with its own problems.[29]

The theory of induction contains two competing sub-theories, which deal with the question, what kind of evidence confirms a given theory? They both violate the only rule of science universally endorsed within science since its enactment in the early days of the scientific revolution: both sub-theories do not confine their discussion to repeatable, (allegedly) repeated observations, but rather they refer to unique items of experience. In addition to this, each of these sub-theories is easily refuted by very simple arguments. A vast literature is devoted to these refutations in an effort to get rid of them; worse, still, as usual with public-relations spokespeople in a defensive mood, they do not state the difficulties they struggle with and so sound arcane.

The first of these two sub-theories of inductive evidence is the instantiation theory of inductive evidence: a scientific theory is confirmed by instances to it. What then, is an instance to a given theory? What is an instance to a theory of gravity? Anything falling? Decidedly not: a falling feather disobeys even Galileo's theory of gravity. What then counts? Rather than discuss gravity, the public-relations spokespeople of science discuss such generalizations as, 'All ravens are black', forgetting that when asserted, these are items of evidence, not theories. What, then, counts as an instance? Every item that does not contradict a theory is an instance of it, since theories can be stated as prohibitions: there exists no perpetual-motion machine, for example; no gas deviates from the gas-law equation, etc. And then every item that is not a perpetual motion machine instantiates the law of conservation of energy! It sounds very counter-intuitive to admit every non-refutation as an instance, since this invites all irrelevancies into the picture. This is known as Hempel's paradoxes (in the plural) of confirmation. The counter-intuitive character of this fact is taken to be powerful criticism of the theory, despite the obvious fact that the theory is anti-intuitionist and so its advocates should not be disturbed in the least by its counter-intuitive character. For, were it permitted to rely on intuition, then the intuition that the world is law-governed is strongest, and so it dispenses with the problem of induction *ab initio*. A vast literature is devoted to efforts to rescue the instantiation theory of induction from its (seemingly?) counter-intuitive character.[30]

The second sub-theory of inductive evidence has for its background the musing that the function describing confirmation is a unique [!] function of both theory and all [!] extant evidence and of nothing more – or, if not uniquely determined, at least all such functions must [!] conform to the mathematical calculus of probability.[31] The theory, if it can be called that, is that the desired evidence is that which renders a theory probable in accord with this musing. The musing has two advantages. First, it identifies the vague concept of probable hypothesis with the clear concept of conformity to the mathematical calculus of probability. Second, it offers a clear-cut estimate of probability – on the further musing that the probability of an event equals the distribution to which it belongs. Except that this musing has no room for distributions other than those offered by theories whose probability this musing should help us estimate.

But evidence does play a great role both in research and in practical life, the self-appointed public-relations spokespeople of science exclaim in exasperation. Indeed, this is so, and from the very start; what they have promised to expose us to is not this profundity but the answer to the questions how and why? They even overlook the more basic question, which is, does evidence play the same role in research as in practical life? It is more than reasonable to assume that the answer to this question is in the negative. The public-relations spokespeople of science take it for granted that the answer is in the affirmative. So much so, that they refuse to ask it – or to hear anyone who asks it. For, clearly, investigators, be they detectives or scientists – from popular fiction or from real life – do pay great attention to minute details, as they must, and then, when their search is concluded, they ignore most of the minute details and blow up the others. How else can the small details of scientific discovery grow so large as to cover the whole of our city-scape?

When researchers – detectives or scientists – follow a clue, they do so at their own risk. Hence, science is not as successful as it looks. Even in fiction detectives do lots and lots of legwork that ends up in blind alleys. But when successful, results have to be confirmed, and their confirmations have to be easily repeatable. When the success in question is scientific, it matters little to the practical world what these are.

When the success is claimed to be worldly, then there are legal standards for confirmation, that philosophers of science assiduously ignore. In medicine, for example, a claim for success has to be repeated *in vitro*, then *in vivo* on laboratory animals, then on human specimens under specified controls, and then proved satisfactory by some complex standards.[32]

Is this not the inductive canon that the philosophers of science seek? No. It is not any philosopher's stone, but the real, human, limited, at times highly defective system. The established philosophers of science ignore it as it is no use to them in their self-appointed function as public-relations spokespeople of science, as self-appointed bouncers of the haughty club of science.

POPPER'S CRITIQUE OF INDUCTIVISM IS OVERKILL

Popper's critique of the instantiation theory of induction is simple: there are practices accepted in the scientific community concerning what counts there as confirmation, and these should be taken into account when a theory of confirmation is presented: not all instances confirm theories but, at most, those which were expected to refute it and failed. This is admitted obliquely by Carl G. Hempel, the chief discussant of the matter of instantiation and its afflictions, but not openly. Yet, he is not satisfied with the situation as he seeks a formal criterion for confirmation. He thus cannot fully admit Popper's (empirical) assertion that at most only failed refutations of a theory confirm it, as failure is not a formal criterion.[33]

The more extensive criticism of Popper is directed against the identification of confirmation with some function abiding by the calculus of probability. This is surprising, since the probability sub-theory of confirming evidence and the instantiation sub-theory of confirming evidence are, of course, but variants of the theory of induction. (Indeed, the common way to dismiss the paradoxes is to dismiss most of the confirming instances as practically irrelevant by the claim that they scarcely raise the probability of the theory which, strictly speaking, they hardly confirm.) Perhaps he does so on account of its lingering popularity. For decades Popper presented criticisms of this idea, and it would have been dropped from the agenda, were the public-relations spokespeople of science able to exhibit some sensitivity to devastating criticism.[34]

First, says Popper, confirmation cannot be probability as it reflects the force of the evidence and not the informative content of the theory prior to evidence. Therefore, at least confirmation should be probability increase, not probability. (This, he embarrassingly adds, resembles Galileo's announcement that gravity is proportional not to velocity but to its increase.) And probability increase is certainly not a function abiding by the formal calculus of probability. The point is easy to demonstrate. Here is Popper's demonstration.

Let us write '$P(h) = r$' and '$P(h, e) = r$' to denote absolute and relative probability in the usual way; suppose a theory h_1 is absolutely probable and some evidence e_1 reduces its probability, whereas h_2 is improbable yet some evidence e_2 (which may be the same as e_1 if you wish) raises its probability, but not much, so that

$$P(h_1) \geq P(h_1, e),$$
$$P(h_2) \leq P(h_2, e),$$

yet

$$P(h_1, e) \geq (h_2, e).$$

Clearly, though h_1 is more probable than h_2 it is more confirmed by the evidence. The objection that this is impossible is groundless. Moreover, a model for it is easy to construct. Here is one.

Consider event E which is the next throw of a die. Take the following cases:

h_1: E is not a 1.
h_2: E is a 2.
e: E is 1 or 2 or 3 or 4.

and

$e_1 = e_2 = e.$

Now,

$\qquad P(h_1) = 5/6,$

and

$\qquad P(h_2) = 1/6,$

so that

$\qquad P(h_1) \geq P(h_2)$

and

$\qquad P(h_1, e) = 1/2.$

and

$\qquad P(h_2, e) = 1/4,$

Now,

$\qquad P(h_1) \geq P(h_1, e).$

so that the evidence undermines h_1, whereas

$\qquad P(h_2) \leq P(h_2, e).$

so that the evidence supports h_2, yet

$\qquad P(h_1, e) \geq P(h_2, e).$

Hence, h_2 is supported by the evidence yet is less probable than h_1, which is undermined by the evidence.

This elaborate proof is superfluous, as is the model for it. It is merely a tedious if striking application of the point made by Popper in 1935 and since then generally received: probability is the inverse of informative content and science is the search for content; hence, science is not a search for probability.[35]

The more serious criticism of the identification of confirmation with probability is directed at the identification of probability with distributions. The probability of a hypothesis concerning a distribution cannot possibly be the same as the distribution it depicts, since we have competing hypotheses concerning a given distribution, and the sum of their probabilities is a fraction, but they can each ascribe a high distribution so that the sum of their distributions will exceed unity. Attempting to escape this criticism one may seek refuge in the preference for equi-distribution. This lands one in the classical paradoxes of probability. Attempting to escape this criticism one may seek refuge in the preference for confirmed distributions. This not only begs the question: it raises the paradox of perfect evidence: the evidence that fits a given distribution perfectly both raises its probability and keeps it intact – which is absurd.

How can one go on examining the defunct option that science equals probability? Only on the supposition that science is a success story and the public-relations spokespeople of science are convinced that the difficulties piled on their road to present science as a success story are marginal.

Is science a success story? Decidedly yes. What kind of success story? It is hard to specify exactly in all detail, but the first details are clear: science is a success story in that it needs no public-relations spokespeople and it is a success story not in their (vulgar) sense of the word.

❧ SCIENCE IS MORE THAN SCIENTIFIC ❧ TECHNOLOGY

The vulgar view of science as success is the view of the scientist as a person with a powerful insight, a sort of a magician. Surprisingly, this view does not conflict with the view of science as esoteric, since it alleges that only scientific research is esoteric, not the fruits of science, which are for all to see. The idea that scientific research is somewhat mysterious does conflict with the inductivist idea that research, too, is open to all. This is the idea that science is open to a simple algorithm that can be mastered by everybody. This view of science is dismissed by Popper derisively as the idea of 'science-making sausage machine'. Under the influence of Einstein it is now generally rejected as too simplistic – by all except some zealous adherents to the original idea of artificial intelligence. Today, there is a vast and exciting literature on techniques to aid the process of developing ideas that may lead to discovery ('heuristic', is the Greek word for this, which was coined by William Whewell, the great nineteenth-century philosopher who was the first to criticize the idea that there can be a science-producing algorithm). (There are examples of supposedly useful heuristic computer programs, but they are far from having been tested in the field and, anyway, heuristic is the very opposite of an algorithm proper.)[36]

The idea of a science-producing algorithm proper was recently replaced by, or rather modified as, the idea of normal science, so-called, developed around 1960 by Thomas S. Kuhn. The popularity of his philosophy, if it can be called that, rests on his conception of science, normal and exceptional. The exceptional scientist is the leader who prescribes a paradigm, namely a chief example, and a normal scientist solves problems following it. This suggests that the real magic rests in the leadership, the scientific character of the enterprise they lead rests on the obedience of their followers, the normal scientists, and the problems the normal scientists solve are quasi-algorithmically soluble: they are not so simple that a computer or a simple mind can solve, but they are not so difficult as to defy solution.

It is easy to see the allure of this philosophy: it balances a few ideas that seemingly conflict with each other but which share the goodness of being both popular and useful for the celebrated self-appointed public-relations spokespeople of science; it presents science as assured but not without some expertise and hard work; it assures science its openness to a reasonable degree, so that the public-relations spokespeople of science can see a little of the mystery involved – just enough to advocate it but not enough to partake in it actively.

What is missing in the concoction is the mystery – not the alleged mystery of the leaders of science who cannot and would not divulge the secrets of their craft, but the unmistakable mystery that is the secret of the universe.

It is not that the self-appointed public-relations spokespeople of science are not willing to praise science as the big search; after all they will say anything to glorify it. But they will use the public-relations criteria to judge when it is advisable to praise the search as the intellectual frontier and when to present it in a mundane fashion. Except that they claim to be philosophers, and thus bolster each move with a principle, and thus render complementary compliments into contradictory credentials.

Let us see if this serious matter cannot be approached somewhat more seriously and without the tricks of the trade of the public-relations spokespeople of science.

❧ SCIENCE IS A NATURAL RELIGION ❧

There is so much to do other than gate-keeping. Certain grounds may perhaps be cleared. Certain assertions should be endorsed as a matter of course or clearly dissented from, though, of course, we may also examine them in great detail if we wish. It should be conceded that traditionally science admits as evidence only repeatable evidence, though we may examine this characteristic in great detail if we wish. It should be admitted that traditionally science admits only items open to the general public, though we may examine this characteristic in great detail, too, if we wish. It should be admitted that some of the evidence which science traditionally admits as true is later on deemed false, but not overlooked; rather they are qualified and readjusted. Though we may examine all this in great detail, if we wish, we may want to know right now why these rules are deemed obligatory. The answer to this question is simple: it is taken to be the role of empirical science to explain known facts.[37]

More should be stressed at once: the rules are introduced not as taboos but as reasonable commonsense ideas. It should be clear that one may break any of these rules, but openly and at one's own risk.

The paradigm is Max Planck, who took upon himself a most unusual research project and voluntarily and as much as he could ignored all items that he could not square with it. This was his own private road to quantization.[38]

Past this we are ignorant, and it is advisable to admit ignorance in many areas and open them up for genuine research that may get the philosophy of science out of its recently acquired role as gate-keeper and bouncer and into a proliferation of researches. We do not know how empirical empirical science is, though we have the feel that some technologically oriented researches are much nearer to common experience than some speculative studies of first principles. We do not know how a research report is judged scientific and/or deserving of publication. We know that some erroneous criteria are used, and that much latitude is exercised in the matter; but more information is needed and more deliberation and experimentation.[39] We do not know how much of science is empirical and how much is guided by general principles, by the culture at large and even by politics – international, national or of the local chapter of a scientific society or the local department in the university.[40] We simply do not know enough about how science intertwines with other activities, and we only have an inkling as to what is the minimum requirement for a society that wishes to allow it to flourish, namely, freedom of speech and of dissent and of criticism and of organization to that effect.

It is hard to say what other item, if any, is generally admitted as a basic tradition.

This invites one to scout beyond the current horizon, and seek in the past some heuristic that might be helpful. And the point to start with should, perhaps, be the roots of the unbecoming hostility to metaphysics and to religion that is so characteristic of contemporary philosophy of science that induces its practitioners to undertake the lowly task of bouncers-with-a-sense-of-mission. The rise of modern science is the starting point, as the heritage from that noble period is in great need for revision.

Here, only one aspect of that period will be mentioned, the idea of natural religion. It is the idea that religion comprises a doctrine plus a ritual, that the doctrine is either revealed or natural to all thinking humans as such, and that ritual is prescribed in accord with doctrine. All of these items are nowadays known to be false, but let us overlook this for a while.

The idea of natural religion was that it is supplemented by revealed religion, not inconsistent with it. This cannot be admitted without some qualification on the religion under discussion, but here no specific religion is discussed.[41] The idea of natural religious doctrine, natural theology or rational theology, so-called, is the proof of the existence of God. This proof is now dead. The idea of the natural or rational ritual is the idea of research as worship. This idea has a tremendous attraction to some researchers, including Einstein, and other researchers consider it silly. The main obstacle in this matter is not the item under consideration, but the idea of religion as belief. The involvement of belief as a central item in any religion is a very strong item of all Western religions – not of all Eastern ones. It also led to the idea that superstitions are prejudices, namely beliefs in ideas that are objectionable or at least not warranted. It is well-known that superstitious people are sceptical, not dogmatic as the philosophers of science describe them, though, of course, what they particularly lack is the ability to be critically minded about their guiding ideas.[42]

Traditional philosophy of science took it for granted that the dogmatic and the superstitious share the errors of clinging to erroneous metaphysical systems, now better known as intellectual frameworks. It recommended not to endorse any unless it is proven. Then Kant proved that a proven intellectual framework is a set of synthetic propositions a priori proven. Then Russell and Einstein between them proved that such propositions do not exist, and the gate-keepers decided to oust all intellectual frameworks. These were reintroduced by social anthropologists and by the posthumous writings of Ludwig Wittgenstein, who spoke of them, somewhat enigmatically, as of 'forms of life'. As far as science is concerned, they were discovered by various historians of science of the Koyré school, and were then sanctified by those who identified them with Kuhnian paradigms. This is a gross error, of course, since the whole point of Kuhn's idea of the scientific paradigms is to prevent the conflict between the diverse scientific systems, especially the classical Newtonian and the modern. To use the jargon expression, he insists that paradigms are incommensurable. (They can be compared, he stresses, but not contrasted.) The whole confusion, and the bouncing that goes with it, will be cleared once we notice that intellectual frameworks do compete, and that science may both use some of them and be used as arguments for and against some of them.[43]

Obviously, a researcher may consciously and clearly follow two different guiding ideas, employ competing intellectual frameworks – from not knowing which of them is true. Taking notice of this simple, commonsense fact will free the theory of scientific research from its obsession with rational belief.[44] Current philosophy of science is fixated on the study of rational belief without any criticism of traditional ideas of belief in general and of scientific or rational belief in particular. The source of this idea was Sir Francis Bacon's superbly intelligent and highly influential doctrine of prejudice: the prejudiced cannot be productive researchers, since theories colour the way facts are observed, so that facts cease to act as refutations and as correctives of views, so that the prejudiced are blinded to contrary evidence and can only perpetrate their prejudices by endlessly multiplying evidence in their favour. This theory still animates the pseudo-researches of the self-appointed gate-keepers, even though it is amply refuted.[45] The worst of it is that philosophy of science centres on the problem, what theory deserves acceptance, where acceptance means credence. Yet it is well known that we are unable to control our credence, certainly not to confine it to a simple algorithm. It is here that the roots of the erroneous view of science as a competitor of religion can be found and corrected. This is not to deny that scientific research can be a thoroughly religious affair, a dedication to the search of the secret of the universe. This is not to deny that the religious aspect of research is not obligatory either.

Once this is realized, the avenue is open to the study of science as a central item in our culture and to see the interaction of other items in our culture with science. It is interesting to view the philosophy of science as part-and-parcel of our culture rather than as an isolated item in philosophy. What isolates the philosophy of science from the philosophy of human culture in general is the idea of the gate-keepers that any item not quite scientific is beneath the dignity of the philosopher. This idea is not quite philosophical. Nothing human is alien to any philosopher – of science or of any other aspect of human culture.

❧❧ NOTES ❧❧

1 See for more details my 'Between Science and Technology', *Philosophy of Science* 47 (1980): 82–99.

2 For the best presentation of this image of Kant see Stanley Jaki's edition of Kant's writings on cosmology.

3 For more details see my review of David Stove, *Popper and After*, *Philosophy of the Social Sciences* 15 (1985): 368–9.

4 See my 'On Explaining the Trial of Galileo', repr. in [7.4].

5 For this task of sifting the grain from the chaff in the claims of the ecological and the peace movements, see my *Technology: Philosophical and Social Aspects*, Dordrecht, London and Boston, Kluwer, 1985.

6 For more details see my 'The Functions of Intellectual Rubbish', *Research in the Sociology of Knowledge, Science and Art* 2 (1979): 209–27.

7 For more details see my 'On Pursuing the Unattainable', in R. S. Cohen and M. W. Wartofsky (eds) *Boston Studies in the Philosophy of Science*, 11, Dordrecht, London and Boston, Kluwer, 1974, pp. 249–57; repr. in [7.4].

8 References to Max Born's writings will not convey the definiteness and decisiveness with which he said this as he explained to me his refusal to gratify my request for his help in my struggle with the philosophical problems of quantum theory.

9 See Max Born's review of vol. II of Sir Edmund Whittaker's *A History of*

the Theories of the Aether and Electricity, The Modern Theories, 1900–1926 (Edinburgh, Nelson, 1953) in *The British Journal for the Philosophy of Science,* 5 (1953): 261–5.

10 In the original 'monkey trial' matters stood quite differently: not dogmatism but obscurantism was at issue, as the contested demand (of the state of Tennessee) was to forbid the teaching of evolutionism in school, not the demand (of a sect) to allow schools to teach creationism. The original defence was run by Clarence Darrow, who would not dream of inviting expert scientists, as his attitude was old-fashioned, as is clear from his autobiography.

A curious example of the use of an expert in science occurred when Faraday introduced his theory of ionization: he introduced a new terminology and this aroused displeasure which he dispelled by reporting that the terminology was suggested by William Whewell. Faraday stressed on that occasion that science is one thing and words are another. See my *Faraday as a Natural Philosopher,* Chicago IL, Chicago University Press, 1971.

11 It was Samuel Butler who asked, at the end of his classic *The Way of All Flesh,* how do we survive the educational system? His answer is tremendously intelligent: he says, we owe the survival of our culture to the imperfections of the educational system. (This explains his attitude to Matthew Arnold, the leading educationist and educational reformer of his age.)

12 For more details see my 'Science in Schools', a discussion note in *Science, Technology and Human Values,* 8 (1983): 66–7. As far as I know there was no response to this note of mine, especially not by the expert witness in the Arkansas court, whom I criticized there. That expert obviously relied on his (mis)reading of the works of Karl Popper, which he found necessary to ridicule on other occasions. This, I suppose, exempts him from the charge of dogmatism: the practice of public relations is hardly an expression of a dogma.

13 For more details about cargo cults see I.C. Jarvie, *The Revolution in Anthropology,* London, Routledge, 1964, and other editions.

14 This is questionable, as the reason Maimonides claimed that Moses was a scientist was more in order to boost science than to boost religion. See for more details my 'Reason within the Limits of Religion Alone: the Case of Maimonides', forthcoming.

15 For details and references concerning the controversial status of the works of Claude Levi-Strauss, see my [7.3], ch. 2.

16 Sir Francis Bacon introduced 'the mark of science' (*Novum Organu,* Bk. I, Aph. 124: 'the goal and mark of knowledge which I myself set up'; 'Truth . . . and utility are here the very same thing'; see also his *Works,* 1857–74, 3, 232: 'I found that those who sought knowledge for itself, and not for benefit or ostentation or any practical enablement . . . have nevertheless propounded to themselves the wrong mark, namely satisfaction (which men call truth) and not operation.' Unfortunately this was often read as relativist, despite clear anti-relativist remarks of Bacon, say, in his *Novum Organum,* Bk. I, Aph. 129 and throughout his writings, from his early manuscript, *Valerius Terminus,* onwards. Yet he clearly said, the mark of science is its success: alchemy promises the philosopher's stone and science proper will deliver the goods.

17 The exception is Popper's criterion of demarcation which is within language rather than of language, so that he could afford the luxury of ascribing scientific

status to some theories and not to their negations. For more details see my 'Ixmann and the Gavagai', *Zeitschrift für allgemeine Wissenschaftstheorie* 19 (1988): 104–16.

18 For more details see [7.31].

19 It certainly is important, both theoretically and practically, to find out as best we can, which of the regularities we observe is due to changeable local conditions and which is unalterable. The relativists cannot even pose this question intelligibly. See my *Technology*. (note 5).

20 For all this see Karl Popper, *Objective Knowledge*, Oxford, Clarendon Press, 1972, Ch. 1.

21 There is precious little discussion of these two points, of the openness of science and of the repeatability of scientific experiment, and these are brief, as if to intimate that these matters are both too obvious and non-negotiable. Though they appear originally as one in the writings of Robert Boyle, such as the Preface to his *The Skeptical Chymist*, they usually appear as separate if at all. The attempt to (re)unify them occurs first in Karl Popper, *Logik der Forschung*, Vienna, 1935, and later in the writings of Robert K. Merton.

22 Einstein asked, in his preface to Stillman Drak's translation of Galileo's *Dialogue on the Two World Systems*, why did it matter to Galileo that the Church of Rome rejected Copernicanism? There are two sufficient reasons for that, I think, one that he was an obedient son of that Church, and the other is that science at the time was under attack and had to fight back. This does not constrain, however, the correctness of the distaste towards bouncers that Einstein exhibited in that discussion.

23 Sir John Herschel suggested in the early nineteenth century that scientific evidence is *bona fide*. This is wonderful but no longer valid, as so many court cases testify. For more details see my 'Sir John Herschel's Philosophy of Success', *Historical Studies in the Physical Sciences* 1 (1969): 1–36, reprinted in [7.4].

24 This was stressed in Robert Eisler, 'Astrology: The Royal Science of Babylon', which has since gained significance despite its defects from the studies of Derek J. de Solla Price's studies of the import of Babylonian science for the rise of Greek science. See [7.21].

25 See my 'Theoretical Bias in Evidence: A Historical Sketch', *Philosophica*, 31 (1983): 7–24.

26 For more details see my 'The Role of the Philosopher Among the Scientists: Nuisance or Necessary?' *Social Epistemology* 4 (1989): 297–30 and 319.

27 See for all this my 'Sociologism in Philosophy of Science', *Metaphilosophy* 3 (1972): 103–22, reprinted in [7.4].

28 For the difference between criteria of demarcation and touchstones see [7.2].

29 For more details concerning the fact that the contents of some theories but not of all of them are read as a *façon de parler*, see my 'Ontology and Its Discontents' in Paul Weingartner and Georg Dorn (eds) *Studies in Bunge's Treatize*, Amsterdam, Rodopi, 1990, pp. 105–22. (This book appeared also as a special issue of *Poznan Studies*, Vol. 18).

30 For details see my 'The Mystery of the Ravens', *Philosophy of Science*, 33 (1966): 395–402, reprinted in my *The Gentle Art of Philosophical Polemics: Selected Reviews*, LaSalle, Ill., Open Court, 1988.

31 The demand that all (relevant) information be considered is a safeguard against

prejudice. It does not work, since it permits the refraining from the search for instances to the contrary. In the absence of any background knowledge, the demand that all competing hypotheses be examined nullifies their initial probabilities, since there are infinitely many hypotheses and the sum of their probabilities is unity. The introduction of any background hypotheses may easily alter this and render the problem very easily soluble. The literature debates the principle of simplicity (John Stuart Mill), otherwise known as the principle of limited variety (John Maynard Keynes), or of the redistribution of initial probabilities (Sir Harold Jeffreys). These do not work, but other hypotheses work very comfortably. For example, analytic chemistry works inductively very nicely against the background of the table of elements – provided its refutations are ignored, and to the extent that this is possible. Nuclear chemistry, of course, requires different background hypothesis.

The amazing thing is that a whole movement in the philosophy of science evolved when a suggestion was made to study the problem not in the abstract but as against given background hypothesis.

32 For all this see my *Technology* (note 5).

33 See my 'The Mystery of the Ravens' (note 30). In that essay I did not discuss the folly of the requirement that the criterion of confirmation should be formal. It clearly has to do with the theory of demarcation of science by meaning, presented above, which presents science as in principle utterly decidable and the competition as unable to articulate except by either endorsing or rejecting some scientific verdict or another. In brief, it is the idea that a formal criterion makes the life of a bouncer easy. In a public discussion at the end of a session of the Eastern Division of the American Philosophical Association in Boston some years ago, devoted to the contributions of C.G. Hempel to the philosophy of science, I said that researchers do not require licence from the philosopher before they dare employ a metaphysical theory in their researches. To this Hempel answered that at least his theory of confirmation was intended to oust theology, and did so rather well.

34 For the critique here cited see Popper's 'Degree of Confirmation', 1955, reprinted in [7.45], Appendix IX and many later editions.

35 This should be stressed. Popper's point is that informative content (not in the sense of information theory but in Tarski's sense) is the reciprocal of probability. R. Carnap and Y. Bar-Hillel have endorsed it and yet Carnap insisted on the identification of confirmation with probability.

36 For more detail, see my 'Heuristic Computer-Assisted, not Computerized: Comments on Simon's Project', *Journal of Epistemological and Social Studies on Science and Technology* 6 (1992): 15–18.

37 See [7.2].

38 See my *Radiation Theory and the Quantum Revolution*, Basel, Birkhäuser, 1993.

39 For the question of refereeing see my essay on it in my [7.4].

40 See my 'The Politics of Science', *J. Applied Philosophy* 3 (1986): 35–48.

41 See my 'Faith in the Open Society: the End of Hermeneutics', *Methodology and Science* 22 (1989): 183–200.

42 See my review of *Recent Advances in Natal Astrology*, 'Towards a Rational Theory of Superstition', *Zetetic Scholar* 3/4 (1979): 107–20. See also my review

of H. P. Duerr's, *Dreamtime*, 'The Place of Sparks in the World of Blah', *Inquiry* 24 (1980): 445–69.

43 See for more details my 'The Nature of Scientific Problems and Their Roots in Metaphysics', in [7.13], 189–211. Repr. [7.2] See also my *Faraday as a Natural Philosopher* (note 10).

44 For more details see my 'The Structure of the Quantum Revolution' *Philosophy of the Social Sciences* 13 (1983): 367–81.

45 See my 'The Riddle of Bacon', *Studies in Early Modern Philosophy* 2 (1988): 103–36.

～ BIBLIOGRAPHY ～

7.1 Agassi, J. *Towards an Historiography of Science*, Beiheft 2, *Theory and History*, 1963. Facsimile reprint, 1967, Middletown, Wesleyan University Press.

7.2 —— *Science in Flux*, Dordrecht, Kluwer, 1975.

7.3 —— *Towards a Rational Philosophical Anthropology*, Dordrecht, Kluwer, 1977.

7.4 —— *Science and Society*, Dordrecht, Kluwer, 1981.

7.5 Andersson, G. *Criticism and the History of Science*, Leiden, Brill, 1994.

7.6 Ayer, A. J. *The Problem of Knowledge*, London, Macmillan, 1956.

7.7 Bachelard, G. *The New Scientific Spirit*, Boston, Beacon Press, 1984.

7.8 Bohm, D. *Truth and Actuality*, San Francisco, Harper, 1980.

7.9 Born, M. *Natural Philosophy of Cause and Chance*, Oxford, Clarendon Press, 1949.

7.10 Braithwaite, R. B. *Scientific Explanation: A Study of the Function of Theory, Probability and Law*, Cambridge, Cambridge University Press, 1953.

7.11 Bromberger, S. *On What We Know We Don't Know: Explanation, Theory, Linguistics, and How Questions Shape Them*, Chicago IL, Chicago University Press, 1992.

7.12 Bunge, M. *Metascientific Queries*, Springfield IL, C. C. Thomas, 1959.

7.13 —— (ed.) *The Critical Approach: Essays in Honor of Karl Popper*, New York, Free Press, 1964.

7.14 —— *The Philosophy of Science and Technology*, Dordrecht, Kluwer, 1985.

7.15 Burtt, E. A. *The Metaphysical Foundations of Modern Physical Science: A Historical Critical Essay*, London, Routledge, (1924), 1932.

7.16 Carnap R. *Testability and Meaning*, 1936, repr. in [7.25].

7.17 —— *An Introduction to the Philosophy of Science*, New York, Basic Books, 1974.

7.18 Cohen, L. J. *An Essay on Belief and Acceptance*, Oxford, Clarendon Press, 1992.

7.19 Cohen, M. R. *Reason and Nature: An Essay on the Meaning of Scientific Method*, London, Routledge, 1931.

7.20 Colodny, R. G. (ed.) *Beyond the Edge of Certainty: Essays in Contemporary Science and Philosophy*, Englewood Cliffs NJ, Prentice Hall, 1965.

7.21 de Solla Price, D. J. *Science Since Babylon*, New Haven, CT., Yale University Press, 1960.

7.22 Duhem P. *The Aim and Structure of Scientific Theory*, Princeton NJ, Princeton University Press, 1954.

7.23 Einstein, A. 1947, 'Scientific Autobiography', see [7.57].

7.24 —— *Ideas and Opinions*, New York, Modern Library, 1994.

7.25 Feigl, H. and Brodbeck, M. *Readings in the Philosophy of Science*, New York, Appleton, Century, Croft, 1953.

7.26 Feuer, L. *The Scientific intellectual: The Psychological and Sociological Origins of Modern Science*, New York, Basic Books, 1963.

7.27 Feyerabend, P. *Science without Foundations*, Oberlin OH, Oberlin College, 1962.

7.28 Fløistad, G. (ed.) *Contemporary Philosophy*, vol. 2, Dordrecht, Kluwer, 1982.

7.29 Hamlyn, D. W. *Sensation and Perception: A History of the Philosophy of Perception*, New York, Humanities, 1961.

7.30 Hanson, N. R. *Patterns of Discovery*, Cambridge, Cambridge University Press, 1965.

7.31 Harel, D. *Algorithmics: The Spirit of Computing*, Reading MA, Addison-Wesley, (1987), 1992.

7.32 Hempel, C. G. *Aspects of Scientific Explanation and Other Essays*, New York, Free Press, 1968.

7.33 Holton, G. *Thematic Origins of Scientific Thought: Kepler to Einstein*, Cambridge MA, Harvard University Press, (1973), 1988.

7.34 —— *The Scientific Imagination*, Cambridge, Cambridge University Press, 1978.

7.35 Hospers, J. *Introduction to Philosophical Analysis*, Englewood Cliffs NJ, Prentice Hall, 1988.

7.36 Jarvie, I. C. *Concepts and Society*, London, Routledge, 1972.

7.37 Kemeny, J. G. *A Philosopher Looks at Science*, New York, Van Nostrand, 1959.

7.38 Kuhn, T. S., *The Structure of Scientific Revolutions*, Chicago IL, Chicago University Press, (1962), 1976.

7.39 Lakatos, I. and Musgrave, A. (eds) *Problems in the Philosophy of Science*, Amsterdam, North Holland, 1968.

7.40 Mises, R. von *Positivism: A Study in Human Understanding*, New York, Brazilier, 1956.

7.41 Morgenbesser, S. *Philosophy of Science Today*, New York, Basic Books, 1967.

7.42 Poincaré, H. *The Foundations of Science*, New York, Science Press, 1913.

7.43 Planck, M. *Scientific Autobiography and Other Essays*, London, Williams and Norgate, 1950.

7.44 Polanyi, M. *Personal Knowledge: Towards a Post-Critical Philosophy*, Cambridge, Cambridge University Press, (1958), 1974.

7.45 Popper, K. *The Logic of Scientific Discovery*, London, Hutchinson, 1959.

7.46 —— *Conjectures and Refutations*, London, Routledge, 1963.

7.47 —— *The Myth of the Framework: In Defence of Science and Rationality*, London, Routledge, 1994

7.48 Quine, W. V. O. *From a Logical Point of View*, Cambridge MA, Harvard University Press, 1953.

7.49 Reichenbach, H. *The Rise of Scientific Philosophy*, Berkeley CA, University of California Press, 1951.

7.50 Russell, B. *Problems of Philosophy*, New York, Holt, 1912.

7.51 —— *Icarus or The Future of Science*, London, Kegan Paul, (1924), 1927.

7.52 —— *Skeptical Essays*, London, Allen and Unwin, 1928.

7.53 —— *The Scientific Outlook*, London, Allen and Unwin, 1931.

7.54 —— *Human Knowledge. Its Scope and Limits*, London, Allen and Unwin, 1948.

7.55 Salmon, W. *Four Decades of Scientific Explanation*, Minneapolis, University of Minnesota Press, 1990.

7.56 Scheffler, I. *Science and Subjectivity*, Indianapolis, Bobb-Merrill, 1967.

7.57 Schilpp, P. A., (ed.) *Albert Einstein: Philosopher–Scientist*, Evanston, North Western University Press, 1947.

7.58 Schrödinger, E. *Science, Theory and Man*, New York, Dover, 1957.

7.59 Shimony, A. *Search for a Naturalistic World View*, Cambridge, Cambridge University Press.

7.60 Van Fraasen, B. *The Scientific Image*, London, Oxford University Press, 1980.

7.61 Wartofsky, M. W. *The Conceptual Foundations of Scientific Thought*, New York, Macmillan, 1968.

7.62 Whittaker, Sir E. T. *From Euclid to Eddington: A Study of the Conception of the External World*, Cambridge, Cambridge University Press, 1949.

CHAPTER 8

Chance, cause and conduct: probability theory and the explanation of human action
Jeff Coulter

～ INTRODUCTION ～

Human actions remain at the core of most serious explanatory work undertaken within the behavioural sciences, but there still remain major obstacles blocking an appreciation of the truly unique status of the phenomena we subsume under this rubric. In particular, an abiding theme in explanatory strategies continues to be the objective of explaining human actions by invoking *probabilistic causality* as an epistemic solution to the problem of the failure of deductive–nomological causal schemata in this domain.[1]

Deductive–nomological explanation takes the form of the logical derivation of a statement depicting the phenomenon to be explained (the *explanandum*) from a set of statements specifying the conditions under which the phenomenon is encountered and the laws of nature applicable to it (the *explanans*). A typical example of such a form of explanation would be: The occurrence of photosynthesis in plants with green leaves is explained by (i) the law which states that sunlight interacting with chlorophyll (the active agent in the leaves) generates complex organic materials including carbohydrates; and (ii) the actual conditions which obtain, viz., the exposure of green leaves to sunlight. The *explanandum* (e.g., an instance of photosynthesis) is thus a conclusion strictly deducible from a set of premises which state the relevant law(s) and the antecedent condition(s). Despite its limitations as a model for many natural–scientific causal (deterministic) generalisations, this conception of explanation became a model for social–scientific emulation.[2]

Explanatory research in the contemporary human sciences concerning human behaviour rarely employs the terminology of *determinism*: categories such as 'causes' or 'determines' are routinely eschewed or modified in favour of such 'quasi-causal' contenders as: 'shapes', 'affects' or, perhaps the favourite contender, 'influences'. In a widely used text on social research, Earl Babbie observes: 'Most explanatory social research utilizes a *probabilistic* model of causation. *X* may be said to *cause Y* if it is seen to have *some* influence on *Y*.'[3]

Although Babbie is not primarily thinking of human *actions* as explananda here, it is apparent that they are included in the scope of probabilistic-causal reasoning in the behavioural sciences. This conceptual move requires a serious reappraisal. There are many alternative theoretical resources for explaining human conduct which neither require nor employ causal or 'quasi-causal' constructions, and this will be the theme of the closing section of this chapter. However, the continued appeal of 'quasi-causal' models, schemata and theory-building enterprises obscures the relevance and adequacy of *procedural explanation* as an alternative theoretical objective. It is the primary purpose of this discussion to document the *logical* obstacles which prevent explanatory programmatic ambitions in probabilistic clothing from achieving fruition. The prospects for the acceptance of procedural explanation as a (uniquely) appropriate goal for the behavioural sciences clearly depend upon the demonstration of the logical inadequacy of nomological *and* probabilistic approaches to the project of explanation in this domain.

I shall not belabour here the many arguments designed to demonstrate that there are fundamental logical incompatibilities between the grammar of the concepts of human action and the grammar of deductive–nomological (or 'covering law') explanatory propositions.[4] Suffice to say for the purposes of this discussion that very few contemporary theorists and researchers would follow a Homans[5] or a Lundberg[6] in advocating a strictly deductive–nomological programme of enquiry into human social behaviour. The issue I seek to engage in this essay is the idea that a subsidiary form of 'quasi'-causal explanation – a version of what is sometimes called 'weak causality' – can be made intelligible in the explanation of human conduct.

The idea that causation can be conceptualized probabilistically has been the subject of much discussion in the philosophy of the social sciences in recent years. There are two principal positions at stake in the field. Some propose a version of probabilistic causation as an attenuated version of what they consider to constitute 'full-fledged' nomological causation. That is, nomological causation is conceived of as consisting in any contingent relationship between an antecedent event/state-of-affairs and a subsequent event/state-of-affairs which is *invariant* within 'scope modifiers' (*ceteris paribus* conditions which are determinately circumscribable for most practical purposes), while some probabilists claim that *all* causal connections in nature are species of conditional probabilities such that all 'causes' merely probabilify their effects to a degree that is statistically significant. In what follows, the former point of view will be considered most extensively, since this is the position which has been thought to justify a range of theoretical claims about human conduct in the non-biological human sciences. I shall, however, also make some comments about the latter position.

Hempel argued that there exists a logical alternative to the deductive–nomological (D–N) model of explanation in scientific work, and he referred to this as the 'inductive–statistical' (I–S) model.[7] According to Hempel, we can explain some particular action/event by showing that a statement which predicts it is supported with a high degree of inductive probability by some set of antecedent conditions. The burden of this chapter will be to show that this conception of 'probabilistic explanation' is defective, and that human actions, for reasons to be laid out, are not susceptible to *explanation* by *any* 'probabilistic' account. Before we can appreciate the point of such a demonstration, however, some historical ground must first be covered.

☙ BASIC ASSUMPTIONS IN THE ☙ APPLICATION OF PROBABILISTIC ANALYSIS

A central axiom of classical probability theory holds that if any event can occur in X ways and fail to occur in Y ways, where all possible ways are assumed to be equally likely, then the probability of its actual occurrence can be computed according to the formula $X/(X + Y)$ and the probability of its non-occurrence is given by $Y/(X + Y)$.[8] An alternative formulation makes reference to relative frequencies of events defined in advance as successes and failures: the probability of a given event's occurrence (success) is given by *the limit of its relative frequency* approached as the number of trials, samples, draws, etc., increases (approaches infinity). Jakob Bernoulli's golden theorem suggests that the relative frequency of successes continually approaches a stable value as the number of trials (experiments, samples taken, draws made, coins tossed, etc.) increases and that this stable value is equal to the probability of success in a single trial.[9] Bernoulli drew strikingly *deterministic* metaphysical conclusions from the applicability of his theorem:

> If thus all events through all eternity could be repeated, by which we could go from probability to certainty, one would find that everything in the world happens from definite causes

and according to definite rules, and that we would be forced to assume amongst the most apparently fortuitous things a certain necessity.[10]

This kind of reasoning has come to be known as an 'order from disorder' principle, and it has received modern support of sorts from considerations of the following kind. If you time the decay of the nucleus of a radioactive isotope, it can be determined that its radiation decreases by exactly one half every N seconds. For example, thorium C has a 'half-life' (the time it takes for a 50 per cent reduction of its radiation decay) of exactly 60.5 minutes. However, the actual emission of any particular ray/particle by the radioactive isotope is an utterly unpredictable, singular event. It appears that Bernoulli's theorem provides for exactly this sort of determinacy-from-indeterminacy reasoning, and many quantum theorists have projected probabilistic or 'stochastic' attributes to the sub-atomic domain itself as among its 'intrinsic properties'.[11]

The invocation of 'order-from-disorder' reasoning was to play a very significant intellectual role in the social and behavioural sciences. Indeed, Adolphe Quetelet, Durkheim's illustrious nineteenth-century precursor and the founder of 'social physics', sought to argue that while individual social acts (such as committing a crime) cannot be predicted, or perhaps even explained at all, social *regularities* can be detected in rates of crime for a given population. The stability of aggregated statistics, and hence of mean values, encouraged Quetelet to pronounce the possibility of a quantitative social science according to which an abstraction, *l'homme moyen*, or 'the average person', was to figure as the fundamental theoretical concept. As Gigerenzer *et al.* put it:

> Quetelet and his successors believed that large-scale regularities were quite reliable enough to serve as the basis of science. Skilled statisticians would naturally continue to make use of analysis to find how crime or fertility or mortality varied with wealth, occupation, age, marital status, and the like. But even these figures would be averages whose reliability would not grow but decline when the numbers became too small. Quetelet's statistical approach was the purest form of positivism, requiring no knowledge of actual causes, but only the identification of regularities and, if possible, their antecedents. *Such causation was much like the imaginary urn drawings posited by Jakob Bernoulli to model contingent events of all sorts.*[12]

So powerful was the 'order-from-disorderly-events' ontology projected from the tenets of probability theory that James Clerk Maxwell and

Ludwig Boltzmann came to embrace 'statistical laws' in formulating new theoretical foundations for gas physics. Gigerenzer *et al.*, again, document the way in which both Maxwell and Boltzmann 'independently invoked the well-known regularities shown by Buckle and Quetelet to justify their statistical interpretation of the gas laws'.[13] Francis Galton was also employing 'normal curve' conceptions derived from Quetelet. 'Both Galton and the gas theorists also derived their use of the astronomer's error law, or normal curve, indirectly from Quetelet. This is a striking instance of the importance of social science for the natural sciences.'[14] For the *social* sciences, however, it was to be Emile Durkheim who most forcefully propounded a conception of social causation of individual human actions on the basis of Quetelet's achievements.[15] Durkheim's *Suicide* (1897) was to become the *locus classicus* of a newly-forming statistical social science – sociology. The Durkheimian model for sociological explanation exemplified in that work became so influential that even Auguste Comte's contribution was rapidly eclipsed as a resource for the actual conduct of sociological enquiry. Comte had been the actual founder of 'sociology' whose opposition to statistical reasoning had led him to abandon the earlier nomenclature which he had shared with Quetelet ('social physics'), but it was Durkheim and his successors (especially in the United States) who were to assume the mantle of a 'scientific sociology'.

While it is true that Quetelet's 'moral statistics' and 'social physics' played a major role in the formation of the idea that social conditions predetermine differential rates of human actions, and that Durkheim's work on suicide clearly embodied such reasoning, Durkheim distanced himself from Quetelet's assumption of the intervening variable of *l'homme moyen*.[16] None the less, he elevated to the status of a new paradigm of enquiry the precept of 'order-from-disorder' by repudiating individual-level explanations of suicide (e.g., suicidees' reasons as available in, e.g., suicide notes and/or other pre-suicidal communications, or within the terms of some purely 'psychological' theory) in favour of an approach to explaining the *rates* of suicide in given populations, rates which Quetelet and others had determined to exhibit certain regularities.

An important question in interpreting the specifically Durkheimian appeal to the 'order-from-disorder' principle – the claim that macro-level regularities emerge from micro-level unpredictabilities – has been that of whether or not we must construe his resulting explanatory propositions about suicide rates to be *causal* in form. From Durkheim's writings, especially his *Rules of Sociological Method* (1895), it was clear that what he sought were nomological – causal – laws of social behaviour. In *Suicide*, there are references to the necessity of producing 'real laws ... [the better to demonstrate] the possibility of sociology',[17] and elsewhere in that text we encounter frequent allusions to 'social causes', 'real, living active forces' and even 'suicidogenic currents'.[18] However, many commentators select as his central explanatory proposition the following: 'Suicide varies inversely with the degree of [social] integration of the social groups of which the individual forms a part.'[19] Indeed, in a paper written in 1948, the influential American sociologist Robert Merton sought to codify Durkheim's sociological explanation in a classical deductive-nomological format.[20] Others followed this lead.

Although much has been made (and rightly) of Durkheim's neglect of the role of coroners' judgments and the decisions of other public officials in the 'construction' of a statistical rate of suicides,[21] and of his occasional tendency to commit the 'ecological fallacy' of inferring individual-level causation from aggregated data,[22] the more fundamental question of the logical status of any such 'sociological law' of human action has less often attracted the same intensity of critical attention. The fundamental equivocality of Durkheim's formulation has been masked by invocations of what has come to be known as 'probabilistic causality', and this is espoused as a more reasonable/attainable objective for the social sciences than nomological explanation.

Recall Durkheim's major theoretical proposition: suicide varies inversely with the degree of integration of the social groups of which an individual forms a part. From here it is concluded that, for example, anomie (lack of social integration) is a causal factor in explaining suicides. Irrespective of the purely empirical and methodological questions of data selection and interpretation, what could this proposition *mean*? As noted, Durkheim and many subsequent interpreters conceived of it as akin to what we would characterize today as a 'deductive–nomological' explanation, some even comparing it to the laws of thermodynamics, but it clearly cannot satisfy the rigorous prerequisites of a *causal* law. As it stands, it states what amounts to a relationship of co-variation: Durkheim did not have access to the modern statistical tool of the correlation coefficient,[23] but even if he had possessed such a tool and had been able to compute, say, a Pearson r from his data, the gulf which logically separates correlation from causation still looms large.

In recent years, then, a kind of 'fall-back' position has been developed within the social and behavioural sciences to cover Durkheim's and much contemporary macro-level explanatory work of a statistical type, whatever the precise statistical tool in use. This is the conception of 'probabilistic causation'. The use of this theoretical construct is supposed to achieve several objectives. First, and most importantly, it is claimed to preserve the *explanatory point* of behavioural research. Second, it is supposed to facilitate a symmetry of explanation and prediction, construed as an especially strong form of theoretical objective already widely achieved in the natural sciences. Third, it relaxes the demands made by the pursuit of deductive–nomological explanation, the only other form of explanation which carries predictive power. Fourth, it preserves the sanctity (and supremacy) of statistical methods of investigation, of quantitative modes of data gathering and presentation, within the behavioural sciences. Fifth, it makes an appeal to what it construes as cognate forms of explanation elsewhere in the sciences, especially in micro-physics, epidemiology and biomedical science.

In considering the claims made on behalf of the conception of 'probabilistic causality', then, much is at stake. In what follows, a detailed exploration of the logical problems attendant upon the use of 'probabilistic causality', as either a goal or a claim, will be undertaken.

❧ THE INDUCTIVE–STATISTICAL ❧ APPROACH TO THE EXPLANATION OF HUMAN ACTIONS

Keat and Urry, in their well-known work, *Social Theory as Science*,[24] point out several obstacles to a full-fledged *explanatory* role for probabilistic statements in relation to events. They observe that, according to Hempel's conception of inductive–statistical explanation, one can:

> explain some particular event by showing that a statement describing it is supported with a high degree of inductive probability by a set of premises, at least one of which is a statement of the statistical probability that an event of one kind will be followed by, or associated with, an event of another kind.[25]

Drawing upon a discussion of this issue by Donagan,[26] they argue that such an account conflates the distinction between what it is to have a *reasonable expectation* that an event E will occur and what it is to have *an explanation* for event E. Suppose, they suggest, that we are drawing a marble from an urn that contains a thousand marbles, one of which is black and the rest are white. We draw a white one, and then try to 'explain' this event by reference to the high inductive probability of so doing ($p = 0.999$). As Donagan remarks, however, reasonable expectations differ fundamentally from explanations:

> It is more reasonable to expect at the first attempt to toss heads with a coin than to win at roulette on a given number; but the grounds why it is more reasonable do not *explain* why you succeeded in tossing heads and failed to win at roulette. After

all, you might have won at roulette and tossed tails. *With respect to explanation*, chance situations where the odds are equal do not differ from those where the odds are fifty to one or a thousand to one.[27]

Any actual *explanation* of the drawing of the white marble from the urn in our example will have to include such considerations as the spatial distribution of the marbles in the urn *vis-à-vis* the angle of trajectory of the fingers of the one seeking to make a draw, the degree of friction of fingers in relation to marbles with respect to the possibility of grasping any given marble, and so on, none of which is given in the probabilistic analysis of the draw. Hempel had assumed that there is a symmetry between the capacity to predict an event and the capacity to *explain* that event. This example shows that the relationship *cannot* be symmetrical, since while a prediction may be forthcoming, explanation is not yet in sight. Notice, in all of this, that the *explanandum* is an *event* – the selection of a white marble. Are human actions properly conceived of, for purposes of explanation, as events? Was the 'selection of a white marble' an action or an event? This will be an issue to which we shall return further on. For the moment, though, I shall focus upon a somewhat different although related conception of 'probabilistic explanation'.

Many commentators have compared, *inter alia*, Durkheim's explanatory proposition about suicide, that anomie is a cause of suicide, to what they conceive of as a comparable one from medical science, that smoking cigarettes is a cause of lung cancer. This comparison is made because in both cases something 'short of' a nomological law appears to be at issue. Lung cancers can occur in cases when the victim has never smoked a cigarette in his/her life, and some heavy cigarette smokers fail to contract lung cancer in their natural lifetimes.[28] Similarly, some very 'highly socially integrated' people (by reasonable measures) have committed suicide and some exceptionally anomically situated folk have died purely of natural causes. Cases can be ramified: throughout modern criminology, educational psychology, family sociology, psychopathology and related disciplines, one encounters propositions purporting to explain specific forms of human conduct in terms which fall short of lawfulness but which are still displayed as having explanatory power. The device frequently employed is to invoke probabilistic causality. A transition is made from a statement such as: Under conditions $C_1 \ldots$ n, there is a probability of $O.N$ that persons P will engage in action/activity A, to one such as: Conditions $C_1 \ldots$ n cause persons P to engage in action/activity A with a probability of $O.N$. Or, if the conditional probability $p\,(X/Y)$ is significant on the basis of a sufficiently large number of cases of x-type events, given y-type conditions, then Y is causally implicated in the production of X. (Whether specific probability values are actually computed is a separate issue). A standard way of 'interpreting' multiple-regressions or path-analytic models is to extrapolate a 'probabilistic causal' statement of the form: a person's educational level of attainment is a (determinate) probabilistic-causal function of father's educational level, family income, etc., through a range of 'variables'. 'Educability' is assumed to be, thereby, an *equipossible* property. Rom Harré made a very important but often neglected comment upon the problems raised in trying to justify such a theoretical transition from a probability frequency to an explanatory proposition:

> It has long been pointed out (though the phenomenon has only recently been named) that statistical generalizations can lead to two distinct conclusions. For instance, if it is known that 80 per cent of a population have developed property A in certain circumstances and that 20 per cent have not, this can imply:
>
> 1 the probability law that every individual is 0.8 likely to develop the property A in the circumstances; or
> 2 the two non-probabilistic laws that every individual of the domain A determinatively develops A, while every individual of the domain B determinatively develops some property which excludes A, or perhaps no determinate at all of the determinable over A.[29]

Harré's argument proceeds to note that case (1) involves properties which are said to be *distributively reliable*. This means that the propensity to develop the property A can be attributed as an objective property to every member of the original domain. 'The probabilistic distribution is explained as an effect of individual fluctuation.'[30] Adopting this approach presupposes that '*every member of the domain has A amongst its repertoire of possible properties*'.[31] By contrast, case (2) involves properties that are *distributively unreliable*. '*Frequency cannot be automatically transformed into an individual propensity.*'[32] Statistical frequency is to be understood as a measure of the relative size of two or more domains in each of which the mode of manifestation of the property/properties under study is determinate. If a specific property is distributively unreliable, then 'individuals in that domain might not have that property in their repertoire of *possible* properties'.[33]

Now let us reconsider Durkheim's suicide example (although it is to be understood here that *many* other human actions might be equally considered in this context, such as, for example, raping, murdering, behaving 'schizophrenically', selecting occupation O, asking for a divorce, studying successfully, etc.). Is the capacity to 'commit suicide' a distributively reliable property of persons in any sampling domain? Since probabilities presuppose possibilities, the question may be recast as: is the *possibility of committing suicide* equally distributed throughout any given sampled population? How could *that* be determined a priori? To vary the case for a moment in order to get a better perspective on its significance, is it true, as some radical feminist theorists have argued, that it is possible for *any* adult male of reasonable physiological fitness to rape a female? Is that *possibility* equally distributed throughout a population of physiologically capable males?[34] Is 'physiological capacity' itself a sufficient indicator of the existence of the 'capacity to rape' as a part of adult males' repertoire of *possible* properties? Would 'moral values' have to be added in? And what about educational level? How could they be weighted? Remember that we are not yet dealing with probabilities, but with possibilities. The point here is surely that such a 'possible property' (i.e., the capacity to commit rape or to commit suicide) cannot be *determined empirically* in advance *either way*. It cannot be determined that such possibilities are equally distributed in any population by any method. *A priori* specifications of *possibilities* undergird *any* meaningful application of probabilistic reasoning, especially the derivation of probabilities for individual events. Thus, as far as the applicability of probabilistic reasoning to human behaviour is concerned, we confront a problem here which does not arise in those much more familiar cases in which prior possibilities *can* be determined empirically; for example, the number of sides of a coin, the number of marbles in the urn, the physically possible outcomes of a critical experiment, etc. The assumption that, for example, the capacity to commit suicide under some conditions is equipossible, is non-demonstrable, and thus a central requirement for the derivation of a determinate conclusion from the application of probabilistic reasoning to a sample of such cases is not satisfied *and not satisfiable*.

Although, as Pollock has remarked, '[i]t is generally recognised that existing theories of probability do not provide us with an account of a kind of probability adequate for the formulation of probabilistic laws',[35] none the less some philosophers continue to pursue such a theoretical formulation. One interesting theme has been to reformulate *causality* itself in wholly probabilistic terms, thereby denying that causal laws are ever genuinely specifiable as invariances within scope modifiers. Instead, 'the idea is that a cause should raise the probability of the effect; or in other words, that an instance of the type taken to be the cause should increase the probability that an instance of the effect type will occur.'[36] A problem with any such formulation is that the concepts of 'cause' and 'causal' (as well as 'effect') are not given any independent specification apart from their putative 'probability-raising' function. The analysis thus tends to assume what it needs to demonstrate, namely that the meaning of 'cause' is wholly explicable within the language of probability theory without illegitimate conflation with other, well-established probabilistic concepts and without circularity. What is also being assumed is the *invariant* inapplicability of the concept of 'certainty' to *all* causal propositions, an assumption which places a strange restriction upon our use of the word.[37]

Wittgenstein's exploration of the logical grammar of the concepts of 'certain' and 'certainty' is usually ignored in this context.[38] However, a serious problem confronting efforts to analyse all lawful, causal relationships into stochastic ones involves the presupposition of a causal field about which one may be 'certain' in the sense that 'doubt' is *logically* excluded. For example, the proposition that the probability value of getting heads in one toss of a coin is 0.5 itself depends upon the indubitability (certainty) of the causal effects of the gravitational field as a component of the conditions within which any such toss is to be made (or envisaged, to cover the possible-worlds extension of the case in point). To use a Wittgensteinian argument, one cannot treat as hypothetical, as subject to doubt, as *merely probable, every* facet of a system or field of operations within which a probability is being estimated.[39] Thus, *some* causal relationships must be assumed as beyond doubt, as not themselves susceptible to merely probabilistic formulation: attempts to characterise *all* causal relations in probabilistic terms, therefore, subvert the very possibility of establishing a stable domain within which any *particular* probability can be computed.

❧ HUMAN ACTIONS AND NATURAL ❧ EVENTS

The abiding assumption of almost all of the work in the field which employs probabilistic concepts in the context of formulating theoretical explanations of human conduct is the equation of 'human action' with 'event'. It will be remembered that probability theory was formed as a device (or array of devices) for facilitating predictions – of events, outcomes, consequences, successes/failures, states of affairs, etc., with numerical indices informing our degree of confidence, level of (legitimate) expectation, etc. Its extension in the service of ruling out *null hypotheses* or 'chance set-ups' by Fisher and his successors in the conduct of agricultural and subsequent modes of experimentation still rested upon the deployment of the concept of 'expectation'. Explanation, itself, was to be a subsequent matter of interpreting the results, using the alternative-to-null hypothesis, given an achieved 'significance level' (expressing the probability that the outcome occurred 'by chance' or not).[40] However, the appeal to 'probabilistic causation' has encouraged behavioural scientists to conceptualise human actions of various kinds as *in principle* amenable to treatment as 'events' or 'occurrences' to which the concept of 'chance' (and 'chance distribution') might be a priori applicable.

The idea that someone *did* something 'by chance' is often confused with the ordinary notion of someone *achieving* something in, through or by their action (some (unintended) outcome, result, transformation, upshot, effect, consequence etc.)[41] 'by chance'. The intelligible claim that people can do some particular sort of thing *arbitrarily* is, in turn, sometimes confused with the notion that people who have behaved arbitrarily in some sense have thereby behaved *randomly*. However, even the 'random murder' committed by the psychopath is scarcely comparable to the random emission of a particle by an isotope: the probabilistic concept of 'randomness' does not fully reduce to that of 'arbitrariness',[42] any more than the concept of a human action reduces to that of an event in nature.

An event is something that *happens* (sometimes *to* someone), whereas an action is something that someone *does*.[43] Events do not have motives or intentions, whilst actions (routinely) do: events occurring in nature, independently of human agency, are not governed by social rules, norms, conventions or stipulations, whereas most of the actions of human agents are.[44] Zeno Vendler has observed that 'the breaking of the window' may be *either* simply an event description (amenable to a causal explanation) *or* a description of something that someone did. What decides the matter is whether the case being described is one in which the window breaks or one in which someone breaks the window. Compare this case with one such as 'the walking of the dog' in which the potential event/doing ambiguity can be brought out more sharply: either the dog was walking (intransitive) or someone was walking him (transitive). Vendler comments that some verbs exhibit a morphological transformation in the verb root which marks the purely transitive occurrence (e.g., rise–raise, fall–fell, lie–lay), and he concludes that 'the rising of the flag is not the same thing as the raising of the flag, the falling of the tree is a different thing from the felling of the tree'.[45] The falling of the tree may have been (probabilistically) predicted, or even given a causal explanation, but my felling of the tree is to be explained in wholly other terms.

Now let us reconsider the earlier case of 'selecting a white marble'. This can, as it stands, be construed in at least two ways: either the agent intentionally selected a white marble, or he selected a marble 'blindly' and it turned out to be a white one. It is clearly the latter case alone which is the relevant case for a probabilistic analysis. The former case may properly be considered, *in its entirety*, to be an (intentional) action. The latter case, however, differs significantly (grammatically) from it. There, the agent's *action* may be described as, for example, making a random selection. The *outcome* of this action (and it is *this* which is the exclusive target of the probabilistic analysis) was that *a white marble was drawn*. The *event* is the *outcome*, and this is detachable, for the purposes of the analysis of reasonable expectation, from the agent's action. After all, one could say that whether or not the outcome of the act of selecting had been a white *or* a black marble, i.e., if the (target) *events* had differed, the same act of 'randomly selecting' had been performed. While the universe of possible event outcomes may be determinable in advance, the universe of possible actions cannot be. This is not because there is an *infinite* number of possible actions which human beings can perform or undertake: rather, it is because the number of possible human actions is *indefinite*: there is no *closed set* whose elements contain every possible human action, and no set containing as elements every situatedly possible option, even though there are *preferred* options, *rule-ordered* options, and the like. The magician who requests of an audience-member that he 'select a card from the pack' cannot *determine the possibility* of his or her compliance to his request in advance in the way in which he could determine the domain of outcome possibilities (and hence the probability of *any* particular outcome as 1/52).

Because there *are* patterns, regularities, orderlinesses, in human conduct (over and above the mechanistically analyseable *biological* processes subserving such conduct, though not identical to it), the failure of nomological explanation in the social and behavioural sciences has been compensated for by invoking probabilistic causation: but the alternatives are not restricted to 'cause' or 'chance'. The actions in which people engage are differentially amenable to characterisation in terms of a very large set of assessment options in respect of their contingencies of production. A given action of a specific sort may be undertaken as a matter of rule, convention, habit, obligation, preference, disposition, coercion, spontaneity or caprice, among many other contextually relevant dimensions. There are many gross and subtle distinctions to be observed between these characterizations, and even caprice and spontaneity will not reduce to 'pure chance' nor coercion to strict nomological causality. One's expectations may be raised about the prospect of someone's doing something if it can be said of him that he 'is liable to' do such-and-such as distinct from merely 'tends to' or even 'is disposed to' do it, but such a raising of one's expectations hardly qualifies for analysis in terms of a calculus of probabilities.

~~ STATISTICAL METHODS PRESUPPOSING ~~ CAUSALITY DO NOT DEMONSTRATE IT

There are many critical treatments of the application of statistical methods of analysis and explanation in the non-biological human sciences, and it is not the purpose of this essay to review these arguments. Most of them focus upon the problems involved in relating the demands or assumptive requirements of statistical analysis to the actual 'data' or empirical observations and their conceptualizations provided by researchers,[46] or upon the vexed question of the *relevance to agents* of correctly identified 'variables'.[47] These are deep issues, but proponents of quantitative inquiries in the behavioural sciences have become accustomed to treat them as technical ones, assuming that the fundamental logical appropriateness of statistical inference in the domain of explaining human behaviour emerges unscathed.

The transition from the original loci of inferential–statistical applications to their modern fields of use is sometimes treated as a process of successful intellectual cross-fertilization. The 'fertilization' metaphor is apt: some of Fisher's most important work was undertaken 'in the context of the practical demands of agricultural research'.[48] Indeed, genetics and agriculture were the two chief domains for the development and application of mathematical statistical theory in the early twentieth century. Francis Galton and Karl Pearson were primarily concerned with the analysis of genetic inheritance.[49] The founder of 'path analysis', Sewell Wright, was concerned with problems of population genetics. Biological and medical applications became increasingly common, and immensely productive, but it was through the transposition of inferential–statistical analysis to problems in psychology that the first link with the study of human conduct was established.[50]

In the domains for which inferential statistics had been developed and employed, 'causality' and 'chance' were two epistemic axes for thinking about event *explananda*. During the transposition to the study of human behaviour, these epistemic axes or presuppositions were preserved intact, just as, earlier, with classical mechanics as the model for emulation, a search for 'laws' had been the primary explanatory objective in the behavioural sciences. B. F. Skinner, for example, reacted negatively to the introduction of inferential statistics into psychological methodology, insisting upon the formulation of 'functional laws' governing organism–environment transactions as the proper goal for experimental psychological research. Rapidly, however, one inferential–statistical technique, *the analysis of variance*, rose to prominence as perhaps the most widely used of the battery of methodological devices in the behavioural sciences.

The deployment of the 'analysis-of-variance' (ANOVA) technique is designed to show whether or not a 'null hypothesis' about the *effect* of some 'treatment' variable (e.g., a pre-specified level of alcohol consumption) *upon* some 'statistical population' (e.g., a set of scores of measured reaction times) should be *rejected*. This depends upon the satisfaction of a range of assumptions, including the possibility of conducting a rigorous experiment in which the variables under study can be manipulated; the assumption of a 'normal' distribution (bell-shaped distribution) of trial scores were there an infinite number of such experiments conducted, and the assumption of 'variance homogeneity', i.e., the assumption that each set of scores has the same variance or 'dispersion about the mean'. To test the null hypothesis (e.g., that the given level of alcohol consumption has no effect upon reaction times), we compute two estimates of score variance, one of which is independent of the truth or falsity of the null hypothesis while the other is dependent upon it. If the two estimates concur, then we have no reason for rejecting the null hypothesis, whereas if they disagree, we may reject the null hypothesis and are entitled to infer a *causal contribution from the underlying 'treatment differences'* (e.g., the level of alcohol consumption) to our second estimate.

Reaction-time studies were among the earliest to be conducted using the ANOVA technique. However, they posed few epistemological difficulties: the effect of a given fertilizer upon a given crop yield is a problem with a sufficiently similar conceptual structure to the problem of the effect of a given level of human alcohol consumption upon reaction times as measures of alertness. It is when human *actions* are the explicit *or, more commonly, implicit*, focus of explanatory attention that problems arise. Many explananda in the behavioural sciences are thought to comprise discrete *states* or measurable *properties* of persons whereas in fact they comprise arrays of *human actions and their socially ascribed adverbial qualifiers* (often with only 'family resemblances' between them). This shows itself most forcefully in the area of studies of human intelligence.[51]

Considering the claim that differences in 'IQ' ('measured intelligence quotient') are caused by genetic differences,[52] a typical interpretation of the results of some ANOVA studies of this presumed relationship, Alan Garfinkel has argued that special consequences, often overlooked, ensue from the fact that the concept of 'heritability' being used is a statistical one.

> The heritability of a trait in a population is defined as the amount of variation in that trait which is due to genetic variation. The trouble with this definition is that it uses the concept 'due to', a causal concept. This causality is analyzed away statistically

by talking instead about correlations between genetic variation, on the one hand, and variation in the trait, on the other.[53]

What Garfinkel characterizes as the 'slide into correlationism' is problematic here: in the case of a society which discriminates against red-haired people, poverty has a high 'heritability' because it is highly correlated with a genetic trait, red hair:

> But this is obviously misleading. Intuitively, there are two
> distinct types of situation: on the one hand, the situation where
> there really is some genetic cause of poverty, and on the other,
> the type above, where the cause of poverty is social
> discrimination. *By its nature the concept of heritability cannot
> distinguish between the two.* Since it is a correlational notion,
> it cannot distinguish between two different causal configurations
> underlying the same covariance of the genetic trait and the
> social property.[54]

'Intelligence' would seem to be a concept of an *intrinsic* property, closer perhaps to 'having red hair' than to 'being poor' on a scale of biological-to-sociological attributes. Granting Garfinkel's point about the suppression of 'the true causalities which underlie these correlations' by the invocation of ANOVA studies of 'heritability', the question appears to remain: what is the 'true causality' for a given variation in levels of intelligence? The problem, however, is with the phenomenon of 'amount of/level of intelligence' conceptualized as an intrinsic property of a person: this is not just a function of overlooking the tenuous connections between 'intelligence quotients' and 'actual intelligence'; it is a more basic function of overlooking the fact that *any* ascription of 'intelligence' whatsoever, lay *and* 'professional', is predicated upon normative assessments of situated *actions*, their modalities and their consequences. 'Intelligence' decomposes into a variety of *praxiological* phenomena. One's intelligence is not a concrete endowment like one's nervous system. It is that which is attributable to someone who does certain things 'intelligently', or who does 'intelligent things'. Activities performed intelligently are very diverse, but even if we restricted ourselves to those activities performed as constituents of 'IQ tests' (e.g., basic arithmetical calculations, precising/paraphrasing texts, matching words to pictures, etc.), it is clear that one cannot sensibly seek to partition them into biological and cultural 'components' any more than one could determine 'how much' of what a person says is 'due to' his vocal chords and how much is 'due to' his knowledge of the language he speaks. Assuming that 'intelligence' or 'amount of intelligence' are phenomena which *could* be *causally* explained (by genetic, environmental or conjoint genetic–environmental 'factors'), as ANOVA studies routinely do, simply *presupposes* the chief point of contention, viz., that *human actions can be causally explained.*

Let us consider more closely the capacity to 'speak intelligently' as a feature of someone's 'intelligence'. In exhibiting this capacity, in saying something 'intelligent' or in 'speaking intelligently', a person can be said to be doing something, engaging in the production of a rule-governed communicative activity (a speech act of a specific sort, or series of such speech acts) with its attendant, ascribable possibilities of evaluation from among which 'intelligently/unintelligently' may be appropriately selected as relevant assessment options. (Contrast this with an action such as 'tying his shoelaces', for which the options 'deftly/clumsily' might apply, but hardly those of 'intelligently/unintelligently': the actions assessable as 'intelligent/unintelligent' are restricted by both natural *and* conventional criteria). To be able to speak in a manner which qualifies for assessment in these terms, the speaker must be saying something in a natural language (or derivative system), and this obviously means that a constitutive component of his behaviour, his grasp of English, for example, is a product of socialization. His range of vocabulary and command of syntactical complexity also are contingent upon the kinds of life experiences in a society to which he has been exposed (e.g., educational opportunities and encouragement, level of educational attainment, distribution of fluent speakers *vis-à-vis* non-fluent ones in his biographical history, their differential impact upon him as models for emulation, etc.). The topic of his discourse must be recognizably of a type which can be assessed in terms of the relevant dimensions ('intelligent/unintelligent') and not be one that is *not* susceptible to the use of such criteria (e.g., coining a quip, as distinct from repeating a joke: developing an argument, as distinct from hurling an insult). Consider these features – vocabulary, syntax, topic (and many related ones) – as 'environmentally derived'. Now consider the following. To be able to speak at all requires a vocal apparatus, a functioning laryngeal system with intact motor functions in the mouth and throat. There is a complex physiological apparatus, extending deep into the cortex, which *facilitates* (but does not cause)[55] the production of normal speech, most of which may be thought of as components of a person's genetic endowment. Consider these features as 'genetically derived'. Now, for any case *or sequence of cases* in which a person can be *interpersonally assessed* as 'speaking intelligently', itself a common (although by no means exclusive or necessary) criterion for 'having intelligence', how is one to proceed to *partition* and *weight* those contributions made by an 'environment' and those made by 'genetic endowment' to the action or sequence of actions so assessed? Remember that, for the purposes of defining 'intelligence', an 'environment' has been argued to include not only the activity (activities) of the target individual(s) but also the evaluative assessment of others, made against a background of conventional criteria of complex kinds.

'Intelligent discourse' is hardly the sort of 'phenomenon' which can be analysed into discrete 'components' making their 'causal contributions' in a linear, additive manner. Should the amount of variation between people with respect to their 'speaking intelligently' be parcelled out into the amount due to 'genetic' variation (80 per cent? 40 per cent?) and that due to 'environmental' differences (20 per cent? 60 per cent?)? Even now to reconsider the question is to see that its basis is entirely wrong, and the mistake is a function either of failing to appreciate the complexity of human conduct, the varieties and range of human actions with their adverbial potentials, which are glossed by categories such as 'intelligence', *or* of presupposing without question the applicability of causal reasoning to, *inter alia*, rule-governed behaviour. Usually, the one error is committed *pari passu* with the other.

Inferential–statistical studies of the kind known as 'analysis of variance' have been exceptionally illuminating in their domains of proper application, but the extension of this technique into the field of human conduct is fraught with logical difficulties and anomalies which are only obscured by treating human actions as phenomena of the same fundamental logical types as natural events, discrete states, quantifiable differences or fixed or variable properties/attributes.

❧ CONCLUDING REMARKS ❧

The uses (and abuses) of probability theory are many and varied. In this discussion, I have restricted myself to the consideration of some fundamental but interrelated issues which are not often addressed directly by proponents of inferential–statistical analysis as the *sine qua non* of explanatory work in the sciences of human action. Convinced that the conceptual or logical credentials of probabilistic reasoning about human behaviour are impeccable, theorists and researchers alike tend to give much less credence to alternative, non-statistical, approaches to the study of human conduct. It is high time that this unfortunate proclivity were abandoned: the logical foundations of statistical–inferential work in the social sciences are not nearly as impeccable as some of its influential champions would have us believe, and the detailed investigation of the properties, logical and empirical, of *in situ* human conduct which have been conducted over the past twenty or thirty years in more 'qualitative' areas of the behavioural sciences attest to the comparative crudity of the models of behaviour which have been constructed solely to facilitate a preferred methodological strategy of an inferential–statistical sort. Reifications of the kind seen above in the statistical study of the heritability of 'intelligence' are partly a function of insensitivity to the properties of the praxiological phenomena glossed by such categories and partly a function of the over-extension of techniques such as ANOVA to domains for which it had not originally been developed.

If the arguments presented here are correct, then the project of formulating probabilistic–causal explanations is indeed questionable. The further point could be made that it is largely irrelevant. Explanation is a motley affair: if probabilistic–causal explanation is the poor step-child of nomological explanation, then it is time to look again at the explanatory project and ask: what *sort* of scientific (abstract, general, observationally based) explanations are logically appropriate, methodologically defensible and manageable for the scientific study of the domain of human conduct?

One very important alternative contender for the explanatory stakes these days is *procedural* explanation. Here, the theorist or researcher seeks to develop an empirically grounded characterization of *how* human beings produce whatever forms of conduct they produce, including their behaviour of 'explaining their behaviour', of producing 'reasons-for-their-actions'. The form of scientific explanation here is basically a *grammatical* one. That is, the objective becomes to specify a set of abstract rules, principles, procedures or 'methods' (not necessarily of an *algorithmic* kind) which explain how conduct is (re)produceable in its details, to any desired level of such detail.[56]

Advocating the pursuit of alternative forms of explanation is not an invitation to endlessly 'reflexive' self-examination or 'deconstructive' nihilism: the fundamental goals of any empirical science of human action worth its salt should remain those of illuminating the nature of the phenomena and relating any such insights to relevant areas of interest and significance in the other life sciences. Anything less would be to substitute for the demanding project of truly scientific inquiry the fads and vagaries of an ideological quest.

❧ NOTES ❧

1 Carl Hempel, *Aspects of Scientific Explanation*, New York, Free Press, 1965.
2 See [8.6], 4–24.
3 Earl Babbie, *The Practice of Social Research*, 4th édn, California, Wardsworth Publishing Company, 1986, p. 65 (émphasis in original). Babbie also remarks: 'A perfect statistical relationship between two variables is *not* an appropriate criterion for causation in social research. We may say that a causal relationship exists between X and Y, then, even though X is not the *total* cause of Y' (Ibid.). The idea that a probabilistic cause is expressible as a fraction (e.g., the idea

of something like a 'two-thirds cause' of a given variable) is a function of extrapolating theoretically from path-analytical models, as we shall see later on.

4 I shall assume, for the purposes of this essay, that Humean–Hempelian causal programmes for the explanation of human actions have been shown to be incapable of coming to terms with many of the constitutive properties of *praxis*. For an early, but still pertinent, treatment of some of the central problems in this area, see [8.31]. Also, see Hanna F. Pitkin's excellent review of the issues in her 'Explanation, Freedom and the Concepts of Social Science', [8.35], ch. 10. Some more recent issues, especially those associated with Putnam, Dennett and Davidson and are discussed in my *Rethinking Cognitive Theory* New York, St Martin's Press, 1983, ch. 1 and 5 and *Mind in Action*, New Jersey, Humanities Press, 1989, ch. 7.

5 George C. Homans, *The Nature of Social Science*, New York, Harcourt Brace Jovanovich, 1967.

6 G. A. Lundberg, *Foundations of Sociology*, 1939, rev. ed, New York, David McKay 1964.

7 See note 1.

8 This is the 'classical' interpretation associated with the Marquis de LaPlace whose philosophical essay on probability was first published in 1819. For a thorough review of the problems raised by extending the scope of application of the classical interpretation, see W. C. Salmon, *The Foundations of Scientific Inference*, Pittsburgh, University of Pittsburgh Press, 1966. In this chapter, I do not discuss 'subjective' probability. In particular, I shall not be concerned with the assessment of the claim that human agents are crypto-Bayesians. For a good introduction to Bayesian probability, along with some comments on the use of Bayes' theorem as a standard by which to assess 'intuitive probability judgements' made by non-specialists, see Ronald N. Giere, 'Scientific Judgment', ch. 6 of his *Explaining Science: A Cognitive Approach*, Chicago, University of Chicago Press, 1988. For an extensive discussion of the Kahneman–Tversky thesis about putative 'biases' in ordinary human reasoning, informed by the Bayesian model as a criterion, see [8.20] 214–33.

9 The derived binomial theorem holds that the probability of X successes in N trials is given by: N factorial over the product of X factorial and $(N - X)$ factorial, multiplied by the product of (the probability of a success in any single trial raised to the power of X) with (the probability of a failure in any single trial raised to the power of $(N - X)$).

10 Jakob Bernoulli, quoted in F. N. David, *Games, Gods and Gambling*, London, Macmillan, 1962, p. 137.

11 This is the basis of the dispute between the Copenhagen interpretation and its rivals. Some physicists still maintain what could be termed a 'hidden-variable(s)' view of the matter, arguing that the indeterminacies encountered at the subatomic level are functions of our current ignorance of forces yet to be discovered which will, once revealed, enable us to reason causally about the phenomena.

12 [8.20], p. 42, emphasis added.

13 Ibid., p. 45.

14 Ibid.

15 For extensive historical documentation of this claim, see Stephen P. Turner, *The Search for a Methodology of Social Science: Durkheim, Weber, and the Nine-*

teenth-Century Problem of Cause, Probability, and Action, Dordrecht, Reidel, 1986.

16 For some discussion and documentation of this, see Steven Lukes, *Emile Durkheim: His Life and Work*, Stanford, California, Stanford University Press, 1985, p. 194, n. 18. See also Jack D. Douglas, *The Social Meanings of Suicide*, Princeton, Princeton University Press 1967, p. 16. It should also be noted that Quetelet, for his part, was later to become highly critical of 'Durkheimians', to some extent for their espousal of 'causal' forms of explanation.

17 Emile Durkheim, Preface to *Suicide: A Study in Sociology*, trans. J. Spaulding and G. Simpson, London, Routledge and Kegan Paul, 1952.

18 For a detailed and carefully documented discussion of the nature of Durkheim's 'explanation' in *Suicide*, see Steven Lukes, op. cit., pp. 213–22.

19 Ibid., p. 209. Cf. R. W. Maris, *Social Forces in Urban Suicide*, Homewood, Illinois, Dorsey Press, 1969.

20 R. K. Merton, 'The Bearing of Sociological Theory on Empirical Research', in [8.29], 87.

21 There is now quite a large, post-Durkheimian research literature on suicide, much of which begins with criticisms of Durkheim's methodological procedures. For an extensive review of this material, see J. M. Atkinson, *Discovering Suicide*, London, Macmillan, 1978.

22 This is the well-documented and, by now, orthodox, complaint initially made by H. C. Selvin in his well-known paper, 'Durkheim's Suicide and Problems of Empirical Research', *American Journal of Sociology* 63 (1958). 607–19; repr. as rev. in R. A. Nisbet (ed) *Emile Durkheim*, Prentice-Hall Englewood Cliffs, NJ, 1965.

23 This is something noted by Selvin in his critical discussion in Nisbet (ed.), ibid., p. 113.

24 [8.29], 2nd edn.

25 Ibid., p. 12.

26 Alan Donagan, 'The Popper–Hempel Model Reconsidered' in W. H. Dray (ed.) *Philosophical Analysis and History*, New York, Harper and Row, 1966. See Paul Humphreys, 'Why Probability Values Are Not Explanatory' in *The Chances of Explanation*, New Jersey, Princeton University Press, 1989, pp. 109–17, for a more recent statement of this position.

27 Ibid., p. 133.

28 A great deal has been made of these 'shortcomings' in the popular debate about smoking and its relationship to lung cancer, but I do not wish to be understood here as giving credence to any kind of *principled* scepticism about the possibility of a strong, causal relation. Even though it is true that the precise *causal mechanism* involved in the generation of cancerous tumours in lung tissue by the nitrites discovered in cigarette smoke has not yet been determined, the claim for a causal relationship of a nomological kind is still a reasonable hypothesis. The problem arises because of the complexity of the scope modifiers required to buttress the strong nomological claim. That lung cancers can occur in the absence of carcinogenic smoke inhalation only shows that this disease can have more than one kind of cause: it does nothing to limit the generalization that smoking causes lung cancer. The problem with the invocation of 'probabilistic causal statements' as 'explanations' in this domain is precisely that it might

operate to *foreclose* the search for genuine causal mechanisms and hence for genuine causal–explanatory propositions. This presupposes, of course, that the *domain* within which such a type of explanation is being sought is an appropriate one for such a search. In the case of the smoking/cancer relationship, all of the evidence points in that direction. This is not always the case, however.

29 Rom Harré, 'Accounts, Actions and Meanings: The Practice of Participatory Psychology' in M. Brenner *et al.* (eds) *The Social Contexts of Method* New York St Martin's Press, 1978, pp. 53–4. It should be noted here that Harré's use of 'law' in the description of the first conclusion carries no causal implication, and the passage might be paraphrased into the generalization: for every individual in the population sampled there is a probability of 0.8 that he/she will develop property A under conditions C, or: there is an 80 per cent chance that he or she will develop property A under conditions C.

30 Ibid., p. 54.

31 Ibid., emphasis added.

32 Ibid., emphasis added.

33 Ibid.

34 I owe this example to Tim Costelloe.

35 John L. Pollock, 'Nomic Probability' in Peter A. French *et al.* (eds) *Midwest Studies in Philosophy.* vol. IX, Minneapolis, University of Minnesota Press, 1984, p. 177.

36 John Dupré, 'Probabilistic Causality Emancipated', in Peter A. French *et al.* (eds), *op. cit.*, p. 169.

37 For a more technical discussion of these difficulties, see Ellery Eells, *Probabilistic Causality*, Cambridge, Cambridge University Press 1991.

38 L. Wittgenstein, *On Certainty*, G. E. M. Anscombe and G. H. von Wright (eds) Oxford, Blackwell, 1969.

39 Ibid. para. 105.

40 There is a long tradition in the behavioural sciences of insisting upon a significance level of at least 0.05 for results derived from the use of the ANOVA technique as a prerequisite for serious consideration and/or publication. For some critical commentaries upon this practice within the social sciences themselves, see, *inter alia*, J. M. Skipper jnr., A. L. Guenther and G. Nass, 'The Sacredness of .05', *The American Sociologist* 2 (1967): 16–18 and R. P. Carver, 'The Case Against Statistical Significance Testing', *Harvard Educational Review* 48 (1978): 378–99.

41 Part of the difficulty here was noticed by Joel Feinberg who remarked that 'upshots' are sometimes ascribed to persons with the use of singular but complex verbs, such as: 'he frightened him', 'she persuaded you', 'they startled her', etc. This can lead to failures in distinguishing between *actions* and other things 'done' by people. A parallel confusion would be to imagine that 'he slept soundly', being something that he 'did', was an action he undertook. See the treatment of these issues in his 'Action and Responsibility' in Alan R. White (ed.) *The Philosophy of Action*, Oxford, Oxford University Press, 1977. Interestingly, J. L. Austin's category of 'perlocutionary *acts*' appears to suffer from such a conflation of act/upshot, or action/consequence.

42 For an event to be 'random' in the terms of probability theory is for it to be *equally as likely to occur* as any other. As Signorile has remarked, 'what we

discover at work here is the round-robin of using "random" to arrive at the meaning of equiprobability, and equiprobability to arrive at the meaning of "random" ' (Vito Signorile, 'Buridan's Ass: The Statistical Rhetoric of Science and the Problem of Equiprobability' in H. Simon (ed.) *Rhetoric in the Human Sciences*, Newbury Park, California, Sage, 1989, p. 79. Signorile quotes M. G. Kendal and W. R. Buckland (from their *Dictionary of Statistical Terms*, New York, Hafner, 1960) as insisting that: 'Ordinary, haphazard or seemingly purposeless choice is generally insufficient to guarantee randomness when carried out by human beings and devices'. And he adds: 'What the statistician is trying to guarantee is strict equality of opportunity. We all know that this just doesn't happen by chance' (Ibid.).

43 Bearing in mind, of course, the *caveats* in the preceding footnote. Of course, on occasion we can speak of someone's doing something as an 'event' (think of one's child's production of his first word, or of the delivery of an historic speech, etc.). However, *these* 'events' have a different logical status from 'events-in-nature'.

44 This point is worth directing against extrapolating from behaviouristic studies of the conditional probabilities of 'responses' given specific stimuli and conditioning histories to the domain of human actions. Most *actions* are not properly construable as 'responses' to *anything*, and, when they *are* so construable, they cannot be specified in properly behaviouristic terms. How could one analyse, for example, the human action of 'answering a question' (which surely would qualify as a sort of 'response') into bio-behavioural event sequences alone? There are no context-free indicators in the stream of speech which alone specify an utterance as an 'answer to a question'.

45 Zeno Vendler, 'Agency and Causation', in Peter A. French *et al.* (eds), *op. cit.*, p. 371. See note 35.

46 An excellent review of the issues raised by dependent/independent-variable analysis, especially the Lazarsfeldian statistical programme in sociology, is provided by Douglas Benson and John A. Hughes in their chapter, 'Method: Evidence and Inference' in [8.13]. For a discussion of a range of issues involved in implementing quantitative strategies of sociological inquiry, especially as they bear upon the problem of data representation, see Stanley Lieberson, *Making It Count*, Berkeley, University of California Press, 1985.

47 On this issue, Herbert Blumer's classic discussion remains unsurpassed: see his 'Sociological Analysis and the "Variable" ' in his *Symbolic Interactionism: Perspective and Method*, Englewood Cliffs, NJ, Prentice-Hall, 1967.

48 Donald A. MacKenzie, *Statistics in Britain 1865–1930* Edinburgh, Edinburgh University Press, 1981, p. 211.

49 MacKenzie's outstanding study (*Ibid.*) is a rich source of documentation of the stimuli which powered both the initiatives and the disputes characteristic of the developing field of inferential statistics. Especially interesting is his attempt to relate these directly to the growth of the 'eugenics' ideology of human inheritance and its internal controversies.

50 See Gerd Gigerenzer *et al.*, 'The New Tools' in [8.20], 205–11.

51 I have discussed this issue elsewhere. See my 'Intelligence as a Natural Kind' in *Rethinking Cognitive Theory*, London, Macmillan, and New York, St Mar-

tin's Press, 1983 and 'Cognition in an Ethnomethodological Mode' in [8.13], 190–2.

52 It is worth noting at the outset that 'IQ' scores themselves are a function of tests:

> so constructed that the frequency distribution of test scores in the reference population conforms as closely as possible to a normal distribution ... centred on the value of 100 and having a half-width or standard deviation (the square root of the variance) of 15 points. To call IQ a measure of intelligence conforms neither to ordinary educated usage nor to elementary logic.

(David Layzer, 'Science or Superstition? A Physical Scientist Looks at the I.Q. Controversy' in N. J. Block and Gerald Dworkin (eds) *The I.Q. Controversy*, New York, Pantheon Books, 1976, p. 212)

53 [8.19], 119.

54 Ibid., pp. 119–20. Emphasis in original.

55 I mean this in the sense in which my having legs enables me to walk, but my having legs does not *cause* me to walk (or run, hop, etc.).

56 For a representative collection of founding papers in the area of social science called 'ethnomethodology', see my edited volume *Ethnomethodological Sociology*, London, Edward Elgar, 1990. Perhaps the most important contributions to this area of enquiry after Harold Garfinkel's originating work have been the studies of Harvey Sacks. See Gail Jefferson (ed.) *Lectures on Conversation by Harvey Sacks*, vols 1 and 2, Oxford Blackwell, 1992. This set is perhaps misnamed, however: Sacks's investigations ranged over modes of human (largely communicative) *praxis* broader than those glossed by the category 'conversation'.

∞ BIBLIOGRAPHY ∞

8.1 Anderson, R. J., Hughes, J. A. and Sharrock, W. W. *Philosophy and the Human Sciences*, London, Croom Helm, 1986.

8.2 Apel, K-O. *Analytic Philosophy of Language and the Geisteswissenschaften*, trans. H. Holstelilie, Dordrecht, Reidel, 1967.

8.3 Benn, S. and Mortimore, G. (eds) *Rationality and the Social Sciences*, London, Routledge, 1976.

8.4 Benton, T. *Philosophical Foundations of the Three Sociologies*, London, Routledge and Kegan Paul, 1977.

8.5 Bernstein, R. J. *Praxis and Action*, London, Duckworth, 1972.

8.6 —— *The Restructuring of Social and Political Theory*, Pennsylvania, University of Pennsylvania Press, 1978.

8.7 Bhaskar, R. *A Realist Theory of Science*, Leeds, Leeds Books, 1975.

8.8 —— *The Possibility of Naturalism*, Hassocks, Harvester Press, 1979.

8.9 Block, N. (ed.) *Readings in the Philosophy of Psychology*, vols. 1 and 2, Cambridge, Mass., Harvard University Press, 1980.

8.10 Borger, R. and Cioffi, F. (eds) *Explanation in the Behavioral Sciences*, Cambridge, Cambridge University Press, 1970.

8.11 Brodbeck, M. (ed.) *Readings in the Philosophy of the Social Sciences*, New York, Macmillan, 1968.

8.12 Brown, R. *Explanation in Social Science*, London, Routledge and Kegan Paul, 1963.

8.13 Button, G. (ed.) *Ethnomethodology and the Human Sciences*, Cambridge, Cambridge University Press, 1991.

8.14 Care, N. S. and Landesman, C. (eds) *Readings in the Theory of Action*, Bloomington, Ind., Indiana University Press, 1968.

8.15 Cicourel, A. V. *Method and Measurement in Sociology*, New York, Free Press, 1964.

8.16 Coulter, J. *The Social Construction of Mind: Studies in Ethnomethodology and Linguistic Philosophy*, London, Macmillan, (1979), 1987.

8.17 Dallmayr, F. and McCarthy, T. (eds) *Understanding and Social Inquiry*, Notre Dame, University of Notre Dame Press, 1977.

8.18 Emmet, D. M. and MacIntyre, A. (eds) *Sociological Theory and Philosophical Analysis*, London, Macmillan, 1970.

8.19 Garfinkel, A. *Forms of Explanation*, London, Yale University Press, 1981.

8.20 Gigerenzer, G., Swijtink, Z., Porter, T., Daston, L., Beatty, J. and Kruger, L. *The Empire of Chance. How Probability Changed Science and Everyday Life*, Cambridge, Cambridge University Press, 1989.

8.21 Haan, N. *et al.* (eds) *Social Science as Moral Inquiry*, New York, Columbia University Press, 1983.

8.22 Halfpenny, P. *Positivism and Sociology: Explaining Social Life*, London, George Allen and Unwin, 1982.

8.23 Harré, R. *Social Being*, Oxford, Blackwell, 1979.

8.24 Harré, R. and Secord, P. *The Explanation of Social Behavior*, Totowa, N. J., Littlefield Adams, 1973.

8.25 Hollis, M. *Models of Man: Philosophical Thoughts on Social Action*, Cambridge, Cambridge University Press, 1977.

8.26 Hollis, M. and Lukes, S. *Rationality and Relativism*, Oxford, Basil Blackwell, 1982.

8.27 Jarvie, I. C. *The Revolution in Anthropology*, Chicago, Henry Regnery, 1967.

8.28 Kauffmann, F. *Methodology in the Social Sciences*, London, Oxford University Press, 1944.

8.29 Keat, R. N. and Urry, J. R. *Social Theory as Science*, London, Routledge and Kegan Paul, 1975 (2nd edn 1982).

8.30 Laslett, P. and Runciman, W. G. (eds) *Philosophy, Politics and Society*, vol. II, Oxford, Blackwell, 1962; vol. III, Oxford, Blackwell, 1967.

8.31 Louch, A. R. *Explanation and Human Action*, Oxford, Blackwell, 1966.

8.32 Macdonald, G. and Pettit, P. *Semantics and Social Science*, London, Routledge, 1981.

8.33 Natanson, M. (ed.) *Philosophy of the Social Sciences*, New York, Random House, 1963.

8.34 O'Neill, J. (ed.) *Modes of Individualism and Collectivism*, London, Heinemann, 1973.

8.35 Pitkin, H. F. *Wittgenstein and Justice: On the Significance of Ludwig Witt-*

genstein for Social and Political Thought, Berkeley, University of California Press, 1972.

8.36 Popper, K. R. *The Poverty of Historicism*, London, Routledge and Kegan Paul, 1961 (1st edn 1957).

8.37 Putnam, H. *Meaning and the Moral Sciences*, Boston, Routledge, 1978.

8.38 Rudner, R. S. *Philosophy of Social Science*, Englewood Cliffs, N. J., Prentice-Hall, 1966.

8.39 Ryan, A. *The Philosophy of the Social Sciences*, London, Macmillan, 1970.

8.40 —— (ed.) *The Philosophy of Social Explanation*, London, Oxford University Press, 1973.

8.41 Schutz, A. *Collected Papers*, vols. I and II. Evanston, Northwestern University Press (1966), 1971.

8.42 —— *The Phenomenology of the Social World*, trans. G. Walsh and F. Lehnert, London, Heinemann, 1972 (1st English edn., Evanston, Northwestern University Press, 1967).

8.43 Schwayder, D. *The Stratification of Behaviour*, London, Routledge & Kegan Paul, 1965.

8.44 Skinner, Q. (ed.) *The Return of Grand Theory in the Human Sciences*, Cambridge, Cambridge University Press, 1985.

8.45 Taylor, C. *The Explanation of Behaviour*, London, Routledge and Kegan Paul, 1964.

8.46 Taylor, R. *Action and Purpose*, New Jersey, Prentice-Hall, 1966.

8.47 Truzzi, M. (ed.) *Verstehen: Subjective Understanding in the Social Sciences*, New York, Addison-Wesley, 1974.

8.48 von Wright, G. H. *Explanation and Understanding*, Ithaca, N. Y., Cornell University Press, 1971.

8.49 Weber, M. *The Methodology of the Social Sciences*, Glencoe, Ill., Free Press, 1949.

8.50 White, A. R. (ed.) *The Philosophy of Action*, Oxford, Oxford University Press, 1968.

8.51 Wilson, B. R. (ed.) *Rationality*, Oxford, Blackwell, 1970.

8.52 Winch, P. *The Idea of a Social Science and Its Relation to Philosophy*, London, Routledge and Kegan Paul, 1958 (New edn 1988).

8.53 —— *Ethics and Action*, London, Routledge and Kegan Paul, 1972.

CHAPTER 9

Cybernetics

K. M. Sayre

Cybernetics was inaugurated in the 1940s expressly as a field of inter-disciplinary research, in reaction to the specialization that already had begun to encumber the established sciences. Chief among the disciplines initially involved were mathematics (represented by N. Wiener, the leader of the movement), neurophysiology (W. Cannon, A. Rosen-bleuth, later W. McCulloch), and control engineering (J. Bigelow). The interdisciplinary base of the group was soon expanded to include math-ematical logic (W. H. Pitts), automaton theory (J. von Neumann), psychology (K. Lewin) and socioeconomics (O. Morgenstern). While activities of the group at first were centred around Harvard and MIT, its subsequent expansion led to several meetings at other locations along the northeastern seaboard. Notable among these was a conference on teleology and purpose held in New York in 1942 under the auspices of the Josiah Macy Foundation (followed by other meetings under those auspices resuming in 1946), and a meeting on the design of computing machinery held in Princeton in 1944. The role of these early meetings was like that of a community forum, allowing participants to share insights into common problems and jointly to explore novel means of resolution.

Need for a forum of this sort arose first in connection with problems being studied by Wiener and Bigelow in the design of mech-anisms for controlling artillery directed against fast-moving aircraft, which Rosenbleuth saw to be similar to problems he had been studying in the erratic control of goal-directed motor behaviour in human patients. The topic of feedback processes (see below) on which the group subsequently focused attention thus arose from a comparative study of biological and artifactual control systems. Invariably associated with problems in the design of effective control systems are problems of communicating data to the system on which its corrective responses can be based, and of communicating these responses to the appropriate effector mechanisms. In the biological organism these communication functions are served by the afferent and the efferent nervous systems, respectively, parallel to the radar and the aiming mechanisms of the anti-aircraft battery. This joint emphasis upon communication and control systems accounts for the somewhat inelegant subtitle of Wiener's seminal book: *Cybernetics, or Control and Communication in the Animal and the Machine* ([9.5]).

The name 'cybernetics', chosen by Wiener for this new field of study, derives from the Greek *kubernētēs*, meaning steersman or pilot. Inasmuch as 'governor' derives (via the Latin *gubernare*) from the same root, cybernetics was provided with a ready-made technological ancestry, beginning with James Watt's invention in the late eighteenth century of devices (called 'governors') regulating the rotational speed of steam engines. Political antecedents can be traced back to Plato, who several times in the *Republic* and the *Statesman* likened the leader of a well-run political order to the *kubernētēs* of a ship. A recognizably philosophic lineage also goes back to Plato, with his reference in the *Phaedrus* (247C7–8) to reason as the *kubernētēs* of the soul (prefiguring the Phi Beta Kappa motto *philosophia bion kubernētēs* – 'philosophy the guide of life').

Wiener's interest in technical problems of communication had been anticipated by H. Nyquist and R. Hartley, progenitors of the statistical concept of information. Despite Wiener's having numbered C. Shannon among his original group, contributions to this area after publication of the latter's article 'The Mathematical Theory of Communication' ([9.16]) tended to be categorized under the title 'communication theory' (or 'information theory') rather than 'cybernetics'. Another emerging field of research in which cybernetics was initially involved, but soon suffered loss of name-recognition, was the theory of computing machinery. Although Wiener was a key contributor, along with V. Bush (MIT), H. Aiken (Harvard) and J. von Neumann (Princeton), to planning sessions leading to the construction of the first electronic digital computers, he remained more interested in possible neurological parallels with these mechanisms than in their logical design. Subsequent contributions to the field of digital computation owes relatively little to its broadly cybernetic origin.

Cybernetics' early emphasis upon functional parallels between biological and mechanical control systems soon led, in industrial circles, to its identification with factory automation and other forms of robotics. In academic circles, by contrast, cybernetics came to be associated with the then arcane field of artificial intelligence (AI), which took its start as part of an effort to reduce human involvement in the large-scale computer-based air-defence systems under development at MIT's Lincoln Laboratory in the 1950s. Key contributors to AI at this early stage were O. Selfridge, a younger member of Wiener's original group, along with M. Minsky and S. Papert, all of MIT. Philosophers who became involved with AI through their association with MIT in the 1950s included H. Dreyfus, who was generally critical of the enterprise, and K. Sayre, who saw potential in AI as a new approach to traditional problems in the philosophy of mind. The first institutional centre for combined research in philosophy and AI was established by the latter in the early 1960s at the University of Notre Dame.

Despite its history of involvement with technological developments, the major spokesmen of cybernetics from Wiener onward have been explicitly concerned with its broader philosophic implications. The following discussion treats both its philosophic antecedents and its potential for further philosophic contributions. Remarks on the current interaction between AI and cybernetics are reserved for the final section below.

❧ BASIC CONCEPTS ❧

Philosophy before Plato was marked by a series of attempts to find a small set of basic principles in terms of which the manifest variety of the observable world could be understood as coherently integrated. Cybernetics returns to this task with a set of explanatory concepts based upon the presence of variety itself. Primary among these are the concepts of feedback, of entropy and of information.

Feedback

Any operating system functions within a variable environment with which it interacts through its input and output couplings. Feedback occurs whenever variation at the output works upon the environment in such a fashion as to produce a corresponding variation at the input of the system as well. Of primary concern to cybernetics are two kinds of feedback pertaining specifically to deviation from a stable state of the operating system. Positive feedback occurs when deviation from a stable state produces outputs that lead to yet further deviation. An example is an increase in membership of an interbreeding population which produces an even greater increase in subsequent generations. Feedback of this sort is labelled 'positive' because it tends to increase deviation from stability of the system in which it occurs. Negative feedback occurs, by contrast, when momentary deviation from a stable state leads to inputs that counteract further deviation. Common examples of negative feedback are the operations of a thermostat to maintain a steady temperature within an enclosure, and the subtle shifts in bodily posture by which a skier maintains balance on a downhill run.

Types of negative feedback may be further differentiated with respect to the bearing of the regulatory mechanisms that maintain a system in a stable mode of operation. Homeostasis is a type of feedback by which deviation from stability is counteracted by adjustments internal to the system itself. Among familiar forms of homeostasis in biological organisms are mechanisms regulating body temperature and chemical composition of the blood. Another type of negative feedback is exemplified by the heat-seeking missile that changes direction with a manoeuvring target, and by the daisy that aims its blossom to catch the full light of the sun. Feedback of this latter sort has been labelled 'heterotelic', for its role in adjusting the system's external relations to factors in its operating environment.

All organic and most mechanical systems incorporate variables that must be restricted to a narrow range of values if the system is to remain operational. A mammal will soon die, for example, if the oxygen content of its blood falls below a certain level, just as a reciprocating engine will soon freeze if it loses oil pressure. Negative feedback may be conceived generally as a type of regulatory restraint by which the values of a system's crucial variables are maintained within a range compatible with sustained operation. The central role of negative feedback in the economy of an operating system, to paraphrase Ashby ([9.7], 199), thus is to block the transmission of excessive variety to a system's protected variables. An important result of feedback regulation is to maintain the system at a state of low entropy relative to its operating environment.

Entropy

As originally defined by Clausius, entropy measured the proportion of total energy within an isolated system that is available for doing useful work. If part of a system is significantly hotter than another part (e.g., a steam chamber), then work can be done as heat passes from the hotter to the colder part (e.g., the pistons of a steam engine). If all parts of the system are at approximately the same temperature, however, the heat energy within the system is incapable of accomplishing useful work. According to the first law of thermodynamics, the total energy within a closed system remains unchanged through time. But as its energy available for work becomes expended through irreversible physical processes (e.g., discharge of steam into the pistons), its capacity to produce additional work progressively decreases. This means that the entropy of the system, in Clausius's sense, progressively increases. The second law of thermodynamics, originally stating that the energy available for useful work within a closed system tends to decrease with time, thus received concise restatement to the effect that the entropy within a closed system tends always to increase.

The concept of entropy was provided with a statistical basis through the work of Boltzmann and Planck, beginning with Planck's definition of 'complexion' as a specific configuration of its components on the microlevel of a physical system. Boltzmann developed techniques for quantifying the proportion of a system's possible complexions correlated with each of its distinguishable macrostates. Under the assumption that all complexions of a system are equiprobable, he then established the a priori probability of its existing in a given macrostate as equal to the proportion of complexions associated with that macrostate to the total number of possible complexions of the system overall. In this treatment, the greater the proportion of complexions associated with a given macrostate (i.e. the greater its probability), the less highly organized the system will be when existing in that macrostate, and the less capable accordingly of producing useful work. This enabled a redefinition of entropy in terms of probabilities. If P is the probability of a system's existing in a given macrostate, and k is the quantity known as Boltzmann's constant, then the entropy S of the system in that macrostate is given by the equation '$S = k \log P$'. (Logarithms were used in this function to make entropy additive.)

As a result of Boltzmann's treatment, an increase in entropy came to be understood not only as a decrease in energy available for useful work, but also as a decrease in organization (structure, order) of the system concerned. Yet another formulation of the second law of thermodynamics now became appropriate: closed systems tend to become configured into increasingly more probable macrostates, which is to say macrostates exhibiting increasingly less order. What this means in practical terms is familiar to anyone responsible for cleaning house, or for keeping weeds out of a vegetable garden.

Further development of the concept of entropy came with its extension into the mathematical theory of communication. The relevance of this extension appears with the reflection that our information about the specific microstructure of a given system derives largely from observation of its macrostates, and that the more complexions there are that might possibly underlie a given macrostate the less information we have about its actual microstructure in particular. The situation is analogous to that of a detective with a general description only of a wanted person: the more people there are who fit the description, the less information at hand about the actual culprit. When entropy is taken as a measure of the variety of microstates that might underlie an observable macrostate of a system, as in Boltzmann's application, then it also provides a measure of our lack of information about the structure of the system on the microlevel.

Information

Communication theory, pioneered by Nyquist and Hartley in the 1920s and formulated systematically by Shannon in 1948, is the study of the efficient transmission of messages through a communication channel. In its most general form, a communication channel consists of an input ensemble (A) of symbols (a_1, a_2 ... a_r) and an output ensemble (B) of symbols (b_1, b_2, ... b_s), statistically interrelated by a set of conditional probabilities ($P(b_j/a_i)$ specifying for each output b_j the probability of its occurring in association with each input a_i. For purposes of formal descriptions, both A and B are assumed to include a variety of symbol events, one and only one of which occurs at a significant moment of system operation. A simple illustration is a telegraph circuit, where A and B are comprised by events at the key and sounder, respectively, with conditional probabilities $P(b_j/a_i)$ determined by the physical characteristics of transmitting medium.

Because of the variety of symbol events at the input, there is uncertainty in advance (a priori probability less than 1) about what event (E) will actually occur there at a given moment of operation. This uncertainty is removed when E actually occurs (with an a posteriori probability of 1). The removal of this uncertainty is designated 'information'. Information varies in quantity with the amount of uncertainty removed by E's occurrence, according to the formula '$I(E) = \log 1/P(E)$'. (As in the equation defining thermodynamic entropy S, logarithms are employed here to achieve additivity. Logarithms to the base 2 are commonly used for convenience in application to digital computers.) If E has an a priori probability, say, of 50 per cent (think of a flip of an unbiased coin), then the information provided by its occurrence measures $\log 1/0.5$ (= $\log 2$), which amount to 1 bit (for '*bi*nary uni*t*') of information. In general, the amounts of information provided by the occurrence of a given event is identical to the number of times (e.g., 1.74 for an event 30 per cent probable) its a priori probability must be doubled to equal unity.

The average information ($H(A)$) available at A is the sum of the quantities of information provided by its individual events, each multiplied by the event's probability of occurrence. It is easily shown mathematically that $H(A)$ increases both with number of independent events at A and with the approach of these events to randomness, i.e., to equiprobability. Because of this (and because of the similarity of the mathematical definition of H(A) to that of thermodynamic entropy S), the quantity H(A) is often called the 'entropy' of A. A related measure is the 'equivocation' (H(A/B)) of A with respect to B, which is the average amount of uncertainty remaining about events occurring at input A after the occurrence of associated events at output B. This quantity is given by the sum of the conditional probabilities of each event a_i given each event b_j in turn, each probability being multiplied by the logarithm of its reciprocal. This quantity approaches zero as events at B increase in reliability as indicators of events at A, which makes H(A/B) a negative indicator of a channel's reliability as a conveyor of information. The capacity of a channel overall for the conveyance of information is directly proportional to the information available at its input and indirectly proportional to its equivocation. A channel's capacity in this regard is referred to as its 'mutual information' (I(A;B)), and accordingly is measured by the quantity H(A) – H(A/B).

While communication theorists typically are concerned with the design of channels for technological applications, communication channels play prominent roles in many natural processes as well. Communication of information in a natural setting often involves complex sets of channels known as 'cascades'. A cascade of channels consists of a sequence of individual channels so arranged that the output of the first serves as the input of the second, and so on *seriatim*. A perspicuous illustration is the cascade beginning at the cornea, and proceeding serially through the lens, the several layers of the retina, the optic chiasma, and eventually to the optical cortex. Each individual channel along the way has an integral part to play in the information-processing that constitutes visual perception.

A fact stressed by Shannon and other pioneers of communication theory, but too often unheeded by cognitive theorists employing an 'information-processing' vocabulary, is that information in this technical sense (information(t)) has very little to do with meaning or cognitive content. The symbol events with which communication theory deals might receive meaning under interpretation by human users, but by themselves have no semantical characteristics whatever. One of the major challenges of cybernetics is to gain insight into how information(t) can be converted by processes in the nervous system into information with cognitive significance (information(s)) – into information in the sense of knowledge or intelligence. It is no service to clarity to assume, as is common in cognitive theory today, that information(s) appears 'ready-made' at the inputs of the central nervous system.

Negentropy

As entropy is a measure of a relative lack of information(t), so information(t) corresponds to a lack of entropy. The expression 'negative entropy' was used by Wiener ([9.5], 64) in describing information(t) as the absence of entropy, and was later shortened by Brilluoin to 'negentropy'. Other forms of negentropy are structure (departure from random arrangement of a system's components) and productive energy (capacity within a system for useful work). These three forms of negentropy are mutually convertible.

Energy is converted into structure when water is pumped into an elevated reservoir. And structure is converted to energy in turn when water falls to drive the turbines of a generator. Energy is converted into information(t) with the detection of a signal on a modulated radio wave. Structure is convertible to the same effect in the operation of a computer by a coded punch card. Inasmuch as information(t) is basically a statistical quantity, its conversion into structure and energy is harder to illustrate; but an intuitive sense is provided by the thought-experiment known as 'Maxwell's demon'. The 'demon' in question is situated along a passageway connecting two containers of gas, and operates a trapdoor controlling access of individual molecules to either chamber. Initially this (closed) system is in a state of maximum disorder (maximum entropy), with gas molecules distributed randomly from moment to moment. The 'demon', however, is capable of receiving information(t), distinguishing slow- from fast-moving molecules, and of admitting only fast into one chamber and only slow into the other. As an eventual result of the trapdoor's operation, the system reaches a state of maximum structure (segregation of molecules by rate of motion) and of maximum usable energy (temperature difference between chambers due to molecular impact), both purchased by the information(t) that enables the 'demon' to discriminate rates of motion. Entropy re-enters the picture with the observation that actual transformations of this sort among forms of negentropy generally involve some loss of usable energy, in accord with the second law of thermodynamics.

An important principle of communication theory (Shannon's tenth theorem) states that a system can correct all but an arbitrarily small fraction of errors at its input if its equivocation $H(A/B)$ is no greater than the mutual information $I(A;B)$ of its correction channel. An equivalent formulation is Ashby's law of requisite variety, to the effect that a device's capacity to serve as a regulator (to block variations producing instability) cannot exceed its capacity as a communication channel (marshalling variation for the communication of information (t)).

❧ EXPLANATORY PRINCIPLES AND ❧ METHODOLOGY

Cybernetics has been conceived from the start as a unifying discipline, providing continuity across the borderlines of more specialized sciences ([9.5], 2). It has drawn freely upon the explanatory resources of other disciplines, but always with an eye towards applications beyond the boundaries of their original employment. As the biological concept of homeostasis was extended by Ashby ([9.17]) to the design of machines with adaptive capacities (*Design for a Brain*), for instance, so the physical concept of entropy was extended into biology with the work of Schrödinger ([9.14]). Observing that all natural processes produce increases of entropy in their general vicinity, Schrödinger characterized life as the capacity of an organism to resist progressive entropy in the form of structural loss by 'continually sucking orderliness from its environment' (Ibid., 79). The 'essential thing in metabolism' he remarked, 'is that the organism succeeds in freeing itself from ... the entropy it cannot help producing while alive', which it accomplishes by 'feeding' on negentropy at the expense of an accelerated progression of entropy in its immediate locale. This characterization highlights the remarkable ability of living organisms to receive energy from foodstuffs existing at lower energy levels than themselves, comparable in effect to a toaster being warmed by a cold piece of bread. It is by reversing otherwise natural flows of energy in this manner that a living system maintains itself, as Wiener puts it, 'as a local enclave in the general stream of increasing entropy' ([9.6], 95).

Another biological concept with broad application in cybernetics is that of adaptation. Homeostasis itself is an adaptive process, as are other forms of negative feedback. Among organisms functioning in variable environments, moreover, there is a tendency to adjust their feedback capacities in response to pervasive environmental change, which amounts to an adaptation of adaptive capacities. Species evolution itself provides examples of this higher-level adaptation, as in the development of spiny leaf structures by plants adjusting their moisture-conserving procedures to increasing levels of infrared radiation. While the interest of evolutionary biologists in such adjustments is likely to focus upon the underlying genetic mechanisms, however, interest from the cybernetic point of view will lie more with their effect upon the interchange of negentropy between organism and environment. The primary role of such adaptive processes, from this point of view, is to maintain an efficient coupling between organisms and environment by which the organism can gain the negentropy needed to sustain its vital processes. By way of augmenting Schrödinger's characterization, it may be said that a living organism not only is capable of receiving negentropy from its proximate environment, but also belongs to a reproductive group that tends to preserve this capacity throughout its membership by adaptive changes in the feedback mechanisms involved.

While relying upon other disciplines for certain of its explanatory principles, cybernetics also has developed explanatory resources of its own which would not fit comfortably into the specialized sciences. One is the principle of mutual convertability among energy, structure and information, cited above as being due largely to Brillouin. Another is the aforementioned law of requisite variety, in which Ashby reformulated Shannon's tenth theorem of communication theory in terms directly germane to the feedback capacities of living organisms. According to this law, the range of environmental variation to which an organism can adapt is limited by the capacities of its information(t)-processing systems. A consequence is that a large amount of the negentropy received by highly adaptive organisms like the human being must come in the form of information(t), and that a large portion of their physiological structure must be devoted to processing this information(t). This result is basic to a cybernetic analysis of human mental capacities.

These considerations make clear that the sense in which cybernetics is a unifying discipline has little in common with the 'unity of science' projected by logical positivism in the early twentieth century. While this latter was to have been achieved by way of reduction to physics, cybernetic theorists from the beginning have been explicit in denying primacy to the physical sciences ([9.6], 21; [9.7], 1). The biological principles upon which cybernetics relies are no more reducible to physics than its physical principles are reducible to biology; and neither science can deal with information(t) as a form of negentropy. The manner of unification offered by cybernetics is rather that of a context in which comparable phenomena from diverse disciplines can be studied in common terms, without loss of autonomy of the part of the disciplines concerned.

Because of its essentially interdisciplinary character, there is no single method or set of methods by which cybernetics can be distinguished from related fields of enquiry. The experimental techniques of neurophysiology and control engineering were important to cybernetics at its inception, along with the more formal methods of mathematical logic, calculus and the theory of computation. In recent years, cybernetic studies have employed techniques of systems analysis, organizational theory and computer modelling as well. From this it follows not that anyone employing these techniques of investigation *ipso facto* is engaged in cybernetics, nor that being engaged in cybernetics requires employing one or more of these techniques, but only that someone might employ any of these methods in cybernetic inquiry.

What is methodologically distinctive about cybernetics is rather the way in which it undertakes to bring the diverse resources of allied fields of study into mutual relevance. As an integrative discipline, cybernetics is more philosophy than science. In his quasi-autobiographical account of how the discipline came into being, Wiener cites Leibniz time and again (at one point naming him 'patron saint' of the field ([9.5], 12), and mentions the influence of Royce and Russell as former teachers. Among other philosophers favourably noted are Pascal, Locke, Hume and Bergson. While acknowledging debt to these thinkers in various respects, Wiener seems particularly sympathetic with their interest in metascientific issues, and with their sense of how philosophy informs the foundations of science. The way in which cybernetics was pursued by Wiener is not unlike the way philosophy has been pursued by its major exponents throughout the centuries. Its manner of proceeding, in most general terms, was to adopt a few basic concepts and principles of elucidation, and in terms of these to elaborate a coherent picture of the world at large. For Wiener, the basic concept was that of system or organization, and the principles of elucidation those of feedback and communication. Due perhaps to the predominantly scientific orientation of other members of his original group, however, there seems to have been little incentive to work out the ramifications of this methodological perspective in detail.

A specific mode of enquiry that has proven serviceable to cybernetics in its more recent development is patterned after a familiar method of philosophic analysis. In its typical philosophic application, the method begins with a necessary feature of the concept or kind being analysed, and proceeds by adding other features until a combination is found that characterizes all and only instances of the thing in question. Successfully completed, the procedure yields a characterization unique to the thing being analysed, in terms of its necessary and sufficient conditions. In its specifically cybernetic application, the procedure is concerned instead with complex systems and their modes of behaviour, and the techniques of analysis might be experimental (e.g., in mechanical or computer simulations) as well as conceptual; but in other respects the procedure is similar. Beginning with a component of the complex structure under investigation, it proceeds by combining other components in some appropriate order until the structure in question has been exhibited (mechanically or conceptually) as a combination of parts. What marks the procedure as specifically cybernetic is the character of the components with which it deals, and (in application to biological systems especially) the order in which these components are appropriately combined. The components will have to do typically with the regulation of the system, and with its management of information(t) and other forms of negentropy. In biological applications, moreover, and in any other where the structures being studied show signs of having evolved from less complex substructures, the order of combination should follow lines of plausible evolutionary development.

This procedure overall might be characterized as a form of analysis by synthesis, or what in recent philosophy of mind has been called 'bottom-up' (in contrast with 'top-down') analysis. The synthetic or integrative bearing of the method is philosophical in character, and is directed towards understanding a complex structure in terms of its functional components. The components themselves are understood, as indicated above, according to the explanatory resources of the specialized sciences. The methodology of cybernetics thus is both philosophic and scientific, and might be pursued in a study as well as in a laboratory.

❧ ANALYSIS OF GOAL-DIRECTED ❧ BEHAVIOUR

Among the earliest indications of the interdisciplinary and more broadly philosophic implications of the concept of negative feedback was the paper 'Behavior, Purpose, and Teleology' published by Rosenblueth, Wiener and Bigelow in 1943 ([9.12). The seminal idea of this paper, in Wiener's estimation ([9.5], 8), is that the central nervous system does not function as a self-contained organ, taking inputs from the senses and issuing outputs into the musculature, but that it characteristically acts instead as part of a negative feedback loop circling from the effector muscles out through the environment and back again through the sensory system. The neurological research that led to this insight had been concerned with goal-directed behaviour like picking up a pencil, and the authors saw fit accordingly to illustrate the type of feedback involved by the target-seeking missiles being developed as part of the current war effort. Weapons of this sort are guided by some sort of communication link (sounding–echoing, magnetic, thermal, etc.) with the intended object, through which an error-correcting mechanism operates to maintain the missile on a course leading to contact with the target. In their initial enthusiasm for this analogy between human and overtly mechanical feedback operations, the authors proposed target-seeking behaviour of this sort as a model for goal-directed (purposive, teleological) behaviour generally.

A telling difficulty of this model raised in subsequent criticism is that target seeking of this sort requires the physical presence of the intended goal, whereas human purposive behaviour (e.g., searching for a lost earring) is often directed towards goals that are absent. What has been taken as teleological activity in biological processes (e.g., growth of an oak from an acorn), similarly, appears to be directed toward goal states (e.g., the morphology of a mature tree) that are present, if ever, only late in the process. A model of goal-directed behaviour better suited to this wide range of examples is based upon the concept of equilibrium or stability, and stresses the manner of direction rather than the (external) goal itself. The missile is guided to its target by feedback mechanisms designed to maintain a stable correspondence between its actual motion and the path leading to impact with the target; from the guidance system's standpoint (although not the designer's) the resulting impact is coincidental. When loss of an earring disrupts a person's morning toilet, the search-behaviour ensuing is guided by feedback procedures (search patterns) directed towards restoring equilibrium to the person's dressing routines. And when an acorn begins to sprout and sends down its roots, its subsequent growth is guided by genetically established feedback processes towards a state of stable homeostasis (that of a fully leaved tree) within its living environment. Goal-directed behaviour in each case is governed by negative feedback, and is aimed at establishing or maintaining some facet of the operating system in a state of equilibrium.

Sharing this general form of goal-directed behaviour does not relegate either human purpose or biological teleology to the mechanical status of target-seeking missiles. Artifacts like guided missiles typically are engineered to perform certain predetermined operations when functioning properly under certain conditions, such that failure to perform accordingly under those conditions would be an indication of system malfunction. Human acts performed on purpose, however, are to some extent discretionary, which means *inter alia* that failure to perform when conditions warrant does not indicate a breakdown of the feedback systems involved. Human purpose in this sense is not deterministic, and thus is in accord with the general restriction in the cybernetic framework against deterministic explanations of natural processes at large (see below). Teleological growth is distinguished from target-guided behaviour, in turn, not only by being directed toward an absent goal, but also in that the goal-directed activity involved takes the form of morphological change rather than change in vectored motion. At any stage of its morphological development, an organism must relate to its immediate environment with sufficient stability to acquire the negentropy it needs to remain alive. Only at a relatively advanced stage of growth, however, does an organism achieve homeostasis in a form that can be maintained without further morphological change (exfoliation of leafy structure, growth of teeth, etc.). The sense in which biological growth is teleological is that it is directed toward a goal state which arrives literally only towards the end of the growth process itself, which is a state of stable homeostasis within the living environment. In view of the fact that such growth is guided by feedback mechanisms set in place by the organism's genetic structure, however, there is no call to interpret biological teleology as a causal process in which cause follows effect. The biological basis of teleology and its causal structure are examined more fully in [9.9].

➤➤ FORMS OF ADAPTATION ➤➤

Morphological development is guided primarily by the genetic mechanisms of the individual organism. Another form of change to which organisms submit is adaptation, which occurs primarily in response to environmental variations. Among modes of adaptation that had been studied systematically before the advent of cybernetics are evolution and natural selection among biological species, and the behavioural conditioning of individual organisms. Cybernetic analysis of the feedback characteristics shared by these modes of adaptation led to the discovery of another mode pertaining to the formation of perceptual patterns, which appears significant for our understanding of cognitive processes.

Evolution and Natural Selection

A biological species is a group of interbreeding individuals with traits transmitted genetically to succeeding generations. Membership of a local subgroup (deme) of a given species fluctuates with changes in local conditions, as more or fewer members live to maturity in response to variations in food supply, predation, etc. Adjustments to short-term environmental variations of this sort generally occur without significant alteration of the group's genetic pool, and hence without alteration of the traits typically shared by its membership. Adjustment to more pervasive environmental changes like geophysical upheaval or shift in climate, on the other hand, may require alteration of a group's specific traits, enabling its members to take advantage of new food sources (e.g., thicker beaks for cracking seed shells) or new means of protection (e.g., lighter colouration for a snow-covered habitat). Long-term adaptation of this sort may be initiated by a shift in reproductive dominance to individuals within the group already approximating the features in question, which thereby become proliferated among members of subsequent generations. An eventual result may be the emergence of a reproductive group based on a genetic pool sufficiently altered to constitute a new species. Species evolution thus may be viewed as the product of a homeostatic process that enables reproductive groups to maintain stability under changing environmental circumstances. The mechanism of adjustment is alteration of the genetically controlled traits affecting the group's viability within its immediate environment.

Whereas species evolution is an adaptive process operating on the level of the reproductive group, natural selection in turn is an adaptive process on the level of the biota or ecosystem. A biota is a system of species interacting within a shared environment, each occupying a distinctive role or niche in which it can maintain stable relationships with its companion species. Niches are distinguished by the kinds of living space (trees, meadows, etc.) and food source (seeds, insects, etc.) they provide. The normal state of a biota is to provide all the niches needed to keep its community in balance, and at the same time to keep its existing niches full with as many individuals as the negentropic resources of its locale can sustain. Momentary decreases in population within a given niche may be countered by increased reproduction on the part of its occupying species, or by the immigration of competing species from adjacent locales. Excessive increases in population, on the other hand, will be countered by decreased reproduction, perhaps in the form of the extinction (or severe depletion) or one or another competing group. When competition for the limited resources of a niche puts a newly emerged species at hazard, the eventual result will be either its irradication by a more competitive species or its establishment as part of a well-balanced ecosystem. Natural selection thus may be viewed as a homeostatic process by which an ecosystem maintains integrity in a changing environment by changes in relationship among its constituent species.

Learning

Failure of a newly emerged species in its original biota does not preclude success in some other locale to which it may have migrated. Characteristics that enable a group to perform competitively in various locales (part of what above was termed 'negentropic flexibility') thus provide multiple opportunities for success, and are likely to become part of the group's genetic endowment. A major provision of this sort appeared in the course of species evolution with the ability of individual organisms to adapt their behaviour to local changes in their immediate environment. Whereas adaptation of primitive life-forms like bacteria and protozoa depends upon genetic mutations affecting the species at large, and hence requires a period of several generations, adaptation of individual behaviour to immediate contingencies can occur repeatedly within the lifetime of a single organism. This ability is known in behavioural science as 'conditioning' or 'learning'.

Any operating system produces outputs that are conditional to some extent upon its inputs. A system is capable of learning when it can adjust this conditional association between input and output to its own benefit. While a biological system in an entirely fixed environment would gain nothing by such an adjustment, a complex organism in a variable environment will generally benefit from some behaviour patterns and be harmed by others. Organisms capable of learning have been genetically disposed to avoid adversive (painful or 'punishing') stimuli and to seek stimuli they find agreeable (pleasant or 'reinforcing'). Inasmuch as natural selection will favour species whose members are reinforced under beneficial circumstances, and are punished by harmful, the effect of this disposition in an enduring species is to support survival of the individuals in which it operates. Learning then boils down to a process of shaping the behaviour of organisms to elicit predominantly agreeable stimuli from their current environments, and to minimize the occurrence of adversive stimuli, with the long-term result of enhancing the survival probabilities of the species involved.

In favourably conditioned organisms, stimuli indicative of beneficial circumstances will tend to elicit behaviour likely to secure those benefits, while stimuli indicative of harmful circumstances will tend to elicit avoidance behaviour. But when an organism begins to find adversive stimuli associated with previously beneficial circumstances (e.g., a once clear stream showing signs of contamination), or vice versa, the organism will undergo significant changes in the probabilities of its behavioural outputs conditional upon inputs signalling the presence of those circumstances. Inputs previously prompting the organism to take advantage of the circumstances they signify will now tend to elicit avoidance behaviour instead, or perhaps will simply lose their power to elicit any distinctive behaviour whatever. And vice versa for inputs previously leading to avoidance behaviour. By thus adjusting its conditional probabilities between sensory inputs and behavioural output in response to changing 'contingencies of reinforcement' (the phrase comes from Skinner ([9.23])), the organism adapts its behaviour to a changing environment. In its most general cybernetic description, learning is a feedback process in which the environmental effects of an organism's behaviour are channelled back through its sense receptors, and used to shape that behaviour in patterns conducive to the organism's advantage under current environmental circumstances.

Perceptual Patterning

According to Ashby's law of requisite variety, the range of environmental variation to which an organism can adapt its behaviour is limited by its capacities as an information(t)-processing system. A straightforward consequence is that the variety of adaptive responses an organism can make to a fluctuating environment is limited by the variety of circumstances distinguishable within its afferent nervous system. Cybernetically inspired experiments at MIT in the 1950s indicated that frogs, for example, are capable of distinguishing only five or six different patterns of stimulation in their visual environment, one being a spot the size of a fly moving a frog's tongue-length away in front of its eyes. The frog's behaviour in its biotic niche is confined to responses to these distinctive patterns (and a few others like them pertaining to other sense modalities), each of which is communicated through a set of nerve fibres dedicated to that pattern specifically. With this method of information(t)-processing requiring a one-to-one correspondence between message channel and message type, a radical extension in the number of patterns distinguishable by the animal's afferent system would require additional bulk that could impair its mobility. Perceptual patterning of this sort might be described as 'hard-wired', rather than adaptive in the manner of more advanced visual systems.

A major advance in adaptive capacity came with the evolution of organisms able to extend radically their range of discriminable circumstances without corresponding increase in bulk of their afferent nervous systems. The manner of information(t)-processing making this possible permits different stimulus patterns shaped in response to different environmental circumstances to pass through a single integrated network of afferent channels. This expedient of adaptive pattern-formation is similar in its feedback characteristics both to evolution and natural selection (adaptation on the species level) and to behavioural conditioning (adaptation on the level of the individual organism), and might be conceived alternatively as a very rapid evolution of afferent neuronal structures or as a much accelerated learning of the sensory system.

By 'perceptual pattern' here is meant a more or less specific set of neuronal events that occur interactively in response to a more or less specific configuration of external events in the perceptual environment. Between the external configuration and the neuronal pattern will extend a cascade of information (t)-channels (e.g., external object to cornea to lens to retina to optic chiasma, etc.), each serving both to convey relevant information(t) into the upper reaches of the afferent system and to help forge the features of the resulting pattern along the way. The key function of the cascade overall is to fashion a configuration of neuronal events that stands in a relation of high mutual information (see above) with the configuration in the external environment. If the mutual information between external and neuronal configuration is sufficiently high (i.e., they are sufficiently alike in information(t)-structure), then the latter will serve the organism as an effective guide of behaviour it undertakes with respect to the former. The latter in this respect is an adequate 'representation' of the former.

A corollary of Ashby's law cited above is that organisms under selective pressure to increase their variety of adaptive behaviours will be under pressure as well to employ their information(t)-processing channels as efficiently as possible. Efficiency might be served by various 'noise reductions', 'boundary tracing' and other information(t)-processing techniques of sorts well studied by communications engineers, performed at various stages along the cascade (e.g., at the retina or optic chiasma). The result is a neuronal representation of largely 'schematic' character, incorporating less detail than might be had at earlier stages in the cascade. If more detail proves necessary for successful guidance of behaviour undertaken with regard to what is represented, or if different representations are required to guide other behavioural projects, adjustments are made throughout the cascade to produce patterns at the upper afferent levels with informational(t)-features adequate to the task at hand.

Pattern-formation procedures of this general sort join with the efferent faculties of the behaving organism to constitute a homeostatic system, the normal state of which is a series of afferent patterns providing perceptual guidance for the organism's ongoing behaviour. Deviation from the norm is indicated by incipient loss of perceptual control, and the system regains stability by restructuring the representations by which this behaviour is currently being guided. Recent theoretical analysis suggests that perceptual pattern-formation of this sort provides a basis for certain cognitive processes typical of the human organism specifically.

❧ HIGHER COGNITIVE FUNCTIONS ❧

Similarities in feedback characteristics among the processes of natural selection, learning and perceptual patterning, have been extensively explored in cybernetic literature. Parallels in natural selection and learning were pointed out by Wiener [9.5], 181), and were further developed by Skinner ([9.23]). An empirical basis for the account of perceptual patterning outlined above was proposed by Sayre ([9.9]). Extensions of this line of analysis to higher cognitive functions like language use and reason remain more conjectural. The brief discussion following is an indication of potential rather than actual accomplishment.

In a perceptual environment providing regularly recurring stimulus configurations, the afferent system of a perceptually adaptive organism may develop standard representations which find employment time and again in the pursuit of its perceptually guided projects. Such representations, which might be labelled 'percepts', are normally activated by stimulation of the external sense organs, and in this sense are controlled by the external environment. Percepts available to a given organism would typically include representations of familiar plants, animals, etc. Individuals of species capable of language will also form percepts responding to symbol configurations issued by other members of their linguistic community. To learn the language of one's community is to learn to associate percepts representative of familiar objects with other percepts representing the standard symbols of the language (at first vocal, later written, etc.), in such a fashion that the former percepts are capable of being activated by the latter. Percepts that in this fashion have been brought under the control of linguistic symbols, as well as of the objects they standardly represent, may be referred to as 'meanings'.

Meanings in this sense are not abstract entities, but rather well-entrenched neuronal patterns capable of functioning in the actual information(t)-processing activities of linguistically competent organisms. Since the essential feature of a given meaning structure is its relation of mutual information with the object it represents, and since physically different structures can share in this relation with a single given object, the same meanings can be present in different organisms. Linguistic communities emerge as many individuals learn to activate the same meanings upon presentation of the same symbol configurations, and to associate those symbols with the same objects in their shared environment.

Meaning B may be said to be redundant relative to meaning A when all features of the world represented by B are represented by A as well. The meaning 'ripe' applied to grapefruit, for instance, renders the meaning 'yellow' redundant. Conversely, applicability of 'yellow' to a given grapefruit is required for 'ripe' to be correctly applicable. The former controls the latter in this connection by restricting the circumstances of its correct application. Concepts may be conceived as meanings that have been removed from exclusive control of perceptual configurations (either linguistic symbols or objective circumstances), and brought under the control in this fashion of other meanings. While the percept 'yellow' is activated only by yellow objects, and the meaning 'yellow' either by objects or their linguistic symbols, the concept 'yellow' can be activated not only by objects and symbols, but in certain applications also by the meaning 'ripe'. Understood in this fashion, percepts, meanings and concepts are all stable structures of neuronal activity, distinguished with regard to their manner of control.

Concepts may be said to participate in a shared linkage if they are mutually relevant to each other's application, perhaps conditional upon the applicability of other concepts within the same linkage. The concepts 'ripe', 'yellow' and 'soft' thus share linkage with the concept 'grapefruit', reflecting the coincidence of colour and tactual properties discovered through the experience of a linguistic group with palatable grapefruit. If a variety of grapefruit were encountered in which a colour other than yellow (say, pink) turned out to be a more reliable sign of palatability, however, the relevant conceptual linkages of the individuals undertaking to eat this fruit would soon adapt to this novel set of circumstances. Due to the public nature of the language from which these concepts are derived, it would not be necessary for other individuals to undergo the same experiences themselves for their conceptual linkages to be appropriately modified. They can be modified through conversation with the individuals first affected. Conceptual linkages thus serve as facilities of information storage, subject to homeostatic adjustment and augmentation through the experiences of subgroups within the linguistic community. Such linkages in effect are neuronal mappings of regularly associated objective circumstances, subject to adaptation by continued encounters with a shared living environment. By using these maps to chart the course of anticipated behaviour, rational agents can explore alternatives before committing themselves to action.

❧ RELATION TO ALTERNATIVE PARADIGMS ❧

Cybernetics has been guided from the outset by the conviction that a wide range of human mental functions can be reproduced mechanically. Among Wiener's original associates in the 1940s were several figures (e.g., O. G. Selfridge, W. H. Pitts, W. S. McCulloch) who subsequently became known for contributions to AI. Spokesmen for cybernetics up through the late 1970s, (e.g., F. H. George, K. Gunderson, K. M. Sayre) still considered AI to be an integral part of that discipline. The original ties between cybernetics and AI were effectively severed during the 1980s, however, to the extent that early contributors to machine intelligence who had remained closely identified with the former movement (e.g. W. R. Ashby, D. M. MacKay, F. H. George, Wiener himself) are seldom cited in current histories of the latter. This divorce appears to have been due largely to the recent takeover of AI by the computational paradigm, and to an ideological slide towards materialism on the part of its advocates.

Materialism, in its bare essentials, is the doctrine that everything in the universe comes under the purview of physical science. The primacy of physics in this regard was challenged in Wiener's original manifesto ([9.5], ch. 1; see also [9.6], 21), and was explicitly rejected in Ashby ([9.7]). Wiener's disavowal was based in part upon his realization that the determinism implicit in classical physics is incompatible with the variety inherent in biological processes. A theoretical basis for rejecting determinism in the natural world generally lies in the principle (a version of the second law of thermodynamics) that all irreversible processes tend to involve a loss of negentropy, which entails that causes generally tend to be more highly structured (involve less variety) than their effects. A consequence, as Wiener puts it, is that even the most 'complete collection of data for the present and the past is not sufficient to predict the future more than statistically' ([9.5], 37). Ashby's repudiation of materialism was more direct, pointing out ([9.7], 1) that the materiality of the systems studied by cybernetics is simply irrelevant. Some organized systems (e.g., computers) are strictly physical, while others (e.g., linguistic communities) quite probably are not; and the fact that systems of both sorts can perform comparable feedback and information(t)-processing functions is no indication that they share the same ontological status. It should be noted at the same time, however, that the likely non-physical status of some cybernetic systems does not convert automatically into evidence for dualism. Contrary to current dogma in some quarters that materialism and dualism are the only ontological options on the horizon, a more plausible alternative from the cybernetic point of view is some version of neutral monism (as in Spinoza or early Russell). Sayre attempts to articulate a monism in which neither information(t)-functions of cognitive activity nor probabilistic functions at the quantum level of matter are further reducible to mental or physical features, making mathematical (statistical) structures more basic ontologically than either mind or matter [9.9].

The computational paradigm in recent AI and cognitive science rests upon the thesis that cognitive processes are computations performed upon representations, where the computations in question are of the sort typified by a standard digital computer. Barring the arbitrary introduction of randomizing elements, the computations performed by a properly operating digital computer are deterministic in outcome, which means that the same input invariably produces the same output. Even when the machine is computing probabilities, its procedures of computation are deterministic in this fashion. This makes mechanical computation an inappropriate model for indeterministic natural processes in general, and especially so for the highly negentropy-intensive (entropy producing) cognitive functions of human organisms. This difficulty, coupled with the well-known conceptual problems computationalists have encountered trying to account for the semantic properties of mental representations (discussed in [9.22]; [9.21] and elsewhere), should dispose anyone approaching cognition within a cybernetic framework towards disfavour of the computational model.

A more sympathetic reception may be accorded the connectionist paradigm that emerged during the late 1980s, which portrays various forms of cognitive activity as informational exchanges within a network of interconnected nodes with varying weights and excitation levels. Description of these networks is often couched in terms of conditional probabilities, and hence could be recast without distortion in the technical terminology of communication theory. Connectionist researchers have already begun to study certain feedback characteristics of such systems, along with certain ways in which they might function in the control of motor behaviour ([9.19], 84). If attention were directed as well towards how these networks might adjust homeostatically in response to changes in a cognitively stimulating environment, connectionism might produce significant insight into the cybernetic workings of our cognitive faculties.

❧ BIBLIOGRAPHY ❧

General Introductions

9.1 Crosson, F. J. and Sayre, K. M. (eds) *Philosophy and Cybernetics*, Notre Dame University of Notre Dame Press, 1967.
9.2 Gunderson, K. 'Cybernetics', in P. Edwards (ed.) *Encyclopedia of Philosophy*, New York, Macmillan, 1967.
9.3 Sluckin, W. *Minds and Machines*, Baltimore, Penguin Books, 1954.
9.4 von Neumann, J. *The Computer and the Brain*, New Haven, Yale University Press, 1958.
9.5 Wiener, N. *Cybernetics, or Control and Communication in the Animal and the Machine*, Cambridge, MIT Press, 1948 (2nd edn 1961).
9.6 —— *The Human Use of Human Beings: Cybernetics and Society*, Garden City, Doubleday, 1954. (An earlier edition was published by Houghton Mifflin in 1950.)

Technical Introductions

9.7 Ashby, W. R. *An Introduction to Cybernetics*, London, Chapman and Hall, 1956.
9.8 George, F. H. *The Foundations of Cybernetics*, London, Gordon and Breach 1977.
9.9 Sayre, K. M. *Cybernetics and the Philosophy of Mind*, London, Routledge and Kegan Paul, 1976.

Contributions to Specific Problem Areas

9.10 Brillouin, L. *Science and Information Theory*, New York, Academic Press, 1962.
9.11 MacKay, D. M. 'Mindlike Behaviour in Artefacts', *British Journal for the Philosophy of Science* 2 (1951–2): 105–21.
9.12 Rosenblueth, A. Wiener, N. and Bigelow, J. 'Behavior, Purpose, and Teleology', *Philosophy of Science* 10 (1943): 18–24.
9.13 Sayre, K. M. *Consciousness: A Philosophic Study of Minds and Machines*, New York, Random House, 1969.
9.14 Schrödinger, E. *What is Life?*, Cambridge University Press, 1967.
9.15 Shannon C. E. and McCarthy J. (eds) *Automata Studies*, Princeton, Princeton University Press, 1956.
9.16 Shannon C. E. and Weaver, W. *The Mathematical Theory of Communication*, Urbana, University of Illinois Press, 1949. (Shannon's original paper, with comments by Weaver.)

Closely Related Topics

9.17 Ashby, W. R. *Design for a Brain*, London, Chapman and Hall, 1952.
9.18 Feldman J. and Feigenbaum E. A. (eds) *Computers and Thought*, New York, McGraw-Hill, 1963.
9.19 Haugeland, J. 'Representational Genera', in W. Ramsey, S. Stich, and D. Rumelhart (eds) *Philosophy and Connectionist Theory*, Hillsdale, Lawrence Erlbaum, 1991.
9.20 Miller, G., Galanter, E. and Pribram, K. *Plans and the Structure of Behavior*, New York, Holt, Rinehart and Winston, 1960.
9.21 Sayre, K. M. 'Intentionality and Information Processing: An Alternative Model for Cognitive Science', *Behavioral and Brain Science* 9 (1986): 121–38.
9.22 Searle, J. R. 'Minds, Brains, and Programs', *Behavioral and Brain Sciences* 3 (1980): 417–24.
9.23 Skinner, B. F. *Contingencies of Reinforcement: A Theoretical Analysis*, New York, Appleton-Century-Crofts, 1969.

CHAPTER 10

Descartes' legacy: the mechanist/vitalist debates

Stuart G. Shanker

➤ I DESCARTES' DOMINION ➤

Why, man, he doth bestride the narrow world
Like a Colossus, and we petty men
Walk under his huge legs and peep about
To find ourselves dishonourable graves.
Men at some time are masters of their fates.
The fault, dear Brutus, is not in our stars,
But in ourselves, that we are underlings.
(Julius Caesar Act 1, Scene 4)

Rare is the philosopher of psychology who has not felt like Cassius at some point in his career. For there is no other port of entry into the field than through the legs of Descartes. Even those – or perhaps, especially those – who have sought a completely different route have ended up delivering eulogies to Descartes' greatness. Mechanist or vitalist, dualist or materialist, introspectionist, behaviourist, computationalist or cognitivist: succeeding generations have found themselves responding to Cartesianism in one way or another.

It is becoming virtually impossible these days to open a monograph in the philosophy of psychology without beginning with a chapter on Descartes. 'Descartes' Myth', 'Descartes' Dichotomy', 'Descartes' Dream', 'Descartes' Legacy': one begins to yearn for the chapter announcing 'Descartes' Demise'! But the problem is that Descartes really is a Colossus, and the final word in the history of his ideas will belong to a Marc Antony and not to a Brutus.

Descartes epitomises – and was widely seen by his contemporaries as having inspired – the enormous social, scientific and even religious changes taking place in the Enlightenment. When Newton explained to Hooke how it was by standing on the shoulders of giants that he had been able to see further, it was specifically 'further than Descartes'. No doubt when the 'Newton of the mind' longed for by so many contemporary psychologists appears on the scene, he will say much the same thing.

Descartes represents the appeal to reason and self-responsibility over authority. It is in this respect that the *Discourse on Method* is such a revolutionary text: the paradigm of a modern revolutionary text. Not just the content, but even the very style in which it is written marks a radical break from the past. Descartes tells of how:

> returning to the army from the coronation of the Emperor, the onset of winter detained me in quarters where, finding no conversation to divert me and fortunately having no cares or passions to trouble me, I stayed all day shut up alone in a stove-heated room, where I was completely free to converse with myself about my own thoughts.

([10.4], 116)

We have grown so accustomed to the voice in which this is written that it requires a conscious effort to recover the period eye necessary to appreciate the full significance of this 'fragment of autobiography': i.e. that it is a fragment of *autobiography* (see [10.1]). Moreover, the tone of what follows in the text cloaks the extent to which Descartes was deliberately challenging the established order. Far more is at stake here than Descartes' anxiety to avoid a similar fate to that which befell Galileo. Hence, we must be careful not to allow the stories about Descartes' reluctance to publish *The World* to blind us from seeing what an extraordinarily bold work the *Discourse on Method* is: not so much because it provides us with any serious grounds to question Descartes' attitude towards the soul, but because of the truly revolutionary implications of the argument presented at the end of Part Five.

Descartes is here repudiating the orthodox doctrine of the 'Great Chain of Being'. He is insisting that there is a hiatus between animals and man that cannot be filled by any 'missing links'. The body may be a machine (which was itself a heretical view), but man, by his abilities to reason, to speak a language, to direct his actions and to be conscious of his cognitions, is categorically *not* an animal. There is no hint in the *Discourse* that any of these attributes can be possessed in degrees. Rather, Descartes' universe, unlike that of the Ancients, is bifurcated. And at its centre stands neither the Earth, nor the Sun, but the mind of the individual, responding to the world around it.

When Aristotle tells us that 'Man is by nature a political animal', or Seneca that 'Man is a reasoning animal', the emphasis is on *animal*: one analyses man as an *animal species* (see the opening chapter of Aristotle's *Metaphysics*). But all this is changed in the *Discourse*. Here we begin, not with humanity, but with René Descartes: with the thoughts of a solitary individual who has come to distrust the teachings of the finest minds of his time; who has renounced the blind homage to Aristotelian thought which so dominated medieval and Renaissance thought; who decided to continue his studies by reading from the 'great book of the world' rather than from the classics, and whose 'real education' has taught him to accept as certain only those ideas which he himself can see clearly and distinctly: *in his own mind's eye*. Descartes' revolutionary epistemology thus goes hand-in-hand with the social revolution; for what need is there for 'privileged access' when one has the writings of The Philosopher to fall back on?

The shock waves which this argument set off – and which it was intended to set off – were every bit as great as the effect of the *Cogito*: if not more so. What was initially hailed by the Cambridge Platonists as an act of heroism was soon to be castigated as an act of hubris. For the Great Chain of Being was not a doctrine which Western thinkers were about to abandon without a struggle. Gassendi swiftly recounted the classical line (in the Fifth set of Objections), seemingly unaware that Descartes' heresy was intentional (see [10.3], II: 188). Similarly, the objections compiled by Mersenne in the sixth set defend the Great Chain of Being from what he perceived as Descartes' self-defeating sceptical attack (Ibid., 279). And in the third book of *An Essay Concerning Human Understanding* we find Locke arguing that: 'In all the visible corporeal world we see no chasms or gaps. All quite down from us the descent is by easy steps, and a continued series that in each remove differ very little one from the other.' The crucial corollary of this argument is that:

> There are some brutes that seem to have as much reason and knowledge as some that are called men; and the animal and vegetable kingdoms are so nearly joined, that if you will take the lowest of one and the highest of the other, there will scarce be perceived any great difference between them.
>
> ([10.11], III, vi, Section 12)

Significantly, when La Mettrie ridiculed 'all the insignificant philosophers – poor jesters, and poor imitators of Locke', it was not for defending this continuum picture, but for doing so on the wrong terms. He felt that the real lesson to be learnt from Descartes' 'proof that animals are pure machines' is that 'these proud and vain beings, more distinguished by their pride than by the name of men however much they may wish to exalt themselves, are at bottom only animals and machines which, though upright, go on all fours' ([10.10], 142–3).

In other words, the defence of the Great Chain of Being could proceed in either of two directions: show how the behaviour of animals is intelligent, or that of man, mechanical. Two versions of the *continuum picture* thus emerged: the vitalist and the mechanist. The former sought to blur the lines between the higher animals and man via a *continuum of sentience*; the latter sought to reduce man to the level of the beasts by eschewing the appeal to consciousness. What was perhaps the greatest irony in the emerging debate between these two polarities is that both sides were to claim Descartes as their spiritual guide.

For the next two hundred years, the life sciences were dominated by the battle over Descartes' picture of the body. To begin with, the debate centred on Descartes' claim that 'It is an error to believe that the soul gives movement and heat to the body' ([10.6], 329). With the successful mechanist resolution of the theory of heat in the middle of the nineteenth-century (see section 2 below), attention shifted onto Descartes' picture of reflexive behaviour (see section 3), and thence, to psychology (see sections 3–4 below). For Descartes' attack on the Great Chain of Being is grounded in the fundamental distinction which he draws between *actions* and *reactions*.

Despite the common assumption by Cartesians that Descartes intended his argument to be read as an inductive hypothesis, it is never quite clear whether Descartes' denial of the possibility of purposive animal behaviour was meant as an empirical or as a conceptual thesis. Certainly it was interpreted and disputed as a hypothesis. In essence, his argument is that all bodily movements are caused by 'agitations in the brain', which in turn are triggered by two different kinds of event: external objects impinging on the senses, or internal mental acts or states. It is the fate of animals/automatons that they only experience the former phenomena while man experiences the latter phenomena as well.

This argument may seem to be directly opposed to the sentiments expressed in the above quotation from *The Passions of the Soul*, but the point Descartes is making there is simply that reflex movements are not volitional (cf. his reply to Arnauld in [10.3], II: 161). The distinction operating here is that between *voluntary* and *involuntary movements*. Those that are involuntary occur 'without any intervention of the will', while 'the movements which we call "voluntary" ' are those which 'the soul determines' (Ibid, 315). These 'volitions, in their essence (pure acts of the soul, terminating in itself) are limitless and disembodied, but all existing volitions (acts of the soul terminating in the body) are limited by the structure of embodiment' ([10.13], 109). Most important of all: to the eye of the observer, voluntary and involuntary movements *look* exactly the same. It is only because each individual is able to see and report on his own volitions that we are able to make this fundamental distinction between *voluntary* and *involuntary* movements, and because animals lack a similar capacity that they are ruled automata.

The argument that these acts of will are transparent to reason amounts to a doctrine of *epistemological asymmetry*: while I can *know directly* what causes my own actions, I can only *infer* that someone else's bodily movements are brought about by similar mental events. Hence, for all intents and purposes, the behaviour of other human beings stands on the same epistemological footing as that of animals. But the fact that

> There are no men so dull-witted or stupid ... that they are incapable of arranging various words together and forming an utterance from them in order to make their thoughts understood; whereas there is no other animal, however perfect and well-endowed it may be, that can do the like.'
>
> [(10.4], 140)

warrants our adopting a stance of semi-solipsism towards our fellow man, but not towards the beasts. For even madmen can report on their volitions (the bodily movements caused by their will), but no animal possesses such a capacity.

This argument invited the obvious response that animals do indeed communicate, but in a language which we cannot understand (a point which led Gassendi to reiterate the orthodox line that, 'although [animals] do not reason so perfectly or about as many subjects as man, they still reason, and the difference seems to be merely one of degree' ([10.3], II: 189)). But Descartes had already anticipated this objection when he argued that animals lack the sort of creative behaviour necessary to be credited with such an ability ([10.4], 141; cf. [10.2]).

It is highly significant for the history of psychology that Descartes immediately tied this theme in to the claim that reflex movements cannot be adaptive; for from this issue was to ensue the prolonged debate over the purposiveness of reflex behaviour. But before we examine the consequent evolution of mechanism, it is important to see how, despite all the modifications which reflex theory was to undergo, there is a sense in which this entire controversy completely missed Descartes' point.

In the second *Meditation* Descartes remarks how:

> If I look out of the window and see men crossing the square, as I just happen to have done, I normally say that I see the men themselves, just as I say that I see the wax. Yet do I see any more than hats and coats which could conceal automatons?

> I judge that they are men. And so something which I thought I
> was seeing with my eyes is in fact grasped solely by the faculty
> of judgement which is in my mind.
>
> ([10.5], 21)

This last sentence is absolutely crucial to understanding Descartes'
argument, which is that *our minds* assume, on the basis of the similarity
between the observed behaviour and our own, that the men crossing
the square are not automatons. Our minds cannot *see* the causes of
their behaviour, any more than they can see the causes of an animal's
movements. But given the observable disparity between human and
animal behaviour, there is no justifiable ground (psychological
compulsion?) for the mind to extend its mental–causal schemata to the
latter case.

For some idea of the extent to which this argument continues to
dominate modern thought, one need only look at attribution theory.
Heider approached the analysis of social interaction in terms of an
inferential theory of perception: social no less than object judgements
involve the classification of sensory information. Actions are 'stimuli'
which must be 'categorized': they are seen as the effects of external or
internal causes (where the latter are comprised of the mental processes
and states with which the agent is acquainted in the case of his own
actions). Our minds construct and continually revise inchoate theories
as to how attitudes cause intentions and intentions cause actions;
whether we are aware – whether we *could* be aware – of this mental
activity is another matter (see [10.8]).

On this cognitivist reading of the continuum, we begin with the
paradigm of the scientific mind, and work our way backwards through
a descending level of 'cognitive schemes' until we arrive at a brute level
of non-verbal processing. On the converse behaviourist picture of the
continuum, there is no logical need to postulate such 'mental constructs'
to explain the behaviour of other agents or lower organisms. At the
beginning of this century, H. S. Jennings wrote about the continuity
of 'the psychological processes' that constitute 'the bridge which con-
nects the chemical processes of inorganic nature with the mental life of
the highest animals' ([10.12], 508; cf. [10.9], ch. XX). This provoked a
sharp rebuke from the young John Watson:

> Have we any other criterion than that of behavior for assuming
> that our neighbor is conscious? And do we not determine this
> by the complexity of his reactions (including language under
> behavior)? ... If my monkey's adjustments were as complex as
> those of my human subjects in the laboratory, I would have the
> same reason for drawing the conclusion as regards a like
> complexity in the mental processes of the two ... Jennings has

not shown, nor has any one else shown that the behavior of lower organisms is objectively similar to that in man.

([10.14], 289–90)

But that is exactly what Descartes was saying!

To be sure, this does not signify that Watson was really a closet dualist. By 1913 he was arguing that we could eschew the use of 'all subjective terms' in human as well animal contexts (first-person cases included; see [10.15] and [10.17]). But what this parallel does reveal is that, whether or not there is a continuum of purposive reflexive behaviour has no bearing on the question of the criteria that license our judgment that our neighbour – or an animal – is conscious, intends to ϕ, decided to ψ, believes, thinks, sees, feels ξ. At best it merely suggests the thesis that, should we all become familiar with this mechanist explanation of animal/human behaviour, the Cartesian might be forced into a much more extreme form of solipsism in which all human behaviour other than one's own would have to be treated on the same plane as animal.

What this means is that Descartes' attack on the Great Chain of Being is one that no amount of experiments on decerebrated frogs, hungry dogs, chimpanzees, blind interaction tests or learning programs can hope to resolve. This may sound a bizarre claim, given the three centuries of controversy devoted to the exact opposite premisses. Perhaps the reason for this anomaly is that Descartes himself was far from clear on the nature of his argument: is it *a priori* or *a posteriori*, *conceptual* or *empirical*? Hence, all the dissension over his motives in consigning animals to the realm of the mechanical. Many have suspected him of harbouring a hidden materialist agenda, while an equal number have accused him of devising his argument with the sole intention of thwarting such a development. But virtually all parties were agreed that Descartes launched a sceptical attack on the intelligence of animal behaviour which must be scientifically discredited if man's mental processes are to be understood: either by reinstating animals into the cognitive fold, or by redefining 'intelligent behaviour' so as to return man to his proper place among the natural order.

In what follows we shall be concerned with both the historical and the philosophical sides of this issue: viz., how Descartes' attack on the Great Chain of Being influenced the development of the mechanist picture of the continuum, and how, despite the mounting complexity of mechanist theories, culminating with AI, they have come no closer to refuting Descartes' attack on the continuum picture. But the goal here is neither to praise nor to bury Descartes. It is simply to understand the nature of his argument in order to understand the foundations upon which psychology has been built: to clarify the *type of theory* whereby succeeding generations of mechanists, up to and including AI, have sought to free themselves from what they see as the Cartesian yoke that is stifling the science of mind.

❧ II THE ANIMAL HEAT DEBATE ❧

The philosopher of psychology's concern with the mechanist/vitalist debates sparked off by Descartes' attack on the Great Chain of Being is no mere exercise in the history of ideas and/or *Weltanschauungen*. That is not to deny the importance of this topic for the sociology of knowledge. But our immediate philosophical objective is to clarify the conceptual framework in which psychology has evolved, and equally important, the attitudes which we have inherited.

To be branded a vitalist is the ultimate in analytic invective: it is to be found guilty of allowing primitive metaphysical urges to overcome one's scientific rigour. No doubt there were countless country parsons and gentleman scholars who were attracted to vitalism because of their theological anxieties (just as there are many today who misguidedly believe that evolutionary theory has a bearing on the Creation myth). But no such charges could be laid against such scientists as Müller, Liebig or Bernard without grossly distorting their intentions, and thereby misconstruing the very essence of the issues with which they were concerned.

A proper treatment of the complex themes involved in the permutations of mechanist and vitalist thought would undertake to trace their history in light of the development of both the natural and the life sciences, and intimately connected with this, the shifting conceptions of man's nature and autonomy. But in so far as post-computational mechanism represents the culmination of nineteenth-century mathematical, physical, psychological and biological advances, there are strong grounds for confining our attention here to the mechanist/vitalist debates of that period. And yet, the very fact that the question from whence both schools proceed – viz., what is the difference between living and non-living matter? – had been a source of controversy for two millennia should surely give one pause; for much of what follows turns on the question of whether such an issue is to be resolved philosophically or physiologically. Or rather, it turns on the difference between a philosophical and a physiological approach to a question that is far from clear, nor constant in the succession of disputes which it has aroused.

The basic problem here is that philosophical and empirical questions should have been so closely intermingled in the two issues which dominated the period: the debates over the causes of an animal's ability to maintain a state of thermal equilibrium, and the question whether reflex actions are in some sense purposive. Of course, on the scientistic conception of philosophy – the idea that, in Russell's words, 'those questions which are already capable of definite answers are placed in the sciences, while those only to which, at present, no definite answer can be given, remain to form the residue which is called philosophy' ([10. 39], 70) – this is not a problem in the least; if anything, it is one of the primary catalysts for the scientistic outlook.[1]

The point is that the mechanist resolution of these two debates turned on the elimination of spurious a priori theories, which created a momentum that carried over into all remaining aspects of the mind/body problem (as is epitomized, for example, in Russell's *The Analysis of Mind*). This is made clear in Section 3.4 of the *Vienna Circle Manifesto*. Here the overthrowal of vitalist theories in biology is equated with the imminent removal of similar 'metaphysical burdens and logical incongruities' from psychology ([10.36], 314). Thus, if we are to do justice to the scientistic conception of the mind/body problem – the gradual displacement of philosophical theories by psychological theories – we must address both aspects of the historical antecedents on which this view is based: i.e. vitalist as well as mechanist attitudes towards the nature of conceptual versus empirical problems.

It is not difficult to see what position Descartes must take on the above two issues. The whole thrust of his animal automaton thesis demands that he show how animal heat and movement can be explained without appeal to vital forces. Hence, he must show how, in animals, neither the production of heat nor bodily movements depend upon the activities of a soul (see [10.6], 329). In the *Discourse* he introduces his theory of heat as a paradigm for explaining all animal functions. ('[Understand this] and it will readily enable us to decide how we ought to think about all the others' [10.4], 134).) The heart, he argues, is like a furnace which produces its heat by a process similar to 'fires without light' (viz., spontaneous combustion or fermentation). This heat causes the blood entering the ventricles to expand and contract ('just as liquids generally do when they are poured drop by drop into some vessel which is very hot' (Ibid., 135)). Note that the reason why Descartes rejects Harvey's explanation of the contractile nature of the heart muscle is precisely because:

> if we suppose that the heart moves in the way Harvey describes,
> we must imagine some faculty which causes this movement;
> yet the nature of this faculty is much harder to conceive of than
> whatever Harvey purports to explain by invoking it.
>
> ([10.7], 318)

323

Here, Descartes claims, is an explanation that can be seen to follow from

> the mere arrangement of the parts of the heart (which can be seen with the naked eye), from the heat in the heart (which can be felt with the fingers), and from the nature of the blood (which can be known through observation). This movement follows just as necessarily as the movement of a clock follows from the force, position and shape of its counterweights and wheels.

> ([10.4], 136)

Yet few agreed with Descartes' hypothesis. To begin with, his 'fire without light' merely seemed to replace an enigma with a mystery. Second, the heart of a newly dissected animal did not feel as hot as Descartes' theory would suggest. Third, the argument overlooks the fact that the hearts of cold-blooded animals beat in the same way as those of warm-blooded animals. And fourth, the argument does not account for the ability of a warm-blooded animal to maintain a constant heat within a broad range of temperature extremes.

It was precisely in order to account for this last phenomenon that Barthez (re-)introduced the so-called *principio vitalis* in 1773, but in vastly different terms from what one finds in classical writings. Barthez postulated a 'special causal "principle of life", which was not to be confused with the origins of thought' ([10.27], II:87). He specified the 'role of the vital principle in digestion, circulation, the pulse, heat production, secretion, nutrition, respiration, the voice, genital function development, the senses, movement, sleep, perception' (Ibid.). In place of dualism, Barthez distinguished three separate elements: soul, body and vital principle, and thence two separate issues: the mind/body problem and the life/matter problem (Ibid., 89).

At stake for late eighteenth-century biology was the question of whether the so-called 'vital phenomena' were to be explained by special physiological laws or could be subsumed under the general laws of nature. The seventeenth-century search for a mechanical account of matter had obviously received a tremendous impetus from the Newtonian revolution: not simply because Newton had succeeded in presenting a unified account of the physical laws governing both the heavens and the earth, but had done so using concepts whose justification lay in their mathematical consistency and explanatory power. At one and the same time this was to have a profound effect on both mechanist and vitalist thought: the former because it would fix attention on the motion of matter, the latter because it would appear to license the use of 'forces' on a par with gravity to explain vital phenomena.

What was primarily an empirical problem concerning the location and generation of animal heat merged, during the nineteenth century, into a philosophical debate on the mind/body problem, mainly because the amorphous notion of *vital phenomena* indiscriminately grouped together those biological processes which typify living organisms (e.g. reproduction, growth, respiration, metabolism) with the so-called 'psychic processes' experienced by man. To exclude the latter from the biochemical successes that were rapidly eliminating vitalist explanations from physiology seemed, as far as the scientific materialists were concerned, to abandon the mechanist spirit of the age in favour of dualist obscurantism. But we must be careful not to generalize on the basis of their example.

Several historians of science have warned of the dangers of over-simplifying the mechanist/vitalist debate during the nineteenth century. There are subtle but significant distinctions to be drawn between the scientific materialism espoused by Vogt, Moleschott and Büchner (see [10.26]), the reductionist materialism of the mechanist quadrumvirate (Brücke, Du Bois-Reymond, Helmholtz and Ludwig (see [10.21], [10.27])) and Liebig and Bernard's vital materialism (otherwise known as 'physical' or 'descriptive' materialism (see [10.41], [10.25], [10.32])). These differences were a consequence of the fact that the two prevailing theories of mechanism from the seventeenth century to the beginning of the nineteenth century – the physical and the physiological – not only seemed to be independent of one another, but if anything, in opposition to one another.

The former was the direct consequence of the search for the universal laws of nature. The latter saw man, animals and plant life as machines exhibiting a uniquely self-regulating behaviour. This was particularly true of that most quintessential feature of living organisms: their ability to maintain a constant heat (generally) above that of their surroundings, whereas inanimate matter rapidly tends towards thermal equilibrium with its environment. But despite the attention which this issue received, it proved impossible 'to bring a former "vital function", animal heat, into accord with the mechanical theories of heat so prominent in the years following Newton' ([10.34], 91).

The problem of animal heat is important in more ways than one for the foundations of psychology. Not only did it dominate the mechanist/vitalist debate up to the 1870s (cf. [10.33], 6–7), but as a direct result, created a focus which continues to influence critical attitudes towards psychology. This line of thought can be pursued in two different directions. One leads through Helmholtz's work on the conservation of energy to the debate on the second law of thermodynamics, the bearing which the kinetic theory of gas had on vitalist thought, and ultimately to the development of information theory. The reason why Helmholtz's work was so pivotal is partly because of his close relations to the Berlin mechanists, and partly because of his unique position to bridge the physical and the physiological in the theory of heat, as is amply demonstrated by his publication in 1847 of 'Über die Erhaltung der Kraft' and 'Bericht über die Theorie der Physiologischen Wärmeerscheinungen' (see [10.24] and for a reminder of the number of participants involved [10.30]).

For present purposes, we shall concentrate on the consequences of the physico-chemical transformation of physiology. Although this set the stage for the unification of the two species of mechanism, it served in the process to sunder materialist thought. The problem was that animal heat was but one of the vital phenomena which had divided the two schools of mechanism. The Darwinian revolution encouraged a new generation of materialists to assume that the successes demonstrated in the physiological explanation of the theory of heat could be extended to the mechanisms governing growth and reproduction. But what of the host of problems contained under 'psychic processes', for example, conscious and unconscious mental processes, thought, intentions, volition, beliefs, reasoning, problem-solving, insight, memory, perception and sensation?

The answer to this last question lies partly in the changing attitude towards neurophysiology. At the beginning of the century Berzelius had portrayed the brain, not as the last frontier, but rather as inherently impenetrable. Hence, it was natural to respond to the 'Brodie hypothesis' (viz., that animal heat is in some way caused by the nervous system) with the vitalist dogma that the secret causes of animal heat would prove to be equally impenetrable (see [10.25], 98). The rapid development of experimental methodology and technology in physiological studies of respiration dating from the 1830s was matched, however, by a growing interest in anthropometry and the anatomy and pathology of the brain (cf. [10.20], 263–302).

The major breakthroughs which took place independently in both fields in the 1860s not only dealt a devastating blow to vitalist attitudes towards the problem of animal heat (and hence other biological vital phenomena), but also had a dramatic effect on mechanist attitudes towards the brain. While Liebig, Helmholtz and Bernard were successfully identifying the complex mechanisms involved in the organic conservation of energy, Broca, Fritsch, Hitzig and Wernicke were discovering (or at least, were seen as discovering) the neural localization of specific motor and language functions. Thus, it was increasingly tempting to conclude that what was relevant to homeostatic vital phenomena would apply no less forcefully to 'cerebral' vital phenomena. It was the assumption that any explanation of the nature and causes of psychic processes would have to be one which pursued the same lines as the theory of heat which, more than anything else, divided late nineteenth-century materialist thought.

Just as Vogt, Moleschott and Büchner had deliberately distanced themselves from their mechanist predecessors, so, too, the reductionists were to repudiate what they regarded as the excesses of the scientific materialists. To be sure, there is considerable overlap between the writings of La Mettrie and the scientific materialists, if only because of the broad spectrum of activities grouped together under the notion of 'vital phenomena'. But, as even Lange concedes, there is also a marked discontinuity as a result of the revolutions occurring in biology, physiology and chemistry ([10.31], ii:240–1). And the exact same thing can be said of the relationship between the scientific materialists and the reductionist materialists. Although the two groups shared a strongly anti-dualist bias, they evinced very different temperaments and objectives.

Whereas the former saw themselves as popularizers and prosyletizers of a new ethos, the latter were first and foremost experimentalists intent on instituting new technological and methodological principles. For the reductionists, the dualist issue at stake was largely (if not exclusively) confined to the removal of 'vital forces' from biochemical explanations of physiological processes. But for the scientific materialists, this spilled over into mind/body dualism; there could be no categorial distinction between mental causes of animal heat and mental causes of behaviour. This resulted in what has proved the most memorable quotation from scientific materialist writings: Vogt's infamous remark that 'thoughts stand in the same relation to the brain as gall does to the liver or urine to the kidneys' ([10.26], 64).

Vogt may have been satisfied with the reaction which he clearly intended to provoke with this comment (which he did not in fact originate), but the other scientific materialists were far from pleased with the brouhaha that ensued. Büchner could not 'refrain from finding the comparison unsuitable and badly chosen'; thought 'is no excretion, but an activity or motion of the substances and material compounds grouped together in a definite manner in the brain' ([10.20], 303–4). Despite the variations which this theme was to undergo in materialist writings from Cabanis to Czolbe (see [10.35], 469–70), the basic point which remained constant is that cognition, *qua* 'mental' phenomenon, must permit the same type of causal explanation as any of the other biological vital phenomena. And it was ultimately this theme which led to the formal rupture between the two mechanist groups.

As far as the reductionists were concerned, this was to confuse philosophical speculation about an empirical problem with empirical speculation about a philosophical problem. The latent tension between them which was present from the start came to a head in 1872 when

Du Bois-Reymond insisted in his infamous lecture on 'The Limits of our Knowledge of Nature' that the real:

> faultiness with Vogt's expression ... lies in this, that it leaves the impression on the mind that the soul's activity is in its own nature as intelligible from the structure of the brain, as is the secretion from the structure of a gland.
>
> ([10.22], 31–2; cf. [10.28], I, 102–3)

This led Du Bois-Reymond to close on a note that was to prove no less provocative: 'as regards the enigma what matter and force are, and how [the brain gives rise to thought, the scientist] must resign himself once for all to the far more difficult confession – "IGNORABIMUS!" ' (Ibid., 32).

Du Bois-Reymond was not hereby abandoning, but was rather seeking to contain mechanism. His 'Ignorabimus' was putatively set by the bounds of materialism: i.e. what cannot be explained by 'the law of causality' (viz., the nature of matter, force and thought) cannot be explained at all. The argument was thus intended to circumscribe the parameters of the mechanist/vitalist debate.[2] Far from wishing to lend any support to the vitalist approach to 'psychic processes', his intention was rather to remove the latter from the scientist's legitimate concern with 'vital forces' (Ibid., 24). In other words, the mechanist/vitalist debate is strictly confined to the life/matter problem; to conflate this with the mind/body problem is to confuse an empirical with a conceptual issue, which cannot but result in a materialist metaphysics. (Which in turn, as Du Bois-Reymond rightly anticipated, would give rise to idealist responses.) The only issue that involves the mechanist is that:

> What distinguishes living from dead matter, the plant and the animal, as considered only in its bodily functions, from the crystal, is just this: in the crystal the matter is in stable equilibrium, while a stream of matter pours through the organic being, and its matter is in a state of more or less perfect dynamic equilibrium, the balance being now positive, again approaching zero, and again negative.
>
> (Ibid., 23)

This argument draws heavily on Bernard's theory that 'All the vital mechanisms, varied as they are, have only one object, that of preserving constant the conditions of life in the internal environment' ([10.37], 224). This in turn had evolved from Liebig's 'state of equilibrium',[3] demonstrating yet again how difficult it can be to distinguish between the various schools; for Liebig is commonly identified as a vitalist, largely because he was prepared to countenance the presence of vital forces in physiological explanations.

According to Liebig, 'the state of equilibrium [is] determined by a resistance and the dynamics, of the vital force' ([10.25], 136). Like Barthez, however, he divorced this vital–causal agency from the mind/ body problem,[4] and justified its heuristic role by comparing it to the concept of gravity which, 'like light to one born blind, is a mere word, devoid of meaning'. In a passage in *Animal Chemistry* which clearly serves as a precursor for Du Bois-Reymond's 'Ignorabimus', Liebig explicitly drew on the methodological precedent established by gravity in order to defend the explanatory role which vital forces play in physiology:

> Natural science has fixed limits which cannot be passed; and it must always be borne in mind that, with all our discoveries, we shall never know what light, electricity, and magnetism are in their essence, because even of those things which are material, the human intellect has only conceptions. We can ascertain, however, the laws which regulate their motion and rest, because these are manifested in phenomena. In a like manner, the laws of vitality, and of all that disturbs, promotes, or alters it, may certainly be discovered although we shall never learn what life is. Thus the discovery of the laws of gravitation and of the planetary motions led to an entirely new conception of the cause of these phenomena.
>
> ([10.25], 138)

Similarly, Bernard emphasized 'the vital point of view' in contrast to those scientific materialists who 'paid too much attention to the purely physical side of nervous and muscular action' ([10.37], 149). And like Liebig, he maintained that, 'When a physiologist calls in vital force or life he does not see it; he merely pronounces a word' ([10.25], 151). Bernard was careful, however, to chastise those who would invoke 'a vital force in opposition to physicochemical forces, dominating all the phenomena of life, subjecting them to entirely separate laws, and making the organism an organized whole which the experimenter may not touch without destroying the quality of life itself' ([10.37], 132–3). And yet, contemporary physiologists saw in Bernard's *directive idée* which governs the activities of the *milieu intérieure* a return to just such a vitalist position.[5]

To historians of science, the real question which these 'mere words, devoid of meaning' raises is not so much whether Liebig and Bernard's theories should be classified as vitalist or mechanist, as whether they signal the imminent demise of the mechanist/vitalist debate as far as the problem of animal heat was concerned (see [10.32]; [10.21]). Bernard sought to distinguish between organic and inorganic processes without postulating the existence of special laws or kinds of matter to explain the former ([10.25], 158–60; [10.32], 457). The mechanical laws of heat are indeed universal, but 'life cannot be wholly elucidated by the physico-chemical phenomena known in inorganic nature'. But while there are 'vital phenomena [which] differ from those of inorganic bodies in complexity and appearance, this difference obtains only by virtue of determined or determinable conditions proper to themselves' ([10.25], 151). That is, the explanation of these unique biological processes must conform to established 'scientific method': i.e. to the laws of causality.

In an obvious sense this had done nothing to eliminate the core of the mechanist/vitalist debate; rather, its decline *vis-à-vis* the life sciences is to be sought on the sociological, not philosophical grounds that 'Ultimately vitalism di[s]appeared with the emergence of a new set of questions' (Ibid.) in much the same way and at much the same time that

> Physical research had been diverted ... into an entirely new channel. Under the overmastering influence of Helmholtz's discovery of the conservation of energy, its object was henceforward to refer all phenomena in last resort to the laws which govern the transformations of energy.
>
> ([10.29], 46)

Once again we must be careful not to oversimplify the situation. Given the diversity of processes grouped together under 'vital phenomena', the mechanist/vitalist debate was far from curtailed by this development: what occurred was rather a significant realignment in its focus. Animal heat was now relegated to the secondary status of a subsidiary metabolic activity. What took its place as far as the controversy over a 'life force' was concerned was the controlling agency overseeing the various homeostatic mechanisms that sustain life.

The theory of animal heat had left its mark, however; for the very nature of the problem invited the model of a self-regulating system which, as Arbib points out, was instrumental in the evolution of the notions of control mechanism and intelligent automata ([10.18], 80–1). It is thus no coincidence that the thermostat should have come to play such a central role in the elucidation of cybernetics. When Liebig first articulated the principle that all matter is governed by the same thermal laws, he used the example of food and oxygen as the fuel which enable the animal/furnace to maintain a stable temperature. It is also interesting to note that in 1851 Helmholtz and Du Bois-Reymond simultaneously (and independently) compared the nervous system to a telegraph system 'which in an instant transmit[s] intelligence from the outposts to the controlling centres, and then convey[s] its orders back to the outlying posts to be executed there' ([10.29], 72; see Helmholtz's remark about Wagner (Ibid., 87) and Du Bois-Reymond's letters ([10.23], 64)).

This proto-cybernetic picture provided the obvious starting-point for a new generation of mechanists who were eager to respond to the furore provoked by Darwin and, even more importantly, the renewed vitalist attack inspired by Du Bois-Reymond. For Du Bois-Reymond's lectures offered an opportunity which no vitalist was likely to forgo, and a challenge which no mechanist could afford to ignore. Yet another reading of Du Bois-Reymond's *ignorabimus*, therefore, is that while it marked the end of the physiologist's biochemical involvement in the physical/physiological thermal debate, the very terms in which he presented his argument served notice that the issue was shifting to a different arena: one in which physiologists and psychologists would do battle with philosophers over the structure of those teleological and 'psychic' processes which Du Bois-Reymond had dogmatically declared out of materialist bounds.

❧ III THE REFLEX THEORY DEBATE ❧

The debate over the theory of heat established a paradigm for the scientistic outlook. Here was a case where conceptual progress, made possible by technological advances, had enabled scientists to eschew any appeal to 'logical fictions'. The movement in this issue was from the study to the laboratory, as a question in which philosophers had originally played a leading role was ultimately removed altogether from their sphere of influence. Unlike the case of animal heat, however, the philosophical problem in the debate over reflex actions concerns the question whether it *makes any sense* to suppose that these underlying neural processes could explain the nature of purposive behaviour.

At first sight the debate over reflex actions appears to be – or at least was conceived by Descartes to be – of exactly the same order as that over the theory of heat. Behaviourists, and indeed cognitivists, have cast themselves in much the same role as the mechanist reductionists. The whole point of the so-called top-down/bottom-up distinction is to suggest that, as with the case of animal heat, it would be possible to resolve this problem experimentally if only we had sufficient 'information about the physiological states of the *twelve billion neurons* in the human brain, each with up to *five thousand* synapses' ([10.44], 476). But at our present level of understanding:

> This vast amount of information and its fantastic complexity
> would utterly dumbfound us; we could not hope to begin
> creating much order out of such vast quantities of particulate

information. Rather, we would need some very powerful theories or ideas about how the particulate information was to be organized into a hierarchy of higher-level concepts referring to structure and function.

Hence:

> Many psychologists feel that their task is to describe the functional program of the brain at the level of flow-charting information-processing mechanisms. What is important is the logical system of interacting parts – the model – and not the specific details of the machinery that might actually embody it in the nervous system.

(Ibid.)

No better example of the paramount role which the Cartesian framework plays in the evolution and the continuity of mechanist thought can be found than in the persisting mechanist preoccupation with the nature of purposive behaviour. Goals and intentions are more than just an embarrassment for the mechanist thesis. They have become the testing ground which decides the success or failure of entire theories.

The roots of this fixation lie in Descartes' attempt to explain reflex actions in such a way as to encompass all animal behaviour, while excluding a significant portion of human behaviour. According to Descartes, a reflex action is the result of the automatic or machine-like release of animal spirits that are stored in the brain: a point which applies to all reflex movements, whether these be animal or human. But humans, unlike animals, are endowed with a mind that is able to modify the reflection of animal spirits in the pineal gland, thereby resulting in voluntary or conscious actions.

The obvious response for the vitalist champion of the Great Chain of Being to make to this argument was to establish that animals are at least capable of purposive behaviour (or, on the extremist position, that *all* animal behaviour is purposive). There was another option available to the defender of the continuum picture, however, which was certainly not conceivable before Descartes: viz., that all human, as well as all animal behaviour, is automatic, albeit governed by mechanisms that might be vastly more complex than those which occur in simpler life forms. And given the reductionism which defined eighteenth- and nineteenth-century materialism, it was only natural to present this 'mechanist thesis' in the same terms as applied in the animal heat debate, with 'goals', 'purposes', 'intentions' and 'volitions' dismissed as akin to 'vital forces'.

What makes this issue so difficult is that there is an important parallel to be drawn between the debates over animal heat and reflex actions: viz., both were first and foremost biological problems riddled by a priori preconceptions which led into philosophical concerns over the mind/body problem. As we saw in section 1, at the heart of Descartes' attack on the Great Chain of Being is his idea that the subject is conscious of the operations of his mind: of his cognitions, perceptions, sensations, imaginings and affects. We experience these 'actions of the soul', or, in more general terms, 'volitions', as 'proceeding directly from our soul and as seeming to depend on it alone' ([10.6], 335). But although immediately acquainted with the 'actions of our souls', we are not conscious of the intervening mechanisms involved in the bodily movements brought about by our volitions (i.e. the mechanisms activated by the animal spirits that are released when the soul deflects the pineal gland). That does not mean that the processes involved in the maintenance of body heat and in bodily movement are *unconscious*, however; rather, they are *non-conscious*. For to suppose that they might be 'unconscious' would imply that these processes take place beneath the threshold of an animal's – as well as man's – consciousness (where Descartes has already excluded the former possibility a priori).

What we have to remember in the reflex theory debate is that almost everyone was opposed to Descartes' attack on the Great Chain of Being, but not to his presupposition that all actions are the effects of causes. Thus the burden which Descartes' argument imposed on vitalists and mechanists alike was to establish that man and animals are equally capable of purposive behaviour: in significantly different senses. In the case of vitalists, this meant showing how the mental causes of purposive behaviour are shared by animals; for mechanists, that whatever is responsible for the 'purposiveness' of human 'voluntary' behaviour is a feature that is also present in animal movements.

Both sides were agreed, therefore, that the 'purposiveness' of purposive behaviour must lie in the *originating causes* of that behaviour, not in the actual movements of that behaviour. This means that there is nothing in the movements of purposive behaviour to account for the purposiveness of that behaviour; we can at best *infer*, not *observe* that that behaviour is purposive (has such-and-such a cause). Yet, both sides were also (tacitly) agreed that the purposiveness of purposive behaviour must be evident in the behaviour; otherwise, it would make no sense to distinguish between 'purposive' and 'non-purposive' behaviour, and without such a distinction, no sense to speak of 'purposive' behaviour. Hence our 'inability' to observe someone else's, or an animal's, 'originating causes' – either because of the intrinsic privacy of minds (in which case our 'inability' is a priori) or because these causes are neural (in which case our 'inability' is what Russell called 'medical') – has no bearing on the classification of someone or something's behaviour as purposive.

Furthermore, both sides were committed to demonstrating that the various bodily movements which Descartes had identified as reflexes are in fact purposive: again, for vastly different reasons. As far as the vitalists were concerned, this was solely in order to establish that these movements are not mechanical, i.e. that, as Stahl put it, 'the very purposiveness of the so-called "reflex actions" proves that, even if we are unaware of the fact, the soul controls all bodily movements' (see [10.27], ch. 25). For mechanists, the challenge was to show that to describe a reflex action as purposive in no way entails that it must have been brought about by the 'actions of a soul'; i.e. that animals and perhaps even plants are capable of such movements. But before the implications of this issue for dualism could be properly addressed, it was first necessary to confirm that reflex actions are indeed purposive, and to do that required an understanding of the mechanics of automatic behaviour.

Descartes' views had a profound impact on the seventeenth-century conflict between iatro-physicists and iatro-chemists on the life/matter issue. What had hitherto been regarded as a debate over the universality of the laws of mechanics (the question whether the operations of the body are subsumed under the laws of physics, or call for special chemical laws) was now forced to account for the similarities and/or differences between plant, animal, and human 'responses to stimuli'. The emerging consensus accepted a sharp division between the behaviour of living and non-living matter, but as far as the continuity of animal and human life forms was concerned, most 'true philosophers' agreed that 'The transition from animals to man is not violent' ([10.10], 103).

Both sides in this transformed mechanist/vitalist debate accepted that Descartes was wrong, but for vastly different reasons. Apart, that is, from the question of Descartes' remarks on anatomy, which virtually everyone saw as antiquated. The mechanists were of course disturbed by Descartes' commitment to a metaphysical soul; the vitalists by the suggestion that a large element of human and animal behaviour is automatic.

The conflict between the two sides centred on three key problems with Descartes' argument. First, the dubious role assigned to 'animal spirits'. As Stensen put it, 'Animal spirits, the more subtle part of the blood, the vapour of blood, and juice of the nerves, these are names used by man, but they are mere words, meaning nothing' (quoted in [10.45], 8). Second, there was the fact that decerebrated animals can continue to move, which was difficult to reconcile with Descartes' premiss that animal spirits are stored in the brain. And third, the fact that animals are capable of adapting to their environments, which was difficult to reconcile with the seventeenth-century conception of 'machine'.

This last point became the focus of attention throughout the eighteenth century. Vitalist attitudes are summed up by Claude Perrault's belief that:

> although the movements of plants in turning towards the sun, and the flowing of the river which 'seems to seek the valley', appear to indicate choice and desire, in reality these movements are of a wholly different nature than those of animals. In the latter there is a soul which is concerned with sensation and movement.
>
> ([10.47], 33)

The exact same issue – the overriding concern with the mechanics of 'choice and desire' – recurs throughout the ensuing debates over mechanism (and indeed, lie at the heart of Turing's thesis[6] (see [10.55])).

The crux of the vitalist position was that, in the words of Samuel Farr, the body is more than 'a simple machine, instigated by no spiritual agent, and influenced by no stimulus'. Even if 'custom and habit' should have made us oblivious of the fact, all movements – voluntary and involuntary – are 'controlled by the will' ([10.47], 102). The proof lay in the dogmatic *modus tollens* that, if the body were a machine, its movements could not *per definiens* be purposive; but since the latter is patently false, so too must be the premiss. This is the reasoning underlying Alexander Monro the younger's assertion that, 'The more we consider the various spontaneous operations the more fully we shall be convinced that they are the best calculated for the preservation and well-being of the animal' (Ibid., 106). Hence Stahl's conclusion that:

> Vital activities, vital movements, cannot, as some recent crude speculations suppose, have any real likeness to such movements as, in an ordinary way depend on the material condition of a body and take place without any direct use or end or aim.
>
> (Ibid., 32–3)

The mechanist response to this argument received a major boost from Hartley's *Observations on Man*. The strength of Hartley's argument lay in the manner in which he turned a central theme in vitalist thought to mechanist advantage. Perrault and Leibniz had argued that there are two different kinds of movement under the control of the soul: those that are consciously dictated, and those which through habit no longer require an act of choice for their performance, and have thus become unconscious (see [10.47], 33). This, too, is an issue which has remained at the forefront of post-computational mechanist concerns. What is particularly interesting, when tracing the continuity in mechanist thought on the problem of insight, is to locate the origin of Newell and Simon's models of the mechanics of 'pre-conscious selection' in Hartley's account 'Of muscular Motion, and its two Kinds, automatic and voluntary; and of the Use of the Doctrines of Vibrations and Association', for explaining these respectively ([10.50], 85; see [10.54]).

According to Hartley, voluntary movements are brought about by ideas, automatic movements by sensations. Sensations are caused by the vibration of minute particles in the nerves which ascend to the brain where, if repeated a sufficient number of times, frame an image or copy of themselves. These images, or 'simple ideas of sensation', constitute the building material for complex ideas. Images of regularly occurring sensory vibrations can also form in the nerves. These 'vibratiuncles' are 'the physiological counterparts of ideas'. This yields Hartley's famous (isomorphic) laws of association: any sensation/vibration A,B,C, by being associated with one another a sufficient number of times, get such a power over corresponding ideas/vibratiuncles a,b,c that any one of the sensations/vibrations A, when impressed alone, shall be able to excite in the mind/brain b,c the ideas/vibratiuncles of the rest.

Although prepared to describe himself as a mechanist, Hartley was no determinist. The problem posed by his argument was simply that, while voluntary actions are caused by ideas, the latter are themselves the product of experience. (The price he pays for free will is an unconvincing defence of a Cartesian soul that is able to originate causes of actions.) As far as the evolution of mechanism is concerned, the significance of his emphasis on the role of past experience is twofold: first, it opened up the prospect of a scientific study of the laws governing the succession of thoughts; and second, it suggested a method of breaking down the barrier between voluntary and involuntary movements.

On Hartley's account, what were originally voluntary motions can become automatic, and vice versa: 'Association not only converts automatic actions into voluntary, but voluntary ones into automatic' ([10.47], 85). To illustrate the former phenomenon, Hartley cites the example of a baby automatically grasping a rattle:

> after a sufficient repetition of the proper associations, the sound
> of the words *grasp, take, hold*, etc., the sight of the nurse's
> hand in a state of contraction, the idea of a hand, and particularly
> of the child's own hand, in that state, and innumerable other
> associated circumstances, i.e. sensations, ideas, and motions, will
> put the child upon grasping, till, at last, that idea, or state of mind
> which we may call the will to grasp, is generated, and sufficiently

associated with the action to produce it instantaneously. It is therefore perfectly voluntary in this case.

([10.42], 94)

Here is an explanation of what, in the early twentieth century, would be referred to as the 'stamping in' of volitions. To illustrate this phenomenon, Hartley offers the example (now familiar in cognitivist writings) of someone learning how to play the harpsichord: at the beginning he exercises 'a perfectly voluntary command over his fingers', but with time 'the action of volition grow[s] less and less express ... till at last [it] become[s] evanescent and imperceptible' ([10.47], 85).

Hartley made clear that his paramount intention in this argument was to restore the continuum picture. An entire section is devoted to showing how 'If the Doctrines of Vibrations and Association be found sufficient to solve the Phænomena of Sensation, Motion, Ideas, and Affections, in Men, it will be reasonable to suppose, that they will also be sufficient to solve the analogous Phænomena in Brutes' ([10.50], 404). He even went so far as to claim that 'the Laws of Vibrations and Association may be as universal in respect of the nervous Systems of Animals of all Kinds, as the Law of Circulation is with respect to the System of the Heart and Blood-vessels' (Ibid.).

The impetus for this latter argument lay in the fact that eighteenth-century vitalists had based their objection to mechanism on the classical Newtonian exclusion of teleological considerations from mechanical explanations. This had placed the onus on mechanists to account for the organization, adaptativeness and directedness of 'spontaneous movements' in strictly physical terms. And that is exactly what remains most problematic in Hartley's argument; for Hartley had remained enough of a Cartesian to see the progression from voluntary to secondarily automatic actions as the movement from actions caused by volitions to those instigated by mechanical causes (as is brought out by his use of the term 'secondarily *automatic*'). But then, this does nothing to counter the terms of Descartes' attack on the Great Chain of Being, since the objection still remains that behaviour bifurcates into mechanical and volitional.

Fortunately for mechanists, the apparent key to removing the latter obstacle was to be provided, two years after the publication of *Observations on Man*, by Hartley's vitalist peer, Robert Whytt. The central theme in Hartley's account of involuntary movement is given the same prominence in *An Essay on the Vital and other Involuntary Motions of Animals*. Indeed, not only does Whytt emphasize the importance of involuntary actions which we 'acquire through custom and habit,' but he does so using the same example as Hartley. In standard vitalist fashion, Whytt insists that such 'automatic actions' are

337

not mechanical. Hence he warns that the term 'automatic' is danger-
ously misleading, since 'it may seem to convey the *idea* of a mere
inanimate machine, producing such motions purely by virtue of its
mechanical construction' (Ibid., 75). But unlike earlier vitalists, Whytt
was not suggesting that all purposive movements must *ipso facto* be
under the direct control of the will. Rather, these automatic actions –
whether reflex or secondarily automatic – are controlled by a 'sentient
principle' which is co-extensive with the mind but is below the threshold of consciousness, and can thus be neither volitional nor rational.

This third type of causal factor enables Whytt to complete the
anti-Cartesian attack which eluded Hartley. The key to defending
the continuum picture was to define a continuum of voluntary and
involuntary actions. Hartley could only speak of actions 'esteemed less
and less voluntary, semi-voluntary, or scarce voluntary at all' (Ibid.,
84). For the orthodox Cartesian, this would mark the break-off point
between human and animal behaviour. But Whytt could superimpose
on this a continuum of animal and human sentient behaviour. It is
precisely on this basis that we find Whytt emphasizing how:

> It appears, that as in all the works of nature, there is a beautiful
> gradation, and a kind of link, as it were, betwixt each species
> of animals, the lowest of the immediately superior class, different
> little from the highest in the next succeeding order; so in the
> motions of animals . . . the mix'd motion, as they are called, and
> those from habit, being the link between the voluntary and
> involuntary motions.

> (Ibid.)

By thus extending reflex theory to encompass both voluntary and
involuntary movements in such a way as to have the one shade into
the other, Hartley and Whytt had paved the way for what would
henceforth be seen by mechanists as the continuum of unconscious/
conscious purposive behaviour: not just in man, but throughout the
chain of self-regulating life forms. Not the perfect continuum demanded
by the *scala naturae*, however; rather, a continuum made up of a myriad
different branches (as would, of course, become the primary picture at
the end of the nineteenth century with Darwin's tree metaphor).

This provides the (barest fragment of the) background to Marshall
Hall's controversial claim at the beginning of the nineteenth century
that reflex actions are 'independent of both volition and sensation, of
their organ the brain, and of the mind or soul' ([10.47], 139). Hall's
model was highly schematic, leading Sherrington to warn at the end of
the century that 'there are a number of reactions that lie intermediate
between [Hall's] extreme types, "unconscious reflex" and "willed
action"' (Ibid., 140). A large part of the experimental progress made

over the century was stimulated by the obvious need to fill in these lacunae. But even more important, for philosophical purposes, are the misleading terms in which Sherrington described Hall's contribution. In the above quotation Hall stresses that reflex actions take place 'independent of both volition and sensation'. Had he described these movements as 'unconscious', it would certainly not have been in the sense which Pflüger understood when he criticized Hall's theory, nor that which Lotze intended when he responded to Pflüger's attack on Hall (infra).

The use of the term 'unconscious' is a source of endless confusion when discussing the reflex theory debate; for it is indiscriminately applied to those who held that consciousness plays no causal role in involuntary movements and those who insisted that all purposive behaviour must – by definition – be under the control of a 'degenerated will'.[8] Furthermore, we must distinguish within the former category between those who held that it makes no sense to speak of a creature or agent being aware of mechanically responding to a stimulus, and those who regarded reflex and secondarily automatic movements as unconscious sentient reactions. Thus, we must distinguish between two concurrent mechanist/vitalist debates on reflex theory in the nineteenth century: one over the question whether purposive automatic acts are mechanical or sentient, and the other whether the very notion of a *purposive automatic act* is a contradiction in terms.

Bearing in mind its Cartesian antecedents, it is not quite so curious that this issue should have been fought out over the question whether the reflexes of decerebrated animals are voluntary, and thus – contra Hall – under psychic control. In the Pflüger–Lotze version of this debate, the issue was largely confined to the question of whether the reflex movements of a decerebrated frog are conscious. As far as Pflüger was concerned, the very fact that a decerebrated frog can shift from its favoured leg to the other limb in order to remove acid placed on its back renders it self-evident that its actions are intelligent, and hence, that consciousness is co-extensive with the entire nervous system. Lotze's objection to this 'spinal soul' theory turned on the familiar theme that what appear to be voluntary actions are in fact secondarily automatic motions, resulting from originally intelligent actions that were stamped into the frog's brain by previous experiences.[9] In order to constitute genuinely intelligent action, we would need proof that the frog is capable of responding to demonstrably novel circumstances.

Both sides were agreed, however, that such movements are legitimately described as 'purposive': a premise from which much of the confusion sustaining the mechanist/vitalist debate was to follow. Moreover, the very terms of this conflict ensured that such confusion was to follow. For to agree with Pflüger was to concede the applicability of volitional concepts to spinal reflexes, whereas to side with Lotze was to accept, not merely that such movements can be described as 'unconscious' (in the sense that originally mental causes have become automatic), but equally serious, that learning is a form of neurological imprinting.

Boring dismissed this whole controversy as nothing more than a squabble over whether to 'define consciousness so as to exclude spinal reflexes or to include them' ([10.43], 38). Were this simply a dispute over semantic proprieties this issue would now belong to the history of psychological ideas, not philosophy. But this is not at all the pseudo-problem which Boring contended. For the problem was not just concerned with the boundaries of the concept of consciousness: more importantly, it was a debate over the *causes* of the behaviour that had been so delimited (as well, of course, as a debate over the 'nature and location' of consciousness).

From a modern perspective, perhaps the most striking feature of the reflex theory debate is that, the more physiologists began to understand the mechanics of the autonomic nervous system, the more prominent became philosophers' interest in Descartes' attack on the continuum picture. One reason for this reaction was their mounting concern over the determinist implications which scientific materialists were drawing from reflex theory (as is evident, for example, in the writings of Mill, Green, Sedgewick and Spencer). Thus, we find Carpenter insisting in *Principles of Mental Physiology* ([10.46]) that what mechanists had ignored in their quest to 'elucidate the mechanism of Automatic action' were

> the fundamental facts of Consciousness on which Descartes
> himself built up his philosophical fabric, dwelling exclusively on
> Physical action as the only thing with which Science has to do,
> and repudiating the doctrine (based on the universal experience
> of mankind) that the Mental states which we call Volitions and
> Emotions have a causative relation to Bodily changes.
>
> ([10.47], 161)

Well into this century we encounter Descartes' argument for 'semi-solipsism', but with one notable difference: gone is any hint of Descartes' consequent attack on the continuum picture. Herrick, for example, explains in *Neurological Foundations of Animal Behavior* (1924) that:

> Consciousness, then, is a factor in behavior, a real cause of
> human conduct, and probably to some extent in that of other
> animals ... This series of activities as viewed objectively forms
> an unbroken graded series from the lowest to the highest animal

species. And since in myself the awareness of the reaction is an integral part of it, I am justified in extending the belief in the participation of consciousness to other men and to brutes in so far as the similarities of their objective behavior justify the inference.

([10.47], 179)

This overturning of Descartes' intentions was based on an argument which one finds in such self-styled defenders of Descartes' 'animal automata' thesis as Lewes and Huxley: viz., the doctrine that animals, and indeed man, are 'sentient automata' (see [10.51]).[10]

What these neo-Cartesians thought they were doing was correcting an empirical oversight on Descartes' part on the basis of the two centuries of physiological advances that had intervened. They proposed to replace Descartes' *mechanical* distinction between conscious/voluntary and non-conscious/involuntary movements with a *sentient* distinction between conscious/voluntary and unconscious/involuntary movements. The major benefit of this strategy is that it enabled them to reconcile the existence of volitions with the continuum picture, and thus, remain in step with the dawning Darwinian revolution.[11]

This does not mean, however, that they were about to anthropomorphize animals by assigning them voluntary acts as defined by Descartes. The 'similarities of objective behaviour' between animals and man lay rather at the level of sentient – equals unconscious or automatic – reactions. This leads one to suspect that perhaps the real point which Boring was driving at was that this controversy was not so much over the definition of 'consciousness' as over the definition of 'machine'. For both sides of the mechanical/sentient debate were committed to a mechanist framework which was to survive the particulars of the Pflüger–Lotze dispute.

According to the vitalist outlook, secondarily automatic actions are the result of neural mechanisms that had been imprinted in the frog's cerebrum. When the animal was first undergoing these experiences it might have been conscious of its sensations; but consciousness, on this model, is deprived of any causal agency suggested by its inclusion in the group of 'vital phenomena', and reduced to the role of passive bystander.[12] In which case, should this behaviour become habitual, there is no reason to retain this 'ghost in the machine' in order to account for its residual purposive character.

On this argument, the difference 'between conscious, sub-conscious, and unconscious states ... is only of degree of complication in the neural processes' ([10.52], 407). That is, consciousness is an *emergent property*, and 'There is no real and essential distinction between voluntary and involuntary actions. They all spring from Sensibility.

They are all determined by feeling' (Ibid., 420–2). The purposiveness of the behaviour exhibited by decerebrated animals results from the fact that 'sensations excite other sensations'. But while such movements may not be 'stimulated by cerebral incitations, and cannot be regulated or controlled by such incitations – or as the psychologists would say, because Consciousness in the form of Will is no agent prompting and regulating such actions' – they nonetheless 'have the general character of sentient actions' (Ibid., 416). Hence, the flaw in the mechanist argument lies in the fact that reflex acts are 'consentient' and for that reason 'not *physical* but *vital*' (Ibid., 366).

Mechanists were quick to point out that the only rationale for this use of 'vital' is that the laws governing the mechanics of unconscious purposive behaviour are biological rather than physical; and the mechanical sense of 'cause' which underpins this objection was already being replaced by a new conception that could embrace both types of phenomena. But what is perhaps most significant in the reflex theory debate as it stood at the end of the century is the mechanist use of 'unconscious'. Far from considering what it would mean to attribute consciousness to an intact – much less a decerebrated – frog, this was accepted as a question about the 'divisibility' of consciousness. Certainly no one ever considered what sort of actions would license the assertion that these mutilated creatures were conscious or unconscious.[13]

What is not at first clear is why mechanists should have allowed themselves to be coerced into this position, rather than making the entirely sound point (which seems to have been Hall's original intention) that it makes no sense to describe such behaviour in terms of either the presence or suspension of consciousness. To characterize such movements as either *unconscious* or *involuntary* presupposes the logical possibility of consciousness or volition. But that was the last thing that mechanists wanted to suggest: for reasons which had nothing to do with considerations about the rules governing the application of the concepts of consciousness and unconsciousness. Rather, the whole thrust of the mechanist thesis had derived from the pressure to explain how 'purposive actions may take place, without the intervention of consciousness or volition, or even contrary to the latter' ([10.51], 218).

As would soon become apparent, the key word in this passage was 'intervention'. For there was no reason why mechanists should object to epiphenomenalism. Their quarrel was solely with the dualist notion of 'psychic directedness' to account for automatic motions. Thus, as far as the mechanist/vitalist debate over the nature of automatic acts was concerned, this was soon to become a dispute in name only. But then, why not extend exactly the same strategy to the remaining pillar of the vitalist argument: why eschew volitions when all you need to do is redefine them?

Thus it was that from one confused debate was born another. The problem was that all were agreed that the frog was trying to remove the acid placed on its back. But it is not at all clear what it means to speak of a creature trying to accomplish some goal of which it is not – *and could not be* – aware. Nor does it make any sense to suppose that we can at best 'infer' whether such a disfigured creature is or is not aware of a pain sensation and is trying to alleviate its discomfort. This very assumption is a reminder of the Cartesian origins of this debate: of the premiss that it is only our inability to observe the frog's mind (or at least, what was left of it!) which prevents us from resolving this issue.

Our judgements of a frog's sentience or its intentions are based on the rules governing the use of the concepts of consciousness and intention: rules which are grounded in the paradigm of human behaviour. In so far as human beings serve as the paradigm subjects for our use of psychological concepts, any question about the application of these concepts to lower organisms demands that we compare the behaviour of such creatures with the relevant human behaviour which underpins our use of that concept. For example, it is the complexity of the behaviour displayed by an organism which determines whether or not there are sufficient grounds for the attribution of a perceptual faculty. Thus, in order to establish that *Porthesia chrysorrhoea* can *perceive* light, Jacques Loeb had to show, not just that they react to certain stimuli, but that they are able to *discern* various features of their environment, i.e. that these caterpillars are able to employ what is in fact a *perceptual organ* to acquire knowledge about their environment. Otherwise the relevant concept here is not *perception* but rather, what Loeb so aptly described as a 'heliotropic mechanism' (see Section 4 below).

The corollary of this argument is that only of the caterpillar itself would it make sense to say that it 'perceives': not its 'photo-receptive organ' (or, in the case of the Pflüger–Lotze debate, the frog's central nervous system). The same holds true whether we are talking of more complex sensori-motor structures and perceptual organs, or indeed, the 'mind', 'soul' or 'consciousness'. For in none of these cases does it make sense to say that the organ or faculty in question demonstrates its ability to discriminate features of its environment. The rule of logical grammar rendering such a usage meaningless is that, only of the organism as a whole does it make sense to apply our psychological and cognitive concepts.[14]

It was only their preoccupation with salvaging the continuum picture which prevented the various mechanist and vitalist protagonists from realizing from the start just how curious were the questions which had inspired their bizarre debate.[15] It was this common nineteenth-century priority which led them to assume that the difference between sensori-motor excitation, sensations, and perceptions is itself one of degree rather than of kind. But the difference between these three concepts is categorial, not quantitative. Hence, the source of the mechanist version of the continuum picture lay in the distortions which resulted from this illicit attempt to relate the concept of sensation to that of perception on a scale of neural complexity rather than discerning the logico-grammatical distinctions operating here.

There are indeed important lessons to be learnt from this debate: lessons about the application of psychological as well as physiological concepts. Mechanists were quite right to argue that, from the premiss that I can be unconscious of responding to a stimulus, it does not follow that that response was volitional. But exactly the same holds true if I am conscious of an automatic response to a stimulus. Conversely, I can respond mechanically to some signal (e.g. a conversational cue), but it does not follow that my response was determined by a causal mechanism. If my response to a stimulus was 'willed' (e.g. I stifle a yawn), then it was not a reflex. And if this behaviour should become habitual, then it is no longer willed.

Are these empirical observations? A similar question arises with respect to the Pflüger–Lotze debate. What Pflüger's experiments tell us is not that the frog was unconsciously trying to remove the acid placed on its back, but that we must be careful of how we apply the same concepts to a normal frog. For just as the decerebrated frog was neither *responding unconsciously* to a stimulus nor *trying* to remove the acid, so we have to reconsider what it means to say of an ordinary frog that it was *consciously trying* to remove acid placed on its back.[16] (Consider the experiments on the signal detectors in a frog's eye which are activated by any movement at the periphery of its visual field, and not just that of a fly.) That is not to say that we could never attribute such a psychological capacity to a frog but only, that experiments such as those performed by Pflüger and Goltz remind us of the defeasibility of our judgements of animal behaviour, i.e. force us to register the difference between instincts or reflexes and actions.

It was only by treating the categorial distinctions between sensori-motor excitation, sensations and perceptions as gradations on the scale of consciousness that the way was then open to regarding purposive behaviour as an ascending causal mechanism in which the relations to intentions and learning are rendered external rather than internal, and adaptation is misconstrued as a cognitive process. But there is no evolutionary continuum of purposeful behaviour such that, e.g. the contraction of the pupil of the eye belongs to the same category as striving for a goal; for the former is not a more 'primitive' form of purposive behaviour but rather, a reflex movement *as opposed to* purposive behaviour.

With the growing interest in comparative psychology which resulted from the Darwinian revolution, and the emphasis on evolutionary associationism that accompanied this, it was natural for mechanists to proceed from the opposite direction. Thus, it was held that consciousness and volition develop by degrees, and that the resemblance between the behaviour of a decerebrated frog and that of man is not and could not be expected to be pronounced. Rather, the correspondence lies at the sub-behavioural level: in particular, at the neurological structure where associations between sensations are imprinted. But then, such an argument only makes sense against the premiss that this mechanism is that which guides purposive behaviour *simpliciter*, and to *assume* that the reactions of a lower organism are purposive is to presuppose all of the foregoing argument. As indeed it must, for only of a human being and what resembles (behaves like) a human being can one say: it behaves in a purposive manner. Thus the crucial issue which such an argument overlooks is the need to explain in what sense such causal reactions can be termed purposive. And this was an omission which beset both sides of this mechanist/vitalist debate; or rather, a product of the Cartesian framework which governed their outlooks, and those who were about to follow in their footsteps.

❧ IV THE RISE OF A 'NEW OBJECTIVE ❧ TERMINOLOGY'

Lewes once observed that:

> We can conceive an automaton dog that would bark at the presence of a beggar, but not an automaton dog that would bark one day at a beggar, and the next day wag his tail, remembering the food the beggar had bestowed.

> ([10.00], 304)

Well, why not? Does this not reflect the manner in which the currently prevailing techology seems to limit the powers of one's imagination? Certainly, Lewes's objection would pose no formidable obstacle to today's science of robotics. Moreover, from his own point of view, Lewes seems to have succumbed to a vitalist conception of mental states. What could be easier than to expose Lewes's regression by decerebrating a dog and then watching its behaviour after being repeatedly fed (as Goltz had in fact done). No doubt tail-wagging will turn out to have as mechanical (sentient!) an explanation as salivating. And yet, Lewes would seem to have placed his finger on a troubling problem: one which is impervious to conditioning experiments.

In place of Lewes's question we might ask: could an automaton dog *restrain* itself from wagging its tail? Or better still, deliberately wag its tail in order to elicit food when it couldn't care less about seeing the beggar once again, or when it wasn't even hungry? For that matter, how can we be certain that the movements of a decerebrated animal are identical to those of an intact animal without observing its mind: perhaps reflexes step in when the mind ceases to control?

The real problem here is that, while Lewes and Huxley had succeeded in drawing an important distinction between mechanical and animal automata, this does not suffice to silence Descartes' attack on the continuum picture. One would hardly want to argue that the behaviour of a frog (the 'Job of physiology') – with or without its cerebrum – mirrors that of a human being when, for example, he has burnt himself. And while designating consciousness an emergent property may overturn the Cartesian picture of mental states and processes, it does nothing to reduce the Cartesian gulf between voluntary and involuntary behaviour. One can simply argue that voluntary actions are determined by preconscious mental causes.

The only way that the argument that 'There is no real and essential distinction between voluntary and involuntary actions, they all spring from Sensibility, they are all determined by feeling' could remove the Cartesian assumption that man, unlike any of the lower life forms, is endowed with a soul which determines 'those movements which we call "voluntary"', was by abandoning *mental causes* as conceived by Descartes altogether. Thus Huxley argued that:

> volition ... is an emotion *indicative* of physical changes, not a
> *cause* of such changes. [T]he feeling we call volition is not
> the cause of a voluntary act, but the symbol of that state of the
> brain which is the immediate cause of that act.
>
> ([10.51])

But in order to sustain the voluntary/involuntary distinction, it was necessary to superimpose on this the premiss that the former are associated with a distinctive state of consciousness.

In *Hume* Huxley insists that 'volition is the impression which arises when the idea of a bodily or mental action is accompanied by the desire that the action should be accomplished' ([10.51], 184). Hence, the difference between voluntary and involuntary movements is phenomenological, not causal: the former are simply those actions accompanied by a special mental state (which is itself determined by past events). But then, this only serves to revive Descartes' attack on the continuum picture; for animals must also be capable of experiencing these attendant desires ('purposes'), and Huxley remained enough of a Cartesian to embrace the impossibility of knowing whether or not this was the case (see [10.51]). This meant that there was only one direction in which a mechanism committed to continuity could proceed: dispense entirely with any causal distinction between 'voluntary' and 'involuntary' movements, and define the *apparent* difference between them in terms of experience.

Thus it was that the birth of psychology, like that of modern India, was marked by a bloody clash between two rival factions: in effect, those who wanted to confront Descartes' problem and those who wanted to deny it – James versus Loeb. This may seem an oversimplification of the conflict over whether this new science should be governed by physiology or philosophy, especially as far as the fathers of behaviourism are concerned. But the fact is that, one way or another, the prospects of the mechanist thesis depended at this point on the abolition of volitions. And this was precisely the move which Jacques Loeb pursued.

Frustrated with philosophy, Loeb had turned first to neurophysiology, then biology, in his quest to solve the 'problem of will'. Studying under Goltz, he became convinced that consciousness is irrelevant to behaviour, and could be eliminated from an exclusively associationist explanation of the purposiveness of automatic actions. 'What the metaphysician calls consciousness are phenomena determined by the mechanisms of associative memory' ([10.69], 214). He found the tool for implementing this programme in the work of Julius Sachs, who had employed the notion of *tropism* – the explanation of the 'turning' of a plant in terms of its physico-chemical needs in direct response to external stimuli – as a means of extending the reductionist outlook of the mechanistic quadrumvirate to botany. Seeing in tropisms a biological parallel to automatic movements, Loeb undertook to advance mechanism by employing Sachs' approach as a starting-point for the psychology of animal behaviour (Ibid., 1ff, 77).

The aim of Loeb's subsequent research on animal heliotropism was to exhibit various organisms as 'photochemical machines enslaved to the light'. To accomplish this, he demonstrated that when the caterpillars of *Porthesia chrysorrhoea* are exposed to light coming from the opposite direction to a supply of food, they invariably move towards the former, and perish as a result. Such experiments undermined the vitalist premiss that all creatures are governed by an unanalysable instinct for self-preservation: 'In this instance the light is the "will" of the animal which determines the direction of its movement, just as it is gravity in the case of a falling stone or the movement of a planet' ([10.70], 40–1).

Since it was in principle possible to explain 'on a purely physico-chemical basis' a group of 'animal reactions . . . which the metaphysician would classify under the term of animal "will" ' (Ibid., 35), the answer to nothing less than the 'riddle of life' must lie in the fact that 'We eat,

347

drink, and reproduce not because mankind has reached an agreement that this is desirable, but because, machine-like, we are compelled to do so' (Ibid., 33). But surely, one wants to argue, Loeb's experiments had nothing to do with the 'problem of will'; in his own words, 'Heliotropic animals are . . . in reality photometric machines' (Ibid., 41). The fact that the caterpillars expired for want of food was no more a demonstration of (perverse!) purposive behaviour than the converse result would have supported vitalism. To suppose that their motor responses could exhibit the complexity of human purposive behaviour is once again to assume *ab initio* that *intentions* and *volitions* are simply part of a causal chain, from which the ability to choose, decide, select and deliberate are excluded a priori. But that was exactly what Loeb intended! This was not to be an isolated attack on the notion of *will*: all of the 'mentalist' concepts were to be removed from the eliminativist analysis of purposive – equals self-regulating – behaviour.

That is not to say that the distinction between voluntary and involuntary movements would also have to be abandoned: only that it would have to be redefined accordingly. Loeb could only hint at the direction in which he thought this should proceed: it would indeed be in terms of 'associated memories', but Loeb was careful to explain that what he meant by the term was the (experimentally observable) 'mechanism by which a stimulus brings about not only the effects which its nature and the specific structure of the irritable organ call for, but by which it brings about also the effects of other stimuli which formerly acted upon the organism almost or quite simultaneously with the stimulus in question' [10.68], 72). In other words, a conditioned response.

Thus, Loeb, unlike Huxley, was able to salvage the continuum picture precisely because he eschewed the principle of sentient continuity. All that matters is that 'If an animal can be trained, if it can learn, it possesses associative memory' (Ibid., 72). This tied in with the Darwinian shift which occurred in late nineteenth-century mechanism.[17] In the conclusion to *Origin of Species*, Darwin had proclaimed that 'Psychology will be based on a new foundation, that of the necessary acquirement of each mental power and capacity by gradation' ([10], 488). And in *Descent of Man* he declared that 'the difference in mind between man and the higher animals, great as it is, certainly is one of degree and not of kind' [10.6]. Loeb was simply removing the 'mentalist' obstacles to this version of the continuum picture.

Mechanists quickly embraced this explanation of continuity (although there was considerable disagreement over whether this implied a single continuum, such as Spencer favoured,[18] or the picture of branching continuity championed by Darwin). What is perhaps most interesting, when looking at the development of mechanist thought at the beginning of this century, is how quickly and thoroughly Loeb's outlook came to dominate American psychology. That is not to say it went unchallenged. Perhaps the most famous opposition came from Jennings in *The Behavior of the Lower Organisms* ([10.9]). But ironically, even though Jennings may be said to have won the biological battle, this only resulted in the further entrenchment of the mechanist as opposed to the psychic continuum which Jennings advocated (see [10.74]).

Jennings demonstrated, on the basis of Thorndike's trial-and-error experiments on the 'stamping in' of behaviour into cats, how it is possible to overcome tropic through conditioned responses. Hence purposive behaviour should be seen as an ongoing process in which an organism's physico-chemical needs interact with and are shaped by its environment.[19] But whatever damage this might have inflicted on the science of animal tropism, Jennings' opposition only served to promote even further Loeb's definition of purposive behaviour as a species of neurological adaptation and control, and the mechanist expectation that:

> the more complex activities of the body, which are made up by
> a grouping together of the elementary locomotor activities, and
> which enter into the states referred to in psychological
> phraseology as 'playfulness', 'fear', 'anger', and so forth, will
> soon be demonstrated as reflex activities of the subcortical parts
> of the brain.
>
> ([10.75], 4)

This was not intended to be read as a logical behaviourist thesis. Loeb and Pavlov were not urging that propositions about purposive or volitional behaviour can be reduced to or translated into propositions about molar or molecular behaviour. Rather, they were arguing that the former type of constructions are literally *meaningless* (although poetically resonant), while the latter capture the only sense in which the causes of behaviour can be intelligibly explained and thence controlled. The model for this argument was constituted by the mechanist resolution of the animal heat and reflex theory debates. Propositions about the homeostatic mechanisms sustaining thermal equilibrium, or about the sensori-motor system, did not supply the meaning of propositions citing vital forces, but rather, demonstrated the vacuity of the latter.

Pavlov made clear at the start of *Conditioned Reflexes* how his endeavour to 'lay a solid foundation for a future true science of psychology' (Ibid., 4) was the end-result of nineteenth-century mechanist thought: 'such a course is more likely to lead to the advancement of this branch of natural science' if it embraces the conception that:

Reflexes are the elemental units in the mechanism of perpetual equilibration. Physiologists have studied and are studying at the present time these numerous machine-like, inevitable reactions of the organism – reflexes existing from the very birth of the animal, and due therefore to the inherent organization of the nervous system.

(Ibid., 8)

In other words, so-called 'purposive' behaviour should be understood as the physico-chemical balance that an organism maintains by means of a complex system of 'Reflexes [which,] like the driving-belts of machines of human design, may be of two kinds – positive and negative, excitatory and inhibitory' (Ibid., 8).

In Pavlov's eyes, the key to this breakthrough lay in the advance of physiology from the study of bodily reflexes into the operations of the cerebral cortex. Pavlov saw himself as advancing Loeb's work by explaining animal behaviour in terms of what Charles Richet had called 'psychic reflexes' (Ibid., 5). He undertook to extend 'recent physiology['s] ... tendency to regard the highest activities of the hemispheres as an association of the new excitations at any given time with traces left by old ones (associative memory, training, education by experience)' (Ibid.).

Significantly, Pavlov endorsed the 'new objective terminology to describe animal reactions' introduced by Beer, Bethe, and Üxküll, on the grounds that not only is there no justification for ascribing psychic processes to animals: there is simply no need. Hence the term 'purpose' is conspicuously missing from his writings. Indeed, early behaviourist thought was largely governed by this unwritten injunction to ignore and wherever possible redescribe the role of goals and intentions in human and animal behaviour. For the new psychology was to be an engineering science, unconcerned with any of the spurious issues bequeathed by the mind/body problem.

Nevertheless, their commitment to the continuum picture entailed that they could not avoid philosophical involvement, however acerbic their comments on the sterility of a priori reasoning. For the only way a mechanist continuum of purposive behaviour could be instituted was via an implicit analysis of the family of psychological concepts involved, such that the difference between *voluntary* and *involuntary* behaviour could be treated as one of causal complexity rather than kind. Thus, we find the leading behaviourists forced to deal with these philosophical problems which, so they repeatedly claimed, did not concern them in the least.

Watson exemplifies the pattern. In 'Psychology as the Behaviorist Sees It' [10.82] he makes it clear that his sole interest is in the issue of control. This is still the primary focus in *Behavior* [10.83], but subsidiary concerns about the nature of thinking are beginning to creep in. By the time we get to *Behaviorism* [10.85] the book has become a full-scale defence of a 'behaviourist' philosophy of mind (the exact same progression can be traced in both Hull and Skinner's writings).

It may seem that all this was overturned by the transition to cybernetics, but as Volker Henn points out, the history of cybernetics really begins with Maxwell and Bernard [10.64], 174ff; cf. [10.18] 81f). The publication of 'Behavior, Purpose, and Teleology' [10.77] marks the consummation rather than reorientation of a prolonged conceptual evolution: viz., of the notion of machine *qua* homeostatic system that employs negative feedback to regulate its operations. (This is already clearly implicit in the passage from *Conditioned Reflexes* [10.75], quoted above.)

According to cybernetics, purposive behaviour is that which is 'controlled by negative feedback' in the 'attainment of a goal' (see [10.77]). We must be careful here, first, that we do not suppose that this thesis instituted a sharp break from behaviourism,[20] and second, that we do not impute the naive materialist outlook which guided the founders of behaviourism to all of their followers.[21] Nor should we suppose that the central theme of 'Behavior, Purpose, and Teleology' – viz., the relationship of teleological to causal explanation – had never before been broached. In fact, this problem had been a focus of mechanist concern for over three decades. What was primarily unique about 'Behaviour, Purpose, and Teleology' was rather the manner in which the authors sought to render teleological explanation scientifically respectable by rendering the feedback mechanisms in 'purposive' systems subject to the laws of causality. But far from just rewriting the logical form of teleological explanation (in order to bring out what they saw as its fundamental contrast with the antecedent–consequent form of causal laws), there are several points which stand out in the cybernetic analysis of 'purpose' or 'goal'.

To begin with, there are the central claims that 'purposive' behaviour be defined in terms of the goal-directed movements of a system interacting with its environment, where the goal itself is said to be a part of the environment with which the system interacts. The system is thus controlled by internal and external factors, and the existence of a goal is a necessary condition for the attribution of purposive behaviour. But 'goals' on the cybernetic model are simply the 'final condition' towards which a system is directed.

This represents a radical change in the meaning of 'purposive' or 'goal-directed behaviour'. In purposive behaviour, the relevant goal can be far removed, or even non-existent, without undermining the purposiveness of that behaviour. Indeed, it even makes sense to speak

PHILOSOPHY OF SCIENCE, LOGIC AND MATHEMATICS

of purposive behaviour occurring 'for its own sake' (as, e.g., in the case of singing (see [10.79], [10.80])). Moreover, the internal relations which bind the concept of purpose to those of consciousness, cognition, belief and volition, are rendered external. Hence the upshot of Rosenblueth, Wiener and Bigelow's argument is that there is no logical obstacle to describing cybernetic systems as 'purposive', even though they can exercise no choice, cannot be said to be trying to attain their goal, or even aware that such is their goal (as, e.g., in the case of guided missiles).

There is, of course, nothing to stop the mechanist from introducing a technical (cybernetic) notion of 'purpose' or 'goal', by which will be understood the state of equilibrium that the feedback mechanisms of a homeostatic system are designed or have evolved to maintain. But, as with the case of eliminative materialist theories, if the logico-grammatical distinction between 'purposive' and 'caused behaviour' is undermined, the result is not a new understanding of but rather, the abandonment of 'voluntary behaviour' and the creation of yet another misleading homonym.

Perhaps the most important aspect of cybernetics to bear in mind when assessing its significance for psychology is its continuity with behaviourism. Rosenblueth and Wiener insisted that:

> if the term purpose is to have any significance in science, it must be recognizable from the nature of the act, not from the study of or from any speculation on the structure and nature of the acting object ... [Hence] if the notion of purpose is applicable to living organisms, it is also applicable to non-living entities when they show the same observable traits of behavior.
>
> ([10.76], 235)

As a corollary to this, they articulated the standard behaviourist thesis that multiple observations are needed to verify the existence of purposive behaviour (Ibid., 236). The judgement that an agent is φing is said to be an *inductive hypothesis* which, as such, must be supported by evidence. Most importantly, the theory remained committed to the continuum picture of purposive behaviour, now said to be governed by the 'orders of prediction' displayed by a system.

In typical Cartesian fashion, Rosenblueth, Wiener and Bigelow argued that:

> It is possible that one of the features of the discontinuity of behavior observable when comparing humans with other high mammals may lie in that the other mammals are limited to

predictive behavior of low order, whereas man may be capable
potentially of quite high orders of prediction.

([10.77], 223)

Reflex acts and tropisms can indeed be seen to be purposive (albeit of
a lower order), complex actions are treated as nested hierarchies
of bodily movements, and consciousness cannot be a necessary condition for purposive behaviour. For the theory does not distinguish
between mechanical and biological systems; hence consciousness must
be *emergent* and *epiphenomenal* (Ibid., 235; see [10.78]).

There are a number of important objections that have been raised
against the cybernetic analysis of 'purposive behaviour' by AI scientists
as well as philosophers (see [10.55]). From the standpoint of the former,
the root of these problems lies, not in its mechanist orientation but
rather, in the absence of 'a mechanistic analogy of specifically psychological processes, a cybernetic parallel of the mind/body distinction'
([10.57], 107). This lacuna is to be filled by the cognitivist distinction
between embodied schemata and their neurophysiological components.
These 'internal representations' are models of reality which 'mediate
between stimulus and response in determining the behavior of the
organism as a whole' ([10.56], 58). An organism uses these 'encoded
descriptions' of its environment to guide its actions, and it is this which
accounts for the purposiveness of its behaviour: not the misguided
cybernetic supposition that there must be a goal which is a part of the
environment with which a system interacts.

Assuming a fundamental analogy between computer programs
and these 'internal representations', the crux of the post-computational
version of the mechanist thesis lies in the premiss that, 'Insofar as a
machine's performance is guided by its internal, perhaps idiosyncratic
model of the environment, the overall performance is describable in
intensional terms' ([10.57], 128).[22] The AI scientist endeavours to provide a mechanist account of purposive behaviour by postulating a
species of 'action plans', neurally embodied, that are 'closely analogous
to the sets of instructions comprising procedural routines within a
computer program'. That is, internal representations both of 'the goal
or putative end-state of an intention' and a possible plan of action for
bringing about that state ([10.], 134; cf. [10.]).

Although this argument is committed to the (remote) possibility
of discovering the neurophysiological mechanisms of these internal
models, and thus of the discovery of causally sufficient conditions for
purposive behaviour, all of the emphasis is on the manner in which
these models guide an agent's behaviour (see [10.57]). While post-
computational mechanists are committed, therefore, to the logical possibility of reducibility, they need not regard this as anything more than

a distant prospect. Hence, the much-celebrated shift from bottom-up to top-down approaches, i.e., to the computer simulation of the internal representations that guide purposive behaviour. For 'We can only postulate such models on behavioral grounds, and hypothesize that they correspond to actual neurophysiological mechanisms' ([10.56], 60).

On this picture, the 'explanatory power of a machine model of behavior depends on the extent to which the details of the underlying information-processing are functionally equivalent to the psychological processes actually underlying behavior' ([10.57], 144). Once the mechanics of human and animal purposive behaviour have been discovered, it will be seen that philosophical objections to the mechanist analysis of the 'continuum of purposive behaviour' are vacuous. Not because intentional and volitional concepts are eliminable, but because there is room for both purposive and causal categories in the explanation of human behaviour. The problem is, however, that this very premiss is denied by reductionism.

For all the technical sophistication of AI, it is interesting to see how little it has moved beyond the terms of Descartes' original argument. Indeed, so much so that the mentalist overtones of cognitivist theories have already sparked off strong eliminativist counter-movements in connectionism and neuropsychology. But the very fact that, for three centuries now, psychology has been dominated by these ceaseless 'paradigm–revolutions', with neither side able to refute Descartes' attack on the continuum picture, suggests that it is the framework established by Descartes' argument which needs to be addressed, not its results. That is, that the resolution of the problem created by mind/body dualism lies in the province of conceptual clarification *as opposed* to empirical theories: philosophy as opposed to psychology. And philosophy's chief concern here is with the persisting influence of the continuum picture: with the crucial premiss that all actions, animal and human, are complex sequences of movements brought about by hidden causes, the nature of which the science of psychology must discover.

❧ V THEORY OF MIND ❧

The latest effort to deal with the problems raised by Cartesianism involves a subtle attempt to retain the Cartesian picture of cognition while avoiding the eliminativism and reductionism which, as we saw in the preceding sections, has so dominated the evolution of psychology. Consider the case of a child suddenly becoming aware of its mother's feelings and interacting with her accordingly, or a child beginning to use gestures or symbols to signal its intention. Cognitivism has a ready explanation for this type of phenomenon: the child's mind was busy all the while observing and recording regularities. What *looks* like a sudden moment of insight or development is really the end-result of preconscious inferences the child has drawn in which he has mapped causes onto effects. (E.g., 'Whenever S has this look on its face *x* invariably follows', or, 'If I do *x* then *y* will happen', or, 'If S believes *x* then S will φ'.) The argument is not committed to the premiss that beliefs, desires or intentions cause actions; only to the thesis that the child treats beliefs, desires or intentions as the causes of actions, which as such purportedly amounts to the claim that the child has formulated a theory of mind.

We are not supposed to worry overly about the use of *theory* here. Nothing terribly scientistic is intended (although one might feel otherwise when one reads the five points comprising the theory of mind which the child is supposed to have acquired: viz., (1) the mind is private; (2) mind is distinct from body; (3) the mind represents reality; (4) minds are possessed by others; and (5) thoughts are different from things (see [10.89]; [10.86] Wellman 1990)). But really, the use of the term is only meant to draw attention to the fact that in order for a child to be able to predict another agent's actions on the basis of his beliefs, the child must already possess such concepts as *self* and *person* or *desire* and *intention*. And, of course, the child must possess the concept of causation. So why, then, is the theory of mind thesis so drawn to the use of 'theory' to describe its thesis?

The answer is that the argument treats the ability to predict an agent's actions on the basis of his beliefs as a sub-category of the ability to predict events in general. That is, to predict S's actions on the basis of S's intentions, desires or beliefs is just a special case of predicting that *x* will cause *y*. The actual *theory* which the child must construct is simply the framework filling out the conditions of this 'special case'. The emphasis here is on treating human behaviour as a different kind of phenomenon from physical. Intentions, desires and beliefs are postulated because they prove to be such useful constructs for predicting human – and only human – behaviour (where this, too, is something the child must learn; i.e., at first he blurs the lines between human actions and physical events, or between human and animal behaviour, but he soon learns the ineffectiveness of using mental constructs to predict the latter types of phenomena). But prediction is prediction, whether it be in regards to human actions or physical events, i.e., regularities must be observed, causal connections perceived.[23]

This is precisely what the argument is driving at when it talks of how 'a theory provides a causal–explanatory framework to account for, make understandable, and make predictable phenomena in its domain' (Ibid., 7). We can see how this is supposed to work by looking more closely at the actual type of theory which the child is supposed to create.[24] The process of constructing such a theory is said to take place on two planes: the child is making discoveries about itself at the same time that it is observing regularities in the actions of other human beings. So first, the child has to discover that it is a *self*, and then, that another is an *other*. To do this the child has to discover that intentional actions are not reflexes, i.e., that there are two basic kinds of movements in the realm of human behaviour. We get a residue of the orthodox Cartesian account of 'privileged access' in the emphasis on a child's learning that it can manipulate objects – or its caretakers – and extrapolating from this the concepts of *self* and *object*; or learning what its own beliefs, desires or intentions are, and then, what beliefs, desires or intentions are. While all this is going on, the child is busy observing the difference between the way its caretakers and other humans move about and the way inanimate objects are moved. In this sense, the discovery of the distinction between voluntary and involuntary behaviour is seen as a complex synthesis of self, social and object perception.

We should, perhaps, be more careful about using the term 'discover'; for according to the theory of mind, it is not so much that the child observes that voluntary movements are different from involuntary as that the child discovers that it is more useful, when interacting with humans, to make this distinction. That is, it is not so much that the child discovers what intentional behaviour *is* as that it discovers the value of postulating beliefs, desires or intentions for predicting human behaviour. In so doing, the child is said to realize that other agents have minds. For since beliefs, desires and intentions are not visible, the child treats them as hidden causes of behaviour. That is, the child establishes for itself that beliefs, desires and intentions are mental entities. It establishes that the difference between two seemingly identical actions done with different beliefs, desires or intentions must reside in the concealed mental causes.

As we saw in the preceding sections, mechanism soon discovered that the distinction between voluntary and involuntary movement must be more complex than this brief sketch suggests. The child must also discover the importance of postulating purposes, and goals, and decisions, and choice, and effort. The child must discover that voluntary actions, unlike reflexes or accidents, are somehow willed and not externally caused. The child must determine that, like ordinary causes, an agent can have a belief, a desire or an intention in advance of acting on it, but unlike ordinary causes, an agent can form a belief, a desire or an intention without necessarily acting on it; i.e., the child must discover that beliefs, desires and intentions can be treated as causing but not as forcing actions. And unlike the case of ordinary causes, the child must learn that only he can know what his beliefs, desires or intentions are.

The entrance of language – or rather, the entry into language – is thought to add still more complexity into the child's construction of a theory of mind. To begin with, the child must learn how to map his beliefs, desires and intentions onto words. He must learn the effect of using avowals of belief, desire or intention on others. As the child gets more cognitively sophisticated, he learns how to use expressions of belief, desire or intention to conceal his real feelings or intentions. Verbal habits or routines can then begin to take over, so that language becomes, not just a vehicle for deception, but an actual barrier to genuine communication. The child also learns how to read things into other agents' avowals. It must learn that beliefs, desires and intentions can be the grounds for judging the morality of an action: an element which forces the child to sharpen his 'fundamental, ontological distinction... between internal mental phenomena on the one hand and external physical and behavioral phenomena on the other' ([10.89], 13).

The more one reads about this 'fundamental ontological distinction', the more apparent it becomes that the theory of mind thesis rests on a subtle tension. The very premiss that the ability to recognize another agent's beliefs, desires or intentions – to grasp that other agents have beliefs, desires and intentions – amounts to the construction of a *causal–explanatory framework*, turns on the presupposition that the ability to predict an agent's actions on the basis of his beliefs, desires or intentions is a sub-category of prediction in general. But in effect, all of the above contrasts represent an attempt to divorce intention from prediction. That is, the 'theory' which the child must construct is one which carefully marks the various distinctions between predicting an agent's behaviour on the basis of his beliefs, desires or intentions, and predicting causal events.

Thus, the child must learn that when an agent says 'I'm going to φ' he is not making a prediction which is akin to 'It's going to rain'. If an agent says 'I'm going to φ' in all sincerity, and then fails to do so because something prevented him, that doesn't mean his intention was *wrong* (as is the case if he predicts it is going to rain and we get sunny skies instead). More fundamentally, a child does not learn what his beliefs, desires or intentions are inductively. He neither infers from his own behaviour that he had the intention to φ, nor does he observe that whenever he forms the intention to φ he invariably φs (in the way that he observes how the same effects result from the same cause). He does not discover that, should he want to φ, all he has to do is form the intention and the state of his φing will subsequently occur. The child learns that when he says 'I'm going to φ' he is committing himself to a course of action, i.e., that the act of uttering these words arouses certain expectations in his listener as to how he will behave. He learns that, should an agent fail to φ after announcing his intention to do so, this may indicate the presence of countervailing factors, or it might signify that the agent changed his mind, but whatever the reason, it licenses the demand for some explanation as to why the agent failed to φ (without entailing that there must be an answer). That is not to say that one cannot be wrong about one's beliefs, desires or intentions. But the child learns that to be wrong about about one's beliefs, desires or intentions is a very particular language game. It is not at all like being wrong about the weather. It suggests hidden motives, or that one is driven by forces or factors of which one is unconscious, or that one suddenly has a new insight into one's own behaviour or needs.

The theory of mind trades on the fact that there is often (but not necessarily) a temporal relation between intending to φ and φing. If an agent decides at t to φ at t_1 and then does so there is clearly a temporal relation between his initial decision and subsequent behaviour. But that neither entails that there is a causal relation between two events – a mental and a physical – nor that we construe an agent's behaviour in these terms. For we must be careful to distinguish between the temporal relation between the time (if there is one) at which an agent formed the intention and the time at which he acted, and the rule of grammar which stipulates that this action represents the satisfaction of this intention. It is the rule of grammar 'The intention to φ is satisfied by the act of φing' which governs our accounts of what counts as acting in accord with the intention. But on the causal picture embraced by the theory of mind, we would be forced to accept that whatever S does at t_1 must be deemed the consequence of his intention to φ. If S ψs then his intention to φ was satisfied by his act of ψing. Hence the child is conceived as learning, not only that it is highly likely that an agent will φ if he intends to φ, but that it is highly likely that φing represents the satisfaction of the intention to φ! (see [10.55]).

Suppose we view a child's burgeoning social awareness, however, not as a species of causal perception, but something entirely – categorially – different, i.e., a skill which demands a totally different grammar – for example, the grammar of agency and intentionality as opposed to causality – for its proper description. All of the above statements outlining the 'contrasts' between predicting an agent's actions on the basis of his beliefs, desires, or intentions and predicting the effects of a given cause can be seen as the rules which formulate this grammar. For example, the above statement 'The child learns that only he can know what his intentions are' exemplifies what Wittgenstein calls a *grammatical proposition*: ' "Only you can know if you had that intention." One might tell someone this when one was explaining the meaning of the word "intention" to him. For then it means: *that* is how we use it. (And here "know" means that the expression of uncertainty is senseless.)' ([10.91], section 247) Treat this as an *empirical proposition*, however, and you find yourself mired in sceptical problems: not just with regard to third-person knowledge (viz., you can never be certain that you know what another person intends), but even with respect to first-person knowledge (unless one decides to hold fast – despite all the evidence gathered in [10.87] – to the doctrine of privileged access to one's own mental states).

Remove the Cartesian starting point that predicting an agent's actions is a sub-category of prediction in general, and it is no longer tempting to suppose that a child who knows what another agent believes, wants or intends has inferred the existence of an antecedent mental cause guiding that agent's behaviour. That does not vitiate the importance of the larger point that the theory of mind is making, which is that to say that a child grasps another agent's beliefs, desires or intentions is to say that he grasps or even shares what they see or feel, and can thus anticipate what they will do if given the opportunity. But this, too, is a *grammatical*, not an empirical proposition; one might tell someone this when explaining the meaning of the expression 'to grasp another agent's beliefs, desires or intentions'. Likewise, the theory of mind's basic claim that to possess the concept of false belief a child must possess the concepts of self, person, desire and intention is a grammatical, not an empirical proposition or hypothesis. Whether it is the *right* grammatical proposition is another matter: something which can only be resolved by a philosophical, not a psychological investigation.

It is important to note that, to know what another agent believes, wants or intends does not entail that one must know what beliefs, desires, or intentions are; for the criteria for saying 'S knows what R believes' are very different from the criteria for saying that 'S knows what a "belief" is'. As the quotation marks indicate, the latter demands the ability to speak a language. When a child learns how to *describe* the beliefs, desires or intentions which guide an agent's actions, what he learns are the grounds for attributing such a belief, desire or intention when explaining the nature of someone's actions. He learns how appropriate behaviour *justifies* but does not entail the attribution of beliefs, desires or intentions. Thus, the child learns when it is correct to cite those beliefs, desires, or intentions as one's reasons for φing (e.g. when justifying one's actions or explaining someone else's). And he learns that the fact that one can appear to be acting intentionally without having any definite intention in mind, or conversely, conceal one's beliefs, desires, or intentions, merely attests to the fact that such criterial evidence is defeasible: not that in assigning beliefs, desires or intentions one is framing hypotheses or forming inductive generalizations about the probable causes of S's ϕing.

As far as the voluntary/involuntary distinction is concerned, we might say that what the child learns is how, by describing an agent's beliefs, desires or intentions, the possibility that his behaviour was caused or accidental is excluded. The attribution of beliefs, desires and intentions 'explains action', not in the causal sense that it identifies the factors that *brought about* someone's behaviour, but in the *constitutive* sense that it establishes the *meaning* or the *significance* of an action. If beliefs, desires or intentions were hidden causes, then a statement like 'The intention to ϕ is satisfied by the act of ϕing' would be '*hypothetical* in the sense that further experience can confirm or disprove the causal nexus' ([10.90], 120). And if that were the case, then it would indeed make sense to speak, without qualification, of having beliefs, desires or intentions without knowing what they were in the same way that one can be ignorant of the causes of *x*, or of inferring, learning, suspecting or being wrong about what one believes, wants, or intends. But ' "I know what I want, wish, believe, feel, . . ." (and so on through all the psychological verbs) is either philosophers' nonsense, or any rate *not* a judgement *a priori*' ([10.91], 221). That is, apart from such cases as when an agent is undecided (and in that sense uncertain) as to which course of action to pursue, or when prodding someone to question or confront their real desires or beliefs, it is inappropriate to ask someone whether he is certain that he knows what he believes, wants, or intends. For in ordinary circumstances, how else could one respond to such a question other than: my intention to ϕ is the intention that *I* should really ϕ? If a further explanation of this assurance is wanted I would go on to say 'and by "I" I mean myself, and by "ϕ" I mean doing this . . .': 'But these are just grammatical explanations, explanations which *create* language. It is *in language* that it's all done' ([10.], 143).

Wittgenstein's point here is that, in ordinary circumstances, the only response one can make to persistent doubt is to explain or reiterate the rules of grammar which govern the use of *belief, desire* or *intention*. He is not suggesting that an understanding of other agents' beliefs, desires or intentions can only be attributed to creatures that possess the ability to speak a language. Nor is he seeking to inculcate scepticism; quite the contrary, he is seeking to undermine epistemological scepticism by demonstrating that the issue that concerns us here is not *whether we can ever be certain that S can ϕ* (where 'ϕ' might be *think*, or *feel*, or *intend*, or *understand*, or *mean*, etc.), but *how we describe what S is doing* or *what S understands*. In paradigmatic contexts this distinction is (typically) of no concern; it is in the borderline cases, and especially, in primitive contexts, where it becomes easy to confuse the question of whether S's behaviour satisfies the criteria for describing him as φing with the sceptical question of whether we can ever be certain that S is really φing or merely appears to be doing so. This is the reason why Cartesianism has become such a dominant force in comparative primatology and developmental psychology, and why both behaviourism and cognitivism – i.e., the denial of higher mental processes or the assignment of these higher mental processes to the preconscious – have flourished in these domains. But far from lamenting the indecisiveness which seems to characterize these discussions, we might see this uncertainty as a crucial aspect of psychological concepts.

This last point demands clarification. One of the more glaring problems with the theory of mind is that the terms of the discussion seem so remote from the reality of an infant's behaviour. For example, we are asked to accept, not just that a baby observes regularities, but even, that a baby *makes observations*. The baby does not just suck whatever comes into its purview; it *discovers by trial and error* which things in its world are suckable; it *frames hypotheses* as to the *class of suckable objects* and then *performs experiments* to test its hypotheses. The child who is sharing or initiating joint attention is actually *constructing laws* of human behaviour. And indeed, the human infant, virtually from birth, is *predicting* events; what changes as it develops is not this innate scientistic drive, but the power of the constructs whereby it makes its predictions.

It is little wonder that this picture of prediction (of going beyond the information given) summons up a thesis like the theory of mind. For it seems to make little sense to speak of an agent as predicting something unless he possesses the requisite concepts involved. Thus, the theory of mind insists that, if we are dealing with predicting physical events, then at the very least the subject must possess the concepts of causation, object and object permanence; if we are talking about predicting social events, then the subject must possess the concepts of self, agent, intention and desire. But we lose sight here of what a rarefied concept the concept of concept is. A 2-year-old can do some very extraordinary things which, as Tomasello shows, bear fundamentally on what the theory of mind thesis is trying to explain (see [10.88]). For example, a 2-year-old can share and can even direct attention. But does a 2-year-old jointly attending to something possess the concept of *joint attention*? Does he even know or understand that other agents have thoughts or desires which may differ from his own? Does he possess the concepts of *self* and *person* and *intention*? And most important of all, are these sceptical questions?

Once again we are in danger of straying too far from what we are observing: of reading too much into a child's primitive interactive behaviour. To be sure, there are significant events in the child's development, cognitive feats which stand out as 'developmental milestones'.

But does a child's becoming aware of its mother's feelings and interacting with her accordingly satisfy the criteria for saying that it possesses the concept of person? Does 'passing' the Wimmer–Perner test satisfy the criteria for saying that it possesses the concept of false belief? How else, the Cartesian wants to say, could the child perform these acts unless he possessed these concepts, or at the very least, was capable of representing human behaviour in different terms from physical. Granted, it is always possible – irrevocably possible – that we are misrepresenting the child's representation. But the one thing that is certain, according to Cartesianism, is that the child's behaviour must be concept-driven.

It would take us too far outside the scope of this chapter to chart the origins and conceptual problems involved in the view of concepts as the 'repositories of featural analysis' on which this argument rests. What principally matters to us here is that this view of concepts goes hand-in-hand with the view that social awareness is grounded in a theory of mind. Indeed, in recent years concept-formation has itself come to be seen as a species of theory construction. But these problems disappear when we regard an agent's behaviour, not as *evidence* of the concept which he has formed, but as constituting a *criterion* for saying that he possesses the concept ϕ. That is, when we view the statement 'Doing x, y, z constitutes the criterion for saying that "S possesses the concept ϕ" ', or more generally, 'Saying that S possesses the concept ϕ = Saying that S can do x, y, z' is a rule of grammar, not an empirical proposition. For this means that the statement 'S possesses the concept ϕ' does not describe or refer to a mental entity but rather, is used to attribute certain abilities to S.

For example, to say that S possesses the concept *number* is to say that S can do sums, can apply arithmetical operations, can explain what a number is, can correct his own or someone else's mistakes, etc. Doing all these things does not count as evidence that S possesses the (or a) concept of number; rather, it satisfies the criteria for saying 'S possesses the concept *number*'. Similarly, if a child hides the treat which his mother has given him in the hopes of getting another from his father, this is not evidence that he has acquired the concept of *pretence* – which, according to the theory of mind, entails a theoretical understanding of desire and intention, and possibly, of belief – but rather, a criterion for saying that the child is capable of pretence. Where the theory of mind has been so valuable is in drawing attention to the importance of the conceptual relations enshrined in the above statement. For this is not an empirical proposition: a description of the end-result of the step-by-step process whereby a child has built up a complex construct like 'pretence' (in the same way, for example., that one could describe the mechanics of a pattern recognition system). It is rather a grammatical proposition, stipulating that it makes no sense to speak of a child as *pretending to* φ unless it also makes sense to describe the child as *intending to* φ, *wanting* x, etc. Thus, theorists of mind have been actively engaged in a twofold enterprise: that of mapping the conceptual relations entailed by the application of some psychological concept, and then studying a child's behaviour to ascertain whether it satisfies the necessary criteria or perhaps can be said to satisfy a still more primitive version of the concept in question.

To insist that a subject's behaviour fails to satisfy the criteria for applying some concept, for example, that directing its mother's attention to an object does not satisfy the criteria for saying of a 2-year-old child that it possesses the concept of *person*, does not entail that this behaviour can only be described in causal terms, i.e., that the child did not, after all, *direct its mother's attention*. Wittgenstein makes a point about the origins of causal knowledge which is highly pertinent here. There is, Wittgenstein observes, 'a reaction which can be called "reacting to the cause"' ([10.94]). Consider the case of a small child following a string to see who is pulling at it. If he finds him, how does he know that he, his pulling, is the cause of the string's moving? Does he establish this by a series of experiments? The answer is No: this is rather a primitive case of what is called 'seeing that x was the cause of y'. Only a strong Cartesian bias could induce one to construe this phenomenon as a manifestation of a form of induction. But in order to make sense of the notion of the child exhibiting in such behaviour his mind's 'pre-linguistic causal inferences', it would also have to make sense to speak of the child's exhibiting pre-linguistic manifestations of doubt: of making mistakes in his causal reasoning and taking steps to guard against error, of testing, comparing, and correcting previous judgements. But none of his behaviour satisfies the criteria for attributing these abilities: all he did was react to the cause.

The language game played with 'cause' exemplifies Wittgenstein's point in *Last Writings* about how:

> A sharper concept would not be the same concept. That is: the sharper concept wouldn't have the *value* for us that the blurred one does. Precisely because we would not understand people who act with total certainty when we are in doubt and uncertain.
>
> ([10.93], Section 267)

For example, the very notion of *reacting to a cause* is blurred; the child *saw* that x caused y, whereas the caterpillars in Loeb's experiments merely *reacted* to the light. Just as the cases where it is appropriate to speak of a *conditioned response* merge into circumstances where it is appropriate to speak of *seeing that x caused y*, so, too, the cases where

it is appropriate to speak of *seeing that x caused y* merge into circumstances where it is appropriate to speak of *knowing that x will cause
y*. We can indeed speak of a continuum here, therefore, but it is *grammatical*, not cognitive: a language game ranging from *reacting to a cause*
to *counterfactual reasoning*. This grammatical continuum demands ever
more complex behaviour to license the attribution of ever more complex
abilities and skills. At the lowest end of this spectrum is that behaviour
which satisfies the criteria for what is called 'reacting to a cause'. At
this primitive level, S's behaviour satisfies the criteria for describing
him as being aware of the cause of *y*, but his behaviour comes nowhere
close to satisfying the criteria for saying that he possesses the concept
of *cause*. As the child acquires linguistic abilities, we teach him how to
use 'cause' and 'effect'. It is his growing understanding of causal
relations, as reflected in his growing mastery of the family of causal
terms that satisfies the criteria for describing him as possessing the
concept of *cause*, i.e., as possessing the ability to infer and predict
events, to doubt whether *y* was caused by *x* and to verify that *x* causes
y. We continue to move up the grammatical continuum as the subject
learns the importance of observation and experiment, culminating in
the advanced abilities to engage in counterfactual reasoning or *Gedank-
enexperimente*, to construct theories and models, and theories of theory
and model making.

The important point here is that, rather than following Descartes'
lead and beginning with the paradigm of the scientist – of the scientist's
mind – and reading this into all the lower forms of behaviour as we
work our way backwards through a descending level of cognitive abilities, so that the mere reaction to a cause is construed as manifesting a
'pre-conscious causal inference', we proceed by clarifying the relation
between primitive expressive behaviour and primitive uses of psychological concepts, and show how the roots of *causal inference* lie, not in
'mental processing' but rather, in these primitive uses:

> The origin and the primitive form of the language game is a
> reaction; only from this can more complicated forms develop.
> Language – I want to say – is a refinement, 'im Anfang war die
> Tat' ... it is characteristic of our language that the foundation
> on which it grows consists in steady ways of living, regular ways
> of acting ... We have an idea of which ways of living are
> primitive, and which could only have developed out of these
> ... The simple form (and that is the prototype) of the cause-
> effect game is determining the cause, not doubting.

([10.94])

Similarly, the roots of *social understanding* lie in primitive reactions
and interactions, e.g. in the fact that at 9 months old a child can be

conditioned to follow a caregiver's gaze and to share a caregiver's emotions; at 12 months the child begins to follow the caregiver's gaze spontaneously, and shortly after this, to initiate and direct joint attention; while at much the same time it begins to use imperative pointing, and soon after this, declarative pointing. But the fact that the infant is able to look where another agent wants, to attend to directed objects and situations or direct another where to look, or to use certain gestures and then conventionalized sounds to initiate exchanges, does not in itself constitute theoretical or pre-theoretical knowledge. The infant is learning how to participate in very particular kinds of social practices (giving and requesting objects, playing peek-a-boo, asking and answering simple questions). As the child's mastery of these practices advances, it makes increasing sense to describe the child as 'intending or trying to ϕ', as 'looking or hoping for x', as 'thinking or believing p', and so on.

In other words, what people say and do is what constitutes the justifying grounds for psychological ascriptions. Scepticism about other minds stems from misconstruing this logical relation as inductive evidence. It turns on Descartes' idea that what we see are 'colourless movements' from which we infer a hidden cause. But we do not see *mere behaviour*, we see, for example, pain behaviour, i.e., that behaviour which satisfies the criteria governing the application of 'pain'. The sense in which pain behaviour 'falls short of certainty' is solely that it does not *entail* that someone is in pain. But this has nothing to do with perceptual limitations.

Descartes capitalized on the fact that psychological concepts cannot be applied to lower lifeforms. Unfortunately, he misconstrued the nature of this 'cannot'. For these limits are imposed by logical grammar, not experience. Descartes was quite right to draw attention to the importance of the fact that animals do not utter avowals: but for reasons that have nothing to do with his animal automaton hypothesis. The application of psychological concepts is intimately bound up with the ability to speak a language: to describe one's state of mind, express one's desires and intentions, report on one's feelings (or conceal them). But that does not mean that animals are incapable of manifesting primitive expressive behaviour; for a dog's howling, like a baby's, may indeed be a criterion for saying that it is in pain.

The result of misconstruing the grammatical propositions or rules governing the use of psychological concept words as empirical propositions has been three centuries of conflict over whether intentions, desires, beliefs, etc. in some way cause the actions they are thought to accompany or precede, and whether these mental phenomena correspond to or are caused by neural events. The persisting assumption has been that we start off with these mental events and then try to discover the cerebral mechanisms with which they are correlated or by which they are caused. But the lesson to be learnt from studying the mechanist/vitalist debates is that the real evolution of this psycho-physical parallel thesis was the exact opposite: it was by proceeding from the premiss that all involuntary movements are caused by external and internal stimuli, and the persisting desire to restore the continuum picture by reducing voluntary actions to the same terms, that the notion of 'mental cause' was created: the conception of intentions, desires, beliefs as mental events that bring about actions precisely because they initiate or are isomorphic with the cerebral drive train that provides the motor power. The goal of this chapter has been, not just to chart the development of these ideas, but more importantly, to reverse this way of thinking: to establish the unique and non-causal character of mental concepts in order to clarify why it is so misleading to assume that 'psychology treats of processes in the psychical sphere, as does physics in the physical' ([10.91], section 571). Thus, my intention here has been, not to praise Descartes' legacy, but to bury it: to relegate the mechanist/vitalist debates once and for all to the *history* of psychological ideas.

❧ NOTES ❧

1 It is highly significant that Russell should have written an introduction to Lange's *History of Materialism*, in which he states that: 'Ordinary scientific probability suggests ... that the sphere of mechanistic explanation in regard to vital phenomena is likely to be indefinitely extended by the progress of biological knowledge' ([10.38], xvii–xviii).

2 Du Bois-Reymond followed up on his argument with an expanded account in 1880 of the 'seven world problems'. In addition to the matter force and brain thought problems he now included the origins of motion, life, sensation and language, the teleological design of nature and the problem of free will (see [10.23]).

3 Spencer's explanation of the 'continuous adjustment of internal relations to external relations' also reflects the influence of Liebig's views ([10.40]).

4 In *Animal Chemistry* he warned that:

> The higher phenomena of mental existence cannot, in the present state of science, be referred to their proximate, and still less to their ultimate, causes. We only know of them, that they exist; we ascribe them to an immaterial agency, and that, in so far as its manifestations are connected with matter, an agency, entirely distinct from the vital force *with which it has nothing in common.*

> ([10.25], 138)

5 As indeed do cognitivists, albeit for vastly different reasons. In their eyes Bernard's metaphor manifests the latent tendency to regard biological phenomena 'in terms of categories whose primary application is in the domain of

knowledge' [10.19]. It thus illustrates the inadequacy of physico-chemical concepts to explain such biological phenomena as embryological development; for
as Bernard himself was to explain:

> In saying that life is the directive idea or the evolutive force of the living
> being, we express simply the idea of a unity in the succession of all
> the morphological and chemical changes accomplished by the germ
> from the beginning to the end of life. Our mind grasps this unity as a
> conception which is imposed upon it and explains it as a force; but the
> error consists in thinking that this metaphysical force is active in the
> manner of a physical force.
>
> [([10.37], 214)

But where the cognitivist sees the organism itself as the intended bearer of
Bernard's *directive idée*, Bergson had earlier insisted that it is a 'principle
of interpretation': in modern usage, a paradigm whereby a scientific community
construes its data (Ibid., 148–9). As we shall see, this is a recurring theme in
this whole debate. One suspects, however, that for a proper understanding of
how Bernard himself viewed his *directive idée*, one should look at the psychistic
theory of growth whose antecedents date back to Proutt and Bichat (see [10.27],
238–9, 250).

6 Even Turing's attempt to discover the algorithms determining the evolution of
plant life betrays an underlying goal of laying classical vitalist themes to rest.

7 A young player upon the harpsichord or a dancer, is, at first very thoughtful
and solicitous about every motion of his fingers, or every step he makes while
the proficients or masters of these arts perform the very same motions, not
only more dexterously, and with greater agility, but almost without any reflexion
or attention to what they are about' ([10.47], 79).

8 Cf. Herbert Mayo's argument that:

> there are many voluntary actions, which leave no recollection the instant
> afterwards of an act of the will. I allude to those, which from frequent
> repetition have become habits. Philosophers are generally agreed, that
> such actions continue to be voluntary, even when the influence of the
> will is so faint as to wholly escape detection. We are therefore not
> authorized to conclude that instinctive actions are not voluntary
> merely because we are not conscious of willing their performance.
>
> ([10.47], 125)

9 According to Lotze:

> When, under the influence of the soul life an association has once been
> formed between a mere physical impression of a stimulus and a
> movement which is not united with that stimulus by the mere relation
> of structure and function, and when that association has been firmly
> established, this mechanism can continue the activity without requiring
> the actual assistance of intelligence.
>
> ([10.47], 164)

10 After describing in 'The Spinal Cord a Sensational and Volitional Centre' (1858)
how he had replicated Pflüger's experiment, Lewes concluded:

If the animal is such an organized machine that an external impression will produce the same action as would have been produced by sensation and volition, we have absolutely no ground for believing in the sensibility of animals at all, and we may as well at once accept the bold hypothesis of Descartes that they are mere automata. If the frog is so organized, that when he cannot defend himself in one way, the internal mechanisms will set going several other ways – if he can perform, unconsciously, all actions which he performs consciously, it is surely superfluous to assign any consciousness at all. His organism may be called a self-adjusting mechanism, in which consciousness finds no more room than in the mechanism of a watch.

([10.47], 168)

11 Thus Lewes explains:

The Actions cannot belong to the mechanical order so long as they are the actions of a vital mechanism, and so long as we admit the broad distinction between organisms and anorganisms. Whether they have the special character of Consciousness or not, they have the general character of sentient actions, being those of a sentient mechanism. And this becomes the more evident when we consider the gradations of the phenomena. Many, if not all, of those actions which are classed under the involuntary were originally of the voluntary class – either in the individual or his ancestors; but having become permanently organized dispositions – the pathways of stimulation and reaction having been definitely established – they have lost that volitional element (of hesitation and choice) which implies regulation and control.

([10.53], 416–17).

12 Thus William Graham explained how:

consciousness is only, as Professor Tyndall has termed it, an accidental 'bye-product' – something over and above the full and fair physical result, which by an accident, fortunate or otherwise, appeared to watch over and register the whole series of physical processes, though these would have bone on just as well in its absence.

([10.48], 122)

It is noteworthy in light of the interrelatedness of the various issues involved in the mechanist/vitalist debate that he concluded: 'In this case, thought or consciousness would not consume any of the stock of energy; the law of conservation of energy would not be threatened in its generality; and man would be a true automaton, with consciousness added as a spectator, but not as a director of the machinery' (Ibid., 123; cf. [10.51], 240 ff.).

13 The closest one comes to even a hint of awareness of this issue is George Paton's insistence that 'if these movements be not of a perceptive character then there is no meaning in language, and we must give a new definition to the term perception' ([10.47], 154).

14 The failure to grasp this point marred Haller's otherwise penetrating observation in *First Lines of Physiology*:

that the nature of the mind is different from that of the body, appears from numberless observations; more especially from those abstract ideas and affections of the mind which have no correspondence with the organs of sense. For what is the colour of pride? or what the magnitude of envy or curiosity?

([10.49] II, p. 45)

But, of course, it is the human being who feels pride, envy and curiosity, not his mind or brain.

15 The height of this absurdity was reached by T. L. W. Bischoff. Fearing recounts how, in his 'Einige Physiologisch-anatomische Beobachtungen aus einem Enthaupeteten' Bischoff states that:

he was especially concerned with the question of the persistence of consciousness in the head segment [of recently executed criminals]. The experiments were performed during the first minute after decapitation. The results were wholly negative. The fingers of the experimenters were thrust towards the eyes of the decapitated head, the word 'pardon' was called into the ears, tincture of asafoetida was held to the nose, all with negative results. Stimulation of the end of the severed spine did not result in movement.

([10.47], 152)

16 In what reads as the vitalist anticipation of the objection from Watson cited at the beginning of Section 1 above, Lewes maintained:

All inductions warrant the assertion that a bee has thrills propagated throughout its organism by the agency of its nerves; and that some of these thrills are of the kind called sensations – even discriminated sensations. Nevertheless we may reasonably doubt whether the bee has sentient states resembling otherwise than remotely the sensations, emotions, and thoughts which constitute human Consciousness, either in the general or the special sense of that term. The bee feels and reacts on feelings; but its feelings cannot closely resemble our own, because the conditions in the two cases are different. The bee may even be said to think (in so far as Thought means logical combination of feelings), for it appears to form Judgments in the sphere of the Logic of Feeling ... although incapable of the Logic of Signs ... We should therefore say the bee has Consentience, but not Consciousness – unless we accept Consciousness in its *general* signification as the equivalent of Sentience.

([10.53], 409; cf. 434).

17 Interestingly, Erasmus Darwin had argued at the end of the eighteenth century that animals are no less capable than man of reasoning (of concatenating sensory ideas according to the laws of association ([10.62], 15.3). Indeed, the fact that an organism like the fruit fly often mistakes the carrion flower for carrion is proof of its ability to sustain correct reasoning (Ibid., 16.11).

18 'In tracing up the increase we found ourselves passing *without break* from the phenomena of bodily life to the phenomena of mental life' ([10.40], section 13).

19 All of the attention here has been fixed on the notion of purposiveness, but it

bears noting in the sequel how the so-called ambiguity between 'behaviour as movement' and 'behaviour as action' was becoming an established fact. When Rosebleuth, Wiener, and Bigelow introduced cybernetics they could simply assume without qualification that 'By behavior is meant any change of an entity with respect to its surroundings... [A]ny modification of an object, detectable externally, may be denoted as behavior' ([10.77], 18). It should be noted, however, that this long-established usage of 'behaviour' was, in fact, originally regarded as metaphorical.

20 Rosenblueth, Wiener and Bigelow insisted that their goal was 'a uniform behavioristic analysis [which] is applicable to both machines and living organisms, regardless of the complexity of the behavior' ([10.77], 18, 24, 22). Cf. George:

> It must be emphasized very strongly that cybernetics as a scientific discipline is essentially consistent with behaviourism, and is indeed a direct offshoot from it. Behaviourists, in essence, are people who have always treated organisms as if they were machines.
>
> ([10.63], 32)

21 There is a tendency to rule that anyone straying from the orthodox materialist course is automatically excluded from the behaviourist fold; an obvious example is Tolman, but even a figure such as Hull, who expresses cybernetic sentiments in *Principles of Behavior* (see [10.65], 26–7) is often regarded as only a partial (i.e. neo-) behaviourist (and *de facto* 'father' of cybernetics). But what is one to make of a figure such as Lashley (see [10.67])?

22 It should be noted that this argument marks a shift in focus from the subject of machine intelligence to that of cognitive modelling. For the very fact that these internal representations can be mechanically simulated, thereby enabling us to describe cybernetic systems in purposive terms, might also 'provide a key to understanding the way in which the corresponding [human or animal] behavior is actually produced' ([10.57] 142).

23 Since perception can also be treated as a constructive, or an inferential process, this reference to *causal perception* does not need to be qualified.

24 Nativist arguments are ignored in what follows, but really they are just as much a concern of this discussion. For the emphasis here is not on *construction*, it is on *cognition*: on what the child must putatively know in order to display the various abilities recorded by developmentalists.

❧ BIBLIOGRAPHY ❧

Descartes' Dominion

10.1 Cameron, J. M. 'The theory and practice of autobiography', in *Language Meaning and God*, B. Davies (ed.), London, Geoffrey Chapman, 1987.

10.2 Chomsky, N. *Cartesian Linguistics*, New York, Harper and Row, 1966

10.3 Cottingham J., Stoothoff R., and Murdoch D. (trans.) *The Philosophical Writings of Descartes*, 2 vols, Cambridge, Cambridge University Press, 1986.

10.4 Descartes, R. *Discourse on the Method*, 1637, in *The Philosophical Writings of Descartes*, vol. I, J. Cottingham, R. Stoothoff, and D. Murdoch (trans.), Cambridge, Cambridge University Press, 1986.

10.5 —— *Meditations on First Philosophy*, 1641, in *The Philosophical Writings of Descartes*, vol. II, J. Cottingham, R. Stoothoff, and D. Murdoch (trans.), Cambridge, Cambridge University Press, 1986.

10.6 —— *The Passions of the Soul*, 1649, in *The Philosophical Writings of Descartes*, vol. I, J. Cottingham, R. Stoothoff, and D. Murdoch (trans.), Cambridge, Cambridge University Press, 1986.

10.7 —— *Description of the Human Body*, 1664, in *The Philosophical Writings of Descartes*, vol. I, J. Cottingham, R. Stoothoff, and D. Murdoch (trans), Cambridge, Cambridge University Press, 1986.

10.8 Heider, F. *The Psychology of Interpersonal Relations*, Hillsdale, New Jersey, Lawrence Erlbaum Associates, Publishers, 1958.

10.9 Jennings, H. S. *The Behavior of the Lower Organisms*, Bloomington, Indiana, Indiana University Press, 1962.

10.10 La Mettrie, J. O. de *Man a Machine*, 1748, La Salle, Ill., Open Court, 1912.

10.11 Locke, J. *An Essay Concerning Human Understanding*, 1690, J. Yolton (ed.), London, Dent, 1961.

10.12 Pauly, P. J. 'The Loeb–Jennings Debate and the Science of Animal Behavior', *Journal of the History of the Behavioral Sciences* 17 (1981).

10.13 Reed, E. S. 'The Trapped Infinity: Cartesian Volition as Conceptual Nightmare', *Philosophical Psychology*, 3 (1990): 101–21.

10.14 Watson, J. 'Review of H. S. Jennings', *The Behaviour of the Lower Organisms*, Psychological Bulletin 4 (1907): 288–95.

10.15 'Psychology as the Behaviorist Views It', *Psychological Review* 20 (1913): 158–73.

10.16 —— 'The Psychology of Wish Fulfilment', *The Scientific Monthly* (1916).

10.17 Watson, J. *Behaviorism*, London, Kegan Paul: Trench, Trubner and Co., 1925.

The Animal Heat Debate

10.18 Arbib, M. A. 'Cognitive Science: The View from Brain Theory', *The Study of Information*, F. Machlup and U. Mansfield (eds), New York, John Wiley, 1983.

10.19 Boden, M. A. *Minds and Mechanisms*, Ithaca, Cornell University Press, 1981.

10.20 Büchner, L. *Force and Matter*, London, Asher, 1884.

10.21 Coleman, W. *Biology in the Nineteenth Century*, New York, John Wiley, 1971.

10.22 Du Bois-Reymond, E. 'The Limits of our Knowledge of Nature', J. Fitzgerald (trans.), *The Popular Science Monthly* 5 (1874).

10.23 —— 'The Seven World Problems', *Popular Science Monthly* 20 (1882).

10.24 Elkana, Y. 'Helmholtz's "Kraft": An Illustration of concepts in flux', *Historical Studies of the Physical Sciences*, 2 (1970): 263–98.

10.25 Goodfield, G. J. *The Growth of Scientific Physiology*, London, Hutchinson, 1960.

10.26 Gregory, F. *Scientific Materialism in Nineteenth Century Germany*, Boston, Reidel, 1977.

10.27 Hall, T. S. *Ideas of Life and Matter*, 2 vols, Chicago, University of Chicago Press, 1969.

10.28 James, W. *Principles of Psychology*, 1890, 2 vols, New York, Dover, 1950.

10.29 Königsberger, L. *Hermann von Helmholtz*, New York, Dover, 1965.

10.30 Kuhn, T. 'Energy Conservation as An Example of Simultaneous Discovery', in *Critical Problems in the History of Science*, M. Clagett (ed.), Madison, University of Wisconsin Press, 1959.

10.31 Lange, F. *History of Materialism*, 1865, New York, Humanities Press, 1950.

10.32 Lipman, T.O. 'The Response to Liebig's Vitalism', *Bulletin of the History of Medicine* 40 (1966).

10.33 Loeb, J. 'The Significance of Tropisms for Psychology' in *The Mechanistic Conception of Life*, D. Fleming (ed.), Cambridge, Mass., The Belknap Press of Harvard University Press, 1912.

10.34 Mendelsohn, E. *Heat and Life*, Cambridge, Mass., Harvard University Press, 1964.

10.35 Merz, J. T. *A History of European Thought in the Nineteenth-Century*, Edinburgh and London, Blackwood, 1923–50.

10.36 Neurath, O. *The Scientific Conception of the World*, 1929, in *Empiricism and Sociology*, M. Neurath and R. S. Cohen (eds), Dordrecht, Reidel, 1973.

10.37 Olmsted, J. M. D. and Olmsted, E. H., *Claude Bernard*, New York, Henry Schuman, 1953.

10.38 Russell, B. 'Introduction: Materialism, Past and Present', 1925, in F. Lange, *History of Materialism*, New York, Humanities Press, 1950.

10.39 —— *My Philosophical Development*, London, Allen and Unwin, 1959.

10.40 Spencer, H. *Principles of Biology*, 2 vols, New York, Appleton, 1882, section 2, n. 3.

10.41 Temkin, O. 'Materialism in French and German Physiology in the Early Nineteenth Century', *Bulletin of the History of Medicine* 20 (1946).

The Reflex Theory Debate

10.42 Boakes, R. *From Darwin to Behaviourism*, Cambridge, Cambridge University Press, 1984.

10.43 Boring, E. G. *A History of Experimental Psychology*, 2nd edn, Englewood Cliffs, Prentice-Hall, 1950.

10.44 Bower, G. H. and Hilgard, E. R. *Theories of Learning*, 5th edn, Englewood Cliffs, Prentice-Hall, 1981.

10.45 Brazier, M. A. B. 'The Historical Development of Neurophysiology', in J. Field (ed.) *The Handbook of Physiology, Section 1: Neurophysiology*, vol. I, Washington, DC, American Physiological Society, 1959.

10.46 Carpenter, W. *Principles of Mental Physiology*, New York, Appleton, 1874.

10.47 Fearing, R. *Reflex Action: A Study in the History of Physiological Psychology*, New York, Hafner, 1930.

10.48 Graham, W. *The Creed of Science*, London, Kegan Paul, 1881.

10.49 Haller, A. von *First Lines of Physiology*, 1747, New York, Johnson Reprint Corporation, 1966.

10.50 Hartley, D. *Observations on Man*, 1749, Gainesville, Fla, Scholar's Facsimiles and Reprints, 2 vols, 1966.

10.51 Huxley, T. H. 'On the Hypothesis that Animals are Automata, and its History', 1879, in *Collected Essays*, vol. I, New York, Greenwood Press, 1968.

10.52 Lewes, G. H. 'The Spinal Cord a Sensational and Volitional centre', Report of the 28th meeting of the British Association of Advanced Science, James R. Osgood and Co., 1858.

10.53 Lewes, G. H. *The Physical Basis of Mind*, Boston, 1877.

10.54 Newell, A. and Simon, H. A. 'The Processes of Creative Thinking', 1962, in H. A. Simon *Models of Thought*, New Haven, Yale University Press, 1979.

10.55 Shanker, S. G. 'The Enduring Relevance of Wittgenstein's Remarks on Intuition', in John Hyman (ed.), *Investigating Psychology*, London, Routledge, 1991.

The Rise of a 'New Objective Terminology'

10.56 Boden, M. A. 'Intentionality and Physical Systems', 1970, in M. A. Boden, *Minds and Mechanisms*, Ithaca, Cornell University Press, 1981.

10.57 —— *Purposive Explanation in Psychology*, Cambridge, Mass., Harvard. University Press, 1972.

10.58 —— 'The Structure of Intentions', 1973, in M. A. Boden, *Minds and Mechanisms*, Ithaca, Cornell University Press, 1981.

10.59 Billing, S. *Scientific Materialism*, London, Bickers, 1879.

10.60 Darwin, C. *The Origin of Species*, 1859, New York, Norton, 1975.

10.61 Darwin, C. *The Descent of Man*, London, J. Murray, 1871.

10.62 Darwin, E. *Zoonomia: or, the Laws of Organic Life*, 2 vols, Dublin, P. Byrne and W. Jones, 1794.

10.63 George, F. H. *The Brain as a Computer*, Oxford, Pergamon Press, 1962.

10.64 Henn, V. 'History of Cybernetics', in R. Gregory (ed.) *The Oxford Companion to the Mind*, Oxford, Oxford University Press, 1987.

10.65 Hull, C. L. *Principles of Behavior*, New York, Appleton-Century-Crofts, 1943.

10.66 Huxley, T. H. *Hume*, New York, Harper, 1879.

10.67 Lashley, K. 'The Behavioristic Interpretation of Consciousness', *Psychological Review*, 30 (1923): 237–77, 329–53.

10.68 Loeb, J. 'Some Fundamental Facts and Conceptions Concerning the Comparative Physiology of the Central Nervous System', 1899, in *The Mechanistic Conception of Life*, D, Fleming (ed.), Cambridge, Mass., The Belknap Press of Harvard University Press, 1964.

10.69 —— *Comparative Physiology of the Brain and Comparative Psychology*, New York, Putnam, 1900.

10.70 —— 'The Significance of Tropisms for Psychology' 1912, in *The Mechanistic Conception of Life*, D, Fleming (ed.), Cambridge, Mass., The Belknap Press of Harvard University Press, 1964.

10.71 —— *The Mechanistic Conception of Life*, D, Fleming (ed.), Cambridge, Mass., The Belknap Press of Harvard University Press, 1964.

10.72 Miller, G., Galanter, E. and Pribram, K. *Plan and the Structure of Behavior*, New York, Holt, 1960.

10.73 Pauly, P. J. *Jacques Loeb and the Control of Life: Experimental Biology in Germany and America 1890–1920*, Ph.D. thesis, Johns Hopkins University, 1980.

10.74 —— 'The Loeb–Jennings Debate and the Science of Animal Behavior', *Journal of the History of the Behavioral Sciences* 17 (1981): 504–15.

10.75 Pavlov, I. P. *Conditioned Reflexes*, trans. and ed. B. V. Anrep, New York, Dover, 1927.

10.76 Rosenblueth, A. and N. Wiener 'Purposeful and Non-purposeful Behavior', 1950, in W. Buckley (ed.) *Modern Systems Research for the Behavioral Scientist*, Chicago, Aldine, 1968.

10.77 Rosenblueth, A., Wiener, N. and Bigelow, J. 'Behavior, Purpose and Teleology', *Philosophy of Science* 10 (1943): 18–24.

10.78 Sayre, K. M. *Consciousness: A Philosophic Study of Minds and Machines*, New York, Random House, 1969.

10.79 Taylor, R. 'Comments on a Mechanistic Conception of Purposefulness', 1950a, in W. Buckley (ed.), *Modern Systems Research for the Behavioral Scientist*, Chicago, Aldine, 1968.

10.80 —— 'Purposeful and Non-Purposeful Behavior: A Rejoinder', 1950b in W. Buckley (ed.) *Modern Systems Research for the Behavioral Scientist*, Chicago, Aldine, 1968.

10.81 Watson, J. 'Review of H. S. Jennings' *The Behaviour of the Lower Organisms*', *Psychological Bulletin* (4): 1907.

10.82 —— 'Psychology as the Behaviorist views it', *Psychological Review* 20 (1913).

10.83 —— *Behaviour*, New York, Holt Rhinehart and Winston, 1914

10.84 —— 'The Psychology of Wish Fulfilment', *The Scientific Monthly*, 1916.

10.85 —— *Behaviorism*, London, Kegan Paul; Trench, Trubner and Co., 1925.

Theory of Mind

10.86 Astington, J. W. *The Child's Discovery of the Mind*, Cambridge, Mass, Harvard University Press, 1993.

10.87 Nisbett, R. E and T. D. W. Wilson, 'Telling More than We Can Know: Verbal Reports on Mental Processes', *Psychological Review* 84 (1977): 231–59.

10.88 Tomasello, M. 'Joint Attention as Social Cognition', Report 25, Emory Cognition Project, 1993.

10.89 Wellman, H. M. *The Child's Theory of Mind*, Cambridge, Mass, MIT Press, 1990.
10.90 Waismann, F. *Principles of Linguistic Philosophy*, London, Macmillan, 1965.
10.91 Wittgenstein, L. *Philosophical Investigations*, 1953, G. E. M. Anscombe (trans.), 3rd edn, Oxford, Basil Blackwell, 1973.
10.92 —— *Philosophical Grammar*, R. Rhees (ed.), A. Kenny (trans.), Oxford, Blackwell, 1974.
10.93 —— *Last Writings*, G. H. von Wright and H. Nyman (eds), C. G. Luckhardt and A. E. Maximilian (trans.), Oxford, Blackwell, 1982.
10.94 —— *Philosophical Occasions: 1912–1951*, J. Klagge and A. Nordmann (eds), Indianapolis, Hackett Publishing Company, 1993.

Glossary

❧ GENERAL ❧

ab initio – Latin, 'from the beginning'.

absolute – From the Latin *absolutus*, meaning 'the perfect' or 'completed'. The term further means independent, fixed and unqualified, and stands opposed to the relative, often as its negation; i.e., as that which is independent of relation. At various times, principally in METAPHYSICS, it has been used to describe time, space, value, truth and God, or the totality of what really exists as a unitary system somehow both generating and explaining all apparent diversity. It is associated with IDEALISM.

absolute space and time – The view that space and time exist independently of the objects and events in them. This was NEWTON's position which was rejected by EINSTEIN, among others.

absolutist/relativist debate – Relativism is the position that there is no one correct view of things. Relativists argue that views vary among individual people and among cultures ('cultural relativism'), and that there is no reliable way of deciding who is right. This contrasts with absolutism, the view that there is an objectively right view. Although the most common relativist views concern morality, these terms also apply to ONTOLOGY and the question of the nature of reality itself. Ontological relativists hold that there is no external fact about what sorts of basic things exist: we decide how to categorize things, and what will count as basic, depending on the context and manner of thinking that suits us. By contrast, absolutists hold that there is a basic SUBSTANCE which characterizes the unity of reality (i.e. LEIBNIZ's 'simple substances' or 'monads'). See RELATIVE TRUTH/RELATIVISM.

acquaintance and description, knowledge by – Popularized by RUSSELL, the terms used to describe two ways in which objects are known. According to him, we have 'acquaintance' with anything of which we are directly aware (namely sense data). This is to be distinguished from knowledge by description, which includes our knowledge of those whom we would normally call our acquaintances. In the normal sense, I would claim to be acquainted with a colleague; but according to Russell, my colleague is for me the body and mind connected with certain sense data.

ad hoc – Latin, 'to this', i.e., 'specially for this purpose'. An *ad hoc* assumption is one that is introduced illicitly in an attempt to save some position from a contrary argument or counter example, intending to show that the position is false. It is illicit because it is designed especially to accommodate the argument or example, and has no independent support.

aesthetics – From the Greek *aisthesis*, 'sensation'. This term, which was coined by Baumgarten in the eighteenth century, has come to designate not the whole domain of the sensible, but only that portion to which the term beauty may apply. In a more general and contemporary sense, it refers to the philosophical study of art, of our reactions to it, and of similar reactions to things that are not works of art. Typical questions here are: What is the definition of art? How can we judge aesthetic worth? Is this an OBJECTIVE matter?

a fortiori – Latin, 'from the stronger'. A phrase used to signify 'all the more' or 'even more certain'. If all men are mortal, then *a fortiori* all Englishmen – who constitute a small sub-class of all men – must also be mortal.

agent – One who acts, or has acted, or is contemplating action. In ETHICS, it is usually held to be a moral agent, i.e., one to whom moral qualities may be ascribed and treated accordingly. The agent is generally a normal (even ideal) adult: free and responsible with a certain degree of maturity, rationality and sensitivity.

alchemy – The ancient art and science of transmutation; the precursor to modern CHEMISTRY and metallurgy. It is also a mystical art (see MYSTICISM for the transformation of consciousness, symbolized by the transmutation of base metals into gold or silver. Drawing on the Hermetic tradition and Greco-Egyptian ESOTERIC teachings, alchemy assumed its historical form by AD 4, but it did not spread throughout Europe until the twelfth century.

algebra – The study of mathematical structure. Elementary algebra is the study of NUMBER systems and their properties. Algebra solves problems in arithmetic by using letters or SYMBOLS to stand for quantities and includes CALCULUS, LOGIC, the theories of numbers, equations, FUNCTIONS and combinations of these.

algorithm – A systematic procedure for carrying out a computation; any step-by-step method for the solution of a particular type of problem.

analysis of variance (ANOVA) – A statistical method (see STATISTICS) for making simultaneous comparisons between two or more means. An ANOVA yields a series of values (F values) which can be statistically tested to determine whether a significant relation exists between the experimental variables.

analytic/synthetic – These terms were introduced by KANT, referring to the difference between two kinds of judgement. Kant called a judgement analytic when the 'predicate was contained in the subject'; thus, for example, the subject bachelors contains the predicate unmarried. Some might hold that this distinction is better made in terms of sentences: a sentence is analytic when the meaning of the subject of that sentence contains the meaning of the predicate (i.e. is part of the definition of the subject). In other words, an analytic sentence is one that is true merely because of the meanings of the words. A synthetic truth is a sentence that is true but not merely because of the meaning of the words. 'Pigs don't fly' is true partially because of the meaning of the words, of course, but since the definition of pigs says nothing in the first case about flying, the sentence is synthetically true. An analytically false sentence is also possible as in 'There is a married bachelor'.

In another sense, a statement is an analytic truth or falsehood if it can be proved or disproved from definitions by means of only logical laws, and it is synthetic if its truth or falsity can be established by other means. This was the distinction postulated by FREGE, and followed by the logical positivists (see POSITIVISM) for whom all the truths of mathematics and LOGIC are analytic.

analytic philosophy – A term covering a variety of philosophical schools which emphasize language and share the view that the primary function of philosophy is to clarify statements. It is usually associated with English-speaking philosophers, and is contrasted with speculative or continental philosophy. Some philosophers have regarded it as opposed to METAPHYSICS but others have held metaphysical views. This includes RUSSELL, who was one of its earliest adherents when the distinction first arose in the first decades of this century.

anthropometry – Literally, the measurement of man, in terms of anatomical height, girth, width, length, etc.

anti-realism – See REALISM.

a priori/a posteriori – Latin, 'from before/from after'. In the early eighteenth century, knowledge was called a priori if it was acquired by reason, not observation, or by DEDUCTION, not INDUCTION. It is a posteriori if it can be known on the basis of, and hence, after, sense-experience of the fact. The terms are associated with KANT who claimed that a priori knowledge can be known independently of any (particular) experience, i.e., every event has a CAUSE.

Archimedes – (c. 287–212 BC) Greek mathematician, physicist and inventor; generally regarded as the greatest mathematician of antiquity. His rigorous geometrical technique of measuring curved lines, areas and surfaces anticipated modern CALCULUS. He also laid the foundations of mechanics, statics and hydrostatics.

Archimedes' axiom – The order AXIOM for the real line that states that if a and b are real NUMBERS such that $a < b/n$ for all natural numbers n, then $a \leqslant 0$, or equivalently, that for any positive a and b there is a positive integer n such that $a < nb$, and thus that every real number is less than some natural number. This is equivalent to the assertion that the real numbers are conditionally complete. An infinitesimal is non-Archimedean as it is less than any positive non-zero number.

Aristotle – (384–322 BC) Profoundly influential Greek philosopher and scientist. He was PLATO's student; like his teacher, he was centrally concerned with knowledge of reality and of the right way to live. Unlike Plato, however, he accepted the reality of the EMPIRICAL, changing world, and attempted to discover what sort of understanding we must have in order to have knowledge of it. He argued that individual things must be seen as belonging to kinds of things, each of which has essential properties (see ESSENTIALISM) that give it potential for change and development. Investigation into the essential properties of humans can tell us what human good is: he conceived it as a life lived in accord with the moral and intellectual virtues. Although he is recognized for beginning the systematic study of LOGIC, Aristotle's writings cover diverse areas in NATURAL SCIENCE and philosophy.

artificial intelligence (AI) – An area of study in computer science and psychology that involves the building (or imaging) of machines, or programming computers, to mimic certain complex intelligent human activities. AI is of philosophical interest in so far as it might shed light on what the human mind is like, and in so far as its successes and failures enter into arguments about MATERIALISM.

assertion – FREGE introduced the assertion sign to indicate the difference between asserting a PROPOSITION as true and merely naming a proposition (i.e. in order to make an assertion about it, that it has such and such consequences, or the like). RUSSELL and WHITEHEAD adopted the sign in approximately Frege's sense, and from this source, it has come into general use. Russell requires that the sign be followed by a formula denoting a proposition (see DENOTATION), or a truth value, while Frege requires that it be followed by the syntactical name of such a formula. Some recent writers omit the sign, either as understood, or on the grounds that the distinction is illusory.

attribution theory – In social psychology, the study of the factors that determine how people in everyday life situations come to assign CAUSES, particularly for their own actions and those of others, and the HYPOTHESES arising from that study. The analysis of action as analogous to experimental methods, was first suggested by HEIDER, who remains influential on this theory.

Austin, J(ohn) L(angshaw) – English (Oxford) philosopher; a leading figure in ORDINARY LANGUAGE PHILOSOPHY. He drew philosophical conclusions from analyses of our uses of language in general, and of philosophically relevant words.

automaton/automaton theory – From the Greek *automatos*, 'self-moving'. An automaton is a physical mechanism which exhibits seemingly goal-directed behaviour, but is generally construed to be mindless, a mere machine governed by the laws of physics and mechanics (i.e. a robot). The theory holds that living organisms may be considered machines which primarily abide by mechanistic laws. In METAPHYSICS, this theory is also known as automatism and holds that both animal and human are automata. It was propounded by DESCARTES who considered the lower animals to be pure automata, and man, a machine controlled by a rational soul. Pure automatism for both man and animal was advocated by LA METTRIE (1748), and combined with EPIPHENO-MENALISM, found its way into the nineteenth century, in the work of Hodgson, HUXLEY and Clifford.

axiom – A basic statement for which no proof is required, and is a starting point, or premiss, for deriving other statements. An axiomatic theory is one in which all the claims of the theory are presented as theorems derivable from a specified collection, the set (or system) of axioms, which are the axioms of the theory. Axioms are often considered self-evidently true, as those of Euclidean GEOMETRY were for a long time, or as constituting and/or contributing to an implicit definition of its terms.

Ayer, A(lfred) J. – English philosopher, known mainly for his work in EMPIRICISM and linguistic analysis. He rejected METAPHYSICS and confined the function

379

of philosophy to analysis. His *Language, Truth and Logic* (1936) presented logical POSITIVISM in a rigorous and influential way.

Bacon, Francis – English philosopher and scientist. He was also a legalist and political figure (Baron Verulam [1618] and Viscount St Albans [1620]). Best known for his work on scientific method, he is often considered the father of modern science. In his attempts to establish a 'first philosophy', an axiomatic body of truth as the foundation of science, he sought to restore man to mastery over the natural world.

Barthez, Paul Joseph – French physician who introduced the VITALISM principle in 1778.

Bayesian probability – The Bayesian approach to philosophical problems of scientific method is based on the observation that belief is not a simple yes or no matter, but involves gradations. Its fundamental principle can be stated as follows: the degrees of belief of an ideally rational person conform to the mathematical principles of PROBABILITY theory. According to this view, many methodological puzzles (see METHODOLOGY) arise from a preoccupation with all or nothing belief and may be resolved by means of a more inclusive probabilistic LOGIC of partial belief.

behavioural science – A general label pertaining to sciences that study the behaviour of organisms including psychology, sociology, social anthropology, ethology and others. It is often used as synonym for social science.

behaviourism – Early in the twentieth century, many psychologists decided that introspection was not a reliable basis for a science of the mind; instead they decided to concentrate only on external, observable behaviour. METHODOLOGICAL (psychological) behaviourism is the view that only external behaviour should be investigated by science (see METHODOLOGY). METAPHYSICAL or analytical behaviourism is the philosophical view that public behaviour is all there is – that this is what we are talking about when we refer to mental events or characteristics in others, and even ourselves (see METAPHYSICS). It is a form of MATERIALISM. J. B. WATSON and B. F. SKINNER were two American psychologists who were very influential in arguing the first viewpoint.

Bell inequality – The mathematical condition that expresses the principle of no HIDDEN VARIABLES. It was theorized by John Bell in the early 1960s and refers to the lack of full agreement between QUANTUM MECHANICS and a particular class of hidden variable theories. It is a component of 'Bell's theorem' which promoted philosophical questions about hidden variables to the level of experimental verifiability (although it remained difficult to conceive of specific experiments that could be undertaken in order to demonstrate their VALIDITY). The inequalities in question derive from attempts to account for spin CORRELATIONS between particles: if one is up, the other must be down. The difference between such a theory and quantum mechanics is that in the former, the spins are predetermined (by the hidden variables) before any measurement, and hence, are objectively real.

Bergson, Henri – French philosopher. Dynamism characterizes his philosophy; his dualist view posits a vital principle (*élan vital*) in contrast to inert matter; (see DUALISM); he rejects mechanistic or materialistic approaches to understanding reality and any deterministic view of the world, and claims that the creative urge, not natural selection, is at the heart of evolution (see MECHANISM,

MATERIALISM, DETERMINISM). He draws a distinction between the CONCEPT and the experience of time; the former might be subjected to the kind of analysis applied to the concept of space, but 'real time' is experienced as duration and apprehended by INTUITION. He championed the latter against rationalistic 'conceptual' thought.

Berkeley, George – Irish philosopher, Bishop of Cloyne; known for his empiricist and idealist METAPHYSICS and EPISTEMOLOGY. He rejected the idea that a world independent of perceptions can be inferred from them (see EMPIRICISM, IDEALISM, INFERENCE); mental PHENOMENA, the mind and its contents (spirit and idea), are all that exists. These may be external to us, in the universal mind of God, with the ideas it contains constituting the natural world. His views may be construed as a form of PHENOMENALISM.

Bernard, Claude – French physiologist, who established physiology as an exact science and laid the foundations of experimental method in that field.

Bernoulli, Jean – Swiss mathematician; an important figure in the development of the CALCULUS.

Berzelius, Jöns Jacob – Swedish chemist, recognized for determining the direction of CHEMISTRY for nearly a century. Educated in medicine, he brought organic nature within the atomic concept, while maintaining a vitalist position. See VITALISM.

Bohr, Niels – Highly influential Danish theoretical physicist. He formulated the QUANTUM theory of the electronic structure of the hydrogen atom and of the origin of the spectral lines (corresponding to the energy transition levels) of hydrogen and helium. Bohr became the Director of the Institute for Theoretical Physics in the University of Copenhagen, which rapidly became a mecca for physicists from all over the world. A major development of his philosophical views was put forth in a 1927 lecture when he introduced the idea of COMPLEMENTARITY. He pointed out the impossibility of any sharp separation between the behaviour of atomic objects and their interaction with the measuring instruments which define the conditions under which the phenomena appear. This tended to promote a more realistic interpretation of unobservable conditions.

Bohr's principles – See COMPLEMENTARITY, CORRESPONDENCE.

Bohr's theory – A pioneering attempt to apply QUANTUM theory to the study of atomic structure (1913). It postulates an electron moving in one of certain discrete circular orbits about a nucleus with emission or absorption of electromagnetic radiation, necessarily accompanied by transitions of the electron between the allowed orbits (see ELECTROMAGNETISM). This revised the classical electrodynamic model in which the electrons would theoretically irradiate, lose energy and spiral into the nucleus.

Although it was soon shown to be false, Bohr's theory was successfully extended far enough over the next twelve years to suggest that many facts in physics and CHEMISTRY might be explained in these terms, and even led to the modern theory of QUANTUM MECHANICS. Thus, even though it has been superseded, it revolutionized theoretical physics and is today of outstanding historical and philosophical interest.

Boltzmann Ludwig – Vienna-born and educated physicist. He is celebrated for his contribution to the kinetic theory of gases and to statistical mechanics, the latter of which he was the founder. His great talents as a theoretical physicist focused primarily on the kinetic theory of gases, PROBABILITY THEORY and ELECTROMAGNETISM. The beginning of his career in 1866 belonged to the most creative and revolutionary period in physics since NEWTON, two centuries earlier.

Boltzmann, constant – When the ENTROPY of a system, a gas for example, is divided by the natural LOGARITHM of its statistical instability, the result is the constant named after Boltzmann. It is symbolized by k.

Bolyai, Johann – Hungarian mathematician, who at the age of 22 wrote 'Absolute Science of Space', a complete system of GEOMETRY. He showed that EUCLID's parallel postulate was not necessary. Although he was one of the founders of non-Euclidean geometry, he had been preceded (unknown to him) by GAUSS and ŁOBACHEVSKY.

Boole, George – English mathematician responsible for the development of the idea of treating variables in LOGIC in ways analogous to those in ALGEBRA; this was the first real step in the development of modern logic. He was one of the first mathematicians to realize that SYMBOLS of operation could be separated from those of quantity. He showed that classes or sets could be operated on in the same way algebraic symbols or numerical quantities can and applied ordinary algebra to the logic of classes.

Born, Max – German physicist who made fundamental contributions to QUANTUM MECHANICS. He invented matrix mechanics and put forward the statistical interpretation of wave function.

Boring, Edwin Garrigues – American psychologist, who won distinction for his *History of Experimental Psychology* (1929), which traces the genesis of this recent academic discipline from its origins in early nineteenth century philosophy and physiology.

Boyle, Robert – English chemist and physicist. He gave clear qualitative expression to the notion of heat as due to an increase in the motion of the particles of a gas. He is also known for advancing an atomistic theory according to which the ultimate constituents of matter were made up certain primitive, simple and perfectly unmingled bodies, which by combining together gave all the natural variety of matter.

Bradley, F(rancis) H(erbert) – English idealist philosopher, known for his works on LOGIC, METAPHYSICS and ETHICS. Outside the British empiricist tradition, his work is more in the continental Hegelian spirit. His central metaphysical notion is 'the ABSOLUTE' – a coherent and comprehensive whole that harmonizes the diversity and self-contradictions of appearances.

Brouwer, Luitzen Egbertus Jan – Dutch mathematician, the founder of mathematical INTUITIONISM, who did important work in the philosophy of MATHEMATICS.

Bruno, Giordano – Italian philosopher and supporter of the Copernican (heliocentric) system. He was arrested by the inquisition and burned at the stake for his radical scientific and religious views.

Büchner, Ludwing – German philosopher, who through his book *Power and Matter*, made MATERIALISM a popular doctrine in central Europe. He opposed DUALISM, claiming that the soul is merely a function of the brain.

Cabanis, Pierre Jean Georges – French physician and philosopher, who pioneered physiological psychology.

calculus – An abstract system of SYMBOLS, with definitions, AXIOMS and rules of INFERENCE, aimed at calculating something. A calculus is interpreted when its symbols are given meaning by relating them to things in the real world, and some philosophers think of the various sciences as interpreted calculi. Questions of completeness, consistency, decidability and criteria for decisions are among the theoretical considerations of this subject. There are many different kinds of calculus and each symbol system of symbolic LOGIC may be called a calculus: sentential or propositional, quantifier or predicate calculus, as well as the calculus of identity, of classes and of relations. Infinitesimal calculus, an invention of NEWTON and LEIBNIZ in the second half of the seventeenth century, is one of the greatest achievements in the history of mathematics. It is based on the concepts of limits, convergence and infinitesimals (variables which approach zero as a limit). See PROPOSITIONAL/PREDICATE CALCULUS.

Carnap, Rudolf – German-born philosopher who taught at the universities of Vienna, Prague and Chicago. He transplanted logical POSITIVISM when the VIENNA CIRCLE disbanded in pre-World War II Austria. He is important for his work on formal LOGIC, philosophy of SCIENCE and their applications to the problems of epistemology, and helped to develop a new science of logical SYNTAX and SEMANTICS. He espoused the doctrine of PHYSICALISM and sought to construct one common unified language for all branches of empirical science so that problems of language would no longer be an impediment to knowledge.

Cartesian doubt – A philosophical method associated with DESCARTES in which one begins by assuming that any belief which could be doubted is false – even the most ordinary assumptions of common sense. One then searches for a starting point that is indubitable.

Cartesian plane – A two-dimensional flat plane, the points of which are specified by their position relative to orthogonal axes. It is named after DESCARTES, who established the plane and its coordinates as a basis for analytic geometry.

causality – The principle that every effect is a consequence of an antecedent CAUSE or causes. For causality to be true it is not necessary for an effect to be predictable since uncertainty about it may be attributed to the fact that the antecedent causes may be too numerous, too complicated or too interrelated for analysis. In QUANTUM theory, the classical CERTAINTY of causality is replaced at the sub-atomic level by probabilities that specific particles exist in specific positions and take part in specific events. This involves the uncertainty principle which states that the position and MOMENTUM of an electron cannot be established precisely and it is only following consecutive observations of what may be two particles, that probabilities may be determined. See PROBABILITY.

cause – From the Latin *causa*. A term correlative to the term 'effect'. That which occasions, determines, produces or conditions an effect; or is the necessary antecedent of an effect. Long-standing philosophical problems are concerned with the nature of cause, and how we go about establishing it. HUME argued that we think that *A* causes *B* when *A*'s have regularly been followed by *B*'s in the past (i.e. have been 'constantly conjoined' with B's); but the notion that A has a 'power' to produce B 'necessarily', is not something we can observe, such that this is not a legitimate part of the notion of cause. It is argued that this fails to distinguish between causal connections and mere accidental (contingent), but universal regularities.

certainty – From the Latin *certus*, 'sure'. The alleged indubitability of certain truths, especially of LOGIC and mathematics. The concept of certainty plays an important role in the philosophy of DESCARTES, where it applies to a belief or proof which is beyond rational doubt, as in the case of the *COGITO*.

ceteris paribus – Latin, 'other things being equal'. This expression is used in comparing two things, assuming they differ only in the one characteristic under consideration. For example, it could be said that, '*ceteris paribus*, a simple theory is better than a complicated one'; though if everything else is not equal – if, for example, the simpler theory has fewer true predictions – then it might not be better.

(The Great) Chain of Being – A metaphor for the order, unity, and completeness of the created world, thought of as a chain extending from God to the tiniest particle of inanimate matter. The idea has a long history, originating with PLATO's *Timaeus* and forming the basic medieval and Renaissance image for a hierarchical arrangement of the universe. It is also the title of a book written by Arthur Lovejoy (1873–1962) in 1936, which traces, from Plato onwards, the 'principle of plenitude' – the notion that all real possibilities are realized in this world.

chance – This is an uncalculated and possibly incalculable element of existence concerned with its contingent as opposed to necessary aspects. For example, something happens by chance when it is not fully determined by previous events – when previous events do not necessarily bring it about, or make it the way it is; in other words, when it is a random event. Sometimes, however, we speak of chance events as those we are unable to predict with certainty, though they might be determined in unknown ways. We can sometimes know the PROBABILITY of chance events in advance. See NECESSARY/CONTINGENT TRUTH, RANDOMNESS.

channel – In communications, a specified band of frequencies, or a particular path, used in the transmission and reception of electric signals. See COMMUNICATION THEORY.

charge – A property of some elementary particles that causes them to exert forces on one another, in terms of positive and negative (the natural unit of negative charge is that possessed by the electron and the proton has an equal amount of positive charge). Like charges repel and unlike charges attract each other. The force is thought to result from the exchange of PHOTONS between the charged particles. The charge of a body or region arises as a result of an excess or defect of electrons with respect to protons.

chemistry – The scientific discipline concerned with the investigation of many thousands of substances which exist in nature or can be made artificially (synthetic chemistry). Traditionally, it is subdivided into various branches with specific concerns: physical (dealing with the physical laws governing chemical behaviour); organic/inorganic (the study of substances containing/ not containing carbon); nuclear or theoretical (applications of statistical and

QUANTUM MECHANICS); analytic (the detection and estimation of chemical species) and micro-chemistry, a breed of the former (where minute amounts are involved).

circular definition/reasoning – A definition is circular (and thus, useless) when the term to be defined, or a version of it, occurs in the definition; for example, the definition of 'free action' as 'action that is freely done'. Circular reasoning defends some statement by assuming the truth of that statement. It is also known as 'begging the question'.

Clarke, Samuel – English philosopher who championed a Newtonian philosophy in opposition to the prevailing CARTESIAN climate of thought in the Cambridge of his day. In a famous correspondence with LEIBNIZ, he maintained that space and time were INFINITE homogenous entities, as against Leibniz's claim that they were ultimately relational.

Clausius, Rudolf Julius Emmanuel – German theoretical physicist. He ratified Carnot's theory of THERMODYNAMICS which was shown to be inconsistent with the rapidly developing mechanical theory of heat. Preceding Thomson's equivalent formulation, he held that Carnot's theorem could be maintained provided that heat could not by itself pass from one body to another at a higher temperature. As a result, he developed a precise mathematical expression of the second law of thermodynamics in 1854, and later coined the term ENTROPY to express the law of dissipation of energy in terms of its tendency to increase. In 1858, he introduced the important concepts of mean free path and effective radius of a molecule which was later taken over by MAXWELL. Clausius was able to show that these concepts accounted in principle for the observed small values of diffusion rates and heat conductivities in gases in spite of the very large mean speeds of the gas molecules. This theory based on the laws of dynamics and PROBABILITY theory, provided a significant contribution to the kinetic theory of gases. He was one of the most original physicists of the nineteenth century.

Cogito – Latin, 'I think'. An argument of the type employed by DESCARTES (*Meditation II*) to establish the existence of the self. His *Cogito, ergo sum* ('I think, therefore I exist') is an attempt to posit the existence of the self in any act of thinking, including even the act of doubting. It is not so much INFERENCE as a direct appeal to INTUITION, but it has commonly been construed as an argument, because of Descartes' formulation.

cognition – From the Latin *cognitio*, 'knowledge' or 'recognition'. The term refers both to the act or process of knowing and the knowledge itself. Competing theories of knowledge are the subject matter of EPISTEMOLOGY.

cognitivism – Any theory that deals with COGNITION scientifically. Also known as cognitive science, it is an umbrella term for a cluster of disciplines including cognitive psychology, EPISTEMOLOGY, linguistics, computer sciences, ARTIFICIAL INTELLIGENCE, mathematics and NEUROPSYCHOLOGY. As a new approach to psychological problems, usually making use of experimental data, cognitivism attempts to create theories adequate to explain cognitive processes. In that it uses mental concepts, it constitutes a break from BEHAVIOURISM which has come to be viewed as incomplete in the study of cognition.

communication theory – See INFORMATION THEORY.

complementarity – The principle which states that a system, such as an electron, can be described either in terms of particles or in terms of wave motion. According to BOHR these views are complementary. An experiment that demonstrates the particle-like nature of electrons will not also show their wave-like nature, and vice versa.

computation, theory of – See COMPUTATIONALISM.

computationalism – In psychology, this refers to the use of computers as models of human functioning, and to the extended notion that human COGNITION is a computational process of the sort typified by a standard digital computer. See CONNECTIONIST/COMPUTATIONAL PARADIGM.

computer modelling – A method of transferring a relationship or process from its actual situation to a computer. Computer models are selective approximations of a real situation which, because of their simplification, allow those aspects of the real world which are under examination to appear in a generalized form.

Comte, Auguste – French philosopher, the founder of positivistic philosophy. He began his first series of public lectures on POSITIVISM in 1826, the first volume of which appeared in 1830. He traced the development of human thought from its theological and metaphysical stages to its last positive stage: the systematic collection and CORRELATION of observed facts and abandonment of unverifiable speculation about first CAUSES and final ends. He is credited with having coined the terms altruism and sociology.

concept/conceptualism – While some philosophers conceive of a concept as a mental entity, it is generally regarded as the meaning of a word or phrase, as in the 'concept of man'. Conceptualism is a theory about the nature of UNIVERSALS as mental representations. For instance, a universal term such as animal, is not *merely* a word which applies to a number of particular animals, nor a special kind of entity, a 'universal' which exists outside the mind. It does indeed stand for an entity, but an ideational one which exists only in the way that concepts exist.

confirmation theory – This is closely associated with VERIFICATION theory, although it is concerned with the truth of scientific hypotheses, rather than statements. Many philosophical doctrines (e.g., scientific EMPIRICISM) hold that a certain hypothesis is said to be confirmed to a certain degree by a certain amount of evidence. It depends upon inductive reasoning: the fact that every known A is B confirms the hypothesis that every A whatever is B, but does not establish it conclusively, since it is possible that some as yet undiscovered A is not B, and thus that the unrestricted generalization is false. Evidence in this case merely confers PROBABILITY and the degree of confirmation is thus dependent upon the bulk and variety of the evidence. CARNAP has made elaborate attempts to develop comprehensive formal theories of confirmation on the basis of such principles. See HYPOTHESIS, INDUCTION.

connectionist/computational paradigm – 'Connectionism' is Edward Thorndike's term for the analysis of psychological phenomena in terms of association between, not ideas, but situations and responses. Working within a PARADIGM of this sort, recent connectionist theory portrays cognitive activity as information exchanges within a network of interconnected nodes, studied in terms of the FEEDBACK characteristics of such systems. It may provide an alternative to the DETERMINISM of the computational paradigm which bases its study of human cognitive activity on the basis of a digital computation without environmental interaction.

conservation, laws of – These laws deal with the conservation of mass and energy and relate to the principle that in any system the sum of the mass and the energy remains constant. It follows from the special theory of RELATIVITY and is a general statement of two classical laws. The principle of conservation of energy states that the total energy in any system is constant, while the principle of the conservation of mass states that the total mass of any system remains constant. According to the general principle of conservation it is held that mass and energy are interconvertible according to the equation $E = MC^2$, EINSTEIN's law.

constructivism – The view that mathematical entities exist only if they can be constructed (or, intuitively, shown to exist), and that mathematical statements are true only if a constructive proof can be given. It is thus opposed to any view that sees mathematical objects and truths existing or being true independently of (our) apprehension (i.e. PLATONISM). Constructivism encompasses INTUITIONISM, FINITISM and FORMALISM.

contingent truth See NECESSARY/CONTINGENT TRUTH.

continuity in nature, laws of – That by which variable quantities passing from one magnitude to another, pass through all the intermediate magnitudes without passing over any of them abruptly. Many philosophers have asserted the probable conformity of natural operations to this composite law, but Boskovich went so far as to prove it a universal law. Thus, the distances or velocities of two bodies can never be changed without their passing through all the intermediate distances or velocities. The movement of the planets are said to abide by these laws, as well as magnetism, electricity, the passage of time, and strictly speaking, all things in nature.

control engineering – The field of engineering concerned with the establishment of objectives for the manipulation of a system's resources in a rapidly changing environment so that command objectives, in the interests of maintaining the system, may be implemented.

conventionalism – Any doctrine according to which A PRIORI truth, or the truth of PROPOSITIONS (or of sentences) demonstrable by purely logical means, is a matter of linguistic or postulational convention (and thus not ABSOLUTE in character). It entails the view, first expressed by POINCARÉ and developed by MACH and DUHEM, that scientific laws are disguised conventions reflecting the decision to adopt one of various possible descriptions.

Copernicus, Nicolas – Polish astronomer. Architect of the heliocentric theory of the solar system, Copernicus found it necessary to retain seventeen of PTOLEMY's epicycles, while supposing that planetary orbits were circular. The later work of Tycho Brahe and KEPLER dropped these entirely and transformed the orbits into ellipses.

correlation – In STATISTICS, this is a relationship between two or more variables such that systematic increases in the magnitude of one variable are accompanied by systematic increases or decreases in the magnitude of the other. More loosely, it refers to any relationship between things such that some concomitant or dependent changes in one (or more) occur with changes in the other(s). Note that in both of these usages one properly withholds the presumption of CAUSALITY between the variables. Correlations are statements about concomitance; they may suggest but do not necessarily imply that the changes in one variable are producing or causing the changes in the other(s).

correlation coefficient – A number that expresses the degree and direction of relationship between two (or occasionally, more) variables. The correlation coefficient may range from –1.00 (indicating a perfect negative correlation) to + 1.00 (indicating a perfect positive correlation). The higher the value either negative or positive the greater the concomitance between the variables. A value of 0.00 indicates no correlation; changes in one variable are statistically independent of changes in the other. A large number of statistical procedures exists for determining the correlation coefficient between variables, depending on the nature of the data and their methods of collection. See STATISTICS

correspondence – The principle due to BOHR which states that since the classical laws of physics are capable of describing the properties of macroscopic systems, the principles of QUANTUM MECHANICS, which are applicable to microscopic systems, must give the same results when applied to large systems.

co-variance/co-variation – Co-variation is a literal synonym for co-variance which refers to changes in one variable being accompanied by changes in another.

covering law – A general law applying to a particular instance. The covering law theory of explanation states that a particular event is explained when one or more covering laws are given that (together with particular facts) imply the event. For example, we can explain why a piece of metal rusted by appealing to the covering law that iron rusts when exposed to air and moisture, and the facts that this metal is iron, and was exposed to air and moisture. See 'DEDUCTIVE-NOMOLOGICAL MODEL'.

cybernetics – From the Greek *kubernētēs*, meaning 'steersman'. The science of systems of control and communication in animals and machines in terms of FEEDBACK mechanisms. The term was coined by WIENER to designate this field of study, which was a burgeoning interdisciplinary movement led by him in the 1940s. It initially involved mathematics, neurophysiology and CONTROL ENGINEERING, but expanded to include MATHEMATICAL LOGIC, AUTOMATION THEORY, psychology and socioeconomics.

Darwin, Charles – The great English naturalist who gave shape to his evolutionary HYPOTHESIS in *The Origin of Species* (1859). He was not the first to advance the idea of the kinship of all life but is memorable as the expositor of a provocative and simple explanation in his theory of natural selection. He served to establish the fact of evolution firmly in all scientific minds.

Dedekind, Julius William Richard – German mathematician. His major contribution is the 'Dedekind Cut', which allows irrational NUMBERS to be defined in terms of rational numbers, marking the place and filling in the gaps between the set of rational numbers as points on a straight line. It implies that the number series is compact and continuous.

deduction/induction – From the Latin *de*, 'from', and *in* 'in', combined with *ducere* 'to lead'. In an outdated way of speaking, deduction is reasoning from the general to the particular and induction is reasoning from the particular to the general. In a more contemporary way, the distinction between them is made as follows: correct deductive reasoning is such that if the premisses are true, the conclusion must be true; whereas correct inductive reasoning supports the conclusion by showing only that it is more probably true. A common form of induction works by enumeration: as support for the conclusion that all p's are q's, one lists many examples of p's that are q's. It also involves 'ampliative argument' in which the premisses, while not entailing the truth of the conclusion, nevertheless purports good reason for accepting it.

deductive–nomological model – This mode of explanation takes the form of the logical derivation of a statement depicting the phenomenon to be explained (explanandum) from a set of statements specifying the conditions under which the phenomenon is encountered and the laws of nature applicable to it (explanans). It is also known as the 'COVERING LAW' method of explanation.

De Morgan, Augustus – English mathematician and logician; a noted teacher and founder of the London Mathematical Society. He wrote on PROBABILITY, trigonometry and PARADOXES. De Morgan's rule is used in SET THEORY.

denotation/connotation – The denotation or reference of a word is what that word refers to – the things in the world that it 'names'. By contrast, the connotation or sense of a word is its meaning. Thus, a word can have connotation but no denotation: 'unicorn' has meaning but no reference. The distinction is synonomous with EXTENSION/INTENSION. See also SENSE AND REFERENCE.

Descartes, René – French philosopher and mathematician, the founder of modern philosophy. Earlier scholasticism saw the job of philosophy as analysing and proving truths revealed by religion; Descartes' revolutionary view was that philosophy can discover truth. His famous recipe for doing this is the method of systematic doubt; this is necessary to begin the search for the 'indubitable' foundations for knowledge, the first of which is the truth of his own existence as a thinking (not a material) thing. Although he was a champion of mechanistic thinking about the external and material world, and in fact contributed substantially to the new science and mathematics, he was a DUALIST, and believed that minds are non-material. See MECHANISM.

descriptions, theory of – RUSSELL's attempt to show how a definite description can have meaning even when there is nothing that answers to that description. How, for example, can one say meaningfully 'The present King of France is bald'? A non-Russellian analysis of the sentence would attempt to isolate a non-existent individual and predicate baldness of him, giving rise to a descriptive FALLACY. It renders the sentence meaningless because, having failed to perform an act of reference, the sentence could not be said to be either true or false. Russell's strategy is to move the definite description out of the position which it occupies, i.e., that of the subject of the PROPOSITION. So, for 'the present King of France is bald', Russell would substitute, 'There is at least one individual which is at present a King of France, and there is at most one individual which is at present a King of France, and that individual is bald'.

determinism – From the Latin *determinare*, 'to set bounds or limits'. The view that every event has previous CAUSES, such that given its causes, each event must have existed in the form it does. There is some debate about how (and whether) this view can be justified. The view that at least some events are not fully caused is called 'indeterminism'. Determinism is usually a PRESUPPOSITION of science; KANT thought it was necessary; but quantum physics holds that it is false. One of the main areas of concern about determinism arises when it is considered in connection with or in contrast to free will.

dualism/monism – These terms characterize views on the basic kind(s) of things that exist. Dualists hold that there are two sorts of things, neither of which can be understood in terms of the other. In particular, 'dualism' often refers to the view in the philosophy of mind in which the two distinct elements are the mental and the physical. By contrast, monists believe in only one ultimate kind of thing. While the term dualism was initially introduced in 1700 by Thomas Hyde to characterize the good–evil conflict, the term monism was introduced by Christiann Wolff in a discussion of the MIND/BODY PROBLEM.

Duhem, Pierre Maurice Marie – French theoretical physicist.

Du Bois Reymond, Emil – German physiologist, pioneer of the study of the electric phenomena of living tissues.

Durkheim, Emile – French positivistic sociologist. Influencing French sociology in an EMPIRICAL direction, he stressed the importance of the group as the origin of the norms and goals of individuals, and the source and reference of religious symbols. The function of religion in his view is the creation and maintenance of social solidarity. See POSITIVISM.

Eddington, Sir Arthur Stanley – English astronomer and physicist. He is celebrated for his pioneering work on stellar structure (1926) and for his attempts to unify general RELATIVITY and QUANTUM MECHANICS, with a marked ability to convey complex mathematical ideas to the layperson.

effector – Generally, a muscle or gland at the terminal end of an efferent neural process which produces an observed response or effect.

efferent/afferent nervous system – Efferent is from the Latin, meaning 'carry away from'. Hence, in neurophysiology it refers to the conduction of nerve impulses from the central nervous system outward toward the periphery (muscles, glands). Efferent neurons and neural pathways carry information to EFFECTORS and are called motor neurons or pathways. The afferent nervous system, by contrast, refers to the conduction of nerve impulses from the periphery (the sense organs) the central nervous system.

Einstein, Albert – German-born theoretical physicist whose major contribution was the theory of RELATIVITY. He was educated in Zurich and in 1901 he completed his studies, became a Swiss citizen, and made his first contribution to physics. This was followed in 1905 by three important papers: one was on Brownian movement and provided the most direct evidence for the existence of molecules; another dealt with the spectrum of radiation and provided the basis of QUANTUM MECHANICS; and one presented the special theory of relativity. The fundamental paper on general relativity came in 1915, and was followed by a Nobel prize for his work on quantum theory in 1922. He taught in Zurich, Prague and Berlin, but in 1932 found himself in the United States where he spent the rest of his life, eventually becoming a citizen and holding a position at the Princeton Institute of Advanced Study. See QUANTUM FIELD THEORY.

electromagnetism – One of the four fundamental FORCES of nature characterized by the FIELDS produced by the elementary charged particles, i.e. protons and electrons. More generally, it is also one of the main branches of physics, linking the phenomena of electrostatics, electric currents, magnetism and optics into a single conceptual framework. The final form of the theory was devised by MAXWELL and is one of the triumph of the nineteenth century science. See CHARGE.

elementary number theory – A branch of pure mathematics concerned generally with the properties and relationships of integers.

elementary proposition – In WITTGENSTEIN's philosophy these are possible concatenations of simple elements which feature 'states of affairs'. They are composed of strings of names which are ISOMORPHIC to the concatenations of the objects they represent. An elementary PROPOSITION is true, if the objects it mentions are concatenated the way it pictures them, otherwise it is false and the state of affairs does not obtain. The SYNTAX of elementary propositions thus mirrors the geometry of states of affairs.

emotivism – A position in meta-ETHICS that holds that ethical utterances are to be understood not as statements of fact that are either true or false, but rather as expressions of approval or disapproval and invitations to the listener to have the same reactions. HUME might be construed as holding a form of emotivism; in this century, the position is associated with AYER and the American philosopher STEVENSON.

empirical – Relating to sense experience and experiment; having reference to actual facts. In EPISTEMOLOGY, empirical knowledge is not innate, but is knowledge we get through experience of the world; thus it is A POSTERIORI. In scientific method, it is that part of the method of science in which the reference to actuality allows an HYPOTHESIS to be erected into a law or general principle. It is contrasted with NORMATIVE which means regulative or constituting an ideal standard.

empiricism – From the Greek *empeiria*, which is from *empeiros*, meaning 'experienced in', 'acquainted with', 'skilled at'. The doctrine that the source of all knowledge is to be found in experience. One of the major theories of the origin of knowledge, empiricism is usually contrasted with rationalism, the doctrine that reason is the sole, or at least the primary, source of knowledge. Although this term is associated with the denial of innate CONCEPTS and a SYNTHETIC A PRIORI, in general it refers to stressing the role of experience instead of pure reason in the acquisition of knowledge.

entropy/negentropy – Entropy is the measure of the proportion of total energy within a closed system that is available for useful work. If part of the system is hotter than another part then work can be done as the heat energy passes from the hotter to the colder part; but if the temperature is relatively consistent throughout, the system is incapable of accomplishing work. This property follows from the second law of THERMODYNAMICS in that, as a result of irreversible changes to a system in which it expends energy, its capacity to produce additional work decreases and its entropy thereby increases. The absolute value of the entropy of a system – which remains an arbitrary zero with only changes in its value being significant – is a measure of the unavailability of its energy.

    Negentropy is also known as negative entropy and thus refers to the absence of entropy. While entropy is a measure of a relative lack of information, negentropy corresponds to its presence. In the form of structure, it means the departure from the random arrangement of a system's components, to an orderly situation in which is it capable of productive work. See RANDOMNESS.

epiphenomenalism – Theory of the body–mind relation which holds that consciousness is, in relation to the neural processes which underlie it, a mere epiphenomenon, or 'by-product'. This view was advanced by Clifford, HUXLEY and Hodgson.

epistemology – From the Greek *epistēmē*, 'knowledge' or 'science', and *logos*, 'knowledge'. This term designates the theory which investigates the origin, structure, methods and VALIDITY of knowledge. It is one of the main branches of philosophy. Among the central questions studied here are: What is the difference between knowledge and mere belief? Is all (or any) knowledge based on sense perception? How, in general, are our knowledge claims justified?

EPR experiment – The 1935 work of EINSTEIN, Podolsky and Rosen (EPR) which concluded that QUANTUM theory did not constitute a 'complete' theory, the necessary condition of which, according to EPR, being that 'every element of the physical reality must have a counterpart in the physical theory'. The concept of reality was defined with the claim that if we can predict the value of a physical quantity with certainty (i.e., with PROBABILITY equal to unity) and without in any way disturbing a system, then there exists an element of physical reality corresponding to this physical quantity.

    The EPR experiment can be criticized on the ground that 'the system' must be understood in its totality and cannot refer to just one of the particles of a two-particle system. A measurement of one of them does indeed disturb the system and alters the quantum mechanical description. Thus, motivated by the EPR argument one may ask whether it is possible to formulate a theory in which physical quantities do have OBJECTIVELY real values 'out there', independently of whether any measurements are made.

equivocation – From the Latin *aequia-vox* meaning 'same name'. Any FALLACY arising from the ambiguity of a word, or of a phrase playing the role of a single word in the reasoning in question, the word or phrase being used at different places with different meanings. The INFERENCE drawn is formally correct if the word or phrase is treated as being the same word or phrase throughout.

esoteric/exoteric – From the Greek *esōterō*, 'inner'/'interior', and *exōterikos*, 'outside'. The first implies belonging to the inner circle of initiates, or experts, an exclusive system (i.e., the esoteric doctrines of the Stoics, or the esoteric members of Pythagorean brotherhoods). It is contrasted with exoteric, which connotes that a doctrine or system is open to the public.

essence/essentialism – Essentialism may apply to PLATO's philosophy of the Forms, but more generally, it is the metaphysical view dating back to ARISTOTLE, maintaining that some objects – no matter how described – have essences; that is they have, essentially or necessarily, certain properties, without which they could not exist or be the things they are. There is also a related view, originally presented by Locke, that objects must have a 'real' – though as yet unknown – 'essence', which (causally) explains their more readily observable properties (or 'nominal essence'). Recently, essentialist considerations have been applied to problems raised in LOGIC and to issues in the philosophies of science and of language. See also METAPHYSICS, CAUSE.

ethics – From the Greek *éthikos*, which is from *ēthos*, meaning, 'custom' or 'usage'. As employed by ARISTOTLE, the term included both the idea of 'character' and that of 'disposition'. *Morālis*, a term which was considered equivalent to *éthikos*, was introduced by Cicero. Both terms imply connection with practical activity. It is widely understood that ethical behaviour concerns acting in terms of the good and the right, and the philosophical analysis known as ethics tended to centre on these terms.

ethnomethodology – A term originally coined by GARFINKEL to describe the study of the 'resources' available to participants in social interactions and how these are utilized by them, focusing on the practical reasoning processes that ordinary people use in order to understand and act within the social world. The term is generally used to apply to a body of sociological and psychological research on conversational rules, negotiation of property rights and other socially motivated interactions.

Euclid of Alexandria (3rd century BC). – Greek mathematician, founder of Euclidean geometry and probable founder of the Alexandrian School of geometry. For over 2,000 years his work in geometry held unlimited VALIDITY. Even with the development of non-Euclidean systems of geometry, Euclid's work retains great mathematical importance. In modern mathematics, Euclidean space can have any number of dimensions where the distance between two points is interpreted in the same way as that in two or three dimensions. See 'GEOMETRY, EUCLIDEAN'.

explanandum/explanans – See DEDUCTIVE-NOMOLOGICAL MODEL.

extension – From the Latin *ex*, 'out', and *tendere*, 'to stretch'. The extension of something is its dimensions in space. Having extension is characteristic of things composed of extended SUBSTANCE. Mental substance is unextended since it has no spatial dimensions.

extension/intension – In contemporary LOGIC, 'extension' is sometimes used synonymously with 'DENOTATION', and 'intension' with 'connotation'. The extension of a CONCEPT – a term or a predicate – is the set of things to which that concept applies, while its intension is its meaning in the sentence. An extensional context is a referentially transparent context. This occurs in a sentence where the substitution of an expression does not affect the truth value of the sentence: (1) a singular term a, where b for a have the same denotation; (2) a predicate F where G for F have the same extension; (3) a sentence p, where q for p have the same truth value. Contexts which are not extensional, due to the substituted concept's different meaning in the context, are intensional and opaque. For an example, see OPACITY AND TRANSPARENCY, REFERENTIAL.

fallacy – From the Latin *fallacia*, 'deceit', 'trick' or 'fraud'. Any unsound step or process of reasoning, especially one which has a deceptive appearance of soundness or is falsely accepted as sound. The unsoundness may consist either in a mistake of formal LOGIC, or in the suppression of a premiss whose unacceptability might have been recognized if it had been stated, or in a lack of genuine adaptation of the reasoning to its purpose. There are many recognized kinds of fallacies. For examples, see AD HOC, DESCRIPTIONS, THEORY OF, EQUIVOCATION, MODAL LOGIC, POST HOC.

fallibilism – A doctrine of the pragmatist Charles Pierce that ABSOLUTE CERTAINTY, exactitude, or universality is available in no area of human concern or enquiry, but that movement towards these characteristics is available in every case.

family resemblance – By analogy with the ways members of a family resemble each other, this is the sort of similarity that things classified into certain groups share: each shares characteristics with many but not all of the others, and there are no necessary or sufficient conditions for belonging in that classification. WITTGENSTEIN argued that many of our CONCEPTS are family-resemblance concepts, such that they cannot be defined by necessary and sufficient conditions. His best-known example is the concept of a game.

Faraday, Michael – English physicist, the main architect of classical field theory. His work was rejected by his contemporaries and was only later made respectable by MAXWELL. See FIELD.

feedback, positive/negative – While all operating systems function through input and output couplings, feedback is the process of returning a fraction of the output energy or information to the input by producing a corresponding variation between them. Positive feedback occurs when deviation from a stable state produces outputs that lead to yet further deviation, i.e., when an increase in population which produces a greater increase in subsequent generations. With negative feedback, by contrast, the input energy is decreased. It is like a regulatory restraint which tends toward stabilizing the system, as in HOMEOSTASIS.

fideism – The view of Abbé Louis Bautain (the nineteenth-century French Catholic philosopher) that faith precedes reason with respect to knowledge of God, and that in this respect reason is metaphysically incompetent. The doctrine was condemned in an 1855 decretal. See METAPHYSICS.

field – A region under the influence of some physical agency, such as the electric field resulting from an electric CHARGE.

finite – See INFINITE/FINITE.

finitism – An approach to mathematics that admits to its domain only a FINITE number of objects (numbers), each of which must be capable of construction in a finite number of steps. Any general theorem that asserts something of all members of the domain is acceptable only if it can be proven, in a finite number of steps, to hold of each particular member of the domain. HILBERT was the major proponent of finitistic methods in mathematics.

force – Any action that alters or tends to alter a body's state of rest or velocity.

formal/truth/logic – In the traditional use, formal truth means valid independently of the specific subject matter; having a merely logical meaning. In the narrower sense of formal LOGIC which works by exhibiting, often in symbolic notation, the logical form of sentences, it means independent of, without reference to meaning. See VALIDITY, SYMBOLS.

formalism – The tendency to emphasize form as over against content. In ETHICS, the term is sometimes used as equivalent to INTUITIONISM, and is often used to designate any ethical theory, such as KANT's in which the basic principles for determining our duty are purely formal. In mathematics, formalism refers to a programme of deriving all of mathematics from the smallest possible number of AXIOMS by rules of formation and rules of INFERENCE.

formal/material mode of discourse – The distinction put forth by CARNAP to eliminate the necessity of experience in evaluating the truth of statements. By the formal mode he meant a discourse that confined itself to statements and did not try to go beyond these in reference to things, as in the case of the object sentences of the material mode.

Frege, Gottlob (1848–1925). German logician and philosopher of language, the founder of modern MATHEMATICAL LOGIC. He is best known for inventing QUANTIFICATION in logic, for his arguments that mathematics should be understood as an extension of LOGIC, and for his investigations into the relation between SENSE AND REFERENCE in the philosophy of LANGUAGE.

function – Loosely speaking, a correspondence between one group of things and another. The notion is used in arithmetic, where for example, y is said to be a function of x in the formula $y = x^2$. In its applications in LOGIC, the input value (in place of x in this case) is called the 'argument' of the function, and the output (the corresponding value of y) is called the 'value' of the function for that argument. For instance, given the argument 3, the value is 9.

functionalism – In philosophy, this is an approach to the study of mind that views mental states as functional states. Functionalism in this sense is distinguished metaphysically from PHYSICALISM in that rather than arguing that two identical mental states are physically identical, it argues that they should (can) only be viewed as functionally equivalent. In psychology, this is a general and broadly presented point of view that stresses the analysis of mind and behaviour in terms of their functions or utilities rather than contents.

Galilei, Galileo (1564–1642). Italian astronomer and natural philosopher. Among his scientific discoveries are the isochronism of the pendulum, the hydrostatic balance, the principles of dynamics, the proportional compass and thermometer, and although he did not invent it, he is famous for radically improving the telescope. With the aid of this instrument, he described the mountains of the moon, the Milky Way as a vast constellation of stars, the satellites of Jupiter, the phases of Venus and the so-called solar spots. He is also well-known for his innovative work on gravity and the interdependence of motion and FORCE.

Garfinkel, Harold – American sociologist. He is the founder of ETHNOMETHODOLOGY.

Gassendi, Pierre – French philosopher, scientist and mathematician. He argued the impossibility of deriving scientific theory from sensory experience and held an atomistic theory of the universe; but he is principally known for his fifth set of objections to DESCARTES' *Meditations* (1642).

Gauss, Karl Friedrich – German mathematician and astronomer, considered one of the most original mathematicians who ever lived. He was famous for his contributions to number theory, geometry and astronomy. He was first to prove the fundamental theorem of ALGEBRA and was a pioneer in non-

Euclidean GEOMETRY, STATISTICS and PROBABILITY, the theory of FUNCTIONS and the geometry of curved spaces.

genus/species – For philosophers, not just biological hierarchical divisions, but divisions of group and sub-group anywhere. A genus is a general classification; a species subdivides the genus. This nomenclature is especially associated with ARISTOTLE, who thought that a species ought to be defined, by giving the essential characteristics of its genus, plus the *differentia* (Latin, 'difference') that distinguish that species from others in the genus.

geometry, Euclidean – The geometry based on the assumptions of EUCLID and dealing with the study of plane geometry (two-dimensional) and space or solid geometry (three-dimensional). His AXIOMS were developed in *Elements* which was the pre-eminent textbook on the subject for over 2,000 years; it was not until the nineteenth century that the possibility of a non-Euclidean geometry was seriously considered. See GEOMETRY, NON-EUCLIDEAN.

geometry, non-Euclidean – Any geometry not based upon EUCLID's assumptions; in particular, the substitution of a postulate different from 'Euclid's parallel postulate' which said that one and only one line can be drawn through a point outside a line and parallel to the line. Until the nineteenth century, this was accepted as a self-evident truth. The replacement of the postulate (as in spherical and pseudo-spherical geometry) and the development of new geometries led to a new look at the basic assumptions on which mathematics is built. The founders of non-Euclidean geometry were GAUSS, Riemann, BOLYAI and ŁOBACHEVSKI.

Gödel, Kurt – Czech-born American mathematical logician who proved a number of fundamental mathematical results that bear his name; in the course of these proofs he showed the unattainability of the aims of HILBERT's PROGRAMME and (on some interpretations) LOGICISM, and brought about a complete reassessment of the foundations of mathematics. Gödel's theorem is the proof of the existence of formally undecidable PROPOSITIONS in any FORMAL system of arithmetic. See MATHEMATICAL LOGIC.

Harré, Rom (Horace Romano) – New Zealand-born philosopher of SCIENCE and social and BEHAVIOURAL SCIENCES, who currently teaches at Oxford.

Hartley, David – British philosopher and physician. He developed an account of mind based on sound-like vibrations which is highly important in the history of psychology. He used this not only to explain transmission of messages in the nervous system, but also association of ideas by a kind of resonance, as when one vibrating string activates another by sympathy.

Heider, Fritz – Swiss-born social psychologist who also lived in Germany and the United States, where he emigrated in 1930. His main work, *The Psychology of Interpersonal Relations* (1958), was an influential and wide-ranging phenomenal enquiry which sought to explicate how we discern meaning in everyday events and contributed to the development of ATTRIBUTION THEORY.

Helmholtz, Herman Ludwig Ferdinand von (1821–94). – German scientist, one of the most versatile of the nineteenth century. He is celebrated for his contributions to physiology and theoretical physics.

Hempel, Carl Gustav (1905–). German-born and -educated philosopher who also studied mathematics and physics, and taught in the United States. He became a representative of logical POSITIVISM with its EMPIRICISM and scientific framework and is known for his 'COVERING LAW' approach which allowed for statistical explanations. These use probabilistic laws to show that the event to be explained is made highly probable, rather than deductively necessitated, by the explanatory premisses. See DEDUCTION, PROBABILITY, STATISTICS.

Hempel's paradox – The PARADOX, developed by Hempel, which deals with the way in which an observation report confirms a generalization. Observing a black raven ought to confirm the HYPOTHESIS that all ravens are black; equally, observing a non-black raven ought to confirm the hypothesis that all non-black things are non-ravens; yet the second hypothesis is logically equivalent to the first, so observation of a white shoe ought to confirm that all ravens are black. But intuitively, it does not. This is one of the difficulties formal CONFIRMATION THEORY meets.

heuristic – From the Greek *heuriskein*, 'to discover'. Serving to find out, helping to show how the qualities and relations of objects are to be sought. In METHODOLOGY, aiding in the discovery of truth. The heuristic method is the analytic method.

hidden variable – An indeterminate factor of which we are currently ignorant, but which once discovered, would in theory allow for an accurate CAUSAL prediction of the phenomena in question. In QUANTUM MECHANICS, a hidden variable view of matter implies the fundamental CAUSALITY of invisible FORCES at the sub-atomic level.

Hilbert, David – German mathematician. A pioneer, along with PEANO, of the science of axiomatics (see AXIOM). This is the attempt to establish a minimum number of unidentified terms and basic definitions, and from these to deduce rigorously the entire structure of mathematics. Recognizing the assumptions at the basis of EUCLID's geometry, he shifted its foundation from INTUITION to LOGIC.

Hilbert space – A multidimensional space in which the proper (eigen) FUNCTIONS of WAVE MECHANICS are represented by orthogonal unit vectors.

Hilbert's program – Proposed by Hilbert in 1920 in support of his FORMALISM in the foundations of mathematics, this became a motivating problem of metamathematics, showing by purely syntactic means that finitistic methods could never lead to contradiction. This is equivalent to finding a decision ALGORITHM for all of mathematics, and although it was shown unattainable by GÖDEL's proof in 1931, the project nonetheless led to the development of proof theory and computability theory. See FINITISM, SYNTAX.

Homans, George C(aspar) – American sociologist and professor at Harvard, whose interests range from sociological theory and applications of anthropology to industrial relations.

homeostasis – A type of FEEDBACK by which deviation from stability is counteracted by adjustment internal to the system itself. It refers to an adaptive process which is evident among biological organisms in the mechanisms regulating body temperature and chemical composition of blood.

Hooke, Robert – English scientist. He is known as one of the most brilliant and versatile scientists of the seventeenth century, surpassed only by NEWTON. His contributions in optics and gravitation were dwarfed by the latter with whom he engaged in many controversies. His reputation as an inventer of scientific instruments, however, remains unrivalled for that period.

Hume, David – British philosopher, born and educated in Edinburgh, one of the greatest philosophers of all time. A thoroughgoing empiricist, he believed that all our ideas were copies of sense impressions; he argued that many of our notions (such as the continuing 'self', and the necessary connection we suppose exists between CAUSE and effect), since unsupported by perception, are mistaken, and that A PRIORI knowledge must derive merely from logical relations between ideas. He is famous also for sceptical conclusions regarding moral 'knowledge': our ethical reactions, he argued, come merely from the psychological tendency to feel sympathy with others. His scepticism and empiricism were enormously influential in the tradition ANALYTIC PHILOSOPHY.

Huxley, Thomas Henry – British scientist, who was the main supporter of DARWIN, but also a distinguished scientist in his own right. A prolific writer, he produced research papers and books on wide-ranging subjects, mainly zoological and palaeontological, but also geological, anthropological and botanical.

hypothesis/null hypothesis – A tentative suggestion that may be merely a guess or a hunch, or may be based on some sort of reasoning; in any case it needs further evidence to be rationally acceptable as true. Some philosophers think that all scientific enquiry begins with hypotheses. A null hypothesis is one which has been shown to be invalid.

iatrochemistry/iatrophysics – The study of chemical/physical phenomena in order to obtain results of medical value. Iatrochemistry was practised in the sixteenth century, and finds modern equivalents in chemotherapy or pharmacology.

ideal/idealism – From the Greek *idea*, 'vision' or 'contemplation'. Broadly, any theoretical or practical view emphasizing mind (soul, spirit, life) or what is characteristically of pre-eminent value to it. It is the alternative to MATERIALISM, stressing the 'ideal' – supra- or non-spatial, incorporeal, NORMATIVE or valuational, and teleological – over the real – concrete, sensuous, factual and mechanistic. Metaphysical idealism is the view that only minds and their contents really or basically exist – a form of monism; and epistemological idealism is the view that the only things we know (or know directly) are our own ideas. 'Idealism' was first used philosophically by LEIBNIZ at the start of the eighteenth century.

idealism – See IDEAL.

incomplete symbol – RUSSELL's designation for expressions that disappear upon analysis, giving rise to a logical fiction. For example, if a sentence such as 'There is a possibility it will rain' is represented by 'It is possible it will rain', the possibility is said to have been shown to be a logical fiction. His theory of definite DESCRIPTIONS, he believed, showed such descriptions to be incomplete symbols and enabled him to speak of the supposed reference of a non-referring description as a logical fiction. He also aimed to show that symbols for classes were incomplete and that classes were logical fictions.

individuation – Development or determination of a particular (individual) from its corresponding universal form or general type. The principle of individuation refers to the CAUSE (such as matter, God or form) of individuation.

in situ – Latin, meaning in its (original) place.

induction – See DEDUCTION/INDUCTION.

inductive–statistical model – A form of explanation holding that we can explain some particular action or event by showing that a statement which predicts it is supported with a high degree of inductive PROBABILITY by some set of antecedent conditions.

inductivism – The view in philosophy of SCIENCE which privileges INDUCTION as a valid method of establishing scientific proof. With the growth of NATURAL SCIENCE philosophers became increasingly aware that a deductive argument can only bring out what is already implicit in the premises, and hence, became inclined to insist that all new knowledge must come from some form of induction, i.e., an empirically based method of reasoning by which a general law or principle is inferred from observed particular instances. BACON, who believed that the method was infallible if the collection of experimental instances was exhaustive, was the prophet of inductivism. In the twentieth century, analyses of induction have proliferated, and largely due to the work of CARNAP with his concept of 'degree of CONFIRMATION', have coalesced with PROBABILITY theory. See DEDUCTION/INDUCTION, EMPIRICAL, INFERENCE.

inference – From the Latin *in* and *ferre*, 'to carry or bring'. A logical relation that holds between two statements when the second follows deductively from the first. This relation is sometimes called implication, but inference refers to the *act* of inferring, the mode of reasoning involved when moving from one statement to another, which the first statement implies. See DEDUCTION/INDUCTION.

infinite/finite – From the Latin *in*, 'not', and *finis* 'boundary', 'limit', 'end'. Thus, infinite means that without limit, boundary or end. Etymologically, the first term is gained by negation of the latter term, although there are those who would claim that the conception of the infinite is prior to the finite. The infinite has been associated from the start with series of NUMBERS, magnitudes, times and spaces. the endlessness of such series provides one, and the basic, conception of infinity. Yet if one applies the predicates 'finite' and 'infinite' to being, the conception changes; if finite being is limited in extent, properties, etc., infinite being would be unlimited, or perhaps ABSOLUTE, in all of these respects.

infinity, axiom of – An AXIOM of SET THEORY that asserts, in one form or another, that there exists a set with an INFINITE number of members, or that the number of objects in the world is a natural number. The reduction of mathematics to set theory requires the axiom of infinity, which RUSSELL originally and erroneously believed was provable from other accepted assumptions. The axiom is now known to be independent of the other axioms of set theory.

information theory (Also known as **communication theory**) – In CONTROL ENGINEERING, the study treating the problem of transmitting messages: that is, of reproducing at one point either exactly or approximately a message selected at another point. The meaning of the message is irrelevant to the technical problem, and is to be distinguished from a semantical understanding of communication. It is concerned with the ability to encode, transmit, and decode an actual message selected from a set of possible messages with which the communication system claims to deal. Success in this depends on the quantity of information that has to be processed in a unit of time, measured against CHANNEL capacity. Mathematical tools are developed to enable such measurements to be made and compared. The simplest example would be the selection of one out of two equally likely possibilities (one bit, while one out of four requires two bits, etc.). In general, the selective information content measures the statistical unexpectedness of the event in question. The more improbable an event, the larger its selective information content. This way of measuring was developed by SHANNON who inaugurated the study in 1948.

This theory is strongly interdisciplinary and embraces communication processes of all kinds – in human societies, nervous systems and machines. Psychologists and physiologists now make extensive use of its general ideas and it has become commonplace to regard the impulses that flow along nerve fibres as 'conveying information' (although how these are represented in the brain remains unknown). Nonetheless, information theory provides a valuable conceptual bridge between physiology and psychology.

instantiation theory – In the philosophy of SCENCE, a sub-theory of INDUCTIVISM which holds that a scientific theory is confirmed by instances to it. In this sense, every example under consideration that does not contradict a theory or law is an instance of it. However, the reliability of this theory is problematic due to its reliance on INTUITION and the logical paradoxes it gives rise to. See 'HEMPEL'S PARADOX'.

instrumentalism – The view that one should understand scientific theory in terms of experimental procedures and predictions, stressing means over ends. It holds that theoretical entities do not really exist, and that statements about them do not have truth value; they are actually only instruments, tools or calculating devices to relate observations to predictions. Instrumentalism is also the name of the position associated with PRAGMATISM, especially with Dewey, that emphasizes the way our thinking arises through practical experience and represents a way of coping with our environment.

inter alia – Latin, 'amongst other things'.

introspection/introspectionism – From the Latin *intro*, 'within' and *spectare*, 'to look'. Observation directed on the self or its mental states and operations, either through the direct scrutiny of conscious states and processes as they take place, or the recovery of these upon a retrospective act. The term is the modern equivalent of 'reflection' and 'inner sense' as employed by LOCKE and KANT. In psychology, introspectionism is the standpoint which advocates the introspective method.

intuition – From the Latin *intueri*, 'to look at'. As in vision, intuition involves knowledge by which the object (the self, a conscious state, the external world, a universal, rational truth) is immediately apprehended. It can be apprehended directly and completely, in what it is, or it can be apprehended in its concreteness. In the former the intuitive knowledge is opposed to the discursive, in the latter it is opposed to the abstract.

intuitionism – Any theory that holds INTUITION as a valid source of knowledge, as in the philosophies of DESCARTES, SPINOZA and LOCKE. ETHICAL intuitionism is the position that ethical truths are intuited, while mathematical intuitionism holds that any sort of mathematical entity exists only if it is possible to give a constructive existence proof of it (by producing an example of it or providing a method for producing one). See CONSTRUCTIVISM.

invariance – Generally, characteristic of that which does not change. The term is most often used with the qualifier relative since few things are truly invariant. In the psychological study of perception and learning, those aspects of the stimulus world that display higher degrees of invariance, relative to other aspects, are learned most quickly and easily.

ipso facto – Latin, 'by the fact itself', by that very fact or act, thereby.

isomorphism – From the Greek *iso* 'equal' and *morphé* 'form'. The relevance of this term to philosophy derives from the discipline of mathematics, and is related to the close association between mathematics and LOGIC. Any two groups of entities can be said to be isomorphic when they have the same structure, that is, when by a one-to-one correspondence the elements of one group can be correlated with the elements of the other.

James, William – One of the most important and influential American philosophers whose main contribution came through his *Principles of Psychology* (1890). He espoused a doctrine of radical EMPIRICISM, maintaining that experience consists of a plurality, or multiplicity, of reality (real units). He not only doubted consciousness, like HUME, but denied it, holding that reality was nothing but the stream of OBJECTIVE experiences. See also, LANGE.

Kant, Immanuel – German philosopher, one of the most important figures in the history of philosophy. His epistemological concern was with the 'truths of reason' (for example that everything has a CAUSE). Kant thought that such knowledge was A PRIORI and SYNTHETIC, and that it could be accounted for by the way that any rational mind necessarily thinks. Similarly, he argued that the basis of ETHICS is not EMPIRICAL or psychological. Ethical knowledge can be derived merely from the a priori form any ethical assertion must have: it must be universalizable – that is, rationally applicable to everyone (the categorical imperative). Kant argued that this is equivalent to saying that the basic ethical truth was that everyone must be thought of as an end, never merely as a means. Kant's ethical theory has become a major consideration in contemporary ethics.

Kepler, Johannes – German mathematician and one of the founders of modern astronomy. His three laws of planetary motion state: (1) the orbit of each planet is an ellipse, with the centre of the sun at one focus; (2) the imaginary line joining the centre of each planet with the centre of the sun moves over equal areas of the ellipse in equal periods of time; (3) the time each planet takes to complete its journey around the sun is proportional to the cube of its mean distance from the sun.

Keynes, John Maynard – British economist; the most seminal economist of the twentieth century.

Koyré school – A school of thought in the philosophy of SCIENCE led by the Russian philosopher Alexandre Koyré. He held that the great discoveries of the scientific revolution (from COPERNICUS TO NEWTON) were the achievements of truth-loving individuals working in isolation. This 'internalist' interpretation stressed theory over practice and developed in contrast to the Marxist interpretation of modern science as the response to the technological needs of an emerging capitalist economy.

Kronecker Leopold – German mathematician who developed algebraic number theory. He was often *in* debate with WEIERSTRASS and Cantor which gave rise to his system of AXIOMS to support a formalist viewpoint. See ALGEBRA.

Kuhn, Thomas – American philosopher and historian of science. He holds that scientific theories develop around basic PARADIGMS or models which are of central importance in interpreting scientific theories (i.e., the model of atomic theory in terms of a solar system). In his book *The Structure of Scientific Revolutions* (1962), he described how the scientific community determines the line between orthodoxy and heresy at any given time, such that change in the orientation of science depends upon convulsions in that community.

La Mettrie, Julian Offray de – French philosopher and physician, known for the MATERIALISM of his books, and mechanistic view of both animals and man.

Lange, Carl Georg – Danish psychologist and materialist philosopher. Working independently of William JAMES, he developed an almost identical theory of emotion, i.e., that emotion consists of the bodily changes evoked by the perception of external circumstances. It is known as the James–Lange theory.

Laplace, Pierre Simon – French mathematician, remembered for his contributions to mathematical physics and celestial mechanics.

language, philosophy, of – The branch of philosophy concerned with meaning, truth and with the force of utterances. To be distinguished from 'linguistic philosophy' which is wider in scope and entails the general belief that philosophical questions may be approached by asking questions about the use of words. In the first sense, the question as to the justifiability of this approach is central (as with AUSTIN and WITTGENSTEIN), as is the use of key terms as not only 'meaning' and 'truth', but 'reference' and 'use' as well. It may also be a study of the nature and workings of language as a subject in its own right, rather than as a means to the solution of further philosophical problems.

language game – WITTGENSTEIN used this concept, in a broad sense, to refer to language and its uses, including the way our language influences the way we think and act. The emphasis here is on the similarity of a language to a game: both are rule-governed systems of behaviour, and the rules vary over times and contexts. Language games include the 'picturing' of facts, the primary purpose of language, but extend beyond this to prayer and praise, cursing, requesting, and ceremonial greeting. There is no point in attempting to reduce the endless kinds of language game to a single pattern. Each must be understood in its own terms.

least action, law of – Principle stating that the actual motion of a conservative dynamical system between two points takes place in such a way that the action has a minimum value with reference to all other paths between the points which correspond to the same energy.

Leibniz, Gottfried Wilhelm von – German scientist, mathematician and philosopher. He was trained in law, diplomacy, history, mathematics, theology and philosophy, and became the most notable thinker of the seventeenth century. Known for the view that all PROPOSITIONS are necessary in this 'best of all possible worlds', Leibniz's conception of the universe united beauty with mathematical order. He described the vital elements of this world as 'monads' (true atoms that exist metaphysically); their co-existence and relations are regulated by a pre-established harmony, which is the work of God. Leibniz devoted much of his work to the reform of science through the use of a universal scientific language and a CALCULUS of reasoning, a method which was a forerunner to modern symbolic LOGIC. He and NEWTON independently developed the calculus.

Leibniz's law – Also known as 'the indiscernibility of identicals' or its converse 'the identity of indiscernibles', this law states that if x and y are identical, then x has every property y has, and y has every property x has.

Lévi-Strauss, Claude – French structuralist philosopher; known for his application of STRUCTURALISM to anthropology. He investigated the relationship between culture (an exclusive attribute of humanity) and nature, based on the distinguishing characteristic of man: the ability to communicate in a language.

Lewes, George Henry – British psychologist and philosopher. He contributed to the development of EMPIRICAL METAPHYSICS, and stressed introspection in psychology, using both SUBJECTIVE and OBJECTIVE methods; he viewed mind as similar to body, with aspects that can be logically separated yet are not wholly distinct.

Liebig, Baron Justus von – German chemist. An outstanding figure in chemical education, and the greatest chemist of his time.

Łobachevski, Nikolai – Russian mathematician, contemporary of BOLYAI, who also challenged the parallel postulate of EUCLID. He assumed that through a point outside a given line there are at least two lines parallel to the given line. He then constructed a non-Euclidean GEOMETRY in which the sum of the angles of a triangle is not greater than 180°, and the smaller the triangle is in area, the closer to 180° is the sum of the angles.

Locke, John – English philosopher and political theorist. He argued that none of our ideas are innate and therefore all our knowledge must come from experience. This position makes him the first of the three great British EMPIRICISTS (the others are BERKELEY and HUME). Influential also in political theory, he is renowned for his advocacy of (traditional) liberalism and natural rights.

logarithm – The index (exponent) which changes a given number, called the base, into any required number. The solution of the equation $b^x = N$, where b and N are known, is a logarithm.

logic – From the Greek *logos* meaning 'knowledge' as well as 'reason, speech, discourse, definition, principle or ratio'. Generally speaking, something is logical when it makes sense, although more strictly, it refers to the theory of the conditions of valid INFERENCE. The term was first used by Alexander of Aphrodisius (2nd century AD), then developed in ARISTOTLE's logical writings which were called the *Organon*, or instrument of science. Traditional logic included various sorts of categorization of some types of correct and incorrect reasoning, and included the study of the SYLLOGISM. Most logical theory today is done by exhibiting the types of sentences, and giving rules for what correctly may be reasoned on the basis of sentences of different types, in symbolic form; that is, with SYMBOLS taking the place of logically relevant words or connections. This logic, which concentrates on reasoning that is correct because of SYNTAX, is deemed FORMAL, and is contrasted with informal logic which analyses arguments semantically, and relies less heavily on symbols and mathematical procedures.

logical atomism – The position, associated with RUSSELL and WITTGENSTEIN, that language might be analysed into 'atomic propositions', the smallest and simplest sentences, each of which corresponds to an 'atomic fact', one of the simplest bits of reality. See ELEMENTARY PROPOSITION.

logical empiricism – A doctrine of meaning holding that a word or sentence has meaning only if rules involving sense experience can be given for applying or verifying it. ANALYTIC sentences are excepted. Such rules may further constitute the meaning.

logical positivism – See POSITIVISM.

logical truth – A sentence is logically true when it is true merely because of its logical structure. It is distinguished from analytically true sentences which are true merely because of the meaning of the words. Logical truths are also called 'logically necessary' sentences, but these should be distinguished from (metaphysically) necessary truths, since some of these are neither analytically nor logically true (i.e. KANT's belief that 'All events have a cause' is a necessarily true, but not logically nor analytically true). 'TAUTOLOGY' is often used as a synonym for 'logical truth' and sentences that are neither logically true nor logically false – that are merely true or false – are said to be logically contingent truths or falsehoods. See ANALYTIC/SYNTHETIC, NECESSARY/CONTINGENT TRUTH.

logically proper name – A proper name constituting a definite DESCRIPTION of the kind required by Russell's LOGICAL ATOMISM. Such names had meanings that were strictly identifiable with their bearers and were meaningless if their bearers did not exist. RUSSELL thought demonstratives (i.e., 'that' and 'this') were logically proper names. Ordinary names cannot have their meanings strictly identified with their bearers since we associate a variety of descriptions with the proper names we use. They depend upon such descriptions to ensure their meaningfulness.

logicism – The view pioneered by FREGE and RUSSELL, holding that received mathematics, in particular arithmetic, is part of LOGIC. Its aim was to provide a system of primitives and AXIOMS (which upon interpretation yielded logical truths) such that all arithmetical notions were definable in the system and all theorems of arithmetic were theorems of the system. If successful the programme would ensure that our knowledge of mathematical truths was of the same status as our knowledge of logical truths.

Lorentz transformation – This refers to a set of equations for transforming the position–motion parameter from an observer at one point, O (x,y,z), to an observer at O'(x',y',z'), moving relative to one another. The equations replace the Galilean transformation equations of NEWTONIAN MECHANICS in RELATIVITY problems.

Lotze, Rudolf Hermann – German philosopher and psychologist. A mechanist, he elaborated the philosophical system of teleological IDEALISM, and aided in founding the science of physiological psychology.

Lucretius (full name: Titus Lucretius Carus) (96?–55 BC). – Ancient Roman poet/

philosopher. He popularized the scientific and ethical views of the atomists who believed that things are composed of elementary basic parts.

Mach, Ernst – Austrian theoretical physicist; the 'father of logical POSITIVISM'. He fundamentally reappraised the philosophy of SCIENCE with his belief that science, partly for historical reasons, contained abstract and untestable models and concepts, and that it should discard anything that is not observable.

Maimonides (or **Moses ben Maimon**) (1135–1204). – Spanish-born Jewish philosopher and theologian; codifier of the Talmud.

mass – The quantity of matter in a body. It varies with velocity in accordance with the principle of relativity and is controvertible with energy by EINSTEIN's law.

materialism – Any set of doctrines stressing the material over spiritual factors in METAPHYSICS, value theory, physiology, EPISTEMOLOGY or historical explanation. In its extreme form, it is the philosophical position that all that exists is physical. LUCRETIUS and Hobbes are two of the many philosophers associated with this view. Materialists with respect to mind sometimes argue that apparently non-physical things like the soul, mind or thoughts are actually material things. Central-state materialists identify mental events with physical events central in the body (i.e. the nervous system). Some materialists, however, think that categorizing things as mental is altogether mistaken, that mental events do not exist, and that this mode of discourse should be eliminated as science progresses.

mathematical logic – The application of mathematical techniques to LOGIC, in an attempt both to deduce new PROPOSITIONS by formal manipulations, and to detect any underlying inconsistencies. Its study, by many eminent mathematicians and philosophers, as a means of clarifying the basic concepts of mathematics, has revealed a number of PARADOXES, several of which have yet to be resolved. It is also known as symbolic logic.

mathematics, philosophy of – The study of the concepts and justification for the principles used in mathematics. Two central problems concern what, if anything, mathematical statements such as '2 + 2 = 4' are about, and how it is that we come to have knowledge of such statements. Questions as to the origin and nature of our knowledge of them tend to distinguish various positions within the study: realists hold that it derives from the existence of abstract entities, the relations among which mathematical statements describe (also known as PLATONISM); conventionalists hold that such statements are true merely by convention or fiat; intuitionists restrict the scope of mathematical knowledge to that which can be proven by constructive processes alone (also known as CONSTRUCTIVISM); another form of intuitionism is that of KANT who held that this knowledge is self-evident and A PRIORI, logicists, such as FREGE and RUSSELL, who to some extent accept Kant's view, yet are unsatisfied with its SUBJECTIVE bent, hold that our knowledge of mathematical truth, is as certain as that of logical truth; and formalists, like GÖDEL, maintain that mathematical sentences are not about anything, but are rather to be regarded as meaningless marks.

matrix theory – A branch of mechanics that involves the idea that a measurement on a system disturbs, to some extent, the system itself. It originated simultaneously with, but independently of, wave mechanics. It is equivalent to wave mechanics but here the wave functions are replaced by vectors in a suitable space (HILBERT SPACE) and the observable things of the physical world, e.g., energy, momenta, coordinates, etc., are represented by matrices. A matrix is a mathematical concept introduced originally to abbreviate the expression of simultaneous linear equations. It appears as an array of mn numbers set in m rows and n columns and is a matrix of order $m \times n$.

Maxwell, James Clerk – Scottish physicist, the pioneer of electromagnetism. Mathematically interpreting FARADAY's concept of the electromagnetic FIELD, Maxwell successfully developed the revolutionary field equations bearing his name. This was an advance that may be ranked in pre-quantal theoretical physics among NEWTON's dynamics and EINSTEIN's RELATIVITY.

He is also known for his early predictions of the existence of radio waves – the equations of which are fundamental throughout modern telecommunications – as well as, more importantly, his contributions to the kinetic theory of gases. He adopted CLAUSIUS's concept of mean free path and greatly extended the latter's statistical approach to the subject by allowing for all possible speeds in the gas molecules. This resulted in the celebrated Maxwell distribution of molecular velocities, together with important applications of the theory to viscosity, conduction of heat, and diffusion in gases. He also drew upon the work of BOLTZMANN, who took over his approach.

mechanism – From the Greek *mēkhanē*, 'machine'. The theory that all phenomena are explicable by mechanical principles, with the view that all phenomena are the result of matter in motion and can be explained by its laws. Mechanistic doctrine holds that nature, like a machine, is a whole whose single function is served automatically by its parts. As a theory of explanation by efficient as opposed to final CAUSE, it was first put forth by Leucippus and Democritus (460–370 BC) as the view that nature is explicable on the basis of atoms in motion and the void. It was later developed in the seventeenth century as a mechanical philosophy by GALILEO as well as DESCARTES, for whom the ESSENCE of matter is EXTENSION, and all physical phenomena is explicable by mechanical laws.

Meinong, Alexius Meinong – Austrian philosopher who studied under Brentano and developed the latter's views on the different sorts of 'existence' of the objects of thought. He is known for the view that there are three distinct elements in thinking: the mental act, its content and its object. Object is defined as that towards which a mental act can be directed; it may or may not be an existing entity. Content is that attribute of the mental act that enables attention to be directed toward any part.

Mersenne, Marin – Friend and principal correspondent of DESCARTES. Friar Mersenne, a prolific writer himself, was responsible for collecting for publication the first six sets of objections to the *Meditations*.

metalanguage – A language used in talking about another language. In LOGIC, one distinguishes between the object language and the metalanguage. The first refers to the signs which refer to the world, the language in use, while the latter refers to that part of language which refers to the signs of the language itself. Thus, for example, particular INFERENCES are symbolized in the object language, but general forms of valid inference are symbolized in the metalanguage. See SYMBOLS.

metaphysics – From the Greek 'above' or 'beyond' physics. This term, which refers to one of the main branches of philosophy, is said to have been derived from one of ARISTOTLE's books, which having followed his book on physics, was deemed The *Metaphysics* by a later editor. Metaphysics is thought of as a study of ultimates, of first and last things, its content going beyond physics, or any other discipline. It tends toward the building of systems of ideas; and these ideas either give us some judgement about the nature of reality, or a reason why we must be content with knowing something less than the nature of reality, along with a method for taking hold of whatever can be known.

methodology – The systematic analysis and organization of the rational and experimental principles and processes which must guide a scientific enquiry, or which constitute the structure of the special sciences more particularly. Also called scientific method, it is usually considered a branch of LOGIC; in fact, it is the application of the principles and processes of logic to the special objects of science; while science in general is accounted for by the combination of INDUCTION and DEDUCTION as such.

Mill, John Stuart (1806–173) – The most influential English philosopher of his time. He is known for his thoroughgoing EMPIRICISM, his development of utilitarianism, and liberal political views, as well as his work on the principles of scientific enquiry. He held that all INFERENCE is basically INDUCTION on the basis of the uniformity of nature from one particular event to another or a group of others. He holds that the conclusion of syllogistic reasoning always involves the inclusion of the premises, with knowledge of those in turn resting on empirical inductions. He is known for his inductive 'methods of experimental inquiry' which define the CAUSE of an event as the sum total of its necessary conditions positive and negative.

mind/body problem – This involves the question as to the relation between the mental and the physical, i.e., whether they are distinct, or whether events in one can be reducible to those of the other. Until recently most philosophers have held a dualistic view of the relation between mind and body. (See DUALISM). This is in the tradition of DESCARTES who ascribed mental attributes to spiritual substances, logically independent of anything physical, but inhabiting particular bodies in a way not satisfactorily defined. Although attempts are being made to establish a causal affinity between the mental and physical, their theoretical relation remains a problem.

modal logic – The study of the features and relations of sentences which include the following words, and distinctions between types of modal logic: necessary and 'possible' (alethic), 'ought' and 'must' (deontic), 'knows' (epistemic) and 'before' (temporal). The study encompasses the methods of good reasoning involving these sentences in which a modal FALLACY arises when the premises 'It's necessary that: if p then q' and 'p' are used mistakenly to derive 'It's necessary that q'.

modus ponens – Latin, 'method of putting'. A rule for correct DEDUCTION of the form: 'If p then q; p; therefore q'. It is also called 'affirming the antecedent'.

modus tollens – Latin, 'method of taking'. A rule for correct DEDUCTION of the form: 'If p then q; it's not the case that q; therefore it's not the case that p'. It is also called 'denying the consequent'.

Moleschott, Jacob – Dutch physiologist, a leading representative of scientific MATERIALISM.

Müller, Johannes Peter – German physiologist and anatomist, widely regarded as the founder of modern physiology.

momentum – The product of the mass and velocity of a particle.

monism – See DUALISM/MONISM, NEUTRAL MONISM.

Moore, G(eorge) E(dward) (1873–1958). English (Cambridge) philosopher; the father of ANALYTIC PHILOSOPHY, he also led the revolt against IDEALISM early this century. He was a frequent defender of common sense against abstruse philosophical theory and PARADOX, and for a philosophical method based on clarification and analysis of meanings.

moral statistics – The statistical presentation of regularity in free human acts which are posited under the influence of certain psychic, social, cosmic and other conditions (i.e. STATISTICS on marriage, suicide, crime, birth, automobile accidents). The philosophical meaning of such statistics lies in the fact that they impressively point up the intimate relationship between a person's motive for acting and the psychological/physiological conditions she finds herself in. They demonstrate the impossibility of unmotivated willing, but they do not prove whether or not, in a particular case, a person acted without freedom (a moderate DETERMINISM). The metaphysical question about the freedom of the will cannot be decided by the use of statistical methods.

morality – From the Latin *moralis*, which is equivalent to *éthikos*, meaning 'custom' or 'usage'. One's morality is one's tendency to do right or wrong, or one's beliefs about what is right and wrong, good or evil. In many usages, it is a synonym of 'ETHICS', although the latter term is generally used to designate the philosophical study of these matters. The term was introduced to philosophy by Cicero (106–43 BC), the Roman statesman, orator and political writer.

morphology – From the Greek *morphé*, 'form', and *logos*, 'knowledge'. In biology, this is the study of the form and structure of plants and animals considered apart from function; while in linguistics, it is the formal arrangement and interrelationship of morphemes or the branch of this discipline which studies these, the smallest meaningful units of language.

multiple regression – A technique which determines the optimum weighting of a number of independent variables in order to predict a single dependent variable.

mysticism – From the Greek *mystés* meaning 'one initiated into the mysteries'. A variety of religious practice that relies on direct experience, supposedly of God and of supernatural truths. Mystics often advocate exercises or rituals designed to induce the abnormal psychological states in which these experiences occur. They commonly hold that in these experiences we achieve union with God or with the divine ground of all being.

natural/artificial language – A natural language is one used by an actual group of people, that has developed on its own, culturally and historically. An artificial language, by contrast, is one developed for some purpose. Philosophers use the term to refer especially to ideal languages, the development of which is one of the aims of symbolic LOGIC. Computer languages are also examples of artificial language.

natural science – The collective sciences or any science that deals with the physical universe, such as biology, CHEMISTRY and physics.

necessary/contingent truth – According to conditions of modality (concerning the mode – actuality, possibility, or necessity – in which anything exists) a PROPOSITION is necessarily true if it is certifiable on A PRIORI grounds, or on purely logical grounds. It is a stronger kind of truth than a contingent truth of a proposition which could have been otherwise, but is not as a mere matter of fact. Many philosophers think that the necessity or contingency of some fact is a metaphysical matter – a matter of the way the way the external world is – while others think that this difference is merely a matter of the way we think and conceive of the world – that a truth taken to be necessary is merely a conceptual or logical or ANALYTIC truth. See LOGIC, METAPHYSICS, CONCEPT/CONCEPTUAL.

Neurath, Otto – Austrian philosopher; one of the original members of the VIENNA CIRCLE. With CARNAP, he invented the doctrine of PHYSICALISM, stressing the role of PROTOCOL STATEMENTS, i.e. statements based on observation and referring to SPACE–TIME states.

neuropsychology – A sub-discipline within physiological psychology that focuses on the interrelationships between neurological processes and behaviour.

neutral monism – A theory of mind–body relations, found in the philosophies of JAMES and RUSSELL, which is not dualistic, nor monistic in the conventional sense. According to this theory, minds and bodies do not differ in their intrinsic nature; the difference between them lies in the way that a common ('neutral') material is arranged. This material is not one entity (monism), but consists of many entities (i.e., experiences) of the same fundamental kind.

Newton, Sir Isaac (1642–1727) – Renowned English mathematician and scientist. In his *Mathematical Principles of Natural Philosophy* (1685–87), he not only announced his discovery of the Law of Gravity but also presented a new system of mechanics by which the structure of the universe was to be understood. He sought the true mechanical laws of nature not on the basis of A PRIORI principles but on the basis of the most precise observation of phenomena in nature. One of the important consequences of this work lay in his development of the proper methods of reasoning; he claimed that philosophy's error in seeking the nature of reality was in its insistence on making DEDUCTIONS from phenomena without knowing first the CAUSES of phenomena.

Newtonian mechanics – The basis of Newtonian mechanics consists of three fundamental laws of motion: Law I, every body perseveres in its state of rest or uniform motion in a straight line except in so far as it is compelled to change that state by forces impressed on it (the Principle of Inertia). Law II, the rate of change of linear MOMENTUM is proportional to the force applied, and takes place in the straight line in which that force acts. Law III, an action is always opposed by an equal reaction: the mutual actions of two bodies are always equal an act in opposite directions.

It was Newton's great achievement to have worked out the mechanics of celestial and terrestrial motion which gave modern science a solid basis for the continual development which has since occurred. A more general system of mechanics has been given by Einstein in his theory of RELATIVITY.

This reduces to Newtonian mechanics when all velocities relative to the observer are small compared with those of light.

nihilism – From the Latin *nihil*, 'nothing'. A doctrine denying VALIDITY to any positive alternative, the term has been applied to METAPHYSICS, EPISTEMOLOGY, ETHICS, politics and theology. It is the name of various sorts of negative belief: that nothing can be known, or that nothing generally accepted in science or religion is correct or that the current social order is worthless, or that nothing in our lives has any value.

nomological – From the Greek *nomos* 'law' and *logos*, 'knowledge'. It is synonymous with 'nomic', meaning having to with law. A nomological regularity is distinguished from a mere (accidental) regularity or coincidence, in that the first represents a law of nature.

normative – Tending to establish a standard of correctness by prescription of rules; evaluative rather than descriptive. Normative ETHICS – any system dictating morally correct conduct – is distinguished from meta-ethics – the discussion of the meanings of moral terms without issuing directives.

number – A concept of quantity. Natural numbers: $\{1,2,3,4\ldots\}$; whole numbers: $\{0,1,2,3,4\ldots\}$; integers: $\{-3,-2,-1,0,+1,+2,+3\}$. There is also the set of real numbers which is composed of both rational and irrational numbers: the former are expressed as fractions (i.e., $\frac{1}{2}$), while the latter are non-rational, and not expressible as an integer (i.e., $\sqrt{2}$). A complex number is the sum of a real number and an imaginary one (i.e., $3+2i$, where i is imaginary). A cardinal number describes how many members are in a set of things, which could be either INFINITE (i.e. $\{2,4,6,\ldots\}$) with no last number in the sequence, or finite (i.e., $\{2,4,6,8\}$).

null hypothesis – See HYPOTHESIS.

objective – (1) Possessing the character of a real object existing independently of the knowing mind, in contrast with SUBJECTIVE, as that within a subject. (2) In scholastic terminology, beginning with Duns Scotus (1266/74–1308) and continuing into the seventeenth and eighteenth centuries, objective designated anything existing as idea or representation in the mind, without independent existence. The change from sense (2) to (1) was made by KANT, who understood objective as in the first sense.

Occam's razor (or **Ockham's**) – A general principle of ontological economy that states that, everything else being equal, the correct or preferable explanation is the one that is simpler, i.e., that needs fewer basic principles or fewer explanatory entities. It was named after William of Occam (1285?–?1349), the English theologian whose work was largely in LOGIC and theory of meaning. See ONTOLOGY.

ontology/ontological – From the Greek *ontos*, 'of being' and *logos*, 'knowledge'. The term thus means 'knowledge of being' and refers to the philosophical study of being or existence. Although the relation between METAPHYSICS and ontology is unclear, typical questions which concern the latter are: What basic sorts of things exist? What are the basic things out of which others are composed? How are things related to each other? The ontology of a theory consists of the things which are presupposed by that theory. Simply put, 'ontological' means 'having to do with existence'.

opacity and transparency, referential – The distinction that expresses that Leibniz's law is not universally applicable. For example, 'Cicero' and 'Tully' have the same reference in that they are two names for the same man. But suppose that someone, X, does not know this: then it might be true (a) that Cicero is believed by X to have denounced Catiline, and (b) that Tully is believed by X not to have denounced Catiline. In other words, although they are the same man, contrary to Leibniz's law, Cicero does not appear to have every property that Tully has. It is usual to call ' ... is believed by X to have denounced Cataline' the context of the use of the term 'Cicero'; in the case considered, the context is said to be 'referentially opaque'. In cases where Leibniz's law is satisfied, the context is said to be 'referentially transparent'. This distinction refers to terms, predicates or PROPOSITIONS and the wider distinction between intensional or extensional contexts which are created upon their removal from a sentence. See LEIBNIZ'S LAW, EXTENSION/ INTENSION.

operationism – The view that scientific concepts are to be defined in terms of experimental operations, and that the meaning of these terms is given by these procedures. Operationists argue that any terms not definable in this way should be eliminated from science as meaningless. With respect to QUANTUM physics, this would mean referring to the existence of particles as visual effects which exist under certain conditions, when certain measurements are carried out. However, they are realists in that they hold that the objects science theorizes about are (sometimes) true. It is contrasted with the anti-REALISM of INSTRUMENTALISM, although they share an emphasis on understanding science in terms of its experimental means.

operator/logical operator – That which effects an operation and in LOGIC is usually expressed as a SYMBOL. Corresponding to each FUNCTION on objects there is a symbolic operation effected by the symbol for that function. Thus, if $f(x)$ is a function and a an object, $f(a)$ is an object – the object generated from a by application of $f(x)$. But '$f(a)$' is a name formed by conjoining the symbol 'f' for the function with the name 'a', 'f' is then an operator on names of objects, and is a name-forming operator; that is, when applied to the name of an object, the result is another name. Logical operators are the truth-functional operators and quantifiers. (see QUANTIFICATION). The former are also called sentential operators because, when applied to sentences, they yield another sentence.

'order from disorder' principle – The idea that all events happen from definite causes, according to definite laws and a certain necessity, if only our knowledge could encompass the full scope of these seemingly random events throughout eternity. It entails reasoning from indeterminacy to determinacy and the methodological movement from CHANCE and PROBABILITY to CERTAINTY. See METHODOLOGY, RANDOMNESS.

ordinary language philosophy – A branch of twentieth-century philosophy (most closely associated with WITTGENSTEIN, AUSTIN and RYLE) that held that philosophical problems arise because of confusions about, or complexities in, ordinary language. These might be solved (or dissolved) by attention to the ways the language is used. Thus, for example, problems about free will might be solved (or shown to be empty) by close examination of the actual use in English of such words as 'free', 'will', 'responsible', and so on.

organizational theory – Generally, this is the sociological study dealing with the patterned behaviour of interacting individuals or groups. More specifically, it may refer to the interaction between people in a particular organization, e.g. in industry, the armed forces, etc. It is usually undertaken with a view to making the organization more efficient and concerns itself with issues like improving relations between management and workers, improving communication channels or improving decision-making procedures.

orientalism – A general designation used loosely to cover the philosophical tradition of the Orient, extending far into antiquity and to some extent characterizing early Greek thinking. Oriental philosophy, though by no means homogeneous, nevertheless shares one characteristic: the practical outlook on life (ETHICS linked with METAPHYSICS), involving an absence of clear-cut distinctions between pure speculation and religious motivation, often combining folklore, folk etymology, practical wisdom, pre-scientific speculation, even magic, with flashes of philosophical insight.

oscillator – A system which rhythmically stores and releases energy at a particular frequency (e.g., an electric circuit in which electrical oscillations occur freely and which is usually designed specifically for this purpose).

paradigm – From the Greek *paradeigma* 'a pattern, model or plan'. A completely clear, typical and indisputable example of a kind of thing.

paradox – A clearly false or self-contradictory conclusion deduced apparently correctly from apparently true assumptions. There are many kinds of paradoxes and philosophers often find principles of wide-ranging importance while trying to discover what has gone wrong in a paradox. There is a whole family of them known as the self-referential paradoxes which has been of particular concern to philosophers and logicians, and some of which have played a crucial role in the historical development of the foundations of mathematics. One example is the well-known statement of a Cretan that 'All Cretans are liars', the Liar paradox, while another is Russell's paradox which had serious repercussions in the theory of classes and thus also in the foundations of mathematics. See RUSSELL'S PARADOX, TYPES, THEORY OF.

parapsychology – The investigation of prescience, telepathy and other alleged psychical phenomena which seem to elude ordinary physical and physiological explanation.

pari passu – Latin, meaning 'with equal pace'; simultaneously and equally.

Pascal, Blaise – French philosopher, mathematician and physicist, who made great contributions to science through his studies in hydrodynamics and the mathematical theory of PROBABILITY. Dissatisfied with experimentation, he turned to the study of man and spiritual problems.

path analysis – The analysis of relationships among a series of variables which attempts to establish a CAUSAL chain between them, usually by the use of MULTIPLE-REGRESSION – a technique which determines the optimum weighting of a number of independent variables in order to predict a single dependent variable. The method is generally presented in path diagrams in which asymmetric (one-way) relations between variables are represented by arrows.

Pavlov, Ivan Petrovich – Russian physiologist and pioneer of the study of conditioning. In his study of digestion which won him a Nobel Prize, he observed that dogs salivated in anticipation of receiving food, a response which by 1901, he had named a 'conditioned REFLEX'. This became a cornerstone of American BEHAVIOURISM before World War I and is now regarded as a fundamental aspect of learning.

Peano, Guiseppe (1858–1932). – Italian mathematician who made several contributions to MATHEMATICAL LOGIC. He developed a logical system which permits the writing of every PROPOSITION exclusively in SYMBOLS, in an attempt to emancipate the strict logical part of reasoning from verbal language and its vagueness. Among his contributions to the field of mathematics was a postulate system known as Peano's Postulates, from which the entire arithmetic of natural NUMBERS can be derived. See 'PEANO'S ARITHMETIC'.

Peano's arithmetic – This designates Peano's five postulates for the arithmetic of natural NUMBERS. In the first version, the first postulate referred to 1 as the first number, while in the later versions, as here, he began with o as the first number: (P1) o is a number (P2). The successor of any number is a number (P3). No two numbers have the same successor. (P4) o is not the successor of any number (P5). If P is a property such that: (a) o has the property P; (b) whenever a number n has the property P, then the successor of n also has the property P, then every number has the property P. The last AXIOM is the famous 'principle of mathematical induction'.

Pearson chi-square (x^2) tests – There are several statistical tests included here, all of the them variations of the basic chi-square statistic (the use of a theoretical model to determine expected results and to gauge the differences between expectation and observation). They are used as tests of the amount of data conformity between a large sample and a population and as tests of association between two samples.

Peirce, Charles Sanders (Santiago) – American philosopher and logician. Very little of his work was published during his life, and his views were, until recently, unknown except in the version popularized by JAMES. Today, however, he is recognized as a metaphysician of considerable power, the father of PRAGMATISM, and a significant contributor to philosophy of SCIENCE and LOGIC.

phenomenalism – Literally, a theory based on appearances. This is a doctrine which holds that the knowledge man can reach is never more than the knowledge of phenomena, because man's limited ability to know necessarily deforms objects according to one's own SUBJECTIVE nature.

phenomenology – A school of philosophy deriving from the thought of Husserl (1859–1938). Phenomenologists generally believe that INTUITIONS or direct awarenesses form the basis of truth, and the foundation on which philosophy should proceed: by introspection, bracketing, and exploration of the 'inner', SUBJECTIVE world of experiences. This takes the form of a phenomenological reduction in which normal assumptions and PRESUPPOSITIONS (particularly those of science and including belief in the external world) are suspended and we attempt to see things purely, as they fundamentally appear to consciousness.

phenomenon – From the Greek *phainomenon*, meaning 'that which appears'. Philosophers sometimes use this term in the ordinary sense, referring merely to something that happens, but often it is used in a more technical way, referring to the way a thing seems to us – to something as we perceive it. It is contrasted with noumena which are insensible and perhaps rationally ascertainable things as they really are, i.e., things-in-themselves.

photon – The QUANTUM of electromagnetic radiation. For some purposes photons can be considered as elementary particles travelling at the velocity of light. See ELECTROMAGNETISM.

philosophy of mathematics – see MATHEMATICS, PHILOSOPHY OF.

physicalism – Although this term is usually taken to be synonymous with MATERIALISM – which refers to the philosophical position that all that exists is physical – it may also refer to the position that everything is explainable by physics. It constitutes a doctrine of the VIENNA CIRCLE of logical positivists requiring that PROTOCOL STATEMENTS of any HYPOTHESIS be expressed in a physicalistic language.

picture theory – WITTGENSTEIN's theory of language which holds that the primary purpose of language is to state facts. When a fact is pictured there is a structural similarity between the language used and what is pictured. A secondary purpose of language is to state tautologies, which are true but empty. They tell us nothing but that their use is necessary. The operations of both LOGIC and mathematics are series of tautologies. Any statement which fails to picture a fact, or to express a tautology, is nonsense. Statements of both METAPHYSICS and ETHICS fall into this category. See TAUTOLOGY.

Planck, Max Carl Ernst Ludwig (1858–1947). – German physicist, famous for his enunciation of QUANTUM theory. He introduced the findings of his early work on THERMODYNAMICS into the problem of black-body radiation, in search for a theoretical explanation for the equilibrium reached within a heated cavity based on temperature only, independent of wall density. Drawing upon the relationship between ENTROPY and PROBABILITY put forth by BOLTZMANN, Planck introduced a quantum variable of action (h) with a discrete spectrum for radiation into his account. The result was his celebrated formula for radiation density as a function of frequency and temperature, from which he was able to calculate BOLTZMANN'S CONSTANT and his own quantum of action.

Plato (428?–348? BC) Ancient Greek philosopher, student of SOCRATES, possibly the greatest philosopher of all time. His writings, which often take the form of dialogues with Socrates, contain the first substantial statements of many of the questions and answers in philosophy. His best-known doctrine is the theory of the 'forms' or 'ideas': these are the innate, general or perfect versions of characteristics we ordinarily encounter. They are eternal and unchanging and exist independently of any earthly thing that participates in them.

Platonism – Various sorts of views growing from aspects of PLATO's thought. Platonists tend to emphasize Plato's notion of a transcendent reality, believing that the visible world is not the real world, and Plato's rationalism – that the important truths about reality and about how we ought to live are truths of reason. In the philosophy of MATHEMATICS, Platonism designates the belief that mathematical objects exist independently of our thought; that mathematical statements are true (or false) independently of our ability to prove them; and often includes the view that the subjects of these statements

(NUMBERS) are abstract entities, the relations of which true mathematical statements describe.

pluralism – The view that the world contains many kinds of basic entities, which in their uniqueness cannot be reduced to just one (MONISM) or two (DUALISM). The doctrine of LOGICAL ATOMISM developed by RUSSELL is perhaps the most thoroughgoing pluralism in the history of philosophy.

Poincaré, (Jules) Henri (1854–1912). – French mathematician, engineer and philosopher of SCIENCE. He is often labelled a conventionalist because he argued that the fundamental AXIOMS of geometrical systems express neither A PRIORI necessities nor CONTINGENT TRUTHS, and because he detected important definitional elements in physics. In mathematical philosophy he was an intuitionist, attacking the LOGICISM of RUSSELL and PEANO. See CONVENTIONALISM, INTUITIONISM.

Popper, Karl Raimund – Austrian philosopher of SCIENCE, famous for his emphasis on falsifiability rather than on verifiability in science. This means that the most reliable criterion for truth lies in hypotheses which can be disproved by negative instances. He is also known for his defence of liberalism in social theory. See HYPOTHESIS.

positivism/logical positivism – The philosophy associated with Auguste COMTE, which holds that scientific knowledge is the only valid kind of knowledge, and that anything else is idle speculation. In its earlier versions, the methods of science were held to have the potential not only of reforming philosophy, but society as well. Sometimes this term is loosely used to refer to logical positivism which is a twentieth-century outgrowth of more general nineteenth-century positivism.

post hoc – Latin, 'after that'. A mistaken kind of reasoning, also known as false CAUSE, which states '*post hoc ergo propter hoc*' ('after that, therefore because of that'). It involves the misidentification of *x* as the cause of *y* because *x* happens before *y* (for example, if one supposed that a falling barometer caused it to rain).

pragmatism/neo-pragmatism – From the Greek *pragma*, 'thing, fact, matter, affair'. A philosophical movement in the nineteenth and twentieth centuries whose emphasis lay in interpreting ideas through their consequences. As a school of philosophy, it is associated mainly with American philosophers in the beginning of the twentieth-century, especially PEIRCE, JAMES and Dewey. Peirce, who adapted the term from KANT in 1878, later called his version 'pragmaticism' in order to distinguish the original philosophy from the neo-pragmatism which was less strictly defined. The early pragmatists emphasized the relevance of the practical application of things, their connections to our lives, our activities and values. They demanded instrumental definitions of philosophically relevant terms, deeming much of the language of METAPHYSICS meaningless, and urged that we judge beliefs on the basis of their benefit to the believer.

praxis – In general this term means 'accepted practice or custom' or 'practical human activity', but more particularly, as it was used by Marx, it refers to the union of theory and practice.

predicate calculus – See PROPOSITIONAL/PREDICATE CALCULUS.

presupposition – Something assumed beforehand, for example, as the basis of an argument. The statement 'He has stopped drinking excessively' presupposes that at one time he was drinking excessively.

prima facie – Latin, 'at first appearance'. Based on the first impression: what would be true, or seem to be true, in general, or before additional information is added about the particular case. Thus, philosophers speak of '*prima facie* obligations', those things that by and large people ought to do, but that might not be real duties in particular cases, given additional considerations.

private language argument – WITTGENSTEIN'S argument which states that if there were private events we would be unable to categorize or talk about them. In order for it to be possible to name or categorize something, there must exist rules of correct naming and categorization. Without the possibility of public check, there would be no distinction between our feeling that we reported them accurately and our really doing so, such that nothing could count as our doing so correctly or incorrectly. Thus, there could be no such thing as a 'private language' – a language naming private events.

probability – From the Latin *probare*, 'to prove, to approve', which is related to the Greek *eulogon* meaning 'reasonable or sensible'. The term thus refers to the likelihood of the happening of an event, or of the truth of a PROPOSITION. Where conclusions follow by necessity in deductive INFERENCE they follow only by probability in INDUCTION. Probability theory has been developed into a very sophisticated theory in modern mathematics. When probability is represented by a given number, it is usually on a scale from 0 (impossible) to 1 (definite). To say that something is probable may be to say that it has a probability of more than 0.5. There has been philosophical controversy about what it really means to say that an event has a certain probability. Some philosophers argue that saying a die has a probability of $\frac{1}{6}$ of coming up six means that one is justified in expecting it to come up six only to the degree $\frac{1}{6}$, or that this number should measure the strength of this belief.

problem of 'other minds' – The problem which questions the ground (if any) there is for thinking that anyone else has a mind, and is not, for example, just a body with external appearance and behaviour like one's own. It hinges on the fact that a person's mind and its contents can only be 'perceived' by that person who is thus unable to perceive anyone else's. Some philosophers (RYLE, for example) think that the absurdity of this problem shows that there is something wrong with the view of the mental that leads to it.

procedural explanation – A type of explanation that uses simulation to arrive at solutions to problems. Central to this approach is the idea of representational knowledge about the world as procedures within a system. In behavioural science it provides an alternative to causal or quasi-causal modes of explanation. It may also refer to programs in a computer language in which the meanings of words and sentences are conveniently expressed, and the execution of these programs corresponds to reasoning from the meanings.

proposition – From the Latin *proponere*, 'to set forth or propose'. This term has been used in a variety of ways. Sometimes it means merely a sentence or a statement. Perhaps the most common modern use is the one in which a proposition is what is expressed by a (declarative) sentence: an English sentence and its French translation express the same proposition, and so do 'Steven is Ed's father' and 'Ed's male parent is Steven'.

propositional function – A technical term due to RUSSELL, used to denote that for which a predicate of predicate LOGIC stands. An n-place predicate, when complemented by n singular terms, yields a sentence that expresses a PROPOSITION about the objects denoted by those terms. The n-place propositional function for which the predicate stands is such that when applied to n objects, the result is a proposition concerning those objects. Just as two different sentences may express the same proposition, two different predicates may stand for the same propositional function.

propositional/predicate calculus – The two logical calculi most commonly encountered. Any FORMAL system of LOGIC can be called a propositional calculus if it consists of a specification of a formal language, the SYMBOLS of which are either propositional variables or connectives (where the latter represent such connectives as 'and', 'or', 'not', 'if... then'), and a set of AXIOMS and/or rules governing the connectives of the language. 'Propositional calculus' usually refers to any system in which the formally VALID arguments can be shown to be valid by application to the standard two-valued truth-table definitions of the logical connectives. It is also known as 'sentential' logic or calculus (see VALIDITY).

Used without qualification, predicate calculus usually means 'classical first-order predicate calculus'. This is the system obtained by extending the axioms and/or rules of propositional calculus by adding similar ones for the quantifiers which are designed to treat universally quantified sentences as INFINITE conjunctions and existentially quantified sentences as infinite disjunctions. It deals with sentences using logical terms such as 'all', 'some', 'no', or 'there exists at least one'. It is also known as 'quantifier' logic or calculus. See QUANTIFICATION, UNIVERSAL/EXISTENTIAL.

protocol statement – A statement consisting of an observation report describing directly given experience or sense data. Also called 'basic sentences', these were regarded by logical positivists of the VIENNA CIRCLE as the basis of all science, and of intelligibility in any field. CARNAP argued that protocol statements can be expressed in the language of physics.

Ptolemy, Claudius – (second century AD) Hellenic scientist and philosopher. His great work in astronomy dealing with all of the planets and 1,022 stars, published around AD 150, held the earth to be a globe in the centre of the world system, and the heavens to make a diurnal revolution around an axis passing through the centre of the earth. This system was accepted until COPERNICUS in the sixteenth century. His philosophy was influenced by Platonism, Stoicism and neo-Pythagoreanism, as well as by ARISTOTLE.

quantification, universal/existential – In traditional LOGIC, quantification is the consideration of the totality of objects under discussion in a statement, which necessarily precedes the assessment of its truth or falsity. Universal quantifier is the name given to the notation (x) prefixed to a logical formula A (containing the free variable x) to express that A holds for all values of x – usually, for all values of x within a certain range or domain of values, which either is implicit in the context or is indicated by the notation through some convention. Similarly, existential quantifier is the name given to the notation

Ex prefixed to a logical formula *E* (containing the free variable *x*) to express that *E* holds for some (i.e. at least one) value of *x* – usually, for some value of *x* within a certain range or domain. The *E* which forms part of the notation is often inverted, and various alternative notations also occur.

quantum field theory – A quantum mechanical theory in which particles are represented by FIELDS whose normal modes of oscillation are quantized. Elementary particle interactions are described by relativistically invariant theories of quantized fields. In QUANTUM ELECTRODYNAMICS, for example, charged particles can emit or absorb a PHOTON, the quantum of the electromagnetic field. Quantum field theories naturally predict the existence of antiparticles and both particles and antiparticles can be created or destroyed; a photon can be converted into an electron plus its antiparticle, the positron. These theories provide a proof of the connection between spin and the STATISTICS underlying the Pauli exclusion principle.

quantum/quanta – From the Latin *quantum*, 'how much'. Used in philosophy to refer to a FINITE and determinate quantity, the term has passed into physics where its reference is to the packets of energy, or quanta, the basic indivisible units of QUANTUM MECHANICS.

quantum electrodynamics – A relativistic theory of QUANTUM MECHANICS concerned with the motions and interactions of electrons, muons and PHOTONS, i.e., with electromagnetic interactions. Its predictions have proven highly accurate.

quantum mechanics – A system of mechanics used to explain the behaviour of atoms, molecules, and elementary particles. In 1901 PLANCK suggested that energy must be radiated in discrete units or quanta. In 1913 BOHR applied this theory to the structure of the atom; later his 'solar system' model of the atom was superseded by the formal equations of Heisenberg and SCHRÖDINGER. These yield the required predictions of the frequency and amplitude of radiation emitted by the atom. But one consequence, the uncertainty principle, discovered by Heisenberg in 1927, is that the variables usually interpreted as specifying the position and the MOMENTUM of sub-atomic particles cannot both take definite values simultaneously. This places severe limits on the degree to which these particles or wave-packets can be interpreted as ordinary spatio-temporal objects. The problem thus becomes a locus of dispute between realist and formalist philosophies of science. In addition the conception of fundamental particles as more like disembodied waves than particles challenges a simple material view of the world.

Quetelet, Lambert Adolphe Jacques – Belgian statistician and astronomer. He was DURKHEIM's predecessor and the founder of social physics. In his greatest book, *Sur L'Homme* (1835), he showed the use that may be made of the theory of probabilities, as applied to '*l'homme moyen*' or average person.

Quine, Willard Van Orman (1908–) – Contemporary American philosopher, professor at Harvard since 1946. Known primarily as a logician, his interests and important works extend over many of the basic problems in SEMANTICS, EPISTEMOLOGY and METAPHYSICS.

Ramsey, Frank Plumpton – English mathematical philosopher. Expanding upon the logical problems raised by RUSSELL and WITTGENSTEIN, he made a fundamental distinction between *human* LOGIC, which deals with useful mental habits and is applicable to the realm of practical probability, and *formal* logic, which is concerned exclusively with the rules of consistent thought.

randomness – In common usage something happens randomly when it is not determined by previous events. In PROBABILITY theory, though, in order for an event to be random it must be equally as likely to occur as any other. It defines equiprobability just as it is defined by it. With respect to human action it must be distinguished from arbitrariness as this applies to the random behaviour of unpredictable particles in QUANTUM MECHANICS.

realism/anti-realism – From the Latin *res* meaning 'thing', from which *realitas* is also derived. Realism is, in general, the view that some sort of entity has external existence, independent of the mind. Anti-realists think that that sort of entity is only a product of our thought, perhaps only as a result of an artificial convention. Realists quarrel with anti-realists in many philosophical areas: in METAPHYSICS, about the reality of UNIVERSALS, and in ETHICS, about the reality of the moral categories. Scientific realists sometimes hold that theoretical entities are mind-independent, or that laws in science reflect external realities (i.e. are not merely humanly constructed), or that the universals discovered by science are real and mind independent.

reducibility, axiom of – Russell's axiom, necessary in connection with the ramified theory of types, if that theory is to be adequate for classical mathematics, but the admissibility of which has been much disputed. An exact statement of the axiom can only be made in the context of a detailed formulation of the ramified theory of types, although it might be said that it cancels a large part of the restrictive consequence of the prohibition against impredicative definition, and reduces that theory to the simple theory of types. See TYPES, THEORY OF.

reductionism – The attempt to reduce one science to another by demonstrating that the key terms of the one are definable in the language of the other, and that the conclusions of the one are derivable from the PROPOSITIONS of the other. Reductionism about some notion is the idea that that notion can be reduced – can be given a 'reductive analysis' – and perhaps that it thus can be eliminated. In the social sciences, it operates by holding that social phenomena can be defined in terms of the sum of individuals' behaviour, such that any statement about a social phenomena may be reduced to what individual people do, and social theory may be in principle be reduced to psychology.

reflex/reflex theory – A reflex is an immediate, unlearned response to a specific stimulus. The reflex theory of action was proposed by DESCARTES (1650); Marshall Hall (1833) and CABANIS (1802) were among the first to relate the concept to the nervous system. PAVLOV's work on reflex-action, which has become a standard topic in psychology, is often associated with reflexology. This is a mechanistic, behaviouristic point of view that argues that all psychological processes may be represented as reflexes and combinations of reflexes. See MECHANISM.

refutation – The demonstration by means of argument that some position is mistaken. This is not merely an attempt at rebuttal, but properly speaking, a demonstration successfully showing that a claim is false or position untenable.

relative truth/relativism – Truth which may vary from individual to individual, group to group, time to time, having no OBJECTIVE standard and usually implicated in a subjectivistic theory of knowledge. In EPISTEMOLOGY and ETHICS, relativism denotes the theoretical position which emphasizes this kind of truth. See ABSOLUTIST/RELATIVIST DEBATE.

relativity, special/general theories of – The former contains the famous $E = MC^2$ formula, while the latter deals with SPACE–TIME curvature. The special theory of 1905, entails EINSTEIN's rejection of the notion of an ABSOLUTE SPACE AND TIME. The new view holds that SIMULTANEITY can be established only within a given inertial system, and will not be valid for observers in systems which are in motion relative to the given system. According to this demonstrable theory, mass increases and time slows down as velocity increases, and time is regarded as a fourth dimension. The consequences are such that the same event, viewed from inertial systems in motion with respect to each other will occur at different times, bodies will measure out at different lengths, and clocks will run at different speeds.

The general theory of 1916 generalized the results of the special theory from inertial systems to non-linear transformations of co-ordinates. This was necessary in order to account for the proportionality between gravitational mass and inert mass. In the theory, gravitation is reduced to or is an effect of space–time curvature, and depends upon the masses distributed through the universe. Thus, the concept of action at a distance is discarded. Confirmation of the general theory is much weaker than that of the special theory, but the bending of light rays as they pass through a strong FIELD of gravitation has apparently been observed. One consequence of this theory is that the universe is FINITE but unbounded and it is thus consonant with the cosmological picture of an expanding universe.

Royce, Josiah – American philosopher, influenced by Hegel, who developed his own philosophy of absolute IDEALISM. He argued that to have a conception of an orderly continuous world it is necessary to assume that there is an 'absolute experience to which all facts are known and all facts are subject to universal law'.

Russell, Bertrand (Arthur William) (1872–1970). British philosopher. He is perhaps the best-known philosopher of the twentieth century, as well as the founder (with WHITEHEAD) of contemporary symbolic LOGIC. He was also the leader (with MOORE) of the twentieth century revolt against IDEALISM, though some of his views – for example, on our knowledge of externals – tended to be less in accord with common sense than Moore's. Owing to his pacifism, his criticism of Christianity and his advocacy of freer sexual morality, he was a controversial public figure; his views even led him to be fired from teaching positions and jailed.

Russell's paradox – The PARADOX concerned with the set of sets which are not members of themselves (i.e., is a set a member of itself? If it is, it isn't. If is isn't, it is). It has resulted in some complications in set theory. See SET THEORY, TYPES, THEORY OF.

Ryle, Gilbert – English (Oxford) philosopher and leading early figure in ANALYTIC PHILOSOPHY and ORDINARY LANGUAGE PHILOSOPHY. He did important work in philosophy of LOGIC and of mind; in *The Concept of Mind* (1949), his key work, he argued that cartesian DUALISM was based on a category mistake.

Saussure, Ferdinand De – Swiss linguist and philosopher, known for his work on structural linguistics and his influence on contemporary French STRUC-TURALISM.

scepticism – From the Greek *skepsis*, 'consideration' or 'doubt'. The view that reason has no capacity to come to any conclusions at all, or else that reason is capable of nothing beyond very modest results. This position questions not so much the truth of a particular belief, but the VALIDITY of the justifications for it. In fact, consistent scepticism is close to agnosticism and NIHIL-ISM. The more extreme sceptics are often called Pyrrhonists, after Pyrrho the founder of the sceptical tradition. HUME is known as a champion of modern scepticism.

Schlick, Moritz (1882–1936). – German founder of the VIENNA CIRCLE, leading figure in the development of logical POSITIVISM. His own view was called 'Consistent Empiricism'.

Schröder, Ernst – German logician and mathematician. He systematized and completed the work begun by BOOLE and DE MORGAN in the ALGEBRA of LOGIC. His contributions to the algebra of relations have particular importance.

Schrödinger, Erwin (1887–1961). – Austrian physicist, born and educated in Vienna. He was the founder of WAVE-MECHANICS and originator in 1926 of the Schrödinger equation describing the QUANTUM behaviour of electrons and other particles. This PRESUPPOSED EINSTEIN'S treatment of light as PHOTONS associated with electromagnetic waves, but taken one step further to the development of a fundamental differential equation which was seen to govern particle behaviour in a wave FIELD. He also proved that this theory was mathematically equivalent to matrix mechanics and along with Heisenberg, BOHR, Pauli and Dirac, played a vital role in the in the creation of modern quantum theory.

science, philosophy of – A discipline which attempts to relate philosophy to the fields of scientific enquiry. Depending upon the philosopher and the area of science, its goal is to discover the nature of science, or the nature of scientific method, or the LOGIC of science, or to explore the interfaces of the fields of science, or to axiomatize the sciences. It involves the question of what constitutes genuine science from pseudo-science, and considers the empirical collection of data and inductive extrapolations, as well as the role of valid explanations, models and theories, and to what extent these correspond to objective reality (realism vs. anti-realism and instrumentalism). Although the philosophy of science extends back to the origins of Western philosophy, when emphasis was on scientific knowledge, it is more appropriate to regard it as beginning with the remarkable development of the sciences in the modern period.

semantics – From the Greek *sēmantikos*, 'significant meaning', which is from *sema*, 'sign'. Semantics is that part of language which has to do with meaning and reference. The term was first used in a technical sense in philology, where it stands for the historical study, empirically oriented, of the changes of meanings in words. In philosophy, semantics is usually considered as the study and interpretation of formal SYMBOLS. It is concerned with the relations between signs and the objects which they designate, mostly in contrast with SYNTAX which designates the rules of FORMALISM in themselves.

sensationalism – From the Latin *sensatio*, which is from *sentire*, 'to feel or perceive'. Subvariety of EMPIRICISM which asserts that all knowledge is ultimately derived form sensations. Hobbes is considered the founder of modern sensationalism and Condillac is its most typical exponent.

sense and reference – These terms render a distinction drawn by FREGE. The 'sense' (*Sinn*) of an expression is its meaning, as opposed to that which the expression names, its 'reference' (*Bedeutung*). Expressions can have different meanings, but the same reference: e.g. 'the Morning Star' does not mean the same as 'the Evening Star', but both have the same reference, the planet Venus. The terms are synonomous with connotation and DENOTATION.

sense modality – In BEHAVIOURAL SCIENCE, under the general heading of sense, there are its primary modalities. Five criteria distinguish these: they have (1) different receptive organs, that (2) respond to characteristic stimuli. Each set of receptive organs has (3) its own nerve that goes to (4) a different part of the brain, and (5) the resultant sensations are different on the basis of these criteria. Nine senses have been identified: vision, audition, kinesthesis, vestibular, tactile, temperature, pain, taste and smell.

set theory – Sets (or classes) occur naturally in mathematics, but their importance was only appreciated after G. Cantor (1845–1918) had developed the theory of INFINITE sets. His ideas formed the basis for the LOGIC of FREGE and RUSSELL. The discovery of various PARADOXes showed that the naive theory of classes is contradictory (i.e., sets which are, and at the same time, are not, members of themselves). Cantor himself made a distinction between collections (such as the totality of all abstract objects) which are too all-embracing to be treated as wholes and smaller totalities (such as the set of all real NUMBERS) which can be regarded as single objects; nowadays the former are called proper classes, the latter are called sets.

Shannon, C(laude) E(lwood) – American applied mathematician, engineer and pioneer of COMMUNICATION THEORY.

Sherrington, Sir Charles Scott – British physiologist and philosopher. He did his epoch-making work on the REFLEX response of the spinal cord, with a detailed anatomical study of the structure of the nervous system. It has been said that modern neurophysiology owes not only its basic theories but also its nomenclature to Sherrington. As a philosopher, he was concerned with the 'mind–brain' problem, taking a firmly dualistic line, but imposed on it his own concept of integrative function by which the action of the nervous system is coordinated.

simpliciter – Latin, meaning 'simply'. Without qualification, not just in certain respects.

simultaneity – To be truly simultaneous events must occur not only at the same time but also at the same place. For example, an event on Jupiter might be observed to occur simultaneously with an event on Earth. However, as the two events occur in different frames of reference, and as the information cannot travel from one frame to the other faster than the speed of light, the two events would not, in fact, have occurred simultaneously.

sine qua non – Latin, meaning 'without which not'; indispensable condition or qualification.

Sinn – See SENSE AND REFERENCE.

Skinner, B(urrhus) F(rederic) – American psychologist; the developer of operant-conditioning techniques. He showed that animal and human behaviour could be modified by reinforcement and that animals could in this way be trained to carry out particular tasks to obtain reward, or avoid punishment. These came to be widely used in the training and studying of animals, and in the modification of human behaviour in teaching and clinical situations. He promulgated a philosophy of BEHAVIOURISM.

social anthropology – Also known as cultural anthropology, the study of the culture and social structure of a community or society including its psychological factors. It emphasizes the understanding of the total configuration and interrelationships of cultural traits, complexes, and social relationships in a particular geographic environment and historical context. There has been a tendency in recent years to extend its range of study from non-Western societies to modern Western culture.

sociology – From the Greek *socio*, 'to associate', and *logos*, 'knowledge'. The term is taken to refer to a study of the forms, institutions, functions, and inter-relations of human groups. The term was introduced by Auguste COMTE to designate a new science, the most comprehensive of all, dealing with social phenomena. The character he expected of the discipline is suggested by the term 'social physics', his original name for the subject.

Socrates (470?–399 BC). – Athenian philosopher whose debates were chronicled by PLATO. Extremely influential for his 'dialectical' method of debate in which he led his opponents to analyse their own assumptions and reveal their inadequacy. He rejected the sceptical and relativistic views of the professional rhetoricians of the day, urging a return to ABSOLUTE ideals. He was condemned to death for impiety and corrupting the youth.

solipsism – From the Latin *solus*, 'alone' and *ipse*, 'self'. The doctrine that the individual human mind has no grounds for believing in anything but itself. The consequence is sometimes drawn that the mind coming to that conclusion constitutes all there is of reality. The first claim may be termed 'epistemological solipsism', while the latter view, often drawn as a *reductio ad absurdum* of the first, may be called 'metaphysical solipsism'.

space–time – A four dimensional order with four coordinates, three of them spatial (length, width, height) and one temporal; the unity of space and time. Specification of the coordinates precisely locates any physical magnitude whatever. The concept was first suggested by Minkowski and soon after adopted by EINSTEIN. While in classical or Newtonian theory, space–time is separable in an ABSOLUTE way, in Einstein's RELATIVITY theory, this is impossible in an absolute sense but is relative to a choice of a coordinate system.

Spinoza, Benedict (or **Baruch**) (1632–77). – Dutch Jewish philosopher. He argued that nature is a unity, equivalent to a highly abstract and all-pervasive God, and that its facts are necessary and can be derived by a method of rigourous 'proof' (as in geometry). Believing that humans were part of nature, Spinoza was a thoroughgoing determinist.

spiritualism – From the Latin *spiritus*, 'breath, life, soul, mind, spirit'. This term has both philosophical and religious meanings. In the first sense, spiritualism is the doctrine that the ultimate reality in the universe is Spirit (*Pneuma*,

Nous, Reason, *Logos*), akin to human spirit, but pervading the entire universe as its ground and rational explanation. It is sometimes used to denote the IDEALISTIC view that only an ABSOLUTE Spirit and FINITE spirits exist, and that the world of sense is a realm of ideas. Religious spiritualism emphasizes the direct influence of the Holy Spirit in the sphere of religion, indicating especially the teaching that God is spirit, and that worship is direct correspondence of Spirit with spirit.

'states of affairs' – See ELEMENTARY PROPOSITION.

statistics – Very generally, this is the branch of mathematics, pure and applied, which deals with collecting, classifying and analysing data. More specifically, in terms of its various breeds in psychology (i.e. descriptive, inferential), statistics refers to sets of procedures developed to describe and analyse particular types of data and enable a researcher to draw various kinds of conclusions on their basis. While in popular usage, it refers to numbers used to represent facts or data.

Stevenson, C(harles) L. – American philosopher, known for his work in ETHICS, and particularly for his views on ethical language. He held that ethical terms have emotive as well as cognitive meaning and have the power to produce affective responses in those who hear and use them. What is involved in ethical discourse, in his view, is the reinforcing or redirecting of attitudes through the affective power of emotive meaning.

stochastic – Meaning 'having to do with PROBABILITY'. A stochastic (as opposed to deterministic) law predicts outcomes as only probable.

structuralism – A method of approach with wide-ranging applications, rather than a distinct philosophy. Its focus is the irreducible structural units that constitute the MORPHOLOGY of a system (i.e., phonology of language, the formal structure of mathematics, the underlying organization of society). The central ideal of structuralism is that cultural phenomena should be understood as manifesting unchanging and universal abstract structures or forms, the meaning of which can be understood only when these forms are revealed.

sub specie aeternitatis – Latin, 'under the view or aspect of eternity'. The phrase used to signify the attempt to see things at once in one thought without any past or future, as a species of eternity – as God might grasp them. The term is commonly associated with SPINOZA.

subjective/subjectivism – Any variety of views that claim that something is subjective – that is, a feature of our minds only, not of the external 'OBJECTIVE' world. Ethical subjectivism, for example, holds that our ethical judgements reflect our own feelings only, not facts about externals.

substance – From the Latin *sub* 'under' and *stare* 'to stand'. Generally, the stuff out of which things are made. The term refers to both the underlying, supporting substratum of something, as well as the individual subject which remains the same through time despite changes in characteristics. It may also mean 'ESSENCE', as that which something really is, despite the way that it appears. In terms of LOGIC, substance is defined according to the notions of subject and predicate; regarded this way S is a substance if S is a subject of predicates, but cannot be predicated in turn of any other subject. This conception can be traced back to ARISTOTLE and plays an important part in the philosophy of LEIBNIZ.

sufficient reason, principle of – A principle of LEIBNIZ, stating that for every fact there is a reason why it is so and not otherwise. Thus, reason takes the form of an A PRIORI proof founded on the nature of the subject and predicate terms used in stating the fact. Leibniz used the principle freely; to prove, for example, that there could not be two identical atoms (for there would be no reason for one to be in one place and the other somewhere else, rather than vice versa) or that the world did not begin at a moment in time (for there would be no reason for it to have begun at one moment rather than another).

syllogism – A form of deductive argument, in which one PROPOSITION, the conclusion, is inferred from two other propositions, the premises. For example, 'All Greeks are rational, all Athenians are Greek, therefore all Athenians are rational'. A syllogism has only three terms; the subject term and the predicate term, called 'minor' and 'major', respectively; the other term, which occurs only in the premises, is called the 'middle' term. The forms of a valid syllogism were first studied systematically by ARISTOTLE, and the theory of the syllogism forms a large part of what is termed 'traditional LOGIC.'

symbols – Philosophers often use symbols to abbreviate logical connections, with letters standing for terms or sentences. For instance, suppose B stands for property of being bald. If f stands for Fred, Bf stands for the sentence 'Fred is bald'. With respect to quantifier LOGIC in which A, the universal quantifier, signifies 'all', the formula $(Ax)(Bx)$ means 'Everything is bald'; or likewise, in the case of the existential quantifier E, $(Ex)(Bx)$ means 'Something is bald'. The equals sign (=) means 'is identical with'.

   In sentential logic, there are many symbols that refer to logical connections between sentences, the latter of which are usually abbreviated by capital letters. Here are some examples: the ampersand (&) and the dot ($\cdot$) are commonly used to stand for 'and'; the horseshoe on its side and the arrow ($\rightarrow$) are used for 'if ... then'; the wedge or vee (V) stands for the inclusive 'or'; the tilde or curl ($\sim$) stands for 'not', where $\sim P$ means 'it is not the case that P'; another negation symbol is '–'; the triple bar ($\equiv$) or the double arrow ($\leftrightarrow$) stands for 'if and only if'; etc.

synapse – From the Greek for 'juncture' or 'point of contact'. The functional junction between the axon and the dendrite of two neurons by which nerve impulses flow. The term was coined by SHERRINGTON in 1906.

syntax – The aspect of language which has to do with grammar or logical form. It can tell you whether a sentence is formed correctly but cannot tell you what a correctly formed sentence means, which is the realm of SEMANTICS. The study of syntax, which is part of the general theory of signs, is called syntactics.

synthetic – See ANALYTIC/SYNTHETIC.

systems analysis – Generally and collectively, the processes and operations involved in the designing, implementing and coordinating of the various components of any complex system. More specifically, it is characterized by the use of systematic analytical procedures derived from industrial/organization psychology and assisted by the techniques of computer science to understand the workings of complex organizations, to identify problems and sources of error and to make recommendations for more efficient and effective structures.

Tarski, Alfred (1902–) Polish–American mathematician and logician. He is the founder of SEMANTICS.

tautology – In ordinary language a tautology says the same thing twice, but in LOGIC, it is used to describe a PROPOSITION which is true by virtue of its form alone. It is sometimes used as a synonym for logical truth, and for some, every definition is tautological. In terms of truth tables a tautology is a statement form, all of whose substitution instances are true. While one might say then that a tautology is necessarily true, some might hold that although this is true, the truth in question is vacuous. WITTGENSTEIN divided meaningful propositions into two classes: those which picture facts, and those which express tautologies.

taxonomy – From the Greek meaning 'laws of arrangement'. Any systematic set of principles for classification and arrangement.

teleology – From the Greek *telos*, 'end', and *logos*, 'discourse' or 'doctrine'. The study of aims, purposes or functions as well as the doctrine that ends, final CAUSES or purposes are to be invoked as principles of explanation. In general, much of traditional philosophy viewed nature and the universe in terms of teleology. The term itself was introduced in the eighteenth century by Christian Wolff.

Theaetetus (*c.* 414–369 BC) – Theaetetus was a Greek mathematician who joined PLATO in founding the Academy of Athens and whose work was later used by EUCLID. Plato's dialogue *Theaetetus* is devoted to the question of the definition of knowledge.

thermodynamics, first and second law of – The study of the interrelation between heat and other forms of energy. The first law of thermodynamics states simply that heat is a form of energy and that in a closed system the total amount of energy of all kinds remains constant through time. It is therefore the application of the principle of CONSERVATION of energy to include heat energy. The second law deals with the direction in which any chemical or physical process involving energy takes place: it is impossible to construct a continuously operating machine which does mechanical work and which cools a source of heat without producing any other effects. The energy in a closed system tends to decrease with time, while the ENTROPY tends to increase.

transcendental – The sort of thought that attempts to discover the (perhaps universal and necessary) laws of reason, and to deduce consequences from this about how reality must be understood by any mind. KANT used this kind of reasoning – the 'transcendental argument' – to argue in favour of A PRIORI metaphysical truths.

transparency, referential – See OPACITY AND TRANSPARENCY, REFERENTIAL.

truth function – A PROPOSITION is a truth function if, and only if, its truth or falsity is determined by the truth or falsity of its component propositions. For example, to say that 'p and q' is a truth function is to say that, once we can answer the questions (1) 'Is p true? (2) 'Is q true?' we are in a position to answer the question 'Is "p and q" true?'. See FUNCTION.

Turing, Alan Mathison – British mathematician, biologist and philosopher. He was the key figure, along with VON NEUMANN, in the conception of electronic digital computers and ARTIFICIAL INTELLIGENCE, as well as the concepts of mind that arose alongside of these. He developed the Turing machine, a computer prototype, and queried whether the human mind functioned in an analogous manner or could be simulated by such a machine. He claimed that the success of such a simulation of mind could be gauged, and developed an intelligence test for this purpose. It is known as the 'Turing Test', in which a man's responses to a series of questions is measured against those of a computer (responding by teletype) in an attempt to distinguish which is which. Given that only mental attributes can be questioned in this behaviour-istic model, the computer's superior mathematical skills may provide an objection to the test. Turing left the question of whether the machine was conscious open.

types, theory of – A theory devised by RUSSELL to avoid the logical PARADOXes and antinomies which arise from self-reference. Deciding that no class could be a member of itself, he concluded that the class is of a higher type than its members. In the assertion 'Socrates is human', the predicate is thus of a higher type than the subject. In the simple theory of types, the initial type level is that of individuals followed by properties of individuals, properties of properties, etc. While this solved the logical paradoxes, it did not touch certain semantical paradoxes (i.e. the Grelling paradox which distinguished between predicates which have the properties they DENOTE (autological) and those that do not (heterological). The paradoxical question is whether the predicate 'heterological' is autological or heterological). These led Russell, along with WHITEHEAD, to develop the ramified theory of types. Here atten-tion is given not only to the elements of the simple theory but also to the hierarchy of orders – first/second/third . . . order FUNCTIONS, each function quantifying over a lower type. A 'type fallacy' occurs when this logical hierarchy is disregarded.

universals – These are 'abstract' things – beauty, courage, redness, etc. The problem of universals is, at core, the question of whether these exist in the external world – whether they are real things, or merely the result of our classification (non-existent if there were no minds). Thus, one may be a realist or anti-realist about universals. PLATO's theory of forms is an early example of REALISM in this sense, while ARISTOTLE and the empiricists are associated with anti-realism. Nominalism is a variety of anti-realism that claims that such abstractions are merely the result of the way we use language.

validity – In common usage an argument is valid if it is permitted by the laws of LOGIC. In fact, the question of the validity of a conclusion is independent of the question of the truth of the premises, which bears upon the 'sound-ness' of an argument. In deductive arguments, the conclusion is sound given the truth of the premises, while in inductive arguments, the truth of the premises only makes the conclusion more probable. Although in both cases, with the proper logical connections intact, the arguments may be valid. See DEDUCTION/INDUCTION.

verification principle/criterion of verifiability – Advocated by the logical positivi-sts, this criterion states that any statement that is not verifiable is meaningless. For example, since it might be thought impossible to find evidence for or against the statement that 'God loves us', they would deem this statement not false (or true), but meaningless. Empiricists in general tend to share this position. Some logical positivists used this criterion to argue that statements in METAPHYSICS and ETHICS were meaningless. Further, some of them, including A. J. SAYER, thought that the verification principle provided the definitive answer to questions about meaning. This holds that the meaning of a sentence can only be specified by giving its procedures of verification.

verificationism – In this position, it is argued that scientific work consists of the attempt to substantiate (verify) the correctness of a theory by logical and EMPIRICAL means. It is usually contrasted with falsification, a younger point of view associated with POPPER, that holds that scientific theories cannot be proven to be true but only subjected to attempts at REFUTATION. From this point of view, a scientific theory is accepted, not because it is demonstrably a correct codification of a class of phenomena, but because it has not yet been shown to be false.

Vienna Circle – A group of philosophers who met in Vienna and elsewhere during the 1920 and 1930s. It included SCHLICK, CARNAP, and GÖDEL, among others, and was deeply influenced by WITTGENSTEIN. Reacting against the continental ways of thought that surrounded them, these philosophers produced the groundwork of logical POSITIVISM and proved very influential on future ANALYTIC PHILOSOPHY, especially in Britain and the United States, where many members moved during the rise of Hitler.

virtual particle – A particle which is created for short periods of time where its creation would normally violate the CONSERVATION law of energy and mass. This is due to the uncertainty principle, the consequence of which states that any measurement of a subatomic system must disturb the system under investigation. There is a resulting lack of precision, particularly when the lifetime of a particle is short, and a high degree of uncertainty with respect to its energy.

vitalism – From the Latin *vita*, 'life'. The doctrine that phenomena of life possess a particular character by virtue of which they are distinct from the physico-chemical phenomena of the body and from the mind. Vitalists ascribe the activities of living organisms to the operation of a 'vital force' and are opposed to biological MECHANISTS who assert that living phenomena can be explained exclusively in physico-chemical terms.

volition – The exercise of the will – the power of deciding, desiring, or wanting.

von Neumann, John – Hungarian-born Princeton professor, one of the outstanding mathematicians of this century. He contributed to the development of atomic energy, built one of the first electronic computers, designed many nuclear devices and contributed to game theory – a branch of mathematics concerned with PROBABILITY in its approach to the problem of strategy.

Waisman, Friedrich (1896–1959). – Austrian- born philosopher. Assistant to SCHLICK in Vienna, he moved to Cambridge to study with WITTGENSTEIN where he later taught. Beginning as a logical POSITIVIST committed to mathematical rigour, he came to hold the position that linguistic methods held more promise in dealing with the problems of philosophy.

Watson, John Broadus (1878–1958). – American psychologist, the founder of BEHAVIOURISM. Influenced by SKINNER, and in response to the introspectionist psychology of his day, Watson held that psychology could only become a productive science, like other NATURAL SCIENCES, if it was OBJECTIVE and dealt with the observable. He launched the movement with his 1913 paper 'Psychology as the Behaviourist Sees It', which was followed by numerous influential articles and books.

wave mechanics – One of the forms of QUANTUM MECHANICS that developed from the theory that a particle can also be regarded as a wave. Wave mechanics is based on the SCHRÖDINGER wave equation describing the wave properties of matter. It relates the energy of a system to a wave function, and in general it is found that a system (such as an atom or molecule) can only have certain allowed wave functions and certain allowed energies. In wave mechanics the QUANTUM conditions arise in a natural way from the basic postulates as solutions of the wave equation.

weak/strong interaction – The interactions between elementary particles at the subatomic level which are, along with gravity and ELECTROMAGNETISM, two of the fundamental FORCES of nature. The weak force produces radioactive decay and the strong force permanently binds quarks (the three known basic particles). Weak interaction, compared with strong, is a trillion times weaker, and when strong interactions take place the weak are unimportant.

Weierstrass, Karl – One of the greatest German mathematicians of the nineteenth century; a teacher of Cantor. He worked in mathematical analysis, in the theory of FUNCTIONS and on ideas that had troubled mathematicians since ancient times: INFINITY and irrational NUMBERS.

Weltanschauung – German, meaning 'world-view, perspective of life, conception of things'.

Weyl, Hermann – German–American scientist and philosopher. Making contributions to both geometry and RELATIVITY theory, his philosophical interest was in philosophy of MATHEMATICS and PHILOSOPHY of science.

Whewell, William (1794–1866). English philosopher. Interested in the methods of the INDUCTIVE sciences, he suggested the importance of 'colligation' in the ordering of scientific data – i.e., finding the conception which allows one to see the facts as connected – and thereby assimilating induction to the hypothetico-deductive method.

Whitehead, Alfred North (1861–1947). – English (Cambridge) philosopher and logician, who developed, with RUSSELL, the first modern systematic symbolic LOGIC. He is also known for his 'process' philosophy in which change, not SUBSTANCE, is fundamental, and in which purpose is a feature of the external world.

Wiener, Norbert (1894–1964). – American mathematician and founder of CYBERNETICS. He joined the faculty of MIT at twenty-five and later, with Arturo Rosenblueth formed an interdisciplinary group in the late 1930s, whose meetings were concerned with scientific method and the unification of science, and from which the concept of cybernetics emerged. The central core of his theories which were inspired by the development of the computer have been developed under the label 'ARTIFICIAL INTELLIGENCE'. This has taken over the concept of man as 'machine-like' and revolutionized the terms in which perception, learning, thinking and language have been conceived of since. He wrote a number of articles with Rosenblueth and Julian Bigelow on the philosophical aspects of cybernetics, involving VITALISM and Bergsonian time and was concerned with the social dangers of this viewpoint in terms of the need for social evolution to accommodate the rapid technological advances.

Wittgenstein, Ludwig (Josef Johann) (1889–1951). – Austrian-born, he taught at Cambridge and did much of his work in England, where his thought was greatly influential on recent philosophical trends. This is especially true of logical POSITIVISM and ORDINARY LANGUAGE PHILOSOPHY the latter of which he may be seen as the father. His *Tractatus Logico-Philosophicus* (1922) became of immediate consequence to philosophy and drew him permanently into the discipline. He engaged many of the technical problems of contemporary philosophy but is best known for his view of philosophy as therapy, designed to cure puzzles and confusions resulting from misunderstandings of the function of parts of language. He set up a system of linguistic analysis by which any statement must satisfy certain logical conditions before being admitted as a proper philosophical statement. The tools of his system are symbols, which enable a thing to be *shown* in the event that it cannot, because of the limitations of language, be *said*.

Logic

algorithm – See DECISION PROCEDURE.

ampliative argument – An argument or inference whose conclusion goes beyond the information contained in its premisses; an argument in which the premisses fail to provide conclusive evidence for the conclusion. Ampliative arguments include inductive (or non-monotonic) inferences as well as inferences to the best explanation. They may be either acceptable or unacceptable depending upon their strength or weakness.

antinomy – Any paradoxical statement such that its truth leads to a contradiction and the truth of its denial leads to a contradiction; a paradox.

argument – The inference of a conclusion from premisses; a set of sentences (or propositions) supporting or purporting to justify such an inference.

axiomatic system – A logistic system or logical calculus which includes a set of axioms as part of its primitive basis; to be contrasted with a natural deduction system.

belief dynamics – The standard name for theories of belief revision, which are designed in such a way as to model changes in one's belief set which come about both as a result of the acceptance of new beliefs and the revision of old beliefs.

bivalence – The property of a logic in which each well-formed formula has one of exactly two possible truth values: truth and falsehood.

Boolean algebra – A formal system introduced by George Boole which models logical relations algebraically by defining the operations, ∩ (or ×, representing intersection), ∪ (or +, representing union) and ' (or –, representing complementation) over a set of elements representing propositions.

bound variable – A variable which falls within the scope of a quantifier; a variable, x, to which a quantifier, such as ∃ or ∀, applies.

calculus – Another name for a logistic system.

Cantor's theorem – The theorem, proved by Georg Cantor in 1891, that the cardinality of the set of all subsets of a given set (the power set of that set) is always greater than that of the set itself. Alternatively, the theorem that the set of real numbers is non-denumerable (or, equivalently, that the cardinality of the set of real numbers is greater than that of the set of natural numbers). Cantor proved both versions of the theorem by means of a diagonal argument.

cardinality – The property of a set associated with the cardinal (or counting) number that measures the number of its members.

category theory – The mathematical study of structures and structure-preserving mappings (or morphisms); the study of mathematical categories, which are defined as sets of objects together with associated sets of morphisms (or arrows) which satisfy certain conditions.

Church's theorem – The metatheorem, proved by Alonzo Church in 1936, that there is no effective decision procedure for determining whether an arbitrary well-formed formula of first-order logic is a theorem. Equivalently, the theorem that the valid formulas of the predicate calculus do not form a general recursive set. Also called the Church–Turing theorem.

Church's thesis – The thesis, suggested by Alonzo Church, that every effectively calculable function (or equivalently, every decidable predicate) is general recursive. Also called the Church–Turing thesis.

classical logic – Any logic for which bivalence holds; alternatively, the propositional and predicate logics originally developed by Gottlob Frege and modified over the years by his successors.

closed sentence – A well-formed formula or sentence in which all variables are bound; to be compared with an open sentence.

combinatory logic – A branch of formal logic which contains functions capable of playing the role of variables in ordinary logic; hence, a branch of logic in which variables are eliminated.

compactness theorem – The metatheorem, proved by Kurt Gödel in 1930, stating that in first-order logic any collection of well-formed formulas of a given language has a model if every finite subset of the collection has a model.

completeness – The property of a logistic system, introduced by E. L. Post, in which for any well-formed formula, either that formula is a theorem of the system or, if added to the system as an axiom, the resulting system would be inconsistent. Alternatively (but not equivalently), the property of a logistic system, introduced by Kurt Gödel, in which all valid well-formed formulas expressible in the system are theorems of the system. In the former sense, the classical propositional calculus but not the pure first-order predicate calculus is complete; in the latter sense, both are complete.

computability – Intuitively, the property of being able to compute a function. A computable function is thus any function for which there exists an effective, finite, mechanical procedure (or algorithm) for calculating a solution. One precise notion of effective computability is that given by the notion of a Turing machine; another is that of a general recursive function.

conclusion – That which is inferred from or purportedly justified by the premisses of an argument.

confirmation theory – The theory of the degree to which evidence supports (or confirms) a given hypothesis; the theory of rational degrees of confidence that a cognitive agent should have in favour of a hypothesis, given some body of evidence.

connective – A symbol used to join one or more propositional constants or forms. The result is a new constant or form. Standard connectives include symbols representing negation ($\sim$), conjunction (&), (inclusive) disjunction ($\lor$), material implication ($\rightarrow$), and material equivalence ($\leftrightarrow$).

consistency – The property of a set of statements or propositions or of a logistic system in which no contradiction (the joint assertion of a proposition and its denial) can be derived. Alternatively (but not equivalently), the property, introduced by Alfred Tarski, of a logistic system that not every well-formed formula is a theorem. Alternatively (but not equivalently), the property, introduced by E. L. Post, of a logistic system that no well-formed formula consisting of only a propositional variable is a theorem. Alternatively (but not equivalently), the property of a logistic system of having a model. This last is called the semantic definition of consistency.

constructivism – The view that satisfactory proofs (and definitions) refer only to entities which can be successfully constructed or discovered. Thus, constructive proofs, unlike indirect proofs or proofs by *reductio ad absurdum*, are ones which allow us to find examples, or to find algorithms for finding examples, of each set of objects which purportedly have some given property, *P*.

continuum hypothesis – The hypothesis, suggested by Georg Cantor, that there is no set with cardinality greater than that of the natural numbers but less than that of the power set of the natural numbers. When generalized, the hypothesis states that there is no set with cardinality greater than a given infinite set but less than that of the power set of that set.

Cook's theorem – The theorem, proved by Stephen Cook in 1971, that the problem of satisfiability is at least as difficult to solve as is any NP-complete problem.

counterfactual – A conditional sentence in which the antecedent is false.

decision problem – The problem of finding an effective, finite, mechanical decision procedure (or algorithm) for arriving at an answer to a given question. Typically, the most common decision problem with regard to logistic systems is the problem of determining whether an arbitrary, well-formed formula of the system is a theorem of the system. A positive solution to a decision problem is a proof that an effective decision procedure exists. A negative solution to a decision problem is a proof that an effective decision procedure does not exist. An example of a positive solution is the proof that truth tables provide an effective decision procedure for the propositional calculus. An example of a negative solution is Church's theorem for the predicate calculus.

decision procedure – A procedure for coming to a decision with regard to a given question. The procedure is said to be effective, or to be an algorithm, provided that it results in the correct answer following a finite number of mechanical steps.

decision theory – The theory of selection under various conditions of risk and uncertainty; the theory of rational choice, given that each option has associated with it an expected probability distribution of outcomes, gains and losses. Decision theory, together with game theory, is often called the theory of practical rationality.

deducibility – The relation, symbolized ⊢ and contrasted with entailment, that holds between a statement (or proposition), C, and a set of statements (or propositions), P, provided that C is provable from P.

deduction – An argument or inference in which the conclusion, C, is provable from the premises, P. Alternatively, but less commonly, an argument or inference in which the premises provide conclusive evidence for the conclusion; a valid argument or entailment.

deduction theorem – The metatheorem that states that, in a given logistic system, if $s_1, s_2, \ldots, s_n \vdash s_{n+1}$, then $s_1, s_2, \ldots, s_{n-1} \vdash s_n \rightarrow s_{n+1}$.

deductive logic – The formal study of deductions or of arguments or inferences in which the premises provide conclusive evidence for the conclusion.

default logic – A form of nonmonotonic logic which permits the acceptance or rejection of certain types of default propositions simply in the absence of information to the contrary.

denumerable – A denumerable set is any set whose cardinality is equal to that of the natural numbers, the smallest of infinite sets. A non-denumerable set is one whose cardinality is greater than that of the natural numbers; to be contrasted with an enumerable set.

deontic logic – Any logic emphasizing inferential relations and entailments which result from deontic properties of sentences, such as obligation and permission, and obtained from a classical logic, such as the propositional calculus or the predicate calculus, by the addition of axioms and rules of inference governing operators such as O and P in 'Op' ('it ought to be the case that p') and 'Pp' ('it is permissible that p').

detachment – The rule of inference (also called *modus ponens*) that, given well-formed formulas of the form p and $p \rightarrow q$, one can infer a well-formed formula of the form q.

diagonal argument – An argument introduced by Georg Cantor to show that certain sets have distinct cardinalities; a method or procedure for constructing objects on the basis of other objects in such a way that the new objects are guaranteed to differ from the old. When generalized, this method becomes one of the most powerful tools in metamathematics.

entailment – The relation, symbolized ⊨ and contrasted with deducibility, that holds between a statement (or proposition), C, and a set of statements (or propositions), P, provided that C follows from P. Alternatively, an argument or inference in which the conclusion, C, follows from the premises, P, or in which the premises provide conclusive evidence for the conclusion. In this sense, entailment is often identified with validity, the property of being logically impossible that the premises should be true while at the same time the conclusion be false. Others suggest it be identified with a stronger relation in order to avoid the paradoxes of strict implication.

enumerable – An enumerable set is any set whose cardinality is equal to that of some (finite) natural number or to the cardinality of the set of natural numbers as a whole. A synonym of 'countable'; to be contrasted with a denumerable set.

433

epistemic logic – Any logic emphasizing inferential relations and entailments which result from epistemic properties of sentences and obtained from a classical logic, such as the propositional calculus or the predicate calculus, by the addition of axioms and/or rules of inference governing operators such as K and B in 'Kp' ('it is known that p') and 'Bp' ('it is believed that p').

erotetic logic – Any logic emphasizing inferential relations and entailments pertaining to questions and answers.

existential quantifier – A symbol such as '$\exists$' which is used in combination with a variable to represent the notion 'there exists'. For example, under the appropriate interpretation '$(\exists x)(x = x)$' could be used to symbolize 'There exists an x, such that x is identical with itself' or, more informally, 'Something is identical with itself'.

fallacy – An argument which although neither valid nor inductively strong is nevertheless persuasive; any error in reasoning.

finitary method (finitism) – A method of metamathematical research adhered to by David Hilbert and his followers which emphasizes the use of only finite, well-defined and constructible objects. Like constructivism, finitism holds that we cannot assert the existence of a mathematical object unless we can also indicate how to go about constructing it. Unlike constructivism, it also requires that one should never refer to completed infinite totalities.

finitism – See FINITARY METHOD.

first-order language – A language whose quantifiers and functions are allowed to range over only individuals. In contrast, the quantifiers and functions of higher-order languages may range over properties and functions as well as individuals.

first-order logic – The logic of valid inferences carried out in first-order languages; also called first-order predicate (or functional) logic. See predicate logic.

formal language – A collection of well-formed formulas together with an interpretation.

formal logic – The study of arguments whose validity or inductive strength depends exclusively or primarily upon the form or structure, rather than the material content, of their component statements or propositions.

formal system – Another name for a logical calculus.

formalism – A programme of research into the foundations of mathematics initiated by David Hilbert and using the finitary method.

formation rule – Any rule of a logistic system governing which combinations of (primitive) symbols constitute well-formed formulas.

formula – Any sequence of primitive symbols; sometimes used as a synonym for well-formed formula.

free logic – Any logic in which it is not assumed that names successfully refer; a logic without existence assumptions.

free variable – A variable which is not bound by a quantifier.

function – A many-one correspondence. Also called a map or mapping, a function is a relation which associates members, x, of one set, X, with some unique member, y, of another set, Y. We write $f(x) = y$, or $f: X \rightarrow Y$, and name X the domain and Y the range of the function f.

functional logic – Another name for predicate logic.

future contingents, problem of – The problem, first raised by Aristotle but popularized by Jan Łukasiewicz, of whether contingent statements concerning the future have truth-values prior to the time to which they refer.

fuzzy logic – An extension of logic which attempts to deal with imprecise information such as information conveyed through vague predicates or information associated with so-called fuzzy sets, sets in which membership is a matter of degree.

game theory – The mathematical theory of selection by two or more agents (or players) when the outcome is a function, not just of one's own choice or strategy, but the choices or strategies of other agents as well. Game theory, together with decision theory, is often called the theory of practical rationality.

general recursive function – A type of recursive function definable in terms of primitive recursive functions together with minimization.

Gentzen's consistency proof – The 1936 proof by Gerhard Gentzen, using transfinite induction up to the ordinal ε_0, that classical pure number theory is consistent.

Gödel numbering – The systematic assignment of natural numbers to the components and formulas of a formal system in such a way that, by studying the properties and relations of the correlated numbers, one is able to infer information about the syntax of the underlying formal system.

Gödel's completeness theorem – The metatheorem, proved by Kurt Gödel in 1930, that every valid well-formed formula of (pure) first-order predicate logic is a theorem of that system.

Gödel's incompleteness theorems – The two 1931 theorems of Kurt Gödel relating to the incompleteness of systems of elementary number theory. The first theorem states that any ω-consistent system adequate to express elementary number theory is incomplete in the sense that there is a valid well-formed formula of the system that is not provable within the system. (In 1936 this theorem was extended by J. B. Rosser to apply to any consistent system.) The second theorem states that no consistent system adequate to express elementary number theory can contain a proof of a sentence which states the system's own consistency.

halting problem – The problem of discovering an effective procedure for determining whether a computational device (such as a Turing machine) will ever halt, given arbitrary input.

higher-order language – A language whose quantifiers and functions are allowed to range over properties and functions as well as individuals.

higher-order logic – The logic of valid inferences carried out in higher-order languages.

imperative logic – Any logic emphasizing inferential relations and entailments which result from imperatives.

induction – An ampliative argument from empirical premises to an empirical conclusion. For example, in induction by simple enumeration, given observed objects a, b and c of some kind, G, if it turns out that a, b, and c also all have property F, then one might conclude that all future observed Gs will be F, or perhaps that all Gs are F. Inductions may be either acceptable or unacceptable depending upon their inductive strength or weakness.

inductive logic – The formal study of inductions, of ampliative arguments or inferences from empirical premisses to empirical conclusions, in which the premisses fail to provide conclusive evidence for the conclusion.

inductive strength – The degree of support a non-conclusive argument's premisses give to its conclusion. In cases where the conclusion is likely to be true given the premisses, the argument is said to be inductively strong. In cases where the conclusion is not likely to be true given the premisses, the argument is said to be inductively weak.

inference rule – Also known as a transformation rule, any justification of a well-formed formula within a logistic system of the form, 'Given well-formed formulas of the form $s_1, \ldots s_n$, infer a well-formed formula of the form s_m'.

informal logic – The study of arguments whose validity or inductive strength depends exclusively or primarily upon the material content, rather than the form or structure, of their component statements or propositions.

interpretation – The meanings of, or alternatively a method of assigning meanings to, a set of well-formed formulas or to a formal system. Thus, given a set, S, of well-formed formulas, an interpretation consists of a non-empty set (or domain), together with a function which (i) assigns to each individual constant found in members of S an element of the domain; (ii) assigns to each n-place predicate found in members of S an n-place relation of the domain; (iii) assigns to each n-place function-name found in members of S a function whose arguments are n-tuples of elements of the domain and whose values are also elements of the domain; and (iv) assigns to each sentence letter a truth value. Logical constants, such as those representing truth functions and quantifiers, are assigned standard meanings using rules (such as truth tables) which specify how well-formed formulas containing them are to be evaluated.

interrogative logic – Another name for erotetic logic.

intuitionism – A program of research into the foundations of mathematics initiated by L. E. J. Brouwer; a species of constructivism.

intuitionistic logic – A logic which formalizes the 'intuitionistic' view that the subject matter of mathematics consists of mental constructions made by mathematicians. Classical proofs (such as those which rely upon indirect proof or *reductio ad absurdum* arguments) are therefore not admissible since they do not contain the appropriate constructions. In intuitionistic logic, the sentence '$p \lor \neg p$' is not a theorem and the inferences from $\neg\neg p$ to p and from $\neg(\forall x)Fx$ to $(\exists x)\neg Fx$ are not allowed.

lambda calculus A logic governing the manipulation of functions, which gains its name from the notation used to name functions. Terms such as '$f(x)$' or the 'successor of y' are used to refer to objects obtained from x or y by the appropriate functions. To refer to the functions themselves, Alonzo Church introduced the notation which yields, respectively, '$(\lambda x)(f(x))$' and '(λy) (successor of y)'.

logic – The study of correct inference. Alternatively, the science of validity and of inductive strength, and of all formal structures and informal properties relating to correct inference. The term is also used as a synonym for 'logical calculus'.

logical calculus – Any systematic treatment of logical inference in which a primitive basis – consisting of a formal language, including a vocabulary of primitive elements and a set of formation rules (or grammar), and a logic, including a (possibly empty) set of axioms and a set of transformation rules – is explicitly stated in the system's metalanguage. Also called a formal system or a logistic system. The two most important classical logical calculi are the propositional (or sentential) calculus and the predicate (or functional) calculus.

logical constant – A symbol used to represent topic-neutral expressions which are relevant to a sentence's logical form. Standard logical constants include symbols used to represent truth-functions such as negation ($\sim$), conjunction (&), (inclusive) disjunction ($\vee$), material implication ($\rightarrow$), and material equivalence ($\leftrightarrow$), the universal and existential quantifiers ($\forall$ and $\exists$), the identity relation (=), and scope indicators (such as '('and')').

logical form – The structure of a sentence or argument relevant to that sentence or argument's logical relations. The logical form of an expression is typically obtained by making explicit the expression's logical constants and by substituting free variables for its non-logical constants. Logical form is contrasted with the material content (or subject matter) of the non-logical constants for which the free variables are substituted.

logical paradox – A paradox not involving semantic notions such as reference or truth; to be contrasted with a semantic paradox.

logicism – The doctrine, variously advanced by Gottlob Frege, Bertrand Russell, Alfred North Whitehead and others, that (some or all branches of) mathematics can reduced to logic. Specifically, it is the view that the concepts of (some or all branches of) mathematics can be defined in terms of purely logical concepts and that the theorems of (these same branches of) mathematics can in turn be deduced from purely logical axioms.

logistic system – Another name for a logical calculus.

Löwenheim–Skolem theorems – Any of a series of metatheorems relating to Leopold Löwenheim's 1915 theorem, that if there is an interpretation in which a well-formed formula is true, then there is an interpretation in which the formula is true and whose domain is enumerable, and to Thoralf Skolem's 1920 extension of this theorem.

many-valued logic – Any logic, such as that developed by Jan Łukasiewicz, which countenances more than the two possible classical truth values: truth and falsity.

material content – The subject matter of a sentence or argument, in contrast to the sentence or argument's logical form.

material implication – The truth function, normally written $p \rightarrow q$ or $p \supset q$, which is false if and only if p (its antecedent) is true but q (its consequent) is false.

material implication, paradoxes of – Any of a number of unintuitive (but, strictly speaking, non-contradictory) results to the effect that whenever the antecedent is false or the consequent is true in a material implication, the resulting implication will be true, regardless of its content; to be contrasted with the paradoxes of strict implication.

mathematical logic – Another name for formal logic, particularly for those branches of formal logic which rely upon mathematical tools and concepts, or which are suitable for expressing mathematical theories.

mereology – A logic emphasizing inferential relations and entailments which result from the relationship of whole and part.

437

metalanguage – A language used to talk about a (usually separate) language called an object language.

metalogic – A logical theory whose subject matter is a particular logical calculus or logistic system; the study of logical calculi from the point of view of a separate metalanguage.

metamathematics – The study of logistic systems used to model mathematical theories and in which formulas of the theory (such as axioms, theorems and proofs) are themselves assumed to be mathematical objects. Sometimes the term is restricted to proof theory, or to proof theory using only finitary methods.

metatheorem – A theorem proved in a metalanguage; a theorem of metalogic or metamathematics.

metatheory – A theory in a metalanguage concerning a separate theory or logistic system.

modal logic – Any logic emphasizing inferential relations and entailments which result from alethic modalities such as necessity, possibility and impossibility, and obtained from a classical logic, such as the propositional calculus or the predicate calculus, by the addition of axioms and rules of inference governing operators such as $\Box$ and $\Diamond$ in '$\Box p$' ('it is necessary that p') and '$\Diamond p$' ('it is possible that p').

model – An interpretation of a set of sentences (or of a logistic system) under which all sentences (or theorems) turn out to be true.

model theory – The study of interpretations of formal systems; the study of relations of (semantic) consequence between sentences (and sets of sentences) within an interpreted logistic system.

modus ponens – Another name for the rule of detachment.

multi-valued logic – A synonym for many-valued logic.

natural deduction system – A logistic system or logical calculus which avoids the use of axioms, relying instead upon a sufficiently powerful set of rules of inference; to be contrasted with an axiomatic system.

non-monotonic logic – The formal study of ampliative reasoning; a type of logic which is sensitive to changing evidence and so allows for the revision or overturning of previously proved theorems.

NP-complete – An abbreviation for 'non-deterministic, polynomial-time-complete', the property of the most difficult class of problems for which there is no polynomial time solution but whose solutions, if they exist, are checkable within polynomial time.

object language – A language referred to by a metalanguage. Alternatively, a language used to talk about (usually non-linguistic) objects.

ω-completeness – The property of a formal system in which, if it has as theorems that a given property, P, holds of all individual natural numbers, then it also has as a theorem that P holds of all numbers.

ω-consistency – The property of a formal system in which, if it has as theorems that a given property, P, holds of all individual natural numbers, then it fails to have as a theorem that P fails to hold of all numbers.

open sentence – A formula or sentence in which not all variables are bound. Alternatively, a predicate; to be contrasted with a closed sentence.

paraconsistent logic – Any logical calculus which is inconsistent in the sense that a contradiction (the joint assertion of a proposition and its denial) can be derived; but consistent in the sense (introduced by Alfred Tarski) that not every well-formed formula is a theorem.

paradox – The existence of apparently conclusive arguments in favour of contradictory propositions. Equivalently, the existence of apparently conclusive arguments both in favour of accepting, and in favour of rejecting, the same proposition. The distinction between logical paradoxes (such as Russell's paradox) and semantic paradoxes (such as the liar paradox) is due to Guiseppe Peano and Frank Ramsey.

Peano's postulates – A set of postulates introduced by Richard Dedekind and popularized by Guiseppe Peano which defines the set of natural numbers as a series of successors to the number zero.

pleonotetic logic – A synonym for plurality logic.

plurality logic – Any logic emphasizing inferential relations and entailments pertaining to relations of quantity and using plurality quantifiers such as most and few.

plurative logic – A synonym for plurality logic.

Polish notation – A logical notation devised by Jan Łukasiewicz which avoids the need for scope indicators (such as parentheses) in formal languages by using an unambiguous system of ordering. Thus, letting N represent negation, K represent conjunction, A represent disjunction (or alternation), R represent exclusive disjunction, C represent material implication, E represent material equivalence, L represent necessity, and M represent possibility, sentences such as $\sim (p \rightarrow (p \,\&\, q))$ and $\Box(p \rightarrow p)$ can be represented as $NCpKpq$ and $LCpp$, respectively.

predicate – An expression representing a condition or relation and which, when connected with one or more referring terms, forms a sentence. The resulting sentence is taken to be true when the predicate expresses a condition or relation that is satisfied by the referred-to entities, and false otherwise.

predicate logic – A logical calculus which analyses the relations between individuals and predicates within propositions (or statements), in additional to the truth-functional relations between propositions (or statements) that are analyzed within propositional logic. Each such system is based upon a set of individual and predicate (or functional) constants, individual (and sometime predicate) variables, and quantifiers (such as $\exists$ and $\forall$) which range over (some of) these variables, as well as the standard constants and connectives of the propositional calculus.

preference logic – Any logic emphasizing inferential relations and entailments which result from preferences.

premiss – One of a set of sentences (or propositions) which support or purport to justify a conclusion.

primitive basis – A set of primitive symbols, formation rules, axioms and inference rules (transformation rules) used to characterize a logicist system.

primitive recursive function – A type of recursive function definable by recursion and substitution from a set of fundamental functions including the constant functions, the projection (or identity) functions, and the successor function.

primitive symbols – A set of undefined symbols, including constants, variables, connectives and operators, used as the basic vocabulary of a language.

probability – A measure of the acceptability of a statement or proposition; a measure of likelihood.

probability theory – A mathematical theory of the acceptability of a statement or proposition, or of likelihood, axiomatized by Andrej Kolmogorov in 1933 as a non-negative real-value additive set function with a maximum value of unity.

proof – Any finite list of well-formed formulas in a logistic system, each of which is either an axiom of the system or results from the previous members of the list together with the inference rules of the system. The final formula in the list is said to be a theorem of the system.

proof theory – The study of the syntax of formal systems; the study of relations of (syntactic) deducibility between formulas (and sets of formulas) within a logistic system. Sometimes the term is restricted to the study of formal systems using only the finitary methods suggested by David Hilbert.

propositional function – A notion introduced by Gottlob Frege as a formal equivalent to that of a property; a function having as its domain a set of referring terms (such as individual constants) and as its range a set of propositions or truth values.

propositional logic – A logical calculus which analyses the truth-functional relations between propositions (or statements). Each such system is based upon a set of propositional (or sentential) constants and connectives (or operators) which are combined in various ways to produce sentences of greater complexity. Standard connectives include those representing negation (~), conjunction (&), (inclusive) disjunction (∨), material implication (→), and material equivalence (↔).

quantification theory – Another name for predicate logic.

quantifier – An operator, such as the existential or universal quantifiers, ∃ and ∀, first introduced by Gottlob Frege to indicate what was traditionally called the quantity of a proposition, namely, whether it was universal or particular.

quantum logic – A logic in which the law of distributivity fails; any logic designed to take account of the unusual entailment relations between propositions in theories of contemporary quantum physics.

recursion theory – The theory of recursive functions.

recursive function – Any of a set of functions which are said to be either primitive recursive or general recursive, and which are constructed from a set of fundamental functions by a series of fixed procedures. Specifically, a function is primitive recursive if it is definable by recursion and substitution from a set of fundamental functions including the constant functions, the projection (or identity) functions, and the successor function. A function is general recursive (or simply recursive) if it is definable in terms of the primitive recursive functions together with minimization.

recursive procedure – A procedure which is applied iteratively in such a way that each non-initial application is applied to the result of the previous application.

recursive set – Any set such that both it and its complement can be enumerated by recursive functions.

relevance logic – Any logic emphasizing inferential relations and entailments which involve connections of relevance between premises and conclusions, rather than simple classical derivability conditions; a type of paraconsistent logic involving an implication relation stronger than strict implication and designed to avoid the paradoxes of implication and of strict implication.

Russell's paradox – The most famous of the logical or set-theoretical paradoxes. The paradox comes from considering the set of all sets which are not members of themselves, since this set appears to be a member of itself if and only if it is not a member of itself. Discovered by Russell in 1901, the paradox prompted much work in logic and set theory during the early part of this century.

satisfiability – The property of an open sentence such that, given some non-empty domain of individuals, there is a possible assignment of individuals to the formula's free variables such that the resulting formula is true. Alternatively, the property of any set of sentences which can be given an interpretation, relative to a domain, such that all of the sentences turn out to be true. Thus, the problem of satisfiability is the problem, given an arbitrary set of sentences, of determining whether the set is satisfiable.

scope (of a quantifier) – The part of an expression to which a quantifier, such as $\exists$ or $\forall$, applies. Thus, a variable, x, falls within the scope of a quantifier provided that the quantifier applies to it.

second-order language – The most elementary of higher-order languages, in which quantifiers and functions are allowed to range over properties and functions of individuals, as well as individuals.

second-order logic – The logic of valid inferences carried out in second-order languages; the most elementary of higher-order logics.

semantic paradox – A paradox involving semantic notions such as reference or truth; to be contrasted with a logical paradox.

semantics – The meanings of the symbols of a formal system and the study of their properties and relations, including the theory of reference (or denotation) and the theory of meaning (or connotation).

sentential logic – Another name for propositional logic.

set – Intuitively, any collection of well-defined, distinct objects. The objects which determine a set are called the elements or members of the set. The symbol '$\in$' is regularly used to denote the relation of membership or elementhood. Thus '$a \in A$' is read 'a is an element (or member) of A' or 'a belongs to A'. Two sets are identical if and only if they contain exactly the same elements.

set theory – The systematic study of sets, their properties and relations. Motivated both by Georg Cantor's discovery of the set-theoretic hierarchy and by the paradoxes of naive set theory which accompanied it, the first standard axiomatization, Z, of the theory was provided by Ernst Zermelo in 1908.

Skolem–Löwenheim theorems – Another name for the Löwenheim–Skolem theorems.

Skolem's paradox – The unintuitive (but ultimately non-contradictory) result that systems for which Cantor's theorem is provable, and hence which must contain non-denumerable sets, nevertheless must be satisfiable, because of the Löwenheim-Skolem theorems, in an enumerably infinite domain.

soundness – The property of a logistic system in which all theorems of the system are valid well-formed formulas.

strict implication – A relation between two formulas, p and q, such that it is not possible that both p and $\sim q$. In such cases p is said to strictly imply q.

strict implication, paradoxes of – The unintuitive (but, strictly speaking, non-contradictory) results that a necessary proposition is strictly implied by any proposition and that an impossible proposition strictly implies all propositions, regardless of their content; to be contrasted with the paradoxes of material implication.

substitution – The rule of inference that, given one well-formed formula, one can infer a second well-formed formula from the first by uniformly replacing every variable of a given kind by some distinct variable.

successor – For a given member of an ordering, the member of the ordering which next follows.

symbolic logic – Another name for formal logic.

syntax – The symbols of a formal system and the study of their properties and relations, including the distinction between well-formed and ill-formed formulas.

tautology – Any compound sentence or formula of the propositional calculus which, because of its logical structure, is true regardless of the truth values of its constituent sentences.

temporal logic – Any logic which is sensitive to the tense of sentences and to the changing truth values of sentences over time; a logic emphasizing inferential relations and entailments which result from properties of tensed sentences.

tense logic – Another name for temporal logic.

theorem – Any well-formed formula of a logistic system which is provable within the system.

theory – Any set of well-formed formulas. Alternatively, a set of well-formed formulas closed under logical entailment.

transformation rule – Another name for an inference rule.

truth function – Any function whose arguments and values are truth values.

truth table – A matrix which lists the truth value of a compound proposition for all possible assignments of truth values to its constituent propositions.

truth value – In classical logic, the two abstract entities which serve as the reference of true and false sentences, respectively, truth and falsehood. In many-valued logics, any values which play similar roles.

Turing-computable – The property of any function capable of being computed by a Turing machine. The set of Turing-computable functions turns out to be identical to the set of general recursive functions. See Church's thesis.

Turing machine – A theoretical machine introduced by Alan Turing in order to make precise the idea of (effective) computability. Intuitively, the machine can be thought of as a computer which manipulates information contained on a linear tape (which is infinite in both directions) according to a series of instructions. More formally, the machine can be thought of as a set of ordered quintuples, $\langle q_i, s_i, s_j, I_i, q_j \rangle$, where q_i is the current state of the machine, s_i is the symbol currently being read on the tape, s_j is the symbol with which the machine replaces S_i, I_i is an instruction to move the tape one unit to the right, to the left, or to remain where it is, and q_j is the machine's next state.

types, theory of – A theory of the correct structure of an ideal language, and introduced by Bertrand Russell as a means of blocking paradoxes such as the paradox of the set of all sets which are not members of themselves (Russell's paradox). Russell's idea was that by ordering the objects (and eventually predicates) of a language or theory into a hierarchy (beginning with individuals at the lowest level, sets of individuals at the next lowest level, etc.), one could avoid reference being made to sets such as the set of all sets, since there would be no level at which such a set appeared.

universal quantifier – A symbol such as '∀' which is used in combination with a variable to represent the notion 'for all'. For example, under the appropriate interpretation '$(\forall x)(x = x)$' could be used to symbolize 'For all x, x is identical with itself' or, more informally, 'Everything is identical with itself'.

validity – The property of any inference such that the joint assertion of its premisses and denial of its conclusion results in a contradiction. Alternatively, the property of any well-formed formula which is true under all interpretations; that is, given any non-empty domain, every possible assignment of values to its free variables results in a true sentence.

well-formed formula – Any formula of a logistic system which is grammatically correct; a sentence.

Index

Bigelow, J. 303, 352–3
biochemistry 327
biological species 305
biology 215, 300, 323–4, 327, 333
bivalence 430
body 316, 318, 324, 334–5
Bohr's principles *see* complementarity,
  correspondence
Bohr's theory 216, 381
Bohr, N. 222, 381
Bois-Reymond, E., Du 325, 328–31, 390
Boltzmann constant 296, 382
Boltzmann, L. 270, 296–7, 381–2
Bolyai, J. 12, 50, 53–4, 382
Boole, G. 10–14, 50, 55, 382
Boolean algebra 11, 430
Boring, E. G. 340–1, 382
Born, M. 242–3, 382
Boscovich, R. J. 225–6
Bostock, D. 89
Bournoulli, J. 175
Boyle, R. 230, 382
Bradley, F. H. 206–7, 382
brain 326–7, 331–2, 338
Bridgman, P. W. 202
Brillouin, L. 299, 301
Broca, A. 326
Brodie hypothesis 326
Brouwer, L. E. J. 16, 18–19, 54, 71–8,
  81, 91, 93–4, 382
Brücke, E. von 325
Bruno, G. 238, 382
Büchner, L. 325, 327, 382
Buckle, H. T. 270
Burali-Forti, C. 17
Bush, V. 293

Cabanis, P. J. G. 327, 383
calculus 225, 251, 301, 383, 430; logical
  23, 436–7; predicate 14, 23, 415, 417;
  propositional 14, 23–4, 417, 440
Cannon, W. 292
Cantor's continuum problem 16–17
Cantor's theorem 25, 431
Cantor, G. 12, 15, 21
cardinality 431
cargo cults 244

Carnap, R. 125, 175, 183, 186, 193–5,
  203–6, 208–9, 241, 383
Carpenter, W. 340
Cartesian doubt 383
category theory 431
caterpillar 343, 347–8, 363
Cauchy, L. 12
causal nexus 360
causal–explanatory framework 355–7
causality 102, 175, 217, 227, 268, 275–6,
  279–83, 328, 330, 346, 348, 351, 383;
  weak 267
cause 267–8, 275–6, 320, 329, 333, 342,
  383–4, 360; hidden 354, 356, 364–5;
  mapping onto effect 355; mental 327,
  346, 356, 359, 366; reacting to 363–4
cerebral cortex 350
certainty 384
ceteris paribus 384
Chain of Being 316–18, 321–2, 332–4,
  337–8, 340–1, 343–4, 346, 348, 350,
  352, 354, 366, 384
chance 279, 384
channel 297–9, 308, 384; cascade of 298
  308
charge 217, 384
chemistry 214–15, 230, 327, 384–5
child 354–65
choice 356
Church's theorem 28–9, 431
Church's thesis *see* Church–Turing
  thesis
Church, A. 16, 28
Church–Turing thesis 31, 431
circular definition/reasoning 385
Clarke, S. 217, 221, 385
classes 137–8
Clausius, R. J. E. 295–6, 385
Clausius–Maxwell theory 216
closed sentence 431
Cogito 317, 385
cognition 316, 327, 333, 352, 385;
  Cartesian picture of 354
cognitive activity 312–13
cognitivism 298, 312, 315, 331, 354–5,
  361, 385
Cohen, P. 25
colour 179–81

gaze 365
Gedankenexperiment 364
genetic difference 280–1
genetic endowment/pool 305
Gentzen's consistency proof 435
Gentzen, G. 28, 84
genus/species 396
geometry, arithmetization of 71;
  asymmetry with arithmetic 53–4,
  56–7, 64, 70–1; Euclidian 52, 215, 396;
  non-Euclidean 12, 15, 50, 55–6, 64,
  70–1, 105–6, 396; necessary 105–6;
  synthetic a priori 71
geophysics 215
George, F. H. 311
gesture 354, 365
ghost in the machine 341
Gigerenzer, G. 269–70
goal 332, 351, 353, 356
God 178, 184, 206–7, 238, 240, 257–8;
  ontological proof 257–8
Gödel numbering 26, 435
Gödel's completeness theorem 435
Gödel's incompleteness theorems 19,
  25–7, 83–4, 107, 435
Gödel, K. 10, 16, 25–7, 83–4, 99–101,
  107, 246, 396
Goethe, J. W. von 75
Goltz, F. 344–5, 347
Goodings, D. 226–7
governor 293
grammar 267, 276, 284; logical 343, 365;
  of agency and intentionality 358;
  rule of 358, 362
grammatical continuum 364
grammatical form 101
Grassmann, H. G. 12
gravity 231, 251, 329
Green, G. 340
Gunderson, K. 311

habit 357
Hall, M. 338–9, 342
halting problem 435
Hamilton, W. 11
Hamilton, W. R. 12
Harré, R. 274, 396
Hartley, D. 293, 297, 335–8, 396

Harvey, W. 323–4
Hausdorff, F. 135
heart 323–4
heat 322–31; laws of 330; location and
  generation of 325; as metabolic
  activity 330; theory of 318, 323–4
Heidegger, M. 206
Heider, F. 320, 396
Heisenberg, W. 226
heliotropism 347–8
Hellmann, G. 102
Helmholtz, H. L. F. von 325–6, 330–1,
  396
Hempel's paradox 397
Hempel, C. G. 200, 251–2, 268, 272–3,
  396–7
Henn, V. 351
heritability 280–1, 284
Herrick, C. J. 340–1
Hertz, H. R. 226
heuristic 255, 397
Heyting, A. 16, 23, 32–3, 93–4
hidden variable theory 227–8
Hilbert space 216, 397
Hilbert's program 397
Hilbert, D. 16–19, 23, 25–7, 54, 56,
  76–88, 104–7, 397
history of ideas 322; of psychological
  ideas 366
Hodes, H. 89–90
Hodgson, P. E. 226
Homans, G. C. 267, 397
homeomorph 223
homeostasis 295, 300, 304–5, 309, 326,
  397
homme moyen, l' 269–70
Hooke, R. 316, 397–8
Hull, C. 351
humankind 223, 315–22, 325, 333–4,
  338, 341, 343, 345–6, 348, 353
Hume, D. 88, 237, 302, 398
Husserl, E. 142, 148
Huxley, T. H. 341, 346, 348, 398
hypothesis 361, 398; inductive 352; null
  276, 280, 398
hypothetical 171

iatrochemistry/iatrophysics 334, 398

Meinong, A. M. 167–9, 406
memory 326; associative 347–8
mental construct 320, 355
mental states 169, 345–6, 359
mereology 36, 438
Mersenne, M. 317, 406
Merton, R. K. 244, 271
metabolism 300
metalanguage 19, 185–6, 406, 438
metalogic 22, 24, 438
metamathematics 438; arithmetization
 of 83; predicates 26
metaphysics 9, 186, 193, 199–200,
 206–8, 230, 235, 237, 243–4, 257–8,
 268, 322–3, 328, 347, 407
metatheorems 25, 438
metatheory 438
methodology 235–7, 283, 326–7, 407
Mettrie, J. O. de la 317, 327, 402
Michelson, A. A. 219, 221
micro-level unpredictability 270, 297
microstate 296
microstructure 296–7
Mill, J. S. 88, 195, 340, 407
mind 51, 70, 94, 169, 171, 196, 317, 320,
 322, 332–3, 338, 343, 346, 355, 364–5,
 407
mind's eye 317
mind/body problem 323–5, 329, 333,
 350, 353, 407
Minkowsky manifold 220
Minkowsky, H. 220
Minsky, M. 294
mistakes 146–7
model 225, 239, 266–7, 274, 330, 354,
 364, 438; in logic 225; quasi-causal
 267; of reality 353; of the world 223–4
model making 364
model theory 22, 364, 438
modus ponens 14, 184, 407, 438
modus tollens 407
Moleschott, J. 325, 327, 408
momentum 217, 221, 408
monism 408
monkey trial 243
Monro, A. 335
Moore, G. E. 178, 205, 408
morality 209–10, 357, 408

Morgan, A. de 10–11, 55, 389
Morgenstern, O. 292
Morley, E. W. 219, 221
morphology 305, 408
Morse–Kelly class theory 32
Moses 244
movement *see* action
Müller, J. P. 322, 408
multiple regression 408
mysticism 184, 186, 207, 408

name 126, 157–9, 165, 170, 179, 181–3,
 185, 196; proper 137, 404; simple 179
natural selection 305–7, 309
nature 239, 330; laws of 176–9, 218–21,
 324–5, 387
necessity 161
neo-Cartesianism 341
neo-pragmatism 224
nervous system 293, 298, 303, 308, 330,
 332, 336, 337, 339, 350; autonomic
 340; efferent/afferent 390
Neumann, J. von 21, 292–3, 428
Neurath, O. 195, 203–4, 409
neurological imprinting 340
neurology 303
neurophysiology 292, 301, 326, 347, 353
neuropsychology 354, 409
neutral monism 312, 409
Newell, A. 336
Newton, I. 230, 232, 258, 316, 324–5,
 337, 409
Newtonian matter theory 216
niche 306, 308
nihilism 410
nomological 410
nonsense 169–70, 172, 185, 360
normal curve 270
normal distribution 280
normative 410
NP-complete 438
number 104, 134–5, 137–8, 175, 410; as
 sets 137; complex 12; concept 60–2,
 138; definition of 132–3; finitary
 number theory 100, 104; ontological
 characteristics 103; reference of, 143;
 science of 104; zero 133–4, 144; *see
 also* arithmetic

number theory, elementary 26, 391;
  predicates 26
Nyquist, H. 293, 297

object 79, 103, 131, 135, 141, 158–60,
  165, 167, 169–70, 178–83, 185, 196,
  356; constitution of 143; logical 60–1,
  64; of direct acquaintance 178;
  properties/features of 180–2; quasi-
  concrete 104
Objective 167, 169–70
objective 410
objectivity 77
observation 279, 361, 364; statements
  203
observer 318–19
Occam's/Ockham's razor 410
Ogden, C. K. 157
Olbers, H. W. M. 53
ontological commitment 168
ontology/ontological 169–70, 185,
  221–3, 226, 269, 357, 410
opacity and transparency, referential
  410–11
operationism 202, 411
operator see logical operator
option, possible, preferred, rule-
  ordered 278
order from disorder principle 269–70,
  411
ordinary language philosophy 411
organism 293, 295, 300–1, 305, 307–10,
  325, 343, 350, 353; genetic structure
  of 304–5
organizational theory 302, 412
orientalism 412
oscillator 412
outcome 276–8
Ozanam, J. 236
ω-completeness 438
ω-consistency 26, 438
ω-particle 228

Papert, S. 294
paradigm 412; revolution 354
paradox 412, 439; distinction between
  set-theoretic and semantic 20–1
paramorph 223

parapsychology 247, 249, 412
pari passu 412
Parsons, C. 98–9, 104
Pascal, B. 302, 412
Passmore, J. 193
pattern formation 309
Patzig, G. 129–30
Pavlov, I. P. 349–50, 412–13
Peano's postulates 439
Peano, G. 12, 17, 20, 26, 50, 55, 65, 84,
  413
Pears, D. F. 157
Pearson chi-square 413
Pearson, K. 279
Peirce, C. S. 10, 13, 50, 55, 65, 413
percept 310
perceptible attributes 229
perception 221, 320, 326, 333, 344, 356;
  inner 147; theory of 320
perceptual pattern 305, 307–9; hard-
  wired 308
Perrault, C. 335
person 355
Pflüger, E. 339–41, 343–4
Pflüger–Lotze debate 339–41, 344
phenomenalism 413
phenomenology 346, 413
phenomenon 232, 413–14; behavioural
  357; mental 194, 357, 365–6;
  physical 357; physicochemical 330;
  vital see vital force or phenomenon
philosophical reflection 147–8
philosophy 1, 193, 323, 340, 347;
  analytic 378; development 194; non-
  intuitionistic 142; of language 10, 168;
  of logic 9–49; of mathematics see
  mathematics, philosophy of; of mind
  294, 351; of psychology 322; of
  science 10, 157; of unreason 237–9;
  problems in 24, 184, 194; scientific
  237
photon 228, 414
physicalism 205, 414
physics 1, 177, 214–32, 366; and
  philosophy 215; Aristotelian 218–19;
  as phenomenon 226, 228–9; classical
  312; experiments in 216; foundations
  of 226; gas 270; history of 225; is

mechanics 229; laws of 215, 219, 334; methodology of 214; nature of 223; Newtonian 217, 227, 231; philosophy of 214–32; post-Aristotelian 217; social 269
physiology 324–9, 331, 350
pictorial form 185
picture 170
picture theory 159, 164–6, 169, 185, 196, 414
pineal gland 332
Pitts, W. H. 311
Planck, M. C. E. L. 257, 296, 414
plane, Cartesian 218, 383; Euclidian 136
Plato 146, 166, 214, 293–4, 414
Platonism 101–2, 168, 317, 414–15
pluralism 415
Poincaré, J. H. 20, 72–4, 91–2, 94, 415
Polanyi, M. 249
Polish notation 439
Pollock, J. L. 275
Popper, K. R. 224, 232, 238, 247, 252–5, 415
population 306
positivism 224, 269
possible outcomes 278
possible worlds 35, 159–61, 182–3
post hoc 415
Post, E. 28
post-realism 224
pragmatic realism 222
pragmatism/neo-pragmatism 415
praxis 415
preconception, a priori 333
preconscious 361; selection 336
predicate 439
prediction 355, 357–9, 361
premiss 439
presupposition 415–16
prima facie 416
primitive basis 439
primitive lore 240–1
principio vitalis see vitalism
private language argument 205, 416
privileged access 356, 359
probabilistic causation 267, 271–2, 274, 276, 278
probability 174–6, 251, 253–4, 268,

274–5, 296–8, 313, 416, 440; a priori 296–7; conditional 268, 297–8, 313; paradox of 254
probability theory 9, 35, 37, 253, 266–84, 440; classical 268
problem, conceptual versus empirical 323, 328; empirical versus philosophical 322, 327; of other minds 416
process/processing 298, 300, 303; biological 325; cognitive 305, 312, 344; continuity of psychological 320; mental 320–1, 326, 346, 361; neural 331; non-verbal 320; organic versus inorganic 329–30; physical 366; psychic 325–6, 328, 331, 350, 366; psychological 320, 353–4
productivity, epistemic 64
Promethean madness 238, 240
proof 2, 72, 440; canonical 59–60; consistency 84–5; finitary consistency 27; finitary, of real-ideal 87; impossibility 15; mathematical 15; nature of 15; real 79; of standard theorems 86; theory 22
property 217, 232, 274, 281, 311; emergent 341; possible 274–5
proposition 131, 157, 160–76, 184–5, 197–203, 222, 270, 379, 416–17; a priori/a posteriori 51; elementary 157–63, 165–7, 172–6, 179, 181, 183–4, 200–1, 203, 391; empirical 359, 365; experiential 203; explanatory 274; false 166–7, 171; grammatical 358–9, 363, 365; ideal 86; meaning is method of verification 196; meaningless 196–7; pseudo 185; real versus ideal 79–80; type of 65
propositional attitudes 169
protocol statement 203–4, 417
psychic control 339
psychic directedness 342
psychological ascription, grounds for 365
psychological verbs/concept words 360; use of 365
psychology 1, 168, 292, 208, 318–19, 323, 332, 347–9, 354, 366;

157–86, 195–6, 198, 205, 207, 258, 276, 358, 360, 363, 430
words 60, 144, 169, 198, 202, 204, 357
world 166–7, 169, 176–8, 182, 184–5, 222–4, 241, 312; apparatus-world set-up 232

Wright, S. 279

Zermelo, E. 16, 18, 20
Zermelo–Fraenkel set theory (ZF) 21 25; ZFC 21, 31
z particle 228